DATE DUE

A LITERARY HISTORY OF THE ARABS

THE KEGAN PAUL ARABIA LIBRARY

ARABIA AND THE ISLES
HAROLD INGRAMS

STUDIES IN ISLAMIC MYSTICISM
REYNOLD A. NICHOLSON

A LITERARY HISTORY OF THE ARABS
REYNOLD A. NICHOLSON

LORD OF ARABIA: IBN SAUD
H.C. ARMSTRONG

R

A LITERARY HISTORY OF THE ARABS

REYNOLD A. NICHOLSON

THE KEGAN PAUL ARABIA LIBRARY
VOLUME FOUR

KEGAN PAUL INTERNATIONAL
London and New York

30
national Limited in 1998
3 3SW, England
71) 436 0899
mon.co.uk
Internet: http://www.demon.co.uk/keganpaul/
USA: 562 West 113th Street, New York, NY, 10025, USA
Tel: (212) 666 1000 Fax: (212) 316 3100

Distributed by
John Wiley & Sons Ltd
Southern Cross Trading Estate
1 Oldlands Way, Bognor Regis
West Sussex, PO22 9SA, England
Tel: (01243) 779 777 Fax: (01243) 820 250

Columbia University Press
562 West 113th Street
New York, NY 10025. USA
Tel: (212) 666 1000 Fax: (212) 316 3100

Printed in Great Britain by
Antony Rowe Ltd

ISBN 0 7103 0568 0

British Library Cataloguing in Publication Data

Nicholson, Reynold A. (Reynold Alleyne), 1868-1945
A literary history of the Arabs. - (The Kegan Paul Arabia library ; v. 1)
1. Arabic literature - History and criticism
I. Title
892.7'009
ISBN 0-7103-0566-4

Library of Congress Cataloging-in-Publication Data

Nicholson, Reynold Alleyne, 1868-1945.
A literary history of the Arabs / by Reynold A. Nicholson.
p. cm. -- (The Kegan Paul Arabia library ; 1)
Includes bibliographical referneces (p.) and index.
ISBN 0-7103-0566-4 (alk. paper)
1. Arabic literature--History and criticism.
I. Title. II. Series.
PJ510.N5 1997
892'.709--dc20 96-41815
CIP

PREFACE

A Literary History of the Arabs, published by T. Fisher Unwin in 1907 and twice re-issued without alteration, now appears under new auspices, and I wish to thank the Syndics of the Cambridge University Press for the opportunity they have given me of making it in some respects more accurate and useful than it has hitherto been. Since the present edition is printed from the original plates, there could be no question of revising the book throughout and recasting it where necessary; but while only a few pages have been rewritten, the Bibliography has been brought up to date and I have removed several mistakes from the text and corrected others in an appendix which includes a certain amount of supplementary matter. As stated in the preface to the first edition, I hoped "to compile a work which should serve as a general introduction to the subject, and which should be neither too popular for students nor too scientific for ordinary readers. It has been my chief aim to sketch in broad outlines what the Arabs thought, and to indicate as far as possible the influences which moulded their thought....Experience has convinced me that young students of Arabic, to whom this volume is principally addressed, often find difficulty in understanding what they read, since they are not in touch with the political, intellectual, and religious notions which are presented to them. The pages of almost every Arabic book abound in allusions to names, events, movements, and ideas of which Moslems require no explanation, but which puzzle the Western reader unless he have some general knowledge of Arabian history in the widest meaning of the word. Such a survey is not to be found, I believe, in any single European book; and if mine supply the want, however partially and inadequately, I shall feel that my labour has been amply rewarded. . . . As regards the choice of topics, I agree with the author of a famous anthology who declares that it is harder to select than compose (*ikhtiyáru 'l-kalám aṣ'abu min ta'lífihi*). Perhaps an epitomist may be excused for not doing equal justice all round. To me the literary side of the subject appeals more than the historical, and I have followed my bent without hesitation; for in order to interest others a writer must first be interested himself. . . . Considering the importance of Arabic poetry as, in the main, a true mirror of Arabian life, I do not think the space devoted to it is excessive. Other branches of literature could not receive the same attention. Many an eminent writer has been dismissed in a few lines, many well-known names have been passed over. But, as before said, this work is a sketch of ideas in their historical environment rather than a record of authors, books, and dates. The exact transliteration of Arabic words, though superfluous for scholars and for persons entirely ignorant of the language, is an almost indispensable aid to the class of readers whom I have especially in view. My system is that recommended by the Royal Asiatic Society and adopted by Professor Browne in his *Literary History of Persia*; but I use ẓ for the letter which he denotes by dh. The definite article *al*, which is frequently omitted at the beginning of proper names, has been restored in the Index. It may save trouble if I mention here the abbreviations 'b.' for 'ibn' (son of); *J.R.A.S.* for *Journal of the Royal Asiatic Society*; Z.D.M.G. for *Zeitschrift der Deutschen Morgenländischen Gesellschaft*; and *S.B.W.A.* for *Sitzungsberichte der Wiener Akademie*. Finally, it behoves me to make full acknowledgment of my debt to the learned Orientalists whose works I have studied and freely 'conveyed' into these pages. References could not be given in every case, but the reader will see for himself how much is derived from Von Kremer, Goldziher, Nöldeke, and Wellhausen, to mention only a few of the leading authorities. At the same time I have constantly gone back to the native sources of information."

There remains an acknowledgment of a more personal kind. Twenty-two years ago I wrote—"my warmest thanks are due to my friend and colleague, Professor A. A. Bevan, who read the proofs throughout and made a number of valuable remarks which will be found in the footnotes." Happily the present occasion permits me to renew those ties between us; and the book which he helped into the world now celebrates its majority by associating itself with his name.

REYNOLD A. NICHOLSON

November 1, 1929

Contents

Introduction

THE Arabs belong to the great family of nations which on account of their supposed descent from Shem, the son of Noah, are commonly known as the 'Semites.'

The Semites.

This term includes the Babylonians and Assyrians, the Hebrews, the Phœnicians, the Aramæans, the Abyssinians, the Sabæans, and the Arabs, and although based on a classification that is not ethnologically precise—the Phœnicians and Sabæans, for example, being reckoned in Genesis, chap. x, among the descendants of Ham—it was well chosen by Eichhorn († 1827) to comprehend the closely allied peoples which have been named. Whether the original home of the undivided Semitic race was some part of Asia (Arabia, Armenia, or the district of the Lower Euphrates), or whether, according to a view which has lately found favour, the Semites crossed into Asia from Africa,[1] is still uncertain. Long before the epoch when they first appear in history they had branched off from the parent stock and formed separate nationalities. The relation of the Semitic languages to each other cannot be discussed here, but we may arrange them in the chronological order of the extant literature as follows:—[2]

[1] H. Grimme, *Weltgeschichte in Karakterbildern: Mohammed* (Munich, 1904), p. 6 sqq.

[2] *Cf.* Nöldeke, *Die Semitischen Sprachen* (Leipzig, 1899), or the same scholar's article, 'Semitic Languages,' in the *Encyclopædia Britannica*, 11th edition. Renan's *Histoire générale des langues sémitiques* (1855) is now

1. Babylonian or Assyrian (3000–500 B.C.).
2. Hebrew (from 1500 B.C.).
3. South Arabic, otherwise called Sabæan or Ḥimyarite (inscriptions from 800 B.C.).
4. Aramaic (inscriptions from 800 B.C.).
5. Phœnician (inscriptions from 700 B.C.).
6. Æthiopic (inscriptions from 350 A.D.).
7. Arabic (from 500 A.D.).

Notwithstanding that Arabic is thus, in a sense, the youngest of the Semitic languages, it is generally allowed to be nearer akin than any of them to the original archetype, the 'Ursemitisch,' from which they all are derived, just as the Arabs, by reason of their geographical situation and the monotonous uniformity of desert life, have in some respects preserved the Semitic character more purely and exhibited it more distinctly than any people of the same family. From the period of the great Moslem conquests (700 A.D.) to the present day they have extended their language, religion, and culture over an enormous expanse of territory, far surpassing that of all the ancient Semitic empires added together. It is true that the Arabs are no longer what they were in the Middle Ages, the ruling nation of the world, but loss of temporal power has only strengthened their spiritual dominion. Islam still reigns supreme in Western Asia; in Africa it has steadily advanced; even on European soil it has found in Turkey compensation for its banishment from Spain and Sicily. While most of the Semitic peoples have vanished, leaving but a meagre and ambiguous record, so that we cannot hope to become intimately acquainted with them, we possess in the

The Arabs as representatives of the Semitic race.

antiquated. An interesting essay on the importance of the Semites in the history of civilisation was published by F. Hommel as an introduction to his *Semitischen Völker und Sprachen*, vol. i (Leipzig, 1883). The dates in this table are of course only approximate.

case of the Arabs ample materials for studying almost every phase of their development since the sixth century of the Christian era, and for writing the whole history of their national life and thought. This book, I need hardly say, makes no such pretensions. Even were the space at my disposal unlimited, a long time must elapse before the vast and various field of Arabic literature can be thoroughly explored and the results rendered accessible to the historian.

Arabs of the North and South.

From time immemorial Arabia was divided into North and South, not only by the trackless desert (*al-Rub' al-Khálí*, the 'Solitary Quarter') which stretches across the peninsula and forms a natural barrier to intercourse, but also by the opposition of two kindred races widely differing in their character and way of life. Whilst the inhabitants of the northern province (the Ḥijáz and the great central highland of Najd) were rude nomads sheltering in 'houses of hair,' and ever shifting to and fro in search of pasture for their camels, the people of Yemen or Arabia Felix are first mentioned in history as the inheritors of an ancient civilisation and as the owners of fabulous wealth —spices, gold and precious stones—which ministered to the luxury of King Solomon. The Bedouins of the North spoke Arabic—that is to say, the language of the Pre-islamic poems and of the Koran—whereas the southerners used a dialect called by Muḥammadans 'Ḥimyarite' and a peculiar script of which the examples known to us have been discovered and deciphered in comparatively recent times. Of these Sabæans —to adopt the designation given to them by Greek and Roman geographers—more will be said presently. The period of their bloom was drawing to a close in the early centuries of our era, and they have faded out of history before 600 A.D., when their northern neighbours first rise into prominence.

It was, no doubt, the consciousness of this racial distinction that caused the view to prevail among Moslem genealogists that the Arabs followed two separate lines of descent from their common ancestor, Sám b. Núḥ (Shem, the son of Noah). As regards those of the North, their derivation from 'Adnán, a descendant of Ismá'íl (Ishmael) was universally recognised; those of the South were traced back to Qaḥṭán, whom most genealogists identified with Yoqṭán (Joktan), the son of 'Ábir (Eber). Under the Yoqṭánids, who are the elder line, we find, together with the Sabæans and Ḥimyarites, several large and powerful tribes—*e.g.*, Ṭayyi', Kinda, and Tanúkh—which had settled in North and Central Arabia long before Islam, and were in no respect distinguishable from the Bedouins of Ishmaelite origin. As to 'Adnán, his exact genealogy is disputed, but all agree that he was of the posterity of Ismá'íl (Ishmael), the son of Ibráhím (Abraham) by Hájar (Hagar). The story runs that on the birth of Ismá'íl God commanded Abraham to journey to Mecca with Hagar and her son and to leave them there. They were seen by some Jurhumites, descendants of Yoqṭán, who took pity on them and resolved to settle beside them. Ismá'íl grew up with the sons of the strangers, learned to shoot the bow, and spoke their tongue. Then he asked of them in marriage, and they married him to one of their women.[1] The tables on the opposite page show the principal branches of the younger but by far the more important family of the Arabs which traced its pedigree through 'Adnán to Ismá'íl. A dotted line indicates the omission of one or more links in the genealogical chain.[2]

Ishmaelites and Yoqṭánids.

[1] Ibn Qutayba, *Kitábu 'l-Ma'árif*, ed. by Wüstenfeld, p. 18.

[2] Full information concerning the genealogy of the Arabs will be found in Wüstenfeld's *Genealogische Tabellen der Arabischen Stämme und Familien* with its excellent *Register* (Göttingen, 1852–1853).

I.

The Descendants of Rabí'a.

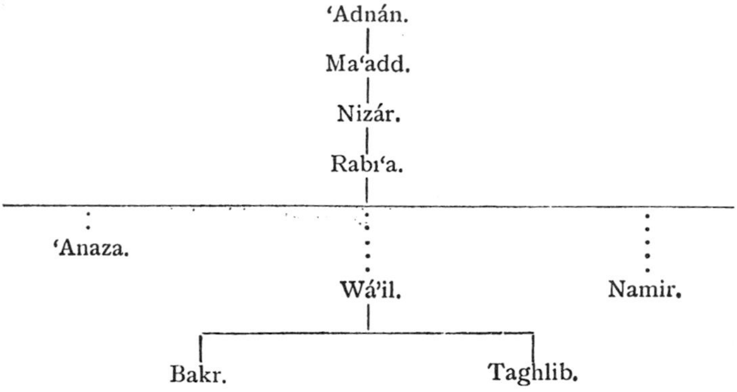

II.

The Descendants of Muḍar.

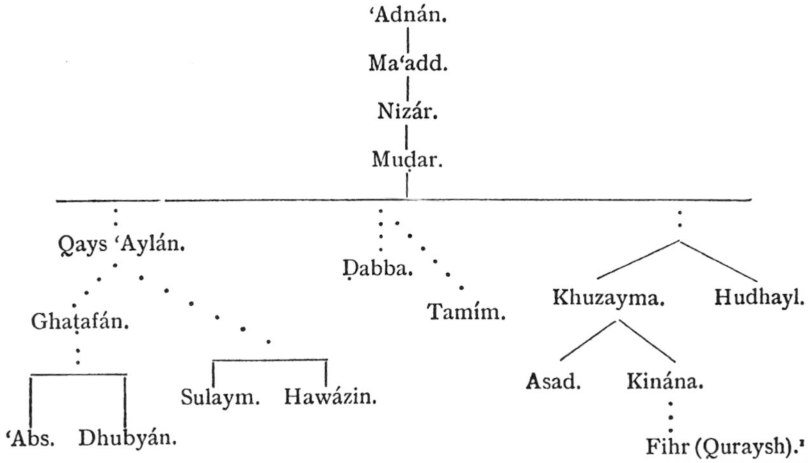

[1] The tribes Ḍabba, Tamím, Khuzayma, Hudhayl, Asad, Kinána, and Quraysh together formed a group which is known as Khindif, and is often distinguished from Qays 'Aylán.

It is undeniable that these lineages are to some extent fictitious. There was no Pre-islamic science of genealogy, so that the first Muḥammadan investigators had only confused and scanty traditions to work on. They were biassed, moreover, by political, religious, and other considerations.[1] Thus their study of the Koran and of Biblical history led to the introduction of the patriarchs who stand at the head of their lists. Nor can we accept the national genealogy beginning with ʿAdnán as entirely historical, though a great deal of it was actually stored in the memories of the Arabs at the time when Islam arose, and is corroborated by the testimony of the Pre-islamic poets.[2] On the other hand, the alleged descent of every tribe from an eponymous ancestor is inconsistent with facts established by modern research.[3] It is probable that many names represent merely a local or accidental union; and many more, *e.g.*, Maʿadd, seem originally to have denoted large groups or confederations of tribes. The theory of a radical difference between the Northern Arabs and those of the South, corresponding to the fierce hostility which has always divided them since the earliest days of Islam,[4] may hold good if we restrict the term 'Yemenite' (Southern) to the civilised Sabæans, Ḥimyarites, &c., who dwelt in Yemen and spoke their own dialect, but can hardly apply to the Arabic-speaking 'Yemenite' Bedouins scattered all over the peninsula. Such criticism, however, does not affect the value of the genealogical documents regarded as an index of the popular mind. From this point of view legend is often superior to fact, and it must be our aim in the following chapters to set forth what

Character of Muḥammadan genealogy.

[1] Goldziher, *Muhammedanische Studien*, Part I, p. 133 sqq., 177 sqq.

[2] Nöldeke in *Z.D.M.G.*, vol. 40, p. 177.

[3] See Margoliouth, *Mohammed and the Rise of Islam*, p. 4.

[4] Concerning the nature and causes of this antagonism see Goldziher, *op. cit.*, Part I, p. 78 sqq.

the Arabs believed rather than to examine whether or no they were justified in believing it.

'Arabic,' in its widest signification, has two principal dialects:—

1. South Arábic, spoken in Yemen and including Sabæan, Ḥimyarite, Minæan, with the kindred dialects of Mahra and Shiḥr.

2. Arabic proper, spoken in Arabia generally, exclusive of Yemen.

South Arabic.

Of the former language, leaving Mahrí, Socotrí, and other living dialects out of account, we possess nothing beyond the numerous inscriptions which have been collected by European travellers and which it will be convenient to discuss in the next chapter, where I shall give a brief sketch of the legendary history of the Sabæans and Ḥimyarites. South Arabic resembles Arabic in its grammatical forms, *e.g.*, the broken plural, the sign of the dual, and the manner of denoting indefiniteness by an affixed *m* (for which Arabic substitutes *n*) as well as in its vocabulary; its alphabet, which consists of twenty-nine letters, *Sin* and *Samech* being distinguished as in Hebrew, is more nearly akin to the Æthiopic. The Ḥimyarite Empire was overthrown by the Abyssinians in the sixth century after Christ, and by 600 A.D. South Arabic had become a dead language. From this time forward the dialect of the North established an almost universal supremacy and won for itself the title of 'Arabic' *par excellence.*[1]

The oldest specimens of Arabic writing.

The oldest monuments of written Arabic are modern in date compared with the Sabæan inscriptions, some of which take us back 2,500 years or thereabout. Apart from the inscriptions of Ḥijr in the northern Ḥijáz, and those of Ṣafá in the neighbourhood of Damascus (which, although written by northern Arabs before the Christian era, exhibit a peculiar character not unlike the

[1] The word 'Arabic' is always to be understood in this sense wherever it occurs in the following pages.

Sabæan and cannot be called Arabic in the usual acceptation of the term), the most ancient examples of Arabic writing which have hitherto been discovered appear in the trilingual (Syriac, Greek, and Arabic) inscription of Zabad,[1] south-east of Aleppo, dated 512 or 513 A.D., and the bilingual (Greek and Arabic) of Ḥarrán,[2] dated 568 A.D. With these documents we need not concern ourselves further, especially as their interpretation presents great difficulties. Very few among the Pre-islamic Arabs were able to read or write.[3] Those who could generally owed their skill to Jewish and Christian teachers, or to the influence of foreign culture radiating from Ḥíra and Ghassán. But although the Koran, which was first collected soon after the battle of Yamáma (633 A.D.), is the oldest Arabic book, the beginnings of literary composition in the Arabic language can be traced back to an earlier period. Probably all the Pre-islamic poems which have come down to us belong to the century preceding Islam (500–622 A.D.), but their elaborate form and technical perfection forbid the hypothesis that in them we have "the first sprightly runnings" of Arabian song. It may be said ot these magnificent odes, as of the Iliad and Odyssey, that "they are works of highly finished art, which could not possibly have been produced until the poetical art had been practised for a long time." They were preserved during hundreds of years by oral tradition, as we shall explain elsewhere, and were committed to writing, for the most part, by the Moslem scholars of the early 'Abbásid age, *i.e.*, between 750 and 900 A.D. It is a noteworthy fact that the language of these poems, the authors of which represent many different tribes and districts of the

The Pre-islamic poems.

[1] First published by Sachau in *Monatsberichte der Kön. Preuss. Akad. der Wissenschaften zu Berlin* (February, 1881), p. 169 sqq.

[2] See De Vogüé, *Syrie Centrale, Inscriptions Sémitiques*, p. 117. Other references are given in *Z.D.M.G.*, vol. 35, p. 749.

[3] On this subject the reader may consult Goldziher, *Muhammedanische Studien*, Part I, p. 110 sqq.

peninsula, is one and the same. The dialectical variations are too trivial to be taken into account. We might conclude that the poets used an artificial dialect, not such as was commonly spoken but resembling the epic dialect of Ionia which was borrowed by Dorian and Æolian bards. When we find, however, that the language in question is employed not only by the wandering troubadours, who were often men of some culture, and the Christian Arabs of Ḥíra on the Euphrates, but also by goat-herds, brigands, and illiterate Bedouins of every description, there can be no room for doubt that in the poetry of the sixth century we hear the Arabic language as it was then spoken throughout the length and breadth of Arabia. The success of Muḥammad and the conquests made by Islam under the Orthodox Caliphs gave an entirely new importance to this classical idiom. Arabic became the sacred language of the whole Moslem world.

The Koran.

This was certainly due to the Koran; but, on the other hand, to regard the dialect of Mecca, in which the Koran is written, as the source and prototype of the Arabic language, and to call Arabic 'the dialect of Quraysh,' is utterly to reverse the true facts of the case. Muḥammad, as Nöldeke has observed, took the ancient poetry for a model; and in the early age of Islam it was the authority of the heathen poets (of whom Quraysh had singularly few) that determined the classical usage and set the standard of correct speech. Moslems, who held the Koran to be the Word of God and inimitable in point of style, naturally exalted the dialect of the Prophet's tribe above all others, even laying down the rule that every tribe spoke less purely in proportion to its distance from Mecca, but this view will not commend itself to the unprejudiced student. The Koran, however, exercised a unique influence on the history of the Arabic language and literature. We shall see in a subsequent chapter that the necessity of preserving the text of the Holy Book uncorrupted, and of elucidating its obscurities, caused the Moslems to invent a science of grammar and lexicography, and to collect the old Pre-Muḥammadan poetry and traditions which must otherwise have perished. When the Arabs settled as conquerors in Syria and Persia and mixed with foreign peoples, the purity of the classical language could no longer be maintained. While in Arabia itself, especially among the nomads of the desert, little difference was felt, in the provincial garrison towns and great centres of industry like Baṣra and Kúfa, where the population largely consisted of aliens who had embraced Islam and were rapidly being Arabicised, the door stood open for all sorts of depravation to creep in. Against this vulgar Arabic the philologists waged unrelenting war, and it was mainly through their exertions that the classical idiom triumphed over the dangers to which it was exposed. Although the language of the pagan Bedouins did not survive intact—or survived, at any rate, only in the mouths of pedants and poets—it became, in a modified form, the universal medium of expression among the upper classes of Muḥammadan society. During the early Middle Ages it was spoken and written by all cultivated Moslems, of whatever nationality they might be, from the Indus to the Atlantic; it was the language of the Court and the Church, of Law and Commerce, of Diplomacy and Literature and Science. When the Mongol invasion in the thirteenth century swept away the 'Abbásid Caliphate, and therewith the last vestige of political unity in Islam, classical Arabic ceased to be the κοινή or 'common dialect' of the Moslem world, and was supplanted in Arabia, Syria, Egypt, and other Arabic-speaking countries by a vulgar colloquial idiom. In these countries, however, it is still the language of business, literature, and education, and we are told on high authority that even now it "is undergoing a renaissance, and there is every likelihood of its again becoming a great literary vehicle."[1] And if, for those

Arabic in the Muḥammadan Empire.

[1] Professor Margoliouth in *J.R.A.S.* for 1905, p. 418

Moslems who are not Arabs, it occupies relatively much the same position as Latin and Greek in modern European culture, we must not forget that the Koran, its most renowned masterpiece, is learned by every Moslem when he first goes to school, is repeated in his daily prayers, and influences the whole course of his life to an extent which the ordinary Christian can hardly realise.

I hope that I may be excused for ignoring in a work such as this the information regarding Ancient Arabian history which it is possible to glean from the Babylonian and Assyrian monuments. Any sketch that might be drawn of the Arabs, say from 2500 B.C. to the beginning of our era, would resemble a map of Cathay delineated by Sir John Mandeville. But amongst the shadowy peoples of the peninsula one, besides Saba and Ḥimyar, makes something more than a transient impression. The Nabaṭæans (*Nabaṭ*, pl. *Anbáṭ*) dwelt in towns, drove a flourishing trade long before the birth of Christ, and founded the kingdom of Petra, which attained a high degree of prosperity and culture until it was annexed by Trajan in 105 A.D. These Nabaṭæans were Arabs and spoke Arabic, although in default of a script of their own they used Aramaic for writing.[1] Muḥammadan authors identify them with the Aramæans, but careful study of their inscriptions has shown that this view, which was accepted by Quatremère,[2] is erroneous. 'The Book of Nabaṭaean Agriculture' (*Kitábu 'l-Faláḥat al-Nabaṭiyya*), composed in 904 A.D. by the Moslem Ibnu 'l-Waḥshiyya, who professed to have translated it from the Chaldæan, is now known to be a forgery. I only mention it here as an instance of the way in which Moslems apply the term 'Nabaṭæan'; for the title in question does not, of course, refer to Petra but to Babylon.

The Nabaṭæans.

[1] Nöldeke, *Die Semitischen Sprachen*, p. 36 sqq. and p. 51.

[2] *Journal Asiatique* (March, 1835), p. 209 sqq.

Three periods of Arabian history.

From what has been said the reader will perceive that the history of the Arabs, so far as our knowledge of it is derived from Arabic sources, may be divided into the following periods :—

I. The Sabæan and Ḥimyarite period, from 800 B.C., the date of the oldest South Arabic inscriptions, to 500 A.D.

II. The Pre-islamic period (500–622 A.D.).

III. The Muḥammadan period, beginning with the Migration (Hijra, or Hegira, as the word is generally written) of the Prophet from Mecca to Medína in 622 A.D. and extending to the present day.

The Sabæans and Ḥimyarites.

For the first period, which is confined to the history of Yemen or South Arabia, we have no contemporary Arabic sources except the inscriptions. The valuable but imperfect information which these supply is appreciably increased by the traditions preserved in the Pre-islamic poems, in the Koran, and particularly in the later Muḥammadan literature. It is true that most of this material is legendary and would justly be ignored by any one engaged in historical research, but I shall nevertheless devote a good deal of space to it, since my principal object is to make known the beliefs and opinions of the Arabs themselves.

The pagan Arabs.

The second period is called by Muḥammadan writers the *Jáhiliyya*, *i.e.*, the Age of Ignorance or Barbarism.[1] Its characteristics are faithfully and vividly reflected in the songs and odes of the heathen poets which have come down to us. There was no prose literature at that time : it was the poet's privilege to sing the history of his own people, to record their genealogies, to celebrate their feats of arms, and to extol their virtues. Although an immense quantity of Pre-islamic verse has been lost for ever,

[1] Strictly speaking, the *Jáhiliyya* includes the whole time between Adam and Muḥammad, but in a narrower sense it may be used, as here, to denote the Pre-islamic period of Arabic Literature.

we still possess a considerable remnant, which, together with the prose narratives compiled by Moslem philologists and antiquaries, enables us to picture the life of those wild days, in its larger aspects, accurately enough.

The last and by far the most important of the three periods comprises the history of the Arabs under Islam. It falls naturally into the following sections, which are enumerated in this place in order that the reader may see at a glance the broad political outlines of the complex and difficult epoch which lies before him.

The Moslem Arabs.

A. The Life of Muḥammad.

About the beginning of the seventh century of the Christian era a man named Muḥammad, son of 'Abdulláh, of the tribe Quraysh, appeared in Mecca with a Divine revelation (Koran). He called on his fellow-townsmen to renounce idolatry and worship the One God. In spite of ridicule and persecution he continued for several years to preach the religion of Islam in Mecca, but, making little progress there, he fled in 622 A.D. to the neighbouring city of Medína. From this date his cause prospered exceedingly. During the next decade the whole of Arabia submitted to his rule and did lip-service at least to the new Faith.

Life of Muḥammad.

B. The Orthodox Caliphate (632–661 A.D.).

On the death of the Prophet the Moslems were governed in turn by four of the most eminent among his Companions—Abú Bakr, 'Umar, 'Uthmán, and 'Alí—who bore the title of *Khalífa* (Caliph), *i.e.*, Vicegerent, and are commonly described as the Orthodox Caliphs (*al-Khulafá al-Ráshidún*). Under their guidance Islam was firmly established in the peninsula and was spread far beyond its borders. Hosts of Bedouins settled as military colonists in the fertile plains of Syria and Persia. Soon, however, the

The Orthodox Caliphs.

recently founded empire was plunged into civil war. The murder of 'Uthmán gave the signal for a bloody strife between rival claimants of the Caliphate. 'Alí, the son-in-law of the Prophet, assumed the title, but his election was contested by the powerful governor of Syria, Mu'áwiya b. Abí Sufyán.

C. The Umayyad Dynasty (661–750 A.D.).

'Alí fell by an assassin's dagger, and Mu'áwiya succeeded to the Caliphate, which remained in his family for ninety years.

The Umayyad dynasty.

The Umayyads, with a single exception, were Arabs first and Moslems afterwards. Religion sat very lightly on them, but they produced some able and energetic princes, worthy leaders of an imperial race. By 732 A.D. the Moslem conquests had reached the utmost limit which they ever attained. The Caliph in Damascus had his lieutenants beyond the Oxus and the Pyrenees, on the shores of the Caspian and in the valley of the Nile. Meantime the strength of the dynasty was being sapped by political and religious dissensions nearer home. The Shí'ites, who held that the Caliphate belonged by Divine right to 'Alí and his descendants, rose in revolt again and again. They were joined by the Persian Moslems, who loathed the Arabs and the oppressive Umayyad government. The 'Abbásids, a family closely related to the Prophet, put themselves at the head of the agitation. It ended in the complete overthrow of the reigning house, which was almost exterminated.

D. The 'Abbásid Dynasty (750–1258 A.D.).

Hitherto the Arabs had played a dominant rôle in the Moslem community, and had treated the non-Arab Moslems

The 'Abbásid dynasty.

with exasperating contempt. Now the tables were turned. We pass from the period of Arabian nationalism to one of Persian ascendancy and cosmopolitan culture. The flower of the 'Abbásid troops were Persians from Khurásán; Baghdád, the wonderful

'Abbásid capital, was built on Persian soil; and Persian nobles filled the highest offices of state at the 'Abbásid court. The new dynasty, if not religious, was at least favourable to religion, and took care to live in the odour of sanctity. For a time Arabs and Persians forgot their differences and worked together as good Moslems ought. Piety was no longer its own reward. Learning enjoyed munificent patronage. This was the Golden Age of Islam, which culminated in the glorious reign of Hárún al-Rashíd (786–809 A.D.). On his death peace was broken once more, and the mighty empire began slowly to collapse. As province after province cut itself loose from the Caliphate, numerous independent dynasties sprang up, while the Caliphs became helpless puppets in the hands of Turkish mercenaries. Their authority was still formally recognised in most Muḥammadan countries, but since the middle of the ninth century they had little or no real power.

E. From the Mongol invasion to the present day (1258 A.D. —).

The Post-Mongolian period.

The Mongol hordes under Húlágú captured Baghdád in 1258 A.D. and made an end of the Caliphate. Sweeping onward, they were checked by the Egyptian Mamelukes and retired into Persia, where, some fifty years afterwards, they embraced Islam. The successors of Húlágú, the Íl-kháns, reigned in Persia until a second wave of barbarians under Tímúr spread devastation and anarchy through Western Asia (1380–1405 A.D.). The unity of Islam, in a political sense, was now destroyed. Out of the chaos three Muḥammadan empires gradually took shape. In 1358 the Ottoman Turks crossed the Hellespont, in 1453 they entered Constantinople, and in 1517 Syria, Egypt, and Arabia were added to their dominions. Persia became an independent kingdom under the Ṣafawids (1502–1736); while in India the empire of the Great Moguls was founded by Bábur, a descendant of Tímúr, and gloriously maintained by his successors, Akbar and Awrangzíb (1525–1707).

Some of the political events which have been summarised above will be treated more fully in the body of this work; others will receive no more than a passing notice.

Arabian literary history.

The ideas which reveal themselves in Arabic literature are so intimately connected with the history of the people, and so incomprehensible apart from the external circumstances in which they arose, that I have found myself obliged to dwell at considerable length on various matters of historical interest, in order to bring out what is really characteristic and important from our special point of view. The space devoted to the early periods (500–750 A.D.) will not appear excessive if they are seen in their true light as the centre and heart of Arabian history. During the next hundred years Moslem civilisation reaches its zenith, but the Arabs recede more and more into the background. The Mongol invasion virtually obliterated their national life, though in Syria and Egypt they maintained their traditions of culture under Turkish rule, and in Spain we meet them struggling desperately against Christendom. Many centuries earlier, in the palmy days of the 'Abbásid Empire, the Arabs *pur sang* contributed only a comparatively small share to the literature which bears their name. I have not, however, enforced the test of nationality so strictly as to exclude all foreigners or men of mixed origin who wrote in Arabic. It may be said that the work of Persians (who even nowadays are accustomed to use Arabic when writing on theological and philosophical subjects) cannot illustrate the history of Arabian thought, but only the influence exerted upon Arabian thought by Persian ideas, and that consequently it must stand aside unless admitted for this definite purpose. But what shall we do in the case of those numerous and celebrated authors who are neither wholly

Writers who are wholly or partly of foreign extraction.

Arab nor wholly Persian, but unite the blood of both races? Must we scrutinise their genealogies and try to discover which strain preponderates? That would be a tedious and unprofitable task. The truth is that after the Umayyad period no hard-and-fast line can be drawn between the native and foreign elements in Arabic literature. Each reacted on the other, and often both are combined indissolubly. Although they must be distinguished as far as possible, we should be taking a narrow and pedantic view of literary history if we insisted on regarding them as mutually exclusive.

CHAPTER I

SABA AND ḤIMYAR

WITH the Sabæans Arabian history in the proper sense may be said to begin, but as a preliminary step we must take account of certain races which figure more or less prominently in legend, and are considered by Moslem chroniclers to have been the original inhabitants of the country. Among these are the peoples of 'Ád and Thamúd, which are constantly held up in the Koran as terrible examples of the pride that goeth before destruction. The home of the 'Ádites was in Ḥaḍramawt, the province adjoining Yemen, on the borders of the desert named *Aḥqáfu 'l-Raml.* It is doubtful whether they were Semites, possibly of Aramaic descent, who were subdued and exterminated by invaders from the north, or, as Hommel maintains,[1] the representatives of an imposing non-Semitic culture which survives in the tradition of 'Many-columned Iram,'[2] the Earthly Paradise built by Shaddád, one of their kings. The story of their destruction is related as follows:[3] They were a people of gigantic strength and stature, worshipping idols and committing all

Primitive races.

Legend of 'Ad.

[1] *Die Namen der Säugethiere bei den Südsemitischen Völkern,* p. 343 seq.

[2] *Iramu Dhátu 'l-'Imád* (Koran, lxxxix, 6). The sense of these words is much disputed. See especially Ṭabarí's explanation in his great commentary on the Koran (O. Loth in *Z.D.M.G.*, vol. 35, p. 626 sqq.).

[3] I have abridged Ṭabarí, *Annals,* i, 231 sqq. *Cf.* also chapters vii, xi, xxvi, and xlvi of the Koran.

manner of wrong; and when God sent to them a prophet, Húd by name, who should warn them to repent, they answered: "O Húd, thou hast brought us no evidence, and we will not abandon our gods for thy saying, nor will we believe in thee. We say one of our gods hath afflicted thee with madness." [1] Then a fearful drought fell upon the land of 'Ád, so that they sent a number of their chief men to Mecca to pray for rain. On arriving at Mecca the envoys were hospitably received by the Amalekite prince, Mu'áwiya b. Bakr, who entertained them with wine and music—for he had two famous singing-girls known as *al-Jarádatán*; which induced them to neglect their mission for the space of a whole month. At last, however, they got to business, and their spokesman had scarce finished his prayer when three clouds appeared, of different colours—white, red, and black—and a voice cried from heaven, "Choose for thyself and for thy people!" He chose the black cloud, deeming that it had the greatest store of rain, whereupon the voice chanted—

> "Thou hast chosen embers dun | that will spare of 'Ád not one | that will leave nor father nor son | ere him to death they shall have done."

Then God drove the cloud until it stood over the land of 'Ád, and there issued from it a roaring wind that consumed the whole people except a few who had taken the prophet's warning to heart and had renounced idolatry.

From these, in course of time, a new people arose, who are called 'the second 'Ád.' They had their settlements in Yemen, in the region of Saba. The building of the great Dyke of Ma'rib is commonly attributed to their king, Luqmán b. 'Ád, about whom many fables are told. He was surnamed 'The Man of the Vultures' (*Dhu 'l-Nusúr*), because it had been granted to him that he should live as long as seven vultures, one after the other.

[1] Koran, xi, 56–57.

In North Arabia, between the Ḥijáz and Syria, dwelt the kindred race of Thamúd, described in the Koran (vii, 72) as inhabiting houses which they cut for themselves in the rocks. Evidently Muḥammad did not know the true nature of the hewn chambers which are still to be seen at Ḥijr (Madá'in Ṣáliḥ), a week's journey northward from Medína, and which are proved by the Nabaṭæan inscriptions engraved on them to have been sepulchral monuments.[1] Thamúd sinned in the same way as 'Ád, and suffered a like fate. They scouted the prophet Ṣáliḥ, refusing to believe in him unless he should work a miracle. Ṣáliḥ then caused a she-camel big with young to come forth from a rock, and bade them do her no hurt, but one of the miscreants, Qudár the Red (al-Aḥmar), hamstrung and killed her. "Whereupon a great earthquake overtook them with a noise of thunder, and in the morning they lay dead in their houses, flat upon their breasts."[2] The author of this catastrophe became a byword: Arabs say, "More unlucky than the hamstringer of the she-camel," or "than Aḥmar of Thamúd." It should be pointed out that, unlike the 'Ádites, of whom we find no trace in historical times, the Thamúdites are mentioned as still existing by Diodorus Siculus and Ptolemy; and they survived down to the fifth century A.D. in the corps of *equites Thamudeni* attached to the army of the Byzantine emperors.

Legend of Thamúd.

Besides 'Ád and Thamúd, the list of primitive races includes the 'Amálíq (Amalekites)—a purely fictitious term under which the Moslem antiquaries lumped together several peoples of an age long past, *e.g.*, the Canaanites and the Philistines. We hear of Amalekite settlements in the Tihána (Netherland) of Mecca and in other parts of the peninsula. Finally, mention should

'Amálíq.

[1] See Doughty's *Documents Epigraphiques recueillis dans le nord de l'Arabie*, p. 12 sqq.

[2] Koran, vii, 76.

be made of Ṭasm and Jadís, sister tribes of which nothing is recorded except the fact of their destruction and the events that brought it about. The legendary narrative in which these are embodied has some archæological interest as showing the existence in early Arabian society of a barbarous feudal custom, 'le droit du seigneur,' but it is time to pass on to the main subject of this chapter.

Ṭasm and Jadís.

The Pre-islamic history of the Yoqṭánids, or Southern Arabs, on which we now enter, is virtually the history of two peoples, the Sabæans and the Ḥimyarites, who formed the successive heads of a South Arabian empire extending from the Red Sea to the Persian Gulf.

History of the Yoqṭánids.

Saba[1] (Sheba of the Old Testament) is often incorrectly used to denote the whole of Arabia Felix, whereas it was only one, though doubtless the first in power and importance, of several kingdoms, the names and capitals of which are set down in the works of Greek and Roman geographers. However exaggerated may be the glowing accounts that we find there of Sabæan wealth and magnificence, it is certain that Saba was a flourishing commercial state many centuries before the birth of Christ.[2] "Sea-traffic between the ports of East Arabia and India was very early established, and Indian products, especially spices and rare animals (apes and peacocks) were conveyed to the coast of 'Umán. Thence, apparently even in the tenth century B.C., they went overland to the Arabian Gulf, where they

The Sabæans.

[1] Properly Saba' with *hamza*, both syllables being short.

[2] The oldest record of Saba to which a date can be assigned is found in the Assyrian cuneiform inscriptions. We read in the Annals of King Sargon (715 B.C.), "I received the tribute of Pharaoh, the King of Egypt, of Shamsiyya, the Queen of Arabia, of Ithamara the Sabæan—gold, spices, slaves, horses, and camels." Ithamara is identical with Yatha'amar, a name borne by several kings of Saba.

were shipped to Egypt for the use of the Pharaohs and grandees. . . . The difficulty of navigating the Red Sea caused the land route to be preferred for the traffic between Yemen and Syria. From Shabwat (Sabota) in Ḥaḍramawt the caravan road went to Ma'rib (Mariaba), the Sabæan capital, then northward to Macoraba (the later Mecca), and by way of Petra to Gaza on the Mediterranean."[1] The prosperity of the Sabæans lasted until the Indian trade, instead of going overland, began to go by sea along the coast of Ḥaḍramawt and through the straits of Báb al-Mandab. In consequence of this change, which seems to have taken place in the first century A.D., their power gradually declined, a great part of the population was forced to seek new homes in the north, their cities became desolate, and their massive aqueducts crumbled to pieces. We shall see presently that Arabian legend has crystallised the results of a long period of decay into a single fact—the bursting of the Dyke of Ma'rib.

The Ḥimyarites.

The disappearance of the Sabæans left the way open for a younger branch of the same stock, namely, the Ḥimyarites, or, as they are called by classical authors, Homeritæ, whose country lay between Saba and the sea. Under their kings, known as Tubba's, they soon became the dominant power in South Arabia and exercised sway, at least ostensibly, over the northern tribes down to the end of the fifth century A.D., when the latter revolted and, led by Kulayb b. Rabí'a, shook off the suzerainty of Yemen in a great battle at Khazázá.[2] The Ḥimyarites never flourished like the Sabæans. Their maritime situation exposed them more to attack, while the depopulation of the country had seriously weakened their military strength. The Abyssinians—originally colonists from Yemen—made repeated attempts to gain a

[1] A. Müller, *Der Islam im Morgen und Abendland*, vol. i, p. 24 seq.

[2] Nöldeke, however, declares the traditions which represent Kulayb as leading the Rabí'a clans to battle against the combined strength of Yemen to be entirely unhistorical (*Fünf Mo'allaqát*, i, 44).

foothold, and frequently managed to instal governors who were in turn expelled by native princes. Of these Abyssinian viceroys the most famous is Abraha, whose unfortunate expedition against Mecca will be related in due course. Ultimately the Ḥimyarite Empire was reduced to a Persian dependency. It had ceased to exist as a political power about a hundred years before the rise of Islam.

Sources of information.

The chief Arabian sources of information concerning Saba and Ḥimyar are (1) the so-called 'Ḥimyarite' inscriptions, and (2) the traditions, almost entirely of a legendary kind, which are preserved in Muḥammadan literature.

The South Arabic or Sabæan inscriptions.

Although the South Arabic language may have maintained itself sporadically in certain remote districts down to the Prophet's time or even later, it had long ago been superseded as a medium of daily intercourse by the language of the North, the Arabic *par excellence*, which henceforth reigns without a rival throughout the peninsula. The dead language, however, did not wholly perish. Already in the sixth century A.D. the Bedouin rider made his camel kneel down while he stopped to gaze wonderingly at inscriptions in a strange character engraved on walls of rock or fragments of hewn stone, and compared the mysterious, half-obliterated markings to the almost unrecognisable traces of the camping-ground which for him was fraught with tender memories. These inscriptions are often mentioned by Muḥammadan authors, who included them in the term *Musnad*. That some Moslems—probably very few—could not only read the South Arabic alphabet, but were also acquainted with the elementary rules of orthography, appears from a passage in the eighth book of Hamdání's *Iklíl;* but though they might decipher proper names and make out the sense of words here and there, they had no real knowledge of the language. How the inscriptions were discovered anew by the enterprise of European travellers, gradually deciphered and interpreted until they became capable of serving as a basis for historical research, and what results the study of them has produced, this I shall now set forth as briefly as possible. Before doing so it is necessary to explain why instead of 'Ḥimyarite inscriptions' and 'Ḥimyarite language' I have adopted the less familiar designations 'South Arabic' or 'Sabæan.' 'Ḥimyarite' is equally misleading, whether applied to the language of the inscriptions or to the inscriptions themselves. As regards the language, it was spoken in one form or another not by the Ḥimyarites alone, but also by the Sabæans, the Minæans, and all the different peoples of Yemen. Muḥammadans gave the name of 'Ḥimyarite' to the ancient language of Yemen for the simple reason that the Ḥimyarites were the most powerful race in that country during the last centuries preceding Islam. Had all the inscriptions belonged to the period of Ḥimyarite supremacy, they might with some justice have been named after the ruling people; but the fact is that many date from a far earlier age, some going back to the eighth century B.C., perhaps nearly a thousand years before the Ḥimyarite Empire was established. The term 'Sabæan' is less open to objection, for it may fairly be regarded as a national rather than a political denomination. On the whole, however, I prefer 'South Arabic' to either.

Objections to the term 'Ḥimyarite.'

Among the pioneers of exploration in Yemen the first to interest himself in the discovery of inscriptions was Carsten Niebuhr, whose *Beschreibung von Arabien*, published in 1772, conveyed to Europe the report that inscriptions which, though he had not seen them, he conjectured to be 'Ḥimyarite,' existed in the ruins of the once famous city of Ẓafár. On one occasion a Dutchman who had turned Muḥammadan showed him the copy of an inscription in a completely unknown alphabet, but "at that time (he says) being very ill with a violent fever, I had more reason to prepare myself for death

Discovery and decipherment of the South Arabic inscriptions.

than to collect old inscriptions."[1] Thus the opportunity was lost, but curiosity had been awakened, and in 1810 Ulrich Jasper Seetzen discovered and copied several inscriptions in the neighbourhood of Ẓafár. Unfortunately these copies, which had to be made hastily, were very inexact. He also purchased an inscription, which he took away with him and copied at leisure, but his ignorance of the character led him to mistake the depressions in the stone for letters, so that the conclusions he came to were naturally of no value.[2] The first serviceable copies of South Arabic inscriptions were brought to Europe by English officers employed on the survey of the southern and western coasts of Arabia. Lieutenant J. R. Wellsted published the inscriptions of Ḥiṣn Ghuráb and Naqb al-Ḥajar in his *Travels in Arabia* (1838).

Meanwhile Emil Rödiger, Professor of Oriental Languages at Halle, with the help of two manuscripts of the Berlin Royal Library containing 'Ḥimyarite' alphabets, took the first step towards a correct decipherment by refuting the idea, for which De Sacy's authority had gained general acceptance, that the South Arabic script ran from left to right[3]; he showed, moreover, that the end of every word was marked by a straight perpendicular line.[4] Wellsted's inscriptions, together with those which Hulton and Cruttenden brought to light at Ṣan'á, were deciphered by Gesenius and Rödiger working independently (1841). Hitherto England and Germany had shared the

[1] *Op. cit.*, p. 94 seq. An excellent account of the progress made in discovering and deciphering the South Arabic inscriptions down to the year 1841 is given by Rödiger, *Excurs ueber himjaritische Inschriften*, in his German translation of Wellsted's *Travels in Arabia*, vol. ii, p. 368 sqq.

[2] Seetzen's inscriptions were published in *Fundgruben des Orients*, vol. ii (Vienna, 1811), p. 282 sqq. The one mentioned above was afterwards deciphered and explained by Mordtmann in the *Z.D.M.G.*, vol. 31, p. 89 seq.

[3] The oldest inscriptions, however, run from left to right and from right to left alternately (βουστροφηδόν).

[4] *Notiz ueber die himjaritische Schrift nebst doppeltem Alphabet derselben* in *Zeitschrift für die Kunde des Morgenlandes*, vol. i (Göttingen, 1837), p. 332 sqq.

credit of discovery, but a few years later France joined hands with them and was soon leading the way with characteristic brilliance. In 1843 Th. Arnaud, starting from Ṣan'á, succeeded in discovering the ruins of Ma'rib, the ancient Sabæan metropolis, and in copying at the risk of his life between fifty and sixty inscriptions, which were afterwards published in the *Journal Asiatique* and found an able interpreter in Osiander.[1] Still more important were the results of the expedition undertaken in 1870 by the Jewish scholar, Joseph Halévy, who penetrated into the Jawf, or country lying east of Ṣan'á, which no European had traversed before him since 24 B.C., when Ælius Gallus led a Roman army by the same route. After enduring great fatigues and meeting with many perilous adventures, Halévy brought back copies of nearly seven hundred inscriptions.[2] During the last twenty-five years much fresh material has been collected by E. Glaser and Julius Euting, while study of that already existing by Prætorius, Halévy, D. H. Müller, Mordtmann, and other scholars has substantially enlarged our knowledge of the language, history, and religion of South Arabia in the Pre-islamic age.

Neither the names of the Ḥimyarite monarchs, as they appear in the lists drawn up by Muḥammadan historians, nor the order in which these names are arranged can pretend to accuracy. If they are historical persons at all they must have reigned in fairly recent times, perhaps a short while before the rise of Islam, and probably they were unimportant princes whom the legend has thrown back into the ancient epoch, and has invested with heroic attributes. Any one who doubts this has only to compare the modern lists with those which have been made from the material in the inscriptions.[3] D. H.

[1] See Arnaud's *Relation d'un voyage à Mareb (Saba) dans l'Arabie méridionale* in the *Journal Asiatique*, 4th series, vol. v (1845), p. 211 sqq. and p. 309 sqq.

[2] See *Rapport sur une mission archéologique dans le Yémen* in the *Journal Asiatique*, 6th series, vol. xix (1872), pp. 5–98, 129–266, 489–547.

[3] See D. H. Müller, *Die Burgen und Schlösser Südarabiens* in *S.B.W.A.*, vol. 97, p. 981 sqq.

Müller has collected the names of thirty-three Minæan kings. Certain names are often repeated—a proof of the existence of ruling dynasties—and ornamental epithets are usually attached to them. Thus we find Dhamar-'alí Dhirríḥ (Glorious), Yatha'amar Bayyin (Distinguished), Kariba'íl Watár Yuhan'im (Great, Beneficent), Samah'alí Yanúf (Exalted). Moreover, the kings bear different titles corresponding to three distinct periods of South Arabian history, viz., 'Priest-king of Saba' (*Mukarrib Saba*),[1] 'King of Saba' (*Malk Saba*), and 'King of Saba and Raydán.' In this way it is possible to determine approximately the age of the various buildings and inscriptions, and to show that they do not belong, as had hitherto been generally supposed, to the time of Christ, but that in some cases they are at least eight hundred years older.

The historical value of the inscriptions.

How widely the peaceful, commerce-loving people of Saba and Ḥimyar differed in character from the wild Arabs to whom Muḥammad was sent appears most strikingly in their submissive attitude towards their gods, which forms, as Goldziher has remarked, the key-note of the South Arabian monuments.[2] The prince erects a thank-offering to the gods who gave him victory over his enemies; the priest dedicates his children and all his possessions; the warrior who has been blessed with "due man-slayings," or booty, or escape from death records his gratitude, and piously hopes for a continuance of favour. The dead are conceived as living happily under divine protection; they are venerated and sometimes deified.[3] The following inscription,

Votive inscriptions.

[1] The title *Mukarrib* combines the significations of prince and priest.

[2] Goldziher, *Muhammedanische Studien*, Part I, p. 3.

[3] See F. Prætorius, *Unsterblichkeitsglaube und Heiligenverehrung bei den Himyaren* in *Z.D.M.G.*, vol. 27, p. 645. Hubert Grimme has given an interesting sketch of the religious ideas and customs of the Southern Arabs in *Weltgeschichte in Karakterbildern : Mohammed* (Munich, 1904), p. 29 sqq.

translated by Lieut.-Col. W. F. Prideaux, is a typical example of its class :—

"Sa'd-iláh and his sons, Benú Marthad^{im}, have endowed Il-Maḳah of Hirrán with this tablet, because Il-Maḳah, lord of Awwám Dhú-'Irán Alú, has favourably heard the prayer addressed to him, and has consequently heard the Benú Marthad^{im} when they offered the first-fruits of their fertile lands of Arhaḳim in the presence of Il-Maḳah of Hirrán, and Il-Maḳah of Hirrán has favourably heard the prayer addressed to him that he would protect the plains and meadows and this tribe in their habitations, in consideration of the frequent gifts throughout the year ; and truly his (Sa'd-iláh's) sons will descend to Arhaḳim, and they will indeed sacrifice in the two shrines of 'Athtor and Shams^{im}, and there shall be a sacrifice in Hirrán—both in order that Il-Maḳah may afford protection to those fields of Bin Marthad^{im} as well as that he may favourably listen—and in the sanctuary of Il-Maḳah of Ḥarwat, and therefore may he keep them in safety according to the sign in which Sa'd-iláh was instructed, the sign which he saw in the sanctuary of Il-Maḳah of Na'mán ; and as for Il-Maḳah of Hirrán, he has protected those fertile lands of Arhaḳim from hail and from all misfortune (*or,* from cold and from all extreme heat).[1]

In concluding this very inadequate account of the South Arabic inscriptions I must claim the indulgence of my readers, who are aware how difficult it is to write clearly and accurately upon any subject without first-hand knowledge, in particular when the results of previous research are continually being transformed by new workers in the same field.

Literary sources.

Fortunately we possess a considerable literary supplement to these somewhat austere and meagre remains. Our knowledge of South Arabian geography, antiquities, and legendary history is largely derived from the works of two natives of Yemen, who were filled with enthusiasm for its ancient glories, and whose writings, though different as fact and fable, are from the present point of view equally instructive—Ḥasan b. Aḥmad al-Hamdání and

[1] *Transactions of the Society of Biblical Archæology*, vol. 5, p. 409.

Nashwán b. Sa'íd al-Ḥimyarí. Besides an excellent geography of Arabia (*Ṣifatu Jazírat al-'Arab*), which has been edited by D. H. Müller, Hamdání left a great work on the history and antiquities of Yemen, entitled *al-Iklíl* ('The Crown'), and divided into ten books under the following heads :—[1]

Hamdání († 945 A.D.).

Book I. *Compendium of the beginning and origins of genealogy.*
Book II. *Genealogy of the descendants of al-Hamaysa' b. Ḥimyar.*
Book III. *Concerning the pre-eminent qualities of Qaḥṭán.*
Book IV. *Concerning the first period of history down to the reign of Tubba' Abú Karib.*
Book V. *Concerning the middle period from the accession of As'ad Tubba' to the reign of Dhú Nuwás.*
Book VI. *Concerning the last period down to the rise of Islam.*
Book VII. *Criticism of false traditions and absurd legends.*
Book VIII. *Concerning the castles, cities, and tombs of the Ḥimyarites; the extant poetry of 'Alqama,[2] the elegies, the inscriptions, and other matters.*
Book IX. *Concerning the proverbs and wisdom of the Ḥimyarites in the Ḥimyarite language, and concerning the alphabet of the inscriptions.*
Book X. *Concerning the genealogy of Ḥáshid and Bakíl* (the two principal tribes of Hamdán).

The same intense patriotism which caused Hamdání to devote himself to scientific research inspired Nashwán b. Sa'íd, who descended on the father's side from one of the ancient princely families of Yemen, to recall the legendary past and become the laureate of a long vanished and well-nigh forgotten empire. In 'The Ḥimyarite Ode' (*al-Qaṣídatu 'l-Ḥimyariyya*) he sings the might and grandeur of the monarchs who ruled over his people, and moralises in true Muḥammadan spirit upon the

Nashwán b. Sa'íd al-Ḥimyarí († 1177 A.D.).

[1] This table of contents is quoted by D. H. Müller (*Südarabische Studien*, p. 108, n. 2) from the title-page of the British Museum MS. of the eighth book of the *Iklíl*. No complete copy of the work is known to exist, but considerable portions of it are preserved in the British Museum and in the Berlin Royal Library.

[2] The poet 'Alqama b. Dhí Jadan, whose verses are often cited in the commentary on the 'Ḥimyarite Ode.'

fleetingness of life and the futility of human ambition.[1] Accompanying the Ode, which has little value except as a comparatively unfalsified record of royal names,[2] is a copious historical commentary either by Nashwán himself, as Von Kremer thinks highly probable, or by some one who lived about the same time. Those for whom history represents an aggregate of naked facts would find nothing to the purpose in this commentary, where threads of truth are almost inextricably interwoven with fantastic and fabulous embroideries. A literary form was first given to such legends by the professional story-tellers of early Islam. One of these, the South Arabian 'Abíd b. Sharya, visited Damascus by command of the Caliph Mu'áwiya I, who questioned him "concerning the ancient traditions, the kings of the Arabs and other races, the cause of the confusion of tongues, and the history of the dispersion of mankind in the various countries of the world,"[3] and gave orders that his answers should be put together in writing and published under his name. This work, of which unfortunately no copy has come down to us, was entitled 'The Book of the Kings and the History of the Ancients' (*Kitábu 'l-Mulúk wa-akhbáru 'l-Máḍín*). Mas'údí (†956 A.D.) speaks of it as a well-known book, enjoying a wide circulation.[4] It was used by the commentator of the Ḥimyarite Ode, either at first hand or through the medium of Hamdání's *Iklíl*. We may regard it, like the commentary itself, as a historical romance in which most of the characters and some of the events are real, adorned with fairy-tales, fictitious verses,

'Abíd b. Sharya.

[1] *Die Himjarische Kasideh* herausgegeben und übersetzt von Alfred von Kremer (Leipzig, 1865). *The Lay of the Himyarites*, by W. F. Prideaux (Sehore, 1879).

[2] Nashwán was a philologist of some repute. His great dictionary, the *Shamsu 'l-'Ulúm*, is a valuable aid to those engaged in the study of South Arabian antiquities. It has been used by D. H. Müller to fix the correct spelling of proper names which occur in the Ḥimyarite Ode (*Z.D.M.G.*, vol. 29, p. 620 sqq.; *Südarabische Studien*, p. 143 sqq.).

[3] *Fihrist*, p. 89, l. 26.

[4] *Murúju 'l-Dhahab*, ed. by Barbier de Meynard, vol. iv, p. 89.

and such entertaining matter as a man of learning and story-teller by trade might naturally be expected to introduce. Among the few remaining Muḥammadan authors who bestowed special attention on the Pre-islamic period of South Arabian history, I shall mention here only Ḥamza of Iṣfahán, the eighth book of whose Annals (finished in 961 A.D.) provides a useful sketch, with brief chronological details, of the Tubba'ʻs or Ḥimyarite kings of Yemen.

Ḥamza of Iṣfahán.

Qaḥṭán, the ancestor of the Southern Arabs, was succeeded by his son Yaʻrub, who is said to have been the first to use the Arabic language, and the first to receive the salutations with which the Arabs were accustomed to address their kings, viz., "*Inʻim ṣabáḥan*" ("Good morning!") and "*Abayta 'l-laʻna*" ("Mayst thou avoid malediction!"). His grandson, ʻAbd Shams Saba, is named as the founder of Ma'rib and the builder of the famous Dyke, which, according to others, was constructed by Luqmán b. ʻÁd. Saba had two sons, Ḥimyar and Kahlán. Before his death he deputed the sovereign authority to Ḥimyar, and the task of protecting the frontiers and making war upon the enemy to Kahlán. Thus Ḥimyar obtained the lordship, assumed the title Abú Ayman, and abode in the capital city of the realm, while Kahlán took over the defence of the borders and the conduct of war.[1] Omitting the long series of mythical Sabæan kings, of whom the legend has little or nothing to relate, we now come to an event which fixed itself ineffaceably in the memory of the Arabs, and which is known in their traditions as *Saylu 'l-ʻArim*, or the Flood of the Dyke.

Yaʻrub.

Ḥimyar and Kahlán.

[1] Von Kremer, *Die Südarabische Sage*, p. 56. Possibly, as he suggests (p. 115), the story may be a symbolical expression of the fact that the Sabæans were divided into two great tribes, Ḥimyar and Kahlán, the former of which held the chief power.

Some few miles south-west of Ma'rib the mountains draw together leaving a gap, through which flows the River Adana. During the summer its bed is often dry, but in the rainy season the water rushes down with such violence that it becomes impassable. In order to protect the city from floods, and partly also for purposes of irrigation, the inhabitants built a dam of solid masonry, which, long after it had fallen into ruin, struck the imagination of Muḥammad, and was reckoned by Moslems among the wonders of the world.[1] That their historians have clothed the bare fact of its destruction in ample robes of legendary circumstance is not surprising, but renders abridgment necessary.[2]

The Dam of Ma'rib.

Towards the end of the third century of our era, or possibly at an earlier epoch,[3] the throne of Ma'rib was temporarily occupied by 'Amr b. 'Ámir Má' al-Samá, surnamed Muzayqiyá.[4] His wife, Ẓarífa, was skilled in the art of divination. She dreamed dreams and saw visions which announced the impending calamity. "Go to the Dyke," she said to her husband, who doubted her clairvoyance, "and if thou see a rat digging holes in the Dyke with its paws and moving huge boulders with its hind-legs, be assured that the woe hath come upon us." So 'Amr went to

Its destruction announced by portents.

[1] *Cf.* Koran xxxiv, 14 sqq. The existing ruins have been described by Arnaud in the *Journal Asiatique*, 7th series, vol. 3 (1874), p. 3 sqq.

[2] I follow Mas'údí, *Murúju 'l-Dhahab* (ed. by Barbier de Meynard), vol. iii, p. 378 sqq., and Nuwayrí in Reiske's *Primæ lineæ Historiæ Rerum Arabicarum*, p. 166 sqq.

[3] The story of the migration from Ma'rib, as related below, may have some historical basis, but the Dam itself was not finally destroyed until long afterwards. Inscriptions carved on the existing ruins show that it was more or less in working order down to the middle of the sixth century A.D. The first recorded flood took place in 447–450, and on another occasion (in 539–542) the Dam was partially reconstructed by Abraha, the Abyssinian viceroy of Yemen. See E. Glaser, *Zwei Inschriften über den Dammbruch von Mârib* (*Mitteilungen der Vorderasiatischen Gesellschaft*, 1897, 6).

[4] He is said to have gained this sobriquet from his custom of tearing to pieces (*mazaqa*) every night the robe which he had worn during the day.

the Dyke and looked carefully, and lo, there was a rat moving an enormous rock which fifty men could not have rolled from its place. Convinced by this and other prodigies that the Dyke would soon burst and the land be laid waste, he resolved to sell his possessions and depart with his family; and, lest conduct so extraordinary should arouse suspicion, he had recourse to the following stratagem. He invited the chief men of the city to a splendid feast, which, in accordance with a preconcerted plan, was interrupted by a violent altercation between himself and his son (or, as others relate, an orphan who had been brought up in his house). Blows were exchanged, and 'Amr cried out, "O shame! on the day of my glory a stripling has insulted me and struck my face." He swore that he would put his son to death, but the guests entreated him to show mercy, until at last he gave way. "But by God," he exclaimed, "I will no longer remain in a city where I have suffered this indignity. I will sell my lands and my stock." Having successfully got rid of his encumbrances—for there was no lack of buyers eager to take him at his word—'Amr informed the people of the danger with which they were threatened, and set out from Ma'rib at the head of a great multitude. Gradually the waters made a breach in the Dyke and swept over the country, spreading devastation far and wide. Hence the proverb *Dhahabú* (or *tafarraqú*) *aydí Saba*, "They departed" (or "dispersed") "like the people of Saba." [1]

This deluge marks an epoch in the history of South Arabia.

Fall of the Sabæan Empire.

The waters subside, the land returns to cultivation and prosperity, but Ma'rib lies desolate, and the Sabæans have disappeared for ever, except "to point a moral or adorn a tale." Al-A'shá sang:—

Metre *Mutaqárib*: (⏑ — ⏓ | ⏑ — ⏓ | ⏑ — ⏓ | ⏑ —).

[1] Freytag, *Arabum Proverbia*, vol. i, p. 497.

"Let this warn whoever a warning will take—
And Ma'rib withal, which the Dam fortified.
Of marble did Ḥimyar construct it, so high,
The waters recoiled when to reach it they tried.
It watered their acres and vineyards, and hour
By hour, did a portion among them divide.
So lived they in fortune and plenty until
Therefrom turned away by a ravaging tide.
Then wandered their princes and noblemen through
Mirage-shrouded deserts that baffle the guide."[1]

The poet's reference to Ḥimyar is not historically accurate. It was only after the destruction of the Dyke and the dispersion of the Sabæans who built it[2] that the Ḥimyarites, with their capital Ẓafár (at a later period, Ṣan'á) became the rulers of Yemen.

The first Tubba', by which name the Ḥimyarite kings are known to Muḥammadan writers, was Ḥárith, called al-Rá'ish, *i.e.*, the Featherer, because he 'feathered' his people's nest with the booty which he brought home as a conqueror from India and Ádharbayján.[3] Of the Tubba's who come after him some obviously owe their place in the line of Ḥimyar to genealogists whose respect for the Koran was greater than their critical acumen. Such a man of straw is Ṣa'b Dhu 'l-Qarnayn (Ṣa'b the Two-horned).

The Tubba's.

The following verses show that he is a double of the mysterious Dhu 'l-Qarnayn of Koranic legend, supposed by most commentators to be identical with Alexander the Great[4]:—

Dhu 'l-Qarnayn.

[1] Hamdání, *Iklíl*, bk. viii, edited by D. H. Müller in *S.B.W.A.* (Vienna, 1881), vol. 97, p. 1037. The verses are quoted with some textual differences by Yáqút, *Mu'jam al-Buldán*, ed. by Wüstenfeld, vol. iv, 387, and Ibn Hishám, p. 9.

[2] The following inscription is engraved on one of the stone cylinders described by Arnaud: "Yatha'amar Bayyin, son of Samah'alí Yanúf, Prince of Saba, caused the mountain Balaq to be pierced and erected the flood-gates (called) Raḥab for convenience of irrigation." I translate after D. H. Müller, *loc. laud.*, p. 965.

[3] The words *Ḥimyar* and *Tubba'* do not occur at all in the older inscriptions, and very seldom even in those of a more recent date.

[4] See Koran, xviii, 82–98.

"Ours the realm of Dhu 'l-Qarnayn the glorious,
Realm like his was never won by mortal king.
Followed he the Sun to view its setting
When it sank into the sombre ocean-spring;
Up he clomb to see it rise at morning,
From within its mansion when the East it fired;
All day long the horizons led him onward,[1]
All night through he watched the stars and never tired.
Then of iron and of liquid metal
He prepared a rampart not to be o'erpassed,
Gog and Magog there he threw in prison
Till on Judgment Day they shall awake at last."[2]

Bilqís.

Similarly, among the Tubba's we find the Queen of Sheba, whose adventures with Solomon are related in the twenty-seventh chapter of the Koran. Although Muḥammad himself did not mention her name or lineage, his interpreters were equal to the occasion and revealed her as Bilqís, the daughter of Sharáḥíl (Sharaḥbíl).

The national hero of South Arabian legend is the Tubba'

[1] Dhu 'l-Qarnayn is described as "the measurer of the earth" (*Massáḥu 'l-arḍ*) by Hamdání, *Jazíratu 'l-'Arab*, p. 46, l. 10. If I may step for a moment outside the province of literary history to discuss the mythology of these verses, it seems to me more than probable that Dhu 'l-Qarnayn is a personification of the Sabæan divinity 'Athtar, who represents "sweet Hesper-Phosphor, double name" (see D. H. Müller in *S.B.W.A.*, vol. 97, p. 973 seq.). The Minæan inscriptions have "'Athtar of the setting and 'Athtar of the rising" (*ibid.*, p. 1033). Moreover, in the older inscriptions 'Athtar and Almaqa are always mentioned together; and Almaqa, which according to Hamdání is the name of Venus (*al-Zuhara*), was identified by Arabian archæologists with Bilqís. For *qarn* in the sense of 'ray' or 'beam' see Goldziher, *Abhand. zur Arab. Philologie*, Part I, p. 114. I think there is little doubt that Dhu 'l-Qarnayn and Bilqís may be added to the examples (*ibid.*, p. 111 sqq.) of that peculiar conversion by which many heathen deities were enabled to maintain themselves under various disguises within the pale of Islam.

[2] The Arabic text will be found in Von Kremer's *Altarabische Gedichte ueber die Volkssage von Jemen*, p. 15 (No. viii, l. 6 sqq.). Ḥassán b. Thábit, the author of these lines, was contemporary with Muḥammad, to whose cause he devoted what poetical talent he possessed. In the verses immediately preceding those translated above he claims to be a descendant of Qaḥṭán.

Asʿad Kámil, or, as he is sometimes called, Abú Karib. Even at the present day, says Von Kremer, his memory is kept alive, and still haunts the ruins of his palace at Ẓafár. "No one who reads the Ballad of his Adventures or the words of exhortation which he addressed on his death-bed to his son Ḥassán can escape from the conviction that here we have to do with genuine folk-poetry—fragments of a South Arabian legendary cycle, the beginnings of which undoubtedly reach back to a high antiquity."[1] I translate here the former of these pieces, which may be entitled

As'ad Kámil.

THE BALLAD OF THE THREE WITCHES.[2]

"Time brings to pass full many a wonder
Whereof the lesson thou must ponder.
Whilst all to thee seems ordered fair,
Lo, Fate hath wrought confusion there.
Against a thing foredoomed to be
Nor cunning nor caution helpeth thee.
Now a marvellous tale will I recite;
Trust me to know and tell it aright!

Once on a time was a boy of Asd
Who became the king of the land at last,
Born in Hamdán, a villager;
The name of that village was Khamir.
This lad in the pride of youth defied
His friends, and they with scorn replied.
None guessed his worth till he was grown
Ready to spring.

[1] Von Kremer, *Die Südarabische Sage*, p. vii of the Introduction.

[2] A prose translation is given by Von Kremer, *ibid.*, p. 78 sqq. The Arabic text which he published afterwards in *Altarabische Gedichte ueber die Volkssage von Jemen*, p. 18 sqq., is corrupt in some places and incorrect in others. I have followed Von Kremer's interpretation except when it seemed to me to be manifestly untenable. The reader will have no difficulty in believing that this poem was meant to be recited by a wandering minstrel to the hearers that gathered round him at nightfall. It may well be the composition of one of those professional story-tellers who flourished in the first century after the Flight, such as 'Abíd b. Sharya (see p. 13 *supra*), or Yazíd b. Rabí'a b. Mufarrigh († 688 A.D.), who is said to have invented the poems and romances of the Ḥimyarite kings (*Aghání*, xvii, 52).

One morn, alone
On Hinwam hill he was sore afraid.[1]
(His people knew not where he strayed;
They had seen him only yesternight,
For his youth and wildness they held him light.
The wretches! Him they never missed
Who had been their glory had they wist).

O the fear that fell on his heart when he
Saw beside him the witches three!
The eldest came with many a brew—
In some was blood, blood-dark their hue.
'Give me the cup!' he shouted bold;
'Hold, hold!' cried she, but he would not hold.
She gave him the cup, nor he did shrink
Tho' he reeled as he drained the magic drink.

Then the second yelled at him. Her he faced
Like a lion with anger in his breast.
'These be our steeds, come mount,' she cried,
'For asses are worst of steeds to ride.'
''Tis sooth,' he answered, and slipped his flank
O'er a hyena lean and lank,
But the brute so fiercely flung him away,
With deep, deep wounds on the earth he lay.
Then came the youngest and tended him
On a soft bed, while her eyes did swim
In tears; but he averted his face
And sought a rougher resting-place:
Such paramour he deemed too base.
And himthought, in anguish lying there,
That needles underneath him were.[2]

Now when they had marked his mien so bold,
Victory in all things they foretold.
'The wars, O As'ad, waged by thee
Shall heal mankind of misery.

---

[1] Instead of Hinwam the original has Hayyúm, for which Von Kremer reads Ahnúm. But see Hamdání, *Jazíratu 'l-'Arab*, p. 193, last line and fol.

[2] I read *al-jahdi* for *al-jahli*.

Thy sword and spear the foe shall rue
When his gashes let the daylight through;
And blood shall flow on every hand
What time thou marchest from land to land.
By us be counselled: stay not within
Khamir, but go to Ẓafár and win!
To thee shall dalliance ne'er be dear,
Thy foes shall see thee before they hear.
Desire moved to encounter thee,
Noble prince, us witches three.
Not jest, but earnest on thee we tried,
And well didst thou the proof abide.'

As'ad went home and told his folk
What he had seen, but no heed they took.
On the tenth day he set out again
And fared to Ẓafár with thoughts in his brain.
There fortune raised him to high renown:
None swifter to strike ever wore a crown.[1]

* * * * *

Thus found we the tale in memory stored.
And Almighty is the Lord.
Praise be to God who liveth aye,
The Glorious to whom all men pray!"

Legend makes As'ad the hero of a brilliant expedition to Persia, where he defeated the general sent against him by the Arsacids, and penetrated to the Caspian Sea. On his way home he marched through the Ḥijáz, and having learned that his son, whom he left behind in Medína, had been treacherously murdered, he resolved to take a terrible vengeance on the people of that city.

"Now while the Tubba' was carrying on war against them, there came to him two Jewish Rabbins of the Banú Qurayẓa, men deep in knowledge, who when they heard that he wished to destroy the

---

[1] I omit the following verses, which tell how an old woman of Medína came to King As'ad, imploring him to avenge her wrongs, and how he gathered an innumerable army, routed his enemies, and returned to Ẓafár in triumph.

city and its people, said to him: 'O King, forbear! Verily, if thou wilt accept nothing save that which thou desirest, an intervention will be made betwixt thee and the city, and we are not sure but that sudden chastisement may befall thee.' 'Why so?' he asked. They answered: ''Tis the place of refuge of a prophet who in the after time shall go forth from the sacred territory of Quraysh: it shall be his abode and his home.' So the king refrained himself, for he saw that those two had a particular knowledge, and he was pleased with what they told him. On departing from Medína he followed them in their religion.[1] . . . And he turned his face towards Mecca, that being his way to Yemen, and when he was between 'Usfán and Amaj some Hudhalites came to him and said: 'O King, shall we not guide thee to a house of ancient treasure which the kings before thee neglected, wherein are pearls and emeralds and chrysolites and gold and silver?' He said, 'Yea.' They said: 'It is a temple at Mecca which those who belong to it worship and in which they pray.' Now the Hudhalites wished to destroy him thereby, knowing that destruction awaited the king who should seek to violate its precinct. So on comprehending what they proposed, he sent to the two Rabbins to ask them about the affair. They replied: 'These folk intend naught but to destroy thee and thine army; we wot not of any house in the world that God hath chosen for Himself, save this. If thou do that to which they invite thee, thou and those with thee will surely perish together.' He said: 'What then is it ye bid me do when I come there?' They said: 'Thou wilt do as its people do—make the circuit thereof, and magnify and honour it, and shave thy head, and humble thyself before it, until thou go forth from its precinct.' He said: 'And what hinders you from doing that yourselves?' 'By God,' said they, 'it is the temple of our father Abraham, and verily it is even as we told thee, but we are debarred therefrom by the idols which its people have set up around it and by the blood-offerings which they make beside it; for they are vile polytheists,' or words to the same effect. The king perceived that their advice was good and their tale true. He ordered the Hudhalites to approach, and cut off their hands and feet. Then he continued his march to Mecca, where he made the circuit of the temple, sacrificed camels, and shaved his head. According to what is told, he stayed six days at Mecca, feasting the inhabitants with the flesh of camels

As'ad Kámil and the two Rabbins of Medína.

As'ad Kámil at Mecca.

---

[1] Ibn Hishám, p. 13, l. 14 sqq.

and letting them drink honey.[1] . . . Then he moved out with his troops in the direction of Yemen, the two Rabbins accompanying him; and on entering Yemen he called on his subjects to adopt the religion which he himself had embraced, but they refused unless the question were submitted to the ordeal of fire which at that time existed in Yemen; for as the Yemenites say, there was in their country a fire that gave judgment between them in their disputes: it devoured the wrong-doer but left the injured person unscathed. The Yemenites therefore came forward with their idols and whatever else they used as a means of drawing nigh unto God, and the two Rabbins came forward with their scriptures hung on their necks like necklaces, and both parties seated themselves at the place from which the fire was wont to issue. And the fire blazed up, and the Yemenites shrank back from it as it approached them, and were afraid, but the bystanders urged them on and bade them take courage. So they held out until the fire enveloped them and consumed the idols and images and the men of Ḥimyar, the bearers thereof; but the Rabbins came forth safe and sound, their brows moist with sweat, and the scriptures were still hanging on their necks. Thereupon the Ḥimyarites consented to adopt the king's religion, and this was the cause of Judaism being established in Yemen."[2]

He seeks to establish Judaism in Yemen.

The ordeal of fire.

The poem addressed to his son and successor, Ḥassán, which tradition has put into his mouth, is a sort of last will and testament, of which the greater part is taken up with an account of his conquests and with glorification of his family and himself.[3] Nearly all that we find in the way of maxims or injunctions suitable to the solemn occasion is contained in the following verses:—

As'ad's farewell to his son.

"O Ḥassán, the hour of thy father's death has arrived at last:
Look to thyself ere yet the time for looking is past.
Oft indeed are the mighty abased, and often likewise
Are the base exalted: such is Man who is born and dies.

---

[1] Ibn Hishám, p. 15, l. 1 sqq. [2] *Ibid.*, p. 17, l. 2 sqq.

[3] Arabic text in Von Kremer's *Altarabische Gedichte ueber die Volkssage von Jemen*, p. 20 seq.; prose translation by the same author in *Die Südarabische Sage*, p. 84 sqq.

Bid ye Ḥimyar know that standing erect would I buried be,
And have my wine-skins and Yemen robes in the tomb with
 me.[1]
And hearken thou to my Sibyl, for surely can she foresay
The truth, and safe in her keeping is castle Ghaymán aye.[2]

The castles of Yemen.

In connection with Ghaymán a few words may be added respecting the castles in Yemen, of which the ruined skeletons rising from solitary heights seem still to frown defiance upon the passing traveller. Two thousand years ago, and probably long before, they were occupied by powerful barons, more or less independent, who in later times, when the Ḥimyarite Empire had begun to decline, always elected, and occasionally deposed, their royal master. Of these castles the geographer Hamdání has given a detailed account in the eighth book of his great work on the history and antiquities of Yemen entitled the *Iklíl*, or 'Crown.'[3] The oldest and most celebrated was Ghumdán, the citadel of Ṣanʿá. It is described as a huge edifice of twenty stories, each story ten cubits high. The four façades were built with stone of different colours, white, black, green, and red. On the top story was a chamber which had windows of marble framed with ebony and planewood. Its roof was a slab of pellucid marble, so that when the lord of Ghumdán lay on his couch he saw the birds fly overhead, and could distinguish a raven from a kite. At each corner stood a brazen lion, and when the wind blew

Ghumdán.

[1] The second half of this verse is corrupt. Von Kremer translates (in his notes to the Arabic text, p. 26): "And bury with me the camel stallions *(al-khílán)* and the slaves *(al-ruqqán)*." Apart, however, from the fact that *ruqqán* (plural of *raqíq*) is not mentioned by the lexicographers, it seems highly improbable that the king would have commanded such a barbarity. I therefore take *khílán* (plural of *khál*) in the meaning of 'soft stuffs of Yemen,' and read *zuqqán* (plural of *ziqq*).

[2] Ghaymán or Miqláb, a castle near Ṣanʿá, in which the Ḥimyarite kings were buried.

[3] The text and translation of this section of the *Iklíl* have been published by D. H. Müller in *S.B.W.A.*, vols. 94 and 97 (Vienna, 1879–1880).

it entered the hollow interior of the effigies and made a sound like the roaring of lions.

The adventure of As'ad Kámil with the three witches must have recalled to every reader certain scenes in *Macbeth*. Curiously enough, in the history of his son Ḥassán an incident is related which offers a striking parallel to the march of Birnam Wood. Ṭasm and Jadís have already been mentioned. On the massacre of the former tribe by the latter, a single Ṭasmite named Ribáḥ b. Murra made his escape and took refuge with the Tubba' Ḥassán, whom he persuaded to lead an expedition against the murderers. Now Ribáḥ's sister had married a man of Jadís. Her name was Zarqá'u 'l-Yamáma—*i.e.*, the Blue-eyed Woman of Yamáma—and she had such piercing sight that she was able to descry an army thirty miles away. Ḥassán therefore bade his horsemen hold in front of them leafy branches which they tore down from the trees. They advanced thus hidden, and towards evening, when they had come within a day's journey, Zarqá said to her people: "I see trees marching." No one believed her until it was too late. Next morning Ḥassán fell upon them and put the whole tribe to the sword.

Zarqá'u 'l-Yamáma.

The warlike expeditions to which Ḥassán devoted all his energy were felt as an intolerable burden by the chiefs of Ḥimyar, who formed a plot to slay him and set his brother 'Amr on the throne. 'Amr was at first unwilling to lend himself to their designs, but ultimately his scruples were overcome, and he stabbed the Tubba' with his own hand. The assassin suffered a terrible punishment. Sleep deserted him, and in his remorse he began to execute the conspirators one after another. There was, however, a single chief called Dhú Ru'ayn, who had remained loyal and had done his best to save 'Amr from the guilt of fratricide. Finding his efforts fruitless, he requested 'Amr to take charge of a sealed

Ḥassán murdered by his brother.

Dhú Ru'ayn.

paper which he brought with him, and to keep it in a safe place until he should ask for it. 'Amr consented and thought no more of the matter. Afterwards, imagining that Dhú Ru'ayn had joined in the fatal plot, he gave orders for his execution. "How!" exclaimed Dhú Ru'ayn, "did not I tell thee what the crime involved?" and he asked for the sealed writing, which was found to contain these verses—

> "O fool to barter sleep for waking! Blest
> Is he alone whose eyelids close in rest.
> Hath Ḥimyar practised treason, yet 'tis plain
> That God forgiveness owes to Dhú Ru'ayn.[1]"

On reading this, 'Amr recognised that Dhú Ru'ayn had spoken the truth, and he spared his life.

With 'Amr the Tubba' dynasty comes to an end. The succeeding kings were elected by eight of the most powerful barons, who in reality were independent princes, each ruling in his strong castle over as many vassals and retainers as he could bring into subjection. During this period the Abyssinians conquered at least some part of the country, and Christian viceroys were sent by the Najáshí (Negus) to govern it in his name. At last Dhú Nuwás, a descendant of the Tubba' As'ad Kámil, crushed the rebellious barons and made himself unquestioned monarch of Yemen. A fanatical adherent of

Dhú Nuwás.

Judaism, he resolved to stamp out Christianity in Najrán, where it is said to have been introduced from Syria by a holy man called Faymiyún (Phemion). The Ḥimyarites flocked to his standard, not so much from religious motives as from hatred of the Abyssinians. The pretended murder of two Jewish children gave Dhú Nuwás a plausible *casus belli*. He marched against Najrán with an overwhelming

Massacre of the Christians in Najrán (523 A.D.).

force, entered the city, and bade the inhabitants choose between Judaism and death. Many perished by the sword; the rest were thrown into a trench which the king ordered to be dug and filled with

[1] *Aghání*, xx, 8, l. 14 seq.

blazing fire. Nearly a hundred years later, when Muḥammad was being sorely persecuted, he consoled and encouraged his followers by the example of the Christians of Najrán, who suffered "*for no other reason but that they believed in the mighty, the glorious God.*"[1] Dhú Nuwás paid dearly for his triumph. Daws Dhú Tha'labán, one of those who escaped from the massacre, fled to the Byzantine emperor and implored him, as the head of Christendom, to assist them in obtaining vengeance. Justinus accordingly wrote a letter to the Najáshí, desiring him to take action, and ere long an Abyssinian army, 70,000 strong, under the command of Aryáṭ, disembarked in Yemen. Dhú Nuwás could not count on the loyalty of the Ḥimyarite nobles; his troops melted away. "When he saw the fate that had befallen himself and his people, he turned to the sea and setting spurs to his horse, rode through the shallows until he reached the deep water. Then he plunged into the waves and nothing more of him was seen."[2]

Death of Dhú Nuwás.

Thus died, or thus at any rate should have died, the last representative of the long line of Ḥimyarite kings. Henceforth Yemen appears in Pre-islamic history only as an Abyssinian dependency or as a Persian protectorate. The events now to be related form the prologue to a new drama in which South Arabia, so far from being the centre of interest, plays an almost insignificant rôle.[3]

On the death of Dhú Nuwás, the Abyssinian general Aryáṭ continued his march through Yemen. He slaughtered a third part of the males, laid waste a third part of the land, and sent a third part of the women and children to the Najáshí as slaves. Having reduced the Yemenites to submission and re-established order, he held the position of viceroy

Yemen under Abyssinian rule.

---

[1] Koran, lxxxv, 4 sqq. [2] Ṭabarí, i, 927, l. 19 sqq.

[3] The following narrative is abridged from Ṭabarí, i, 928, l. 2 sqq. = Nöldeke, *Geschichte der Perser and Araber zur Zeit der Sasaniden*, p. 192 sqq.

for several years. Then mutiny broke out in the Abyssinian army of occupation, and his authority was disputed by an officer, named Abraha. When the rivals faced each other, Abraha said to Aryáṭ: "What will it avail you to engage the Abyssinians in a civil war that will leave none of them alive? Fight it out with me, and let the troops follow the victor." His challenge being accepted, Abraha stepped forth. He was a short, fleshy man, compactly built, a devout Christian, while Aryáṭ was big, tall, and handsome. When the duel began, Aryáṭ thrust his spear with the intention of piercing Abraha's brain, but it glanced off his forehead, slitting his eyelid, nose, and lip—hence the name, *al-Ashram*, by which Abraha was afterwards known; and ere he could repeat the blow, a youth in Abraha's service, called 'Atwada, who was seated on a hillock behind his master, sprang forward and dealt him a mortal wound. Thus Abraha found himself commander-in-chief of the Abyssinian army, but the Najáshí was enraged and swore not to rest until he set foot on the soil of Yemen and cut off the rebel's forelock. On hearing this, Abraha wrote to the Najáshi: "O King, Aryáṭ was thy servant even as I am. We quarrelled over thy command, both of us owing allegiance to thee, but I had more strength than he to command the Abyssinians and keep discipline and exert authority. When I heard of the king's oath, I shore my head, and now I send him a sack of the earth of Yemen that he may put it under his feet and fulfil his oath." The Najáshí answered this act of submission by appointing Abraha to be his viceroy. . . . Then Abraha built the church (*al-Qalís*) at Ṣan'á, the like of which was not to be seen at that time in the whole world, and wrote to the Najáshí that he would not be content until he had diverted thither every pilgrim in Arabia. This letter made much talk, and a man of the Banú Fuqaym, one of those who arranged the calendar, was angered by what he learned of Abraha's purpose; so he went into the church and defiled it. When Abraha heard that the author of the outrage belonged to the people of the Temple in Mecca, and that he meant to show thereby his scorn and contempt for the new foundation, he waxed wroth and swore that he would march against the Temple and lay it in ruins.

Abraha and Aryáṭ.

Abraha viceroy of Yemen.

The disastrous failure of this expedition, which took place in the year of the Elephant (570 A.D.), did not at once free Yemen from the Abyssinian yoke. The sons of Abraha, Yaksúm and Masrúq, bore heavily on the Arabs. Seeing no help among his own people, a noble Ḥimyarite named Sayf b. Dhí Yazan resolved to seek foreign intervention. His choice lay between the Byzantine and Persian empires, and he first betook himself to Constantinople. Disappointed there, he induced the Arab king of Ḥíra, who was under Persian suzerainty, to present him at the court of Madá'in (Ctesiphon). How he won audience of the Sásánian monarch, Núshírwán, surnamed the Just, and tempted him by an ingenious trick to raise a force of eight hundred condemned felons, who were set free and shipped to Yemen under the command of an aged general; how they literally 'burned their boats' and, drawing courage from despair, routed the Abyssinian host and made Yemen a satrapy of Persia[1]—this forms an almost epic narrative, which I have omitted here (apart from considerations of space) because it belongs to Persian rather than to Arabian literary history, being probably based, as Nöldeke has suggested, on traditions handed down by the Persian conquerors who settled in Yemen to their aristocratic descendants whom the Arabs called *al-Abná* (the Sons) or *Banu 'l-Aḥrár* (Sons of the Noble).

Sayf b. Dhí Yazan.

The Persians in Yemen (*circa* 572 A.D.).

Leaving the once mighty kingdom of Yemen thus pitiably and for ever fallen from its high estate, we turn northward into the main stream of Arabian history.

[1] The reader will find a full and excellent account of these matters in Professor Browne's *Literary History of Persia*, vol. i, pp. 178–181.

CHAPTER II

THE HISTORY AND LEGENDS OF THE PAGAN ARABS

The Age of Barbarism (al-Jáhiliyya).

MUḤAMMADANS include the whole period of Arabian history from the earliest times down to the establishment of Islam in the term *al-Jáhiliyya*, which was used by Muḥammad in four passages of the Koran and is generally translated 'the state of ignorance' or simply 'the Ignorance.' Goldziher, however, has shown conclusively that the meaning attached to *jahl* (whence *Jáhiliyya* is derived) by the Pre-islamic poets is not so much 'ignorance' as 'wildness,' 'savagery,' and that its true antithesis is not *'ilm* (knowledge), but rather *ḥilm*, which denotes the moral reasonableness of a civilised man. "When Muḥammadans say that Islam put an end to the manners and customs of the *Jáhiliyya*, they have in view those barbarous practices, that savage temper, by which Arabian heathendom is distinguished from Islam and by the abolition of which Muḥammad sought to work a moral reformation in his countrymen : the haughty spirit of the *Jáhiliyya* (*ḥamiyyatu 'l-Jáhiliyya*), the tribal pride and the endless tribal feuds, the cult of revenge, the implacability and all the other pagan characteristics which Islam was destined to overcome." [1]

Our sources of information regarding this period may be classified as follows :—

(1) *Poems and fragments of verse*, which though not written

[1] Goldziher, *Muhammedanische Studien*, Part I, p. 225.

down at the time were preserved by oral tradition and committed to writing, for the most part, two or three hundred years afterwards. The importance of this, virtually the sole contemporary record of Pre-islamic history, is recognised in the well-known saying, "Poetry is the public register of the Arabs (*al-shi'ru díwánu 'l-'Arab*); thereby genealogies are kept in mind and famous actions are made familiar." Some account of the chief collections of old Arabian poetry will be given in the next chapter.

Sources of information concerning the Jáhiliyya.

(2) *Proverbs.* These are of less value, as they seldom explain themselves, while the commentary attached to them is the work of scholars bent on explaining them at all costs, though in many cases their true meaning could only be conjectured and the circumstances of their origin had been entirely forgotten. Notwithstanding this very pardonable excess of zeal, we could ill afford to lose the celebrated collections of Mufaḍḍal b. Salama († *circa* 900 A.D.) and Maydání († 1124 A.D.),[1] which contain so much curious information throwing light on every aspect of Pre-islamic life.

(3) *Traditions and legends.* Since the art of writing was neither understood nor practised by the heathen Arabs in general, it was impossible that Prose, as a literary form, should exist among them. The germs of Arabic Prose, however, may be traced back to the *Jáhiliyya.* Besides the proverb (*mathal*) and the oration (*khuṭba*) we find elements of history and romance in the prose narratives used by the rhapsodists to introduce and set forth plainly the matter of their songs, and in the legends which recounted the glorious deeds of tribes and individuals. A vast number of such stories—some unmistakably genuine, others bearing the stamp of fiction—are preserved in various literary, historical, and geographical works composed under the 'Abbásid Caliphate, especially in the *Kitábu 'l-Aghání* (Book

[1] Maydání's collection has been edited, with a Latin translation by Freytag, in three volumes (*Arabum Proverbia*, Bonn, 1838–1843).

of Songs) by Abu 'l-Faraj of Iṣfahán († 967 A.D.), an invaluable compilation based on the researches of the great Humanists as they have been well named by Sir Charles Lyall, of the second and third centuries after the Hijra.[1] The original writings of these early critics and scholars have perished almost without exception, and beyond the copious citations in the *Aghání* we possess hardly any specimens of their work. "The *Book of Songs*," says Ibn Khaldún, "is the Register of the Arabs. It comprises all that they had achieved in the past of excellence in every kind of poetry, history, music, *et cetera*. So far as I am aware, no other book can be put on a level with it in this respect. It is the final resource of the student of belles-lettres, and leaves him nothing further to desire." [2]

The *Book of Songs.*

In the following pages I shall not attempt to set in due order and connection the confused mass of poetry and legend in which all that we know of Pre-islamic Arabia lies deeply embedded. This task has already been performed with admirable skill by Caussin de Perceval in his *Essai sur l'histoire des Arabes avant l'Islamisme*,[3] and it could serve no useful purpose to inflict a dry summary of that famous work upon the reader. The better course, I think, will be to select a few typical and outstanding features of the time and to present them, wherever possible, as they have been drawn—largely from imagination—by the Arabs themselves. If the Arabian traditions are wanting in historical accuracy they are nevertheless, taken as a whole, true in spirit to the Dark Age which they call up from the dead and reverently unfold beneath our eyes.

Scope of this chapter.

[1] The *Kitábu 'l-Aghání* has been published at Buláq (1284–1285 A.H.) in twenty volumes. A volume of biographies not contained in the Buláq text was edited by R. E. Brünnow (Leiden, 1888).

[2] *Muqaddima* of Ibn Khaldún (Beyrout, 1900), p. 554, ll. 8–10; *Les Prolégomènes d' Ibn Khaldoun traduits par M. de Slane* (Paris, 1863–68) vol. iii, p. 331.

[3] Published at Paris, 1847–1848, in three volumes.

About the middle of the third century of our era Arabia was enclosed on the north and north-east by the rival empires of Rome and Persia, to which the Syrian desert, stretching right across the peninsula, formed a natural termination. In order to protect themselves from Bedouin raiders, who poured over the frontier-provinces, and after laying hands on all the booty within reach vanished as suddenly as they came, both Powers found it necessary to plant a line of garrisons along the edge of the wilderness. Thus the tribesmen were partially held in check, but as force alone seemed an expensive and inefficient remedy it was decided, in accordance with the well-proved maxim, *divide et impera*, to enlist a number of the offending tribes in the Imperial service. Regular pay and the prospect of unlimited plunder—for in those days Rome and Persia were almost perpetually at war—were inducements that no true Bedouin could resist. They fought, however, as free allies under their own chiefs or phylarchs. In this way two Arabian dynasties sprang up—the Ghassánids in Syria and the Lakhmites at Ḥíra, west of the Euphrates—military buffer-states, always ready to collide even when they were not urged on by the suzerain powers behind them. The Arabs soon showed what they were capable of when trained and disciplined in arms. On the defeat of Valerian by the Chosroes Sábúr I, an Arab chieftain in Palmyra, named Udhayna (Odenathus), marched at the head of a strong force against the conqueror, drove him out of Syria, and pursued him up to the very walls of Madá'in, the Persian capital (265 A.D.). His brilliant exploits were duly rewarded by the Emperor Gallienus, who bestowed on him the title of Augustus. He was, in fact, the acknowledged master of the Roman legions in the East when, a year later, he was treacherously murdered. He found a worthy successor in his wife, the noble and ambitious Zenobia, who set herself the task of building up a great Oriental Empire. She fared, however, no

The Arab dynasties of Ḥíra and Ghassán.

Odenathus and Zenobia.

better than did Cleopatra in a like enterprise. For a moment the issue was doubtful, but Aurelian triumphed and the proud 'Queen of the East' was led a captive before his chariot through the streets of Rome (274 A.D.).

These events were not forgotten by the Arabs. It flattered their national pride to recall that once, at any rate, Roman armies had marched under the flag of an Arabian princess. But the legend, as told in their traditions, has little in common with reality. Not only are names and places freely altered—Zenobia herself being confused with her Syrian general, Zabdai—but the historical setting, though dimly visible in the background, has been distorted almost beyond recognition: what remains is one of those romantic adventures which delighted the Arabs of the *Jáhiliyya*, just as their modern descendants are never tired of listening to the *Story of 'Antar* or to the *Thousand Nights and a Night.*

The first king of the Arab settlers in 'Iráq (Babylonia)[1] is said to have been Málik the Azdite, who was accidentally

Málik the Azdite.

shot with an arrow by his son, Sulayma. Before he expired he uttered a verse which has become proverbial:—

> *U'allimuhu 'l-rimáyata kulla yawm*[in]
> *falamma 'stadda sá'iduhú ramání.*
>
> "I taught him every day the bowman's art,
> And when his arm took aim, he pierced my heart."

Málik's kingdom, if it can properly be described as such, was consolidated and organised by his son, Jadhíma, surnamed

Jadhíma al-Abrash.

al-Abrash (the Speckled)—a polite euphemism for al-Abraṣ (the Leprous). He reigned as the vassal of Ardashír Bábakán, the founder (226 A.D.) of the Sásánian dynasty in Persia, which thereafter continued to dominate the Arabs of 'Iráq during the whole Pre-islamic

[1] These are the same Bedouin Arabs of Tanúkh who afterwards formed part of the population of Ḥíra. See p. 38 *infra.*

period. Jadhíma is the hero of many fables and proverbs. His pride, it is said, was so overweening that he would suffer no boon-companions except two stars called *al-Farqadán*, and when he drank wine he used to pour out a cup for each of them. He had a page, 'Adí b. Naṣr, with whom his sister fell in love; and in a moment of intoxication he gave his consent to their marriage. Next morning, furious at the trick which had been played upon him, he beheaded the unlucky bridegroom and reviled his sister for having married a slave. Nevertheless, when a son was born, Jadhíma adopted the boy, and as he grew up regarded him with the utmost affection. One day the youthful 'Amr suddenly disappeared. For a long time no trace of him could be found, but at last he was discovered, running wild and naked, by two brothers, Málik and 'Aqíl, who cared for him and clothed him and presented him to the king. Overjoyed at the sight, Jadhíma promised to grant them whatever they asked. They chose the honour, which no mortal had hitherto obtained, of being his boon-companions, and by this title (*nadmáná Jadhíma*) they are known to fame.

Jadhíma was a wise and warlike prince. In one of his expeditions he defeated and slew 'Amr b. Ẓarib b. Ḥassán b. Udhayna, an Arab chieftain who had brought part of Eastern Syria and Mesopotamia under his sway, and who, as the name Udhayna indicates, is probably identical with Odenathus, the husband of Zenobia. This opinion is confirmed by the statement of Ibn Qutayba that "Jadhíma sought in marriage Zabbá, the daughter of the King of Mesopotamia, who became queen after her *husband*."[1] According to the view generally held by Muḥammadan authors Zabbá[2] was the daughter of 'Amr b. Ẓarib and was

The story of Zabbá.

[1] Ibn Qutayba in Brünnow's *Chrestomathy*, p. 29.

[2] Properly *al-Zabbá*, an epithet meaning 'hairy.' According to Ṭabarí (i, 757) her name was Ná'ila. It is odd that in the Arabic version of the story the name Zenobia (Zaynab) should be borne by the heroine's sister.

elected to succeed him when he fell in battle. However this may be, she proved herself a woman of extraordinary courage and resolution. As a safeguard against attack she built two strong castles on either bank of the Euphrates and connected them by a subterranean tunnel; she made one fortress her own residence, while her sister, Zaynab, occupied the other.

Having thus secured her position she determined to take vengeance on Jadhíma. She wrote to him that the sceptre was slipping from her feeble grasp, that she found no man worthy of her except himself, that she desired to unite her kingdom with his by marriage, and begged him to come and see her. Jadhíma needed no urging. Deaf to the warnings of his friend and counsellor, Qaṣír, he started from Baqqa, a castle on the Euphrates. When they had travelled some distance, Qaṣír implored him to return. "No," said Jadhíma, "the affair was decided at Baqqa"—words which passed into a proverb. On approaching their destination the king saw with alarm squadrons of cavalry between him and the city, and said to Qaṣír, "What is the prudent course?" "You left prudence at Baqqa," he replied; "if the cavalry advance and salute you as king and then retire in front of you, the woman is sincere, but if they cover your flanks and encompass you, they mean treachery. Mount al-'Aṣá"—Jadhíma's favourite mare—"for she cannot be overtaken or outpaced, and rejoin your troops while there is yet time." Jadhíma refused to follow this advice. Presently he was surrounded by the cavalry and captured. Qaṣír, however, sprang on the mare's back and galloped thirty miles without drawing rein.

When Jadhíma was brought to Zabbá she seated him on a skin of leather and ordered her maidens to open the veins in his arm, so that his blood should flow into a golden bowl. "O Jadhíma," said she, "let not a single drop be lost. I want it as a cure for madness." The dying man suddenly moved his arm and sprinkled with his blood one of the marble pillars of the hall—an evil portent for Zabbá, inasmuch as it had been prophesied by a certain soothsayer that unless every drop of the king's blood entered the bowl, his murder would be avenged.

Now Qaṣír came to 'Amr b. 'Adí, Jadhíma's nephew and son by adoption, who has been mentioned above, and engaged to win over the army to his side if he would take vengeance on Zabbá. "But how?" cried 'Amr; "for she is more inaccessible than the eagle of the air." "Only help me," said Qaṣír, "and you will be clear of blame." He cut off his nose and ears and betook himself to Zabbá, pretending that he had been mutilated by 'Amr. The queen believed what she saw, welcomed him, and gave him money to trade on her behalf. Qaṣír hastened to the palace of 'Amr at Ḥíra, and, having obtained permission to ransack the royal treasury, he returned laden with riches. Thus he gradually crept into the confidence of Zabbá, until one day he said to her: "It behoves every king and queen to provide themselves with a secret passage wherein to take refuge in case of danger." Zabbá answered: "I have already done so," and showed him the tunnel which she had constructed underneath the Euphrates. His project was now ripe for execution. With the help of 'Amr he fitted out a caravan of a thousand camels, each carrying two armed men concealed in sacks. When they drew near the city of Zabbá, Qaṣír left them and rode forward to announce their arrival to the queen, who from the walls of her capital viewed the long train of heavily burdened camels and marvelled at the slow pace with which they advanced. As the last camel passed through the gates of the city the janitor pricked one of the sacks with an ox-goad which he had with him, and hearing a cry of pain, exclaimed, "By God, there's mischief in the sacks!" But it was too late. 'Amr and his men threw themselves upon the garrison and put them to the sword. Zabbá sought to escape by the tunnel, but Qaṣír stood barring the exit on the further side of the stream. She hurried back, and there was 'Amr facing her. Resolved that her enemy should not taste the sweetness of vengeance, she sucked her seal-ring, which contained a deadly poison, crying, "By my own hand, not by 'Amr's!"[1]

In the kingdoms of Ḥíra and Ghassán Pre-islamic culture attained its highest development, and from these centres it diffused itself and made its influence felt throughout Arabia. Some account, therefore, of their history and of the circumstances which enabled them to assume a civilising rôle will not be superfluous.[2]

[1] The above narrative is abridged from *Aghání*, xiv, 73, l. 20–75, l. 25. *Cf.* Ṭabarí, i, 757–766; Mas'údí, *Murúju 'l-Dhahab* (ed. by Barbier de Meynard), vol. iii, pp. 189–199.

[2] Concerning Ḥíra and its history the reader may consult an admirable monograph by Dr. G. Rothstein, *Die Dynastie der Laḫmiden in al-Ḥíra* (Berlin, 1899), where the sources of information are set forth (p. 5 sqq.). The incidental references to contemporary events in Syriac and Byzantine writers, who often describe what they saw with their own eyes, are

About the beginning of the third century after Christ a number of Bedouin tribes, wholly or partly of Yemenite origin, who had formed a confederacy and called themselves collectively Tanúkh, took advantage of the disorder then prevailing in the Arsacid Empire to invade 'Iráq (Babylonia) and plant their settlements in the fertile country west of the Euphrates. While part of the intruders continued to lead a nomad life, others engaged in agriculture, and in course of time villages and towns grew up. The most important of these was Ḥíra (properly, al-Ḥíra, *i.e.*, the Camp), which occupied a favourable and healthy situation a few miles to the south of Kúfa, in the neighbourhood of ancient Babylon.[1] According to Hishám b. Muḥammad al-Kalbí (†819 or 821 A.D.), an excellent authority for the history of the Pre-islamic period, the inhabitants of Ḥíra during the reign of Ardashír Bábakán, the first Sásánian king of Persia (226–241 A.D.), consisted of three classes, viz. :—

The foundation of Ḥíra.

(1) The *Tanúkh*, who dwelt west of the Euphrates between Ḥíra and Anbár in tents of camel's hair.

(2) The *'Ibád*, who lived in houses in Ḥíra.

(3) The *Aḥláf* (Clients), who did not belong to either of the above-mentioned classes, but attached themselves to the people of Ḥíra and lived among them—blood-guilty fugitives

extremely valuable as a means of fixing the chronology, which Arabian historians can only supply by conjecture, owing to the want of a definite era during the Pre-islamic period. Muḥammadan general histories usually contain sections, more or less mythical in character, "On the Kings of Ḥíra and Ghassán." Attention may be called in particular to the account derived from Hishám b. Muḥammad al-Kalbí, which is preserved by Ṭabarí and has been translated with a masterly commentary by Nöldeke in his *Geschichte der Perser und Araber zur Zeit der Sasaniden.* Hishám had access to the archives kept in the churches of Ḥíra, and claims to have extracted therefrom many genealogical and chronological details relating to the Lakhmite dynasty (Ṭabarí, i, 770, 7).

[1] Ḥíra is the Syriac *ḥértá* (sacred enclosure, monastery), which name was applied to the originally mobile camp of the Persian Arabs and retained as the designation of the garrison town.

pursued by the vengeance of their own kin, or needy emigrants seeking to mend their fortunes.

Naturally the townsmen proper formed by far the most influential element in the population. Hishám, as we have seen, calls them 'the 'Ibád.' His use of this term, however, is not strictly accurate. The 'Ibád are exclusively the *Christian Arabs of Ḥíra*, and are so called in virtue of their Christianity; the pagan Arabs, who at the time when Ḥíra was founded and for long afterwards constituted the bulk of the citizens, were never comprised in a designation which expresses the very opposite of paganism. *'Ibád* means 'servants,' *i.e.*, those who serve God or Christ. It cannot be determined at what epoch the name was first used to distinguish the religious community, composed of members of different tribes, which was dominant in Ḥíra during the sixth century. Dates are comparatively of little importance; what is really remarkable is the existence in Pre-islamic times of an Arabian community that was not based on blood-relationship or descent from a common ancestor, but on a spiritual principle, namely, the profession of a common faith. The religion and culture of the 'Ibád were conveyed by various channels to the inmost recesses of the peninsula, as will be shown more fully in a subsequent chapter. They were the schoolmasters of the heathen Arabs, who could seldom read or write, and who, it must be owned, so far from desiring to receive instruction, rather gloried in their ignorance of accomplishments which they regarded as servile. Nevertheless, the best minds among the Bedouins were irresistibly attracted to Ḥíra. Poets in those days found favour with princes. A great number of Pre-islamic bards visited the Lakhmite court, while some, like Nábigha and 'Abíd b. al-Abraṣ, made it their permanent residence.

The 'Ibád.

It is unnecessary to enter into the vexed question as to the origin and rise of the Lakhmite dynasty at Ḥíra. According to Hishám b. Muḥammad al-Kalbi, who gives a list of twenty kings, covering a period of 522 years and eight months, the first Lakhmite ruler was 'Amr b. 'Adí b. Naṣr b. Rabí'a b. Lakhm, the same who was adopted by Jadhíma, and afterwards avenged his death on Queen Zabbá. Almost nothing is known of his successors until we come to Nu'mán I, surnamed al-A'war (the One-eyed), whose reign falls in the first quarter of the fifth century. Nu'mán is renowned in legend as the builder of Khawarnaq, a famous castle near Ḥíra. It was built at the instance of the Sásánian king, Yazdigird I, who desired a salubrious residence for his son, Prince Bahrám Gór. On its completion, Nu'mán ordered the architect, a 'Roman' (*i.e.*, Byzantine subject) named Sinimmár, to be cast headlong from the battlements, either on account of his boast that he could have constructed a yet more wonderful edifice "which should turn round with the sun," or for fear that he might reveal the position of a certain stone, the removal of which would cause the whole building to collapse. One spring day (so the story is told) Nu'mán sat with his Vizier in Khawarnaq, which overlooked the Fen-land (al-Najaf), with its neighbouring gardens and plantations of palm-trees and canals, to the west, and the Euphrates to the east. Charmed by the beauty of the prospect, he exclaimed, "Hast thou ever seen the like of this?" "No," replied the Vizier, "if it would but last." "And what is lasting?" asked Nu'mán. "That which is with God in heaven." "How can one attain to it?" "By renouncing the world and serving God, and striving after that which He hath." Nu'mán, it is said, immediately resolved to abandon his kingdom; on the same night he clad himself in sack-cloth, stole away unperceived, and became a wandering devotee (*sá'iḥ*). This legend seems to have grown out of the following verses by 'Adí b. Zayd, the 'Ibádite:—

The Lakhmites.

Nu'mán I. (*circa* 400 A.D.).

The Castle of Khawarnaq.

Nu'mán becomes an anchorite.

"Consider thou Khawarnaq's lord—and oft
Of heavenly guidance cometh vision clear—
Who once, rejoicing in his ample realm,
Surveyed the broad Euphrates, and Sadír;[1]
Then sudden terror struck his heart: he cried,
'Shall Man, who deathward goes, find pleasure here?'
They reigned, they prospered; yet, their glory past,
In yonder tombs they lie this many a year.
At last they were like unto withered leaves
Whirled by the winds away in wild career."[2]

The opinion of most Arabian authors, that Nu'mán embraced Christianity, is probably unfounded, but there is reason to believe that he was well disposed towards it, and that his Christian subjects—a Bishop of Ḥíra is mentioned as early as 410 A.D.—enjoyed complete religious liberty.

Nu'mán's place was filled by his son Mundhir, an able and energetic prince. The power of the Lakhmites at this time may be inferred from the fact that on the death of Yazdigird I Mundhir forcibly intervened in the dispute as to the Persian succession and procured the election of Bahrám Gór, whose claims had previously been rejected by the priesthood.[3] In the war which broke out shortly afterwards between Persia and Rome, Mundhir proved himself a loyal vassal, but was defeated by the Romans with great loss (421 A.D.). Passing over several obscure reigns, we arrive at the beginning of the sixth century, when another Mundhir, the third and most illustrious of his name, ascended the throne. This is he whom the Arabs called Mundhir b. Má' al-samá.[4] He had a long and brilliant reign, which, however, was temporarily

Mundhir I.

Mundhir III, b. Má' al-samá.

[1] Sadír was a castle in the vicinity of Ḥíra. [2] Ṭabarí, i, 853, 20 sqq.

[3] Bahrám was educated at Ḥíra under Nu'mán and Mundhir. The Persian grandees complained that he had the manners and appearance of the Arabs among whom he had grown up (Ṭabarí, i, 858, 7).

[4] Má' al-samá (*i.e.*, Water of the sky) is said to have been the sobriquet of Mundhir's mother, whose proper name was Máriya or Máwiyya.

clouded by an event that cannot be understood without some reference to the general history of the period. About 480 A.D. the powerful tribe of Kinda, whose princes appear to have held much the same position under the Tubba'ś of Yemen as the Lakhmites under the Persian monarchs, had extended their sway over the greater part of Central and Northern Arabia.

Rise of Kinda.

The moving spirit in this conquest was Ḥujr, surnamed Ákilu 'l-Murár, an ancestor of the poet Imru'u 'l-Qays. On his death the Kindite confederacy was broken up, but towards the year 500 it was re-established for a brief space by his grandson, Ḥárith b. 'Amr, and became a formidable rival to the kingdoms of Ghassán and Ḥíra. Meanwhile, in Persia, the communistic doctrines of Mazdak

Mazdak.

had obtained wide popularity among the lower classes, and were finally adopted by King Kawádh himself.[1] Now, it is certain that at some date between 505 and 529 Ḥárith b. 'Amr, the Kindite, invaded 'Iráq, and drove Mundhir out of his kingdom; and it seems not impossible

Mundhir expelled from Ḥíra by Ḥárith of Kinda.

that, as many historians assert, the latter's downfall was due to his anti-Mazdakite opinions, which would naturally excite the displeasure of his suzerain. At any rate, whatever the causes may have been, Mundhir was temporarily supplanted by Ḥárith, and although he was restored after a short interval, before the accession of Anúshirwán, who, as Crown Prince, carried out a wholesale massacre of the followers of Mazdak (528 A.D.), the humiliation which he had suffered and cruelly avenged was not soon forgotten;[2] the life and poems of Imru'u 'l-Qays

[1] For an account of Mazdak and his doctrines the reader may consult Nöldeke's translation of Ṭabarí, pp. 140–144, 154, and 455–467, and Professor Browne's *Literary History of Persia*, vol. i, pp. 168–172.

[2] Mundhir slaughtered in cold blood some forty or fifty members of the royal house of Kinda who had fallen into his hands. Ḥárith himself was defeated and slain by Mundhir in 529. Thereafter the power of Kinda sank, and they were gradually forced back to their original settlements in Ḥaḍramawt.

bear witness to the hereditary hatred subsisting between Lakhm and Kinda. Mundhir's operations against the Romans were conducted with extraordinary vigour; he devastated Syria as far as Antioch, and Justinian saw himself obliged to entrust the defence of these provinces to the Ghassánid Ḥárith b. Jabala (Ḥárith al-Aʿraj), in whom Mundhir at last found more than his match. From this time onward the kings of Ḥíra and Ghassán are continually raiding and plundering each other's territory. In one of his expeditions Mundhir captured a son of Ḥárith, and "immediately sacrificed him to Aphrodite"—*i.e.*, to the Arabian goddess al-ʿUzzá;[1] but on taking the field again in 554 he was surprised and slain by stratagem in a battle which is known proverbially as 'The Day of Ḥalíma.'[2]

Death of Mundhir III.

On the whole, the Lakhmites were a heathen and barbarous race, and these epithets are richly deserved by Mundhir III. It is related in the *Aghání* that he had two boon-companions, Khálid b. al-Muḍallil and ʿAmr b. Masʿúd, with whom he used to carouse; and once, being irritated by words spoken in wine, he gave orders that they should be buried alive. Next morning he did not recollect what had passed and inquired as usual for his friends. On learning the truth he was filled with remorse. He caused two obelisks to be erected over their graves, and two days in every year he would come and sit beside these obelisks, which were called *al-Ghariyyán*—*i.e.*, the Blood-smeared. One day was the Day of Good (*yawmu naʿím*^{in}), and whoever first encountered him on that day received a hundred black camels. The other day was the Day of Evil (*yawmu bu's*^{in}), on which he would present the first-comer with the head of a black polecat (*ẓaribán*), then sacrifice him and smear the obelisks with his blood.[3] The

Mundhir's "Good Day and Evil Day."

[1] On another occasion he sacrificed four hundred Christian nuns to the same goddess.

[2] See p. 50 *infra*.

[3] *Aghání*, xix, 86, l. 16 sqq.

poet 'Abíd b. al-Abraṣ is said to have fallen a victim to this horrible rite. It continued until the doom fell upon a certain Ḥanẓala of Ṭayyi', who was granted a year's grace in order to regulate his affairs, on condition that he should find a surety. He appealed to one of Mundhir's suite, Sharík b. 'Amr, who straightway rose and said to the king, "My hand for his and my blood for his if he fail to return at the time appointed." When the day came Ḥanẓala did not appear, and Mundhir was about to sacrifice Sharík, whose mourning-woman had already begun to chant the dirge. Suddenly a rider was seen approaching, wrapped in a shroud and perfumed for burial. A mourning-woman accompanied him. It was Ḥanẓala. Mundhir marvelled at their loyalty, dismissed them with marks of honour, and abolished the custom which he had instituted.[1]

Ḥanẓala and Sharík.

He was succeeded by his son 'Amr, who is known to contemporary poets and later historians as 'Amr, son of Hind.[2] During his reign Ḥíra became an important literary centre. Most of the famous poets then living visited his court; we shall see in the next chapter what relations he had with Ṭarafa, 'Amr b. Kulthúm, and Ḥárith b. Ḥilliza. He was a morose, passionate, and tyrannical man. The Arabs stood in great awe of him, but vented their spite none the less. "At Ḥíra," said Dahháb al-'Ijlí, "there are mosquitoes and fever and lions and 'Amr b. Hind, who acts unjustly and wrongfully."[3] He was slain by the chief of Taghlib, 'Amr b. Kulthúm, in vengeance for an insult offered to his mother, Laylá.

'Amr b. Hind (554–569 A.D.).

It is sufficient to mention the names of Qábús and

[1] *Aghání*, xix, 87, l. 18 sqq.

[2] Hind was a princess of Kinda (daughter of the Ḥárith b. 'Amr mentioned above), whom Mundhir probably captured in one of his marauding expeditions. She was a Christian, and founded a monastery at Ḥíra. See Nöldeke's translation of Ṭabarí, p. 172, n. 1.

[3] *Aghání*, xxi, 194, l. 22.

Mundhir IV, both of whom were sons of Hind, and occupied the throne for short periods. We now come to the last Lakhmite king of Ḥíra, and by far the most celebrated in tradition, Nu'mán III, son of Mundhir IV, with the *kunya* (name of honour) Abú Qábús, who reigned from 580 to 602 or from 585 to 607. He was brought up and educated by a noble Christian family in Ḥíra, the head of which was Zayd b. Ḥammád, father of the poet 'Adí b. Zayd. 'Adí is such an interesting figure, and his fortunes were so closely and tragically linked with those of Nu'mán, that some account of his life and character will be acceptable. Both his father and grandfather were men of unusual culture, who held high posts in the civil administration under Mundhir III and his successors. Zayd, moreover, through the good offices of a *dihqán*, or Persian landed proprietor, Farrukh-máhán by name, obtained from Khusraw Anúshirwán an important and confidential appointment—that of Postmaster—ordinarily reserved for the sons of satraps.[1] When 'Adí grew up, his father sent him to be educated with the son of the *dihqán*. He learned to write and speak Persian with complete facility and Arabic with the utmost elegance; he versified, and his accomplishments included archery, horsemanship, and polo. At the Persian court his personal beauty, wit, and readiness in reply so impressed Anúshirwán that he took him into his service as secretary and interpreter—Arabic had never before been written in the Imperial Chancery—and accorded him all the privileges of a favourite. He was entrusted with a mission to Constantinople, where he was honourably received; and on his departure the Qayṣar,[2] following an excellent custom, instructed the officials in charge of the post-routes to provide horses and

Nu'mán Abú Qábús.

'Adí b. Zayd.

[1] Zayd was actually Regent of Ḥíra after the death of Qábús, and paved the way for Mundhir IV, whose violence had made him detested by the people (Nöldeke's translation of Ṭabarí, p. 346, n. 1).

[2] The Arabs called the Byzantine emperor '*Qayṣar*,' *i.e.*, Cæsar, and the Persian emperor '*Kisrá*,' *i.e.*, Chosroes.

every convenience in order that the ambassador might see for himself the extent and resources of the Byzantine Empire. 'Adí passed some time in Syria, especially at Damascus, where his first poem is said to have appeared. On his father's death, which happened about this time, he renounced the splendid position at Ḥíra which he might have had for the asking, and gave himself up to hunting and to all kinds of amusement and pleasure, only visiting Madá'in (Ctesiphon) at intervals to perform his secretarial duties. While staying at Ḥíra he fell in love with Nu'mán's daughter Hind, who was then eleven years old. The story as told in the *Book of Songs* is too curious to be entirely omitted, though want of space prevents me from giving it in full.[1]

'Adí meets the Princess Hind in church.

It is related that Hind, who was one of the fairest women of her time, went to church on Thursday of Holy Week, three days after Palm Sunday, to receive the sacrament. 'Adí had entered the church for the same purpose. He espied her—she was a big, tall girl—while she was off her guard, and fixed his gaze upon her before she became aware of him. Her maidens, who had seen him approaching, said nothing to their mistress, because one of them called Máriya was enamoured of 'Adí and knew no other way of making his acquaintance. When Hind saw him looking at herself, she was highly displeased and scolded her handmaidens and beat some of them. 'Adí had fallen in love with her, but he kept the matter secret for a whole year. At the end of that time Máriya, thinking that Hind had forgotten what passed, described the church of Thómá (St. Thomas) and the nuns there and the girls who frequented it, and the beauty of the building and of the lamps, and said to her, "Ask thy mother's leave to go." As soon as leave was granted, Máriya conveyed the intelligence to 'Adí, who immediately dressed himself in a magnifi-

[1] My friend and colleague, Professor A. A. Bevan, writes to me that "the story of 'Adí's marriage with the king's daughter is based partly on a verse in which the poet speaks of himself as connected by marriage with the royal house (*Aghání*, ii, 26, l. 5), and partly on another verse in which he mentions 'the home of Hind' (*ibid.*, ii, 32, l. 1). But this Hind was evidently a Bedouin woman, not the king's daughter."

cent gold-embroidered Persian tunic (*yalmaq*) and hastened to the rendezvous, accompanied by several young men of Ḥíra. When Máriya perceived him, she cried to Hind, "Look at this youth: by God, he is fairer than the lamps and all things else that thou seest." "Who is he?" she asked. "'Adí, son of Zayd." "Do you think," said Hind, "that he will recognise me if I come nearer?" Then she advanced and watched him as he conversed with his friends, outshining them all by the beauty of his person, the elegance of his language, and the splendour of his dress. "Speak to him," said Máriya to her young mistress, whose countenance betrayed her feelings. After exchanging a few words the lovers parted. Máriya went to 'Adí and promised, if he would first gratify her wishes, to bring about his union with Hind. She lost no time in warning Nu'mán that his daughter was desperately in love with 'Adí and would either disgrace herself or die of grief unless he gave her to him. Nu'mán, however, was too proud to make overtures to 'Adí, who on his part feared to anger the prince by proposing an alliance. The ingenious Máriya found a way out of the difficulty. She suggested that 'Adí should invite Nu'mán and his suite to a banquet, and having well plied him with wine should ask for the hand of his daughter, which would not then be refused. So it came to pass. Nu'mán gave his consent to the marriage, and after three days Hind was brought home to her husband.[1]

His marriage to Hind.

On the death of Mundhir IV 'Adí warmly supported the claims of Nu'mán, who had formerly been his pupil and was now his father-in-law, to the throne of Ḥíra. The ruse which he employed on this occasion was completely successful, but it cost him his life.[2] The partisans of Aswad b. Mundhir, one of the defeated candidates, resolved on vengeance. Their intrigues awakened

'Adí secures the election of Nu'mán as King of Ḥíra.

[1] *Aghání*, ii, 22, l. 3 sqq.

[2] When Hurmuz summoned the sons of Mundhir to Ctesiphon that he might choose a king from among them, 'Adí said to each one privately, "If the Chosroes demands whether you can keep the Arabs in order, reply, 'All except Nu'mán.'" To Nu'mán, however, he said: "The Chosroes will ask, 'Can you manage your brothers?' Say to him: 'If I am not strong enough for them, I am still less able to control other folk!'" Hurmuz was satisfied with this answer and conferred the crown upon Nu'mán.

the suspicions of Nu'mán against the 'King-maker.' 'Adí was cast into prison, where he languished for a long time and was finally murdered by Nu'mán when the Chosroes (Parwéz, son of Hurmuz) had already intervened to procure his release.[1]

He is imprisoned and put to death by Nu'mán.

'Adí left a son named Zayd, who, on the recommendation of Nu'mán, was appointed by Khusraw Parwéz to succeed his father as Secretary for Arabian Affairs at the court of Ctesiphon. Apparently reconciled to Nu'mán, he was none the less bent on vengeance, and only waited for an opportunity. The kings of Persia were connoisseurs in female beauty, and when they desired to replenish their harems they used to circulate an advertisement describing with extreme particularity the physical and moral qualities which were to be sought after;[2] but hitherto they had neglected Arabia, which, as they supposed, could not furnish any woman possessed of these perfections. Zayd therefore approached the Chosroes and said: "I know that Nu'mán has in his family a number of women answering to the description. Let me go to him, and send with me one of thy guardsmen who understands Arabic." The Chosroes complied, and Zayd set out for Ḥíra. On learning the object of his mission, Nu'mán exclaimed with indignation: "What! are not the gazelles of Persia sufficient for your needs?" The comparison of a beautiful woman to a gazelle is a commonplace in Arabian poetry, but the officer accompanying Zayd was ill acquainted with Arabic, and asked the meaning of the word (*'ín* or *mahá*) which Nu'mán had employed. "Cows," said Zayd. When Parwéz heard from his guardsman that Nu'mán had said, "Do not the cows of Persia content him?" he could scarcely suppress his rage. Soon afterwards he sent for Nu'mán,

The vengeance of Zayd b. 'Adí.

Death of Nu'mán III.

[1] A full account of these matters is given by Ṭabarí, i, 1016–1024 = Nöldeke's translation, pp. 314–324.

[2] A similar description occurs in Freytag's *Arabum Proverbia*, vol. ii. p. 589 sqq.

threw him into chains, and caused him to be trampled to pieces by elephants.[1]

Nu'mán III appears in tradition as a tyrannical prince, devoted to wine, women, and song. He was the patron of many celebrated poets, and especially of Nábigha Dhubyání, who was driven from Ḥíra in consequence of a false accusation. This episode, as well as another in which the poet Munakhkhal was concerned, gives us a glimpse into the private life of Nu'mán. He had married his step-mother, Mutajarrida, a great beauty in her time; but though he loved her passionately, she bestowed her affections elsewhere. Nábigha was suspected on account of a poem in which he described the charms of the queen with the utmost minuteness, but Munakhkhal was the real culprit. The lovers were surprised by Nu'mán, and from that day Munakhkhal was never seen again. Hence the proverb, "Until Munakhkhal shall return," or, as we might say, "Until the coming of the Coqcigrues."

Character of Nu'mán III.

Although several of the kings of Ḥíra are said to have been Christians, it is very doubtful whether any except Nu'mán III deserved even the name; the Lakhmites, unlike the majority of their subjects, were thoroughly pagan. Nu'mán's education would naturally predispose him to Christianity, and his conversion may have been wrought, as the legend asserts, by his mentor 'Adí b. Zayd.

Nu'mán's conversion to Christianity.

According to Muḥammadan genealogists, the Ghassánids, both those settled in Medína and those to whom the name is consecrated by popular usage—the Ghassánids of Syria—are descended from 'Amr b. 'Ámir al-Muzayqiyá, who, as was related in the last chapter, sold his possessions in Yemen and quitted the country, taking with him a great number of its inhabitants, shortly before the Bursting of

The Ghassánids or Jafnites.

[1] Ṭabarí, i, 1024–1029 = Nöldeke's translation, pp. 324–331. Ibn Qutayba in Brünnow's *Chrestomathy*, pp. 32–33.

the Dyke of Ma'rib. His son Jafna is generally regarded as the founder of the dynasty. Of their early history very few authentic facts have been preserved. At first, we are told, they paid tribute to the Ḍajá'ima, a family of the stock of Salíḥ, who ruled the Syrian borderlands under Roman protection. A struggle ensued, from which the Ghassánids emerged victorious, and henceforth we find them established in these regions as the representatives of Roman authority with the official titles of Patricius and Phylarch, which they and the Arabs around them rendered after the simple Oriental fashion by 'King' (*malik*).

Ibn Qutayba's account of the Ghassánids.

The first (says Ibn Qutayba) that reigned in Syria of the family of Jafna was Ḥárith b. 'Amr Muḥarriq, who was so called because he burnt (*ḥarraqa*) the Arabs in their houses. He is Ḥárith the Elder (*al-Akbar*), and his name of honour (*kunya*) is Abú Shamir. After him reigned Ḥárith b. Abí Shamir, known as Ḥárith the Lame (*al-A'raj*), whose mother was Máriya of the Ear-rings. He was the best of their kings, and the most fortunate, and the craftiest; and in his raids he went the farthest afield. He led an expedition against Khaybar[1] and carried off a number of prisoners, but set them free after his return to Syria. When Mundhir b. Má' al-samá marched against him with an army 100,000 strong, Ḥárith sent a hundred men to meet him—among them the poet Labíd, who was then a youth—ostensibly to make peace. They surrounded Mundhir's tent and slew the king and his companions; then they took horse, and some escaped, while others were slain. The Ghassánid cavalry attacked the army of Mundhir and put them to flight. Ḥárith had a daughter named Ḥalíma, who perfumed the hundred champions on that day and clad them in shrouds of white linen and coats of mail. She is the heroine of the proverb, "The day of Ḥalíma is no secret."[2] Ḥárith was succeeded by his son, Ḥárith the Younger. Among his other sons were 'Amr b. Ḥárith (called Abú Shamir the Younger), to whom Nábigha came on leaving Nu'mán b. Mundhir; Mundhir b. Ḥárith; and al-Ayham b. Ḥárith. Jabala, the son of al-Ayham, was the last of the kings of Ghassán.

Ḥárith the Lame.

[1] A town in Arabia, some distance to the north of Medína.
[2] See Freytag, *Arabum Proverbia*, vol. ii, p. 611.

He was twelve spans in height, and his feet brushed the ground when he rode on horseback. He reached the Islamic period and became a Moslem in the Caliphate of 'Umar b. al-Khaṭṭáb, but afterwards he turned Christian and went to live in the Byzantine Empire. The occasion of his turning Christian was this: In passing through the bazaar of Damascus he let his horse tread upon one of the bystanders, who sprang up and struck Jabala a blow on the face. The Ghassánís seized the fellow and brought him before Abú 'Ubayda b. al-Jarráḥ,[1] complaining that he had struck their master. Abú 'Ubayda demanded proof. "What use wilt thou make of the proof?" said Jabala. He answered: "If he has struck thee, thou wilt strike him a blow in return." "And shall not he be slain?" "No." "Shall not his hand be cut off?" "No," said Abú 'Ubayda; "God has ordained retaliation only—blow for blow." Then Jabala went forth and betook himself to Roman territory and became a Christian; and he stayed there all the rest of his life.[2]

Jabala b. al-Ayham.

The Arabian traditions respecting the dynasty of Ghassán are hopelessly confused and supply hardly any material even for the rough historical sketch which may be pieced together from the scattered notices in Byzantine authors.[3] It would seem that the first unquestionable Ghassánid prince was Ḥárith b. Jabala ('Αρέθας τοῦ Γαβάλα), who figures in Arabian chronicles as 'Ḥárith the Lame,' and who was appointed by Justinian (about 529 A.D.) to balance, on the Roman side, the active and enterprising King of Ḥíra, Mundhir b. Má' al-samá. During the greater part of his long reign (529–569 A.D.) he was engaged in war with this dangerous rival, to whose defeat and death in the decisive battle of Ḥalíma we have already referred. Like all his line, Ḥárith was a Christian of the Monophysite Church, which he defended with equal zeal and success at a time when its very existence

Ḥárith the Lame.

[1] A celebrated Companion of the Prophet. He led the Moslem army to the conquest of Syria, and died of the plague in 639 A.D.

[2] Ibn Qutayba in Brünnow's *Chrestomathy*, pp. 26–28.

[3] The following details are extracted from Nöldeke's monograph: *Die Ghassânischen Fürsten aus dem Hause Gafna's*, in *Abhand. d. Kön. Preuss. Akad. d. Wissenschaften* (Berlin, 1887).

was at stake. The following story illustrates his formidable character. Towards the end of his life he visited Constantinople to arrange with the Imperial Government which of his sons should succeed him, and made a powerful impression on the people of that city, especially on the Emperor's nephew, Justinus. Many years afterwards, when Justinus had fallen into dotage, the chamberlains would frighten him, when he began to rave, with "Hush! Arethas will come and take you."[1]

Ḥárith was succeeded by his son, Mundhir, who vanquished the new King of Ḥíra, Qábús b. Hind, on Ascension Day, 570 A.D., in a battle which is perhaps identical with that celebrated by the Arabs as the Battle of 'Ayn Ubágh. The refusal of the Emperor Justinus to furnish him with money may have prevented Mundhir from pursuing his advantage, and was the beginning of open hostility between them, which culminated about eleven years later in his being carried off to Constantinople and forced to reside in Sicily.

Mundhir b. Ḥárith.

From this time to the Persian conquest of Palestine (614 A.D.) anarchy prevailed throughout the Ghassánid kingdom. The various tribes elected their own princes, who sometimes, no doubt, were Jafnites; but the dynasty had virtually broken up. Possibly it was restored by Heraclius when he drove the Persians out of Syria (629 A.D.), as the Ghassánians are repeatedly found fighting for Rome against the Moslems, and according to the unanimous testimony of Arabian writers, the Jafnite Jabala b. al-Ayham, who took an active part in the struggle, was the last king of Ghassán. His accession may be placed about 635 A.D. The poet Ḥassán b. Thábit, who as a native of Medína could claim kinship with the Ghassánids, and visited their court in his youth, gives a glowing description of its luxury and magnificence.

[1] Nöldeke, *op. cit.*, p. 20, refers to John of Ephesus, iii, 2. See *The Third Part of the Ecclesiastical History of John, Bishop of Ephesus*, translated by R. Payne Smith, p. 168.

"I have seen ten singing-girls, five of them Greeks, singing Greek songs to the music of lutes, and five from Ḥíra who had been presented to King Jabala by Iyás b. Qabíṣa,[1] chanting Babylonian airs. Arab singers used to come from Mecca and elsewhere for his delight; and when he would drink wine he sat on a couch of myrtle and jasmine and all sorts of sweet-smelling flowers, surrounded by gold and silver vessels full of ambergris and musk. During winter aloes-wood was burned in his apartments, while in summer he cooled himself with snow. Both he and his courtiers wore light robes, arranged with more regard to comfort than ceremony,[2] in the hot weather, and white furs, called *fanak*,[3] or the like, in the cold season; and, by God, I was never in his company but he gave me the robe which he was wearing on that day, and many of his friends were thus honoured. He treated the rude with forbearance; he laughed without reserve and lavished his gifts before they were sought. He was handsome, and agreeable in conversation: I never knew him offend in speech or act."[4]

Ḥassán b. Thábit's picture of the Ghassánid court.

Unlike the rival dynasty on the Euphrates, the Ghassánids had no fixed residence. They ruled the country round Damascus and Palmyra, but these places were never in their possession. The capital of their nomad kingdom was the temporary camp (in Aramaic, *ḥértá*) which followed them to and fro, but was generally to be found in the Gaulonitis

[1] Iyás b. Qabíṣa succeeded Nu'mán III as ruler of Ḥíra (602–611 A.D.). He belonged to the tribe of Ṭayyi'. See Rothstein, *Laḫmiden*, p. 119.

[2] I read *yatafaḍḍalu* for *yanfaṣilu*. The arrangement which the former word denotes is explained in Lane's Dictionary as "the throwing a portion of one's garment over his left shoulder, and drawing its extremity under his right arm, and tying the two extremities together in a knot upon his bosom."

[3] The *fanak* is properly a kind of white stoat or weasel found in Abyssinia and northern Africa, but the name is also applied by Muḥammadans to other furs.

[4] *Aghání*, xvi, 15, ll. 22–30. So far as it purports to proceed from Ḥassán, the passage is apocryphal, but this does not seriously affect its value as evidence, if we consider that it is probably compiled from the poet's *díwán* in which the Ghassánids are often spoken of. The particular reference to Jabala b. al-Ayham is a mistake. Ḥassán's acquaintance with the Ghassánids belongs to the pagan period of his life, and he is known to have accepted Islam many years before Jabala began to reign.

(al-Jawlán), south of Damascus. Thus under the quickening impulse of Hellenistic culture the Ghassánids developed a civilisation far superior to that of the Lakhmites, who, just because of their half-barbarian character, were more closely in touch with the heathen Arabs, and exercised a deeper influence upon them. Some aspects of this civilisation have been indicated in the description of Jabala b. al-Ayham's court, attributed to the poet Ḥassán. An earlier bard, the famous Nábigha, having fallen out of favour with Nu'mán III of Ḥíra, fled to Syria, where he composed a splendid eulogy of the Ghassánids in honour of his patron, King 'Amr, son of Ḥárith the Lame. After celebrating their warlike prowess, which he has immortalised in the oft-quoted verse—

Ghassánid civilisation.

Nábigha's encomium.

"One fault they have: their swords are blunt of edge
Through constant beating on their foemen's mail,"

he concludes in a softer strain:

"Theirs is a liberal nature that God gave
To no men else; their virtues never fail.
Their home the Holy Land: their faith upright:
They hope to prosper if good deeds avail.
Zoned in fair wise and delicately shod,
They keep the Feast of Palms, when maidens pale,
Whose scarlet silken robes on trestles hang,
Greet them with odorous boughs and bid them hail.
Long lapped in ease tho' bred to war, their limbs
Green-shouldered vestments, white-sleeved, richly veil."[1]

The Pre-islamic history of the Bedouins is mainly a record of wars, or rather guerillas, in which a great deal of raiding and plundering was accomplished, as a rule without serious bloodshed. There was no lack of shouting; volleys of vaunts

[1] Nábigha, ed. by Derenbourg, p. 78; Nöldeke's *Delectus*, p. 96. The whole poem has been translated by Sir Charles Lyall in his *Ancient Arabian Poetry*, p. 95 sqq.

and satires were exchanged; camels and women were carried off; many skirmishes took place but few pitched battles: it was an Homeric kind of warfare that called forth individual exertion in the highest degree, and gave ample opportunity for single-handed deeds of heroism. "To write a true history of such Bedouin feuds is well-nigh impossible. As comparatively trustworthy sources of information we have only the poems and fragments of verse which have been preserved.

Character of Bedouin history.

According to Suyúṭí, the Arabian traditionists used to demand from any Bedouin who related an historical event the citation of some verses in its support; and, in effect, all such stories that have come down to us are crystallised round the poems. Unfortunately these crystals are seldom pure. It appears only too often that the narratives have been invented, with abundant fancy and with more or less skill, to suit the contents of the verses."[1] But although what is traditionally related concerning the Battle-days of the Arabs (*Ayyámu 'l-'Arab*) is to a large extent legendary, it describes with sufficient fidelity how tribal hostilities generally arose and the way in which they were conducted. The following account of the War of Basús—the most famous of those waged in Pre-islamic times—will serve to illustrate this important phase of Bedouin life.[2]

War of Basús.

Towards the end of the fifth century A.D. Kulayb, son of Rabí'a, was chieftain of the Banú Taghlib, a powerful tribe which divided with their kinsmen, the Banú Bakr, a vast tract in north-eastern Arabia, extending from the central highlands to the Syrian desert. His victory at the head of a confederacy formed by these tribes and others over the Yemenite Arabs made him the first man in the peninsula, and soon his pride became no less proverbial than his power.[3] He was

---

[1] Thorbecke, *'Antarah, ein vorislamischer Dichter*, p. 14.

[2] The following narrative is an abridgment of the history of the War of Basús as related in Tibrízí's commentary on the *Ḥamása* (ed. by Freytag), pp. 420–423 and 251–255. *Cf.* Nöldeke's *Delectus*, p. 39 sqq.

[3] See p. 5 *supra*.

married to Ḥalíla, daughter of Murra, of the Banú Bakr, and dwelt in a 'preserve' (*ḥimá*), where he claimed the sole right of pasturage for himself and the sons of Murra. His brother-in-law, Jassás, had an aunt named Basús. While living under her nephew's protection she was joined by a certain Sa'd, a client of her own people, who brought with him a she-camel called Sarábi.

Kulayb b. Rabí'a and Jassás b. Murra.

Now it happened that Kulayb, seeing a lark's nest as he walked on his land, said to the bird, which was screaming and fluttering distressfully over her eggs, "Have no fear! I will protect thee." But a short time afterwards he observed in that place the track of a strange camel and found the eggs trodden to pieces. Next morning when he and Jassás visited the pasture ground, Kulayb noticed the she-camel of Sa'd among his brother-in-law's herd, and conjecturing that she had destroyed the eggs, cried out to Jassás, "Take heed thou! Take heed! I have pondered something, and were I sure, I would have done it! May this she-camel never come here again with this herd!" "By God," exclaimed Jassás, "but she shall come!" and when Kulayb threatened to pierce her udder with an arrow, Jassás retorted, "By the stones of Wá'il,[1] fix thine arrow in her udder and I will fix my lance in thy backbone!" Then he drove his camels forth from the *ḥimá*. Kulayb went home in a passion, and said to his wife, who sought to discover what ailed him, "Knowest thou any one who durst defend his client against me?" She answered, "No one except my brother Jassás, if he has given his word." She did what she could to prevent the quarrel going further, and for a time nothing worse than taunts passed between them, until one day Kulayb went to look after his camels which were being taken to water, and were followed by those of Jassás. While the latter were waiting their turn to drink, Sa'd's she-camel broke loose and ran towards the water. Kulayb imagined that Jassás had let her go deliberately, and resenting the supposed insult, he seized his bow and shot her through the udder. The beast lay down, moaning loudly, before the tent of Basús, who in vehement indignation at the wrong suffered by her friend, Sa'd, tore the veil from her head, beating her face and crying, "O shame, shame!" Then, addressing Sa'd, but raising her voice so that Jassás might

The wounding of Sa'd's she-camel.

[1] Wá'il is the common ancestor of Bakr and Taghlib. For the use of stones (*anṣáb*) in the worship of the Pagan Arabs see Wellhausen, *Reste Arabischen Heidentums* (2nd ed.), p. 101 sqq. Robertson Smith, *Lectures on the Religion of the Semites* (London, 1894), p. 200 sqq.

hear, she spoke these verses, which are known as 'The Instigators' (*al-Muwaththibát*):—

Verses spoken by Basús.

"O Sa'd, be not deceived! Protect thyself!
This people for their clients have no care.
Look to my herds, I charge thee, for I doubt
Even my little daughters ill may fare.
By thy life, had I been in Minqar's house,
Thou would'st not have been wronged, my client, there!
But now such folk I dwell among that when
The wolf comes, 'tis my sheep he comes to tear!"[1]

Jassás was stung to the quick by the imputation, which no Arab can endure, that injury and insult might be inflicted upon his guest-friend with impunity. Some days afterwards, having ascertained that Kulayb had gone out unarmed, he followed and slew him, and fled in haste to his own people. Murra, when he heard the news, said to his son, "Thou alone must answer for thy deed: thou shalt be put in chains that his kinsmen may slay thee. By the stones of Wá'il, never will Bakr and Taghlib be joined together in welfare after the death of Kulayb. Verily, an evil thing hast thou brought upon thy people, O Jassás! Thou hast slain their chief and severed their union and cast war into their midst." So he put Jassás in chains and confined him in a tent; then he summoned the elders of the families and asked them, "What do ye say concerning Jassás? Here he is, a prisoner, until the avengers demand him and we deliver him unto them." "No, by God," cried Sa'd b. Málik b. Ḍubay'a b. Qays, "we will not give him up, but will fight for him to the last man!" With these words he called for a camel to be sacrificed, and when its throat was cut they swore to one another over the blood. Thereupon Murra said to Jassás:—

Kulayb murdered by Jassás.

Verses of Murra, the father of Jassás.

"If war thou hast wrought and brought on me,
No laggard I with arms outworn.
Whate'er befall, I make to flow
The baneful cups of death at morn.

When spear-points clash, my wounded man
Is forced to drag the spear he stained.
Never I reck, if war must be,
What Destiny hath preordained.

---

[1] *Ḥamása*, 422, 14 sqq. Nöldeke's *Delectus*, p. 39, last line and foll.

Donning war's harness, I will strive
To fend from me the shame that sears.
Already I thrill and my lust is roused
For the shock of the horsemen against the spears!" [1]

Thus began the War of Basús between Taghlib on the one side and the clan of Shaybán, to which Murra belonged, on the other; for at first the remaining divisions of Bakr held aloof from the struggle, considering Shaybán to be clearly in the wrong. The latter were reduced to dire straits, when an event occurred which caused the Bakrites to rise as one man on behalf of their fellows. Ḥárith b. 'Ubád, a famous knight of Bakr, had refused to take part in the contest, saying in words which became proverbial, "I have neither camel nor she-camel in it," *i.e.*, "it is no affair of mine." One day his nephew, Bujayr, encountered Kulayb's brother, Muhalhil, on whom the mantle of the murdered chief had fallen; and Muhalhil, struck with admiration for the youth's comeliness, asked him who he was. "Bujayr," said he, "the son of 'Amr, the son of 'Ubád." "And who is thy uncle on the mother's side?" "My mother is a captive" (for he would not name an uncle of whom he had no honour). Then Muhalhil slew him, crying, "Pay for Kulayb's shoe-latchet!" On hearing this, Ḥárith sent a message to Muhalhil in which he declared that if vengeance were satisfied by the death of Bujayr, he for his part would gladly acquiesce. But Muhalhil replied, "I have taken satisfaction only for Kulayb's shoe-latchet." Thereupon Ḥárith sprang up in wrath and cried:—

Outbreak of war between Taghlib and Bakr.

"God knows, I kindled not this fire, altho'
I am burned in it to-day.
A lord for a shoe-latchet is too dear:
To horse! To horse! Away!" [2]

And al-Find, of the Banú Bakr, said on this occasion:—

"We spared the Banú Hind [3] *and said, 'Our brothers they remain:*
It may be Time will make of us one people yet again.'

[1] *Ḥamása*, 423, 11 sqq. Nöldeke's *Delectus*, p. 41, l. 3 sqq.

[2] *Ḥamása*, 252, 8 seq. Nöldeke's *Delectus*, p. 44, l. 3 seq.

[3] Hind is the mother of Bakr and Taghlib. Here the Banú Hind (Sons of Hind) are the Taghlibites.

But when the wrong grew manifest, and naked Ill stood plain,
And naught was left but ruthless hate, we paid them bane with bane!

Verses by al-Find.

As lions marched we forth to war in wrath and high disdain:
Our swords brought widowhood and tears and wailing in their train,
Our spears dealt gashes wide whence blood like water spilled amain.
No way but Force to weaken Force and mastery obtain;
'Tis wooing contumely to meet wild actions with humane:
By evil thou may'st win to peace when good is tried in vain." [1]

The Banú Bakr now prepared for a decisive battle. As their enemy had the advantage in numbers, they adopted a stratagem devised by Ḥárith. "Fight them," said he, "with your women. Equip every woman with a small waterskin and give her a club. Place the whole body of them behind you—this will make you more resolved in battle—and wear some distinguishing mark which they will recognise, so that when a woman passes by one of your wounded she may know him by his mark and give him water to drink, and raise him from the ground; but when she passes by one of your foes she will smite him with her club and slay him." So the Bakrites shaved their heads, devoting themselves to death, and made this a mark of recognition between themselves and their women, and this day was called the Day of Shearing. Now Jaḥdar b. Ḍubay'a was an ill-favoured, dwarfish man, with fair flowing love-locks, and he said, "O my people, if ye shave my head ye will disfigure me, so leave my locks for the first horseman of Taghlib that shall emerge from the hill-pass on the morrow" (meaning "I will answer for him, if my locks are spared"). On his request being granted, he exclaimed :—

The Day of Shearing.

"To wife and daughter
Henceforth I am dead:
Dust for ointment
On my hair is shed.

Let me close with the horsemen
Who hither ride,
Cut my locks from me
If I stand aside!

The vow of Jaḥdar b. Ḍubay'a.

[1] *Ḥamása*, 9, 17 seq. Nöldeke's *Delectus*, p. 45, l. 10 sqq.

Well wots a mother
If the son she bore
And swaddled on her bosom
And smelt him o'er,

Whenever warriors
In the mellay meet,
Is a puny weakling
Or a man complete!" [1]

He kept his promise but in the course of the fight he fell, severely wounded. When the women came to him, they saw his love-locks and imagining that he was an enemy despatched him with their clubs.

Women as combatants.

The presence of women on the field and the active share they took in the combat naturally provoked the bitterest feelings. If they were not engaged in finishing the bloody work of the men, their tongues were busy inciting them. We are told that a daughter of al-Find bared herself recklessly and chanted :—

"*War! War! War! War!*
It has blazed up and scorched us sore.
The highlands are filled with its roar.
Well done, the morning when your heads ye shore!" [2]

The mothers were accompanied by their children, whose tender age did not always protect them from an exasperated foe. It is related that a horseman of the Banú Taghlib transfixed a young boy and lifted him up on the point of his spear. He is said to have been urged to this act of savagery by one al-Bazbáz, who was riding behind him on the crupper. Their triumph was short; al-Find saw them, and with a single spear-thrust pinned them to each other—an exploit which his own verses record.

On this day the Banú Bakr gained a great victory, and broke the power of Taghlib. It was the last battle of note in the Forty Years' War, which was carried on, by raiding and plundering, until the exhaustion of both tribes and the influence of King Mundhir III of Ḥíra brought it to an end.

Not many years after the conclusion of peace between

[1] *Ḥamása*, 252, 14 seq. Nöldeke's *Delectus*, p. 46, l. 16 sqq.
[2] *Ḥamása*, 254, 6 seq. Nöldeke's *Delectus*, p. 47, l. 2 seq.

Bakr and Taghlib, another war, hardly less famous in tradition than the War of Basús, broke out in Central Arabia. The combatants were the tribes of 'Abs and Dhubyán, the principal stocks of the Banú Ghaṭafán, and the occasion of their coming to blows is related as follows:—

The War of Dáḥis and Ghabrá.

Qays, son of Zuhayr, was chieftain of 'Abs. He had a horse called Dáḥis, renowned for its speed, which he matched against Ghabrá, a mare belonging to Ḥudhayfa b. Badr, the chief of Dhubyán. It was agreed that the course should be a hundred bow-shots in length, and that the victor should receive a hundred camels. When the race began Ghabrá took the lead, but as they left the firm ground and entered upon the sand, where the 'going' was heavy, Dáḥis gradually drew level and passed his antagonist. He was nearing the goal when some Dhubyánites sprang from an ambuscade prepared beforehand, and drove him out of his course, thus enabling Ghabrá to defeat him. On being informed of this foul play Qays naturally claimed that he had won the wager, but the men of Dhubyán refused to pay even a single camel. Bitterly resenting their treachery, he waylaid and slew one of Ḥudhayfa's brothers. Ḥudhayfa sought vengeance, and the murder of Málik, a brother of Qays, by his horsemen gave the signal for war. In the fighting which ensued Dhubyán more than held their own, but neither party could obtain a decisive advantage. Qays slew the brothers Ḥudhayfa and Ḥamal—

"Ḥamal I slew and eased my heart thereby,
Ḥudhayfa glutted my avenging brand;
But though I slaked my thirst by slaying them,
I would as lief have lost my own right hand." [1]

After a long period—forty years according to the traditional computation—'Abs and Dhubyán were reconciled by the exertions of two chieftains of the latter tribe, Ḥárith b. 'Awf and Harim b.

---

[1] *Ḥamása*, 96. Ibn Nubáta, cited by Rasmussen, *Additamenta ad Historiam Arabum ante Islamismum*, p. 34, remarks that before Qays no one had ever lamented a foe slain by himself (*wa-huwa awwalu man rathá maqtúlahu*).

Sinán, whose generous and patriotic intervention the poet Zuhayr has celebrated. Qays went into exile. "I will not look," he said, "on the face of any woman of Dhubyán whose father or brother or husband or son I have killed." If we may believe the legend, he became a Christian monk and ended his days in 'Umán.

The Hijáz.

Descending westward from the highlands of Najd the traveller gradually approaches the Red Sea, which is separated from the mountains running parallel to it by a narrow strip of coast-land, called the Tiháma (Netherland). The rugged plateau between Najd and the coast forms the Ḥijáz (Barrier), through which in ancient times the Sabæan caravans laden with costly merchandise passed on their way to the Mediterranean ports. Long before the beginning of our era two considerable trading settlements had sprung up in this region, viz., Macoraba (Mecca) and, some distance farther north, Yathrippa (Yathrib, the Pre-islamic name of Medína). Of their early inhabitants and history we know nothing except what is related by Muḥammadan writers, whose information reaches back to the days of Adam and Abraham. Mecca was the cradle of Islam, and Islam, according to Muḥammad, is the religion of Abraham, which was corrupted by succeeding generations until he himself was sent to purify it and to preach it anew. Consequently the Pre-islamic history of Mecca has all been, so to speak, 'Islamised.' The Holy City of Islam is made to appear in the same light thousands of years before the Prophet's time: here, it is said, the Arabs were united in worship of Allah, hence they scattered and fell into idolatry, hither they return annually as pilgrims to a shrine which had been originally dedicated to the One Supreme Being, but which afterwards became a Pantheon of tribal deities. This theory lies at the root of the Muḥammadan legend which I shall now recount as briefly as possible, only touching on the salient points of interest.

In the Meccan valley—the primitive home of that portion

of the Arab race which claims descent from Ismá'íl (Ishmael), the son of Ibráhím (Abraham) by Hájar (Hagar)—stands an irregular, cube-shaped building of small dimensions —the Ka'ba. Legend attributes its foundation to Adam, who built it by Divine command after a celestial archetype. At the Deluge it was taken up into heaven, but was rebuilt on its former site by Abraham and Ishmael. While they were occupied in this work Gabriel brought the celebrated Black Stone, which is set in the south-east corner of the building, and he also instructed them in the ceremonies of the Pilgrimage. When all was finished Abraham stood on a rock known to later ages as the *Maqámu Ibráhím*, and, turning to the four quarters of the sky, made proclamation: "O ye people! The Pilgrimage to the Ancient House is prescribed unto you. Hearken to your Lord!" And from every part of the world came the answer: "*Labbayka 'lláhumma, labbayka*"—*i.e.*, "We obey, O God, we obey."

Foundation of the Ka'ba.

The descendants of Ishmael multiplied exceedingly, so that the barren valley could no longer support them, and a great number wandered forth to other lands. They were succeeded as rulers of the sacred territory by the tribe of Jurhum, who waxed in pride and evil-doing until the vengeance of God fell upon them. Mention has frequently been made of the Bursting of the Dyke of Ma'rib, which caused an extensive movement of Yemenite stocks to the north. The invaders halted in the Ḥijáz and, having almost exterminated the Jurhumites, resumed their journey. One group, however—the Banú Khuzá'a, led by their chief Luḥayy—settled in the neighbourhood of Mecca. 'Amr, son of Luḥayy, was renowned among the Arabs for his wealth and generosity. Ibn Hishám says: 'I have been told by a learned man that 'Amr b. Luḥayy went from Mecca to Syria on some business and when he arrived at Má'ab, in the land of al-Balqá, he found the inhabitants, who were 'Amálíq, worshipping idols. "What are these idols?" he in-

Idolatry introduced at Mecca.

quired. "They are idols that send us rain when we ask them for rain, and help us when we ask them for help." "Will ye not give me one of them," said 'Amr, "that I may take it to Arabia to be worshipped there?" So they gave him an idol called Hubal, which he brought to Mecca and set it up and bade the people worship and venerate it.'[1] Following his example, the Arabs brought their idols and installed them round the sanctuary. The triumph of Paganism was complete. We are told that hundreds of idols were destroyed by Muḥammad when he entered Mecca at the head of a Moslem army in 8 A.H. = 629 A.D.

The Quraysh.

To return to the posterity of Ismá'íl through 'Adnán: the principal of their descendants who remained in the Ḥijáz were the Hudhayl, the Kinána, and the Quraysh. The last-named tribe must now engage our attention almost exclusively. During the century before Muḥammad we find them in undisputed possession of Mecca and acknowledged guardians of the Ka'ba—an office which they administered with a shrewd appreciation of its commercial value. Their rise to power is related as follows:—

The story of Quṣayy.

Kiláb b. Murra, a man of Quraysh, had two sons, Zuhra and Zayd. The latter was still a young child when his father died, and soon afterwards his mother, Fáṭima, who had married again, left Mecca, taking Zayd with her, and went to live in her new husband's home beside the Syrian borders. Zayd grew up far from his native land, and for this reason he got the name of Quṣayy—*i.e.*, 'Little Far-away.' When he reached man's estate and discovered his true origin he returned to Mecca, where the hegemony was wholly in the hands of the Khuzá'ites under their chieftain, Ḥulayl b. Ḥubshiyya, with the determination to procure the superintendence of the Ka'ba for his own people, the Quraysh, who as pure-blooded descendants of Ismá'íl had the best right to that honour. By his marriage with Ḥubbá, the daughter of Ḥulayl, he hoped to inherit the privileges vested in his father-in-law, but Ḥulayl on his death-bed committed the keys of the Ka'ba to a

[1] Ibn Hishám, p. 51, l. 7 sqq.

kinsman named Abú Ghubshán. Not to be baffled, Quṣayy made the keeper drunk and persuaded him to sell the keys for a skin of wine—hence the proverbs "A greater fool than Abú Ghubshán" and "Abú Ghubshán's bargain," denoting a miserable fraud. Naturally the Khuzá'ites did not acquiesce in the results of this transaction; they took up arms, but Quṣayy was prepared for the struggle and won a decisive victory. He was now master of Temple and Town and could proceed to the work of organisation. His first step was to bring together the Quraysh, who had previously been dispersed over a wide area, into the Meccan valley—this earned for him the title of *al-Mujammi'* (the Congregator)—so that each family had its allotted quarter. He built a House of Assembly (*Dáru 'l-Nadwa*), where matters affecting the common weal were discussed by the Elders of the tribe. He also instituted and centred in himself a number of dignities in connection with the government of the Ka'ba and the administration of the Pilgrimage, besides others of a political and military character. Such was his authority that after his death, no less than during his life, all these ordinances were regarded by the Quraysh as sacred and inviolable.

Quṣayy master of Mecca.

The death of Quṣayy may be placed in the latter half of the fifth century. His descendant, the Prophet Muḥammad, was born about a hundred years afterwards, in 570 or 571 A.D. With one notable exception, to be mentioned immediately, the history of Mecca during the period thus defined is a record of petty factions unbroken by any event of importance. The Prophet's ancestors fill the stage and assume a commanding position, which in all likelihood they never possessed; the historical rivalry of the Umayyads and 'Abbásids appears in the persons of their founders, Umayya and Háshim—and so forth. Meanwhile the influence of the Quraysh was steadily maintained and extended. The Ka'ba had become a great national rendezvous, and the crowds of pilgrims which it attracted from almost every Arabian clan not only raised the credit of the Quraysh, but also materially contributed to their commercial prosperity. It has already been related how Abraha, the Abyssinian viceroy of Yemen, resolved to march against

Mecca in the sixth century after Christ.

Mecca with the avowed purpose of avenging upon the Ka'ba a sacrilege committed by one of the Quraysh in the church at Ṣan'á. Something of that kind may have served as a pretext, but no doubt his real aim was to conquer Mecca and to gain control of her trade.

The Year of the Elephant.

This memorable expedition[1] is said by Moslem historians to have taken place in the year of Muḥammad's birth (about 570 A.D.), usually known as the Year of the Elephant—a proof that the Arabs were deeply impressed by the extraordinary spectacle of these huge animals, one or more of which accompanied the Abyssinian force. The report of Abraha's preparations filled the tribesmen with dismay. At first they endeavoured to oppose his march, regarding the defence of the Ka'ba as a sacred duty, but they soon lost heart, and Abraha, after defeating Dhú Nafar, a Ḥimyarite chieftain, encamped in the neighbourhood of Mecca without further resistance. He sent the following message to 'Abdu 'l-Muṭṭalib, the Prophet's grandfather, who was at that time the most influential personage in Mecca: "I have not come to wage war on you, but only to destroy the Temple. Unless you take up arms in its defence, I have no wish to shed your blood." 'Abdu 'l-Muṭṭalib replied: "By God, we seek not war, for which we are unable. This is God's holy House and the House of Abraham, His Friend; it is for Him to protect His House and Sanctuary; if He abandons it, we cannot defend it."

The Abyssinians at Mecca.

Then 'Abdu 'l-Muṭṭalib was conducted by the envoy to the Abyssinian camp, as Abraha had ordered. There he inquired after Dhú Nafar, who was his friend, and found him a prisoner. "O Dhú Nafar," said he, "can you do aught in that which has befallen us?" Dhú Nafar answered, "What can a man do who is a captive in the hands of a

'Abdu 'l-Muṭṭalib's interview with Abraha.

[1] In the account of Abraha's invasion given below I have followed Ṭabarí, i, 936, 9 – 945, 19 = Nöldeke's translation, pp. 206–220.

king, expecting day and night to be put to death? I can do nothing at all in the matter, but Unays, the elephant-driver, is my friend; I will send to him and press your claims on his consideration and ask him to procure you an audience with the king. Tell Unays what you wish: he will plead with the king in your favour if he can." So Dhú Nafar sent for Unays and said to him, "O Unays, 'Abdu 'l-Muṭṭalib is lord of Quraysh and master of the caravans of Mecca. He feeds the people in the plain and the wild creatures on the mountain-tops. The king has seized two hundred of his camels. Now get him admitted to the king's presence and help him to the best of your power." Unays consented, and soon 'Abdu 'l-Muṭṭalib stood before the king. When Abraha saw him he held him in too high respect to let him sit in an inferior place, but was unwilling that the Abyssinians should see the Arab chief, who was a large man and a comely, seated on a level with himself; he therefore descended from his throne and sat on his carpet and bade 'Abdu 'l-Muṭṭalib sit beside him. Then he said to his dragoman, "Ask him what he wants of me." 'Abdu 'l-Muṭṭalib replied, "I want the king to restore to me two hundred camels of mine which he has taken away." Abraha said to the dragoman, "Tell him: You pleased me when I first saw you, but now that you have spoken to me I hold you cheap. What! do you speak to me of two hundred camels which I have taken, and omit to speak of a temple venerated by you and your fathers which I have come to destroy?" Then said 'Abdu 'l-Muṭṭalib: "The camels are mine, but the Temple belongs to another, who will defend it," and on the king exclaiming, "He cannot defend it from me," he said, "That is your affair; only give me back my camels."

As it is related in a more credible version, the tribes settled round Mecca sent ambassadors, of whom 'Abdu 'l-Muṭṭalib was one, offering to surrender a third part of their possessions to Abraha on condition that he should spare the Temple, but he refused. Having recovered his camels, 'Abdu 'l-Muṭṭalib returned to the Quraysh, told them what had happened, and bade them leave the city and take shelter in the mountains. Then he went to the Ka'ba, accompanied by several of the Quraysh, to pray for help against Abraha and his army. Grasping the ring of the door, he cried:—

"O God, defend Thy neighbouring folk even as a man his gear[1] defendeth!
Let not their Cross and guileful plans defeat the plans Thyself intendeth!
But if Thou make it so, 'tis well: according to Thy will it endeth."[2]

[1] I read *ḥilálak.* See Glossary to Ṭabarí. [2] Ṭabarí, i, 940, 13.

Next morning, when Abraha prepared to enter Mecca, his elephant knelt down and would not budge, though they beat its head with an axe and thrust sharp stakes into its flanks; but when they turned it in the direction of Yemen, it rose up and trotted with alacrity. Then God sent from the sea a flock of birds like swallows every one of which carried three stones as large as a chick-pea or a lentil, one in its bill and one in each claw, and all who were struck by those stones perished.[1] The rest fled in disorder, dropping down as they ran or wherever they halted to quench their thirst. Abraha himself was smitten with a plague so that his limbs rotted off piecemeal.[2]

Rout of the Abyssinians.

These details are founded on the 105th chapter of the Koran, entitled 'The Súra of the Elephant,' which may be freely rendered as follows:—

"Hast not thou seen the people of the Elephant, how dealt with them the Lord?
Did not He make their plot to end in ruin abhorred?—
When He sent against them birds, horde on horde,
And stones of baked clay upon them poured,
And made them as leaves of corn devoured."

The part played by 'Abdu 'l-Muṭṭalib in the story is, of course, a pious fiction designed to glorify the Holy City and to claim for the Prophet's family fifty years before Islam a predominance which they did not obtain until long afterwards; but equally of course the legend reflects Muḥammadan belief, and may be studied with advantage as a characteristic specimen of its class.

"When God repulsed the Abyssinians from Mecca and smote them with His vengeance, the Arabs held the Quraysh

[1] Another version says: "Whenever a man was struck sores and pustules broke out on that part of his body. This was the first appearance of the small-pox" (Ṭabarí, i, 945, 2 sqq.). Here we have the historical fact—an outbreak of pestilence in the Abyssinian army—which gave rise to the legend related above.

[2] There is trustworthy evidence that Abraha continued to rule Yemen for some time after his defeat.

in high respect and said, 'They are God's people: God hath fought for them and hath defended them against their enemy;' and made poems on this matter."[1] The following verses, according to Ibn Isḥáq, are by Abu 'l-Ṣalt b. Abí Rabí'a of Thaqíf; others more reasonably ascribe them to his son Umayya, a well-known poet and monotheist (*Ḥaníf*) contemporary with Muḥammad:—

Verses by Umayya b. Abi 'l-Ṣalt.

"Lo, the signs of our Lord are everlasting,
None disputes them except the unbeliever.
He created Day and Night: unto all men
Is their Reckoning ordained, clear and certain.
Gracious Lord! He illumines the daytime
With a sun widely scattering radiance.
He the Elephant stayed at Mughammas
So that sore it limped as though it were hamstrung,
Cleaving close to its halter, and down dropped,
As one falls from the crag of a mountain.
Gathered round it were princes of Kinda,
Noble heroes, fierce hawks in the mellay.
There they left it: they all fled together,
Every man with his shank-bone broken.
Vain before God is every religion,
When the dead rise, except the Ḥanífite.[2]"

The patriotic feelings aroused in the Arabs of the Ḥijáz by the Abyssinian invasion—feelings which must have been shared to some extent by the Bedouins generally—received a fresh stimulus through events which occurred about forty years after this time on the other side of the peninsula. It will be remembered that the Lakhmite dynasty at Ḥíra came to an end with Nu'mán III, who was cruelly executed by Khusraw Parwéz (602 or 607 A.D.).[3] Before his death he had deposited his arms and other property with Háni', a chieftain of the Banú Bakr. These were claimed by Khusraw, and as Háni' refused to give them up, a Persian army was sent to Dhú Qár,

[1] Ibn Hishám, p. 38, l. 14 sqq. [2] *Ibid.*, p. 40, l. 12 sqq.
[3] See pp. 48–49 *supra*.

a place near Kúfa abounding in water and consequently a favourite resort of the Bakrites during the dry season. A desperate conflict ensued, in which the Persians were completely routed.[1] Although the forces engaged were comparatively small,[2] this victory was justly regarded by the Arabs as marking the commencement of a new order of things; *e.g.*, it is related that Muḥammad said when the tidings reached him: "This is the first day on which the Arabs have obtained satisfaction from the Persians." The desert tribes, hitherto overshadowed by the Sásánian Empire and held in check by the powerful dynasty of Ḥíra, were now confident and aggressive. They began to hate and despise the Colossus which they no longer feared, and which, before many years had elapsed, they trampled in the dust.

Battle of Dhú Qár (*circa* 610 A.D.).

[1] Full details are given by Ṭabarí, i, 1016–1037 = Nöldeke's translation, pp. 311–345.

[2] A poet speaks of three thousand Arabs and two thousand Persians (Ṭabarí, i, 1036, 5–6).

CHAPTER III

PRE-ISLAMIC POETRY, MANNERS, AND RELIGION

"WHEN there appeared a poet in a family of the Arabs, the other tribes round about would gather together to that family and wish them joy of their good luck. Feasts would be got ready, the women of the tribe would join together in bands, playing upon lutes, as they were wont to do at bridals, and the men and boys would congratulate one another; for a poet was a defence to the honour of them all, a weapon to ward off insult from their good name, and a means of perpetuating their glorious deeds and of establishing their fame for ever. And they used not to wish one another joy but for three things—the birth of a boy, the coming to light of a poet, and the foaling of a noble mare." [1]

As far as extant literature is concerned—and at this time there was only a spoken literature, which was preserved by oral tradition, and first committed to writing long afterwards—the *Jáhiliyya* or Pre-islamic Age covers scarcely more than a century, from about 500 A.D., when the oldest poems of which we have any record were composed, to the year of Muḥammad's Flight to Medína (622 A.D.), which is the starting-point of a new era in Arabian history. The influence of these hundred and twenty years was great and lasting.

[1] Ibn Rashíq in Suyúṭí's *Muzhir* (Buláq, 1282 A.H.), Part II, p. 236, l. 22 sqq. I quote the translation of Sir Charles Lyall in the Introduction to his *Ancient Arabian Poetry*, p. 17, a most admirable work which should be placed in the hands of every one who is beginning the study of this difficult subject.

They saw the rise and incipient decline of a poetry which most Arabic-speaking Moslems have always regarded as a model of unapproachable excellence; a poetry rooted in the life of the people, that insensibly moulded their minds and fixed their character and made them morally and spiritually a nation long before Muḥammad welded the various conflicting groups into a single organism, animated, for some time at least, by a common purpose. In those days poetry was no luxury for the cultured few, but the sole medium of literary expression. Every tribe had its poets, who freely uttered what they felt and thought. Their unwritten words "flew across the desert faster than arrows," and came home to the hearts and bosoms of all who heard them. Thus in the midst of outward strife and disintegration a unifying principle was at work. Poetry gave life and currency to an ideal of Arabian virtue (*muruwwa*), which, though based on tribal community of blood and insisting that only ties of blood were sacred, nevertheless became an invisible bond between diverse clans, and formed, whether consciously or not, the basis of a national community of sentiment.

Origins of Arabian poetry

In the following pages I propose to trace the origins of Arabian poetry, to describe its form, contents, and general features, to give some account of the most celebrated Pre-islamic poets and collections of Pre-islamic verse, and finally to show in what manner it was preserved and handed down.

By the ancient Arabs the poet (*shá‘ir*, plural *shu‘ará*), as his name implies, was held to be a person endowed with supernatural knowledge, a wizard in league with spirits (*jinn*) or satans (*shayáṭín*) and dependent on them for the magical powers which he displayed. This view of his personality, as well as the influential position which he occupied, are curiously indicated by the story of a certain youth who was refused the hand of his beloved on the ground that he was neither a poet nor a soothsayer nor a water-diviner.[1] The idea of poetry as an art was developed afterwards; the pagan *shá'ir* is the oracle of his tribe, their guide in peace and their champion in war. It was to him they turned for counsel when they sought new pastures, only at his word would they pitch or strike their 'houses of hair,' and when the tired and thirsty wanderers found a well and drank of its water and washed themselves, led by him they may have raised their voices together and sung, like Israel—

"Spring up, O well, sing ye unto it."[2]

Besides fountain-songs, war-songs, and hymns to idols, other kinds of poetry must have existed in the earliest times—*e.g.*, the love-song and the dirge. The powers of the *shá'ir*, however, were chiefly exhibited in Satire (*hijá*), which in the oldest known form "introduces and accompanies the tribal feud, and is an element of war just as important as the actual fighting."[3] The menaces which he hurled against the foe were believed to be inevitably fatal. His rhymes, often compared to arrows, had all the effect of a solemn curse spoken by a divinely inspired prophet or priest,[4] and their pronunciation was attended with peculiar ceremonies of a symbolic character, such as anointing the hair on one side of the head, letting the mantle hang down loosely, and wearing only one sandal.[5] Satire retained something of these ominous associations at a much later period when the magic utterance of the *shá'ir* had long given place to the lampoon

Satire.

[1] Freytag, *Arabum Proverbia*, vol. ii, p. 494.

[2] Numb. xxi, 17. Such well-songs are still sung in the Syrian desert (see Enno Littmann, *Neuarabische Volkspoesie*, in *Abhand. der Kön. Gesellschaft der Wissenschaften, Phil.-Hist. Klasse*, Göttingen, 1901), p. 92. In a specimen cited at p. 81 we find the words *witla yā dlēwēna*—*i.e.*, "Rise, O bucket!" several times repeated.

[3] Goldziher, *Ueber die Vorgeschichte der Higâ'-Poesie* in his *Abhand. zur Arab. Philologie*, Part I (Leyden, 1896), p. 26.

[4] *Cf.* the story of Balak and Balaam, with Goldziher's remarks thereon, *ibid.*, p. 42 seq.

[5] *Ibid.*, p. 46 seq.

by which the poet reviles his enemies and holds them up to shame.

The obscure beginnings of Arabian poetry, presided over by the magician and his familiar spirits, have left not a rack behind in the shape of literature, but the task of reconstruction is comparatively easy where we are dealing with a people so conservative and tenacious of antiquity as the Arabs. Thus it may be taken for certain that the oldest form of poetical speech in Arabia was rhyme without metre (*Saj'*), or, as we should say, 'rhymed prose,' although the fact of Muḥammad's adversaries calling him a poet because he used it in the Koran shows the light in which it was regarded even after the invention and elaboration of metre. Later on, as we shall see, *Saj'* became a merely rhetorical ornament, the distinguishing mark of all eloquence whether spoken or written, but originally it had a deeper, almost religious, significance as the special form adopted by poets, soothsayers, and the like in their supernatural revelations and for conveying to the vulgar every kind of mysterious and esoteric lore.

Saj'.

Out of *Saj'* was evolved the most ancient of the Arabian metres, which is known by the name of *Rajaz*.[1] This is an irregular iambic metre usually consisting of four or six—an Arab would write 'two or three'—feet to the line; and it is a peculiarity of *Rajaz*, marking its affinity to *Saj'*, that all the lines rhyme with each other, whereas in the more artificial metres only the opening verse[2]

Rajaz.

[1] *Rajaz* primarily means "a tremor (which is a symptom of disease) in the hind-quarters of a camel." This suggested to Dr. G. Jacob his interesting theory that the Arabian metres arose out of the camel-driver's song (*ḥidá*) in harmony with the varying paces of the animal which he rode (*Studien in arabischen Dichtern*, Heft III, p. 179 sqq.).

[2] The Arabic verse (*bayt*) consists of two halves or hemistichs (*miṣrá'*). It is generally convenient to use the word 'line' as a translation of *miṣrá'*, but the reader must understand that the 'line' is not, as in English poetry, an independent unit. *Rajaz* is the sole exception to this rule, there being here no division into hemistichs, but each line (verse) forming an unbroken whole and rhyming with that which precedes it.

is doubly rhymed. A further characteristic of *Rajaz* is that it should be uttered extempore, a few verses at a time—commonly verses expressing some personal feeling, emotion, or experience, like those of the aged warrior Durayd b. Zayd b. Nahd when he lay dying :—

> "The house of death[1] is builded for Durayd to-day.
> Could Time be worn out, sure had I worn Time away.
> No single foe but I had faced and brought to bay.
> The spoils I gathered in, how excellent were they !
> The women that I loved, how fine was their array !"[2]

Other metres.

Here would have been the proper place to give an account of the principal Arabian metres—the 'Perfect' (*Kámil*), the 'Ample' (*Wáfir*), the 'Long' (*Ṭawíl*), the 'Wide' (*Basíṭ*), the 'Light' (*Khafíf*), and several more—but in order to save valuable space I must content myself with referring the reader to the extremely lucid treatment of this subject by Sir Charles Lyall in the Introduction to his *Ancient Arabian Poetry*, pp. xlv–lii. All the metres are quantitative, as in Greek and Latin. Their names and laws were unknown to the Pre-islamic bards : the rules of prosody were first deduced from the ancient poems and systematised by the grammarian, Khalíl b. Aḥmad († 791 A.D.), to whom the idea is said to have occurred as he watched a coppersmith beating time on the anvil with his hammer.

The oldest extant poems.

We have now to consider the form and matter of the oldest extant poems in the Arabic language. Between these highly developed productions and the rude doggerel of *Saj'* or *Rajaz* there lies an interval, the length of which it is impossible even to conjecture. The first poets are already consummate masters of the craft. "The number and complexity of the measures which they use, their established laws of quantity and rhyme, and the uniform

[1] In Arabic 'al-bayt,' the tent, which is here used figuratively for the grave.

[2] Ibn Qutayba, *Kitábu 'l-Shi'r wa-'l-Shu'ará*, p. 36, l. 3 sqq.

manner in which they introduce the subject of their poems,[1] notwithstanding the distance which often separated one composer from another, all point to a long previous study and cultivation of the art of expression and the capacities of their language, a study of which no record now remains." [2]

Their date.

It is not improbable that the dawn of the Golden Age of Arabian Poetry coincided with the first decade of the sixth century after Christ. About that time the War of Basús, the chronicle of which has preserved a considerable amount of contemporary verse, was in full blaze; and the first Arabian ode was composed, according to tradition, by Muhalhil b. Rabí'a the Taghlibite on the death of his brother, the chieftain Kulayb, which caused war to break out between Bakr and Taghlib. At any rate, during the next hundred years in almost every part of the peninsula we meet with a brilliant succession of singers, all using the same poetical dialect and strictly adhering to the same rules of composition. The fashion which they set maintained itself virtually unaltered down to the end of the Umayyad period (750 A.D.), and though challenged by some daring spirits under the 'Abbásid Caliphate, speedily reasserted its supremacy, which at the present day is almost as absolute as ever.

This fashion centres in the *Qaṣída*,[3] or Ode, the only form, or rather the only finished type of poetry that existed

[1] Already in the sixth century A.D. the poet 'Antara complains that his predecessors have left nothing new for him to say (*Mu'allaqa*, v. 1).

[2] *Ancient Arabian Poetry*, Introduction, p. xvi.

[3] *Qaṣída* is explained by Arabian lexicographers to mean a poem with an artistic purpose, but they differ as to the precise sense in which 'purpose' is to be understood. Modern critics are equally at variance. Jacob (*Stud. in Arab. Dichtern*, Heft III, p. 203) would derive the word from the principal motive of these poems, namely, to gain a rich reward in return for praise and flattery. Ahlwardt (*Bemerkungen über die Aechtheit der alten Arab. Gedichte*, p. 24 seq.) connects it with *qaṣada*, *to break*, "because it consists of verses, every one of which is divided into two halves, with a common end-rhyme: thus the whole poem is *broken*, as it were, into two halves;" while in the *Rajaz* verses, as we have seen (p. 74 *supra*), there is no such break.

in what, for want of a better word, may be called the classical period of Arabic literature. The verses (*abyát*, singular *bayt*) of which it is built vary in number, but are seldom less than twenty-five or more than a hundred; and the arrangement of the rhymes is such that, while the two halves of the first verse rhyme together, the same rhyme is repeated once in the second, third, and every following verse to the end of the poem. Blank-verse is alien to the Arabs, who regard rhyme not as a pleasing ornament or a "troublesome bondage," but as a vital organ of poetry. The rhymes are usually feminine, *e.g.*, sa*khìná*, tu*llná*, mu*hìná*; mukh*lidí*, *yadí*, 'uw*wadí*; ri*jámuhá*, si*lámuhá*, ḥa*rámuhá*. To surmount the difficulties of the monorhyme demands great technical skill even in a language of which the peculiar formation renders the supply of rhymes extraordinarily abundant. The longest of the *Mu'allaqát*, the so-called 'Long Poems,' is considerably shorter than Gray's *Elegy*. An Arabian Homer or Chaucer must have condescended to prose. With respect to metre the poet may choose any except *Rajaz*, which is deemed beneath the dignity of the Ode, but his liberty does not extend either to the choice of subjects or to the method of handling them: on the contrary, the course of his ideas is determined by rigid conventions which he durst not overstep.

The Qaṣída.

"I have heard," says Ibn Qutayba, "from a man of learning that the composer of Odes began by mentioning the deserted dwelling-places and the relics and traces of habitation. Then he wept and complained and addressed the desolate encampment, and begged his companion to make a halt, in order that he might have occasion to speak of those who had once lived there and afterwards departed; for the dwellers in tents were different from townsmen or villagers in respect of coming and going, because they moved from one water-spring to another, seeking pasture and searching out the places where rain had fallen. Then to this he linked the erotic prelude (*nasíb*), and bewailed the violence of his love and the anguish of separation from his mistress and the extremity of his passion and desire, so as to win the hearts of his hearers and divert

Ibn Qutayba's account of the contents and divisions of the Ode.

their eyes towards him and invite their ears to listen to him, since the song of love touches men's souls and takes hold of their hearts, God having put it in the constitution of His creatures to love dalliance and the society of women, in such wise that we find very few but are attached thereto by some tie or have some share therein, whether lawful or unpermitted. Now, when the poet had assured himself of an attentive hearing, he followed up his advantage and set forth his claim : thus he went on to complain of fatigue and want of sleep and travelling by night and of the noonday heat, and how his camel had been reduced to leanness. And when, after representing all the discomfort and danger of his journey, he knew that he had fully justified his hope and expectation of receiving his due meed from the person to whom the poem was addressed, he entered upon the panegyric (*madíḥ*), and incited him to reward, and kindled his generosity by exalting him above his peers and pronouncing the greatest dignity, in comparison with his, to be little." [1]

Hundreds of Odes answer exactly to this description, which must not, however, be regarded as the invariable model. The erotic prelude is often omitted, especially in elegies ; or if it does not lead directly to the main subject, it may be followed by a faithful and minute delineation of the poet's horse or camel which bears him through the wilderness with a speed like that of the antelope, the wild ass, or the ostrich : Bedouin poetry abounds in fine studies of animal life.[2] The choice of a motive is left open. Panegyric, no doubt, paid better than any other, and was therefore the favourite ; but in Pre-islamic times the poet could generally please himself. The *qaṣída* is no organic whole : rather its unity resembles that of a series of pictures by the same hand or, to employ an Eastern trope, of pearls various in size and quality threaded on a necklace.

The ancient poetry may be defined as an illustrative criti-

[1] *Kitábu 'l-Shi'r wa-'l-Shu'ará*, p. 14, l. 10 sqq.

[2] Nöldeke (*Fünf Mo'allaqát*, i, p. 3 sqq.) makes the curious observation, which illustrates the highly artificial character of this poetry, that certain animals well known to the Arabs (*e.g.*, the panther, the jerboa, and the hare) are seldom mentioned and scarcely ever described, apparently for no reason except that they were not included in the conventional repertory.

cism of Pre-islamic life and thought. Here the Arab has drawn himself at full length without embellishment or extenuation.

It is not mere chance that Abú Tammám's famous anthology is called the *Ḥamása*, *i.e.*, 'Fortitude,' from the title of its first chapter, which occupies nearly a half of the book. 'Ḥamása' denotes the virtues most highly prized by the Arabs—bravery in battle, patience in misfortune, persistence in revenge, protection of the weak and defiance of the strong; the will, as Tennyson has said,

"To strive, to seek, to find, and not to yield."

The ideal Arab hero.

As types of the ideal Arab hero we may take Shanfará of Azd and his comrade in foray, Ta'abbaṭa Sharr^an^. Both were brigands, outlaws, swift runners, and excellent poets. Of the former

Shanfará.

"it is said that he was captured when a child from his tribe by the Banú Salámán, and brought up among them: he did not learn his origin until he had grown up, when he vowed vengeance against his captors, and returned to his own tribe. His oath was that he would slay a hundred men of Salámán; he slew ninety-eight, when an ambush of his enemies succeeded in taking him prisoner. In the struggle one of his hands was hewn off by a sword stroke, and, taking it in the other, he flung it in the face of a man of Salámán and killed him, thus making ninety-nine. Then he was overpowered and slain, with one still wanting to make up his number. As his skull lay bleaching on the ground, a man of his enemies passed by that way and kicked it with his foot; a splinter of bone entered his foot, the wound mortified, and he died, thus completing the hundred."[1]

The following passage is translated from Shanfará's splendid Ode named *Lámiyyatu 'l-'Arab* (the poem rhymed in *l* of the

[1] *Ancient Arabian Poetry*, p. 83.

Arabs), in which he describes his own heroic character and the hardships of a predatory life:—[1]

"And somewhere the noble find a refuge afar from scathe,
The outlaw a lonely spot where no kin with hatred burn.
Oh, never a prudent man, night-faring in hope or fear,
Hard pressed on the face of earth, but still he hath room to
turn.

To me now, in your default, are comrades a wolf untired,
A sleek leopard, and a fell hyena with shaggy mane :[2]
True comrades: they ne'er let out the secret in trust with them,
Nor basely forsake their friend because that he brought them
bane.

And each is a gallant heart and ready at honour's call,
Yet I, when the foremost charge, am bravest of all the brave ;
But if they with hands outstretched are seizing the booty won,
The slowest am I whenas most quick is the greedy knave.

By naught save my generous will I reach to the height of worth
Above them, and sure the best is he with the will to give.
Yea, well I am rid of those who pay not a kindness back,
Of whom I have no delight though neighbours to me they live.

Enow are companions three at last: an intrepid soul,
A glittering trenchant blade, a tough bow of ample size,
Loud-twanging, the sides thereof smooth-polished, a handsome
bow
Hung down from the shoulder-belt by thongs in a comely wise,
That groans, when the arrow slips away, like a woman crushed
By losses, bereaved of all her children, who wails and cries."

---

[1] Verses 3–13. I have attempted to imitate the 'Long' (*Ṭawíl*) metre of the original, viz. :—

⏑ — ⏓ | ⏑ — ⏓ — | ⏑ — ⏓ | ⏑ — ⏑ —

The Arabic text of the *Lámiyya*, with prose translation and commentary, is printed in De Sacy's *Chrestomathie Arabe* (2nd ed.), vol. ii[2], p. 134 sqq., and vol. ii, p. 337 sqq. It has been translated into English verse by G. Hughes (London, 1896). Other versions are mentioned by Nöldeke, *Beiträge zur Kenntniss d. Poesie d. alten Araber*, p. 200.

[2] The poet, apparently, means that his three friends are *like* the animals mentioned. Prof. Bevan remarks, however, that this interpretation is doubtful, since an Arab would scarcely compare his *friend* to a hyena.

On quitting his tribe, who cast him out when they were threatened on all sides by enemies seeking vengeance for the blood that he had spilt, Shanfará said :—

"Bury me not! Me you are forbidden to bury,
But thou, O hyena, soon wilt feast and make merry,
When foes bear away mine head, wherein is the best of me,
And leave on the battle-field for thee all the rest of me.
Here nevermore I hope to live glad—a stranger
Accurst, whose wild deeds have brought his people in danger."[1]

Ta'abbaṭa Sharran.

Thábit b. Jábir b. Sufyán of Fahm is said to have got his nickname, Ta'abbaṭa Sharr^{an}, because one day his mother, who had seen him go forth from his tent with a sword under his arm, on being asked, "Where is Thábit?" replied, "I know not: he put a mischief under his arm-pit (*ta'abbaṭa sharr^{an}*) and departed." According to another version of the story, the 'mischief' was a Ghoul whom he vanquished and slew and carried home in this manner. The following lines, which he addressed to his cousin, Shams b. Málik, may be applied with equal justice to the poet himself :—

"Little he complains of labour that befalls him; much he wills;
Diverse ways attempting, mightily his purpose he fulfils.
Through one desert in the sun's heat, through another in star-light,
Lonely as the wild ass, rides he bare-backed Danger noon and night.
He the foremost wind outpaceth, while in broken gusts it blows,
Speeding onward, never slackening, never staying for repose.
Prompt to dash upon the foeman, every minute watching well—
Are his eyes in slumber lightly sealed, his heart stands sentinel.
When the first advancing troopers rise to sight, he sets his hand
From the scabbard forth to draw his sharp-edged, finely-mettled brand.

---

[1] *Ḥamása*, 242.

When he shakes it in the breast-bone of a champion of the foe,
How the grinning Fates in open glee their flashing side-teeth show!
Solitude his chosen comrade, on he fares while overhead
By the Mother of the mazy constellations he is led."[1]

These verses admirably describe the rudimentary Arabian virtues of courage, hardness, and strength. We must now take a wider survey of the moral ideas on which pagan society was built, and of which Pre-islamic poetry is at once the promulgation and the record. There was no written code, no legal or religious sanction—nothing, in effect, save the binding force of traditional sentiment and opinion, *i.e.*, Honour. What, then, are the salient points of honour in which Virtue (*Muruwwa*), as it was understood by the heathen Arabs, consists?

The old Arabian points of honour.

Courage has been already mentioned. Arab courage is like that of the ancient Greeks, "dependent upon excitement and vanishing quickly before depression and delay."[2] Hence the Arab hero is defiant and boastful, as he appears, *e.g.*, in the *Mu'allaqa* of 'Amr b. Kulthúm. When there is little to lose by flight he will ride off unashamed; but he will fight to the death for his womenfolk, who in serious warfare often accompanied the tribe and were stationed behind the line of battle.[3]

Courage.

"When I saw the hard earth hollowed
By our women's flying footprints,
And Lamís her face uncovered
Like the full moon of the skies,
Showing forth her hidden beauties—
Then the matter was grim earnest:
I engaged their chief in combat,
Seeing help no other wise."[4]

[1] *Ḥamâsa*, 41–43. This poem has been rendered in verse by Sir Charles Lyall, *Ancient Arabian Poetry*, p. 16, and by the late Dr. A. B. Davidson, *Biblical and Literary Essays*, p. 263.

[2] Mahaffy, *Social Life in Greece*, p. 21.

[3] See pp. 59–60 *supra*.

[4] *Ḥamâsa*, 82–83. The poet is 'Amr b. Ma'díkarib, a famous heathen knight who accepted Islam and afterwards distinguished himself in the Persian wars.

The tribal constitution was a democracy guided by its chief men, who derived their authority from noble blood, noble character, wealth, wisdom, and experience. As a Bedouin poet has said in homely language—

"A folk that hath no chiefs must soon decay,
And chiefs it hath not when the vulgar sway.
Only with poles the tent is reared at last,
And poles it hath not save the pegs hold fast.
But when the pegs and poles are once combined,
Then stands accomplished that which was designed."[1]

The chiefs, however, durst not lay commands or penalties on their fellow-tribesmen. Every man ruled himself, and was free to rebuke presumption in others. "*If you are our lord*" (*i.e.*, if you act discreetly as a *sayyid* should), "*you will lord over us, but if you are a prey to pride, go and be proud!*" (*i.e.*, we will have nothing to do with you).[2] Loyalty in the mouth of a pagan Arab did not mean allegiance to his superiors, but faithful devotion to his equals; and it was closely connected with the idea of kinship. The family and the tribe, which included strangers living in the tribe under a covenant of protection—to defend these, individually and collectively, was a sacred duty. Honour required that a man should stand by his own people through thick and thin.

Loyalty.

"I am of Ghaziyya: if she be in error, then I will err;
And if Ghaziyya be guided right, I go right with her!"

sang Durayd b. Ṣimma, who had followed his kin, against his better judgment, in a foray which cost the life of his brother ʻAbdulláh.[3] If kinsmen seek help it should be given promptly, without respect to the merits of the case; if they do wrong

[1] Al-Afwah al-Awdí in Nöldeke's *Delectus*, p. 4, ll. 8–10. The poles and pegs represent lords and commons.

[2] *Ḥamása*, 122.

[3] *Ibid.*, 378.

it should be suffered as long as possible before resorting to violence.[1] The utilitarian view of friendship is often emphasised, as in these verses :—

"Take for thy brother whom thou wilt in the days of peace,
But know that when fighting comes thy kinsman alone is near.
Thy true friend thy kinsman is, who answers thy call for aid
With good will, when deeply drenched in bloodshed are sword and spear.
Oh, never forsake thy kinsman e'en tho' he do thee wrong,
For what he hath marred he mends thereafter and makes sincere."[2]

At the same time, notwithstanding their shrewd common sense, nothing is more characteristic of the Arabs—heathen and Muḥammadan alike—than the chivalrous devotion and disinterested self-sacrifice of which they are capable on behalf of their friends. In particular, the ancient poetry affords proof that they regarded with horror any breach of the solemn covenant plighted between patron and client or host and guest. This topic might be illustrated by many striking examples, but one will suffice :—

The story of Samaw'al b. 'Adiyá.

The Arabs say : "*Awfá mina 'l-Samaw'ali*"—"More loyal than al-Samaw'al" ; or *Wafá*un *ka-wafá'i 'l-Samaw'ali*"—"A loyalty like that of al-Samaw'al." These proverbs refer to Samaw'al b. 'Ádiyá, an Arab of Jewish descent and Jew by religion, who lived in his castle, called al-Ablaq (The Piebald), at Taymá, some distance north of Medína. There he dug a well of sweet water, and would entertain the Arabs who used to alight beside it ; and they supplied themselves with provisions from his castle and set up a market. It is related that the poet Imru'u 'l-Qays, while fleeing, hotly pursued by his enemies, towards Syria, took refuge with Samaw'al, and before proceeding on his way left in charge of his host five coats of mail which had been handed down as heirlooms by the princes of his family. Then he departed, and in due course arrived at Constantinople, where he besought the Byzantine emperor to help him to

[1] *Cf.* the verses by al-Find, p. 58 *supra*.

[2] *Ḥamása*, 327.

recover his lost kingdom. His appeal was not unsuccessful, but he died on the way home. Meanwhile his old enemy, the King of Ḥíra, sent an army under Ḥárith b. Ẓálim against Samaw'al, demanding that he should surrender the coats of mail. Samaw'al refused to betray the trust committed to him, and defended himself in his castle. The besiegers, however, captured his son, who had gone out to hunt. Ḥárith asked Samaw'al: "Dost thou know this lad?" "Yes, he is my son." "Then wilt thou deliver what is in thy possession, or shall I slay him?" Samaw'al answered: "Do with him as thou wilt. I will never break my pledge nor give up the property of my guest-friend." So Ḥárith smote the lad with his sword and clove him through the middle. Then he raised the siege. And Samaw'al said thereupon:—

"I was true with the mail-coats of the Kindite,[1]
I am true though many a one is blamed for treason.
Once did 'Ádiyá, my father, exhort me:
'O Samaw'al, ne'er destroy what I have builded.'
For me built 'Ádiyá a strong-walled castle
With a well where I draw water at pleasure;
So high, the eagle slipping back is baffled.
When wrong befalls me I endure not tamely."[2]

The Bedouin ideal of generosity and hospitality is personified in Ḥátim of Ṭayyi', of whom many anecdotes are told. We may learn from the following one how extravagant are an Arab's notions on this subject:—

Ḥátim of Ṭayyi'.

When Ḥátim's mother was pregnant she dreamed that she was asked, "Which dost thou prefer?—a generous son called Ḥátim, or ten like those of other folk, lions in the hour of battle, brave lads and strong of limb?" and that she answered, "Ḥátim." Now, when Ḥátim grew up he was wont to take out his food, and if he found any one to share it he would eat, otherwise he threw it away. His father, seeing that

[1] Imru'u 'l-Qays was one of the princes of Kinda, a powerful tribe in Central Arabia.

[2] *Aghání*, xix, 99. The last two lines are wanting in the poem as there cited, but appear in the Selection from the *Aghání* published at Beyrout in 1888, vol. ii, p. 18.

he wasted his food, gave him a slave-girl and a mare with her foal and sent him to herd the camels. On reaching the pasture, Ḥátim began to search for his fellows, but none was in sight; then he came to the road, but found no one there. While he was thus engaged he descried a party of riders on the road and went to meet them. "O youth," said they, "hast thou aught to entertain us withal?" He answered: "Do ye ask me of entertainment when ye see the camels?" Now, these riders were 'Abíd b. al-Abraṣ and Bishr b. Abí Kházim and Nábigha al-Dhubyání, and they were on their way to King Nu'mán.[1] Ḥátim slaughtered three camels for them, whereupon 'Abíd said: "We desired no entertainment save milk, but if thou must needs charge thyself with something more, a single young she-camel would have sufficed us." Ḥátim replied: "That I know, but seeing different faces and diverse fashions I thought ye were not of the same country, and I wished that each of you should mention what ye saw, on returning home." So they spoke verses in praise of him and celebrated his generosity, and Ḥátim said: "I wished to bestow a kindness upon you, but your bounty is greater than mine. I swear to God that I will hamstring every camel in the herd unless ye come forward and divide them among yourselves." The poets did as he desired, and each man received ninety-nine camels; then they proceeded on their journey to Nu'mán. When Ḥátim's father heard of this he came to him and asked, "Where are the camels?" "O my father," replied Ḥátim, "by means of them I have conferred on thee everlasting fame and honour that will cleave to thee like the ring of the ringdove, and men will always bear in mind some verse of poetry in which we are praised. This is thy recompense for the camels." On hearing these words his father said, "Didst thou with my camels thus?" "Yes." "By God, I will never dwell with thee again." So he went forth with his family, and Ḥátim was left alone with his slave-girl and his mare and the mare's foal.[2]

We are told that Ḥátim's daughter was led as a captive before the Prophet and thus addressed him: "'O Muḥammad, my sire is dead, and he who would have come to plead for me is gone. Release me, if it seem good to thee, and do not let the Arabs rejoice at my misfortune; for I am the daughter of the chieftain of my people. My father was wont to free the captive, and protect those near and dear to him, and entertain

[1] See p. 45 sqq. [2] *Aghání*, xvi, 98, ll. 5–22.

the guest, and satisfy the hungry, and console the afflicted, and give food and greeting to all; and never did he turn away any who sought a boon. I am Ḥátim's daughter.' The Prophet (on whom be the blessing and peace of God) answered her: 'O maiden, the true believer is such as thou hast described. Had thy father been an Islamite, verily we should have said, "God have mercy upon him!" Let her go,' he continued, 'for her sire loved noble manners, and God loves them likewise.'"[1]

Ḥátim's daughter before the Prophet.

Ḥátim was a poet of some repute.[2] The following lines are addressed to his wife, Máwiyya:—

"O daughter of 'Abdulláh and Málik and him who wore
The two robes of Yemen stuff—the hero that rode the roan,
When thou hast prepared the meal, entreat to partake thereof
A guest—I am not the man to eat, like a churl, alone—:
Some traveller thro' the night, or house-neighbour; for in sooth
I fear the reproachful talk of men after I am gone.
The guest's slave am I, 'tis true, as long as he bides with me,
Although in my nature else no trait of the slave is shown."[3]

Here it will be convenient to make a short digression in order that the reader may obtain, if not a complete view, at least some glimpses of the position and influence of women in Pre-islamic society. On the whole, their position was high and their influence great. They were free to choose their husbands, and could return, if ill-treated or displeased, to their own people; in some cases

Position of women.

[1] *Aghání*, xvi, 97, l. 5 sqq.

[2] His *Díwán* has been edited with translation and notes by F. Schulthess (Leipzig, 1897).

[3] *Ḥamása*, 729. The hero mentioned in the first verse is 'Ámir b. Uḥaymir of Bahdala. On a certain occasion, when envoys from the Arabian tribes were assembled at Ḥíra, King Mundhir b. Má' al-samá produced two pieces of cloth of Yemen and said, "Let him whose tribe is noblest rise up and take them." Thereupon 'Ámir stood forth, and wrapping one piece round his waist and the other over his shoulders, carried off the prize unchallenged.

they even offered themselves in marriage and had the right of divorce. They were regarded not as slaves and chattels, but as equals and companions. They inspired the poet to sing and the warrior to fight. The chivalry of the Middle Ages is, perhaps, ultimately traceable to heathen Arabia. "Knight-errantry, the riding forth on horseback in search of adventures, the rescue of captive maidens, the succour rendered everywhere to women in adversity—all these were essentially Arabian ideas, as was the very name of *chivalry*, the connection of honourable conduct with the horse-rider, the man of noble blood, the cavalier."[1] But the nobility of the women is not only reflected in the heroism and devotion of the men; it stands recorded in song, in legend, and in history. Fáṭima, the daughter of Khurshub, was one of three noble matrons who bore the title *al-Munjibát*, 'the Mothers of Heroes.' She had seven sons, three of whom, viz., Rabí' and 'Umára and Anas, were called 'the Perfect' (*al-Kamala*). One day Ḥamal b. Badr the Fazárite raided the Banú 'Abs, the tribe to which Fáṭima belonged, and made her his prisoner. As he led away the camel on which she was mounted at the time, she cried: "Man, thy wits are wandering. By God, if thou take me captive, and if we leave behind us this hill which is now in front of us, surely there will never be peace between thee and the sons of Ziyád" (Ziyád was the name of her husband), "because people will say what they please, and the mere suspicion of evil is enough." "I will carry thee off," said he, "that thou mayest herd my camels." When Fáṭima knew that she was certainly his prisoner she threw herself headlong from her camel and died; so did she fear to bring dishonour on her sons.[2] Among the names which have become proverbial for loyalty we find

Arabian heroines.

Fáṭima, daughter of Khurshub.

[1] Lady Anne and Mr. Wilfrid Blunt, *The Seven Golden Odes of Pagan Arabia*, Introduction, p. 14.

[2] *Aghání* xvi, 22, ll. 10–16.

those of two women, Fukayha and Umm Jamíl. As to Fukayha, it is related that her clansmen, having been raided by the brigand Sulayk b. Sulaka, resolved to attack him; but since he was a famous runner, on the advice of one of their shaykhs they waited until he had gone down to the water and quenched his thirst, for they knew that he would then be unable to run. Sulayk, however, seeing himself caught, made for the nearest tents and sought refuge with Fukayha. She threw her smock over him, and stood with drawn sword between him and his pursuers; and as they still pressed on, she tore the veil from her hair and shouted for help. Then her brothers came and defended Sulayk, so that his life was saved.[1] Had space allowed, it would have been a pleasant task to make some further extracts from the long Legend of Noble Women. I have illustrated their keen sense of honour and loyalty, but I might equally well have chosen examples of gracious dignity and quick intelligence and passionate affection. Many among them had the gift of poetry, which they bestowed especially on the dead; it is a final proof of the high character and position of women in Pre-islamic Arabia that the hero's mother and sisters were deemed most worthy to mourn and praise him. The praise of living women by their lovers necessarily takes a different tone; the physical charms of the heroine are fully described, but we seldom find any appreciation of moral beauty. One notable exception to this rule occurs at the beginning of an ode by Shanfará. The passage defies translation. It is, to quote Sir Charles Lyall, with whose faithful and sympathetic rendering of the ancient poetry every student of Arabic literature should be acquainted, "the most lovely picture of womanhood which heathen Arabia has left us, drawn by the same hand that has given us, in the unrivalled *Lâmîyah*, its highest ideal of heroic hardness and virile strength."[2]

Fukayha.

[1] *Aghání*, xviii, 137, ll. 5–10. Freytag, *Arabum Proverbia*, vol. ii, p. 834.
[2] *Ancient Arabian Poetry*, p. 81.

UMAYMA.

"She charmed me, veiling bashfully her face,
Keeping with quiet looks an even pace;
Some lost thing seem to seek her downcast eyes:
Aside she bends not—softly she replies.
Ere dawn she carries forth her meal—a gift
To hungry wives in days of dearth and thrift.
No breath of blame up to her tent is borne,
While many a neighbour's is the house of scorn.
Her husband fears no gossip fraught with shame,
For pure and holy is Umayma's name.
Joy of his heart, to her he need not say
When evening brings him home—'Where passed the day?'
Slender and full in turn, of perfect height,
A very fay were she, if beauty might
Transform a child of earth into a fairy sprite!"[1]

Only in the freedom of the desert could the character thus exquisitely delineated bloom and ripen. These verses, taken by themselves, are a sufficient answer to any one who would maintain that Islam has increased the social influence of Arabian women, although in some respects it may have raised them to a higher level of civilisation.[2]

There is, of course, another side to all this. In a land where might was generally right, and where

"the simple plan
That he should take who has the power
And he should keep who can,"

was all but universally adopted, it would have been strange if the weaker sex had not often gone to the wall. The custom which prevailed in the *Jáhiliyya* of burying female infants alive, revolting as it appears to us, was due partly to the frequent famines with which Arabia is afflicted through lack of rain, and partly to a perverted sense of honour. Fathers

[1] *Mufaḍḍaliyyát*, ed. Thorbecke, p. 23.
[2] See Goldziher, *Muhammedanische Studien*, Part II, p. 295 sqq.

feared lest they should have useless mouths to feed, or lest they should incur disgrace in consequence of their daughters being made prisoners of war. Hence the birth of a daughter was reckoned calamitous, as we read in the Koran: "*They attribute daughters unto God—far be it from Him!—and for themselves they desire them not. When a female child is announced to one of them, his face darkens wrathfully: he hides himself from his people because of the bad news, thinking—'Shall I keep the child to my disgrace or cover it away in the dust?'*"[1] It was said proverbially, "The despatch of daughters is a kindness" and "The burial of daughters is a noble deed."[2] Islam put an end to this barbarity, which is expressly forbidden by the Koran: "*Kill not your children in fear of impoverishment: we will provide for them and for you: verily their killing was a great sin.*"[3] Perhaps the most touching lines in Arabian poetry are those in which a father struggling with poverty wishes that his daughter may die before him and thus be saved from the hard mercies of her relatives:—

Infanticide.

THE POOR MAN'S DAUGHTER.

"But for Umayma's sake I ne'er had grieved to want nor braved
Night's blackest horror to bring home the morsel that she craved.
Now my desire is length of days because I know too well
The orphan girl's hard lot, with kin unkind enforced to dwell.
I dread that some day poverty will overtake my child,
And shame befall her when exposed to every passion wild.[4]

---

[1] Koran, xvi, 59-61.

[2] Freytag, *Arabum Proverbia*, vol. i, p. 229.

[3] Koran, xvii, 33. *Cf.* lxxxi, 8-9 (a description of the Last Judgment): "*When the girl buried alive shall be asked for what crime she was killed.*"

[4] Literally: "And tear the veil from (her, as though she were) flesh on a butcher's board," *i.e.*, defenceless, abandoned to the first-comer.

She wishes me to live, but I must wish her dead, woe's me:
Death is the noblest wooer a helpless maid can see.
I fear an uncle may be harsh, a brother be unkind,
When I would never speak a word that rankled in her mind."[1]

And another says:—

"Were not my little daughters
Like soft chicks huddling by me,
Through earth and all its waters
To win bread would I roam free.

Our children among us going,
Our very hearts they be;
The wind upon them blowing
Would banish sleep from me."[2]

Treatment of enemies.

"Odi et amo": these words of the poet might serve as an epitome of Bedouin ethics. For, if the heathen Arab was, as we have seen, a good friend to his friends, he had in the same degree an intense and deadly feeling of hatred towards his enemies. He who did not strike back when struck was regarded as a coward. No honourable man could forgive an injury or fail to avenge it. An Arab, smarting under the loss of some camels driven off by raiders, said of his kin who refused to help him:—

"For all their numbers, they are good for naught,
My people, against harm however light:
They pardon wrong by evildoers wrought,
Malice with lovingkindness they requite."[3]

The last verse, which would have been high praise in the

[1] *Ḥamása*, 140. Although these verses are not Pre-islamic, and belong in fact to a comparatively late period of Islam, they are sufficiently pagan in feeling to be cited in this connection. The author, Isḥáq b. Khalaf, lived under the Caliph Ma'mún (813–833 A.D.). He survived his adopted daughter—for Umayma was his sister's child—and wrote an elegy on her, which is preserved in the *Kámil* of al-Mubarrad, p. 715, l. 7 sqq., and has been translated, together with the verses now in question, by Sir Charles Lyall, *Ancient Arabian Poetry*, p. 26.

[2] *Ḥamása*, 142. Lyall, *op. cit.*, p. 28.

[3] *Ḥamása*, 7.

mouth of a Christian or Muḥammadan moralist, conveyed to those who heard it a shameful reproach. The approved method of dealing with an enemy is set forth plainly enough in the following lines :—

"Humble him who humbles thee, close tho' be your kindred-
ship:
If thou canst not humble him, wait till he is in thy grip.
Friend him while thou must; strike hard when thou hast him
on the hip."[1]

Above all, blood called for blood. This obligation lay heavy on the conscience of the pagan Arabs. Vengeance, with them, was "almost a physical necessity, which if it be not obeyed will deprive its subject of sleep, of appetite, of health." It was a tormenting thirst which nothing would quench except blood, a disease of honour which might be described as madness, although it rarely prevented the sufferer from going to work with coolness and circumspection. Vengeance was taken upon the murderer, if possible, or else upon one of his fellow-tribesmen. Usually this ended the matter, but in some cases it was the beginning of a regular blood-feud in which the entire kin of both parties were involved; as, *e.g.*, the murder of Kulayb led to the Forty Years' War between Bakr and Taghlib.[2] The slain man's next of kin might accept a blood-wit (*diya*), commonly paid in camels—the coin of the country—as atonement for him. If they did so, however, it was apt to be cast in their teeth that they preferred milk (*i.e.*, she-camels) to blood.[3] The true Arab feeling is expressed in verses like these :—

Blood-revenge.

"With the sword will I wash my shame away,
Let God's doom bring on me what it may!"[4]

---

[1] *Ḥamâsa*, 321. [2] See p. 55 sqq.
[3] *Cf.* Rückert's *Hamâsa*, vol. i, p. 61 seq. [4] *Ḥamâsa*, 30.

It was believed that until vengeance had been taken for the dead man, his spirit appeared above his tomb in the shape of an owl (*háma* or *ṣadá*), crying "*Isqúní*" ("Give me to drink"). But pagan ideas of vengeance were bound up with the Past far more than with the Future. The shadowy after-life counted for little or nothing beside the deeply-rooted memories of fatherly affection, filial piety, and brotherhood in arms.

Though liable to abuse, the rough-and-ready justice of the vendetta had a salutary effect in restraining those who would otherwise have indulged their lawless instincts without fear of punishment. From our point of view, however, its interest is not so much that of a primitive institution as of a pervading element in old Arabian life and literature. Full, or even adequate, illustration of this topic would carry me far beyond the limits of my plan. I have therefore selected from the copious material preserved in the *Book of Songs* a characteristic story which tells how Qays b. al-Khaṭím took vengeance on the murderers of his father and his grandfather.[1]

The story of the vengeance of Qays b. al-Khaṭím.

It is related on the authority of Abú 'Ubayda that 'Adí b. 'Amr, the grandfather of Qays, was slain by a man named Málik belonging to the Banú 'Amr b. 'Ámir b. Rabí'a b. 'Ámir b. Ṣa'ṣa'a; and his father, Khaṭím b. 'Adí, by one of the Banú 'Abd al-Qays who were settled in Hajar. Khaṭím died before avenging his father, 'Adí, when Qays was but a young lad. The mother of Qays, fearing that he would sally forth to seek vengeance for the blood of his father and his grandfather and perish, went to a mound of dust beside the door of their dwelling and laid stones on it, and began to say to Qays, "This is the grave of thy father and thy grandfather;" and Qays never doubted but that it was so. He grew up strong in the arms, and one day he had a tussle with a youth of the Banú Ẓafar, who said to him: "By God, thou would'st do better to turn the strength of thine arms against the slayers of thy father and grandfather instead of putting it forth upon me." "And who are their slayers?" "Ask thy mother, she will tell thee." So Qays

[1] *Aghání*, ii, 160, l. 11–162, l. 1 = p. 13 sqq. of the Beyrout Selection.

took his sword and set its hilt on the ground and its edge between his two breasts, and said to his mother: "Who killed my father and my grandfather?" "They died as people die, and these are their graves in the camping-ground." "By God, verily thou wilt tell me who slew them or I will bear with my whole weight upon this sword until it cleaves through my back." Then she told him, and Qays swore that he would never rest until he had slain their slayers. "O my son," said she, "Málik, who killed thy grandfather, is of the same folk as Khidásh b. Zuhayr, and thy father once bestowed a kindness on Khidásh, for which he is grateful. Go, then, to him and take counsel with him touching thine affair and ask him to help thee." So Qays set out immediately, and when he came to the garden where his water-camel was watering his date-palms, he smote the cord (of the bucket) with his sword and cut it, so that the bucket dropped into the well. Then he took hold of the camel's head, and loaded the beast with two sacks of dates, and said: "Who will care for this old woman" (meaning his mother) "in my absence? If I die, let him pay her expenses out of this garden, and on her death it shall be his own; but if I live, my property will return to me, and he shall have as many of its dates as he wishes to eat." One of his folk cried, "I am for it," so Qays gave him the garden and set forth to inquire concerning Khidásh. He was told to look for him at Marr al-Ẓahrán, but not finding him in his tent, he alighted beneath a tree, in the shade of which the guests of Khidásh used to shelter, and called to the wife of Khidásh, "Is there any food?" Now, when she came up to him, she admired his comeliness—for he was exceeding fair of countenance—and said: "By God, we have no fit entertainment for thee, but only dates." He replied, "I care not, bring out what thou hast." So she sent to him dates in a large measure (*qubá'*), and Qays took a single date and ate half of it and put back the other half in the *qubá'*, and gave orders that the *qubá'* should be brought in to the wife of Khidásh; then he departed on some business. When Khidásh returned and his wife told him the news of Qays, he said, "This is a man who would render his person sacred."[1] While he sat there with his wife eating fresh ripe dates, Qays returned on camel-back; and Khidásh, when he saw the foot of the approaching rider, said to his wife, "Is this thy guest?" "Yes." "'Tis as though his foot were the foot of

[1] The Bedouins consider that any one who has eaten of their food or has touched the rope of their tent is entitled to claim their protection. Such a person is called *dakhíl*. See Burckhardt, *Notes on the Bedouins and Wahábys* (London, 1831), vol. i, p. 160 sqq. and 329 sqq.

my good friend, Khaṭím the Yathribite." Qays drew nigh, and struck the tent-rope with the point of his spear, and begged leave to come in. Having obtained permission, he entered to Khidásh and told his lineage and informed him of what had passed, and asked him to help and advise him in his affair. Khidásh bade him welcome, and recalled the kindness which he had of his father, and said, "As to this affair, truly I have been expecting it of thee for some time. The slayer of thy grandfather is a cousin of mine, and I will aid thee against him. When we are assembled in our meeting-place, I will sit beside him and talk with him, and when I strike his thigh, do thou spring on him and slay him." Qays himself relates: "Accompanied by Khidásh, I approached him until I stood over his head when Khidásh sat with him, and as soon as he struck the man's thigh I smote his head with a sword named *Dhu 'l-Khurṣayn*" (the Two-ringed). "His folk rushed on me to slay me, but Khidásh came between us, crying, 'Let him alone, for, by God, he has slain none but the slayer of his grandfather.'" Then Khidásh called for one of his camels and mounted it, and started with Qays to find the 'Abdite who killed his father. And when they were near Hajar Khidásh advised him to go and inquire after this man, and to say to him when he discovered him: "I encountered a brigand of thy people who robbed me of some articles, and on asking who was the chieftain of his people I was directed to thee. Go with me, then, that thou mayest take from him my property. If," Khidásh continued, "he follow thee unattended, thou wilt gain thy desire of him; but should he bid the others go with thee, laugh, and if he ask why thou laughest, say, 'With us, the noble does not as thou dost, but when he is called to a brigand of his people, he goes forth alone with his whip, not with his sword; and the brigand when he sees him gives him everything that he took, in awe of him.' If he shall dismiss his friends, thy course is clear; but if he shall refuse to go without them, bring him to me nevertheless, for I hope that thou wilt slay both him and them." So Khidásh stationed himself under the shade of a tree, while Qays went to the 'Abdite and addressed him as Khidásh had prompted; and the man's sense of honour was touched to the quick, so that he sent away his friends and went with Qays. And when Qays came back to Khidásh, the latter said to him, "Choose, O Qays! Shall I help thee or shall I take thy place?" Qays answered, "I desire neither of these alternatives, but if he slay me, let him not slay thee!" Then he rushed upon him and wounded him in the flank and drove his lance through the other side, and he fell dead on the spot. When Qays had finished with him, Khidásh said, "If we flee just now, his folk will pursue us; but let us go somewhere not far off, for they will never think that thou hast slain him and stayed in the neighbourhood. No; they will miss him and follow his track, and when they find him slain they will start to pursue us in every direction, and will only return when they have lost hope." So those two entered some hollows of the sand, and after staying there several days (for it happened exactly as Khidásh had foretold), they came forth when the pursuit was over, and did not exchange a word until they reached the abode of Khidásh. There Qays parted from him and returned to his own people.

The poems relating to blood-revenge show all that is best and much that is less admirable in the heathen Arab—on the one hand, his courage and resolution, his contempt of death and fear of dishonour, his single-minded devotion to the dead as to the living, his deep regard and tender affection for the men of his own flesh and blood; on the other hand, his implacable temper, his perfidious cruelty and reckless ferocity in hunting down the slayers, and his savage, well-nigh inhuman exultation over the slain. The famous Song or Ballad of Vengeance that I shall now attempt to render in English verse is usually attributed to Ta'abbaṭa Sharr^{an},[1] although some pronounce it to be a forgery by Khalaf al-Aḥmar, the reputed author of Shanfará's masterpiece, and beyond doubt a marvellously skilful imitator of the ancient bards. Be that as it may, the ballad is utterly pagan in tone and feeling. Its extraordinary merit was detected by Goethe, who, after reading it in a Latin translation, published a German rendering, with some fine criticism of the poetry, in his *West-oestlicher Divan*.[2] I have endeavoured to suggest as far as possible the metre and rhythm of the original,

Song of Vengeance by Ta'abbaṭa Sharran.

[1] See p. 81 *supra*.

[2] Stuttgart, 1819, p. 253 sqq. The other renderings in verse with which I am acquainted are those of Rückert (*Hamâsa*, vol. i, p. 299) and Sir Charles Lyall (*Ancient Arabian Poetry*, p. 48). I have adopted Sir Charles Lyall's arrangement of the poem, and have closely followed his masterly interpretation, from which I have also borrowed some turns of phrase that could not be altered except for the worse.

since to these, in my opinion, its peculiar effect is largely due. The metre is that known as the 'Tall' (*Madíd*), viz. :—

⏓ ⏑ – – | ⏓ ⏑ – | – ⏑ – –

Thus the first verse runs in Arabic :—

Inna bi'l-shi' | *bi 'lladhí* | *'inda Sal*[in]
la-qatíl[an] | *damuhú* | *má yuṭallu.*

Of course, Arabic prosody differs radically from English, but *mutatis mutandis* several couplets in the following version (*e.g.* the third, eighth, and ninth) will be found to correspond exactly with their model. As has been said, however, my object was merely to suggest the abrupt metre and the heavy, emphatic cadences, so that I have been able to give variety to the verse, and at the same time to retain that artistic freedom without which the translator of poetry cannot hope to satisfy either himself or any one else.

The poet tells how he was summoned to avenge his uncle, slain by the tribesmen of Hudhayl: he describes the dead man's heroic character, the foray in which he fell, his former triumphs over the same enemy, and finally the terrible vengeance taken for him.[1]

"In the glen there a murdered man is lying—
Not in vain for vengeance his blood is crying.
He hath left me the load to bear and departed;
I take up the load and bear it true-hearted.
I, his sister's son, the bloodshed inherit,
I whose knot none looses, stubborn of spirit;[2]
Glowering darkly, shame's deadly out-wiper,
Like the serpent spitting venom, the viper.

---

[1] The Arabic text will be found in the *Ḥamása*, p. 382 sqq.

[2] This and the following verse are generally taken to be a description not of the poet himself, but of his nephew. The interpretation given above does no violence to the language, and greatly enhances the dramatic effect.

Hard the tidings that befell us, heart-breaking;
Little seemed thereby the anguish most aching.
Fate hath robbed me—still is Fate fierce and froward—
Of a hero whose friend ne'er called him coward:
As the warm sun was he in wintry weather,
'Neath the Dog-star shade and coolness together:
Spare of flank—yet this in him showed not meanness;
Open-handed, full of boldness and keenness:
Firm of purpose, cavalier unaffrighted—
Courage rode with him and with him alighted:
In his bounty, a bursting cloud of rain-water;
Lion grim when he leaped to the slaughter.
Flowing hair, long robe his folk saw aforetime,
But a lean-haunched wolf was he in war-time.
Savours two he had, untasted by no men:
Honey to his friends and gall to his foemen.
Fear he rode nor recked what should betide him:
Save his deep-notched Yemen blade, none beside him.

Oh, the warriors girt with swords good for slashing,
Like the levin, when they drew them, outflashing!
Through the noonday heat they fared: then, benighted,
Farther fared, till at dawning they alighted.[1]
Breaths of sleep they sipped; and then, while they nodded,
Thou didst scare them: lo, they scattered and scudded.
Vengeance wreaked we upon them, unforgiving:
Of the two clans scarce was left a soul living.[2]

Ay, if *they* bruised his glaive's edge 'twas in token
That by him many a time their own was broken.
Oft he made them kneel down by force and cunning—
Kneel on jags where the foot is torn with running.
Many a morn in shelter he took them napping;
After killing was the rieving and rapine.

They have gotten of me a roasting—I tire not
Of desiring them till me they desire not.
First, of foemen's blood my spear deeply drinketh,
Then a second time, deep in, it sinketh.

---

[1] In the original this and the preceding verse are transposed.

[2] Although the poet's uncle was killed in this onslaught, the surprised party suffered severely. "The two clans" belonged to the great tribe of Hudhayl, which is mentioned in the penultimate verse.

Lawful now to me is wine, long forbidden:
Sore my struggle ere the ban was o'erridden.[1]
Pour me wine, O son of 'Amr! I would taste it,
Since with grief for mine uncle I am wasted.
O'er the fallen of Hudhayl stands screaming
The hyena; see the wolf's teeth gleaming!
Dawn will hear the flap of wings, will discover
Vultures treading corpses, too gorged to hover."

Honour conferred by noble ancestry.

All the virtues which enter into the Arabian conception of Honour were regarded not as personal qualities inherent or acquired, but as hereditary possessions which a man derived from his ancestors, and held in trust that he might transmit them untarnished to his descendants. It is the desire to uphold and emulate the fame of his forbears, rather than the hope of winning immortality for himself, that causes the Arab "to say the say and do the deeds of the noble." Far from sharing the sentiment of the Scots peasant—"a man's a man for a' that"—he looks askance at merit and renown unconsecrated by tradition.

"The glories that have grown up with the grass
Can match not those inherited of old."[2]

Ancestral renown (*ḥasab*) is sometimes likened to a strong castle built by sires for their sons, or to a lofty mountain which defies attack.[3] The poets are full of boastings (*mafákhir*) and revilings (*mathálib*) in which they loudly proclaim the nobility of their own ancestors, and try to blacken those of their enemy without any regard to decorum.

It was my intention to add here some general remarks on Arabian poetry as compared with that of the Hebrews, the

[1] It was customary for the avenger to take a solemn vow that he would drink no wine before accomplishing his vengeance.

[2] *Ḥamása*, 679.

[3] *Cf.* the lines translated below from the *Mu'allaqa* of Ḥárith.

Persians, and our own, but since example is better than precept I will now turn directly to those celebrated odes which are well known by the title of *Mu'allaqát*, or 'Suspended Poems,' to all who take the slightest interest in Arabic literature.[1]

The Mu'allaqát, or 'Suspended Poems.'

Mu'allaqa (plural, *Mu'allaqát*) "is most likely derived from the word *'ilq*, meaning 'a precious thing or a thing held in high estimation,' either because one 'hangs on' tenaciously to it, or because it is 'hung up' in a place of honour, or in a conspicuous place, in a treasury or store-house."[2] In course of time the exact signification of *Mu'allaqa* was forgotten, and it became necessary to find a plausible explanation. Hence arose the legend, which frequent repetition has made familiar, that the 'Suspended Poems' were so called from having been hung up in the Ka'ba on account of their merit; that this distinction was awarded by the judges at the fair of 'Ukáẓ, near Mecca, where poets met in rivalry and recited their choicest productions; and that the successful compositions, before being affixed to the door of the Ka'ba, were transcribed in letters of gold upon pieces of fine Egyptian linen.[3] Were these state-

[1] The best edition of the *Mu'allaqát* is Sir Charles Lyall's (*A Commentary on Ten Ancient Arabic Poems*, Calcutta, 1894), which contains in addition to the seven *Mu'allaqát* three odes by A'shá, Nábigha, and 'Abíd b. al-Abraṣ. Nöldeke has translated five Mu'allaqas (omitting those of Imru' u' l-Qays and Ṭarafa) with a German commentary, *Sitzungsberichte der Kais. Akad. der Wissenschaften in Wien, Phil.-Histor. Klasse*, vols. 140–144 (1899–1901); this is by far the best translation for students. No satisfactory version in English prose has hitherto appeared, but I may call attention to the fine and original, though somewhat free, rendering into English verse by Lady Anne Blunt and Wilfrid Scawen Blunt (*The Seven Golden Odes of Pagan Arabia*, London, 1903).

[2] *Ancient Arabian Poetry*, Introduction, p. xliv. Many other interpretations have been suggested—*e.g.*, 'The Poems written down from oral dictation' (Von Kremer), 'The richly bejewelled' (Ahlwardt), 'The Pendants,' as though they were pearls strung on a necklace (A. Müller).

[3] The belief that the *Mu'allaqát* were written in letters of gold seems to have arisen from a misunderstanding of the name *Mudhhabát* or *Mudhahhabát* (*i.e.*, the Gilded Poems) which is sometimes given to them in token of their excellence, just as the Greeks gave the title χρύσεα ἔπη

ments true, we should expect them to be confirmed by some allusion in the early literature. But as a matter of fact nothing of the kind is mentioned in the Koran or in religious tradition, in the ancient histories of Mecca, or in such works as the *Kitábu 'l-Aghání*, which draw their information from old and trustworthy sources.[1] Almost the first authority who refers to the legend is the grammarian Aḥmad al-Naḥḥás († 949 A.D.), and by him it is stigmatised as entirely groundless. Moreover, although it was accepted by scholars like Reiske, Sir W. Jones, and even De Sacy, it is incredible in itself. Hengstenberg, in the Prolegomena to his edition of the *Mu'allaqa* of Imru'u 'l-Qays (Bonn, 1823) asked some pertinent questions: Who were the judges, and how were they appointed? Why were only these seven poems thus distinguished? His further objection, that the art of writing was at that time a rare accomplishment, does not carry so much weight as he attached to it, but the story is sufficiently refuted by what we know of the character and customs of the Arabs in the sixth century and afterwards. Is it conceivable that the proud sons of the desert could have submitted a matter so nearly touching their tribal honour, of which they were jealous above all things, to external arbitration, or meekly acquiesced in the partial verdict of a court sitting in the neighbourhood of Mecca, which would certainly have shown scant consideration for competitors belonging to distant clans? [2]

However *Mu'allaqa* is to be explained, the name is not contemporary with the poems themselves. In all probability they were so entitled by the person who first chose them

to a poem falsely attributed to Pythagoras. That some of the *Mu'allaqát* were recited at 'Ukáẓ is probable enough and is definitely affirmed in the case of 'Amr b. Kulthúm (*Aghání*, ix, 182).

[1] The legend first appears in the *'Iqd al-Faríd* (ed. of Cairo, 1293 A.H., vol. iii, p. 116 seq.) of Ibn 'Abdi Rabbihi, who died in 940 A.D.

[2] See the Introduction to Nöldeke's *Beiträge zur Kenntniss der Poesie der alten Araber* (Hannover, 1864), p. xvii sqq., and his article 'Mo'allaḳát' in the *Encyclopædia Britannica*.

out of innumerable others and embodied them in a separate collection. This is generally allowed to have been Ḥammád al-Ráwiya, a famous rhapsodist who flourished in the latter days of the Umayyad dynasty, and died about 772 A.D., in the reign of the 'Abbásid Caliph Mahdí. What principle guided Ḥammád in his choice we do not know. Nöldeke conjectures that he was influenced by the fact that all the *Mu'allaqát* are long poems—they are sometimes called 'The Seven Long Poems' (*al-Sab' al-Ṭiwál*) —for in Ḥammád's time little of the ancient Arabian poetry survived in a state even of relative completeness.

Origin of the collection.

It must be confessed that no rendering of the *Mu'allaqát* can furnish European readers with a just idea of the originals, a literal version least of all. They contain much that only a full commentary can make intelligible, much that to modern taste is absolutely incongruous with the poetic style. Their finest pictures of Bedouin life and manners often appear uncouth or grotesque, because without an intimate knowledge of the land and people it is impossible for us to see what the poet intended to convey, or to appreciate the truth and beauty of its expression; while the artificial framework, the narrow range of subject as well as treatment, and the frank realism of the whole strike us at once. In the following pages I shall give some account of the *Mu'allaqát* and their authors, and endeavour to bring out the characteristic qualities of each poem by selecting suitable passages for translation.[1]

Difficulty of translating the Mu'allaqát.

The oldest and most famous of the *Mu'allaqát* is that of Imru'u 'l-Qays, who was descended from the ancient kings of Yemen. His grandfather was King Ḥárith of Kinda, the antagonist of Mundhir III, King of Ḥíra, by whom he was

[1] It is well known that the order of the verses in the *Mu'allaqát*, as they have come down to us, is frequently confused, and that the number of various readings is very large. I have generally followed the text and arrangement adopted by Nöldeke in his German translation.

defeated and slain.[1] On Ḥárith's death, the confederacy which he had built up split asunder, and his sons divided among themselves the different tribes of which it was composed. Ḥujr, the poet's father, ruled for some time over the Banú Asad in Central Arabia, but finally they revolted and put him to death. "The duty of avenging his murder fell upon Imru'u 'l-Qays, who is represented as the only capable prince of his family; and the few historical data which we have regarding him relate to his adventures while bent upon this vengeance."[2] They are told at considerable length in the *Kitábu 'l-Aghání*, but need not detain us here. Suffice it to say that his efforts to punish the rebels, who were aided by Mundhir, the hereditary foe of his house, met with little success. He then set out for Constantinople, where he was favourably received by the Emperor Justinian, who desired to see the power of Kinda re-established as a thorn in the side of his Persian rivals. The emperor appointed him Phylarch of Palestine, but on his way thither he died at Angora (about 540 A.D.). He is said to have perished, like Nessus, from putting on a poisoned robe sent to him as a gift by Justinian, with whose daughter he had an intrigue. Hence he is sometimes called 'The Man of the Ulcers' (*Dhu 'l-Qurúḥ*).

Imru'u 'l-Qays.

Many fabulous traditions surround the romantic figure of Imru'u 'l-Qays.[3] According to one story, he was banished by his father, who despised him for being a poet and was enraged by the scandals to which his love adventures gave rise. Imru'u 'l-Qays left his home and wandered from tribe to tribe with a company of outcasts like himself, leading a wild life, which caused him to be known as 'The Vagabond Prince' (*al-Malik al-Ḍillíl*). When the news of his father's death

[1] See p. 42 *supra*.

[2] *Ancient Arabian Poetry*, p. 105.

[3] See the account of his life (according to the *Kitábu' l-Aghání*) in *Le Diwan d'Amro'lkaïs*, edited with translation and notes by Baron MacGuckin de Slane (Paris, 1837), pp. 1–51; and in *Amrilkais, der Dichter und König* by Friedrich Rückert (Stuttgart and Tübingen, 1843).

reached him he cried, "My father wasted my youth, and now that I am old he has laid upon me the burden of blood-revenge. Wine to-day, business to-morrow!" Seven nights he continued the carouse; then he swore not to eat flesh, nor drink wine, nor use ointment, nor touch woman, nor wash his head until his vengeance was accomplished. In the valley of Tabála, north of Najrán, there was an idol called Dhu 'l-Khalaṣa much reverenced by the heathen Arabs. Imru'u 'l-Qays visited this oracle and consulted it in the ordinary way, by drawing one of three arrows entitled 'the Commanding,' 'the Forbidding,' and 'the Waiting.' He drew the second, whereupon he broke the arrows and dashed them on the face of the idol, exclaiming with a gross imprecation, "If *thy* father had been slain, thou would'st not have hindered me!"

Imru'u 'l-Qays is almost universally reckoned the greatest of the Pre-islamic poets. Muḥammad described him as 'their leader to Hell-fire,' while the Caliphs 'Umar and 'Alí, *odium theologicum* notwithstanding, extolled his genius and originality.[1] Coming to the *Mu'allaqa* itself, European critics have vied with each other in praising its exquisite diction and splendid images, the sweet flow of the verse, the charm and variety of the painting, and, above all, the feeling by which it is inspired of the joy and glory of youth. The passage translated below is taken from the first half of the poem, in which love is the prevailing theme:—[2]

"Once, on the hill, she mocked at me and swore,
'This hour I leave thee to return no more.'

[1] That he was not, however, the inventor of the Arabian *qaṣída* as described above (p. 76 sqq.) appears from the fact that he mentions in one of his verses a certain Ibn Ḥumám or Ibn Khidhám who introduced, or at least made fashionable, the prelude with which almost every ode begins: a lament over the deserted camping-ground (Ibn Qutayba, *K. al-Shi'r wa-'l-Shu'ará*, p. 52).

[2] The following lines are translated from Arnold's edition of the *Mu'allaqát* (Leipsic, 1850), p. 9 sqq., vv. 18–35.

Soft! if farewell is planted in thy mind,
Yet spare me, Fáṭima, disdain unkind.
Because my passion slays me, wilt thou part?
Because thy wish is law unto mine heart?
Nay, if thou so mislikest aught in me,
Shake loose my robe and let it fall down free.
But ah, the deadly pair, thy streaming eyes!
They pierce a heart that all in ruin lies.

How many a noble tent hath oped its treasure
To me, and I have ta'en my fill of pleasure,
Passing the warders who with eager speed
Had slain me, if they might but hush the deed,
What time in heaven the Pleiades unfold
A belt of orient gems distinct with gold.
I entered. By the curtain there stood she,
Clad lightly as for sleep, and looked on me.
'By God,' she cried, 'what recks thee of the cost?
I see thine ancient madness is not lost.'
I led her forth—she trailing as we go
Her broidered skirt, lest any footprint show—
Until beyond the tents the valley sank
With curving dunes and many a pilèd bank.
Then with both hands I drew her head to mine,
And lovingly the damsel did incline
Her slender waist and legs more plump than fine;—
A graceful figure, a complexion bright,
A bosom like a mirror in the light;
A white pale virgin pearl such lustre keeps,
Fed with clear water in untrodden deeps.
Now she bends half away: two cheeks appear,
And such an eye as marks the frighted deer
Beside her fawn; and lo, the shapely neck
Not bare of ornament, else without a fleck;
While from her shoulders in profusion fair,
Like clusters on the palm, hangs down her coal-dark hair."

In strange contrast with this tender and delicate idyll are the wild, hard verses almost immediately following, in which the poet roaming through the barren waste hears the howl of a starved wolf and hails him as a comrade:—

"Each one of us what thing he finds devours:
Lean is the wretch whose living is like ours." [1]

The noble qualities of his horse and its prowess in the chase are described, and the poem ends with a magnificent picture of a thunder-storm among the hills of Najd.

Ṭarafa.

Ṭarafa b. al-'Abd was a member of the great tribe of Bakr. The particular clan to which he belonged was settled in Baḥrayn on the Persian Gulf. He early developed a talent for satire, which he exercised upon friend and foe indifferently; and after he had squandered his patrimony in dissolute pleasures, his family chased him away as though he were 'a mangy camel.' At length a reconciliation was effected. He promised to mend his ways, returned to his people, and took part, it is said, in the War of Basús. In a little while his means were dissipated once more and he was reduced to tend his brother's herds. His *Mu'allaqa* composed at this time won for him the favour of a rich kinsman and restored him to temporary independence. On the conclusion of peace between Bakr and Taghlib the youthful poet turned his eyes in the direction of Ḥíra, where 'Amr b. Hind had lately succeeded to the throne (554 A.D.). He was well received by the king, who attached him, along with his uncle, the poet Mutalammis, to the service of the heir-apparent. But Ṭarafa's bitter tongue was destined to cost him dear. Fatigued and disgusted by the rigid ceremony of the court, he improvised a satire in which he said—

"Would that we had instead of 'Amr
A milch-ewe bleating round our tent!"

Shortly afterwards he happened to be seated at table opposite the king's sister. Struck with her beauty, he exclaimed—

[1] The native commentators are probably right in attributing this and the three preceding verses (48–51 in Arnold's edition) to the brigand-poet, Ta'abbaṭa Sharr^{an}.

"Behold, she has come back to me,
My fair gazelle whose ear-rings shine;
Had not the king been sitting here,
I would have pressed her lips to mine!"

'Amr b. Hind was a man of violent and implacable temper. Ṭarafa's satire had already been reported to him, and this new impertinence added fuel to his wrath. Sending for Ṭarafa and Mutalammis, he granted them leave to visit their homes, and gave to each of them a sealed letter addressed to the governor of Baḥrayn. When they had passed outside the city the suspicions of Mutalammis were aroused. As neither he nor his companion could read, he handed his own letter to a boy of Ḥíra[1] and learned that it contained orders to bury him alive. Thereupon he flung the treacherous missive into the stream and implored Ṭarafa to do likewise. Ṭarafa refused to break the royal seal. He continued his journey to Baḥrayn, where he was thrown into prison and executed.

Thus perished miserably in the flower of his youth—according to some accounts he was not yet twenty—the passionate and eloquent Ṭarafa. In his *Mu'allaqa* he has drawn a spirited portrait of himself. The most striking feature of the poem, apart from a long and, to us who are not Bedouins, painfully tedious description of the camel, is its insistence on sensual enjoyment as the sole business of life:—

"Canst thou make me immortal, O thou that blamest me so
For haunting the battle and loving the pleasures that fly?
If thou hast not the power to ward me from Death, let me go
To meet him and scatter the wealth in my hand, ere I die.

Save only for three things in which noble youth take delight,
I care not how soon rises o'er me the coronach loud:
Wine that foams when the water is poured on it, ruddy, not bright,
Dark wine that I quaff stol'n away from the cavilling crowd;

[1] We have already (p. 39) referred to the culture of the Christian Arabs of Ḥíra.

"And second, my charge at the cry of distress on a steed
Bow-legged like the wolf you have startled when thirsty he cowers;
And third, the day-long with a lass in her tent of goat's hair
To hear the wild rain and beguile of their slowness the hours."[1]

Keeping, as far as possible, the chronological order, we have now to mention two *Mu'allaqas* which, though not directly related to each other,[2] are of the same period—the reign of 'Amr b. Hind, King of Ḥíra (554–568 A.D.). Moreover, their strong mutual resemblance and their difference from the other *Mu'allaqas*, especially from typical *qaṣídas* like those of 'Antara and Labíd, is a further reason for linking them together. Their distinguishing mark is the abnormal space devoted to the main subject, which leaves little room for the subsidiary motives.

'Amr b. Kulthúm.

'Amr b. Kulthúm belonged to the tribe of Taghlib. His mother was Laylá, a daughter of the famous poet and warrior Muhalhil. That she was a woman of heroic mould appears from the following anecdote, which records a deed of prompt vengeance on the part of 'Amr that gave rise to the proverb, "Bolder in onset than 'Amr b. Kulthúm"[3]:—

One day 'Amr. b. Hind, the King of Ḥíra, said to his boon-companions, "Do ye know any Arab whose mother would disdain to serve mine?" They answered, "Yes, the mother of 'Amr b.

[1] Vv. 54–59 (Lyall); 56–61 (Arnold).

[2] See Nöldeke, *Fünf Mu'allaqát*, i, p. 51 seq. According to the traditional version (*Aghání*, ix, 179), a band of Taghlibites went raiding, lost their way in the desert, and perished of thirst, having been refused water by a sept of the Banú Bakr. Thereupon Taghlib appealed to King 'Amr to enforce payment of the blood-money which they claimed, and chose 'Amr b. Kulthúm to plead their cause at Ḥíra. So 'Amr recited his *Mu'allaqa* before the king, and was answered by Ḥárith on behalf of Bakr.

[3] Freytag, *Arabum Proverbia*, vol. ii, p. 233.

Kulthúm." "Why so?" asked the king. "Because," said they, "her father is Muhalhil b. Rabí'a and her uncle is Kulayb b. Wá'il, the most puissant of the Arabs, and her husband is Kulthúm b. Málik, the knightliest, and her son is 'Amr, the chieftain of his tribe." Then the king sent to 'Amr b. Kulthúm, inviting him to pay a visit to himself, and asking him to bring his mother, Laylá, to visit his own mother, Hind. So 'Amr came to Ḥíra with some men of Taghlib, and Laylá came attended by a number of their women; and while the king entertained 'Amr and his friends in a pavilion which he had caused to be erected between Ḥíra and the Euphrates, Laylá found quarters with Hind in a tent adjoining. Now, the king had ordered his mother, as soon as he should call for dessert, to dismiss the servants, and cause Laylá to wait upon her. At the pre-arranged signal she desired to be left alone with her guest, and said, "O Laylá, hand me that dish." Laylá answered, "Let those who want anything rise up and serve themselves." Hind repeated her demand, and would take no denial. "O shame!" cried Laylá. "Help! Taghlib, help!" When 'Amr heard his mother's cry the blood flew to his cheeks. He seized a sword hanging on the wall of the pavilion—the only weapon there—and with a single blow smote the king dead.[1]

How 'Amr avenged an insult to his mother.

'Amr's *Mu'allaqa* is the work of a man who united in himself the ideal qualities of manhood as these were understood by a race which has never failed to value, even too highly, the display of self-reliant action and decisive energy. And if in 'Amr's poem these virtues are displayed with an exaggerated boastfulness which offends our sense of decency and proper reserve, it would be a grave error to conclude that all this sound and fury signifies nothing. The Bedouin poet deems it his bounden duty to glorify to the utmost himself, his family, and his tribe; the Bedouin warrior is never tired of proclaiming his unshakable valour and recounting his brilliant feats of arms: he hurls menaces and vaunts in the same breath, but it does not follow that he is a *Miles Gloriosus.* 'Amr certainly was not: his *Mu'allaqa* leaves a vivid impression of conscious and exultant strength. The first eight verses seem

[1] *Aghání*, ix, 182.

to have been added to the poem at a very early date, for out of them arose the legend that 'Amr drank himself to death with unmixed wine. It is likely that they were included in the original collection of the *Mu'allaqát*, and they are worth translating for their own sake:—

"Up, maiden! Fetch the morning-drink and spare not
The wine of Andarín,
Clear wine that takes a saffron hue when water
Is mingled warm therein.
The lover tasting it forgets his passion,
His heart is eased of pain;
The stingy miser, as he lifts the goblet,
Regardeth not his gain.

Pass round from left to right! Why let'st thou, maiden,
Me and my comrades thirst?
Yet am I, whom thou wilt not serve this morning,
Of us three not the worst!
Many a cup in Baalbec and Damascus
And Qáṣirín I drained,
Howbeit we, ordained to death, shall one day
Meet death, to us ordained." [1]

In the next passage he describes his grief at the departure of his beloved, whom he sees in imagination arriving at her journey's end in distant Yamáma:—

"And oh, my love and yearning when at nightfall
I saw her camels haste,
Until sharp peaks uptowered like serried sword-blades,
And me Yamáma faced!
Such grief no mother-camel feels, bemoaning
Her young one lost, nor she,
The grey-haired woman whose hard fate hath left her
Of nine sons graves thrice three." [2]

Now the poet turns abruptly to his main theme. He

[1] Vv. 1–8 (Arnold); in Lyall's edition the penultimate verse is omitted.
[2] Vv. 15–18 (Lyall); 19–22 (Arnold).

addresses the King of Ḥíra, 'Amr b. Hind, in terms of defiance, and warns the foes of Taghlib that they will meet more than their match :—

"Father of Hind,[1] take heed and ere thou movest
Rashly against us, learn
That still our banners go down white to battle
And home blood-red return.
And many a chief bediademed, the champion
Of the outlaws of the land,
Have we o'erthrown and stripped him, while around him
Fast-reined the horses stand.
Our neighbours lopped like thorn-trees, snarls in terror
Of us the demon-hound ;[2]
Never we try our hand-mill on the foemen
But surely they are ground.
We are the heirs of glory, all Ma'add knows,[3]
Our lances it defend,
And when the tent-pole tumbles in the foray,
Trust us to save our friend ![4]

O 'Amr, what mean'st thou ? Are we, we of Taghlib,
Thy princeling's retinue ?
O 'Amr, what mean'st thou, rating us and hearkening
To tale-bearers untrue ?
O 'Amr, ere thee full many a time our spear-shaft
Has baffled foes to bow ;[5]
Nipped in the vice it kicks like a wild camel
That will no touch allow—
Like a wild camel, so it creaks in bending
And splits the bender's brow !"[6]

The *Mu'allaqa* ends with a eulogy, superb in its extravagance, of the poet's tribe :—

[1] The Arabs use the term *kunya* to denote this familiar style of address in which a person is called, not by his own name, but 'father of So-and-so' (either a son or, as in the present instance, a daughter).

[2] *I.e.*, even the *jinn* (genies) stand in awe of us.

[3] Here Ma'add signifies the Arabs in general.

[4] Vv. 20–30 (Lyall), omitting vv. 22, 27, 28.

[5] This is a figurative way of saying that Taghlib has never been subdued

[6] Vv. 46–51 (Lyall), omitting v. 48.

"Well wot, when our tents rise along their valleys,
The men of every clan
That we give death to them that durst attempt us,
To friends what food we can;
That staunchly we maintain a cause we cherish,
Camp where we choose to ride,
Nor will we aught of peace, when we are angered,
Till we be satisfied.
We keep our vassals safe and sound, but rebels
We soon force to their knees;
And if we reach a well, we drink pure water,
Others the muddy lees.
Ours is the earth and all thereon: when *we* strike,
There needs no second blow;
Kings lay before the new-weaned boy of Taghlib
Their heads in homage low.
We are called oppressors, being none, but shortly
A true name shall it be![1]
We have so filled the earth 'tis narrow for us,
And with our ships the sea![2]

Ḥárith b. Ḥilliza.

Less interesting is the *Mu'allaqa* of Ḥárith b. Ḥilliza of Bakr. Its inclusion among the *Mu'allaqát* is probably due, as Nöldeke suggested, to the fact that Ḥammád, himself a client of Bakr, wished to flatter his patrons by selecting a counterpart to the *Mu'allaqa* of 'Amr b. Kulthúm, which immortalised their great rivals, the Banú Taghlib. Ḥárith's poem, however, has some historical importance, as it throws light on feuds in Northern Arabia connected with the antagonism of the Roman and Persian Empires. Its purpose is to complain of unjust accusations made against the Banú Bakr by a certain group of the Banú Taghlib known as the Aráqim:—

[1] *I.e.*, we will show our enemies that they cannot defy us with impunity. This verse, the 93rd in Lyall's edition, is omitted by Arnold.

[2] Vv. 94–104 (Arnold), omitting vv. 100 and 101. If the last words are anything more than a poetic fiction, 'the sea' must refer to the River Euphrates.

"Our brothers the Aráqim let their tongues
Against us rail unmeasuredly.
The innocent with the guilty they confound:
Of guilt what boots it to be free?
They brand us patrons of the vilest deed,
Our clients in each miscreant see." [1]

A person whom Ḥárith does not name was 'blackening' the Banú Bakr before the King of Ḥíra. The poet tells him not to imagine that his calumnies will have any lasting effect: often had Bakr been slandered by their foes, but (he finely adds):—

"Maugre their hate we stand, by firm-based might
Exalted and by ancestry—
Might which ere now hath dazzled men's eyes: thence scorn
To yield and haughty spirit have we.
On us the Days beat as on mountain dark
That soars in cloudless majesty,
Compact against the hard calamitous shocks
And buffetings of Destiny." [2]

He appeals to the offenders not wantonly to break the peace which ended the War of Basús:—

"Leave folly and error! If ye blind yourselves,
Just therein lies the malady.
Recall the oaths of Dhu 'l-Majáz [3] for which
Hostages gave security,
Lest force or guile should break them: can caprice
Annul the parchments utterly? [4]

'Antara.

'Antara b. Shaddád, whose father belonged to the tribe of 'Abs, distinguished himself in the War of Dáḥis.[5] In modern times it is not as a poet that he is chiefly remembered, but as a hero of romance—the Bedouin Achilles. Goddess-born, however, he could not be called by

[1] Vv. 16–18.
[2] Vv. 23–26.
[3] A place in the neighbourhood of Mecca.
[4] Vv. 40–42 (Lyall); 65–67 (Arnold).
[5] See *'Antarah, ein vorislamischer Dichter*, by H. Thorbecke (Leipzig, 1867).

any stretch of imagination. His mother was a black slave, and he must often have been taunted with his African blood, which showed itself in a fiery courage that gained the respect of the pure-bred but generally less valorous Arabs. 'Antara loved his cousin 'Abla, and following the Arabian custom by which cousins have the first right to a girl's hand, he asked her in marriage. His suit was vain—the son of a slave mother being regarded as a slave unless acknowledged by his father—until on one occasion, while the 'Absites were hotly engaged with some raiders who had driven off their camels, 'Antara refused to join in the mêlée, saying, "A slave does not understand how to fight; his work is to milk the camels and bind their udders." "Charge!" cried his father, "thou art free." Though 'Antara uttered no idle boast when he sang—

> "On one side nobly born and of the best
> Of 'Abs am I: my sword makes good the rest!"

his contemptuous references to 'jabbering barbarians,' and to 'slaves with their ears cut off, clad in sheepskins,' are characteristic of the man who had risen to eminence in spite of the stain on his scutcheon. He died at a great age in a foray against the neighbouring tribe of Ṭayyi'. His *Mu'allaqa* is famous for its stirring battle-scenes, one of which is translated here:—[1]

> "Learn, Málik's daughter, how
> I rush into the fray,
> And how I draw back only
> At sharing of the prey.
>
> I never quit the saddle,
> My strong steed nimbly bounds;
> Warrior after warrior
> Have covered him with wounds.

[1] I have taken some liberties in this rendering, as the reader may see by referring to the verses (44 and 47–52 in Lyall's edition) on which it is based.

Full-armed against me stood
  One feared of fighting men:
He fled not oversoon
  Nor let himself be ta'en.

With straight hard-shafted spear
  I dealt him in his side
A sudden thrust which opened
  Two streaming gashes wide,

Two gashes whence outgurgled
  His life-blood: at the sound
Night-roaming ravenous wolves
  Flock eagerly around.

So with my doughty spear
  I trussed his coat of mail—
For truly, when the spear strikes,
  The noblest man is frail—

And left him low to banquet
  The wild beasts gathering there;
They have torn off his fingers,
  His wrist and fingers fair!"

Zuhayr.

While 'Antara's poem belongs to the final stages of the War of Dáḥis, the *Mu'allaqa* of his contemporary, Zuhayr b. Abí Sulmá, of the tribe of Muzayna, celebrates an act of private munificence which brought about the conclusion of peace. By the self-sacrificing intervention of two chiefs of Dhubyán, Harim b. Sinán and Ḥárith b. 'Awf, the whole sum of blood-money to which the 'Absites were entitled on account of the greater number of those who had fallen on their side, was paid over to them. Such an example of generous and disinterested patriotism—for Harim and Ḥárith had shed no blood themselves—was a fit subject for one of whom it was said that he never praised men but as they deserved:—

Noble pair of Ghayẓ ibn Murra,[1] well ye laboured to restore
Ties of kindred hewn asunder by the bloody strokes of war.
Witness now mine oath the ancient House in Mecca's hallowed bound,[2]
Which its builders of Quraysh and Jurhum solemnly went round,[3]
That in hard or easy issue never wanting were ye found!
Peace ye gave to 'Abs and Dhubyán when each fell by other's hand
And the evil fumes they pestled up between them filled the land." [4]

At the end of his panegyric the poet, turning to the lately reconciled tribesmen and their confederates, earnestly warns them against nursing thoughts of vengeance:—

"Will ye hide from God the guilt ye dare not unto Him disclose?
Verily, what thing soever ye would hide from God, He knows.
Either it is laid up meantime in a scroll and treasured there
For the day of retribution, or avenged all unaware.[5]
War ye have known and war have tasted: not by hearsay are ye wise.
Raise no more the hideous monster! If ye let her raven, she cries
Ravenously for blood and crushes, like a mill-stone, all below,
And from her twin-conceiving womb she brings forth woe on woe." [6]

After a somewhat obscure passage concerning the lawless deeds of a certain Ḥusayn b. Ḍamḍam, which had well-nigh

[1] Ghayẓ b. Murra was a descendant of Dhubyán and the ancestor of Harim and Ḥárith.

[2] The Ka'ba.

[3] This refers to the religious circumambulation (*ṭawáf*).

[4] Vv. 16–19 (Lyall).

[5] There is no reason to doubt the genuineness of this passage, which affords evidence of the diffusion of Jewish and Christian ideas in pagan Arabia. Ibn Qutayba observes that these verses indicate the poet's belief in the Resurrection (*K. al-Shi'r wa-'l-Shu'ará*, p. 58, l. 12).

[6] Vv. 27–31.

caused a fresh outbreak of hostilities, Zuhayr proceeds, with a natural and touching allusion to his venerable age, to enforce the lessons of conduct and morality suggested by the situation :—

"I am weary of life's burden : well a man may weary be
After eighty years, and this much now is manifest to me :
Death is like a night-blind camel stumbling on :—the smitten die
But the others age and wax in weakness whom he passes by.
He that often deals with folk in unkind fashion, underneath
They will trample him and make him feel the sharpness of their teeth.
He that hath enough and over and is niggard with his pelf
Will be hated of his people and left free to praise himself.
He alone who with fair actions ever fortifies his fame
Wins it fully : blame will find him out unless he shrinks from blame.
He that for his cistern's guarding trusts not in his own stout arm
Sees it ruined : he must harm his foe or he must suffer harm.
He that fears the bridge of Death across it finally is driven,
Though he span as with a ladder all the space 'twixt earth and heaven.
He that will not take the lance's butt-end while he has the chance
Must thereafter be contented with the spike-end of the lance.
He that keeps his word is blamed not ; he whose heart repaireth straight
To the sanctuary of duty never needs to hesitate.
He that hies abroad to strangers doth account his friends his foes ;
He that honours not himself lacks honour wheresoe'er he goes.
Be a man's true nature what it will, that nature is revealed
To his neighbours, let him fancy as he may that 'tis concealed." [1]

The ripe sententious wisdom and moral earnestness of Zuhayr's poetry are in keeping with what has been said

[1] The order of these verses in Lyall's edition is as follows : 56, 57, 54, 50, 55, 53, 49, 47, 48, 52, 58.

above concerning his religious ideas and, from another point of view, with the tradition that he used to compose a *qaṣída* in four months, correct it for four months, submit it to the poets of his acquaintance during a like period, and not make it public until a year had expired.

Of his life there is little to tell. Probably he died before Islam, though it is related that when he was a centenarian he met the Prophet, who cried out on seeing him, "O God, preserve me from his demon!"[1] The poetical gifts which he inherited from his uncle Basháma he bequeathed to his son Ka'b, author of the famous ode, *Bánat Su'ád*.

Labíd.

Labíd b. Rabí'a, of the Banú 'Ámir b. Ṣa'ṣa'a, was born in the latter half of the sixth century, and is said to have died soon after Mu'áwiya's accession to the Caliphate, which took place in A.D. 661. He is thus the youngest of the Seven Poets. On accepting Islam he abjured poetry, saying, "God has given me the Koran in exchange for it." Like Zuhayr, he had, even in his heathen days, a strong vein of religious feeling, as is shown by many passages in his Díwán.

Labíd was a true Bedouin, and his *Mu'allaqa*, with its charmingly fresh pictures of desert life and scenery, must be considered one of the finest examples of the Pre-islamic *qaṣída* that have come down to us. The poet owes something to his predecessors, but the greater part seems to be drawn from his own observation. He begins in the conventional manner by describing the almost unrecognisable vestiges of the camping-ground of the clan to which his mistress belonged:—

"Waste lies the land where once alighted and did wone
The people of Miná: Rijám and Ghawl are lone.

[1] Reference has been made above to the old Arabian belief that poets owed their inspiration to the *jinn* (genii), who are sometimes called *shayáṭín* (satans). See Goldziher, *Abhand. zur arab. Philologie*, Part I, pp. 1–14.

The camp in Rayyán's vale is marked by relics dim
Like weather-beaten script engraved on ancient stone.
Over this ruined scene, since it was desolate,
Whole years with secular and sacred months had flown.
In spring 'twas blest by showers 'neath starry influence shed,
And thunder-clouds bestowed a scant or copious boon.
Pale herbs had shot up, ostriches on either slope
Their chicks had gotten and gazelles their young had thrown;
And large-eyed wild-cows there beside the new-born calves
Reclined, while round them formed a troop the calves half-grown.
Torrents of rain had swept the dusty ruins bare,
Until, as writing freshly charactered, they shone,
Or like to curved tattoo-lines on a woman's arm,
With soot besprinkled so that every line is shown.
I stopped and asked, but what avails it that we ask
Dumb changeless things that speak a language all unknown?"[1]

After lamenting the departure of his beloved the poet bids himself think no more about her : he will ride swiftly away from the spot. Naturally, he must praise his camel, and he introduces by way of comparison two wonderful pictures of animal life. In the former the onager is described racing at full speed over the backs of the hills when thirst and hunger drive him with his mate far from the barren solitudes into which they usually retire. The second paints a wild-cow, whose young calf has been devoured by wolves, sleeping among the sand-dunes through a night of incessant rain. At daybreak "her feet glide over the firm wet soil." For a whole week she runs to and fro, anxiously seeking her calf, when suddenly she hears the sound of hunters approaching and makes off in alarm. Being unable to get within bowshot, the hunters loose their dogs, but she turns desperately upon them, wounding one with her needle-like horn and killing another.

Then, once more addressing his beloved, the poet speaks complacently of his share in the feasting and revelling, on which a noble Arab plumes himself hardly less than on his bravery :—

[1] Vv. 1–10 (Lyall), omitting v. 5.

"Know'st thou not, O Nawár, that I am wont to tie
The cords of love, yet also snap them without fear?
That I abandon places when I like them not,
Unless Death chain the soul and straiten her career?
Nay, surely, but thou know'st not I have passed in talk
Many a cool night of pleasure and convivial cheer,
And often to a booth, above which hung for sign
A banner, have resorted when old wine was dear.
For no light price I purchased many a dusky skin
Or black clay jar, and broached it that the juice ran clear;
And many a song of shrill-voiced singing-girl I paid,
And her whose fingers made sweet music to mine ear."[1]

Continuing, he boasts of dangerous service as a spy in the enemy's country, when he watched all day on the top of a steep crag; of his fearless demeanour and dignified assertion of his rights in an assembly at Ḥíra, to which he came as a delegate, and of his liberality to the poor. The closing verses are devoted, in accordance with custom, to matters of immediate interest and to a panegyric on the virtues of the poet's kin.

Besides the authors of the *Muʿallaqát* three poets may be mentioned, of whom the two first-named are universally acknowledged to rank with the greatest that Arabia has produced—Nábigha, Aʿshá, and ʿAlqama.

Nábigha of Dhubyán.

Nábigha[2]—his proper name is Ziyád b. Muʿáwiya, of the tribe Dhubyán—lived at the courts of Ghassán and Ḥíra during the latter half of the century before Islam. His chief patron was King Nuʿmán b. Mundhir Abú Qábús of Ḥíra. For many years he basked in the sunshine of royal favour, enjoying every privilege that Nuʿmán bestowed on his most intimate friends. The occasion of their falling out is differently related. According to one story, the poet described the charms of

[1] Vv. 55–60 (Lyall).

[2] The term *nábigha* is applied to a poet whose genius is slow in declaring itself but at last "jets forth vigorously and abundantly" (*nabagha*).

Queen Mutajarrida, which Nu'mán had asked him to celebrate, with such charm and liveliness as to excite her husband's suspicion; but it is said—and Nábigha's own words make it probable—that his enemies denounced him as the author of a scurrilous satire against Nu'mán which had been forged by themselves. At any rate he had no choice but to quit Ḥíra with all speed, and ere long we find him in Ghassán, welcomed and honoured, as the panegyrist of King 'Amr b. Ḥárith and the noble house of Jafna. But his heart was in Ḥíra still. Deeply wounded by the calumnies of which he was the victim, he never ceased to affirm his innocence and to lament the misery of exile. The following poem, which he addressed to Nu'mán, is at once a justification and an appeal for mercy [1]:—

"They brought me word, O King, thou blamedst me;
For this am I o'erwhelmed with grief and care.
I passed a sick man's night: the nurses seemed,
Spreading my couch, to have heaped up briars there.
Now (lest thou cherish in thy mind a doubt)
Invoking our last refuge, God, I swear
That he, whoever told thee I was false,
Is the more lying and faithless of the pair.
Exiled perforce, I found a strip of land
Where I could live and safely take the air:
Kings made me arbiter of their possessions,
And called me to their side and spoke me fair—
Even as thou dost grace thy favourites
Nor deem'st a fault the gratitude they bear.[2]
O leave thine anger! Else, in view of men
A mangy camel, smeared with pitch, I were.
Seest thou not God hath given thee eminence
Before which monarchs tremble and despair?

---

[1] *Díwán*, ed. by Derenbourg, p. 83; Nöldeke's *Delectus*, p. 96.

[2] He means to say that Nu'mán has no reason to feel aggrieved because he (Nábigha) is grateful to the Ghassánids for their munificent patronage; since Nu'mán does not consider that his own favourites, in showing gratitude to himself, are thereby guilty of treachery towards their former patrons.

All other kings are stars and thou a sun:
When the sun rises, lo, the heavens are bare!
A friend in trouble thou wilt not forsake;
I may have sinned: in sinning all men share.
If I am wronged, thou hast but wronged a slave,
And if thou spar'st, 'tis like thyself to spare."

It is pleasant to record that Nábigha was finally reconciled to the prince whom he loved, and that Ḥíra again became his home. The date of his death is unknown, but it certainly took place before Islam was promulgated. Had the opportunity been granted to him he might have died a Moslem: he calls himself 'a religious man' (*dhú ummatin*),[1] and although the tradition that he was actually a Christian lacks authority, his long residence in Syria and 'Iráq must have made him acquainted with the externals of Christianity and with some, at least, of its leading ideas.

The grave and earnest tone characteristic of Nábigha's poetry seldom prevails in that of his younger contemporary, Maymún b. Qays, who is generally known by his surname, al-A'shá—that is, 'the man of weak sight.' A professional troubadour, he roamed from one end of Arabia to the other, harp in hand, singing the praises of those who rewarded him; and such was his fame as a satirist that few ventured to withhold the bounty which he asked. By common consent he stands in the very first rank of Arabian poets. Abu 'l-Faraj, the author of the *Kitábu 'l-Aghání*, declares him to be superior to all the rest, adding, however, "this opinion is not held unanimously as regards A'shá or any other." His

A'shá.

[1] *Díwán*, ed. by Derenbourg, p. 76, ii, 21. In another place (p. 81, vi, 6) he says, addressing his beloved:—

"Wadd give thee greeting! for dalliance with women is lawful to me no more,
Since Religion has become a serious matter."

Wadd was a god worshipped by the pagan Arabs. Derenbourg's text has *rabbí*, *i.e.*, Allah, but see Nöldeke's remarks in *Z.D.M.G.*, vol. xli (1887), p. 708.

wandering life brought him into contact with every kind of culture then existing in Arabia. Although he was not an avowed Christian, his poetry shows to what an extent he was influenced by the Bishops of Najrán, with whom he was intimately connected, and by the Christian merchants of Ḥíra who sold him their wine. He did not rise above the pagan level of morality.

It is related that he set out to visit Muḥammad for the purpose of reciting to him an ode which he had composed in his honour. When the Quraysh heard of this, they feared lest their adversary's reputation should be increased by the panegyric of a bard so famous and popular. Accordingly, they intercepted him on his way, and asked whither he was bound. "To your kinsman," said he, "that I may accept Islam." "He will forbid and make unlawful to thee certain practices of which thou art fond." "What are these?" said A'shá. "Fornication," said Abú Sufyán. "I have not abandoned it," he replied, "but it has abandoned me. What else?" "Gambling." "Perhaps I shall obtain from him something to compensate me for the loss of gambling. What else?" "Usury." "I have never borrowed nor lent. What else?" "Wine." "Oh, in that case I will drink the water I have left stored at al-Mihrás." Seeing that A'shá was not to be deterred, Abú Sufyán offered him a hundred camels on condition that he should return to his home in Yamáma and await the issue of the struggle between Muḥammad and the Quraysh. "I agree," said A'shá. "O ye Quraysh," cried Abú Sufyán, "this is A'shá, and by God, if he becomes a follower of Muḥammad, he will inflame the Arabs against you by his poetry. Collect, therefore, a hundred camels for him." [1]

A'shá excels in the description of wine and wine-parties. One who visited Manfúḥa in Yamáma, where the poet was buried, relates that revellers used to meet at his grave and pour out beside it the last drops that remained in their cups. As an example of his style in this *genre* I translate a few lines from the most celebrated of his poems, which is included by some critics among the *Mu'allaqát*:—

[1] *Aghání*, viii, 85, last line–86, l. 10.

"Many a time I hastened early to the tavern—while there ran
At my heels a ready cook, a nimble, active serving-man—
'Midst a gallant troop, like Indian scimitars, of mettle high;
Well they know that every mortal, shod and bare alike, must die.
Propped at ease I greet them gaily, them with myrtle-boughs I greet,
Pass among them wine that gushes from the jar's mouth bitter-sweet.
Emptying goblet after goblet—but the source may no man drain—
Never cease they from carousing save to cry, 'Fill up again!'
Briskly runs the page to serve them: on his ears hang pearls: below,
Tight the girdle draws his doublet as he bustles to and fro.
'Twas the harp, thou mightest fancy, waked the lute's responsive note,
When the loose-robed chantress touched it and sang shrill with quavering throat.
Here and there among the party damsels fair superbly glide:
Each her long white skirt lets trail and swings a wine-skin at her side."[1]

Very little is known of the life of 'Alqama b. 'Abada, who was surnamed *al-Faḥl* (the Stallion). His most famous poem is that which he addressed to the Ghassánid Ḥárith al-A'raj after the Battle of Ḥalíma, imploring him to set free some prisoners of Tamím—the poet's tribe—among whom was his own brother or nephew, Shás. The following lines have almost become proverbial:—

'Alqama.

"Of women do ye ask me? I can spy
Their ailments with a shrewd physician's eye.
The man whose head is grey or small his herds
No favour wins of them but mocking words.
Are riches known, to riches they aspire,
And youthful bloom is still their heart's desire."[2]

---

[1] Lyall, *Ten Ancient Arabic Poems*, p. 146 seq., vv. 25–31.
[2] Ahlwardt, *The Divans*, p. 106, vv. 8–10.

In view of these slighting verses it is proper to observe that the poetry of Arabian women of the Pre-islamic period is distinctly masculine in character. Their songs are seldom of Love, but often of Death. Elegy (*rithá* or *marthiya*) was regarded as their special province. The oldest form of elegy appears in the verses chanted on the death of Ta'abbaṭa Sharr^{an} by his sister :—

Elegiac poetry.

"O the good knight ye left low at Rakhmán,
Thábit son of Jábir son of Sufyán !
He filled the cup for friends and ever slew his man." [1]

"As a rule the Arabian dirge is very simple. The poetess begins with a description of her grief, of the tears that she cannot quench, and then she shows how worthy to be deeply mourned was he whom death has taken away. He is described as a pattern of the two principal Arabian virtues, bravery and liberality, and the question is anxiously asked, 'Who will now make high resolves, overthrow the enemy, and in time of want feed the poor and entertain the stranger ?' If the hero of the dirge died a violent death we find in addition a burning lust of revenge, a thirst for the slayer's blood, expressed with an intensity of feeling of which only women are capable." [2]

Among Arabian women who have excelled in poetry the place of honour is due to Khansá—her real name was Tumáḍir—who flourished in the last years before Islam. By far the most famous of her elegies are those in which she bewailed her valiant brothers, Mu'áwiya and Ṣakhr, both of whom were struck down by sword or spear. It is impossible to translate the poignant and vivid emotion, the energy of passion and noble simplicity of style which distinguish the poetry of Khansá, but here are a few verses :—

Khansá.

[1] *Ḥamása*, p. 382, l. 17.
[2] Nöldeke, *Beiträge zur Kenntniss der Poesie der alten Araber*, p. 152.

Death's messenger cried aloud the loss of the generous one,
So loud cried he, by my life, that far he was heard and wide.
Then rose I, and scarce my soul could follow to meet the news,
For anguish and sore dismay and horror that Ṣakhr had died.
In my misery and despair I seemed as a drunken man,
Upstanding awhile—then soon his tottering limbs subside."[1]

*Yudhakkiruní ṭulú'u 'l-shamsi Ṣakhr*an
wa-adhkuruhú likulli ghurúbi shamsi.

"Sunrise awakes in me the sad remembrance
Of Ṣakhr, and I recall him at every sunset."

The last poets born in the Age of Paganism.

To the poets who have been enumerated many might be added—*e.g.*, Ḥassán b. Thábit, who was 'retained' by the Prophet and did useful work on his behalf; Ka'b b. Zuhayr, author of the famous panegyric on Muḥammad beginning "*Bánat Su'ád*" (Su'ád has departed); Mutammim b. Nuwayra, who, like Khansá, mourned the loss of a brother; Abú Miḥjan, the singer of wine, whose devotion to the forbidden beverage was punished by the Caliph 'Umar with imprisonment and exile; and al-Ḥuṭay'a (the Dwarf), who was unrivalled in satire. All these belonged to the class of *Mukhaḍramún*, *i.e.*, they were born in the Pagan Age but died, if not Moslems, at any rate after the proclamation of Islam.

Collections of ancient poetry.

The grammarians of Baṣra and Kúfa, by whom the remains of ancient Arabian poetry were rescued from oblivion, arranged and collected their material according to various principles. Either the poems of an individual or those of a number of individuals belonging to the same tribe or class were brought together—such a collection was called *Díwán*, plural *Dawáwín*; or, again, the compiler edited a certain number of *qaṣídas* chosen for their fame or

[1] Nöldeke, *ibid.*, p. 175.

excellence or on other grounds, or he formed an anthology of shorter pieces or fragments, which were arranged under different heads according to their subject-matter.

Díwáns.

Among *Díwáns* mention may be made of *The Díwáns of the Six Poets*, viz. Nábigha, 'Antara, Ṭarafa, Zuhayr, 'Alqama, and Imru'u 'l-Qays, edited with a full commentary by the Spanish philologist al-A'lam (†1083 A.D.) and published in 1870 by Ahlwardt; and of *The Poems of the Hudhaylites* (*Ash'áru 'l-Hudhaliyyín*) collected by al-Sukkarí († 888 A.D.), which have been published by Kosegarten and Wellhausen.

The chief Anthologies, taken in the order of their composition, are :—

Anthologies. 1. The *Mu'allaqát*.

1. *The Mu'allaqát*, which is the title given to a collection of seven odes by Imru'u 'l-Qays, Ṭarafa, Zuhayr, Labíd, 'Antara, 'Amr b. Kulthúm, and Ḥárith b. Ḥilliza; to these two odes by Nábigha and A'shá are sometimes added. The compiler was probably Ḥammád al-Ráwiya, a famous rhapsodist of Persian descent, who flourished under the Umayyads and died in the second half of the eighth century of our era. As the *Mu'allaqát* have been discussed above, we may pass on directly to a much larger, though less celebrated, collection dating from the same period, viz. :—

2. The *Mufaḍḍaliyyát*.

2. The *Mufaḍḍaliyyát*,[1] by which title it is generally known after its compiler, Mufaḍḍal al-Ḍabbí († *circa* 786 A.D.), who made it at the instance of the Caliph Manṣúr for the instruction of his son and successor, Mahdí. It comprises 128 odes and is extant in two recensions, that of Anbárí († 916 A.D.), which derives from Ibnu 'l-A'rábí, the stepson of Mufaḍḍal, and that of Marzúqí (†1030 A.D.). About a third of the *Mufaḍḍaliyyát* was pub-

[1] The original title is *al-Mukhtárát* (The Selected Odes) or *al-Ikhtiyárát* (The Selections).

lished in 1885 by Thorbecke, and Sir Charles Lyall has recently edited the complete text with Arabic commentary and English translation and notes.[1]

All students of Arabian poetry are familiar with—

3. The Ḥamása of Abú Tammám Ḥabíb b. Aws, himself a distinguished poet, who flourished under the Caliphs Ma'mún and Mu'taṣim, and died about 850 A.D. Towards the end of his life he visited 'Abdulláh b. Ṭáhir, the powerful governor of Khurásán, who was virtually an independent sovereign. It was on this journey, as Ibn Khallikán relates, that Abú Tammám composed the *Ḥamása*; for on arriving at Hamadhán (Ecbatana) the winter had set in, and as the cold was excessively severe in that country, the snow blocked up the road and obliged him to stop and await the thaw. During his stay he resided with one of the most eminent men of the place, who possessed a library in which were some collections of poems composed by the Arabs of the desert and other authors. Having then sufficient leisure, he perused those works and selected from them the passages out of which he formed his *Ḥamása*.[2] The work is divided into ten sections of unequal length, the first, from which it received its name, occupying (together with the commentary) 360 pages in Freytag's edition, while the seventh and eighth require only thirteen pages between them. These sections or chapters bear the following titles:—

3. The *Ḥamása* of Abú Tammám.

I. The Chapter of Fortitude (*Bábu 'l-Ḥamása*).
II. The Chapter of Dirges (*Bábu 'l-Maráthí*).
III. The Chapter of Good Manners (*Bábu 'l-Adab*).
IV. The Chapter of Love-Songs (*Bábu 'l-Nasíb*).
V. The Chapter of Satire (*Bábu 'l-Hijá*).
VI. The Chapter of Guests (Hospitality) and Panegyric (*Bábu 'l-Aḍyáf wa'-l-Madíḥ*).

---

[1] Oxford, 1918–21. The Indexes of personal and place-names, poetical quotations, and selected words were prepared by Professor Bevan and published in 1924 in the E. J. W. Gibb Memorial Series.

[2] Ibn Khallikán, ed. by Wüstenfeld, No. 350 = De Slane's translation, vol. ii, p. 51.

VII. The Chapter of Descriptions (*Bábu 'l-Ṣifát*).
VIII. The Chapter of Travel and Repose (*Bábu 'l-Sayr wa-'l-Nu'ás*).
IX. The Chapter of Facetiæ (*Bábu 'l-Mulaḥ*).
X. The Chapter of Vituperation of Women (*Bábu Madhammati 'l-Nisá*).

The contents of the *Ḥamása* include short poems complete in themselves as well as passages extracted from longer poems; of the poets represented, some of whom belong to the Pre-islamic and others to the early Islamic period, comparatively few are celebrated, while many are anonymous or only known by the verses attached to their names. If the high level of excellence attained by these obscure singers shows, on the one hand, that a natural genius for poetry was widely diffused and that the art was successfully cultivated among all ranks of Arabian society, we must not forget how much is due to the fine taste of Abú Tammám, who, as the commentator Tibrízí has remarked, "is a better poet in his *Ḥamása* than in his poetry."

4. The *Ḥamása* of Buḥturí († 897 A.D.), a younger contemporary of Abú Tammám, is inferior to its model.[1] However convenient from a practical standpoint, the division into a great number of sections, each illustrating a narrowly defined topic, seriously impairs the artistic value of the work; moreover, Buḥturí seems to have had a less catholic appreciation of the beauties of poetry—he admired, it is said, only what was in harmony with his own style and ideas.

4. The *Ḥamása* of Buḥturí.

5. The *Jamharatu Ash'ári 'l-'Arab*, a collection of forty-nine odes, was put together probably about 1000 A.D. by Abú Zayd Muḥammad al-Qurashí, of whom we find no mention elsewhere.

5. The *Jamhara*.

[1] See Nöldeke, *Beiträge*, p. 183 sqq. There would seem to be comparatively few poems of Pre-islamic date in Buḥturí's anthology.

Apart from the *Díwáns* and anthologies, numerous Pre-islamic verses are cited in biographical, philological, and other works, *e.g.*, the *Kitábu 'l-Aghání* by Abu 'l-Faraj of Iṣfahán († 967 A.D.), the *Kitábu 'l-Amálí* by Abú 'Alí al-Qálí († 967 A.D.), the *Kámil* of Mubarrad († 898 A.D.), and the *Khizánatu 'l-Adab* of 'Abdu 'l-Qádir of Baghdád († 1682 A.D.).

Prose sources.

We have seen that the oldest existing poems date from the beginning of the sixth century of our era, whereas the art of writing did not come into general use among the Arabs until some two hundred years afterwards. Pre-islamic poetry, therefore, was preserved by oral tradition alone, and the question arises, How was this possible? What guarantee have we that songs living on men's lips for so long a period have retained their original form, even approximately? No doubt many verses, *e.g.*, those which glorified the poet's tribe or satirised their enemies, were constantly being recited by his kin, and in this way short occasional poems or fragments of longer ones might be perpetuated. Of whole *qaṣídas* like the *Mu'allaqát*, however, none or very few would have reached us if their survival had depended solely on their popularity. What actually saved them in the first place was an institution resembling that of the Rhapsodists in Greece. Every professed poet had his *Ráwí* (reciter), who accompanied him everywhere, committed his poems to memory, and handed them down, as well as the circumstances connected with them, to others. The characters of poet and *ráwí* were often combined; thus Zuhayr was the *ráwí* of his step-father, Aws b. Ḥajar, while his own *ráwí* was al-Ḥuṭay'a. If the tradition of poetry was at first a labour of love, it afterwards became a lucrative business, and the *Ráwís*, instead of being attached to individual poets, began to form an independent class, carrying in their memories a prodigious

The tradition of Pre-islamic poetry.

The Ráwís.

stock of ancient verse and miscellaneous learning. It is related, for example, that Ḥammád once said to the Caliph Walíd b. Yazíd: "I can recite to you, for each letter of the alphabet, one hundred long poems rhyming in that letter, without taking into count the short pieces, and all that composed exclusively by poets who lived before the promulgation of Islamism." He commenced and continued until the Caliph, having grown fatigued, withdrew, after leaving a person in his place to verify the assertion and hear him to the last. In that sitting he recited two thousand nine hundred *qaṣídas* by poets who flourished before Muḥammad. Walíd, on being informed of the fact, ordered him a present of one hundred thousand dirhems.[1] Thus, towards the end of the first century after the Hijra, *i.e.*, about 700 A.D., when the custom of *writing* poetry began, there was much of Pre-islamic origin still in circulation, although it is probable that far more had already been irretrievably lost. Numbers of *Ráwís* perished in the wars, or passèd away in the course of nature, without leaving any one to continue their tradition. New times had brought new interests and other ways of life. The great majority of Moslems had no sympathy whatever with the ancient poetry, which represented in their eyes the unregenerate spirit of heathendom. They wanted nothing beyond the Koran and the Ḥadíth. But for reasons which will be stated in another chapter the language of the Koran and the Ḥadíth was rapidly becoming obsolete as a spoken idiom outside of the Arabian peninsula: the 'perspicuous Arabic' on which Muḥammad prided himself had ceased to be fully intelligible to the Moslems settled in 'Iráq and Khurásán, in Syria, and in Egypt. It was essential that the Sacred Text should be explained, and this necessity gave birth to the sciences of Grammar and Lexi-

[1] Ibn Khallikán, ed. by Wüstenfeld, No. 204 = De Slane's translation, vol. i, p. 470.

cography. The Philologists, or, as they have been aptly designated, the Humanists of Baṣra and Kúfa, where these studies were prosecuted with peculiar zeal, naturally found their best material in the Pre-islamic poems—a well of Arabic undefiled. At first the ancient poetry merely formed a basis for philological research, but in process of time a literary enthusiasm was awakened. The surviving *Ráwís* were eagerly sought out and induced to yield up their stores, the compositions of famous poets were collected, arranged, and committed to writing, and as the demand increased, so did the supply.[1]

The Humanists.

In these circumstances a certain amount of error was inevitable. Apart from unconscious failings of memory, there can be no doubt that in many cases the *Ráwís* acted with intent to deceive. The temptation to father their own verses, or centos which they pieced together from sources known only to themselves, upon some poet of antiquity was all the stronger because they ran little risk of detection. In knowledge of poetry and in poetical talent they were generally far more than a match for the philologists, who seldom possessed any critical ability, but readily took whatever came to hand. The stories which are told of Ḥammád al-Ráwiya, clearly show how unscrupulous he was in his methods, though we have reason to suppose that he was not a typical example of his class. His contemporary, Mufaḍḍal al-Ḍabbí, is reported to have said that the corruption which poetry suffered through Ḥammád could never be repaired, "for," he added, "Ḥammád is a man skilled in the language and poesy of the Arabs and in the styles and ideas of the poets, and he is always making verses in imitation of some

Corrupt tradition of the old poetry.

Ḥammád al-Ráwiya.

[1] Many interesting details concerning the tradition of Pre-islamic poetry by the *Ráwís* and the Philologists will be found in Ahlwardt's *Bemerkungen ueber die Aechtheit der alten Arabischen Gedichte* (Greifswald, 1872), which has supplied materials for the present sketch.

one and introducing them into genuine compositions by the same author, so that the copy passes everywhere for part of the original, and cannot be distinguished from it except by critical scholars—and where are such to be found?"[1] This art of forgery was brought to perfection by Khalaf al-Aḥmar († about 800 A.D.), who learned it in the school of Ḥammád. If he really composed the famous *Lámiyya* ascribed to Shanfará, his own poetical endowments must have been of the highest order. In his old age he repented and confessed that he was the author of several poems which the scholars of Baṣra and Kúfa had accepted as genuine, but they laughed him to scorn, saying, "What you said then seems to us more trustworthy than your present assertion."

Khalaf al-Aḥmar.

Besides the corruptions due to the *Ráwís*, others have been accumulated by the philologists themselves. As the Koran and the Ḥadíth were, of course, spoken and afterwards written in the dialect of Quraysh, to whom Muḥammad belonged, this dialect was regarded as the classical standard;[2] consequently the variations therefrom which occurred in the ancient poems were, for the most part, 'emended' and harmonised with it. Many changes were made under the influence of Islam, *e.g.*, 'Allah' was probably often substituted for the pagan goddess 'al-Lát.' Moreover, the structure of the *qaṣída*, its disconnectedness and want of logical cohesion, favoured the omission and transposition of whole passages or single verses. All these modes of depravation might be illustrated in detail, but from what has been said the reader can judge for himself how far the poems, as they now stand, are likely to have retained the form in which they were first uttered to the wild Arabs of the Pre-islamic Age.

Other causes of corruption.

[1] *Aghání*, v, 172, l. 16 sqq.

[2] This view, however, is in accordance neither with the historical facts nor with the public opinion of the Pre-islamic Arabs (see Nöldeke, *Die Semitischen Sprachen*, p. 47).

Religion had so little influence on the lives of the Pre-islamic Arabs that we cannot expect to find much trace of it in their poetry. They believed vaguely in a supreme God, Allah, and more definitely in his three daughters—al-Lát, Manát, and al-'Uzzá—who were venerated all over Arabia and whose intercession was graciously accepted by Allah. There were also numerous idols enjoying high favour while they continued to bring good luck to their worshippers. Of real piety the ordinary Bedouin knew nothing. He felt no call to pray to his gods, although he often found them convenient to swear by. He might invoke Allah in the hour of need, as a drowning man will clutch at a straw; but his faith in superstitious ceremonies was stronger. He did not take his religion too seriously. Its practical advantages he was quick to appreciate. Not to mention baser pleasures, it gave him rest and security during the four sacred months, in which war was forbidden, while the institution of the Meccan Pilgrimage enabled him to take part in a national fête.

Religion.

Commerce went hand in hand with religion. Great fairs were held, the most famous being that of 'Ukáẓ, which lasted for twenty days. These fairs were in some sort the centre of old Arabian social, political, and literary life. It was the only occasion on which free and fearless intercourse was possible between the members of different clans.[1]

The Fair of 'Ukáẓ.

Plenty of excitement was provided by poetical and oratorical displays—not by athletic sports, as in ancient Greece and modern England. Here rival poets declaimed their verses and submitted them to the judgment of an acknowledged master. Nowhere else had rising talents such an opportunity of gaining wide reputation: what 'Ukáẓ said to-day all Arabia would repeat to-morrow. At 'Ukáẓ, we are told, the youthful Muḥammad listened, as though spellbound, to

[1] See Wellhausen, *Reste Arab. Heidentums* (2nd ed.), p. 88 seq.

the persuasive eloquence of Quss b. Sá'ida, Bishop of Najrán; and he may have contrasted the discourse of the Christian preacher with the brilliant odes chanted by heathen bards.

The Bedouin view of life was thoroughly hedonistic. Love, wine, gambling, hunting, the pleasures of song and romance, the brief, pointed, and elegant expression of wit and wisdom—these things he knew to be good. Beyond them he saw only the grave.

> "Roast meat and wine: the swinging ride
> On a camel sure and tried,
> Which her master speeds amain
> O'er low dale and level plain:
> Women marble-white and fair
> Trailing gold-fringed raiment rare:
> Opulence, luxurious ease,
> With the lute's soft melodies—
> Such delights hath our brief span;
> Time is Change, Time's fool is Man.
> Wealth or want, great store or small,
> All is one since Death's are all."[1]

It would be a mistake to suppose that these men always, or even generally, passed their lives in the aimless pursuit of pleasure. Some goal they had—earthly, no doubt—such as the accumulation of wealth or the winning of glory or the fulfilment of blood-revenge. "*God forbid*," says one, "*that I should die while a grievous longing, as it were a mountain, weighs on my breast!*"[2] A deeper chord is touched by Imru'u 'l-Qays: "*If I strove for a bare livelihood, scanty means would suffice me and I would seek no more. But I strive for lasting renown, and 'tis men like me that sometimes attain lasting renown. Never, while life endures, does a man reach the summit of his ambition or cease from toil.*"[3]

[1] *Ḥamása*, 506. [2] *Ibid.*, 237.

[3] *Díwán* of Imru'u 'l-Qays, ed. by De Slane, p. 22 of the Arabic text, l. 17 sqq. = No. 52, ll. 57–59 (p. 154) in Ahlwardt's *Divans of the Six Poets*.

These are noble sentiments nobly expressed. Yet one hears the sigh of weariness, as if the speaker were struggling against the conviction that his cause is already lost, and would welcome the final stroke of destiny. It was a time of wild uproar and confusion. Tribal and family feuds filled the land, as Zuhayr says, with evil fumes. No wonder that earnest and thoughtful minds asked themselves—What worth has our life, what meaning? Whither does it lead? Such questions paganism could not answer, but Arabia in the century before Muḥammad was not wholly abandoned to paganism. Jewish colonists had long been settled in the Ḥijáz. Probably the earliest settlements date from the conquest of Palestine by Titus or Hadrian. In their new home the refugees, through contact with a people nearly akin to themselves, became fully Arabicised, as the few extant specimens of their poetry bear witness. They remained Jews, however, not only in their cultivation of trade and various industries, but also in the most vital particular—their religion. This, and the fact that they lived in isolated communities among the surrounding population, marked them out as the salt of the desert. In the Ḥijáz their spiritual predominance was not seriously challenged. It was otherwise in Yemen. We may leave out of account the legend according to which Judaism was introduced into that country from the Ḥijáz by the Tubba' As'ad Kámil. What is certain is that towards the beginning of the sixth century it was firmly planted there side by side with Christianity, and that in the person of the Ḥimyarite monarch Dhú Nuwás, who adopted the Jewish faith, it won a short-lived but sanguinary triumph over its rival. But in Yemen, except among the highlanders of Najrán, Christianity does not appear to have flourished as it did in the extreme north and north-east, where the Roman and

Judaism and Christianity in Arabia.

With the last line, however, *cf.* the words of Qays b. al-Khaṭím on accomplishing his vengeance: "*When this death comes, there will not be found any need of my soul that I have not satisfied*" (*Ḥamása*, 87).

Persian frontiers were guarded by the Arab levies of Ghassán and Ḥíra. We have seen that the latter city contained a large Christian population who were called distinctively

The 'Ibád of Ḥíra.

'Ibád, *i.e.*, Servants (of God). Through them the Aramaic culture of Babylonia was transmitted to all parts of the peninsula. They had learned the art of writing long before it was generally practised in Arabia, as is shown by the story of Ṭarafa and Mutalammis, and they produced the oldest *written* poetry in the Arabic language—a poetry very different in character from that which forms the main subject of this chapter. Unfortunately the bulk of it has perished, since the rhapsodists, to whom we owe the preservation of so much Pre-islamic verse, were devoted to the traditional models and would not burden their memories with anything new-fashioned. The most famous of the 'Ibádí poets is 'Adí b. Zayd, whose adventurous career as a politician has been sketched above. He is not reckoned by Muḥammadan critics among the *Fuḥúl* or poets of the first rank, because he was a townsman (*qarawí*). In this connec-

'Adí b. Zayd.

tion the following anecdote is instructive. The poet al-'Ajjáj († about 709 A.D.) said of his contemporaries al-Ṭirimmáḥ and al-Kumayt: "They used to ask me concerning rare expressions in the language of poetry, and I informed them, but afterwards I found the same expressions wrongly applied in their poems, the reason being that they were townsmen who described what they had not seen and misapplied it, whereas I who am a Bedouin describe what I have seen and apply it properly."[1] 'Adí is chiefly remembered for his wine-songs. Oriental Christianity has always been associated with the drinking and selling of wine. Christian ideas were carried into the heart of Arabia by 'Ibádí wine merchants, who are said to have taught their religion to the celebrated A'shá. 'Adí drank and was merry like the rest, but the underlying thought, 'for to-morrow we die,' repeatedly

[1] *Aghání*, ii, 18, l. 23 sqq.

makes itself heard. He walks beside a cemetery, and the voices of the dead call to him—[1]

"Thou who seëst us unto thyself shalt say,
'Soon upon me comes the season of decay.'
Can the solid mountains evermore sustain
Time's vicissitudes and all they bring in train?
Many a traveller lighted near us and abode,
Quaffing wine wherein the purest water flowed—
Strainers on each flagon's mouth to clear the wine,
Noble steeds that paw the earth in trappings fine!
For a while they lived in lap of luxury,
Fearing no misfortune, dallying lazily.
Then, behold, Time swept them all, like chaff, away:
Thus it is men fall to whirling Time a prey.
Thus it is Time keeps the bravest and the best
Night and day still plunged in Pleasure's fatal quest."

It is said that the recitation of these verses induced Nuʿmán al-Akbar, one of the mythical pagan kings of Ḥíra, to accept Christianity and become an anchorite. Although the story involves an absurd anachronism, it is *ben trovato* in so far as it records the impression which the graver sort of Christian poetry was likely to make on heathen minds.

The courts of Ḥíra and Ghassán were well known to the wandering minstrels of the time before Muḥammad, who flocked thither in eager search of patronage and remuneration. We may be sure that men like Nábigha, Labíd, and Aʿshá did not remain unaffected by the culture around them, even if it seldom entered very deeply into their lives. That considerable traces of religious feeling are to be found in Pre-islamic poetry admits of no denial, but the passages in question were formerly explained as due to interpolation. This view no longer prevails. Thanks mainly to the arguments of Von Kremer, Sir Charles Lyall, and Wellhausen, it has come to be recognised (1) that in many cases the above-mentioned religious feeling is not Islamic in tone; (2) that the passages in which it occurs

Pre-islamic poetry not exclusively pagan in sentiment.

[1] *Aghání*, ii, 34, l. 22 sqq.

are not of Islamic origin ; and (3) that it is the natural and necessary result of the widely spread, though on the whole superficial, influence of Judaism, and especially of Christianity.[1] It shows itself not only in frequent allusions, *e.g.*, to the monk in his solitary cell, whose lamp serves to light belated travellers on their way, and in more significant references, such as that of Zuhayr already quoted, to the Heavenly Book in which evil actions are enscrolled for the Day of Reckoning, but also in the tendency to moralise, to look within, to meditate on death, and to value the life of the individual rather than the continued existence of the family. These things are not characteristic of old Arabian poetry, but the fact that they do appear at times is quite in accord with the other facts which have been stated, and justifies the conclusion that during the sixth century religion and culture were imperceptibly extending their sphere of influence in Arabia, leavening the pagan masses, and gradually preparing the way for Islam.

[1] See Von Kremer, *Ueber die Gedichte des Labyd* in *S.B.W.A.*, *Phil.-Hist. Klasse* (Vienna, 1881), vol. 98, p. 555 sqq. Sir Charles Lyall, *Ancient Arabian Poetry*, pp. 92 and 119. Wellhausen, *Reste Arabischen Heidentums* (2nd ed.), p. 224 sqq.

CHAPTER IV

THE PROPHET AND THE KORAN

WITH the appearance of Muḥammad the almost impenetrable veil thrown over the preceding age is suddenly lifted and we find ourselves on the solid ground of historical tradition. In order that the reasons for this change may be understood, it is necessary to give some account of the principal sources from which our knowledge of the Prophet's life and teaching is derived.

Sources of information: I. The Koran.

There is first, of course, the Koran,[1] consisting "exclusively of the revelations or commands which Muḥammad professed, from time to time, to receive through Gabriel as a message direct from God; and which, under an alleged Divine direction, he delivered to those about him. At the time of pretended inspiration, or shortly after, each passage was recited by Muḥammad before the Companions or followers who happened to be present, and was generally committed to writing by some one amongst them upon palm-leaves, leather, stones, or such other rude material as conveniently came to hand. These Divine messages continued throughout the three-and-twenty years of his prophetical life, so that the last portion did not appear till the year of his death. The canon was then closed; but the contents were

[1] I prefer to retain the customary spelling instead of Qur'án, as it is correctly transliterated by scholars. Arabic words naturalised in English, like Koran, Caliph, Vizier, &c., require no apology

never, during the Prophet's lifetime, systematically arranged, or even collected together."[1] They were preserved, however, in fragmentary copies and, especially, by oral recitation until the sanguinary wars which followed Muḥammad's death had greatly diminished the number of those who could repeat them by heart. Accordingly, after the battle of Yamáma (633 A.D.) 'Umar b. al-Khaṭṭáb came to Abú Bakr, who was then Caliph, and said: "I fear that slaughter may wax hot among the Reciters on other battle-fields, and that much of the Koran may be lost; so in my opinion it should be collected without delay." Abú Bakr agreed, and entrusted the task to Zayd b. Thábit, one of the Prophet's amanuenses, who collected the fragments with great difficulty "from bits of parchment, thin white stones, leafless palm-branches, and the bosoms of men." The manuscript thus compiled was deposited with Abú Bakr during the remainder of his life, then with 'Umar, on whose death it passed to his daughter Ḥafṣa. Afterwards, in the Caliphate of 'Uthmán, Ḥudhayfa b. al-Yamán, observing that the Koran as read in Syria was seriously at variance with the text current in 'Iráq, warned the Caliph to interfere, lest the Sacred Book of the Moslems should become a subject of dispute, like the Jewish and Christian scriptures. In the year 651 A.D. 'Uthmán ordered Zayd b. Thábit to prepare a Revised Version with the assistance of three Qurayshites, saying to the latter, "If ye differ from Zayd regarding any word of the Koran, write it in the dialect of Quraysh; for it was revealed in their dialect."[2] This has ever since remained the final and standard recension of the Koran. "Transcripts were multiplied and forwarded to the chief cities in the empire, and all previously existing copies were, by the Caliph's com-

How it was preserved.

[1] Muir's *Life of Mahomet*, Introduction, p. 2 seq. I may as well say at once that I entirely disagree with the view suggested in this passage that Muḥammad did not believe himself to be inspired.

[2] The above details are taken from the *Fihrist*, ed. by G. Fluegel, p. 24, l. 14 sqq.

mand, committed to the flames."[1] In the text as it has come down to us the various readings are few and unimportant, and its genuineness is above suspicion. We shall see, moreover, that the Koran is an exceedingly human document, reflecting every phase of Muḥammad's personality and standing in close relation to the outward events of his life, so that here we have materials of unique and incontestable authority for tracing the origin and early development of Islam—such materials as do not exist in the case of Buddhism or Christianity or any other ancient religion. Unfortunately the arrangement of the Koran can only be described as chaotic. No chronological sequence is observed in the order of the Súras (chapters), which is determined simply by their length, the longest being placed first.[2] Again, the chapters themselves are sometimes made up of disconnected fragments having nothing in common except the rhyme; whence it is often impossible to discover the original context of the words actually spoken by the Prophet, the occasion on which they were revealed, or the period to which they belong. In these circumstances the Koran must be supplemented by reference to our second main source of information, namely, Tradition.

Value of the Koran as an authority.

Already in the last years of Muḥammad's life (writes Dr. Sprenger) it was a pious custom that when two Moslems met, one should ask for news (*ḥadíth*) and the other should relate a saying or anecdote of the Prophet. After his death this custom continued, and the name *Ḥadíth* was still applied to sayings and stories which were no longer new.[3] In the course of time an elaborate system of Tradition was built up, as the Koran—originally the sole criterion by which Moslems were guided alike in the

2. Tradition (Ḥadíth).

[1] Muir, *op. cit.*, Introduction, p. 14.

[2] With the exception of the Opening Súra (*al-Fátiḥa*), which is a short prayer.

[3] Sprenger, *Ueber das Traditionswesen bei den Arabern*, *Z.D.M.G.*, vol. x, p. 2.

greatest and smallest matters of public and private interest—was found insufficient for the complicated needs of a rapidly extending empire. Appeal was made to the sayings and practice (*sunna*) of Muḥammad, which now acquired "the force of law and some of the authority of inspiration." The Prophet had no Boswell, but almost as soon as he began to preach he was a marked man whose *obiter dicta* could not fail to be treasured by his Companions, and whose actions were attentively watched. Thus, during the first century of Islam there was a multitude of living witnesses from whom traditions were collected, committed to memory, and orally handed down. Every tradition consists of two parts: the text (*matn*) and the authority (*sanad*, or *isnád*), *e.g.*, the relater says, "I was told by *A*, who was informed by *B*, who had it from *C*, that the Prophet (God bless him!) and Abú Bakr and 'Umar used to open prayer with the words 'Praise to God, the Lord of all creatures.'" Written records and compilations were comparatively rare in the early period. Ibn Isḥáq († 768 A.D.) composed the oldest extant Biography of the Prophet, which we do not possess, however, in its original shape but only in the recension of Ibn Hishám († 833 A.D.). Two important and excellent works of the same kind are the *Kitábu 'l-Maghází* ('Book of the Wars') by Wáqidí († 822 A.D.) and the *Kitábu 'l-Ṭabaqát al-Kabír* ('The Great Book of the Classes,' *i.e.*, the different classes of Muḥammad's Companions and those who came after them) by Ibn Sa'd († 844 A.D.). Of miscellaneous traditions intended to serve the Faithful as a model and rule of life in every particular, and arranged in chapters according to the subject-matter, the most ancient and authoritative collections are those of Bukhárí († 870 A.D.) and Muslim († 874 A.D.), both of which bear the same title, viz., *al-Ṣaḥíḥ*, 'The Genuine.' It only remains to speak of Commentaries on the Koran. Some passages were explained by Muḥammad himself, but the real founder of

Biographies of Muḥammad.

General collections.

Koranic Exegesis was 'Abdulláh b. 'Abbás, the Prophet's cousin. Although the writings of the early interpreters have entirely perished, the gist of their researches is embodied in the great commentary of Ṭabarí († 922 A.D.), a man of encyclopædic learning who absorbed the whole mass of tradition existing in his time. Subsequent commentaries are largely based on this colossal work, which has recently been published at Cairo in thirty volumes. That of Zamakhsharí († 1143 A.D.), which is entitled the *Kashsháf*, and that of Bayḍáwí († 1286 A.D.) are the best known and most highly esteemed in the Muḥammadan East. A work of wider scope is the *Itqán* of Suyúṭí († 1505 A.D.), which takes a general survey of the Koranic sciences, and may be regarded as an introduction to the critical study of the Koran.

Commentaries on the Koran.

While every impartial student will admit the justice of Ibn Qutayba's claim that no religion has such historical attestations as Islam—*laysa li-ummat^in mina 'l-umami asnád^un ka-asnádihim* [1]—he must at the same time cordially assent to the observation made by another Muḥammadan: "In nothing do we see pious men more given to falsehood than in Tradition" (*lam nara 'l-ṣáliḥína fí shay'^in akdhaba minhum fí 'l-ḥadíth*).[2] Of this severe judgment the reader will find ample confirmation in the Second Part of Goldziher's *Muhammedanische Studien*.[3] During the first century of Islam the forging of Traditions became a recognised political and religious weapon, of which all parties availed themselves. Even men of the strictest piety practised this species of fraud (*tadlís*), and maintained that the end justified the means. Their point of view is well expressed in the following words which are supposed to have been spoken by the Prophet: "You must compare the sayings attributed

Character of Moslem tradition.

[1] Quoted by Sprenger, *loc. cit.*, p. 1.

[2] Quoted by Nöldeke in the Introduction to his *Geschichte des Qorâns*, p 22.

[3] See especially pp. 28–130.

to me with the Koran; what agrees therewith is from me, whether I actually said it or no;" and again, "Whatever good saying has been said, I myself have said it." [1] As the result of such principles every new doctrine took the form of an Apostolic *Ḥadíth*; every sect and every system defended itself by an appeal to the authority of Muḥammad. We may see how enormous was the number of false Traditions in circulation from the fact that when Bukhárí († 870 A.D.) drew up his collection entitled 'The Genuine' (*al-Ṣaḥíḥ*), he limited it to some 7,000, which he picked out of 600,000.

The credibility of Tradition, so far as it concerns the life of the Prophet, cannot be discussed in this place.[2] The oldest and best biography, that of Ibn Isḥáq, undoubtedly contains a great deal of fabulous matter, but his narrative appears to be honest and fairly authentic on the whole.

Birth of Muḥammad.

If we accept the traditional chronology, Muḥammad, son of 'Abdulláh and Ámina, of the tribe of Quraysh, was born at Mecca on the 12th of Rabí' al-Awwal, in the Year of the Elephant (570–571 A.D.). His descent from Quṣayy is shown by the following table:—

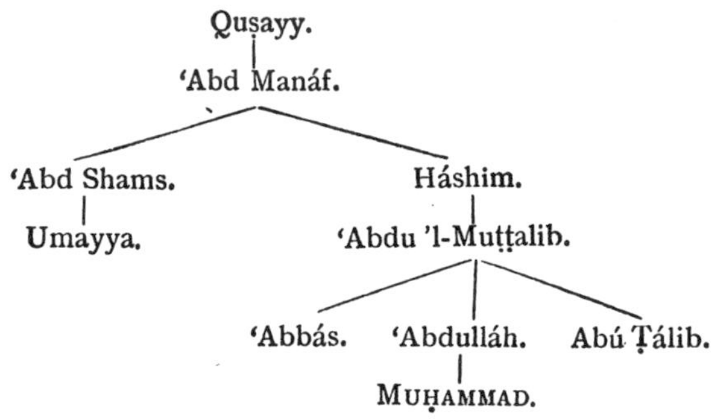

[1] *Muhamm. Studien*, Part II, p. 48 seq.

[2] The reader may consult Muir's Introduction to his *Life of Mahomet*, pp. 28–87.

Shortly after his birth he was handed over to a Bedouin nurse—Ḥalíma, a woman of the Banú Sa'd—so that until he was five years old he breathed the pure air and learned to speak the unadulterated language of the desert. One marvellous event which is said to have happened to him at this time may perhaps be founded on fact:—

His childhood.

"He and his foster-brother" (so Ḥalíma relates) "were among the cattle behind our encampment when my son came running to us and cried, 'My brother, the Qurayshite! two men clad in white took him and laid him on his side and cleft his belly; and they were stirring their hands in it.' When my husband and I went out to him we found him standing with his face turned pale, and on our asking, 'What ails thee, child?' he answered, 'Two men wearing white garments came to me and laid me on my side and cleft my belly and groped for something, I know not what.' We brought him back to our tent, and my husband said to me, 'O Ḥalíma, I fear this lad has been smitten (*uṣíba*); so take him home to his family before it becomes evident.' When we restored him to his mother she said, 'What has brought thee, nurse? Thou wert so fond of him and anxious that he should stay with thee.' I said, 'God has made him grow up, and I have done my part. I feared that some mischance would befall him, so I brought him back to thee as thou wishest.' 'Thy case is not thus,' said she; 'tell me the truth,' and she gave me no peace until I told her. Then she said, 'Art thou afraid that he is possessed by the Devil?' I said, 'Yes.' 'Nay, by God,' she replied, 'the Devil cannot reach him; my son hath a high destiny.'"[1]

Muḥammad and the two angels.

Other versions of the story are more explicit. The angels, it is said, drew forth Muḥammad's heart, cleansed it, and removed the black clot—*i.e.*, the taint of original sin.[2] If these inventions have any basis at all beyond the desire to glorify the future Prophet, we must suppose that they refer

[1] Ibn Hishám, p. 105, l. 9 sqq.

[2] This legend seems to have arisen out of a literal interpretation of Koran, xciv, 1, "*Did we not open thy breast?*"—*i.e.*, give thee comfort or enlightenment.

to some kind of epileptic fit. At a later period he was subject to such attacks, which, according to the unanimous voice of Tradition, often coincided with the revelations sent down from heaven.

'Abdulláh had died before the birth of his son, and when, in his sixth year, Muḥammad lost his mother also, the charge of the orphan was undertaken first by his grandfather, the aged 'Abdu 'l-Muṭṭalib, and then by his uncle, Abú Ṭálib, a poor but honourable man, who nobly fulfilled the duties of a guardian to the last hour of his life. Muḥammad's small patrimony was soon spent, and he was reduced to herding sheep—a despised employment which usually fell to the lot of women or slaves. In his twelfth year he accompanied Abú Ṭálib on a trading expedition to Syria, in the course of which he is said to have encountered a Christian monk called Baḥírá, who discovered the Seal of Prophecy between the boy's shoulders, and hailed him as the promised apostle. Such anticipations deserve no credit whatever. The truth is that until Muḥammad assumed the prophetic rôle he was merely an obscure Qurayshite; and scarcely anything related of him anterior to that event can be deemed historical except his marriage to Khadíja, an elderly widow of considerable fortune, which took place when he was about twenty-five years of age.

His meeting with the monk Baḥírá.

During the next fifteen years of his life Muḥammad was externally a prosperous citizen, only distinguished from those around him by an habitual expression of thoughtful melancholy. What was passing in his mind may be conjectured with some probability from his first utterances when he came forward as a preacher. It is certain, and he himself has acknowledged, that he formerly shared the idolatry of his countrymen. "*Did not He find thee astray and lead thee aright?*" (Kor. xciii, 7). When and how did the process of conversion begin? These questions cannot be answered, but it is natural to suppose that the all-important result, on which

Muḥammad's biographers concentrate their attention, was preceded by a long period of ferment and immaturity. The idea of monotheism was represented in Arabia by the Jews, who were particularly numerous in the Ḥijáz, and by several gnostic sects of an ascetic character—*e.g.*, the Ṣábians[1] and the Rakúsians. Furthermore, "Islamic tradition knows of a number of religious thinkers before Muḥammad who are described as Ḥanífs,"[2] and of whom the best known are Waraqa b. Nawfal of Quraysh; Zayd b. 'Amr b. Nufayl, also of Quraysh; and Umayya b. Abi 'l-Ṣalt of Thaqíf. They formed no sect, as Sprenger imagined; and more recent research has demonstrated the baselessness of the same scholar's theory that there was in Pre-islamic times a widely-spread religious movement which Muḥammad organised, directed, and employed for his own ends. His Arabian precursors, if they may be so called, were merely a few isolated individuals. We are told by Ibn Isḥáq that Waraqa and Zayd, together with two other Qurayshites, rejected idolatry and left their homes in order to seek the true religion of Abraham, but whereas Waraqa is said to have become a Christian, Zayd remained a pious dissenter unattached either to Christianity or to Judaism; he abstained from idol-worship, from eating that which had died of itself, from blood, and from the flesh of animals offered in sacrifice to idols; he condemned the barbarous custom of burying female infants alive, and said,

The Ḥanífs.

[1] This name, which may signify 'Baptists,' was applied by the heathen Arabs to Muḥammad and his followers, probably in consequence of the ceremonial ablutions which are incumbent upon every Moslem before the five daily prayers (see Wellhausen, *Reste Arab. Heid.*, p. 237).

[2] Sir Charles Lyall, *The Words 'Ḥaníf' and 'Muslim,' J.R.A.S.* for 1903, p. 772. The original meaning of *ḥaníf* is no longer traceable, but it may be connected with the Hebrew *ḥánéf*, 'profane.' In the Koran it generally refers to the religion of Abraham, and sometimes appears to be nearly synonymous with *Muslim*. Further information concerning the Ḥanífs will be found in Sir Charles Lyall's article cited above; Sprenger, *Das Leben und die Lehre des Moḥammed*, vol. i, pp. 45–134; Wellhausen, *Reste Arab. Heid.*, p. 238 sqq.; Caetani, *Annali dell' Islam*, vol. i, pp. 181–192.

"I worship the Lord of Abraham."[1] As regards Umayya b. Abi 'l-Ṣalt, according to the notice of him in the *Aghání*, he had inspected and read the Holy Scriptures; he wore sackcloth as a mark of devotion, held wine to be unlawful, was inclined to disbelieve in idols, and earnestly sought the true religion. It is said that he hoped to be sent as a prophet to the Arabs, and therefore when Muḥammad appeared he envied and bitterly opposed him.[2] Umayya's verses, some of which have been translated in a former chapter,[3] are chiefly on religious topics, and show many points of resemblance with the doctrines set forth in the early Súras of the Koran. With one exception, all the Ḥanífs whose names are recorded belonged to the Ḥijáz and the west of the Arabian peninsula. No doubt Muḥammad, with whom most of them were contemporary, came under their influence, and he may have received his first stimulus from this quarter.[4] While they, however, were concerned only about their own salvation, Muḥammad, starting from the same position, advanced far beyond it. His greatness lies not so much in the sublime ideas by which he was animated as in the tremendous force and enthusiasm of his appeal to the universal conscience of mankind.

In his fortieth year, it is said, Muḥammad began to dream dreams and see visions, and desire solitude above all things else.

Muḥammad's vision.

He withdrew to a cave on Mount Ḥirá, near Mecca, and engaged in religious austerities (*taḥannuth*). One night in the month of Ramaḍán[5] the Angel[6] appeared to him and said, "Read!" (*iqra'*). He

[1] Ibn Hishám, p. 143, l. 6 sqq.

[2] *Aghání*, iii, 187, l. 17 sqq.

[3] See p. 69 *supra*.

[4] Tradition associates him especially with Waraqa, who was a cousin of his first wife, Khadíja, and is said to have hailed him as a prophet while Muḥammad himself was still hesitating (Ibn Hishám, p. 153, l. 14 sqq.).

[5] This is the celebrated 'Night of Power' (*Laylatu 'l-Qadr*) mentioned in the Koran, xcvii, 1.

[6] The Holy Ghost (*Rúḥu'l-Quds*), for whom in the Medína Súras Gabriel (Jibríl) is substituted.

answered, "I am no reader" (*má ana bi-qári'in*).[1] Then the Angel seized him with a strong grasp, saying, "Read!" and, as Muḥammad still refused to obey, gripped him once more and spoke as follows:—

THE SÚRA OF COAGULATED BLOOD (XCVI).

(1) Read in the name of thy Lord[2] who created,
(2) Who created Man of blood coagulated.
(3) Read! Thy Lord is the most beneficent,
(4) Who taught by the Pen,[3]
(5) Taught that which they knew not unto men.

On hearing these words Muḥammad returned, trembling, to Khadíja and cried, "Wrap me up! wrap me up!" and remained covered until the terror passed away from him.[4] Another tradition relating to the same event makes it clear

[1] But another version (Ibn Hishám, p. 152, l. 9 sqq.) represents Muḥammad as replying to the Angel, "What am I to read?" (*má aqra'u* or *má dhá aqra'u*). Professor Bevan has pointed out to me that the tradition in this form bears a curious resemblance, which can hardly be accidental, to the words of Isaiah xl. 6: "The voice said, Cry. And he said, What shall I cry?" The question whether the Prophet could read and write is discussed by Nöldeke (*Geschichte des Qorâns*, p. 7 sqq.), who leaves it undecided. According to Nöldeke (*loc. cit.*, p. 10), the epithet *ummí*, which is applied to Muḥammad in the Koran, and is commonly rendered by 'illiterate,' does not signify that he was ignorant of reading and writing, but only that he was unacquainted with the ancient Scriptures; *cf.* 'Gentile.' However this may be, it appears that he wished to pass for illiterate, with the object of confirming the belief in his inspiration: "*Thou*" (Muḥammad) "*didst not use to read any book before this*" (the Koran) "*nor to write it with thy right hand; else the liars would have doubted* (Koran, xxix, 47).

[2] The meaning of these words (*iqra' bismi rabbika*) is disputed. Others translate, "Preach in the name of thy Lord" (Nöldeke), or "Proclaim the name of thy Lord" (Hirschfeld). I see no sufficient grounds for abandoning the traditional interpretation supported by verses 4 and 5. Muḥammad dreamed that he was commanded to read the Word of God inscribed in the Heavenly Book which is the source of all Revelation.

[3] Others render, "who taught (the use of) the Pen."

[4] This account of Muḥammad's earliest vision (Bukhárí, ed. by Krehl, vol. iii, p. 380, l. 2 sqq.) is derived from 'Á'isha, his favourite wife, whom he married after the death of Khadíja.

that the revelation occurred in a dream.[1] "I awoke," said the Prophet, "and methought it was written in my heart." If we take into account the notions prevalent among the Arabs of that time on the subject of inspiration,[2] it will not appear surprising that Muḥammad at first believed himself to be possessed, like a poet or soothsayer, by one of the spirits called collectively *Jinn*. Such was his anguish of mind that he even meditated suicide, but Khadíja comforted and reassured him, and finally he gained the unalterable conviction that he was not a prey to demoniacal influences, but a prophet divinely inspired. For some time he received no further revelation.[3] Then suddenly, as he afterwards related, he saw the Angel seated on a throne between earth and heaven. Awe-stricken, he ran into his house and bade them wrap his limbs in a warm garment (*dithár*). While he lay thus the following verses were revealed :—

THE SÚRA OF THE ENWRAPPED (LXXIV).

(1) O thou who enwrapped dost lie!
(2) Arise and prophesy,[4]
(3) And thy Lord magnify,
(4) And thy raiment purify,
(5) And the abomination fly![5]

Muḥammad no longer doubted that he had a divinely ordained mission to preach in public. His feelings of relief and thankfulness are expressed in several Súras of this period, *e.g.*—

THE SÚRA OF THE MORNING (XCIII).

(1) By the Morning bright
(2) And the softly falling Night,
(3) Thy Lord hath not forsaken thee, neither art thou hateful in His sight.

---

[1] Ibn Hishám, p. 152, l. 9 sqq.
[2] See p. 72 *supra*.
[3] This interval is known as the Fatra.
[4] Literally, 'warn.'
[5] 'The abomination' (*al-rujz*) probably refers to idolatry.

(4) Verily, the Beginning is hard unto thee, but the End shall be light.[1]
(5) Thou shalt be satisfied, the Lord shall thee requite.
(6) Did not He shelter thee when He found thee in orphan's plight?
(7) Did not He find thee astray and lead thee aright?
(8) Did not He find thee poor and make thee rich by His might?
(9) Wherefore, the orphan betray not,
(10) And the beggar turn away not,
(11) And tell of the bounty of thy Lord.

According to his biographers, an interval of three years elapsed between the sending of Muḥammad and his appearance as a public preacher of the faith that was in him. Naturally, he would first turn to his own family and friends, but it is difficult to accept the statement that he made no proselytes openly during so long a period. The contrary is asserted in an ancient tradition related by al-Zuhrí († 742 A.D.), where we read that the Prophet summoned the people to embrace Islam[2] both in private and public; and that those who responded to his appeal were, for the most part, young men belonging to the poorer class.[3] He found, however, some influential adherents. Besides Khadíja, who was the first to believe, there were his cousin ʿAlí, his adopted son, Zayd b. Ḥáritha, and, most important of all, Abú Bakr b. Abí Quḥáfa, a leading merchant of the Quraysh, universally respected and beloved for his integrity, wisdom, and kindly disposition. At the outset Muḥammad seems to have avoided everything calculated to offend the heathens, confining himself to moral and religious generalities,

The first Moslems.

[1] Literally, "The Last State shall be better for thee than the First," referring either to Muḥammad's recompense in the next world or to the ultimate triumph of his cause in this world.

[2] *Islám* is a verbal noun formed from *Aslama*, which means 'to surrender' and, in a religious sense, 'to surrender one's self to the will of God.' The participle, *Muslim* (Moslem), denotes one who thus surrenders himself.

[3] Sprenger, *Leben des Mohammad*, vol. i, p. 356.

so that many believed, and the Meccan aristocrats themselves regarded him with good-humoured toleration as a harmless oracle-monger. "Look!" they said as he passed by, "there goes the man of the Banú 'Abd al-Muṭṭalib who tells of heaven." But no sooner did he begin to emphasise the Unity of God, to fulminate against idolatry, and to preach the Resurrection of the dead, than his followers melted away in face of the bitter antagonism which these doctrines excited amongst the Quraysh, who saw in the Ka'ba and its venerable cult the mainspring of their commercial prosperity, and were irritated by the Prophet's declaration that their ancestors were burning in hell-fire. The authority of Abú Ṭálib secured the personal safety of Muḥammad; of the little band who remained faithful some were protected by the strong family feeling characteristic of old Arabian society, but many were poor and friendless; and these, especially the slaves, whom the levelling ideas of Islam had attracted in large numbers, were subjected to cruel persecution.[1] Nevertheless Muḥammad continued to preach. "I will not forsake this cause" (thus he is said to have answered Abú Ṭálib, who informed him of the threatening attitude of the Quraysh and begged him not to lay on him a greater burden than he could bear) "until God shall make it prevail or until I shall perish therein—not though they should set the sun on my right hand and the moon on my left!"[2] But progress

Hostility of the Quraysh.

[1] It must be remembered that this branch of Muḥammadan tradition derives from the pietists of the first century after the Flight, who were profoundly dissatisfied with the reigning dynasty (the Umayyads), and revenged themselves by painting the behaviour of the Meccan ancestors of the Umayyads towards Muḥammad in the blackest colours possible. The facts tell another story. It is significant that hardly any case of real persecution is mentioned in the Koran. Muḥammad was allowed to remain at Mecca and to carry on, during many years, a religious propaganda which his fellow-citizens, with few exceptions, regarded as detestable and dangerous. We may well wonder at the moderation of the Quraysh, which, however, was not so much deliberate policy as the result of their indifference to religion and of Muḥammad's failure to make appreciable headway in Mecca.

[2] Ibn Hishám, p. 168, l. 9. sqq.

was slow and painful: the Meccans stood obstinately aloof, deriding both his prophetic authority and the Divine chastisement with which he sought to terrify them. Moreover, they used every kind of pressure short of actual violence in order to seduce his followers, so that many recanted, and in the fifth year of his mission he saw himself driven to the necessity of commanding a general emigration to the Christian kingdom of Abyssinia, where the Moslems would be received with open arms [1] and would be withdrawn from temptation.[2] About a hundred men and women went into exile, leaving their Prophet with a small party of staunch and devoted comrades to persevere in a struggle that was daily becoming more difficult. In a moment of weakness Muḥammad resolved to attempt a compromise with his countrymen. One day, it is said, the chief men of Mecca, assembled in a group beside the Ka'ba, discussed as was their wont the affairs of the city, when Muḥammad appeared and, seating himself by them in a friendly manner, began to recite in their hearing the 53rd Súra of the Koran. When he came to the verses (19–20)—

Emigration to Abyssinia.

Temporary reconciliation with the Quraysh.

"Do ye see Al-Lát and Al-'Uzzá, and Manát, the third and last?"

Satan prompted him to add:—

"These are the most exalted Cranes (or Swans),
And verily their intercession is to be hoped for."

The Quraysh were surprised and delighted with this acknowledgment of their deities; and as Muḥammad wound up the Súra with the closing words—

"Wherefore bow down before God and serve Him,"

---

[1] At this time Muḥammad believed the doctrines of Islam and Christianity to be essentially the same.

[2] Ṭabarí, i, 1180, 8 sqq. *Cf.* Caetani, *Annali dell' Islam*, vol. i, p. 267 sqq.

the whole assembly prostrated themselves with one accord on the ground and worshipped.[1] But scarcely had Muḥammad returned to his house when he repented of the sin into which he had fallen. He cancelled the idolatrous verses and revealed in their place those which now stand in the Koran—

> "Shall yours be the male and his the female?[2]
> This were then an unjust division!
> They are naught but names which ye and your fathers
> have named."

Muḥammad's concession to the idolaters.

We can easily comprehend why Ibn Hishám omits all mention of this episode from his Biography, and why the fact itself is denied by many Moslem theologians.[3] The Prophet's friends were scandalised, his enemies laughed him to scorn. It was probably no sudden lapse, as tradition represents, but a calculated endeavour to come to terms with the Quraysh; and so far from being immediately annulled, the reconciliation seems to have lasted long enough for the news of it to reach the emigrants in Abyssinia and induce some of them to return to Mecca. While putting the best face on the matter, Muḥammad felt keenly both his own disgrace and the public discredit. It speaks well for his sincerity that, as soon as he perceived any compromise with idolatry to be impossible—to be, in fact, a surrender of the great principle by which he was inspired—he frankly confessed his error and delusion.

[1] Muir, *Life of Mahomet*, vol. ii, p. 151.

[2] We have seen (p. 91 *supra*) that the heathen Arabs disliked female offspring, yet they called their three principal deities the daughters of Allah.

[3] It is related by Ibn Isḥáq (Ṭabarí, i, 1192, 4 sqq.). In his learned work, *Annali dell' Islam*, of which the first volume appeared in 1905, Prince Caetani impugns the authenticity of the tradition and criticises the narrative in detail (p. 279 sqq.), but his arguments do not touch the main question. As Muir says, "it is hardly possible to conceive how the tale, if not founded in truth, could ever have been invented."

Henceforth he "wages mortal strife with images in every shape"—there is no god but Allah.

The further course of events which culminated in Muḥammad's Flight to Medína may be sketched in a few words. Persecution now waxed hotter than ever, as the Prophet, rising from his temporary vacillation like a giant refreshed, threw his whole force into the denunciation of idolatry. The conversion of 'Umar b. al-Khaṭṭáb, the future Caliph, a man of 'blood and iron,' gave the signal for open revolt. "The Moslems no longer concealed their worship within their own dwellings, but with conscious strength and defiant attitude assembled in companies about the Ka'ba, performed their rites of prayer and compassed the Holy House. Their courage rose. Dread and uneasiness seized the Quraysh." The latter retaliated by cutting off all relations with the Háshimites, who were pledged to defend their kinsman, whether they recognised him as a prophet or no. This ban or boycott secluded them in an outlying quarter of the city, where for more than two years they endured the utmost privations, but it only cemented their loyalty to Muḥammad, and ultimately dissensions among the Quraysh themselves caused it to be removed. Shortly afterwards the Prophet suffered a double bereavement—the death of his wife, Khadíja, was followed by that of the noble Abú Ṭálib, who, though he never accepted Islam, stood firm to the last in defence of his brother's son. Left alone to protect himself, Muḥammad realised that he must take some decisive step. The situation was critical. Events had shown that he had nothing to hope and everything to fear from the Meccan aristocracy. He had warned them again and again of the wrath to come, yet they gave no heed. He was now convinced that they would not and could not believe, since God in His inscrutable wisdom had predestined them to eternal damnation. Consequently he resolved on a bold and, according to Arab ways of thinking, abominable expedient,

Death of Khadíja and Abú Ṭálib.

namely, to abandon his fellow-tribesmen and seek aid from strangers.[1] Having vainly appealed to the inhabitants of Ṭá'if, he turned to Medína, where, among a population largely composed of Jews, the revolutionary ideas of Islam might more readily take root and flourish than in the Holy City of Arabian heathendom. This time he was not disappointed. A strong party in Medína hailed him as the true Prophet, eagerly embraced his creed, and swore to defend him at all hazards. In the spring of the year 622 A.D. the Moslems of Mecca quietly left their homes and journeyed northward. A few months later (September, 622) Muḥammad himself, eluding the vigilance of the Quraysh, entered Medína in triumph amidst the crowds and acclamations due to a conqueror.

The *Hijra* or Migration to Medina (622 A.D.).

This is the celebrated Migration or Hegira (properly *Hijra*) which marks the end of the Barbaric Age (*al-Jáhiliyya*) and the beginning of the Muḥammadan Era. It also marks a new epoch in the Prophet's history; but before attempting to indicate the nature of the change it will be convenient, in order that we may form a juster conception of his character, to give some account of his early teaching and preaching as set forth in that portion of the Koran which was revealed at Mecca.

[1] The Meccan view of Muḥammad's action may be gathered from the words uttered by Abú Jahl on the field of Badr—"O God, bring woe upon him who more than any of us hath severed the ties of kinship and dealt dishonourably!" (Ṭabarí, i, 1322, l. 8 seq.). Alluding to the Moslems who abandoned their native city and fled with the Prophet to Medína, a Meccan poet exclaims (Ibn Hishám, p. 519, ll. 3–5):—

They (the Quraysh slain at Badr) *fell in honour. They did not sell their kinsmen for strangers living in a far land and of remote lineage;*
Unlike you, who have made friends of Ghassán (the people of Medína), *taking them instead of us—O, what a shameful deed!*
Tis an impiety and a manifest crime and a cutting of all ties of blood: your iniquity therein is discerned by men of judgment and understanding.

Koran (Qur'án) is derived from the Arabic root *qara'a*, 'to read,' and means 'reading aloud' or 'chanting.' This term may be applied either to a single Revelation or to several recited together or, in its usual acceptation, to the whole body of Revelations which are thought by Moslems to be, actually and literally, the Word of God; so that in quoting from the Koran they say *qála 'lláhu*, *i.e.*, 'God said.' Each Revelation forms a separate *Súra* (chapter)[1] composed of verses of varying length which have no metre but are generally rhymed. Thus, as regards its external features, the style of the Koran is modelled upon the *Saj'*,[2] or rhymed prose, of the pagan soothsayers, but with such freedom that it may fairly be described as original. Since it was not in Muḥammad's power to create a form that should be absolutely new, his choice lay between *Saj'* and poetry, the only forms of elevated style then known to the Arabs. He himself declared that he was no poet,[3] and this is true in the sense that he may have lacked the technical accomplishment of verse-making. It must, however, be borne in mind that his disavowal does not refer primarily to the poetic art, but rather to the person and character of the poets themselves. He, the divinely inspired Prophet, could have nothing to do with men who owed their inspiration to demons and gloried in the ideals of paganism which he was striving to overthrow. "*And the poets do those follow who go astray! Dost thou not see that they wander distraught in every vale? and that they say that which they do not?*" (Kor. xxvi, 224–226). Muḥammad was not of these; although he was not so unlike them as he pretended. His kinship with the pagan *Shá'ir* is clearly shown, for example, in the 113th and 114th Súras, which are charms against magic and *diablerie*, as well as in the solemn imprecation calling down destruction upon the head of his uncle, 'Abdu 'l-'Uzzá, nicknamed Abú Lahab (Father of Flame).

The Koran.

Was Muḥammad poet?

[1] *Súra* is properly a row of stones or bricks in a wall.

[2] See p. 74 *supra*.

[3] Koran, lxix, 41.

THE SÚRA OF ABÚ LAHAB (CXI).

(1) Perish the hands of Abú Lahab and perish he!
(2) His wealth shall not avail him nor all he hath gotten in fee.
(3) Burned in blazing fire he shall be!
(4) And his wife, the faggot-bearer, also she.
(5) Upon her neck a cord of fibres of the palm-tree.

If, then, we must allow that Muḥammad's contemporaries had some justification for bestowing upon him the title of poet against which he protested so vehemently, still less can his plea be accepted by the modern critic, whose verdict will be that the Koran is not poetical as a whole; that it contains many pages of rhetoric and much undeniable prose; but that, although Muḥammad needed "heaven-sent moments for this skill," in the early Meccan Súras frequently, and fitfully elsewhere, his genius proclaims itself by grand lyrical outbursts which could never have been the work of a mere rhetorician.

The Meccan Súras.

"Muhammad's single aim in the Meccan Súras," says Nöldeke, "is to convert the people, by means of persuasion, from their false gods to the One God. To whatever point the discourse is directed, this always remains the ground-thought; but instead of seeking to convince the reason of his hearers by logical proofs, he employs the arts of rhetoric to work upon their minds through the imagination. Thus he glorifies God, describes His working in Nature and History, and ridicules on the other hand the impotence of the idols. Especially important are the descriptions of the everlasting bliss of the pious and the torments of the wicked: these, particularly the latter, must be regarded as one of the mightiest factors in the propagation of Islam, through the impression which they make on the imagination of simple men who have not been hardened, from their youth up, by similar theological ideas. The Prophet often attacks his heathen adversaries personally and threatens them with eternal punishment; but while he is living among heathens alone, he seldom assails the Jews who stand much nearer to him, and the Christians scarcely ever." [1]

[1] Nöldeke, *Geschichte des Qorâns*, p. 56.

The preposterous arrangement of the Koran, to which I have already adverted, is mainly responsible for the opinion almost unanimously held by European readers that it is obscure, tiresome, uninteresting; a farrago of long-winded narratives and prosaic exhortations, quite unworthy to be named in the same breath with the Prophetical Books of the Old Testament. One may, indeed, peruse the greater part of the volume, beginning with the first chapter, and find but a few passages of genuine enthusiasm to relieve the prevailing dulness. It is in the short Súras placed at the end of the Koran that we must look for evidence of Muḥammad's prophetic gift. These are the earliest of all; in these the flame of inspiration burns purely and its natural force is not abated. The following versions, like those which have preceded, imitate the original form as closely, I think, as is possible in English. They cannot, of course, do more than faintly suggest the striking effect of the sonorous Arabic when read aloud. The Koran was designed for oral recitation, and it must be *heard* in order to be justly appraised.

THE SÚRA OF THE SEVERING (LXXXII).

(1) When the Sky shall be severèd,
(2) And when the Stars shall be shiverèd,
(3) And when the Seas to mingle shall be sufferèd,
(4) And when the Graves shall be uncoverèd—
(5) A soul shall know that which it hath deferred or deliverèd.[1]
(6) O Man, what beguiled thee against thy gracious Master to rebel,
(7) Who created thee and fashioned thee right and thy frame did fairly build?
(8) He composed thee in whatever form He willed.
(9) Nay, but ye disbelieve in the Ordeal![2]
(10) Verily over you are Recorders honourable,
(11) Your deeds inscribing without fail:[3]

---

[1] *I.e.*, what it has done or left undone.
[2] The Last Judgment.
[3] Moslems believe that every man is attended by two Recording Angels who write down his good and evil actions.

(12) What ye do they know well.
(13) Surely the pious in delight shall dwell,
(14) And surely the wicked shall be in Hell,
(15) Burning there on the Day of Ordeal;
(16) And evermore Hell-fire they shall feel!
(17) What shall make thee to understand what is the Day of Ordeal?
(18) Again, what shall make thee to understand what is the Day of Ordeal?—
(19) A Day when one soul shall not obtain anything for another soul, but the command on that Day shall be with God alone.

THE SÚRA OF THE SIGNS (LXXXV).

(1) By the Heaven in which Signs are set,
(2) By the Day that is promisèd,
(3) By the Witness and the Witnessèd:—
(4) Cursèd be the Fellows of the Pit, they that spread
(5) The fire with fuel fed,
(6) When they sate by its head
(7) And saw how their contrivance against the Believers sped;[1]
(8) And they punished them not save that they believed on God, the Almighty, the Glorified,
(9) To whom is the Kingdom of Heaven and Earth, and He seeth every thing beside.
(10) Verily, for those who afflict believing men and women and repent not, the torment of Gehenna and the torment of burning is prepared.
(11) Verily, for those who believe and work righteousness are Gardens beneath which rivers flow: this is the great Reward.
(12) Stern is the vengeance of thy Lord.
(13) He createth the living and reviveth the dead:
(14) He doth pardon and kindly entreat:
(15) The majestic Throne is His seat:
(16) That he willeth He doeth indeed.
(17) Hath not word come to thee of the multitude
(18) Of Pharaoh, and of Thamúd?[2]

---

[1] This is generally supposed to refer to the persecution of the Christians of Najrán by Dhú Nuwás (see p. 26 *supra*). Geiger takes it as an allusion to the three men who were cast into the fiery furnace (Daniel, ch. iii).

[2] See above, p. 3.

(19) Nay, the infidels cease not from falsehood,
(20) But God encompasseth them about.
(21) Surely, it is a Sublime Koran that ye read,
(22) On a Table inviolate.[1]

THE SÚRA OF THE SMITING (CI).

(1) The Smiting! What is the Smiting?
(2) And how shalt thou be made to understand what is the Smiting?
(3) The Day when Men shall be as flies scatterèd,
(4) And the Mountains shall be as shreds of wool tatterèd.
(5) One whose Scales are heavy, a pleasing life he shall spend,
(6) But one whose Scales are light, to the Abyss he shall descend.
(7) What that is, how shalt thou be made to comprehend?
(8) Scorching Fire without end!

THE SÚRA OF THE UNBELIEVERS (CIX).

(1) Say: 'O Unbelievers,
(2) I worship not that which ye worship,
(3) And ye worship not that which I worship.
(4) Neither will I worship that which ye worship,
(5) Nor will ye worship that which I worship.
(6) Ye have your religion and I have my religion.'

To summarise the cardinal doctrines preached by Muḥammad during the Meccan period:—

The teaching of Muḥammad at Mecca.

1. There is no god but God.

2. Muḥammad is the Apostle of God, and the Koran is the Word of God revealed to His Apostle.

3. The dead shall be raised to life at the Last Judgment, when every one shall be judged by his actions in the present life.

4. The pious shall enter Paradise and the wicked shall go down to Hell.

Taking these doctrines separately, let us consider a little more in detail how each of them is stated and by what arguments it is enforced. The time had not yet come for drawing

[1] According to Muḥammadan belief, the archetype of the Koran and of all other Revelations is written on the Guarded Table (*al-Lawḥ al-Maḥfúẓ*) in heaven.

the sword: Muḥammad repeats again and again that he is only a warner (*nadhîr*) invested with no authority to compel where he cannot persuade.

The Unity of God.

1. The Meccans acknowledged the supreme position of Allah, but in ordinary circumstances neglected him in favour of their idols, so that, as Muḥammad complains, "*When danger befalls you on the sea, the gods whom ye invoke are forgotten except Him alone; yet when He brought you safe to land, ye turned your backs on Him, for Man is ungrateful.*"[1] They were strongly attached to the cult of the Ka'ba, not only by self-interest, but also by the more respectable motives of piety towards their ancestors and pride in their traditions. Muḥammad himself regarded Allah as Lord of the Ka'ba, and called upon the Quraysh to worship him as such (Kor. cvi, 3). When they refused to do so on the ground that they were afraid lest the Arabs should rise against them and drive them forth from the land, he assured them that Allah was the author of all their prosperity (Kor. xxviii, 57). His main argument, however, is drawn from the weakness of the idols, which cannot create even a fly, contrasted with the wondrous manifestations of Divine power and providence in the creation of the heavens and the earth and all living things.[2]

It was probably towards the close of the Meccan period that Muḥammad summarised his Unitarian ideas in the following emphatic formula:—

THE SÚRA OF PURIFICATION (CXII).[3]

(1) Say: 'God is One;
(2) God who liveth on;
(3) Without father and without son;
(4) And like to Him there is none!'

---

[1] Koran, xvii, 69.

[2] See, for example, the passages translated by Lane in his *Selections from the Kur-án* (London, 1843), pp. 100–113.

[3] *Ikhlás* means 'purifying one's self of belief in any god except Allah.'

Muḥammad, the Apostle of God.

2. We have seen that when Muḥammed first appeared as a prophet he was thought by all except a very few to be *majnūn*, *i.e.*, possessed by a *jinnī*, or genie, if I may use a word which will send the reader back to his *Arabian Nights*. The heathen Arabs regarded such persons—soothsayers, diviners, and poets—with a certain respect; and if Muḥammad's 'madness' had taken a normal course, his claim to inspiration would have passed unchallenged. What moved the Quraysh to oppose him was not disbelief in his inspiration—it mattered little to them whether he was under the spell of Allah or one of the *Jinn*—but the fact that he preached doctrines which wounded their sentiments, threatened their institutions, and subverted the most cherished traditions of old Arabian life. But in order successfully to resist the propaganda for which he alleged a Divine warrant, they were obliged to meet him on his own ground and to maintain that he was no prophet at all, no Apostle of Allah, as he asserted, but "an insolent liar," "a schooled madman," "an infatuated poet," and so forth; and that his Koran, which he gave out to be the Word of Allah, was merely "old folks' tales" (*asāṭīru 'l-awwalīn*), or the invention of a poet or a sorcerer. "Is not he," they cried, "a man like ourselves, who wishes to domineer over us? Let him show us a miracle, that we may believe." Muḥammad could only reiterate his former assertions and warn the infidels that a terrible punishment was in store for them either in this world or the next. Time after time he compares himself to the ancient prophets—Noah, Abraham, Moses, and their successors—who are represented as employing exactly the same arguments and receiving the same answers as Muḥammad; and bids his people hearken to him lest they utterly perish like the ungodly before them. The truth of the Koran is proved, he says, by the Pentateuch and the Gospel, all being Revelations of the One God, and therefore identical in substance. He is no mercenary soothsayer, he seeks no

personal advantage: his mission is solely to preach. The demand for a miracle he could not satisfy except by pointing to his visions of the Angel and especially to the Koran itself, every verse of which was a distinct sign or miracle (*áyat*).[1] If he has forged it, why are his adversaries unable to produce anything similar? "*Say: 'If men and genies united to bring the like of this Koran, they could not bring the like although they should back each other up*'" (Kor. xvii, 90).

Resurrection and Retribution.

3. Such notions of a future life as were current in Pre-islamic Arabia never rose beyond vague and barbarous superstition, *e.g.*, the fancy that the dead man's tomb was haunted by his spirit in the shape of a screeching owl.[2] No wonder, then, that the ideas of Resurrection and Retribution, which are enforced by threats and arguments on almost every page of the Koran, appeared to the Meccan idolaters absurdly ridiculous and incredible. "*Does Ibn Kabsha promise us that we shall live?*" said one of their poets. "*How can there be life for the ṣadá and the háma? Dost thou omit to ward me from death, and wilt thou revive me when my bones are rotten?*"[3] God provided His Apostle with a ready answer to these gibes: "*Say: 'He shall revive them who produced them at first, for He knoweth every*

[1] The Prophet's confession of his inability to perform miracles did not deter his followers from inventing them after his death. Thus it was said that he caused the infidels to see "the moon cloven asunder" (Koran, liv, 1), though, as is plain from the context, these words refer to one of the signs of the Day of Judgment.

[2] I take this opportunity of calling the reader's attention to a most interesting article by my friend and colleague, Professor A. A. Bevan, entitled *The Beliefs of Early Mohammedans respecting a Future Existence* (*Journal of Theological Studies*, October, 1904, p. 20 sqq.), where the whole subject is fully discussed.

[3] Shaddád b. al-Aswad al-Laythí, quoted in the *Risálatu 'l-Ghufrán* of Abu 'l-'Alá al-Ma'arrí (see my article in the *J.R.A.S.* for 1902, pp. 94 and 818); *cf.* Ibn Hishám, p. 530, last line. Ibn (Abí) Kabsha was a nickname derisively applied to Muḥammad. *Ṣadá* and *háma* refer to the death-bird which was popularly supposed to utter its shriek from the skull (*háma*) of the dead, and both words may be rendered by 'soul' or 'wraith.'

creation" (Kor. xxxvi, 79). This topic is eloquently illustrated, but Muḥammad's hearers were probably less impressed by the creative power of God as exhibited in Nature and in Man than by the awful examples, to which reference has been made, of His destructive power as manifested in History. To Muḥammad himself, at the outset of his mission, it seemed an appalling certainty that he must one day stand before God and render an account; the overmastering sense of his own responsibility goaded him to preach in the hope of saving his countrymen, and supplied him, weak and timorous as he was, with strength to endure calumny and persecution. As Nöldeke has remarked, the grandest Súras of the whole Koran are those in which Muḥammad describes how all Nature trembles and quakes at the approach of the Last Judgment. "It is as though one actually saw the earth heaving, the mountains crumbling to dust, and the stars hurled hither and thither in wild confusion."[1] Súras lxxxii and ci, which have been translated above, are specimens of the true prophetic style.[2]

The Muḥammadan Paradise.

4. There is nothing spiritual in Muḥammad's pictures of Heaven and Hell. His Paradise is simply a glorified pleasure-garden, where the pious repose in cool shades, quaffing spicy wine and diverting themselves with the Houris (*Ḥúr*), lovely dark-eyed damsels like pearls hidden in their shells.[3] This was admirably calculated to allure his hearers by reminding them of one of their chief enjoyments—the gay drinking parties which occasionally broke the monotony of Arabian life, and which are often described in Pre-islamic poetry; indeed, it is highly probable that Muḥammad drew a good deal of his Paradise from this source. The gross and sensual character of the Muḥammadan Afterworld is commonly thought to betray a particular weak-

[1] Nöldeke, *Geschichte des Qorâns*, p. 78.

[2] *Cf.* also Koran, xviii, 45–47; xx, 102 sqq.; xxxix, 67 sqq.; lxix, 13–37.

[3] The famous freethinker, Abu 'l-'Alá al-Ma'arrí, has cleverly satirised Muḥammadan notions on this subject in his *Risálatu 'l-Ghufrán* (*J.R.A.S.* for October, 1900, p. 637 sqq.).

ness of the Prophet or is charged to the Arabs in general, but as Professor Bevan has pointed out, "the real explanation seems to be that at first the idea of a future retribution was absolutely new both to Muḥammad himself and to the public which he addressed. Paradise and Hell had no traditional associations, and the Arabic language furnished no religious terminology for the expression of such ideas; if they were to be made comprehensible at all, it could only be done by means of precise descriptions, of imagery borrowed from earthly affairs." [1]

Muḥammad was no mere visionary. Ritual observances, vigils, and other austerities entered largely into his religion, endowing it with the formal and ascetic character which it retains to the present day. Prayer was introduced soon after the first Revelations: in one of the oldest (Súra lxxxvii, 14–15) we read, "*Prosperous is he who purifies himself* (or *gives alms*) *and repeats the name of his Lord and prays.*" Although the five daily prayers obligatory upon every true believer are nowhere mentioned in the Koran, the opening chapter (*Súratu 'l-Fátiḥa*), which answers to our Lord's Prayer, is constantly recited on these occasions, and is seldom omitted from any act of public or private devotion. Since the *Fátiḥa* probably belongs to the latest Meccan period, it may find a place here.

Prayer.

THE OPENING SÚRA (I).

(1) In the name of God, the Merciful, who forgiveth aye!
(2) Praise to God, the Lord of all that be,
(3) The Merciful, who forgiveth aye,
(4) The King of Judgment Day!
(5) Thee we worship and for Thine aid we pray.
(6) Lead us in the right way,
(7) The way of those to whom thou hast been gracious, against whom thou hast not waxed wroth, and who go not astray!

[1] *Journal of Theological Studies* for October, 1904, p. 22.

About the same time, shortly before the Migration, Muḥammad dreamed that he was transported from the Ka'ba to the Temple at Jerusalem, and thence up to the seventh heaven. The former part of the vision is indicated in the Koran (xvii, 1): "*Glory to him who took His servant a journey by night from the Sacred Mosque to the Farthest Mosque, the precinct whereof we have blessed, to show him of our signs!*" Tradition has wondrously embellished the *Mi'ráj*, by which name the Ascension of the Prophet is generally known throughout the East; while in Persia and Turkey it has long been a favourite theme for the mystic and the poet. According to the popular belief, which is also held by the majority of Moslem divines, Muḥammad was transported in the body to his journey's end, but he himself never countenanced this literal interpretation, though it seems to have been current in Mecca, and we are told that it caused some of his incredulous followers to abandon their faith.

The Night journey and Ascension of Muḥammad.

Possessed and inspired by the highest idea of which man is capable, fearlessly preaching the truth revealed to him, leading almost alone what long seemed to be a forlorn hope against the impregnable stronghold of superstition, yet facing these tremendous odds with a calm resolution which yielded nothing to ridicule or danger, but defied his enemies to do their worst—Muḥammad in the early part of his career presents a spectacle of grandeur which cannot fail to win our sympathy and admiration. At Medína, whither we must now return, he appears in a less favourable light: the days of pure religious enthusiasm have passed away for ever, and the Prophet is overshadowed by the Statesman. The Migration was undoubtedly essential to the establishment of Islam. It was necessary that Muḥammad should cut himself off from his own people in order that he might found a community in which not blood but religion formed the sole bond that was recognised. This task he

Muḥammad at Medína.

accomplished with consummate sagacity and skill, though some of the methods which he employed can only be excused by his conviction that whatever he did was done in the name of Allah. As the supreme head of the Moslem theocracy both in spiritual and temporal matters—for Islam allows no distinction between Church and State—he exercised absolute authority, and he did not hesitate to justify by Divine mandate acts of which the heathen Arabs, cruel and treacherous as they were, might have been ashamed to be guilty. We need not inquire how much was due to belief in his inspiration and how much to deliberate policy. If it revolts us to see God Almighty introduced in the rôle of special pleader, we ought to remember that Muḥammad, being what he was, could scarcely have considered the question from that point of view.

Medína predisposed to welcome Muḥammad as Legislator and Prophet.

The conditions prevailing at Medína were singularly adapted to his design. Ever since the famous battle of Bu'áth (about 615 A.D.), in which the Banú Aws, with the help of their Jewish allies, the Banú Qurayẓa and the Banú Naḍír, inflicted a crushing defeat upon the Banú Khazraj, the city had been divided into two hostile camps; and if peace had hitherto been preserved, it was only because both factions were too exhausted to renew the struggle. Wearied and distracted by earthly calamities, men's minds willingly admit the consolations of religion. We find examples of this tendency at Medína even before the Migration. Abú 'Ámir, whose ascetic life gained for him the title of 'The Monk' (*al-Ráhib*), is numbered among the *Ḥanífs*.[1] He fought in the ranks of the Quraysh at Uḥud, and finally went to Syria, where he died an outlaw. Another Pre-islamic monotheist of Medína, Abú Qays b. Abí Anas, is said to have turned Moslem in his old age.[2]

"The inhabitants of Medína had no material interest in idol-worship and no sanctuary to guard. Through uninterrupted contact with the Jews of the city and neighbourhood, as also with the Christian tribes settled in the extreme north of Arabia on

[1] Ibn Hishám, p. 411, l. 6 sqq. [2] *Ibid.*, p. 347.

the confines of the Byzantine Empire, they had learned, as it were instinctively, to despise their inherited belief in idols and to respect the far nobler and purer faith in a single God; and lastly, they had become accustomed to the idea of a Divine revelation by means of a special scripture of supernatural origin, like the Pentateuch and the Gospel. From a religious standpoint paganism in Medína offered no resistance to Islam: as a faith, it was dead before it was attacked; none defended it, none mourned its disappearance. The pagan opposition to Muḥammad's work as a reformer was entirely political, and proceeded from those who wished to preserve the anarchy of the old heathen life, and who disliked the dictatorial rule of Muhammad."[1]

Parties in Medína.

There were in Medína four principal parties, consisting of those who either warmly supported or actively opposed the Prophet, or who adopted a relatively neutral attitude, viz., the Emigrants (*Muhájirún*), the Helpers (*Anṣár*), the Hypocrites (*Munáfiqún*), and the Jews (*Yahúd*).

The Emigrants.

The Emigrants were those Moslems who left their homes at Mecca and accompanied the Prophet in his Migration (*Hijra*)—whence their name, *Muhájirún*—to Medína in the year 622. Inasmuch as they had lost everything except the hope of victory and vengeance, he could count upon their fanatical devotion to himself.

The Helpers.

The Helpers were those inhabitants of Medína who had accepted Islam and pledged themselves to protect Muḥammad in case of attack. Together with the Emigrants they constituted a formidable and ever-increasing body of true believers, the first champions of the Church militant.

The Hypocrites.

"Many citizens of Medína, however, were not so well disposed towards Muḥammad, and neither acknowledged him as a Prophet nor would submit to him as their Ruler; but since they durst not come forward against him openly on account of the multitude of his enthusiastic adherents, they met him with a passive resistance which more than once thwarted his plans:

[1] L. Caetani, *Annali dell' Islam*, vol. i, p. 389.

their influence was so great that he, on his part, did not venture to take decisive measures against them, and sometimes even found it necessary to give way." [1]

These are the Hypocrites whom Muḥammad describes in the following verses of the Koran :—

THE SÚRA OF THE HEIFER (II).

(7) And there are those among men who say, 'We believe in God and in the Last Day'; but they do not believe.
(8) They would deceive God and those who do believe; but they deceive only themselves and they do not perceive.
(9) In their hearts is a sickness, and God has made them still more sick, and for them is grievous woe because they lied.[2]

Their leader, 'Abdulláh b. Ubayy, an able man but of weak character, was no match for Muḥammad, whom he and his partisans only irritated, without ever becoming really dangerous.

The Jews, on the other hand, gave the Prophet serious trouble. At first he cherished high hopes that they would accept the new Revelation which he brought to them, and which he maintained to be the original Word of God as it was formerly revealed to Abraham and Moses; but when the Jews, perceiving the absurdity of this idea, plied him with all sorts of questions and made merry over his ignorance, Muḥammad, keenly alive to the damaging effect of the criticism to which he had exposed himself, turned upon his tormentors, and roundly accused them of having falsified and corrupted their Holy Books. Henceforth he pursued them with a deadly hatred against which their political disunion rendered them helpless. A few sought refuge in Islam; the rest were either slaughtered or driven into exile.

The Jews.

It is impossible to detail here the successive steps by which

[1] Nöldeke, *Geschichte des Qorâns*, p. 122.
[2] Translated by E. H. Palmer.

Muḥammad in the course of a few years overcame all opposition and established the supremacy of Islam from one end of Arabia to the other. I shall notice the outstanding events very briefly in order to make room for matters which are more nearly connected with the subject of this History.

Beginnings of the Moslem State.

Muḥammad's first care was to reconcile the desperate factions within the city and to introduce law and order among the heterogeneous elements which have been described. "He drew up in writing a charter between the Emigrants and the Helpers, in which charter he embodied a covenant with the Jews, confirming them in the exercise of their religion and in the possession of their properties, imposing upon them certain obligations, and granting to them certain rights."[1] This remarkable document is extant in Ibn Hishám's *Biography of Muḥammad*, pp. 341–344. Its contents have been analysed in masterly fashion by Wellhausen,[2] who observes with justice that it was no solemn covenant, accepted and duly ratified by representatives of the parties concerned, but merely a decree of Muḥammad based upon conditions already existing which had developed since his arrival in Medína. At the same time no one can study it without being impressed by the political genius of its author. Ostensibly a cautious and tactful reform, it was in reality a revolution. Muḥammad durst not strike openly at the independence of the tribes, but he destroyed it, in effect, by shifting the centre of power from the tribe to the community; and although the community included Jews and pagans as well as Moslems, he fully recognised, what his opponents failed to foresee, that the Moslems were the active, and must soon be the predominant, partners in the newly founded State.

[1] Ibn Hishám, p. 341, l. 5.

[2] *Muḥammad's Gemeindeordnung von Medina* in *Skizzen und Vorarbeiten*, Heft IV, p. 67 sqq.

All was now ripe for the inevitable struggle with the Quraysh, and God revealed to His Apostle several verses of the Koran in which the Faithful are commanded to wage a Holy War against them : "*Permission is given to those who fight because they have been wronged,—and verily God to help them has the might,—who have been driven forth from their homes undeservedly, only for that they said, 'Our Lord is God'*" (xxii, 40–41). "*Kill them wherever ye find them, and drive them out from whence they drive you out*" (ii, 187). "*Fight them that there be no sedition and that the religion may be God's*" (ii, 189). In January, 624 A.D., the Moslems, some three hundred strong, won a glorious victory at Badr over a greatly superior force which had marched out from Mecca to relieve a rich caravan that Muḥammad threatened to cut off. The Quraysh fought bravely, but were borne down by the irresistible onset of men who had learned discipline in the mosque and looked upon death as a sure passport to Paradise. Of the Moslems only fourteen fell; the Quraysh lost forty-nine killed and about the same number of prisoners. But the importance of Muḥammad's success cannot be measured by the material damage which he inflicted. Considering the momentous issues involved, we must allow that Badr, like Marathon, is one of the greatest and most memorable battles in all history. Here, at last, was the miracle which the Prophet's enemies demanded of him : "*Ye have had a sign in the two parties who met; one party fighting in the way of God, the other misbelieving; these saw twice the same number as themselves to the eye-sight, for God aids with His help those whom He pleases. Verily in that is a lesson for those who have perception*" (Kor. iii, 11). And again, "*Ye slew them not, but God slew them*" (Kor. viii, 17). The victory of Badr turned all eyes upon Muḥammad. However little the Arabs cared for his religion, they could not but respect the man who had humbled the lords of Mecca. He was now a power in the land—

Battle of Badr, January, 624 A.D.

"Muḥammad, King of the Ḥijáz."[1] In Medína his cause flourished mightily. The zealots were confirmed in their faith, the waverers convinced, the disaffected overawed. He sustained a serious, though temporary, check in the following year at Uḥud, where a Moslem army was routed by the Quraysh under Abú Sufyán, but the victors were satisfied with having taken vengeance for Badr and made no attempt to follow up their advantage; while Muḥammad, never resting on his laurels, never losing sight of the goal, proceeded with remorseless calculation to crush his adversaries one after the other, until in January, 630 A.D., the Meccans themselves, seeing the futility of further resistance, opened their gates to the Prophet and acknowledged the omnipotence of Allah. The submission of the Holy City left Muḥammad without a rival in Arabia. His work was almost done. Deputations from the Bedouin tribes poured into Medína, offering allegiance to the conqueror of the Quraysh, and reluctantly subscribing to a religion in which they saw nothing so agreeable as the prospect of plundering its enemies.

Battle of Uḥud, 625 A.D.

Submission of Mecca, 630 A.D.

Muḥammad died, after a brief illness, on the 8th of June, 632 A.D. He was succeeded as head of the Moslem community by his old friend and ever-loyal supporter, Abú Bakr, who thus became the first *Khalífa*, or Caliph. It only remains to take up our survey of the Koran, which we have carried down to the close of the Meccan period, and to indicate the character and contents of the Revelation during the subsequent decade.

Death of Muḥammad, 632 A.D.

The Medína Súras faithfully reflect the marvellous change in Muḥammad's fortunes, which began with his flight from Mecca. He was now recognised as the Prophet and Apostle of God, but this recognition made him an earthly potentate and turned his religious activity into secular channels. One

[1] Ibn Hishám, p. 763, l. 12.

who united in himself the parts of prince, legislator, politician, diplomatist, and general may be excused if he sometimes neglected the Divine injunction to arise and preach, or at any rate interpreted it in a sense very different from that which he formerly attached to it.

The Medína Súras.

The Revelations of this time deal, to a large extent, with matters of legal, social, and political interest; they promulgate religious ordinances—*e.g.*, fasting, alms-giving, and pilgrimage—expound the laws of marriage and divorce, and comment upon the news of the day; often they serve as bulletins or manifestoes in which Muḥammad justifies what he has done, urges the Moslems to fight and rebukes the laggards, moralises on a victory or defeat, proclaims a truce, and says, in short, whatever the occasion seems to require. Instead of the Meccan idolaters, his opponents in Medína—the Jews and Hypocrites—have become the great rocks of offence; the Jews especially are denounced in long passages as a stiff-necked generation who never hearkened to their own prophets of old. However valuable historically, the Medína Súras do not attract the literary reader. In their flat and tedious style they resemble those of the later Meccan period. Now and again the ashes burst into flame, though such moments of splendour are increasingly rare, as in the famous 'Throne-verse' (*Áyatu 'l-Kursí*) :—

The 'Throne-verse.'

"God, there is no god but He, the living, the self-subsistent. Slumber takes Him not, nor sleep. His is what is in the heavens and what is in the earth. Who is it that intercedes with Him save by His permission? He knows what is before them and what behind them, and they comprehend not aught of His knowledge but of what He pleases. His throne extends over the heavens and the earth, and it tires Him not to guard them both, for He is high and grand."[1]

The Islam which Muḥammad brought with him to Medína was almost entirely derived by oral tradition from Christianity

[1] Koran, ii, 256, translated by E. H. Palmer.

and Judaism, and just for this reason it made little impression on the heathen Arabs, whose religious ideas were generally of the most primitive kind. Notwithstanding its foreign character and the absence of anything which appealed to Arabian national sentiment, it spread rapidly in Medína, where, as we have seen, the soil was already prepared for it; but one may well doubt whether it could have extended its sway over the peninsula unless the course of events had determined Muḥammad to associate the strange doctrines of Islam with the ancient heathen sanctuary at Mecca, the Ka'ba, which was held in universal veneration by the Arabs and formed the centre of a worship that raised no difficulties in their minds. Before he had lived many months in Medína the Prophet realised that his hope of converting the Jews was doomed to disappointment. Accordingly he instructed his followers that they should no longer turn their faces in prayer towards the Temple at Jerusalem, as they had been accustomed to do since the Flight, but towards the Ka'ba; while, a year or two later, he incorporated in Islam the superstitious ceremonies of the pilgrimage, which were represented as having been originally prescribed to Abraham, the legendary founder of the Ka'ba, whose religion he professed to restore.

The nationalisation of Islam.

These concessions, however, were far from sufficient to reconcile the free-living and free-thinking people of the desert to a religion which restrained their pleasures, forced them to pay taxes and perform prayers, and stamped with the name of barbarism all the virtues they held most dear. The teaching of Islam ran directly counter to the ideals and traditions of heathendom, and, as Goldziher has remarked, its originality lies not in its doctrines, which are Jewish and Christian, but in the fact that it was Muḥammad who first maintained these doctrines with persistent energy against the Arabian view of life.[1] While we must refer the reader to Dr.

[1] *Muhamm. Studien*, Part I, p. 12.

Goldziher's illuminating pages for a full discussion of the conflict between the new Religion (*Dîn*) and the old Virtue (*Muruwwa*), it will not be amiss to summarise the chief points at which they clashed with each other.[1] In the first place, the fundamental idea of Islam was foreign and unintelligible to the Bedouins. "It was not the destruction of their idols that they opposed so much as the spirit of devotion which it was sought to implant in them: the determination of their whole lives by the thought of God and of His pre-ordaining and retributive omnipotence, the prayers and fasts, the renouncement of coveted pleasures, and the sacrifice of money and property which was demanded of them in God's name." In spite of the saying, *Lá dína illá bi 'l-muruwwati* ("There is no religion without virtue"), the Bedouin who accepted Islam had to unlearn the greater part of his unwritten moral code. As a pious Moslem he must return good for evil, forgive his enemy, and find balm for his wounded feelings in the assurance of being admitted to Paradise (Kor. iii, 128). Again, the social organisation of the heathen Arabs was based on the tribe, whereas that of Islam rested on the equality and fraternity of all believers. The religious bond cancelled all distinctions of rank and pedigree; it did away, theoretically, with clannish feuds, contests for honour, pride of race—things that lay at the very root of Arabian chivalry. "*Lo*," cried Muḥammad, "*the noblest of you in the sight of God is he who most doth fear Him*" (Kor. xlix, 13). Against such doctrine the conservative and material instincts of the desert people rose in revolt; and although they became Moslems *en masse*, the majority of them neither believed in Islam nor knew what it meant. Often their motives were frankly utilitarian: they expected that Islam would bring them luck; and so long as they were sound in body, and their mares had fine foals, and

Antagonism of Islamic and Arabian ideals.

[1] See Goldziher's introductory chapter entitled *Muruwwa und Dîn* (*ibid.*, pp. 1–39).

their wives bore well-formed sons, and their wealth and herds multiplied, they said, "We have been blessed ever since we adopted this religion," and were content; but if things went ill they blamed Islam and turned their backs on it.[1] That these men were capable of religious zeal is amply proved by the triumphs which they won a short time afterwards over the disciplined armies of two mighty empires; but what chiefly inspired them, apart from love of booty, was the conviction, born of success, that Allah was fighting on their side.

We have sketched, however barely and imperfectly, the progress of Islam from Muḥammad's first appearance as a preacher to the day of his death. In these twenty years the seeds were sown of almost every development which occurs in the political and intellectual history of the Arabs during the ages to come. More than any man that has ever lived, Muḥammad shaped the destinies of his people; and though they left him far behind as they moved along the path of civilisation, they still looked back to him for guidance and authority at each step. This is not the place to attempt an estimate of his character, which has been so diversely judged. Personally, I feel convinced that he was neither a shameless impostor nor a neurotic degenerate nor a socialistic reformer, but in the beginning, at all events, a sincere religious enthusiast, as truly inspired as any prophet of the Old Testament.

Character of Muḥammad.

"We find in him," writes De Goeje, "that sober understanding which distinguished his fellow-tribesmen: dignity, tact, and equilibrium; qualities which are seldom found in people of morbid constitution: self-control in no small degree. Circumstances changed him from a Prophet to a Legislator and a Ruler, but for himself he sought nothing beyond the acknowledgment that he was Allah's Apostle, since this acknow-

[1] Bayḍáwí on Koran, xxii, 11.

ledgment includes the whole of Islam. He was excitable, like every true Arab, and in the spiritual struggle which preceded his call this quality was stimulated to an extent that alarmed even himself; but that does not make him a visionary. He defends himself, by the most solemn asseveration, against the charge that what he had seen was an illusion of the senses. Why should not we believe him?"[1]

---

[1] *Die Berufung Mohammed's*, by M. J. de Goeje in *Nöldeke-Festschrift* (Giessen, 1906), vol. i, p. 5.

CHAPTER V

THE ORTHODOX CALIPHATE AND THE UMAYYAD DYNASTY

THE Caliphate—*i.e.*, the period of the Caliphs or Successors of Muḥammad—extends over six centuries and a quarter (632–1258 A.D.), and falls into three clearly-marked divisions of very unequal length and diverse character.

The first division begins with the election of Abú Bakr, the first Caliph, in 632, and comes to an end with the assassination of 'Alí, the Prophet's son-in-law and fourth successor, in 661. These four Caliphs are known as the Orthodox (*al-Ráshidún*), because they trod faithfully in the footsteps of the Prophet and ruled after his example in the holy city of Medína, with the assistance of his leading Companions, who constituted an informal Senate.

The Orthodox Caliphate (632–661 A.D).

The second division includes the Caliphs of the family of Umayya, from the accession of Mu'áwiya in 661 to the great battle of the Záb in 750, when Marwán II, the last of his line, was defeated by the 'Abbásids, who claimed the Caliphate as next of kin to the Prophet. According to Moslem notions the Umayyads were kings by right, Caliphs only by courtesy. They had, as we shall see, no spiritual title, and little enough religion of any sort. This dynasty, which had been raised and was upheld by the Syrian Arabs, transferred the seat of government from Medína to Damascus.

The Umayyad Caliphate (661–750 A.D.).

The third division is by far the longest and most important. Starting in 750 with the accession of Abu 'l-'Abbás al-Saffáḥ, it presents an unbroken series of thirty-seven Caliphs of the same House, and culminates, after the lapse of half a millennium, in the sack of Baghdád, their magnificent capital, by the Mongol Húlágú (January, 1258). The 'Abbásids were no less despotic than the Umayyads, but in a more enlightened fashion; for, while the latter had been purely Arab in feeling, the 'Abbásids owed their throne to the Persian nationalists, and were imbued with Persian ideas, which introduced a new and fruitful element into Moslem civilisation.

The 'Abbásid Caliphate (750-1258 A.D.)

From our special point of view the Orthodox and Umayyad Caliphates, which form the subject of the present chapter, are somewhat barren. The simple life of the pagan Arabs found full expression in their poetry. The many-sided life of the Moslems under 'Abbásid rule may be studied in a copious literature which exhibits all the characteristics of the age; but of contemporary documents illustrating the intellectual history of the early Islamic period comparatively little has been preserved, and that little, being for the most part anti-Islamic in tendency, gives only meagre information concerning what excites interest beyond anything else—the religious movement, the rise of theology, and the origin of those great parties and sects which emerge, at various stages of development, in later literature.

Early Islamic literature.

Since the Moslem Church and State are essentially one, it is impossible to treat of politics apart from religion, nor can religious phenomena be understood without continual reference to political events. The following brief sketch of the Orthodox Caliphate will show how completely this unity was realised, and what far-reaching consequences it had.

Unity of Church and State.

That Muḥammad left no son was perhaps of less moment than his neglect or refusal to nominate a successor. The

Arabs were unfamiliar with the hereditary descent of kingly power, while the idea had not yet dawned of a Divine right resident in the Prophet's family. It was thoroughly in accord with Arabian practice that the Moslem community should elect its own leader, just as in heathen days the tribe chose its own chief. The likeliest men—all three belonged to Quraysh—were Abú Bakr, whose daughter 'Â'isha had been Muḥammad's favourite wife, 'Umar b. al-Khaṭṭáb, and 'Alí, Abú Ṭálib's son and Fáṭima's husband, who was thus connected with the Prophet by blood as well as by marriage. Abú Bakr was the eldest, he was supported by 'Umar, and on him the choice ultimately fell, though not without an ominous ebullition of party strife. A man of simple tastes and unassuming demeanour, he had earned the name *al-Ṣiddíq*, *i.e.*, the True, by his unquestioning faith in the Prophet; naturally gentle and merciful, he stood firm when the cause of Islam was at stake, and crushed with iron hand the revolt which on the news of Muḥammad's death spread like wildfire through Arabia. False prophets arose, and the Bedouins rallied round them, eager to throw off the burden of tithes and prayers. In the centre of the peninsula, the Banú Ḥanífa were led to battle by Musaylima, who imitated the early style of the Koran with ludicrous effect, if we may judge from the sayings ascribed to him, *e.g.*, "The elephant, what is the elephant, and who shall tell you what is the elephant? He has a poor tail, and a long trunk: and is a trifling part of the creations of thy God." Moslem tradition calls him the Liar (*al-Kadhdháb*), and represents him as an obscene miracle-monger, which can hardly be the whole truth. It is possible that he got some of his doctrines from Christianity, as Professor Margoliouth has suggested,[1] but we know too little about them to arrive at any conclusion. After a desperate struggle Musaylima was defeated

Abú Bakr elected Caliph (June, 632 A.D.).

Musaylima the Liar.

[1] *On the Origin and Import of the Names Muslim and Ḥaníf* (*J.R.A.S.* for 1903, p. 491)

and slain by 'the Sword of Allah,' Khálid b. Walíd. The Moslem arms were everywhere victorious. Arabia bowed in sullen submission.

Islam a world-religion.

Although Muir and other biographers of Muḥammad have argued that Islam was originally designed for the Arabs alone, and made no claim to universal acceptance, their assertion is contradicted by the unequivocal testimony of the Koran itself. In one of the oldest Revelations (lxviii, 51–52), we read: "*It wanteth little but that the unbelievers dash thee to the ground with their looks* (of anger) *when they hear the Warning* (*i.e.*, the Koran); *and they say, 'He is assuredly mad': but it* (the Koran) *is no other than a* WARNING UNTO ALL CREATURES" (*dhikr*^{un} *li 'l-'álamín*).[1] The time had now come when this splendid dream was to be, in large measure, fulfilled. The great wars of conquest were inspired by the Prophet's missionary zeal and justified by his example. Pious duty coincided with reasons of state. "It was certainly good policy to turn the recently subdued tribes of the wilderness towards an external aim in which they might at once satisfy their lust for booty on a grand scale, maintain their warlike feeling, and strengthen themselves in their attachment to the new faith."[2] The story of their achievements cannot be set down here. Suffice it to say that within twelve years after the Prophet's death the Persian Empire had been reduced to a tributary province, and Syria, together with Egypt, torn away from Byzantine rule. It must not be supposed that the followers of Zoroaster and Christ in these countries were forcibly converted to Islam. Thousands embraced it of free will, impelled by various motives which we have no space to enumerate; those who clung to the religion in which they had been brought up

Conquest of Persia and Syria (633–643 A.D.).

Moslem toleration.

[1] See T. W. Arnold's *The Preaching of Islam*, p. 23 seq., where several passages of like import are collected.

[2] Nöldeke, *Sketches from Eastern History*, translated by J. S. Black, p. 73.

secured protection and toleration by payment of a capitation-tax (*jizya*).[1]

The tide of foreign conquest, which had scarce begun to flow before the death of Abú Bakr, swept with amazing rapidity over Syria and Persia in the Caliphate of 'Umar b. al-Khaṭṭáb (634–644), and continued to advance, though with diminished fury, under the Prophet's third successor, 'Uthmán. We may dwell for a little on the noble figure of 'Umar, who was regarded by good Moslems in after times as an embodiment of all the virtues which a Caliph ought to possess. Probably his character has been idealised, but in any case the anecdotes related of him give an admirable picture of the man and his age. Here are a few, taken almost at random from the pages of Ṭabarí.

The Caliph 'Umar (634-644 A.D.).

One said : "I saw 'Umar coming to the Festival. He walked with bare feet, using both hands (for he was ambidextrous) to draw round him a red embroidered cloth. He towered above the people, as though he were on horseback."[2] A client of (the Caliph) 'Uthmán b. 'Affán relates that he mounted behind his patron and they rode together to the enclosure for the beasts which were delivered in payment of the poor-tax. It was an exceedingly hot day and the simoom was blowing fiercely. They saw a man clad only in a loin-cloth and a short cloak (*ridá*), in which he had wrapped his head, driving the camels into the enclosure. 'Uthmán said to his companion, "Who is this, think you?" When they came up to him, behold, it was 'Umar b. al-Khaṭṭáb. "By God," said 'Uthmán, "this is *the strong, the trusty*."[3]—'Umar used to go round the markets and recite the Koran and judge between disputants wherever he found them.—When Ka'bu 'l-Aḥbár, a well-known Rabbin of Medína, asked how he could obtain access to the Commander of the Faithful,[4] he received this answer : "There

His simple manners.

---

[1] See Professor Browne's *Literary History of Persia*, vol. i, p. 200 sqq.

[2] Ṭabarí, i, 2729, l. 15 sqq.

[3] *Ibid.*, i, 2736, l. 5 sqq. The words in italics are quoted from Koran, xxviii, 26, where they are applied to Moses.

[4] 'Umar was the first to assume this title (*Amíru 'l-Mu'minín*), by which the Caliphs after him were generally addressed.

is no door nor curtain to be passed; he performs the rites of prayer, then he takes his seat, and any one that wishes may speak to him."[1] 'Umar said in one of his public orations: "By Him who sent Muḥammad with the truth, were a single camel to die of neglect on the bank of the Euphrates, I should fear lest God should call the family of al-Khaṭṭáb" (meaning himself) "to account therefor."[2]—"If I live," he is reported to have said on another occasion, "please God, I will assuredly spend a whole year in travelling among my subjects, for I know they have wants which are cut short ere they reach my ears: the governors do not bring the wants of the people before me, while the people themselves do not attain to me. So I will journey to Syria and remain there two months, then to Mesopotamia and remain there two months, then to Egypt and remain there two months, then to Baḥrayn and remain there two months, then to Kúfa and remain there two months, then to Baṣra and remain there two months; and by God, it will be a year well spent!"[3]—One night he came to the house of 'Abdu 'l-Raḥmán b. 'Awf and knocked at the door, which was opened by 'Abdu 'l-Raḥmán's wife. "Do not enter," said she, "until I go back and sit in my place;" so he waited. Then she bade him come in, and on his asking, "Have you anything in the house?" she fetched him some food. Meanwhile 'Abdu 'l-Raḥmán was standing by, engaged in prayer. "Be quick, man!" cried 'Umar. 'Abdu 'l-Raḥmán immediately pronounced the final salaam, and turning to the Caliph said: "O Commander of the Faithful, what has brought you here at this hour?" 'Umar replied: "A party of travellers who alighted in the neighbourhood of the market: I was afraid that the thieves of Medína might fall upon them. Let us go and keep watch." So he set off with 'Abdu 'l-Raḥmán, and when they reached the market-place they seated themselves on some high ground and began to converse. Presently they descried, far away, the light of a lamp. "Have not I forbidden lamps after bedtime?"[4] exclaimed the Caliph. They went to the spot and found a company drinking wine. "Begone," said 'Umar to 'Abdu 'l-Raḥmán; "I know him." Next morning he sent for the culprit and said, addressing him by name, "Last night you were drinking wine with your friends." "O Commander of the Faithful, how did

His sense of personal responsibility.

The Caliph as a policeman.

---

[1] Ṭabarí, i, 2738, 7 sqq. [2] *Ibid.*, i, 2739, 4 sqq. [3] *Ibid.*, i, 2737, 4 sqq.

[4] It is explained that 'Umar prohibited lamps because rats used to take the lighted wick and set fire to the house-roofs, which at that time were made of palm-branches

you ascertain that?" "I saw it with my own eyes." "Has not God forbidden you to play the spy?" 'Umar made no answer and pardoned his offence.[1]—When 'Umar ascended the pulpit for the purpose of warning the people that they must not do something, he gathered his family and said to them: "I have forbidden the people to do so-and-so. Now, the people look at you as birds look at flesh, and I swear by God that if I find any one of you doing this thing, I will double the penalty against him."[2]—Whenever he appointed a governor he used to draw up in writing a certificate of investiture, which he caused to be witnessed by some of the Emigrants or Helpers. It contained the following instructions: That he must not ride on horseback, nor eat white bread, nor wear fine clothes, nor set up a door between himself and those who had aught to ask of him.[3]—It was 'Umar's custom to go forth with his governors, on their appointment, to bid them farewell. "I have not appointed you," he would say, "over the people of Muḥammad (God bless him and grant him peace!) that you may drag them by their hair and scourge their skins, but in order that you may lead them in prayer and judge between them with right and divide (the public money) amongst them with equity. I have not made you lords of their skin and hair. Do not flog the Arabs lest you humiliate them, and do not keep them long on foreign service lest you tempt them to sedition, and do not neglect them lest you render them desperate. Confine yourselves to the Koran, write few Traditions of Muḥammad (God bless him and grant him peace!), and I am your ally." He used to permit retaliation against his governors. On receiving a complaint about any one of them he confronted him with the accuser, and punished him if his guilt were proved.[4]

His strictness towards his own family.

Instructions to his governors.

It was 'Umar who first made a Register (*Díwán*) of the Arabs in Islam and entered them therein according to their tribes and assigned to them their stipends. The following account of its institution is extracted from the charming history entitled *al-Fakhrí*:—

The Register of 'Umar.

In the fifteenth year of the Hijra (636 A.D.) 'Umar, who was then Caliph, seeing that the conquests proceeded without interruption

[1] Ṭabarí, i, 2742, 13 sqq.
[2] *Ibid.*, i, 2745, 15 sqq.
[3] *Ibid.*, i, 2747, 7 sqq.
[4] *Ibid.*, i, 2740, last line and foll.

and that the treasures of the Persian monarchs had been taken as spoil, and that load after load was being accumulated of gold and silver and precious jewels and splendid raiment, resolved to enrich the Moslems by distributing all this wealth amongst them ; but he did not know how he should manage it. Now there was a Persian satrap (*marzubán*) at Medína who, when he saw 'Umar's bewilderment, said to him, "O Commander of the Faithful, the Persian kings have a thing they call a *Díwán*, in which is kept the whole of their revenues and expenditures without exception ; and therein those who receive stipends are arranged in classes, so that no confusion occurs." 'Umar's attention was aroused. He bade the satrap describe it, and on comprehending its nature, he drew up the registers and assigned the stipends, appointing a specified allowance for every Moslem ; and he allotted fixed sums to the wives of the Apostle (on whom be God's blessing and peace !) and to his concubines and next-of-kin, until he exhausted the money in hand. He did not lay up a store in the treasury. Some one came to him and said : "O Commander of the Faithful, you should have left something to provide for contingencies." 'Umar rebuked him, saying, "The devil has put these words into your mouth. May God preserve me from their mischief ! for it were a temptation to my successors. Come what may, I will provide naught except obedience to God and His Apostle. That is our provision, whereby we have gained that which we have gained." Then, in respect of the stipends, he deemed it right that precedence should be according to priority of conversion to Islam and of service rendered to the Apostle on his fields of battle.[1]

Affinity to Muḥammad was also considered. "By God," exclaimed 'Umar, "we have not won superiority in this world, nor do we hope for recompense for our works from God hereafter, save through Muḥammad (God bless him and grant him peace !). He is our title to nobility, his tribe are the noblest of the Arabs, and after them those are the nobler that are nearer to him in blood. Truly, the Arabs are ennobled by God's Apostle. Peradventure some of them have many ancestors in common with him, and we ourselves are only removed by a few forbears from his line of descent, in which we accompany him back to Adam. Notwithstanding this, if the foreigners bring good works and we bring none, by God, they are nearer to Muḥammad on the day of Resurrection than we. Therefore let no man regard affinity, but let him work for that which is in God's

The aristocracy of Islam.

"'Tis only noble to be good."

[1] *Al-Fakhri*, ed. by Derenbourg, p. 116, l. 1 to p. 117, l. 3.

hands to bestow. He that is retarded by his works will not be sped by his lineage." [1]

It may be said of 'Umar, not less appropriately than of Cromwell, that he

"cast the kingdoms old
Into another mould;"

and he too justified the poet's maxim—

"The same arts that did gain
A power, must it maintain."

Under the system which he organised Arabia, purged of infidels, became a vast recruiting-ground for the standing armies of Islam: the Arabs in the conquered territories formed an exclusive military class, living in great camps and supported by revenues derived from the non-Muḥammadan population. Out of such camps arose two cities destined to make their mark in literary history—Baṣra (Bassora) on the delta of the Tigris and Euphrates, and Kúfa, which was founded about the same time on the western branch of the latter stream, not far from Ḥíra.

Foundation of Baṣra and Kúfa (638 A.D.).

'Umar was murdered by a Persian slave named Fírúz while leading the prayers in the Great Mosque. With his death the military theocracy and the palmy days of the Patriarchal Caliphate draw to a close. The broad lines of his character appear in the anecdotes translated above, though many details might be added to complete the picture. Simple and frugal; doing his duty without fear or favour; energetic even to harshness, yet capable of tenderness towards the weak; a severe judge of others and especially of himself, he was a born ruler and every inch a man. Looking back on

Death of 'Umar (644 A.D.)

[1] Ṭabarí, i, 2751, 9 sqq.

the turmoils which followed his death one is inclined to agree with the opinion of a saintly doctor who said, five centuries afterwards, that "the good fortune of Islam was shrouded in the grave-clothes of 'Umar b. al-Khaṭṭáb." [1]

When the Meccan aristocrats accepted Islam, they only yielded to the inevitable. They were now to have an opportunity of revenging themselves. 'Uthmán b. 'Affán, who succeeded 'Umar as Caliph, belonged to a distinguished Meccan family, the Umayyads or descendants of Umayya, which had always taken a leading part in the opposition to Muḥammad, though 'Uthmán himself was among the Prophet's first disciples. He was a pious, well-meaning old man—an easy tool in the hands of his ambitious kinsfolk. They soon climbed into all the most lucrative and important offices and lived on the fat of the land, while too often their ungodly behaviour gave point to the question whether these converts of the eleventh hour were not still heathens at heart. Other causes contributed to excite a general discontent. The rapid growth of luxury and immorality in the Holy Cities as well as in the new settlements was an eyesore to devout Moslems. The true Islamic aristocracy, the Companions of the Prophet, headed by 'Alí, Ṭalḥa, and Zubayr, strove to undermine the rival nobility which threatened them with destruction. The factious soldiery were ripe for revolt against Umayyad arrogance and greed. Rebellion broke out, and finally the aged Caliph, after enduring a siege of several weeks, was murdered in his own house. This event marks an epoch in the history of the Arabs. The ensuing civil wars rent the unity of Islam from top to bottom, and the wound has never healed.

'Uthmán elected Caliph (644 A.D.).

General disaffection.

'Uthmán murdered (656 A.D.).

'Alí, the Prophet's cousin and son-in-law, who had hitherto

[1] Ibn Khallikán (ed. by Wüstenfeld), No. 68, p. 96, l. 3; De Slane's translation, vol. i, p. 152.

remained in the background, was now made Caliph. Although the suspicion that he was in league with the murderers may be put aside, he showed culpable weakness in leaving 'Uthmán to his fate without an effort to save him. But 'Alí had almost every virtue except those of the ruler: energy, decision, and foresight. He was a gallant warrior, a wise counsellor, a true friend, and a generous foe. He excelled in poetry and in eloquence; his verses and sayings are famous throughout the Muḥammadan East, though few of them can be considered authentic. A fine spirit worthy to be compared with Montrose and Bayard, he had no talent for the stern realities of statecraft, and was overmatched by unscrupulous rivals who knew that "war is a game of deceit." Thus his career was in one sense a failure: his authority as Caliph was never admitted, while he lived, by the whole community. On the other hand, he has exerted, down to the present day, a posthumous influence only second to that of Muḥammad himself. Within a century of his death he came to be regarded as the Prophet's successor *jure divino;* as a blessed martyr, sinless and infallible; and by some even as an incarnation of God. The 'Alí of Shí'ite legend is not an historical figure glorified: rather does he symbolise, in purely mythical fashion, the religious aspirations and political aims of a large section of the Moslem world.

'Alí elected Caliph (656 A.D.).

Character of 'Alí.

His apotheosis.

To return to our narrative. No sooner was 'Alí proclaimed Caliph by the victorious rebels than Mu'áwiya b. Abí Sufyán, the governor of Syria, raised the cry of vengeance for 'Uthmán and refused to take the oath of allegiance. As head of the Umayyad family, Mu'áwiya might justly demand that the murderers of his kinsman should be punished, but the con-

'Alí against Mu'áwiya.

test between him and 'Alí was virtually for the Caliphate. A great battle was fought at Ṣiffín, a village on the Euphrates. 'Alí had well-nigh gained the day when Mu'áwiya bethought him of a stratagem. He ordered his troops to fix Korans on the points of their lances and to shout, "Here is the Book of God: let it decide between us!" The miserable trick succeeded. In 'Alí's army there were many pious fanatics to whom the proposed arbitration by the Koran appealed with irresistible force. They now sprang forward clamorously, threatening to betray their leader unless he would submit his cause to the Book. Vainly did 'Alí remonstrate with the mutineers, and warn them of the trap into which they were driving him, and this too at the moment when victory was within their grasp. He had no choice but to yield and name as his umpire a man of doubtful loyalty, Abú Músá al-Ash'arí, one of the oldest surviving Companions of the Prophet. Mu'áwiya on his part named 'Amr b. al-'Áṣ, whose cunning had prompted the decisive manœuvre. When the umpires came forth to give judgment, Abú Músá rose and in accordance with what had been arranged at the preliminary conference pronounced that both 'Alí and Mu'áwiya should be deposed and that the people should elect a proper Caliph in their stead. "Lo," said he, laying down his sword, "even thus do I depose 'Alí b. Abí Ṭálib." Then 'Amr advanced and spoke as follows: "O people! ye have heard the judgment of my colleague. He has called you to witness that he deposes 'Alí. Now I call you to witness that I confirm Mu'áwiya, even as I make fast this sword of mine," and suiting the action to the word, he returned it to its sheath. It is characteristic of Arabian notions of morality that this impudent fraud was hailed by Mu'áwiya's adherents as a diplomatic triumph which gave him a colourable pretext

Battle of Ṣiffín (657 A.D.).

Arbitration.

The award.

for assuming the title of Caliph. Both sides prepared to renew the struggle, but in the meanwhile 'Alí found his hands full nearer home. A numerous party among his troops, including the same zealots who had forced arbitration upon him, now cast him off because he had accepted it, fell out from the ranks, and raised the standard of revolt. These 'Outgoers,' or Khárijites, as they were called, maintained their theocratic principles with desperate courage, and though often defeated took the field again and again.

The Khárijites revolt against 'Alí.

'Alí's plans for recovering Syria were finally abandoned in 660, when he concluded peace with Mu'áwiya, and shortly afterwards he was struck down in the Mosque at Kúfa, which he had made his capital, by Ibn Muljam, a Khárijite conspirator.

Alí assassinated (661 A.D.).

With 'Alí's fall our sketch of the Orthodox Caliphate may fitly end. It was necessary to give some account of these years so vital in the history of Islam, even at the risk of wearying the reader, who will perhaps wish that less space were devoted to political affairs.

The Umayyads came into power, but, except in Syria and Egypt, they ruled solely by the sword. As descendants and representatives of the pagan aristocracy, which strove with all its might to defeat Muḥammad, they were usurpers in the eyes of the Moslem community which they claimed to lead as his successors.[1] We shall see, a little further on, how this opposition expressed itself in two great parties: the Shí'ites or followers of 'Alí, and the radical sect of the Khárijites, who have been mentioned above; and how it was gradually reinforced by the non-Arabian Moslems until it overwhelmed

The Umayyad dynasty.

[1] Mu'áwiya himself said: "I am the first of the kings" (Ya'qúbí, ed. by Houtsma, vol. ii, p. 276, l. 14).

the Umayyad Government and set up the 'Abbásids in their place. In estimating the character of the Umayyads one must bear in mind that the epitaph on the fallen dynasty was composed by their enemies, and can no more be considered historically truthful than the lurid picture which Tacitus has drawn of the Emperor Tiberius. Because they kept the revolutionary forces in check with ruthless severity, the Umayyads pass for bloodthirsty tyrants; whereas the best of them at any rate were strong and singularly capable rulers, bad Moslems and good men of the world, seldom cruel, plain livers if not high thinkers; who upon the whole stand as much above the 'Abbásids in morality as below them in culture and intellect. Mu'áwiya's clemency was proverbial, though he too could be stern on occasion. When members of the house of 'Alí came to visit him at Damascus, which was now the capital of the Muḥammadan Empire, he gave them honourable lodging and entertainment and was anxious to do what they asked; but they (relates the historian approvingly) used to address him in the rudest terms and affront him in the vilest manner: sometimes he would answer them with a jest, and another time he would feign not to hear, and he always dismissed them with splendid presents and ample donations.[1] "I do not employ my sword," he said, "when my whip suffices me, nor my whip when my tongue suffices me; and were there but a single hair (of friendship) between me and my subjects, I would not let it be snapped."[2] After the business of the day he sought relaxation in books. "He consecrated a third part of every night to the history of the Arabs and their famous battles; the history of foreign peoples, their kings, and their government; the biographies of monarchs, including their wars

Moslem tradition hostile to the Umayyads.

Mu'áwiya's clemency.

His hours of study.

[1] *Al-Fakhrí*, ed. by Derenbourg, p. 145
[2] Ya'qúbí, vol. ii, p. 283, l. 8 seq.

and stratagems and methods of rule; and other matters connected with Ancient History." [1]

Mu'áwiya's chief henchman was Ziyád, the son of Sumayya (Sumayya being the name of his mother), or, as he is generally called, Ziyád ibn Abíhi, *i.e.*, 'Ziyád his father's son,' for none knew who was his sire, though rumour pointed to Abú Sufyán; in which case Ziyád would have been Mu'áwiya's half-brother. Mu'áwiya, instead of disavowing the scandalous imputation, acknowledged him as such, and made him governor of Baṣra, where he ruled the Eastern provinces with a rod of iron.

Ziyád ibn Abíhi.

Mu'áwiya was a crafty diplomatist—he has been well compared to Richelieu—whose profound knowledge of human nature enabled him to gain over men of moderate opinions in all the parties opposed to him. Events were soon to prove the hollowness of this outward reconciliation. Yazíd, who succeeded his father, was the son of Maysún, a Bedouin woman whom Mu'áwiya married before he rose to be Caliph. The luxury of Damascus had no charm for her wild spirit, and she gave utterance to her feeling of homesickness in melancholy verse:—

Yazíd (680–683 A.D.).

"A tent with rustling breezes cool
Delights me more than palace high,
And more the cloak of simple wool
Than robes in which I learned to sigh.

The crust I ate beside my tent
Was more than this fine bread to me;
The wind's voice where the hill-path went
Was more than tambourine can be.

And more than purr of friendly cat
I love the watch-dog's bark to hear;
And more than any lubbard fat
I love a Bedouin cavalier." [2]

---

[1] Mas'údí, *Murúju 'l-Dhahab* (ed. by Barbier de Meynard), vol. v. p. 77.
[2] Nöldeke's *Delectus*, p. 25, l. 3 sqq., omitting l. 8.

Mu'áwiya, annoyed by the contemptuous allusion to himself, took the dame at her word. She returned to her own family, and Yazíd grew up as a Bedouin, with the instincts and tastes which belong to the Bedouins—love of pleasure, hatred of piety, and reckless disregard for the laws of religion. The beginning of his reign was marked by an event of which even now few Moslems can speak without a thrill of horror and dismay. The facts are briefly these: In the autumn of the year 680 Ḥusayn, the son of 'Alí, claiming to be the rightful Caliph in virtue of his descent from the Prophet, quitted Mecca with his whole family and a number of devoted friends, and set out for Kúfa, where he expected the population, which was almost entirely Shí'ite, to rally to his cause. It was a foolhardy adventure. The poet Farazdaq, who knew the fickle temper of his fellow-townsmen, told Ḥusayn that although their hearts were with him, their swords would be with the Umayyads; but his warning was given in vain. Meanwhile 'Ubaydulláh b. Ziyád, the governor of Kúfa, having overawed the insurgents in the city and beheaded their leader, Muslim b. 'Aqíl, who was a cousin of Ḥusayn, sent a force of cavalry with orders to bring the arch-rebel to a stand. Retreat was still open to him. But his followers cried out that the blood of Muslim must be avenged, and Ḥusayn could not hesitate. Turning northward along the Euphrates, he encamped at Karbalá with his little band, which, including the women and children, amounted to some two hundred souls. In this hopeless situation he offered terms which might have been accepted if Shamir b. Dhi 'l-Jawshan, a name for ever infamous and accursed, had not persuaded 'Ubaydulláh to insist on unconditional surrender. The demand was refused, and Ḥusayn drew up his comrades—a handful of men and boys—for battle against the host which surrounded them. All the harrowing details invented by grief and passion can scarcely

Ḥusayn marches on Kúfa.

heighten the tragedy of the closing scene. It would appear that the Umayyad officers themselves shrank from the odium of a general massacre, and hoped to take the Prophet's grandson alive. Shamir, however, had no such scruples. Chafing at delay, he urged his soldiers to the assault. The unequal struggle was soon over. Ḥusayn fell, pierced by an arrow, and his brave followers were cut down beside him to the last man.

Massacre of Ḥusayn and his followers at Karbalá (10th Muḥarram, 61 A.H. = 10th October, 680 A.D.).

Muḥammadan tradition, which with rare exceptions is uniformly hostile to the Umayyad dynasty, regards Ḥusayn as a martyr and Yazíd as his murderer; while modern historians, for the most part, agree with Sir W. Muir, who points out that Ḥusayn, "having yielded himself to a treasonable, though impotent design upon the throne, was committing an offence that endangered society and demanded swift suppression." This was naturally the view of the party in power, and the reader must form his own conclusion as to how far it justifies the action which they took. For Moslems the question is decided by the relation of the Umayyads to Islam. Violators of its laws and spurners of its ideals, they could never be anything but tyrants; and being tyrants, they had no right to slay believers who rose in arms against their usurped authority. The so-called verdict of history, when we come to examine it, is seen to be the verdict of religion, the judgment of theocratic Islam on Arabian Imperialism. On this ground the Umayyads are justly condemned, but it is well to remember that in Moslem eyes the distinction between Church and State does not exist. Yazíd was a bad Churchman: therefore he was a wicked tyrant; the one thing involves the other. From our unprejudiced standpoint, he was an amiable prince who inherited his mother's poetic talent, and infin-

Differing views of Muḥammadan and European writers.

The Umayyads judged by Islam.

Character of Yazíd.

itely preferred wine, music, and sport to the drudgery of public affairs. The Syrian Arabs, who recognised the Umayyads as legitimate, thought highly of him: "Jucundissimus," says a Christian writer, "et cunctis nationibus regni ejus subditis vir gratissime habitus, qui nullam unquam, ut omnibus moris est, sibi regalis fastigii causa gloriam appetivit, sed communis cum omnibus civiliter vixit."[1] He deplored the fate of the women and children of Ḥusayn's family, treated them with every mark of respect, and sent them to Medína, where their account of the tragedy added fresh fuel to the hatred and indignation with which its authors were generally regarded.

The Umayyads had indeed ample cause to rue the day of Karbalá. It gave the Shí'ite faction a rallying-cry—"Vengeance for Ḥusayn!"—which was taken up on all sides, and especially by the Persian *Mawálí*, or Clients, who longed for deliverance from the Arab yoke. Their amalgamation with the Shí'a—a few years later they flocked in thousands to the standard of Mukhtár—was an event of the utmost historical importance, which will be discussed when we come to speak of the Shí'ites in particular.

The slaughter of Ḥusayn does not complete the tale of Yazíd's enormities. Medína, the Prophet's city, having expelled its Umayyad governor, was sacked by a Syrian army, while Mecca itself, where 'Abdulláh b. Zubayr had set up as rival Caliph, was besieged, and the Ka'ba laid in ruins. These outrages, shocking to Moslem sentiment, kindled a flame of rebellion. Ḥusayn was avenged by Mukhtár, who seized Kúfa and executed some three hundred of the guilty citizens, including the miscreant Shamir. His troops defeated and slew 'Ubaydulláh b. Ziyád, but he himself was slain, not long afterwards, by

Medína and Mecca desecrated 682–3 A.D.).

Rebellion of Mukhtár (685–6 A.D.).

[1] The *Continuatio* of Isidore of Hispalis, § 27, quoted by Wellhausen, *Das Arabische Reich und sein Sturz*, p. 105.

Muṣʿab, the brother of Ibn Zubayr, and seven thousand of his followers were massacred in cold blood. On Yazíd's death (683) the Umayyad Empire threatened to fall to pieces. As a contemporary poet sang—

> "Now loathed of all men is the Fury blind
> Which blazeth as a fire blown by the wind.
> They are split in sects: each province hath its own
> Commander of the Faithful, each its throne."[1]

Fierce dissensions broke out among the Syrian Arabs, the backbone of the dynasty. The great tribal groups of Kalb and Qays, whose coalition had hitherto maintained the Umayyads in power, fought on opposite sides at Marj Ráhiṭ (684), the former for Marwán and the latter for Ibn Zubayr. Marwán's victory secured the allegiance of Syria, but henceforth Qays and Kalb were always at daggers drawn.[2] This was essentially a feud between the Northern and the Southern Arabs—a feud which rapidly extended and developed into a permanent racial enmity. They carried it with them to the farthest ends of the world, so that, for example, after the conquest of Spain precautions had to be taken against civil war by providing that Northerners and Southerners should not settle in the same districts. The literary history of this antagonism has been sketched by Dr. Goldziher with his wonted erudition and acumen.[3] Satire was, of course, the

Civil war renewed.

Rivalry of Northern and Southern Arabs.

[1] *Ḥamása*, 226. The word translated 'throne' is in Arabic *minbar*, *i.e.*, the pulpit from which the Caliph conducted the public prayers and addressed the congregation.

[2] Kalb was properly one of the Northern tribes (see Robertson Smith's *Kinship and Marriage*, 2nd ed., p. 8 seq.—a reference which I owe to Professor Bevan), but there is evidence that the Kalbites were regarded as 'Yemenite' or 'Southern' Arabs at an early period of Islam. *Cf.* Goldziher, *Muhammedanische Studien*, Part I, p. 83, l. 3 sqq.

[3] *Muhammedanische Studien*, i, 78 sqq.

principal weapon of both sides. Here is a fragment by a Northern poet which belongs to the Umayyad period:—

"Negroes are better, when they name their sires,
Than Qaḥṭán's sons,[1] the uncircumcisèd cowards:
A folk whom thou mayst see, at war's outflame,
More abject than a shoe to tread in baseness;
Their women free to every lecher's lust,
Their clients spoil for cavaliers and footmen."[2]

Thus the Arab nation was again torn asunder by the old tribal pretensions which Muḥammad sought to abolish. That they ultimately proved fatal to the Umayyads is no matter for surprise; the sorely pressed dynasty was already tottering, its enemies were at its gates. By good fortune it produced at this crisis an exceptionally able and vigorous ruler, 'Abdu 'l-Malik b. Marwán, who not only saved his house from destruction, but re-established its supremacy and inaugurated a more brilliant epoch than any that had gone before.

'Abdu 'l-Malik and his successors.

'Abdu 'l-Malik succeeded his father in 685, but required seven years of hard fighting to make good his claim to the Caliphate. When his most formidable rival, Ibn Zubayr, had fallen in battle (692), the eastern provinces were still overrun by rebels, who offered a desperate resistance to the governor of 'Iráq, the iron-handed Ḥajjáj. But enough of bloodshed. Peace also had her victories during the troubled reign of 'Abdu 'l-Malik and the calmer sway of his successors. Four of the next five Caliphs were his own sons—Walíd (705–715), Sulaymán (715–717), Yazíd II (720–724), and Hishám (724–743); the fifth, 'Umar II, was the son of his brother, 'Abdu 'l-'Azíz. For the greater part of this time the Moslem lands enjoyed a well-earned interval of repose and prosperity, which mitigated, though it could not undo, the frightful devastation wrought by

[1] Qaḥṭán is the legendary ancestor of the Southern Arabs.
[2] *Aghání*, xiii, 51, cited by Goldziher, *ibid.*, p. 82.

twenty years of almost continuous civil war. Many reforms were introduced, some wholly political in character, while others inspired by the same motives have, none the less, a direct bearing on literary history. 'Abdu 'l-Malik organised an excellent postal service, by means of relays of horses, for the conveyance of despatches and travellers; he substituted for the Byzantine and Persian coins, which had hitherto been in general use, new gold and silver pieces, on which he caused sentences from the Koran to be engraved; and he made Arabic, instead of Greek or Persian, the official language of financial administration. Steps were taken, moreover, to improve the extremely defective Arabic script, and in this way to provide a sound basis for the study and interpretation of the Koran as well as for the collection of *ḥadīths* or sayings of the Prophet, which form an indispensable supplement thereto. The Arabic alphabet, as it was then written, consisted entirely of consonants, so that, to give an illustration from English, *bnd* might denote *band*, *bend*, *bind*, or *bond*; *crt* might stand for *cart*, *carat*, *curt*, and so on. To an Arab this ambiguity mattered little; far worse confusion arose from the circumstance that many of the consonants themselves were exactly alike: thus, *e.g.*, it was possible to read the same combination of three letters as *bnt*, *nbt*, *byt*, *tnb*, *ntb*, *nyb*, and in various other ways. Considering the difficulties of the Arabic language, which are so great that a European aided by scientific grammars and unequivocal texts will often find himself puzzled even when he has become tolerably familiar with it, one may imagine that the Koran was virtually a sealed book to all but a few among the crowds of foreigners who accepted Islam after the early conquests. 'Abdu'l-Malik's viceroy in 'Iráq, the famous Ḥajjáj, who began life as a schoolmaster, exerted himself to promote the use of vowel-marks (borrowed from the Syriac) and of the diacritical points placed above or below similar consonants. This extraordinary man

Reforms of 'Abdu 'l-Malik.

The writing of Arabic.

deserves more than a passing mention. A stern disciplinarian, who could be counted upon to do his duty without any regard to public opinion, he was chosen by 'Abdu 'l-Malik to besiege Mecca, which Ibn Zubayr was holding as anti-Caliph. Ḥajjáj bombarded the city, defeated the Pretender, and sent his head to Damascus. Two years afterwards he became governor of 'Iráq. Entering the Mosque at Kúfa, he mounted the pulpit and introduced himself to the assembled townsmen in these memorable words:—

Ḥajjáj b. Yúsuf (†714 A.D.).

"I am he who scattereth the darkness and climbeth o'er the summits.
When I lift the turban from my face, ye will know me.[1]

O people of Kúfa! I see heads that are ripe for cutting, and I am the man to do it; and methinks, I see blood between the turbans and beards."[2] The rest of his speech was in keeping with the commencement. He used no idle threats, as the malcontents soon found out. Rebellion, which had been rampant before his arrival, was rapidly extinguished. "He restored order in 'Iráq and subdued its people."[3] For twenty years his despotic rule gave peace and security to the Eastern world. Cruel he may have been, though the tales of his bloodthirstiness are beyond doubt grossly exaggerated, but it should be put to his credit that he established and maintained the settled conditions which afford leisure for the cultivation of learning. Under his protection the Koran and Traditions were diligently studied both in Kúfa and Baṣra, where many Companions of the Prophet had made their home: hence arose in Baṣra the science of Grammar, with which, as we shall see in a subsequent page, the name of that city is peculiarly associated.

His service to literature.

[1] A verse of the poet Suḥaym b. Wathíl.
[2] The *Kámil* of al-Mubarrad, ed. by W. Wright, p. 215, l. 14 sqq.
[3] Ibn Qutayba, *Kitábu 'l-Ma'árif*, p. 202.

Ḥajjáj shared the literary tastes of his sovereign; he admired the old poets and patronised the new; he was a master of terse eloquence and plumed himself on his elegant Arabic style. The most hated man of his time, he lives in history as the savage oppressor and butcher of God-fearing Moslems. He served the Umayyads well and faithfully, and when he died in 714 A.D. he left behind him nothing but his Koran, his arms, and a few hundred pieces of silver.

It was a common saying at Damascus that under Walíd people talked of fine buildings, under Sulaymán of cookery and the fair sex, while in the reign of 'Umar b. 'Abd al-'Azíz the Koran and religion formed favourite topics of conversation.[1] Of Walíd's passion for architecture we have a splendid monument in the Great Mosque of Damascus (originally the Cathedral of St. John), which is the principal sight of the city to this day. He spoke Arabic very incorrectly, and though his father rebuked him, observing that "in order to rule the Arabs one must be proficient in their language," he could never learn to express himself with propriety.[2] The unbroken peace which now prevailed within the Empire enabled Walíd to resume the work of conquest. In the East his armies invaded Transoxania, captured Bokhárá and Samarcand, and pushed forward to the Chinese frontier. Another force crossed the Indus and penetrated as far as Múltán, a renowned centre of pilgrimage in the Southern Punjaub, which fell into the hands of the Moslems after a prolonged siege. But the most brilliant advance, and the richest in its results, was that in the extreme West, which decided the fate of Spain. Although the Moslems had obtained a footing in Northern Africa some thirty years before this time, their position was always precarious, until in 709 Músá

Walíd (705–715 A.D.).

Moslem conquests in the East.

[1] *Al-Fakhrí*, p. 173; Ibnu 'l-Athír, ed. by Tornberg, v, 5.
[2] *Ibid.*, p. 174. *Cf.* Mas'údí, *Murúju l-Dhahab*, v, 412.

b. Nuṣayr completely subjugated the Berbers, and extended not only the dominion but also the faith of Islam to the Atlantic Ocean. Two years later his freedman Ṭáriq crossed the straits and took possession of the commanding height, called by the ancients Calpe, but henceforth known as Jabal Ṭáriq (Gibraltar). Roderic, the last of the West Gothic dynasty, gathered an army in defence of his kingdom, but there were traitors in the camp, and, though he himself fought valiantly, their defection turned the fortunes of the day. The king fled, and it was never ascertained what became of him. Ṭáriq, meeting with feeble resistance, marched rapidly on Toledo, while Músá, whose jealousy was excited by the triumphal progress of his lieutenant, now joined in the campaign, and, storming city after city, reached the Pyrenees. The conquest of Spain, which is told by Moslem historians with many romantic circumstances, marks the nearest approach that the Arabs ever made to World-Empire. Their advance on French soil was finally hurled back by Charles the Hammer's great victory at Tours (732 A.D.).

Conquest of Spain (711–713 A.D.).

Before taking leave of the Umayyads we must not forget to mention 'Umar b. 'Abd al-'Azíz, a ruler who stands out in singular contrast with his predecessors, and whose brief reign is regarded by many Moslems as the sole bright spot in a century of godless and blood-stained tyranny. There had been nothing like it since the days of his illustrious namesake and kinsman,[1] 'Umar b. al-Khaṭṭáb, and we shall find nothing like it in the future history of the Caliphate. Plato desired that every king should be a philosopher: according to Muḥammadan theory every Caliph ought to be a saint. 'Umar satisfied these aspirations. When he came to the throne the following dialogue is said to have occurred between him and one of his favourites, Sálim al-Suddí :—

'Umar b. 'Abd al-'Azíz (717–720 A.D.).

[1] His mother, Umm 'Áṣim, was a granddaughter of 'Umar I.

'Umar: "Are you glad on account of my accession, or sorry?"
Sálim: "I am glad for the people's sake, but sorry for yours."
'Umar: "I fear that I have brought perdition upon my soul."
Sálim: "If you are afraid, very good. I only fear that you may cease to be afraid."
'Umar: "Give me a word of counsel."
Sálim: "Our father Adam was driven forth from Paradise because of one sin."[1]

Poets and orators found no favour at his court, which was thronged by divines and men of ascetic life.[2] He warned his governors that they must either deal justly or go. He would not allow political considerations to interfere with his ideal of righteousness, but, as Wellhausen points out, he had practical ends in view: his piety made him anxious for the common weal no less than for his own salvation. Whether he administered the State successfully is a matter of dispute. It has been generally supposed that his financial reforms were Utopian in character and disastrous to the Exchequer.[3] However this may be, he showed wisdom in seeking to bridge the menacing chasm between Islam and the Imperial house. Thus, *e.g.*, he did away with the custom which had long prevailed of cursing 'Alí from the pulpit at Friday prayers. The policy of conciliation was tried too late, and for too short a space, to be effective; but it was not entirely fruitless. When, on the overthrow of the Umayyad dynasty, the tombs of the hated 'tyrants' were defiled and their bodies disinterred, 'Umar's grave alone was respected, and Mas'údí

[1] Mas'údí, *Murúju 'l-Dhahab*, v, 419 seq.

[2] Ibnu 'l-Athír, ed. by Tornberg, v, 46. *Cf. Aghání*, xx, p. 119, l. 23. 'Umar made an exception, as Professor Bevan reminds me, in favour of the poet Jarír. See Brockelmann's *Gesch. der Arab. Litteratur*, vol. i, p. 57.

[3] The exhaustive researches of Wellhausen, *Das Arabische Reich und sein Sturz* (pp. 169–192) have set this complicated subject in a new light. He contends that 'Umar's reform was not based on purely ideal grounds, but was demanded by the necessities of the case, and that, so far from introducing disorder into the finances, his measures were designed to remedy the confusion which already existed.

(† 956 A.D.) tells us that in his time it was visited by crowds of pilgrims.

The remaining Umayyads do not call for particular notice. Hishám ranks as a statesman with Mu'áwiya and 'Abdu 'l-Malik: the great 'Abbásid Caliph, Manṣúr, is said to have admired and imitated his methods of government.[1] Walíd II was an incorrigible libertine, whose songs celebrating the forbidden delights of wine have much merit. The eminent poet and freethinker, Abu 'l-'Alá al-Ma'arrí, quotes these verses by him[2]:—

Hishám and Walíd II.

Verses by Walíd II (743-4 A.D.).

"The Imám Walíd am I! In all my glory
Of trailing robes I listen to soft lays.
When proudly I sweep on towards her chamber,
I care not who inveighs.

There's no true joy but lending ear to music,
Or wine that leaves one sunk in stupor dense.
Houris in Paradise I do not look for:
Does any man of sense?"

Let us now turn from the monarchs to their subjects.

Political and religious movements of the period.

In the first place we shall speak of the political and religious parties, whose opposition to the Umayyad House gradually undermined its influence and in the end brought about its fall. Some account will be given of the ideas for which these parties fought and of the causes of their discontent with the existing *régime*. Secondly, a few words must be said of the theological and more purely religious sects—the Mu'tazilites, Murjites, and Ṣúfís; and, lastly, of the extant literature, which is almost exclusively poetical, and its leading representatives.

[1] Mas'údí, *Murúju 'l-Dhahab*, v, 479.

[2] The Arabic text and literal translation of these verses will be found in my article on Abu 'l-'Alá's *Risálatu 'l-Ghufrán* (*J.R.A.S.* for 1902, pp. 829 and 342).

The opposition to the Umayyads was at first mainly a question of politics. Mu'áwiya's accession announced the triumph of Syria over 'Iráq, and Damascus, instead of Kúfa, became the capital of the Empire. As Wellhausen observes, "the most powerful risings against the Umayyads proceeded from 'Iráq, not from any special party, but from the whole mass of the Arabs settled there, who were united in resenting the loss of their independence (*Selbstherrlichkeit*) and in hating those into whose hands it had passed."[1] At the same time these feelings took a religious colour and identified themselves with the cause of Islam. The new government fell lamentably short of the theocratic standard by which it was judged. Therefore it was evil, and (according to the Moslem's conception of duty) every right-thinking man must work for its destruction.

The Arabs of 'Iráq.

Among the myriads striving for this consummation, and so far making common cause with each other, we can distinguish four principal classes.

Parties opposed to the Umayyad government.

(1) The religious Moslems, or Pietists, in general, who formed a wing of the Orthodox Party.[2]

(2) The Khárijites, who may be described as the Puritans and extreme Radicals of theocracy.

(3) The Shí'ites, or partisans of 'Alí and his House.

(4) The Non-Arabian Moslems, who were called *Mawálí* (Clients).

It is clear that the Pietists—including divines learned in the law, reciters of the Koran, Companions of the Prophet and

[1] Wellhausen, *Das Arabische Reich und sein Sturz*, p. 38.

[2] *I.e.*, the main body of Moslems—*Sunnís*, followers of the *Sunna*, as they were afterwards called—who were neither Shí'ites nor Khárijites, but held (1) that the Caliph must be elected by the Moslem community, and (2) that he must be a member of Quraysh, the Prophet's tribe. All these parties arose out of the struggle between 'Alí and Mu'áwiya, and their original difference turned solely on the question of the Caliphate.

their descendants—could not but abominate the secular authority which they were now compelled to obey. The conviction that Might, in the shape of the tyrant and his minions, trampled on Right as represented by the Koran and the *Sunna* (custom of Muḥammad) drove many into active rebellion: five thousand are said to have perished in the sack of Medína alone. Others again, like Ḥasan of Baṣra, filled with profound despair, shut their eyes on the world, and gave themselves up to asceticism, a tendency which had important consequences, as we shall see.

The Pietists.

When 'Alí, on the field of Ṣiffín, consented that the claims of Mu'áwiya and himself to the Caliphate should be decided by arbitration, a large section of his army accused him of having betrayed his trust. He, the duly elected Caliph—so they argued—should have maintained the dignity of his high office inviolate at all costs. On the homeward march the malcontents, some twelve thousand in number, broke away and encamped by themselves at Ḥarúrá, a village near Kúfa. Their cry was, "God alone can decide" (*lá ḥukma illá lilláhi*): in these terms they protested against the arbitration. 'Alí endeavoured to win them back, but without any lasting success. They elected a Caliph from among themselves, and gathered at Nahrawán, four thousand strong. On the appearance of 'Alí with a vastly superior force many of the rebels dispersed, but the remainder—about half—preferred to die for their faith. Nahrawán was to the Khárijites what Karbalá afterwards became to the Shí'ites, who from this day were regarded by the former as their chief enemies. Frequent Khárijite risings took place during the early Umayyad period, but the movement reached its zenith in the years of confusion which followed Yazíd's death. The Azraqites, so called after their leader, Náfi' b. al-Azraq, overran 'Iráq and Southern Persia, while another sect, the Najdites, led by

The Khárijites.

Battle of Nahrawán (658 A.D.).

Khárijite risings.

Najda b. 'Ámir, reduced the greater part of Arabia to submission. The insurgents held their ground for a long time against 'Abdu 'l-Malik, and did not cease from troubling until the rebellion headed by Shabíb was at last stamped out by Ḥajjáj in 697.

Meaning of 'Khárijite.'

It has been suggested that the name *Khárijí* (plural, *Khawárij*) refers to a passage in the Koran (iv, 101) where mention is made of "those who go forth (*yakhruj*) from their homes as emigrants (*muhájir^an^*) to God and His Messenger"; so that 'Khárijite' means 'one who leaves his home among the unbelievers for God's sake,' and corresponds to the term *Muhájir*, which was applied to the Meccan converts who accompanied the Prophet in his migration to Medína.[1] Another name by which they are often designated is likewise Koranic in origin, viz., *Shurát* (plural of *Shár^in^*): literally 'Sellers'—that is to say, those who sell their lives and goods in return for Paradise.[2] The Khárijites were mostly drawn from the Bedouin soldiery who settled in Baṣra and Kúfa after the Persian wars. Civil life wrought little change in their unruly temper. Far from acknowledging the peculiar sanctity of a Qurayshite, they desired a chief of their own blood whom they might obey, in Bedouin fashion, as long as he did not abuse or exceed the powers conferred upon him.[3] The mainspring of the movement, however, was pietistic, and can be traced, as Wellhausen has shown, to the Koran-readers who made it a matter of conscience that 'Alí should avow his contrition for the fatal error which their own temporary and deeply regretted infatuation had forced him to commit. They cast off 'Alí for the same

Their political theories.

[1] Brünnow, *Die Charidschiten unter den ersten Omayyaden* (Leiden, 1884), p. 28. It is by no means certain, however, that the Khárijites called themselves by this name. In any case, the term implies *secession* (*khurúj*) from the Moslem community, and may be rendered by 'Seceder' or 'Nonconformist.'

[2] *Cf.* Koran, ix, 112.

[3] Brünnow, *op. cit.*, p. 8.

reason which led them to strike at 'Uthman: in both cases they were maintaining the cause of God against an unjust Caliph.[1] It is important to remember these facts in view of the cardinal Khárijite doctrines (1) that every free Arab was eligible as Caliph,[2] and (2) that an evil-doing Caliph must be deposed and, if necessary, put to death. Mustawrid b. 'Ullifa, the Khárijite 'Commander of the Faithful,' wrote to Simák b. 'Ubayd, the governor of Ctesiphon, as follows: "We call you to the Book of God Almighty and Glorious, and to the *Sunna* (custom) of the Prophet—on whom be peace!—and to the administration of Abú Bakr and 'Umar—may God be well pleased with them!—and to renounce 'Uthmán and 'Alí because they corrupted the true religion and abandoned the authority of the Book."[3] From this it appears that the Khárijite programme was simply the old Islam of equality and fraternity, which had never been fully realised and was now irretrievably ruined. Theoretically, all devout Moslems shared in the desire for its restoration and condemned the existing Government no less cordially than did the Khárijites. What distinguished the latter party was the remorseless severity with which they carried their principles into action. To them it was absolutely vital that the Imám, or head of the com-

[1] Wellhausen, *Die religiös-politischen Oppositionsparteien im alten Islam* (*Abhandlungen der Königl. Gesellschaft der Wissenschaften zu Göttingen, Phil.-Hist. Klasse,* 1901), p. 8 sqq. The writer argues against Brünnow that the oldest Khárijites were not true Bedouins (*A'rábí*), and were, in fact, even further removed than the rest of the military colonists of Kúfa and Baṣra from their Bedouin traditions. He points out that the extreme piety of the Readers—their constant prayers, vigils, and repetitions of the Koran—exactly agrees with what is related of the Khárijites, and is described in similar language. Moreover, among the oldest Khárijites we find mention made of a company clad in long cloaks (*baránis*, pl. of *burnus*), which were at that time a special mark of asceticism. Finally, the earliest authority (Abú Mikhnaf in Ṭabarí, i, 3330, l. 6 sqq.) regards the Khárijites as an offshoot from the Readers, and names individual Readers who afterwards became rabid Khárijites.

[2] Later, when many non-Arab Moslems joined the Khárijite ranks the field of choice was extended so as to include foreigners and even slaves.

[3] Ṭabarí, ii, 40, 13 sqq.

munity, should rule in the name and according to the will of God: those who followed any other sealed their doom in the next world: eternal salvation hung upon the choice of a successor to the Prophet. Moslems who refused to execrate 'Uthmán and 'Alí were the worst of infidels; it was the duty of every true believer to take part in the Holy War against such, and to kill them, together with their wives and children. These atrocities recoiled upon the insurgents, who soon found themselves in danger of extermination. Milder counsels began to prevail. Thus the Ibáḍites (followers of 'Abdulláh b. Ibáḍ) held it lawful to live amongst the Moslems and mix with them on terms of mutual tolerance. But compromise was in truth incompatible with the *raison d'être* of the Khárijites, namely, to establish the kingdom of God upon the earth. This meant virtual anarchy: "their unbending logic shattered every constitution which it set up." As 'Alí remarked, "they say, 'No government' (*lá imára*), but there must be a government, good or bad."[1] Nevertheless, it was a noble ideal for which they fought in pure devotion, having, unlike the other political parties, no worldly interests to serve.

The same fierce spirit of fanaticism moulded their religious views, which were gloomy and austere, as befitted the chosen few in an ungodly world. Shahrastání, speaking of the original twelve thousand who rebelled against 'Alí, describes them as 'people of fasting and prayer' (*ahlu ṣiyám^in wa-ṣalát^in*).[2] The Koran ruled their lives and possessed their imaginations, so that the history of the early Church, the persecutions, martyrdoms, and triumphs of the Faith became a veritable drama which was being enacted by themselves. The fear of hell kindled in them an inquisitorial zeal for righteousness. They scrupulously examined their own belief as well as that of their neighbours, and woe to him that was found wanting! A

Their religion.

[1] Shahrastání, ed. by Cureton, Part I, p. 88, l. 12.

[2] *Ibid.*, p. 86, l. 3 from foot.

single false step involved excommunication from the pale of Islam, and though the slip might be condoned on proof of sincere repentance, any Moslem who had once committed a mortal sin (*kabîra*) was held, by the stricter Khárijites at least, to be inevitably damned with the infidels in everlasting fire.

Much might be written, if space allowed, concerning the wars of the Khárijites, their most famous chiefs, the points on which they quarrelled, and the sects into which they split. Here we can only attempt to illustrate the general character of the movement. We have touched on its political and religious aspects, and shall now conclude with some reference to its literary side. The Khárijites did not produce a Milton or a Bunyan, but as Arabs of Bedouin stock they had a natural gift of song, from which they could not be weaned; although, according to the strict letter of the Koran, poetry is a devilish invention improper for the pious Moslem to meddle with. But these are poems of a different order from the pagan odes, and breathe a stern religious enthusiasm that would have gladdened the Prophet's heart. Take, for example, the following verses, which were made by a Khárijite in prison:—[1]

Khárijite poetry.

"'Tis time, O ye Sellers, for one who hath sold himself
To God, that he should arise and saddle amain.
Fools! in the land of miscreants will ye abide,
To be hunted down, every man of you, and to be slain?
O would that I were among you, armèd in mail,
On the back of my stout-ribbed galloping war-horse again!
And would that I were among you, fighting your foes,
That me, first of all, they might give death's beaker to drain!
It grieves me sore that ye are startled and chased
Like beasts, while I cannot draw on the wretches profane
My sword, nor see them scattered by noble knights
Who never yield an inch of the ground they gain,

[1] Ṭabarí, ii, 36, ll. 7, 8, 11–16.

But where the struggle is hottest, with keen blades hew
Their strenuous way and deem 'twere base to refrain.
Ay, it grieves me sore that ye are oppressed and wronged,
While I must drag in anguish a captive's chain."

Qaṭarí b. al-Fujá'a, the intrepid Khárijite leader who routed army after army sent against him by Ḥajjáj, sang almost as well as he fought. The verses rendered below are included in the *Ḥamása*[1] and cited by Ibn Khallikán, who declares that they would make a brave man of the greatest coward in the world. "I know of nothing on the subject to be compared with them; they could only have proceeded from a spirit that scorned disgrace and from a truly Arabian sentiment of valour."[2]

Qaṭarí b. al-Fujá'a.

"I say to my soul dismayed—
'Courage! Thou canst not achieve,
With praying, an hour of life
Beyond the appointed term.
Then courage on death's dark field,
Courage! Impossible 'tis
To live for ever and aye.
Life is no hero's robe
Of honour: the dastard vile
Also doffs it at last.'"

The murder of 'Uthmán broke the Moslem community, which had hitherto been undivided, into two *shí'as*, or parties —one for 'Alí and the other for Mu'áwiya. When the latter became Caliph he was no longer a party leader, but head of the State, and his *shí'a* ceased to exist. Henceforth 'the Shí'a' *par excellence* was the party of 'Alí, which regarded the House of the Prophet as the legitimate heirs to the succession. Not content, however, with uphold-

The Shí'ites.

[1] *Ḥamása*, 44.
[2] Ibn Khallikán, ed. by Wüstenfeld, No. 555, p. 55, l. 4 seq.; De Slane's translation, vol. ii, p. 523.

ing 'Alí, as the worthiest of the Prophet's Companions and the duly elected Caliph, against his rival, Mu'áwiya, the bolder spirits took up an idea, which emerged about this time, that the Caliphate belonged to 'Alí and his descendants by Divine right. Such is the distinctive doctrine of the Shí'ites to the present day. It is generally thought to have originated in Persia, where the Sásánian kings used to assume the title of 'god' (Pahlaví *bagh*) and were looked upon as successive incarnations of the Divine majesty.

The theory of Divine Right.

"Although the Shí'ites," says Dozy, "often found themselves under the direction of Arab leaders, who utilised them in order to gain some personal end, they were nevertheless a Persian sect at bottom; and it is precisely here that the difference most clearly showed itself between the Arab race, which loves liberty, and the Persian race, accustomed to slavish submission. For the Persians, the principle of electing the Prophet's successor was something unheard of and incomprehensible. The only principle which they recognised was that of inheritance, and since Muḥammad left no sons, they thought that his son-in-law 'Alí should have succeeded him, and that the sovereignty was hereditary in his family. Consequently, all the Caliphs except 'Alí—*i.e.*, Abú Bakr, 'Umar, and 'Uthmán, as well as the Umayyads—were in their eyes usurpers to whom no obedience was due. The hatred which they felt for the Government and for Arab rule confirmed them in this opinion; at the same time they cast covetous looks on the wealth of their masters. Habituated, moreover, to see in their kings the descendants of the inferior divinities, they transferred this idolatrous veneration to 'Alí and his posterity. Absolute obedience to the Imám of 'Alí's House was in their eyes the most important duty; if that were fulfilled all the rest might be interpreted allegorically and violated without scruple. For them the Imám was everything; he was God made man. A servile submission accompanied by immorality was the basis of their system."[1]

Dozy's account of its origin.

[1] Dozy, *Essai sur l'histoire de l'Islamisme* (French translation by Victor Chauvin), p. 219 sqq.

Now, the Shí'ite theory of Divine Right certainly harmonised with Persian ideas, but was it also of Persian origin? On the contrary, it seems first to have arisen among an obscure Arabian sect, the Saba'ites, whose founder, 'Abdulláh b. Sabá (properly, Saba'), was a native of Ṣan'á in Yemen, and is said to have been a Jew.[1] In 'Uthmán's time he turned Moslem and became, apparently, a travelling missionary. "He went from place to place," says the historian, "seeking to lead the Moslems into error."[2] We hear of him in the Ḥijáz, then in Baṣra and Kúfa, then in Syria. Finally he settled in Egypt, where he preached the doctrine of palingenesis (*raj'a*). "It is strange indeed," he exclaimed, "that any one should believe in the return of Jesus (as Messias), and deny the return of Muḥammad, which God has announced (Kor. xxviii, 85).[3] Furthermore, there are a thousand Prophets, every one of whom has an executor (*waṣí*), and the executor of Muḥammad is 'Alí.[4] Muḥammad is the last of the Prophets, and 'Alí is the last of the executors." Ibn Sabá, therefore, regarded Abú Bakr, 'Umar, and 'Uthmán as usurpers. He set on foot a widespread conspiracy in favour of 'Alí, and carried on a secret correspondence with the disaffected in various provinces of the Empire.[5] According

The Saba'ites.

Doctrine of Ibn Sabá.

[1] Wellhausen thinks that the dogmatics of the Shí'ites are derived from Jewish rather than from Persian sources. See his account of the Saba'ites in his most instructive paper, to which I have already referred, *Die religiös-politischen Oppositionsparteien im alten Islam* (*Abh. der König. Ges. der Wissenschaften zu Göttingen, Phil.-Hist. Klasse*, 1901), p. 89 sqq.

[2] Ṭabarí, i, 2942, 2.

[3] "*Verily, He who hath ordained the Koran for thee* (*i.e.*, for Muḥammad) *will bring thee back to a place of return*" (*i.e.*, to Mecca). The ambiguity of the word meaning 'place of return' (*ma'ád*) gave some colour to Ibn Sabá's contention that it alluded to the return of Muḥammad at the end of the world. The descent of Jesus on earth is reckoned by Moslems among the greater signs which will precede the Resurrection.

[4] This is a Jewish idea. 'Alí stands in the same relation to Muḥammad as Aaron to Moses.

[5] Ṭabarí, *loc. cit.*

to Shahrastání, he was banished by 'Alí for saying, "Thou art thou" (*anta anta*), *i.e.*, "Thou art God."[1] This refers to the doctrine taught by Ibn Sabá and the extreme Shí'ites (*Ghulát*) who derive from him, that the Divine Spirit which dwells in every prophet and passes successively from one to another was transfused, at Muḥammad's death, into 'Alí, and from 'Alí into his descendants who succeeded him in the Imámate. The Saba'ites also held that the Imám might suffer a temporary occultation (*ghayba*), but that one day he would return and fill the earth with justice. They believed the millennium to be near at hand, so that the number of Imáms was at first limited to four. Thus the poet Kuthayyir († 723 A.D.) says:—

"Four complete are the Imáms of Quraysh, the lords of Right:
'Alí and his three good sons, each of them a shining light.
One was faithful and devout; Karbalá hid one from sight;
One, until with waving flags his horsemen he shall lead to fight,
Dwells on Mount Raḍwá, concealed: honey he drinks and water bright."[2]

The Messianic idea is not peculiar to the Shí'ites, but was brought into Islam at an early period by Jewish and Christian converts, and soon established itself as a part of Muḥammadan belief. Traditions ascribed to the Prophet began to circulate, declaring that the approach of the Last Judgment would be heralded by a time of tumult and confusion, by the return of Jesus, who would slay the Antichrist (*al-Dajjál*), and finally by the coming of the Mahdí, *i.e.*, 'the God-guided one,' who would fill the earth with justice even as it was then filled with violence and iniquity. This expectation of a Deliverer descended from the

The Mahdí, or Messiah.

[1] Shahrastáni, ed. by Cureton, p. 132, l. 15.
[2] *Aghání*, viii, 32, l. 17 sqq. The three sons of 'Alí are Ḥasan, Ḥusayn, and Muḥammad Ibnu 'l-Ḥanafiyya.

Prophet runs through the whole history of the Shí'a. As we have seen, their supreme religious chiefs were the Imáms of 'Alí's House, each of whom transmitted his authority to his successor. In the course of time disputes arose as to the succession. One sect acknowledged only seven legitimate Imáms, while another carried the number to twelve. The last Imám of the 'Seveners' (*al-Sab'iyya*), who are commonly called Ismá'ílís, was Muḥammad b. Ismá'íl, and of the 'Twelvers' (*al-Ithná-'ashariyya*) Muḥammad b. al-Ḥasan.[1] Both those personages vanished mysteriously about 770 and 870 A.D., and their respective followers, refusing to believe that they were dead, asserted that their Imám had withdrawn himself for a season from mortal sight, but that he would surely return at last as the promised Mahdí. It would take a long while to enumerate all the pretenders and fanatics who have claimed this title.[2] Two of them founded the Fáṭimid and Almohade dynasties, which we shall mention elsewhere, but they generally died on the gibbet or the battle-field. The ideal which they, so to speak, incarnated did not perish with them. Mahdiism, the faith in a divinely appointed revolution which will sweep away the powers of evil and usher in a Golden Age of justice and truth such as the world has never known, is a present and inspiring fact which deserves to be well weighed by those who doubt the possibility of an Islamic Reformation.

The Shí'a began as a political faction, but it could not remain so for any length of time, because in Islam politics always tend to take religious ground, just as the successful religious reformer invariably becomes a ruler. The Saba'ites furnished the Shí'ite movement with a theological basis; and

[1] Concerning the origin of these sects see Professor Browne's *Lit. Hist. of Persia*, vol. i, p. 295 seq.

[2] See Darmesteter's interesting essay, *Le Mahdi depuis les origines de l'Islam jusqu'à nos jours* (Paris, 1885). The subject is treated more scientifically by Snouck Hurgronje in his paper *Der Mahdi*, reprinted from the *Revue coloniale internationale* (1886).

the massacre of Ḥusayn, followed by Mukhtár's rebellion, supplied the indispensable element of enthusiasm. Within a few years after the death of Ḥusayn his grave at Karbalá was already a place of pilgrimage for the Shí'ites. When the 'Penitents' (*al-Tawwábún*) revolted in 684 they repaired thither and lifted their voices simultaneously in a loud wail, and wept, and prayed God that He would forgive them for having deserted the Prophet's grandson in his hour of need. "O God!" exclaimed their chief, "have mercy on Ḥusayn, the Martyr and the son of a Martyr, the Mahdí and the son of a Mahdí, the Ṣiddíq and the son of a Ṣiddíq![1] O God! we bear witness that we follow their religion and their path, and that we are the foes of their slayers and the friends of those who love them."[2] Here is the germ of the *ta'ziyas*, or Passion Plays, which are acted every year on the 10th of Muḥarram, wherever Shí'ites are to be found.

Shí'ite gatherings at Karbalá.

But the Moses of the Shí'a, the man who showed them the way to victory although he did not lead them to it, is undoubtedly Mukhtár. He came forward in the name of 'Alí's son, Muḥammad, generally known as Ibnu 'l-Ḥanafiyya after his mother. Thus he gained the support of the Arabian Shí'ites, properly so called, who were devoted to 'Alí and his House, and laid no stress upon the circumstance of descent from the Prophet, whereas the Persian adherents of the Shí'a made it a vital matter, and held accordingly that only the sons of 'Alí by his wife Fáṭima were fully qualified Imáms. Raising the cry of vengeance for Ḥusayn, Mukhtár carried this party also along with him. In 686 he found himself master of Kúfa. Neither the result of his triumph nor the rapid overthrow of his power concerns us

Mukhtár.

[1] *Ṣiddíq* means 'veracious.' Professor Bevan remarks that in this root the notion of 'veracity' easily passes into that of 'endurance,' 'fortitude.'

[2] Ṭabarí, ii, 546. These 'Penitents' were free Arabs of Kúfa, a fact which, as Wellhausen has noticed, would seem to indicate that the *ta'ziya* is Semitic in origin.

here, but something must be said about the aims and character of the movement which he headed.

"More than half the population of Kúfa was composed of *Mawálí* (Clients), who monopolised handicraft, trade, and commerce. They were mostly Persians in race and language; they had come to Kúfa as prisoners of war and had there passed over to Islam: then they were manumitted by their owners and received as clients into the Arab tribes, so that they now occupied an ambiguous position (*Zwitterstellung*), being no longer slaves, but still very dependent on their patrons; needing their protection, bound to their service, and forming their retinue in peace and war. In these *Mawálí*, who were entitled by virtue of Islam to more than the 'dominant Arabism' allowed them, the hope now dawned of freeing themselves from clientship and of rising to full and direct participation in the Moslem state."[1]

The *Mawálí* of Kúfa.

Mukhtár, though himself an Arab of noble family, trusted the *Mawálí* and treated them as equals, a proceeding which was bitterly resented by the privileged class. "You have taken away our clients who are the booty which God bestowed upon us together with this country. We emancipated them, hoping to receive the Divine recompense and reward, but you would not rest until you made them sharers in our booty."[2] Mukhtár was only giving the *Mawálí* their due—they were Moslems and had the right, as such, to a share in the revenues. To the haughty Arabs, however, it appeared a monstrous thing that the despised foreigners should be placed on the same level with themselves. Thus Mukhtár was thrown into the arms of the *Mawálí*, and the movement now became not so much anti-Umayyad as anti-Arabian. Here is the turning-point in the history of the Shí'a. Its ranks were swelled by thousands of Persians imbued with the extreme doctrines of the Saba'ites which have been

Mukhtár and the *Mawálí*.

Persian influence on the Shí'a.

[1] Wellhausen, *Die religiös-politischen Oppositionsparteien*, p. 79.

[2] Ṭabarí, ii, 650, l. 7 sqq.

sketched above, and animated by the intense hatred of a down-trodden people towards their conquerors and oppressors. Consequently the Shí'a assumed a religious and enthusiastic character, and struck out a new path which led it farther and farther from the orthodox creed. The doctrine of 'Interpretation' (*Ta'wíl*) opened the door to all sorts of extravagant ideas. One of the principal Shí'ite sects, the Háshimiyya, held that "there is an esoteric side to everything external, a spirit to every form, a hidden meaning (*ta'wíl*) to every revelation, and to every similitude in this world a corresponding reality in the other world; that 'Alí united in his own person the knowledge of all mysteries and communicated it to his son Muḥammad Ibnu 'l-Ḥanafiyya, who passed it on to his son Abú Háshim; and that the possessor of this universal knowledge is the true Imám."[1] So, without ceasing to be Moslems in name, the Shí'ites transmuted Islam into whatever shape they pleased by virtue of a mystical interpretation based on the infallible authority of the House of Muḥammad, and out of the ruins of a political party there gradually arose a great religious organisation in which men of the most diverse opinions could work together for deliverance from the Umayyad yoke. The first step towards this development was made by Mukhtár, a versatile genius who seems to have combined the parts of political adventurer, social reformer, prophet, and charlatan. He was crushed and his Persian allies were decimated, but the seed which he had sown bore an abundant harvest when, sixty years later, Abú Muslim unfurled the black standard of the 'Abbásids in Khurásán.

Concerning the origin of the oldest theological sects in Islam, the Murjites and the Mu'tazilites, we possess too little contemporary evidence to make a positive statement. It is probable that the latter at any rate arose, as Von Kremer has suggested, under the influence of Greek theologians,

[1] Shahrastání, Haarbrücker's translation, Part I, p. 169.

especially John of Damascus and his pupil, Theodore Abucara (Abú Qurra), the Bishop of Ḥarrán.[1] Christians were freely admitted to the Umayyad court. The Christian al-Akhṭal was poet-laureate, while many of his co-religionists held high offices in the Government. Moslems and Christians exchanged ideas in friendly discussion or controversially. Armed with the hair-splitting weapons of Byzantine theology, which they soon learned to use only too well, the Arabs proceeded to try their edge on the dogmas of Islam.

The oldest theological sects.

The leading article of the Murjite creed was this, that no one who professed to believe in the One God could be declared an infidel, whatever sins he might commit, until God Himself had given judgment against him.[2] The Murjites were so called because they deferred (*arja'a* = to defer) their decision in such cases and left the sinner's fate in suspense, so long as it was doubtful.[3] This principle they applied in different ways. For example, they refused to condemn 'Alí and 'Uthmán outright, as the Khárijites did. "Both 'Alí and 'Uthmán," they said, "were servants of God, and by God alone must they be judged; it is not for us to pronounce either of them an infidel, notwithstanding that they rent the Moslem people asunder."[4] On the other hand, the Murjites equally rejected the pretensions

The Murjites.

[1] Von Kremer, *Culturgeschicht. Streifzüge*, p. 2 sqq.

[2] The best account of the early Murjites that has hitherto appeared is contained in a paper by Van Vloten, entitled *Irdjâ* (*Z.D.M.G.*, vol. 45, p. 161 sqq.). The reader may also consult Shahrastání, Haarbrücker's trans., Part I, p. 156 sqq.; Goldziher, *Muhammedanische Studien*, Part II, p. 89 sqq.; Van Vloten, *La domination Arabe*, p. 31 seq.

[3] Van Vloten thinks that in the name 'Murjite' (*murji'*) there is an allusion to Koran, ix, 107: "*And others are remanded* (*murjawna*) *until God shall decree; whether He shall punish them or take pity on them—for God is knowing and wise.*"

[4] *Cf.* the poem of Thábit Quṭna (*Z.D.M.G.*, *loc. cit.*, p. 162), which states the whole Murjite doctrine in popular form. The author, who was himself a Murjite, lived in Khurásán during the latter half of the first century A.H.

made by the Shí'ites on behalf of 'Alí and by the Umayyads on behalf of Mu'áwiya. For the most part they maintained a neutral attitude towards the Umayyad Government: they were passive resisters, content, as Wellhausen puts it, "to stand up for the impersonal Law." Sometimes, however, they turned the principle of toleration against their rulers. Thus Ḥárith b. Surayj and other Arabian Murjites joined the oppressed *Mawálí* of Khurásán to whom the Government denied those rights which they had acquired by conversion.[1] According to the Murjite view, these Persians, having professed Islam, should no longer be treated as tax-paying infidels. The Murjites brought the same tolerant spirit into religion. They set faith above works, emphasised the love and goodness of God, and held that no Moslem would be damned everlastingly. Some, like Jahm b. Ṣafwán, went so far as to declare that faith (*ímán*) was merely an inward conviction: a man might openly profess Christianity or Judaism or any form of unbelief without ceasing to be a good Moslem, provided only that he acknowledged Allah with his heart.[2] The moderate school found their most illustrious representative in Abú Ḥanífa († 767 A.D.), and through this great divine—whose followers to-day are counted by millions—their liberal doctrines were diffused and perpetuated.

During the Umayyad period Baṣra was the intellectual capital of Islam, and in that city we find the first traces of a sect which maintained the principle that thought must be free in the search for truth. The origin of the Mu'tazilites (*al-Mu'tazila*), as they are generally called, takes us back to the famous divine and ascetic, Ḥasan of Baṣra (†728 A.D.). One day he was asked to give his opinion on a point regarding which the Murjites and the Khárijites held opposite views, namely, whether those who had committed

The Mu'tazilites.

[1] Van Vloten, *La domination Arabe*, p. 29 sqq.

[2] Ibn Ḥazm, cited in *Z.D.M.G.*, vol. 45, p. 169, n. 7. Jahm († about 747 A.D.) was a Persian, as might be inferred from the boldness of his speculations.

a great sin should be deemed believers or unbelievers. While Ḥasan was considering the question, one of his pupils, Wáṣil b. 'Aṭá (according to another tradition, 'Amr b. 'Ubayd) replied that such persons were neither believers nor unbelievers, but should be ranked in an intermediate state. He then turned aside and began to explain the grounds of his assertion to a group which gathered about him in a different part of the mosque. Ḥasan said: "Wáṣil has separated himself from us" (*i'tazala 'anná*); and on this account the followers of Wáṣil were named 'Mu'tazilites,' *i.e.*, Schismatics. Although the story may not be literally true, it is probably safe to assume that the new sect originated in Baṣra among the pupils of Ḥasan,[1] who was the life and soul of the religious movement of the first century A.H. The Mu'tazilite heresy, in its earliest form, is connected with the doctrine of Predestination. On this subject the Koran speaks with two voices. Muḥammad was anything but a logically exact and consistent thinker. He was guided by the impulse of the moment, and neither he nor his hearers perceived, as later Moslems did, that the language of the Koran is often contradictory. Thus in the present instance texts which imply the moral responsibility of man for his actions—*e.g.*, "*Every soul is in pledge* (with God) *for what it hath wrought*"[2]; "*Whoso does good benefits himself, and whoso does evil does it against himself*"[3]—stand side by side with others which declare that God leads men aright or astray, as He pleases; that the hearts of the wicked are sealed and their ears made deaf to the truth; and that they are certainly doomed to perdition. This fatalistic view prevailed in the first century of Islam, and the dogma of Predestination was almost universally accepted. Ibn Qutayba,

[1] Ḥasan himself inclined for a time to the doctrine of free-will, but afterwards gave it up (Ibn Qutayba, *Kitábu 'l-Ma'árif*, p. 225). He is said to have held that everything happens by fate, except sin (*Al-Mu'tazilah*, ed. by T. W. Arnold, p. 12, l. 3 from foot). See, however, Shahrastání, Haarbrücker's trans., Part I, p. 46.

[2] Koran, lxxiv, 41.

[3] *Ibid.*, xli, 46.

however, mentions the names of twenty-seven persons who held the opinion that men's actions are free.[1] Two among them, Ma'bad al-Juhaní and Abú Marwán Ghaylán, who were put to death by 'Abdu 'l-Malik and his son Hishám, do not appear to have been condemned as heretics, but rather as enemies of the Umayyad Government.[2] The real founder of the Mu'tazilites was Wáṣil b. 'Aṭá († 748 A.D.),[3] who added a second cardinal doctrine to that of free-will. He denied the existence of the Divine attributes—Power, Wisdom, Life, &c.—on the ground that such qualities, if conceived as eternal, would destroy the Unity of God. Hence the Mu'tazilites called themselves 'the partisans of Unity and Justice' (*Ahlu 'l-tawḥíd wa-'l-'adl*): of Unity for the reason which has been explained, and of Justice, because they held that God was not the author of evil and that He would not punish His creatures except for actions within their control. The further development of these Rationalistic ideas belongs to the 'Abbásid period and will be discussed in a subsequent chapter.

Growth of asceticism.

The founder of Islam had too much human nature and common sense to demand of his countrymen such mortifying austerities as were practised by the Jewish Essenes and the Christian monks. His religion was not without ascetic features, *e.g.*, the Fast of Ramaḍán, the prohibition of wine, and the ordinance of the pilgrimage, but these can scarcely be called unreasonable. On the other hand Muḥammad condemned celibacy not only by his personal

[1] *Kitábu 'l-Ma'árif*, p. 301. Those who held the doctrine of free-will were called the Qadarites (*al-Qadariyya*), from *qadar* (power), which may denote (1) the power of God to determine human actions, and (2) the power of man to determine his own actions. Their opponents asserted that men act under compulsion (*jabr*); hence they were called the Jabarites (*al-Jabariyya*).

[2] As regards Ghaylán see *Al-Mu'tazilah*, ed. by T. W. Arnold, p. 15, l. 16 sqq.

[3] Ibn Khallikán, De Slane's translation, vol. iii, p. 642; Shahrastání, trans. by Haarbrücker, Part I, p. 44.

example but also by precept. "There is no monkery in Islam," he is reported to have said, and there was in fact nothing of the kind for more than a century after his death. During this time, however, asceticism made great strides. It was the inevitable outcome of the Muḥammadan conception of Allah, in which the attributes of mercy and love are overshadowed by those of majesty, awe, and vengeance. The terrors of Judgment Day so powerfully described in the Koran were realised with an intensity of conviction which it is difficult for us to imagine. As Goldziher has observed, an exaggerated consciousness of sin and the dread of Divine punishment gave the first impulse to Moslem asceticism. Thus we read that Tamím al-Dárí, one of the Prophet's Companions, who was formerly a Christian, passed the whole night until daybreak, repeating a single verse of the Koran (xlv, 20)—"*Do those who work evil think that We shall make them even as those who believe and do good, so that their life and death shall be equal? Ill do they judge!*"[1] Abu 'l-Dardá, another of the Companions, used to say: "If ye knew what ye shall see after death, ye would not eat food nor drink water from appetite, and I wish that I were a tree which is lopped and then devoured."[2] There were many who shared these views, and their determination to renounce the world and to live solely for God was strengthened by their disgust with a tyrannical and impious Government, and by the almost uninterrupted spectacle of bloodshed, rapine, and civil war. Ḥasan

Ḥasan of Baṣra.

of Baṣra (†728)—we have already met him in connection with the Mu'tazilites—is an outstanding figure in this early ascetic movement, which proceeded on orthodox lines.[3] Fear of God seized on him so mightily that, in the words of his biographer, "it seemed

[1] Sha'ráni, *Lawáqiḥu 'l-Anwár* (Cairo, 1299 A.H.), p. 31. [2] *Ibid.*

[3] See Von Kremer, *Herrschende Ideen*, p. 52 sqq.; Goldziher, *Materialien zur Entwickelungsgesch. des Súfismus* (*Vienna Oriental Journal*, vol. 13, p. 35 sqq.).

as though Hell-fire had been created for him alone."[1] All who looked on his face thought that he must have been recently overtaken by some great calamity.[2] One day a friend saw him weeping and asked him the cause. "I weep," he replied, "for fear that I have done something unwittingly and unintentionally, or committed some fault, or spoken some word which is unpleasing to God: then He may have said, 'Begone, for now thou hast no more honour in My court, and henceforth I will not receive anything from thee.'"[3] Al-Mubarrad relates that two monks, coming from Syria, entered Baṣra and looked at Ḥasan, whereupon one said to the other, "Let us turn aside to visit this man, whose way of life appears like that of the Messiah." So they went, and they found him supporting his chin on the palm of his hand, while he was saying—"How I marvel at those who have been ordered to lay in a stock of provisions and have been summoned to set out on a journey, and yet the foremost of them stays for the hindermost! Would that I knew what they are waiting for!"[4] The following utterances are characteristic:—

> "God hath made fasting a hippodrome (place or time of training) for His servants, that they may race towards obedience to Him.[5] Some come in first and win the prize, while others are left behind and return disappointed; and by my life, if the lid were removed, the well-doer would be diverted by his well-doing, and the evil-doer by his evil-doing, from wearing new garments or from anointing his hair."[6]

---

[1] Sha'rání, *Lawáqiḥ*, p. 38.

[2] Qushayrí's *Risála* (1287 A.H.), p. 77, l. 10.

[3] *Tadhkiratu 'l-Awliyá* of Farídu'ddín 'Aṭṭár, Part I, p. 37, l. 8 of my edition.

[4] *Kámil* (ed. by Wright), p. 57, l. 16.

[5] The point of this metaphor lies in the fact that Arab horses were put on short commons during the period of training, which usually began forty days before the race.

[6] *Kámil*, p. 57, last line.

"You meet one of them with white skin and delicate complexion, speeding along the path of vanity: he shaketh his hips and clappeth his sides and saith, 'Here am I, recognise me!' Yes, we recognise thee, and thou art hateful to God and hateful to good men." [1]

"The bounties of God are too numerous to be acknowledged unless with His help, and the sins of Man are too numerous for him to escape therefrom unless God pardon them." [2]

"The wonder is not how the lost were lost, but how the saved were saved." [3]

"Cleanse ye these hearts (by meditation and remembrance of God), for they are quick to rust; and restrain ye these souls, for they desire eagerly, and if ye restrain them not, they will drag you to an evil end." [4]

Ḥasan of Baṣra not a genuine Ṣúfí.

The Ṣúfís, concerning whom we shall say a few words presently, claim Ḥasan as one of themselves, and with justice in so far as he attached importance to spiritual righteousness, and was not satisfied with merely external acts of devotion. "A grain of genuine piety," he declared, "is better than a thousandfold weight of fasting and prayer." [5] But although some of his sayings which are recorded in the later biographies lend colour to the fiction that he was a full-blown Ṣúfí, there can be no doubt that his mysticism—if it deserves that name—was of the most moderate type, entirely lacking the glow and exaltation which we find in the saintly woman, Rábi'a al-'Adawiyya, with whom legend associates him.[6]

The origin of the name 'Súfí' is explained by the Ṣúfís themselves in many different ways, but of the derivations

[1] *Kámil*, p. 58, l. 14. [2] *Ibid.*, p. 67, l. 9.
[3] *Ibid.*, p. 91, l. 14. [4] *Ibid.*, p. 120, l. 4.
[5] Qushayrí's *Risála*, p. 63, last line.
[6] It is noteworthy that Qushayrí († 1073 A.D.), one of the oldest authorities on Ṣúfiism, does not include Ḥasan among the Ṣúfí Shaykhs whose biographies are given in the *Risála* (pp. 8–35), and hardly mentions him above half a dozen times in the course of his work. The sayings of Ḥasan which he cites are of the same character as those preserved in the *Kámil*.

which have been proposed only three possess any claim to consideration, viz., those which connect it with σοφός (wise) or with *ṣafá* (purity) or with *ṣúf* (wool).[1] The first two are inadmissible on linguistic grounds, into which we need not enter, though it may be remarked that the derivation from *ṣafá* is consecrated by the authority of the Ṣúfí Saints, and is generally accepted in the East.[2] The reason for this preference appears in such definitions as "The Ṣúfí is he who keeps his heart pure (*ṣáfí*) with God,"[3] "Ṣúfiism is 'the being chosen for purity' (*iṣṭifá*): whoever is thus chosen and made pure from all except God is the true Ṣúfí."[4] Understood in this sense, the word had a lofty significance which commended it to the elect. Nevertheless it can be tracked to a quite humble source. Woollen garments were frequently worn by men of ascetic life in the early times of Islam in order (as Ibn Khaldún says) that they might distinguish themselves from those who affected a more luxurious fashion of dress. Hence the name 'Súfí,' which denotes in the first instance an ascetic clad in wool (*ṣúf*), just as the Capuchins owed their designation to the hood (*cappuccio*) which they wore. According to Qushayrí, the term came into common use before the end of the second century of the Hijra (=815 A.D.). By this time, however, the ascetic movement in Islam had to some extent assumed a new character, and the meaning of 'Ṣúfí,' if the word already existed, must have undergone a corresponding change. It seems to me not unlikely that the epithet in question marks the point of

The derivation of 'Ṣúfí.'

[1] See Nöldeke's article, 'Ṣúfí,' in *Z.D.M.G.*, vol. 48, p. 45.

[2] An allusion to *ṣafá* occurs in thirteen out of the seventy definitions of Ṣúfí and Ṣúfiism (*Taṣawwuf*) which are contained in the *Tadhkiratu 'l-Awliyá*, or 'Memoirs of the Saints,' of the well-known Persian mystic, Farídu'ddín 'Aṭṭár († *circa* 1230 A.D.), whereas *ṣúf* is mentioned only twice.

[3] Said by Bishr al-Ḥáfí (the bare-footed), who died in 841–842 A.D.

[4] Said by Junayd of Baghdád († 909–910 A.D.), one of the most celebrated Ṣúfí Shaykhs.

departure from orthodox asceticism and that, as Jámí states, it was first applied to Abú Háshim of Kúfa (*ob.* before 800 A.D.), who founded a monastery (*khánaqáh*) for Ṣúfís at Ramla in Palestine. Be that as it may, the distinction between asceticism (*zuhd*) and Ṣúfiism—a distinction which answers, broadly speaking, to the *via purgativa* and the *via illuminativa* of Western mediæval mysticism—begins to show itself before the close of the Umayyad period, and rapidly develops in the early 'Abbásid age under the influence of foreign ideas and, in particular, of Greek philosophy. Leaving this later development to be discussed in a subsequent chapter, we shall now briefly consider the origin of Ṣúfiism properly so called and the first manifestation of the peculiar tendencies on which it is based.

The beginnings of Ṣúfiism.

As regards its origin, we cannot do better than quote the observations with which Ibn Khaldún († 1406 A.D.) introduces the chapter on Ṣúfiism in the Prolegomena to his great historical work :—

Ibn Khaldún's account of the origin of Ṣúfiism.

"This is one of the religious sciences which were born in Islam. The way of the Ṣúfís was regarded by the ancient Moslems and their illustrious men—the Companions of the Prophet (*al-Ṣaḥába*), the Successors (*al-Tábi'ún*), and the generation which came after them—as the way of Truth and Salvation. To be assiduous in piety, to give up all else for God's sake, to turn away from worldly gauds and vanities, to renounce pleasure, wealth, and power, which are the general objects of human ambition, to abandon society and to lead in seclusion a life devoted solely to the service of God—these were the fundamental principles of Ṣúfiism which prevailed among the Companions and the Moslems of old time. When, however, in the second generation and afterwards worldly tastes became widely spread, and men no longer shrank from such contamination, those who made piety their aim were distinguished by the title of *Ṣúfís* or *Mutaṣawwifa* (aspirants to Súfiism).[1]

[1] Ibn Khaldún's *Muqaddima* (Beyrout, 1900), p. 467 = vol. iii, p. 85 seq. of the French translation by De Slane. The same things are said at greater

From this it is clear that Ṣúfiism, if not originally identical with the ascetic revolt of which, as we have seen, Ḥasan of Baṣra was the most conspicuous representative, at any rate arose out of that movement. It was not a speculative system, like the Mu'tazilite heresy, but a practical religion and rule of life. "We derived Ṣúfiism," said Junayd, "from fasting and taking leave of the world and breaking familiar ties and renouncing what men deem good; not from disputation" (*qíl wa-qál*).[1] The oldest Ṣúfís were ascetics and hermits, but they were also something more. They brought out the spiritual and mystical element in Islam, or brought it in, if they did not find it there already.

The earliest form of Ṣúfiism.

"Ṣúfiism," says Suhrawardí,[2] "is neither 'poverty' (*faqr*) nor asceticism (*zuhd*), but a term which comprehends the ideas of both, together with something besides. Without these superadded qualities a man is not a Ṣúfí, though he may be an ascetic (*záhid*) or a fakír (*faqír*). It is said that, notwithstanding the excellence of 'poverty,' the end thereof is only the beginning of Ṣúfiism." A little further on he explains the difference thus:—

The difference between asceticism and Ṣúfiism.

"The fakír holds fast to his 'poverty' and is profoundly convinced of its superior merit. He prefers it to riches because he longs for the Divine recompense of which his faith assures him . . . and whenever he contemplates the everlasting reward, he abstains from the fleeting joys of this world and embraces poverty and indigence and fears that if he should cease to be 'poor' he will lose both the merit and the prize. Now this is absolutely unsound according to the doctrine of the Ṣúfís, because he hopes for recompense and renounces the world on that account, whereas the Ṣúfí does not renounce it for the sake of promised rewards but, on the contrary,

---

length by Suhrawardí in his *'Awárifu 'l-Ma'árif* (printed on the margin of Ghazálí's *Iḥyá*, Cairo, 1289 A.H.), vol. i, p. 172 *et seqq*. *Cf.* also the passage from Qushayrí translated by Professor E. G. Browne on pp. 297–298 of vol. i. of his *Literary History of Persia*.

[1] Suhrawardí, *loc. cit.*, p. 136 seq. [2] *Loc. cit.*, p. 145.

for the sake of present 'states,' for he is the 'son of his time.' . . .[1] The theory that 'poverty' is the foundation of Ṣúfiism signifies that the diverse stages of Ṣúfiism are reached by the road of 'poverty'; it does not imply that the Ṣúfí is essentially a fakír."

The keynote of Ṣúfiism is disinterested, selfless devotion, in a word, Love. Though not wholly strange, this idea was very far from being familiar to pious Muḥammadans, who were more deeply impressed by the power and vengeance of God than by His goodness and mercy. The Koran generally represents Allah as a stern, unapproachable despot, requiring utter submission to His arbitrary will, but infinitely unconcerned with human feelings and aspirations. Such a Being could not satisfy the religious instinct, and the whole history of Ṣúfiism is a protest against the unnatural divorce between God and Man which this conception involves. Accordingly, I do not think that we need look beyond Islam for the origin of the Ṣúfí doctrines, although it would be a mistake not to recognise the part which Christian influence must have had in shaping their early development. The speculative character with which they gradually became imbued, and which in the course of time completely transformed them, was more or less latent during the Umayyad period and for nearly a century after the accession of the House of 'Abbás. The early Ṣúfís are still on orthodox ground: their relation to Islam is not unlike that of the mediæval Spanish mystics to the Roman Catholic Church. They attach extraordinary value to certain points in Muḥammad's teaching and emphasise them so as to leave the others almost a dead letter. They do not indulge in profound dialectic, but confine themselves to matters bearing on practical theology. Self-abandonment, rigorous self-mortification, fervid piety, and quietism carried to the verge of apathy form the main features of their creed.

The early Ṣúfís.

[1] *I.e.*, he yields himself unreservedly to the spiritual 'states' (*aḥwál*) which pass over him, according as God wills.

A full and vivid picture of early Ṣúfiism might be drawn from the numerous biographies in Arabic and Persian, which supply abundant details concerning the manner of life of these Muḥammadan Saints, and faithfully record their austerities, visions, miracles, and sayings. Here we have only space to add a few lines about the most important members of the group—Ibráhím b. Adham, Abú 'Alí Shaqíq, Fuḍayl b. 'Iyáḍ, and Rábi'a—all of whom died between the middle and end of the second century after the Hijra (767–815 A.D.). Ibráhím belonged to the royal family of Balkh. Forty scimitars of gold and forty maces of gold were borne in front of him and behind. One day, while hunting, he heard a voice which cried, "Awake! wert thou created for this?" He exchanged his splendid robes for the humble garb and felt cap of a shepherd, bade farewell to his kingdom, and lived for nine years in a cave near Naysábúr.[1] His customary prayer was, "O God, uplift me from the shame of disobedience to the glory of submission unto Thee!"

Ibráhím b. Adham.

"O God!" he said, "Thou knowest that the Eight Paradises are little beside the honour which Thou hast done unto me, and beside Thy love, and beside Thy giving me intimacy with the praise of Thy name, and beside the peace of mind which Thou hast given me when I meditate on Thy majesty." And again: "You will not attain to righteousness until you traverse six passes (*'aqabát*): the first is that you shut the door of pleasure and open the door of hardship; the second, that you shut the door of eminence and open the door of abasement; the third, that you shut the door of ease and open the door of affliction; the fourth, that you shut the door of sleep and open the door of wakefulness; the fifth, that you shut the door of riches and open the door of poverty; and the sixth, that you shut the door of expectation and open the door of making yourself ready for death."

---

[1] Possibly Ibráhím was one of the *Shikaftiyya* or 'Cave-dwellers' of Khurásán (*shikaft* means 'cave' in Persian), whom the people of Syria called *al-Jú'iyya*, *i.e.*, 'the Fasters.' See Suhrawardí, *loc. cit.*, p. 171.

Shaqíq, also of Balkh, laid particular stress on the duty of leaving one's self entirely in God's hands (*tawakkul*), a term which is practically synonymous with passivity; *e.g.*, the *mutawakkil* must make no effort to obtain even the barest livelihood, he must not ask for anything, nor engage in any trade: his business is with God alone. One of Shaqíq's sayings was, "Nine-tenths of devotion consist in flight from mankind, the remaining tenth in silence." Similarly, Fuḍayl b. 'Iyáḍ, a converted captain of banditti, declared that "to abstain for men's sake from doing anything is hypocrisy, while to do anything for men's sake is idolatry." It may be noticed as an argument against the Indian origin of Ṣúfiism that although the three Ṣúfís who have been mentioned were natives of Khurásán or Transoxania, and therefore presumably in touch with Buddhistic ideas, no trace can be found in their sayings of the doctrine of dying to self (*faná*), which plays a great part in subsequent Ṣúfiism, and which Von Kremer and others have identified with *Nirvána*. We now come to a more interesting personality, in whom the ascetic and quietistic type of Ṣúfiism is transfigured by emotion and begins clearly to reveal the direction of its next advance. Every one knows that women have borne a distinguished part in the annals of European mysticism: St. Teresa, Madame Guyon, Catharine of Siena, and Juliana of Norwich, to mention but a few names at random. And notwithstanding the intellectual death to which the majority of Moslem women are condemned by their Prophet's ordinance, the Ṣúfís, like the Roman Catholics, can boast a goodly number of female saints. The oldest of these, and by far the most renowned, is Rábi'a, who belonged to the tribe of 'Adí, whence she is generally called Rábi'a al-'Adawiyya. She was a native of Baṣra and died at Jerusalem, probably towards the end of the

Shaqíq of Balkh.

Fuḍayl b. 'Iyáḍ.

Rábi'a al-'Adawiyya.

second century of Islam: her tomb was an object of pilgrimage in the Middle Ages, as we learn from Ibn Khallikán († 1282 A.D.). Although the sayings and verses attributed to her by Ṣúfí writers may be of doubtful authenticity, there is every reason to suppose that they fairly represent the actual character of her devotion, which resembled that of all feminine mystics in being inspired by tender and ardent feeling. She was asked: "Do you love God Almighty?" "Yes." "Do you hate the Devil?" "My love of God," she replied, "leaves me no leisure to hate the Devil. I saw the Prophet in a dream. He said, 'O Rábi'a, do you love me?' I said, 'O Apostle of God, who does not love thee?—but love of God hath so absorbed me that neither love nor hate of any other thing remains in my heart.'" Rábi'a is said to have spoken the following verses:—

"Two ways I love Thee: selfishly,
And next, as worthy is of Thee.
'Tis selfish love that I do naught
Save think on Thee with every thought;
'Tis purest love when Thou dost raise
The veil to my adoring gaze.
Not mine the praise in that or this,
Thine is the praise in both, I wis."[1]

Whether genuine or not, these lines, with their mixture of devotion and speculation—the author distinguishes the illuminative from the contemplative life and manifestly regards the latter as the more excellent way—serve to mark the end of the ascetic school of Ṣúfiism and the rise of a new theosophy which, under the same name and still professing to be in full accord with the Koran and the *Sunna*, was founded to some extent upon ideas of extraneous origin—ideas irreconcilable with any revealed religion, and

[1] Ghazálí, *Iḥyá* (Cairo, 1289 A.H.), vol. iv, p. 298.

directly opposed to the severe and majestic simplicity of the Muḥammadan articles of faith.

Umayyad literature.

The opening century of Islam was not favourable to literature. At first conquest, expansion, and organisation, then civil strife absorbed the nation's energies; then, under the Umayyads, the old pagan spirit asserted itself once more. Consequently the literature of this period consists almost exclusively of poetry, which bears few marks of Islamic influence. I need scarcely refer to the view which long prevailed in Europe that Muḥammad corrupted the taste of his countrymen by setting up the Koran as an incomparable model of poetic style, and by condemning the admired productions of the heathen bards and the art of poetry itself; nor remind my readers that in the first place the Koran is not poetical in form (so that it could not serve as a model of this kind), and secondly, according to Muḥammadan belief, is the actual Word of God, therefore *sui generis* and beyond imitation. Again, the poets whom the Prophet condemned were his most dangerous opponents: he hated them not as poets but as propagators and defenders of false ideals, and because they ridiculed his teaching, while on the contrary he honoured and rewarded those who employed their talents in the right way. If the nomad minstrels and cavaliers who lived, as they sang, the free life of the desert were never equalled by the brilliant laureates of imperial Damascus and Baghdád, the causes of the decline cannot be traced to Muḥammad's personal attitude, but are due to various circumstances for which he is only responsible in so far as he founded a religious and political system that revolutionised Arabian society. The poets of the period with which we are now dealing follow slavishly in the footsteps of the ancients, as though Islam had never been. Instead of celebrating the splendid victories

The decline of Arabian poetry not due to Muḥammad.

and heroic deeds of Moslem warriors, the bard living in a great city still weeps over the relics of his beloved's encampment in the wilderness, still rides away through the sandy waste on the peerless camel, whose fine points he particularly describes; and if he should happen to be addressing the Caliph, it is ten to one that he will credit that august personage with all the virtues of a Bedouin Shaykh. "Fortunately the imitation of the antique *qaṣída*, at any rate with the greatest Umayyad poets, is to some extent only accessory to another form of art that excites our historical interest in a high degree: namely, the occasional poems (very numerous in almost all these writers), which are suggested by the mood of the moment and can shed a vivid light on contemporary history." [1]

The Umayyad poets.

The conquests made by the successors of the Prophet brought enormous wealth into Mecca and Medína, and when the Umayyad aristocracy gained the upper hand in 'Uthmán's Caliphate, these towns developed a voluptuous and dissolute life which broke through every restriction that Islam had imposed. The increase of luxury produced a corresponding refinement of the poetic art. Although music was not unknown to the pagan Arabs, it had hitherto been cultivated chiefly by foreigners, especially Greek and Persian singing-girls. But in the first century after the Hijra we hear of several Arab singers,[2] natives of Mecca and Medína, who set favourite passages to music: henceforth, the words and the melody are inseparably united, as we learn from the *Kitábu 'l-Aghání* or 'Book of Songs,' where hundreds of examples are to be found. Amidst the gay throng of pleasure-seekers women naturally played a prominent part, and love, which had

Music and song in the Holy Cities.

[1] Brockelmann, *Gesch. d. Arab. Litteratur*, vol. i, p. 45.

[2] *E.g.*, Ma'bad, Gharíḍ, Ibn Surayj, Ṭuways, and Ibn 'Á'isha.

hitherto formed in most cases merely the conventional prelude to an ode, now began to be sung for its own sake. In this Peninsular school, as it may be named in contrast with the bold and masculine strain of the great Provincial poets whom we are about to mention, the palm unquestionably belongs to 'Umar b. Abí Rabí'a († 719 A.D.), the son of a rich Meccan merchant. He passed the best part of his life in the pursuit of noble dames, who alone inspired him to sing. His poetry was so seductive that it was regarded by devout Moslems as "the greatest crime ever committed against God," and so charming withal that 'Abdulláh b. 'Abbás, the Prophet's cousin and a famous authority on the Koran and the Traditions, could not refrain from getting by heart some erotic verses which 'Umar recited to him.[1] The Arabs said, with truth, that the tribe of Quraysh had won distinction in every field save poetry, but we must allow that 'Umar b. Abí Rabí'a is a clear exception to this rule. His diction, like that of Catullus, has all the unaffected ease of refined conversation. Here are a few lines :—

'Umar b. Abí Rabí'a.

"Blame me no more, O comrades ! but to-day
Quietly with me beside the howdahs stay.
Blame not my love for Zaynab, for to her
And hers my heart is pledged a prisoner.
Ah, can I ever think of how we met
Once at al-Khayf, and feel no fond regret ?
My song of other women was but jest :
She reigns alone, eclipsing all the rest.
Hers is my love sincere, 'tis she the flame
Of passion kindles—so, a truce to blame ! "[2]

We have no space to dwell on the minor poets of the same school, al-'Arjí (a kinsman of the Umayyads), al-Aḥwaṣ, and many others. It has been pointed out by Dr. C. Brockelmann

[1] *Kámil* of Mubarrad, p. 570 sqq.
[2] *Aghání*, i, 43, l. 15 sqq. ; Nöldeke's *Delectus*, p. 17, last line and foll.

that the love-poetry of this epoch is largely of popular origin; *e.g.*, the songs attributed to Jamíl, in which Buthayna is addressed, and to Majnún—the hero of countless Persian and Turkish romances which celebrate his love for Laylá—are true folk-songs such as occur in the *Arabian Nights*, and may be heard in the streets of Beyrout or on the banks of the Tigris at the present day. Many of them are extremely beautiful. I take the following verses from a poem which is said to have been composed by Jamíl:—

Love-ballads.

"Oh, might it flower anew, that youthful prime,
And restore to us, Buthayna, the bygone time!
And might we again be blest as we wont to be,
When thy folk were nigh and grudged what thou gavest me!

Shall I ever meet Buthayna alone again,
Each of us full of love as a cloud of rain?
Fast in her net was I when a lad, and till
This day my love is growing and waxing still.

I have spent my lifetime, waiting for her to speak,
And the bloom of youth is faded from off my cheek;
But I will not suffer that she my suit deny,
My love remains undying, though all things die!"[1]

The names of al-Akhṭal, al-Farazdaq, and Jarír stand out pre-eminently in the list of Umayyad poets. They were men of a very different stamp from the languishing Minnesingers and carpet-knights who, like Jamíl, refused to battle except on the field of love. It is noteworthy that all three were born and bred in Mesopotamia. The motherland was exhausted; her ambitious and enterprising youth poured into the provinces, which now become the main centres of intellectual activity.

Poetry in the provinces.

Farazdaq and Jarír are intimately connected by a peculiar rivalry—"*Arcades ambo—id est*, blackguards both." For many years they engaged in a public scolding-match (*muháját*), and

[1] Nöldeke's *Delectus*, p. 9, l. 11 sqq., omitting l. 13.

as neither had any scruples on the score of decency, the foulest abuse was bandied to and fro between them—abuse, however, which is redeemed from vulgarity by its literary excellence, and by the marvellous skill which the satirists display in manipulating all the vituperative resources of the Arabic language. Soon these 'Flytings' (*Naqá'iḍ*) were recited everywhere, and each poet had thousands of enthusiastic partisans who maintained that he was superior to his rival.[1] One day Muhallab b. Abí Ṣufra, the governor of Khurásán, who was marching against the Azáriqa, a sect of the Khárijites, heard a great clamour and tumult in the camp. On inquiring its cause, he found that the soldiers had been fiercely disputing as to the comparative merits of Jarír and Farazdaq, and desired to submit the question to his decision. "Would you expose me," said Muhallab, "to be torn in pieces by these two dogs? I will not decide between them, but I will point out to you those who care not a whit for either of them. Go to the Azáriqa! They are Arabs who understand poetry and judge it aright."

The *Naqá'iḍ* of Jarír and Farazdaq.

General interest in poetry.

Next day, when the armies faced each other, an Azraqite named 'Abída b. Hilál stepped forth from the ranks and offered single combat. One of Muhallab's men accepted the challenge, but before fighting he begged his adversary to inform him which was the better poet—Farazdaq or Jarír? "God confound you!" cried 'Abída, "do you ask me about poetry instead of studying the Koran and the Sacred Law?" Then he quoted a verse by Jarír and gave judgment in his favour.[2] This incident affords a striking proof that the taste for poetry, far from being confined to literary circles, was diffused throughout the whole nation, and was cultivated

[1] An edition of the *Naqá'iḍ* by Professor A. A. Bevan has been published at Leyden.

[2] *Aghání*, vii, 55, l. 12 sqq.

even amidst the fatigues and dangers of war. Parallel instances occur in the history of the Athenians, the most gifted people of the West, and possibly elsewhere, but imagine British soldiers discussing questions of that kind over the camp-fires!

Akhṭal joined in the fray. His sympathies were with Farazdaq, and the *naqá'iḍ* which he and Jarír composed against each other have come down to us. All these poets, like their Post-islamic brethren generally, were professional encomiasts, greedy, venal, and ready to revile any one who would not purchase their praise. Some further account of them may be interesting to the reader, especially as the anecdotes related by their biographers throw many curious sidelights on the manners of the time.

Akhṭal.

The oldest of the trio, Akhṭal (Ghiyáth b. Ghawth) of Taghlib, was a Christian, like most of his tribe—they had long been settled in Mesopotamia—and remained in that faith to the end of his life, though the Caliph 'Abdu 'l-Malik is said to have offered him a pension and 10,000 dirhems in cash if he would turn Moslem. His religion, however, was less a matter of principle than of convenience, and to him the supreme virtue of Christianity lay in the licence which it gave him to drink wine as often as he pleased. The stories told of him suggest grovelling devoutness combined with very easy morals, a phenomenon familiar to the student of mediæval Catholicism. It is related by one who was touring in Syria that he found Akhṭal confined in a church at Damascus, and pleaded his cause with the priest. The latter stopped beside Akhṭal and raising the staff on which he leaned—for he was an aged man—exclaimed: "O enemy of God, will you again defame people and satirise them and caluminate chaste women?" while the poet humbled himself and promised never to repeat the offence. When asked how it was that he, who was honoured by the Caliph and feared by all, behaved so submissively to this priest, he answered, "It is religion, it is religion."[1] On another occasion, seeing the Bishop pass, he cried to his wife who was then pregnant, "Run after him and touch his robe." The poor woman only succeeded in touching the tail of the Bishop's ass, but Akhṭal consoled her with the remark, "He and the tail of his ass, there's no difference!"[2] It is characteristic of the anti-Islamic spirit which appears so strongly in the Umayyads that their chosen laureate and champion should have been a Christian who was in truth a lineal descendant of the pagan bards. Pious Moslems might well be scandalised when he burst unannounced into the Caliph's presence, sumptuously attired in silk and wearing a cross of gold which was suspended from his neck by a golden chain, while drops of wine trickled from his beard,[3] but their protests went unheeded at the court of Damascus, where nobody cared whether the author of a fine verse was a Moslem or a Christian, and where a poet was doubly welcome whose religion enabled him to serve his masters without any regard to Muḥammadan sentiment; so that, for example, when Yazíd I wished to take revenge on the people of Medína because one of their poets had addressed amatory verses to his sister, he turned to Akhṭal, who branded the *Anṣár*, the men who had brought about the triumph of Islam, in the famous lines—

"Quraysh have borne away all the honour and glory,
And baseness alone is beneath the turbans of the Anṣár."[4]

We must remember that the poets were leaders of public opinion; their utterances took the place of political pamphlets or of party oratory for or against the Government of the day.

[1] *Aghání*, vii, 182, l. 25 sqq.
[2] *Ibid.*, vii, 183, l. 6 sqq.
[3] *Ibid.*, p. 178, l. 1 seq.
[4] *Ibid.*, xiii, 148, l. 23.

On hearing Akhṭal's ode in praise of the Umayyad dynasty,[1] 'Abdu 'l-Malik ordered one of his clients to conduct the author through the streets of Damascus and to cry out, "Here is the poet of the Commander of the Faithful! Here is the best poet of the Arabs!"[2] No wonder that he was a favourite at court and such an eminent personage that the great tribe of Bakr used to invite him to act as arbitrator whenever any controversy arose among them.[3] Despite the luxury in which he lived, his wild Bedouin nature pined for freedom, and he frequently left the capital to visit his home in the desert, where he not only married and divorced several wives, but also threw himself with ardour into the feuds of his clan. We have already noticed the part which he played in the literary duel between Jarír and Farazdaq. From his deathbed he sent a final injunction to Farazdaq not to spare their common enemy.

Akhṭal is commended by Arabian critics for the number and excellence of his long poems, as well as for the purity, polish, and correctness of his style. Abú 'Ubayda put him first among the poets of Islam, while the celebrated collector of Pre-islamic poetry, Abú 'Amr b. al-'Alá, declared that if Akhṭal had lived a single day in the Pagan Age he would not have preferred any one to him. His supremacy in panegyric was acknowledged by Farazdaq, and he himself claims to have surpassed all competitors in three styles, viz., panegyric, satire, and erotic poetry; but there is more justification for the boast that his satires might be recited *virginibus*—he does not add *puerisque*—without causing a blush.[4]

Hammám b. Ghálib, generally known as Farazdaq, belonged to the tribe of Tamím, and was born at Baṣra towards the end of 'Umar's Caliphate. His grandfather, Ṣa'ṣa'a, won renown

[1] *Encomium Omayadarum*, ed. by Houtsma (Leyden, 1878).
[2] *Aghání*, vii, 172, l. 27 sqq. [3] *Ibid.*, p. 179, l. 25 sqq.
[4] *Ibid.*, p. 178, l. 26 seq.

in Pre-islamic times by ransoming the lives of female infants whom their parents had condemned to die (on account of which he received the title, *Muḥyi 'l-Maw'údát*, 'He who brings the buried girls to life'), and his father was likewise imbued with the old Bedouin traditions of liberality and honour, which were rapidly growing obsolete among the demoralised populace of 'Iráq. Farazdaq was a *mauvais sujet* of the type represented by François Villon, reckless, dissolute, and thoroughly unprincipled: apart from his gift of vituperation, we find nothing in him to admire save his respect for his father's memory and his constant devotion to the House of 'Alí, a devotion which he scorned to conceal; so that he was cast into prison by the Caliph Hishám for reciting in his presence a glowing panegyric on 'Alí's grandson, Zaynu 'l-'Ábidín. The tragic fate of Ḥusayn at Karbalá affected him deeply, and he called on his compatriots to acquit themselves like men—

Farazdaq.

"If ye avenge not him, the son of the best of you,
Then fling, fling the sword away and naught but the spindle ply."[1]

While still a young man, he was expelled from his native city in consequence of the lampoons which he directed against a noble family of Baṣra, the Banú Nahshal. Thereupon he fled to Medína, where he plunged into gallantry and dissipation until a shameless description of one of his intrigues again drew upon him the sentence of banishment. His poems contain many references to his cousin Nawár, whom, by means of a discreditable trick, he forced to marry him when she was on the point of giving her hand to another. The pair were ever quarrelling, and at last Farazdaq consented to an irrevocable divorce, which was witnessed by Ḥasan of Baṣra, the famous theologian. No sooner was

[1] *Aghání*, xix, 34, l. 18.

the act complete than Farazdaq began to wish it undone, and he spoke the following verses :—[1]

> "I feel repentance like al-Kusa'í,[2]
> Now that Nawár has been divorced by me.
> She was my Paradise which I have lost,
> Like Adam when the Lord's command he crossed.
> I am one who wilfully puts out his eyes,
> Then dark to him the shining day doth rise!"

'The repentance of Farazdaq,' signifying bitter regret or disappointment, passed into a proverb. He died a few months before Jarír in 728 A.D., a year also made notable by the deaths of two illustrious divines, Ḥasan of Baṣra and Ibn Sírín.

Jarír.

Jarír b. 'Aṭiyya belonged to Kulayb, a branch of the same tribe, Tamím, which produced Farazdaq. He was the court-poet of Ḥajjáj, the dreaded governor of 'Iráq, and eulogised his patron in such extravagant terms as to arouse the jealousy of the Caliph 'Abdu 'l-Malik, who consequently received him, on his appearance at Damascus, with marked coldness and hauteur. But when, after several repulses, he at length obtained permission to recite a poem which he had composed in honour of the prince, and came to the verse—

> "Are not ye the best of those who on camel ride,
> More open-handed than all in the world beside?"—

the Caliph sat up erect on his throne and exclaimed: "Let

[1] *Kámil* of Mubarrad. p. 70, l. 17 sqq.

[2] Al-Kusa'í broke an excellent bow which he had made for himself. See *The Assemblies of Ḥaríri*, trans. by Chenery, p. 351. Professor Bevan remarks that this half-verse is an almost verbal citation from a verse ascribed to 'Adí b. Mariná of Ḥíra, an enemy of 'Adí b. Zayd the poet (*Aghání*, ii, 24, l. 5).

us be praised like this or in silence !"[1] Jarír's fame as a satirist stood so high that to be worsted by him was reckoned a greater distinction than to vanquish any one else. The blind poet, Bashshár b. Burd († 783 A.D.), said: "I satirised Jarír, but he considered me too young for him to notice. Had he answered me, I should have been the finest poet in the world."[2] The following anecdote shows that vituperation launched by a master like Jarír was a deadly and far-reaching weapon which degraded its victim in the eyes of his contemporaries, however he might deserve their esteem, and covered his family and tribe with lasting disgrace.

There was a poet of repute, well known by the name of Rá'i 'l-ibil (Camel-herd), who loudly published his opinion that Farazdaq was superior to Jarír, although the latter had lauded his tribe, the Banú Numayr, whereas Farazdaq had made verses against them. One day Jarír met him and expostulated with him but got no reply. Rá'i was riding a mule and was accompanied by his son, Jandal, who said to his father: "Why do you halt before this dog of the Banú Kulayb, as though you had anything to hope or fear from him?" At the same time he gave the mule a lash with his whip. The animal started violently and kicked Jarír, who was standing by, so that his cap fell to the ground. Rá'i took no heed and went on his way. Jarír picked up the cap, brushed it, and replaced it on his head. Then he exclaimed in verse:—

> "*O Jandal! what will say Numayr of you*
> *When my dishonouring shaft has pierced thy sire?*"

He returned home full of indignation, and after the evening prayer, having called for a jar of date-wine and a lamp, he set about his work. An old woman in the house heard him muttering, and mounted the stairs to see what ailed him. She found him crawling naked on his bed, by reason of that which was within him; so she ran down, crying "He is mad," and described what she had seen to the people of the house. "Get thee gone," they said, "we know

[1] Ibn Khallikán (ed. by Wüstenfeld), No. 129; De Slane's translation vol. i, p. 298.

[2] *Aghání*, iii, 23, l. 13.

what he is at." By daybreak Jarír had composed a satire of eighty verses against the Banú Numayr. When he finished the poem, he shouted triumphantly, "*Allah Akbar!*" and rode away to the place where he expected to find Rá'i 'l-ibil and Farazdaq and their friends. He did not salute Rá'í but immediately began to recite. While he was speaking Farazdaq and Rá'í bowed their heads, and the rest of the company sat listening in silent mortification. When Jarír uttered the final words—

> "*Cast down thine eyes for shame! for thou art of*
> *Numayr—no peer of Ka'b nor yet Kiláb*"—

Rá'í rose and hastened to his lodging as fast as his mule could carry him. "Saddle! Saddle!" he cried to his comrades; "you cannot stay here longer, Jarír has disgraced you all." They left Baṣra without delay to rejoin their tribe, who bitterly reproached Rá'í for the ignominy which he had brought upon Numayr; and hundreds of years afterwards his name was still a byword among his people.[1]

Dhu 'l-Rumma.

Next, but next at a long interval, to the three great poets of this epoch comes Dhu 'l-Rumma (Ghaylán b. 'Uqba), who imitated the odes of the desert Arabs with tiresome and monotonous fidelity. The philologists of the following age delighted in his antique and difficult style, and praised him far above his merits. It was said that poetry began with Imru'u 'l-Qays and ended with Dhu 'l-Rumma; which is true in the sense that he is the last important representative of the pure Bedouin school.

Prose writers of the Umayyad period.

Concerning the prose writers of the period we can make only a few general observations, inasmuch as their works have almost entirely perished.[2] In this branch of literature the same secular, non-Muḥammadan spirit prevailed which has been mentioned as characteristic of the poets who flourished under the Umayyad dynasty, and of the dynasty itself. Historical studies

[1] *Aghání*, vii, 49, l. 8 sqq.
[2] The following account is mainly derived from Goldziher's *Muhamm. Studien*, Part II, p. 203 sqq.

were encouraged and promoted by the court of Damascus. We have referred elsewhere to 'Abíd b. Sharya, a native of Yemen, whose business it was to dress up the old legends and purvey them in a readable form to the public. Another Yemenite of Persian descent, Wahb b. Munabbih, is responsible for a great deal of the fabulous lore belonging to the domain of *Awá'il* (Origins) which Moslem chroniclers commonly prefix to their historical works. There seems to have been an eager demand for narratives of the Early Wars of Islam (*maghází*). It is related that the Caliph 'Abdu 'l-Malik, seeing one of these books in the hands of his son, ordered it to be burnt, and enjoined him to study the Koran instead. This anecdote shows on the part of 'Abdu 'l-Malik a pious feeling with which he is seldom credited,[1] but it shows also that histories of a legendary and popular character preceded those which were based, like the *Maghází* of Músá b. 'Uqba († 758 A.D.) and Ibn Isḥáq's *Biography of the Prophet*, upon religious tradition. No work of the former class has been preserved. The strong theological influence which asserted itself in the second century of the Hijra was unfavourable to the development of an Arabian prose literature on national lines. In the meantime, however, learned doctors of divinity began to collect and write down the *Ḥadíths*. We have a solitary relic of this sort in the *Kitábu 'l-Zuhd* (Book of Asceticism) by Asad b. Músá († 749 A.D.). The most renowned traditionist of the Umayyad age is Muḥammad b. Muslim b. Shiháb al-Zuhrí († 742 A.D.), who distinguished himself by accepting judicial office under the tyrants; an act of complaisance to which his more stiff-necked and conscientious brethren declined to stoop.

It was the lust of conquest even more than missionary zeal that caused the Arabs to invade Syria and Persia and to settle

[1] Cf. Browne's *Lit. Hist. of Persia*, vol. i, p. 230.

on foreign soil, where they lived as soldiers at the expense of the native population whom they inevitably regarded as an inferior race. If the latter thought to win respect by embracing the religion of their conquerors, they found themselves sadly mistaken. The new converts were attached as clients (*Mawálí*, sing. *Mawlá*) to an Arab tribe: they could not become Moslems on any other footing. Far from obtaining the equal rights which they coveted, and which, according to the principles of Islam, they should have enjoyed, the *Mawálí* were treated by their aristocratic patrons with contempt, and had to submit to every kind of social degradation, while instead of being exempted from the capitation-tax paid by non-Moslems, they still remained liable to the ever-increasing exactions of Government officials. And these 'Clients,' be it remembered, were not ignorant serfs, but men whose culture was acknowledged by the Arabs themselves—men who formed the backbone of the influential learned class and ardently prosecuted those studies, Divinity and Jurisprudence, which were then held in highest esteem. Here was a situation full of danger. Against Shí'ites and Khárijites the Umayyads might claim with some show of reason to represent the cause of law and order, if not of Islam; against the bitter cry of the oppressed *Mawálí* they had no argument save the sword.

The non-Arabian Moslems.

We have referred above to the universal belief of Moslems in a Messiah and to the extraordinary influence of that belief on their religious and political history. No wonder that in this unhappy epoch thousands of people, utterly disgusted with life as they found it, should have indulged in visions of 'a good time coming,' which was expected to coincide with the end of the first century of the Hijra. Mysterious predictions, dark sayings attributed to Muḥammad himself, prophecies of war and deliverance floated to and fro. Men pored over apocry-

Presages of the Revolution.

phal books, and asked whether the days of confusion and slaughter (*al-harj*), which, it is known, shall herald the appearance of the Mahdí, had not actually begun.

The final struggle was short and decisive. When it closed, the Umayyads and with them the dominion of the Arabs had passed away. Alike in politics and literature, the Persian race asserted its supremacy. We shall now relate the story of this Revolution as briefly as possible, leaving the results to be considered in a new chapter.

The 'Abbásids.

While the Shí'ite missionaries (*du'át*, sing. *dá'í*) were actively engaged in canvassing for their party, which, as we have seen, recognised in 'Alí and his descendants the only legitimate successors to Muḥammad, another branch of the Prophet's family—the 'Abbásids—had entered the field with the secret intention of turning the labours of the 'Alids to their own advantage. From their ancestor, 'Abbás, the Prophet's uncle, they inherited those qualities of caution, duplicity, and worldly wisdom which ensure success in political intrigue. 'Abdulláh, the son of 'Abbás, devoted his talents to theology and interpretation of the Koran. He "passes for one of the strongest pillars of religious tradition; but, in the eyes of unprejudiced European research, he is only a crafty liar." His descendants "lived in deep retirement in Ḥumayma, a little place to the south of the Dead Sea, seemingly far withdrawn from the world, but which, on account of its proximity to the route by which Syrian pilgrims went to Mecca, afforded opportunities for communication with the remotest lands of Islam. From this centre they carried on the propaganda in their own behalf with the utmost skill. They had genius enough to see that the best soil for their efforts was the distant Khurásán—that is, the extensive north-eastern provinces of the old Persian Empire." [1] These countries were inhabited by a

'Abbásid propaganda in Khurásán.

[1] Nöldeke, *Sketches from Eastern History*, tr. by J. S. Black, p. 108 seq.

brave and high-spirited people who in consequence of their intolerable sufferings under the Umayyad tyranny, the devastation of their homes and the almost servile condition to which they had been reduced, were eager to join in any desperate enterprise that gave them hope of relief. Moreover, the Arabs in Khurásán were already to a large extent Persianised: they had Persian wives, wore trousers, drank wine, and kept the festivals of Nawrúz and Mihrgán; while the Persian language was generally understood and even spoken among them.[1] Many interesting details as to the methods of the 'Abbásid emissaries will be found in Van Vloten's admirable work.[2] Starting from Kúfa, the residence of the Grand Master who directed the whole agitation, they went to and fro in the guise of merchants or pilgrims, cunningly adapting their doctrine to the intelligence of those whom they sought to enlist. Like the Shí'ites, they canvassed for 'the House of the Prophet,' an ambiguous expression which might equally well be applied to the descendants of 'Alí or of 'Abbás, as is shown by the following table:—

HÁSHIM.

'Abdu 'l-Muttalib.

'Abdulláh. — Abú Tálib. — 'Abbás.

Muhammad (the Prophet). — 'Alí (married to Fátima, daughter of the Prophet).

The Shí'ites join hands with the 'Abbásids.

It was, of course, absolutely essential to the 'Abbásids that they should be able to count on the support of the powerful Shí'ite organisation, which, ever since the abortive rebellion headed by Mukhtár (see p. 218 *supra*) had drawn vast numbers of Persian *Mawálí* into its ranks. Now, of the two main parties of the Shí'a,

[1] Wellhausen, *Das Arabische Reich*, p. 307.
[2] *Recherches sur la domination Arabe*, p. 46 sqq.

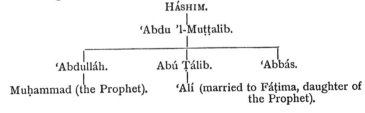

viz., the Háshimites or followers of Muḥammad Ibnu 'l-Ḥanafiyya, and the Imámites, who pinned their faith to the descendants of the Prophet through his daughter Fáṭima, the former had virtually identified themselves with the 'Abbásids, inasmuch as the Imám Abú Háshim, who died in 716 A.D., bequeathed his hereditary rights to Muḥammad b. 'Alí, the head of the House of 'Abbás. It only remained to hoodwink the Imámites. Accordingly the 'Abbásid emissaries were instructed to carry on their propaganda in the name of Háshim, the common ancestor of 'Abbás and 'Alí. By means of this ruse they obtained a free hand in Khurásán, and made such progress that the governor of that province, Naṣr b. Sayyár, wrote to the Umayyad Caliph, Marwán, asking for reinforcements, and informing him that two hundred thousand men had sworn allegiance to Abú Muslim, the principal 'Abbásid agent. At the foot of his letter he added these lines :—

"I see the coal's red glow beneath the embers,
And 'tis about to blaze!
The rubbing of two sticks enkindles fire,
And out of words come frays.
'Oh! is Umayya's House awake or sleeping?'
I cry in sore amaze." [1]

We have other verses by this gallant and loyal officer in which he implores the Arab troops stationed in Khurásán, who were paralysed by tribal dissensions, to turn their swords against "a mixed rabble without religion or nobility" :—

"'Death to the Arabs'—that is all their creed." [2]

These warnings, however, were of no avail, and on June 9th, A.D. 747, Abú Muslim displayed the black banner

[1] Dínawarí, ed. by Guirgass, p. 356.
[2] *Ibid.*, p. 360, l. 15. The whole poem has been translated by Professor Browne in his *Literary History of Persia*, vol. i, p. 242.

of the 'Abbásids at Siqadanj, near Merv, which city he occupied a few months later. The triumphant advance of the armies of the Revolution towards Damascus recalls the celebrated campaign of Cæsar, when after crossing the Rubicon he marched on Rome. Nor is Abú Muslim, though a freedman of obscure parentage—he was certainly no Arab—unworthy to be compared with the great patrician. "He united," says Nöldeke, "with an agitator's adroitness and perfect unscrupulosity in the choice of means the energy and clear outlook of a general and statesman, and even of a monarch."[1] Grim, ruthless, disdaining the pleasures of ordinary men, he possessed the faculty in which Cæsar excelled of inspiring blind obedience and enthusiastic devotion. To complete the parallel, we may mention here that Abú Muslim was treacherously murdered by Manṣúr, the second Caliph of the House which he had raised to the throne, from motives exactly resembling those which Shakespeare has put in the mouth of Brutus—

Declaration of war.

Abú Muslim.

> "So Cæsar may:
> Then, lest he may, prevent. And since the quarrel
> Will bear no colour for the thing he is,
> Fashion it thus: that what he is, augmented,
> Would run to these and these extremities;
> And therefore think him as a serpent's egg
> Which, hatched, would as his kind grow mischievous,
> And kill him in the shell."

The downfall of the Umayyads was hastened by the perfidy and selfishness of the Arabs on whom they relied: the old feud between Muḍar and Yemen broke out afresh, and while the Northern group remained loyal to the dynasty, those of Yemenite stock more or less openly threw in their lot with the Revolution. We need not attempt to trace the course

[1] *Sketches from Eastern History*, p. 111.

of the unequal contest. Everywhere the Arabs, disheartened and divided, fell an easy prey to their adversaries, and all was lost when Marwán, the last Umayyad Caliph, sustained a crushing defeat on the River Záb in Babylonia (January, A.D. 750). Meanwhile Abu 'l-'Abbás, the head of the rival House, had already received homage as Caliph (November, 749 A.D.). In the inaugural address which he delivered in the great Mosque of Kúfa, he called himself *al-Saffáḥ*, *i.e.*, 'the Blood-shedder,'[1] and this title has deservedly stuck to him, though it might have been assumed with no less justice by his brother Manṣúr and other members of his family. All Umayyads were remorselessly hunted down and massacred in cold blood—even those who surrendered only on the strength of the most solemn pledges that they had nothing to fear. A small remnant made their escape, or managed to find shelter until the storm of fury and vengeance, which spared neither the dead nor the living,[2] had blown over. One stripling, named 'Abdu 'l-Raḥmán, fled to North Africa, and after meeting with many perilous adventures founded a new Umayyad dynasty in Spain.

Accession of Abu 'l-'Abbás al-Saffáḥ.

[1] Professor Bevan, to whose kindness I owe the following observations, points out that this translation of *al-Saffáḥ*, although it has been generally adopted by European scholars, is very doubtful. According to Professor De Goeje, *al-Saffáḥ* means 'the munificent' (literally, 'pouring out' gifts, &c.). In any case it is important to notice that the name was given to certain Pre-islamic chieftains. Thus Salama b. Khálid, who commanded the Banú Taghlib at the first battle of al-Kuláb (Ibnu 'l-Athír, ed. by Tornberg, vol. i, p. 406, last line), is said to have been called *al-Saffáḥ* because he 'emptied out' the skin bottles (*mazád*) of his army before a battle (Ibn Durayd, ed. by Wüstenfeld, p. 203, l. 16); and we find mention of a poet named al-Saffáḥ b. 'Abd Manát (*ibid.*, p. 277, penult. line).

[2] See p. 205.

CHAPTER VI

THE CALIPHS OF BAGHDÁD

THE annals of the 'Abbásid dynasty from the accession of Saffáḥ (A.D. 749) to the death of Musta'ṣim, and the destruction of Baghdád by the Mongols (A.D. 1258) make a round sum of five centuries. I propose to sketch the history or this long period in three chapters, of which the first will offer a general view of the more important literary and political developments so far as is possible in the limited space at my command; the second will be devoted to the great poets, scholars, historians, philosophers, and scientists who flourished in this, the Golden Age of Muḥammadan literature; while in the third some account will be given of the chief religious movements and of the trend of religious thought.

The empire founded by the Caliph 'Umar and administered by the Umayyads was essentially, as the reader will have gathered, a military organisation for the benefit of the paramount race. In theory, no doubt, all Moslems were equal, but in fact the Arabs alone ruled—a privilege which national pride conspired with personal interest to maintain. We have seen how the Persian Moslems asserted their right to a share in the government. The Revolution which enthroned the 'Abbásids marks the beginning of a Moslem, as opposed to an Arabian, Empire. The new dynasty, owing its rise to the people of Persia, and especially of Khurásán, could exist only by

Political results of the Revolution.

establishing a balance of power between Persians and Arabs. That this policy was not permanently successful will surprise no one who considers the widely diverse characteristics of the two races, but for the next fifty years the rivals worked together in tolerable harmony, thanks to the genius of Manṣúr and the conciliatory influence of the Barmecides, by whose overthrow the alliançe was virtually dissolved. In the ensuing civil war between the sons of Hárún al-Rashíd the Arabs fought on the side of Amín while the Persians supported Ma'mún, and henceforth each race began to follow an independent path. The process of separation, however, was very gradual, and long before it was completed the religious and intellectual life of both nationalities had become inseparably mingled in the full stream of Moslem civilisation.

The choice of a new capital.

The centre of this civilisation was the province of 'Iráq (Babylonia), with its renowned metropolis, Baghdád, 'the City of Peace' (*Madínatu 'l-Salám*). Only here could the 'Abbásids feel themselves at home. "Damascus, peopled by the dependants of the Omayyads, was out of the question. On the one hand it was too far from Persia, whence the power of the Abbasids was chiefly derived; on the other hand it was dangerously near the Greek frontier, and from here, during the troublous reigns of the last Omayyads, hostile incursions on the part of the Christians had begun to avenge former defeats. It was also beginning to be evident that the conquests of Islam would, in the future, lie to the eastward towards Central Asia, rather than to the westward at the further expense of the Byzantines. Damascus, on the highland of Syria, lay, so to speak, dominating the Mediterranean and looking westward, but the new capital that was to supplant it must face east, be near Persia, and for the needs of commerce have water communication with the sea. Hence everything pointed to a site on either the Euphrates or the Tigris, and the Abbasids were not slow to make their choice."[1] After carefully examining various sites, the Caliph Manṣúr fixed on a little Persian village, on the west bank of the Tigris, called Baghdád, which, being interpreted, means 'given (or 'founded') by God'; and in A.D. 762 the walls of the new city began to rise. Manṣúr laid the first brick with his own hand, and the work was pushed forward with astonishing rapidity under his personal direction by masons, architects, and surveyors, whom he gathered out of different countries, so that 'the Round City,' as he planned it, was actually finished within the short space of four years.

Foundation of Baghdád.

The same circumstances which caused the seat of empire to be transferred to Baghdád brought about a corresponding change in the whole system of government. Whereas the Umayyads had been little more than heads of a turbulent Arabian aristocracy, their successors reverted to the old type of Oriental despotism with which the Persians had been familiar since the days of Darius and Xerxes. Surrounded by a strong bodyguard of troops from Khurásán, on whose devotion they could rely, the 'Abbásids ruled with absolute authority over the lives and properties of their subjects, even as the Sásánian monarchs had ruled before them. Persian fashions were imitated at the court, which was thronged with the Caliph's relatives and freedmen (not to mention his womenfolk), besides a vast array of uniformed and decorated officials. Chief amongst these latter stood two personages who figure prominently in the *Arabian Nights*—the Vizier and the Executioner. The office of Vizier is probably of Persian origin, although in Professor De Goeje's opinion the word itself is Arabic.[2] The first

Despotic character of 'Abbásid rule.

[1] G. Le Strange, *Baghdad under the Abbasid Caliphate*, p. 4 seq.

[2] Professor De Goeje has kindly given me the following references:—Ṭabarí, ii, 78, l. 10, where Ziyád is called the *Wazír* of Mu'áwiya; Ibn

who bore this title in 'Abbásid times was Abú Salama, the minister of Saffáḥ: he was called *Wazíru Áli Muḥammad[in]*, 'the Vizier of Muḥammad's Family.' It was the duty of the Vizier to act as intermediary between the omnipotent sovereign and his people, to counsel him in affairs of State, and, above all, to keep His Majesty in good humour. He wielded enormous power, but was exposed to every sort of intrigue, and never knew when he might be interned in a dungeon or despatched in the twinkling of an eye by the grim functionary presiding over the *naṭ'*, or circular carpet of leather, which lay beside the throne and served as a scaffold.

The Vizier.

We can distinguish two periods in the history of the 'Abbásid House: one of brilliant prosperity inaugurated by Manṣúr and including the reigns of Mahdí, Hárún al-Rashíd, Ma'mún, Mu'taṣim, and Wáthiq—that is to say, nearly a hundred years in all (754–847 A.D.); the other, more than four times as long, commencing with Mutawakkil (847–861 A.D.) —a period of decline rapidly sinking, after a brief interval which gave promise of better things, into irremediable decay.[1]

Two periods of 'Abbásid history.

Sa'd, iii, 121, l. 6 (Abú Bakr the *Wazír* of the Prophet). The word occurs in Pre-islamic poetry (Ibn Qutayba, *K. al-Shi'r wa-'l-Shu'ará*, p. 414, l. 1). Professor De Goeje adds that the 'Abbásid Caliphs gave the name *Wazír* as title to the minister who was formerly called *Kátib* (Secretary). Thus it would seem that the Arabic *Wazír* (literally 'burden-bearer'), who was at first merely a 'helper' or 'henchman,' afterwards became the representative and successor of the *Dapír* (official scribe or secretary) of the Sásánian kings.

[1] This division is convenient, and may be justified on general grounds. In a strictly political sense, the period of decline begins thirty years earlier with the Caliphate of Ma'mún (813–833 A.D.). The historian Abu 'l-Maḥásin († 1469 A.D.) dates the decline of the Caliphate from the accession of Muktafí in 902 A.D. (*al-Nujúm al-Záhira*, ed. by Juynboll, vol. ii, p. 134).

Cruel and treacherous, like most of his family, Abú Ja'far Manṣúr was perhaps the greatest ruler whom the 'Abbásids produced.[1] He had to fight hard for his throne. The 'Alids, who deemed themselves the true heirs of the Prophet in virtue of their descent from Fáṭima, rose in rebellion against the usurper, surprised him in an unguarded moment, and drove him to such straits that during seven weeks he never changed his dress except for public prayers. But once more the 'Alids proved incapable of grasping their opportunity. The leaders, Muḥammad, who was known as 'The Pure Soul' (*al-Nafs al-zakiyya*), and his brother Ibráhím, fell on the battle-field. Under Mahdí and Hárún members of the House of 'Alí continued to 'come out,' but with no better success. In Eastern Persia, where strong national feelings interwove themselves with Pre-Muḥammadan religious ideas, those of Mazdak and Zoroaster in particular, the 'Abbásids encountered a formidable opposition which proclaimed its vigour and tenacity by the successive revolts of Sinbádh the Magian (755–756 A.D.), Ustádhsís (766–768), Muqanna', the 'Veiled Prophet of Khurásán' (780–786), and Bábak the Khurramite (816–838).[2]

Reign of Manṣúr (754–775 A.D.).

Outbreaks in Persia.

Manṣúr said to his son Mahdí, "O Abú 'Abdalláh, when you sit in company, always have divines to converse with you; for Muḥammad b. Shiháb al-Zuhrí said, 'The word *ḥadíth* (Apostolic Tradition) is masculine: only virile men love it, and only effeminate men dislike it'; and he spoke the truth."[3]

Manṣúr's advice to Mahdí.

On one occasion a poet came to Mahdí, who was then heir-apparent, at Rayy, and recited a panegyric in his honour.

[1] See Nöldeke's essay, *Caliph Manṣúr*, in his *Sketches from Eastern History*, trans. by J. S. Black, p. 107 sqq.

[2] Professor Browne has given an interesting account of these ultra-Shí'ite insurgents in his *Lit. Hist. of Persia*, vol. i, ch. ix.

[3] Ṭabarí, iii, 404, l. 5 sqq.

The prince gave him 20,000 dirhems. Thereupon the postmaster of Rayy informed Manṣúr, who wrote to his son reproaching him for such extravagance. "What you should have done," he said, "was to let him wait a year at your door, and after that time bestow on him 4,000 dirhems." He then caused the poet to be arrested and brought into his presence. "You went to a heedless youth and cajoled him?" "Yes, God save the Commander of the Faithful, I went to a heedless, generous youth and cajoled him, and he suffered himself to be cajoled." "Recite your eulogy of him." The poet obeyed, not forgetting to conclude his verses with a compliment to Manṣúr. "Bravo!" cried the Caliph, "but they are not worth 20,000 dirhems. Where is the money?" On its being produced he made him a gift of 4,000 dirhems and confiscated the remainder.[1]

Manṣúr and the poet.

Notwithstanding irreconcilable parties—'Alids, Persian extremists, and (we may add) Khárijites—the policy of *rapprochement* was on the whole extraordinarily effective. In carrying it out the Caliphs received powerful assistance from a noble and ancient Persian family, the celebrated Barmakites or Barmecides. According to Mas'údí,[2] Barmak was originally a title borne by the High Priest (*sádin*) of the great Magian fire-temple at Balkh. Khálid, the son of one of these dignitaries—whence he and his descendants were called Barmakites (*Barámika*)—held the most important offices of state under Saffáḥ and Manṣúr. Yaḥyá, the son of Khálid, was entrusted with the education of Hárún al-Rashíd, and on the accession of the young prince he was appointed Grand Vizier. "My dear father!" said the Caliph, "it is through the blessings and the good fortune which attend you, and through your excellent management, that I am seated on the

The Barmecides.

Yaḥyá b. Khálid.

[1] Ṭabarí, iii, 406, l. 1 sqq.

[2] *Murúju 'l-Dhahab*, ed. by Barbier de Meynard, vol. iv, p. 47 seq.

throne;[1] so I commit to you the direction of affairs." He then handed to him his signet-ring. Yaḥyá was distinguished (says the biographer) for wisdom, nobleness of mind, and elegance of language.[2] Although he took a truly Persian delight in philosophical discussion, for which purpose free-thinking scholars and eminent heretics used often to meet in his house, he was careful to observe the outward forms of piety. It may be said of the 'Abbásids generally that, whatever they might do or think in private, they wore the official badge of Islam ostentatiously on their sleeves. The following verses which Yaḥyá addressed to his son Faḍl are very characteristic:—[3]

"Seek glory while 'tis day, no effort spare,
And patiently the loved one's absence bear;
But when the shades of night advancing slow
O'er every vice a veil of darkness throw,
Beguile the hours with all thy heart's delight:
The day of prudent men begins at night.
Many there be, esteemed of life austere,
Who nightly enter on a strange career.
Night o'er them keeps her sable curtain drawn,
And merrily they pass from eve to dawn.
Who but a fool his pleasures would expose
To spying rivals and censorious foes?"

Fall of the Barmecides (803 A.D.).

For seventeen years Yaḥyá and his two sons, Faḍl and Ja'far, remained deep in Hárún's confidence and virtual rulers of the State until, from motives which have been variously explained, the Caliph resolved to rid himself of the whole family. The story is too well known to need repetition.[4] Ja'far alone was put to death: we may conclude, therefore, that he had specially

[1] When the Caliph Hádí wished to proclaim his son Ja'far heir-apparent instead of Hárún, Yaḥyá pointed out the danger of this course and dissuaded him (*al-Fakhrí*, ed. by Derenbourg, p. 281).

[2] Ibn Khallikán, De Slane's translation, vol. iv, p. 105.

[3] Mas'údí, *Murúju 'l-Dhahab*, vol. vi, p. 364.

[4] See, for example, *Haroun Alraschid*, by E. H. Palmer, in the New Plutarch Series, p. 81 sqq.

excited the Caliph's anger; and those who ascribe the catastrophe to his romantic love-affair with Hárún's sister, 'Abbása, are probably in the right.[1] Hárún himself seems to have recognised, when it was too late, how much he owed to these great Persian barons whose tactful administration, unbounded generosity, and munificent patronage of literature have shed immortal lustre on his reign. Afterwards, if any persons spoke ill of the Barmecides in his presence, he would say (quoting the verse of Ḥuṭay'a):—[2]

> "O slanderers, be your sire of sire bereft![3]
> Give o'er, or fill the gap which they have left."

Hárún al-Rashíd (786–809 A.D.).

Hárún's orthodoxy, his liberality, his victories over the Byzantine Emperor Nicephorus, and last but not least the literary brilliance of his reign have raised him in popular estimation far above all the other Caliphs: he is the Charlemagne of the East, while the entrancing pages of the *Thousand and One Nights* have made his name a household word in every country of Europe. Students of Moslem history will soon discover that "the good Haroun Alraschid" was in fact a perfidious and irascible tyrant, whose fitful amiability and real taste for music and letters hardly entitle him to be described either as a great monarch or a good man. We must grant, however, that he thoroughly understood the noble art of patronage. The poets Abú Nuwás, Abu 'l-'Atáhiya, Di'bil, Muslim b. Walíd, and 'Abbás b. Aḥnaf; the musician Ibráhím of Mosul and his son Isḥáq; the philologists Abú 'Ubayda, Aṣma'í, and Kisá'í; the preacher Ibnu 'l-Sammák; and the historian Wáqidí—these are but a few names in the galaxy of talent which he gathered around him at Baghdád.

[1] *Cf.* A. Müller, *Der Islam*, vol. i, p. 481 seq.
[2] Ibn Khallikán, De Slane's translation, vol. iv, p. 112.
[3] Literally, "No father to your father!" a common form of imprecation.

The fall of the Barmecides revived the spirit of racial antagonism which they had done their best to lay, and an open rupture was rendered inevitable by the short-sighted policy of Hárún with regard to the succession. He had two grown-up sons, Amín, by his wife and cousin Zubayda, and Ma'mún, whose mother was a Persian slave. It was arranged that the Caliphate should pass to Amín and after him to his brother, but that the Empire should be divided between them. Amín was to receive 'Iráq and Syria, Ma'mún the eastern provinces, where the people would gladly welcome a ruler of their own blood. The struggle for supremacy which began almost immediately on the death of Hárún was in the main one of Persians against Arabs, and by Ma'mún's triumph the Barmecides were amply avenged.

Amín and Ma'mún (809–833 A.D.).

The new Caliph was anything but orthodox. He favoured the Shí'ite party to such an extent that he even nominated the 'Alid, 'Alí b. Músá b. Ja'far al-Riḍá, as heir-apparent—a step which alienated the members of his own family and led to his being temporarily deposed. He also adopted the opinions of the Mu'tazilite sect and established an Inquisition to enforce them. Hence the Sunnite historian, Abu 'l-Maḥásin, enumerates three principal heresies of which Ma'mún was guilty: (1) His wearing of the Green (*labsu 'l-Khuḍra*)[1] and courting the 'Alids and repulsing the 'Abbásids; (2) his affirming that the Koran was created (*al-qawl bi-Khalqi 'l-Qur'án*); and (3) his legalisation of the *mut'a*, a loose form of marriage prevailing amongst the Shí'ites.[2] We shall see in due course how keenly and with what fruitful results Ma'mún interested himself in literature and science. Nevertheless, it cannot escape our attention that in this splendid reign there appear ominous signs of political decay. In 822 A.D. Ṭáhir, one of Ma'mún's generals, who

Ma'mún's heresies.

1 Green was the party colour of the 'Alids, black of the 'Abbásids.

2 *Al-Nujúm al-Záhira*, ed. by Juynboll, vol. i, p. 631.

had been appointed governor of Khurásán, omitted the customary mention of the Caliph's name from the Friday sermon (*khuṭba*), thus founding the Ṭahirid dynasty, which, though professing allegiance to the Caliphs, was practically independent. Ṭáhir was only the first of a long series of ambitious governors and bold adventurers who profited by the weakening authority of the Caliphs to carve out kingdoms for themselves. Moreover, the Moslems of 'Iráq had lost their old warlike spirit: they were fine scholars and merchants, but poor soldiers. So it came about that Ma'mún's successor, the Caliph Mu'taṣim (833–842 A.D.), took the fatal step of surrounding himself with a Prætorian Guard chiefly composed of Turkish recruits from Transoxania. At the same time he removed his court from Baghdád sixty miles further up the Tigris to Sámarrá, which suddenly grew into a superb city of palaces and barracks—an Oriental Versailles.[1] Here we may close our brief review of the first and flourishing period of the 'Abbásid Caliphate. During the next four centuries the Caliphs come and go faster than ever, but for the most part their authority is precarious, if not purely nominal. Meanwhile, in the provinces of the Empire petty dynasties arise, only to eke out an obscure and troubled existence, or powerful states are formed, which carry on the traditions of Muḥammadan culture, it may be through many generations, and in some measure restore the blessings of peace and settled government to an age surfeited with anarchy and bloodshed. Of these provincial empires we have now principally to speak, confining our view, for the most part, to the political outlines, and reserving the literary and religious aspects of the period for fuller consideration elsewhere.

Rise of independent dynasties.

Turkish mercenaries introduced.

Decline of the Caliphate.

[1] The court remained at Sámarrá for fifty-six years (836–892 A.D.). The official spelling of Sámarrá was *Surra-man-ra'á*, which may be freely rendered 'The Spectator's Joy.'

The reigns of Mutawakkil (847–861 A.D.) and his immediate successors exhibit all the well-known features of Prætorian rule.

The Second 'Abbásid Period (847–1258 A.D.).

Enormous sums were lavished on the Turkish soldiery, who elected and deposed the Caliph just as they pleased, and enforced their insatiable demands by mutiny and assassination. For a short time (869–907 A.D.) matters improved under the able and energetic Muhtadí and the four Caliphs who followed him; but the Turks soon regained the upper hand. From this date every vestige of real power is centred in the Generalissimo (*Amíru 'l-Umará*) who stands at the head of the army, while the once omnipotent Caliph must needs be satisfied with the empty honour of having his name stamped on the coinage and celebrated in the public prayers. The terrorism of the Turkish bodyguard was broken by the Buwayhids, a Persian dynasty, who ruled in Baghdád from 945 to 1055 A.D. Then the Seljúq supremacy began with Ṭughril Beg's entry into the capital and lasted a full century until the death of Sanjar (1157 A.D.). The Mongols who captured Baghdád in 1258 A.D. brought the pitiable farce of the Caliphate to an end.

Dynasties of the early 'Abbásid Age.

"The empire of the Caliphs at its widest," as Stanley Lane-Poole observes in his excellent account of the Muḥammadan dynasties, "extended from the Atlantic to the Indus, and from the Caspian to the cataracts of the Nile. So vast a dominion could not long be held together. The first step towards its disintegration began in Spain, where 'Abdu 'l-Raḥmán, a member of the suppressed Umayyad family, was acknowledged as an independent sovereign in A.D. 755, and the 'Abbásid Caliphate was renounced for ever. Thirty years later Idrís, a great-grandson of the Caliph 'Alí, and therefore equally at variance with 'Abbásids and Umayyads, founded an 'Alid dynasty in Morocco. The rest of the North African coast was practically lost to the Caliphate when the Aghlabid governor established his authority at Qayrawán in A.D. 800."

Amongst the innumerable kingdoms which supplanted the

decaying Caliphate only a few of the most important can be singled out for special notice on account of their literary or religious interest.[1] To begin with Persia: in 872 A.D. Khurásán, which was then held by the Ṭáhirids, fell into the hands of Ya'qúb b. Layth the Coppersmith (*al-Ṣaffár*), founder of the Ṣaffárids, who for thirty years stretched their sway over a great part of Persia, until they were dispossessed by the Sámánids. The latter dynasty had the seat of its power in Transoxania, but during the first half of the tenth century practically the whole of Persia submitted to the authority of Ismá'íl and his famous successors, Naṣr II and Núḥ I. Not only did these princes warmly encourage and foster the development, which had already begun, of a national literature in the Persian language—it is enough to recall here the names of Rúdagí, the blind minstrel and poet; Daqíqí, whose fragment of a Persian Epic was afterwards incorporated by Firdawsí in his *Sháhnáma;* and Bal'amí, the Vizier of Manṣúr I, who composed an abridgment of Ṭabarí's great history, which is one of the oldest prose works in Persian that have come down to us—but they extended the same favour to poets and men of learning who (though, for the most part, of Persian extraction) preferred to use the Arabic language. Thus the celebrated Rhazes (Abú Bakr al-Rází) dedicated to the Sámánid prince Abú Ṣáliḥ Manṣúr b. Isḥáq a treatise on medicine, which he entitled *al-Kitáb al-Manṣúrí* (the Book of Manṣúr) in honour of his patron. The great physician and philosopher, Abú 'Alí b. Síná (Avicenna) relates that, having been summoned to Bukhárá by King Núḥ, the second of that name (976–997 A.D.), be obtained permission to visit the

Dynasties of the Second Period.

The Sámánids (874–999 A.D.).

[1] My account of these dynasties is necessarily of the briefest and barest character. The reader will find copious details concerning most of them in Professor Browne's *Literary History of Persia:* Ṣaffárids and Sámánids in vol. i, p. 346 sqq.; Fáṭimids in vol. i, pp. 391–400 and vol. ii, p. 196 sqq.; Ghaznevids in vol. ii, chap. ii; and Seljúqs, *ibid.*, chaps. iii to v.

royal library. "I found there," he says, "many rooms filled with books which were arranged in cases row upon row. One room was allotted to works on Arabic philology and poetry; another to jurisprudence, and so forth, the books on each particular science having a room to themselves. I inspected the catalogue of ancient Greek authors and looked for the books which I required: I saw in this collection books of which few people have heard even the names, and which I myself have never seen either before or since." [1]

The Buwayhids (932–1055 A.D.).

The power of the Sámánids quickly reached its zenith, and about the middle of the tenth century they were confined to Khurásán and Transoxania, while in Western Persia their place was taken by the Buwayhids. Abú Shujá' Buwayh, a chieftain of Daylam, the mountainous province lying along the southern shores of the Caspian Sea, was one of those soldiers of fortune whom we meet with so frequently in the history of this period. His three sons, 'Alí, Aḥmad, and Ḥasan, embarked on the same adventurous career with such energy and success, that in the course of thirteen years they not only subdued the provinces of Fárs and Khúzistán, but in 945 A.D. entered Baghdád at the head of their Daylamite troops and assumed the supreme command, receiving from the Caliph Mustakfí the honorary titles of 'Imádu 'l-Dawla, Mu'izzu 'l-Dawla, and Ruknu 'l-Dawla. Among the princes of this House, who reigned over Persia and 'Iráq during the next hundred years, the most eminent was 'Aḍudu 'l-Dawla, of whom it is said by Ibn Khallikán that none of the Buwayhids, notwithstanding their great power and authority, possessed so extensive an empire and held sway over so many kings and kingdoms as he. The chief poets of the day, including Mutanabbí, visited his court at Shíráz and celebrated his praises in magnificent odes. He also built a great hospital in Baghdád, the Bímáristán al-'Aḍudí, which

[1] Ibn Abí Uṣaybi'a, *Ṭabaqátu 'l-Aṭibbá*, ed. by A. Müller, vol. ii, p. 4, l. 4 sqq. Avicenna was at this time scarcely eighteen years of age.

was long famous as a school of medicine. The Viziers of the Buwayhid family contributed in a quite unusual degree to its literary renown. Ibnu 'l-'Amíd, the Vizier of Ruknu 'l-Dawla, surpassed in philology and epistolary composition all his contemporaries; hence he was called 'the second Jáḥiẓ,' and it was a common saying that "the art of letter-writing began with 'Abdu 'l-Ḥamíd and ended with Ibnu 'l-'Amíd."[1] His friend, the Ṣáḥib Ismá'íl b. 'Abbád, Vizier to Mu'ayyidu 'l-Dawla and Fakhru 'l-Dawla, was a distinguished savant, whose learning was only eclipsed by the liberality of his patronage. In the latter respect Sábúr b. Ardashír, the prime minister of Abú Naṣr Bahá'u 'l-Dawla, vied with the illustrious Ṣáḥib. He had so many encomiasts that Tha'álibí devotes to them a whole chapter of the *Yatíma*. The Academy which he founded at Baghdád, in the Karkh quarter, and generously endowed, was a favourite haunt of literary men, and its members seem to have enjoyed pretty much the same privileges as belong to the Fellows of an Oxford or Cambridge College.[2]

Like most of their countrymen, the Buwayhids were Shí'ites in religion. We read in the Annals of Abu 'l-Maḥásin under the year 341 A.H. = 952 A.D. :—

Zeal of the Buwayhids for Shí'ite principles.

"In this year the Vizier al-Muhallabí arrested some persons who held the doctrine of metempsychosis (*tanásukh*). Among them were a youth who declared that the spirit of 'Alí b. Abí Ṭálib had passed into his body, and a woman who claimed that the spirit of Fáṭima was dwelling in her; while another man pretended to be Gabriel. On being flogged, they excused themselves by alleging their relationship to the Family of the Prophet, whereupon Mu'izzu 'l-Dawla ordered them to be set free. This he did because of his attachment to

---

[1] 'Abdu 'l-Ḥamíd flourished in the latter days of the Umayyad dynasty. See Ibn Khallikán, De Slane's translation, vol. ii, p. 173; Mas'údí, *Murúju 'l-Dhahab*, vol. vi, p. 81.

[2] See Professor Margoliouth's Introduction to the *Letters of Abu 'l-'Alá al-Ma'arrí*, p. xxiv.

Shí'ism. It is well known," says the author in conclusion, "that the Buwayhids were Shí'ites and Ráfiḍites."[1]

Three dynasties contemporary with the Buwayhids have still to be mentioned: the Ghaznevids in Afghanistan, the Ḥamdánids in Syria, and the Fáṭimids in Egypt.

The Ghaznevids (976–1186 A.D.).

Sabuktagín, the founder of the first-named dynasty, was a Turkish slave. His son, Maḥmúd, who succeeded to the throne of Ghazna in 998 A.D., made short work of the already tottering Sámánids, and then sweeping far and wide over Northern India, began a series of conquests which, before his death in 1030 A.D., reached from Lahore to Samarcand and Iṣfahán. Although the Persian and Transoxanian provinces of his huge empire were soon torn away by the Seljúqs, Maḥmúd's invasion of India, which was undertaken with the object of winning that country for Islam, permanently established Muḥammadan influence, at any rate in the Panjáb. As regards their religious views, the Turkish Ghaznevids stand in sharp contrast with the Persian houses of Sámán and Buwayh. It has been well said that the true genius of the Turks lies in action, not in speculation. When Islam came across their path, they saw that it was a simple and practical creed such as the soldier requires; so they accepted it without further parley. The Turks have always remained loyal to Islam, the Islam of Abú Bakr and 'Umar, which is a very different thing from the Islam of Shí'ite Persia. Maḥmúd proved his orthodoxy by banishing the Mu'tazilites of Rayy and burning their books together with the philosophical and astronomical works that fell into his hands; but on the same occasion he carried off a hundred camel-loads of presumably harmless literature to his capital. That he had no deep enthusiasm for letters is shown, for

[1] Abu 'l-Maḥásin, *al-Nujúm al-Záhira*, ed. by Juynboll, vol. ii, p. 333. The original Ráfiḍites were those schismatics who rejected (*rafaḍa*) the Caliphs Abú Bakr and 'Umar, but the term is generally used as synonymous with Shí'ite.

example, by his shabby treatment of the poet Firdawsí. Nevertheless, he ardently desired the glory and prestige accruing to a sovereign whose court formed the rallying-point of all that was best in the literary and scientific culture of the day, and such was Ghazna in the eleventh century. Besides the brilliant group of Persian poets, with Firdawsí at their head, we may mention among the Arabic-writing authors who flourished under this dynasty the historians al-'Utbí and al-Bírúní.

The Ḥamdánids (929–1003 A.D.).

While the Eastern Empire of Islam was passing into the hands of Persians and Turks, we find the Arabs still holding their own in Syria and Mesopotamia down to the end of the tenth century. These Arab and generally nomadic dynasties were seldom of much account. The Ḥamdánids of Aleppo alone deserve to be noticed here, and that chiefly for the sake of the peerless Sayfu 'l-Dawla, a worthy descendant of the tribe of Taghlib, which in the days of heathendom produced the poet-warrior, 'Amr b. Kulthúm. 'Abdulláh b. Ḥamdán was appointed governor of Mosul and its dependencies by the Caliph Muktafí in 905 A.D., and in 942 his sons Ḥasan and 'Alí received the complimentary titles of Náṣiru 'l-Dawla (Defender of the State) and Sayfu 'l-Dawla (Sword of the State). Two years later Sayfu 'l-Dawla captured Aleppo and brought the whole of Northern Syria under his dominion. During a reign of twenty-three years he was continuously engaged in harrying the Byzantines on the frontiers of Asia Minor, but although he gained some glorious victories, which his laureate Mutanabbí has immortalised, the fortune of war went in the long run steadily against him, and his successors were unable to preserve their little kingdom from being crushed between the Byzantines in the north and the Fáṭimids in the south. The Ḥamdánids have an especial claim on our sympathy, because they revived for a time the fast-decaying and already almost broken spirit of Arabian nationalism. It is this spirit that speaks with a powerful voice in Mutanabbí and declares itself, for example, in such verses as these :—[1]

> "Men from their kings alone their worth derive,
> But Arabs ruled by aliens cannot thrive :
> Boors without culture, without noble fame,
> Who know not loyalty and honour's name.
> Go where thou wilt, thou seest in every land
> Folk driven like cattle by a servile band."

The circle of Sayfu 'l-Dawla.

The reputation which Sayfu 'l-Dawla's martial exploits and his repeated triumphs over the enemies of Islam richly earned for him in the eyes of his contemporaries was enhanced by the conspicuous energy and munificence with which he cultivated the arts of peace. Considering the brevity of his reign and the relatively small extent of his resources, we may well be astonished to contemplate the unique assemblage of literary talent then mustered in Aleppo. There was, first of all, Mutanabbí, in the opinion of his countrymen the greatest of Moslem poets ; there was Sayfu 'l-Dawla's cousin, the chivalrous Abú Firás, whose war-songs are relieved by many a touch of tender and true feeling ; there was Abu 'l-Faraj of Iṣfahán, who on presenting to Sayfu 'l-Dawla his *Kitábu 'l-Aghání*, one of the most celebrated and important works in all Arabic literature, received one thousand pieces of gold accompanied with an expression of regret that the prince was obliged to remunerate him so inadequately ; there was also the great philosopher, Abú Naṣr al-Fárábí, whose modest wants were satisfied by a daily pension of four dirhems (about two shillings) from the public treasury. Surely this is a record not easily surpassed even in the heyday of 'Abbásid patronage. As for the writers of less note whom Sayfu 'l-Dawla attracted to Aleppo, their name is legion. Space must be found for the poets Sarí al-Raffá, Abu 'l-'Abbás al-Námí, and Abu 'l-Faraj al-Babbaghá ;

[1] Mutanabbí, ed. by Dieterici, p. 148, last line and foll.

for the preacher (*khaṭíb*) Ibn Nubáta, who would often rouse the enthusiasm of his audience while he urged the duty of zealously prosecuting the Holy War against Christian Byzantium; and for the philologist Ibn Khálawayh, whose lectures were attended by students from all parts of the Muḥammadan world. The literary renaissance which began at this time in Syria was still making its influence felt when Tha'álibí wrote his *Yatíma*, about thirty years after the death of Sayfu 'l-Dawla, and it produced in Abu 'l-'Alá al-Ma'arrí (born 973 A.D.) an original and highly interesting personality, to whom we shall return on another occasion.

The Fáṭimids (909–1171 A.D.).

The dynasties hitherto described were political in their origin, having generally been founded by ambitious governors or vassals. These upstarts made no pretensions to the nominal authority, which they left in the hands of the Caliph even while they forced him at the sword's point to recognise their political independence. The Sámánids and Buwayhids, Shí'ites as they were, paid the same homage to the Caliph in Baghdád as did the Sunnite Ghaznevids. But in the beginning of the tenth century there arose in Africa a great Shí'ite power, that of the Fáṭimids, who took for themselves the title and prerogatives of the Caliphate, which they asserted to be theirs by right Divine. This event was only the climax of a deep-laid and skilfully organised plot—one of the most extraordinary in all history. It had been put in train half a century earlier by a certain 'Abdulláh the son of Maymún, a Persian oculist (*qaddáḥ*) belonging to Aḥwáz. Filled with a fierce hatred of the Arabs and with a free-thinker's contempt for Islam, 'Abdulláh b. Maymún conceived the idea of a vast secret society which should be all things to all men, and which, by playing on the strongest passions and tempting the inmost weaknesses of human nature, should unite malcontents of every description in a conspiracy to overthrow the existing *régime.* Modern readers may find a parallel for this romantic project in the pages of Dumas, although the Aramis of *Twenty Years After* is a simpleton beside 'Abdulláh. He saw that the movement, in order to succeed, must be started on a religious basis, and he therefore identified himself with an obscure Shí'ite sect, the Ismá'ílís, who were so called because they regarded Muḥammad, son of Ismá'íl, son of Ja'far al-Ṣádiq, as the Seventh Imám. Under 'Abdulláh the Ismá'ílís developed their mystical and antinomian doctrines, of which an excellent account has been given by Professor Browne in the first volume of his *Literary History of Persia* (p. 405 sqq.). Here we can only refer to the ingenious and fatally insidious methods which he devised for gaining proselytes on a gigantic scale, and with such amazing success that from this time until the Mongol invasion—a period of almost four centuries—the Ismá'ílites (Fáṭimids, Carmathians, and Assassins) either ruled or ravaged a great part of the Muḥammadan Empire. It is unnecessary to discuss the question whether 'Abdulláh b. Maymún was, as Professor Browne thinks, primarily a religious enthusiast, or whether, according to the view commonly held, his real motives were patriotism and personal ambition. The history of Islam shows clearly enough that the revolutionist is nearly always disguised as a religious leader, while, on the other hand, every founder of a militant sect is potentially the head of a state. 'Abdulláh may have been a fanatic first and a politician afterwards; more probably he was both at once from the beginning. His plan of operations was briefly as follows:—

The Ismá'ílite propaganda.

The *dá'í* or missionary charged with the task of gaining adherents for the Hidden Imám (see p. 216 seq.), in whose name allegiance was demanded, would settle in some place, representing himself to be a merchant, Ṣúfí, or the like. By renouncing worldly pleasures, making a show of strict piety, and performing apparent miracles, it was easy for him to pass as a saint with the common folk. As soon as he was assured of his neighbours' confidence and respect, he began to raise doubts in their minds. He would suggest difficult problems of theology or dwell on the mysterious significance of certain passages of the Koran. May there not be (he would ask) in religion itself a deeper meaning than appears on the surface? Then, having excited the curiosity of his hearers, he suddenly breaks off. When pressed to continue his explanation, he declares that such mysteries cannot be communicated save to those who take a binding oath of secrecy and obedience and consent to pay a fixed sum of money in token of their good faith. If these conditions were accepted, the neophyte entered upon the second of the nine degrees of initiation. He was taught that mere observance of the laws of Islam is not pleasing to God, unless the true doctrine be received through the Imáms who have it in keeping. These Imáms (as he next learned) are seven in number, beginning with 'Alí; the seventh and last is Muḥammad, son of Ismá'íl. On reaching the fourth degree he definitely ceased to be a Moslem, for here he was taught the Ismá'ilite system of theology in which Muḥammad b. Ismá'íl supersedes the founder of Islam as the greatest and last of all the Prophets. Comparatively few initiates advanced beyond this grade to a point where every form of positive religion was allegorised away, and only philosophy was left. "It is clear what a tremendous weapon, or rather machine, was thus created. Each man was given the amount of light which he could bear and which was suited to his prejudices, and he was made to believe that the end of the whole work would be the attaining of what he regarded as most desirable."[1] Moreover, the Imám Muḥammad b. Ismá'íl having disappeared long ago, the veneration which sought a visible object was naturally transferred to his successor and representative on earth, viz., 'Abdulláh b. Maymún, who filled the same office in relation to him as Aaron to Moses and 'Alí to Muḥammad.

About the middle of the ninth century the state of the Moslem Empire was worse, if possible, than it had been in the latter days of Umayyad rule. The peasantry of 'Iráq were impoverished by the desolation into which that flourishing province was beginning to fall in consequence of the frequent and prolonged civil wars. In 869 A.D. the negro slaves (*Zanj*) employed in the saltpetre industry, for which Basra was famous, took up arms at the call of an 'Alid Messiah, and

[1] D. B. Macdonald, *Muslim Theology*, p. 43 seq.

during fourteen years carried fire and sword through Khúzistán and the adjacent territory. We can imagine that all this misery and discontent was a godsend to the Ismá'ílites. The old cry, "A deliverer of the Prophet's House," which served the 'Abbásids so well against the Umayyads, was now raised with no less effect against the 'Abbásids themselves.

'Abdulláh b. Maymún died in 875 A.D., but the agitation went on, and rapidly gathered force. One of the leading spirits was Ḥamdán Qarmaṭ, who gave his name to the Carmathian branch of the Ismá'ílís. These Carmathians (*Qarámiṭa*, sing. *Qirmiṭí*) spread over Southern Persia and Yemen, and in the tenth century they threatened Baghdád, repeatedly waylaid the pilgrim-caravans, sacked Mecca and bore away the Black Stone as a trophy; in short, established a veritable reign of terror. We must return, however, to the main Ismá'ílite faction headed by the descendants of 'Abdulláh b. Maymún. Their emissaries discovered a promising field of work in North Africa among the credulous and fanatical Berbers. When all was ripe, Sa'íd b. Ḥusayn, the grandson of 'Abdulláh b. Maymún, left Salamya in Syria, the centre from which the wires had hitherto been pulled, and crossing over to Africa appeared as the long-expected Mahdí under the name of 'Ubaydu'lláh. He gave himself out to be a great-grandson of the Imám Muḥammad b. Ismá'íl and therefore in the direct line of descent from 'Alí b. Abí Ṭálib and Fáṭima the daughter of the Prophet. We need not stop to discuss this highly questionable genealogy from which the Fáṭimid dynasty derives its name. In 910 A.D. 'Ubaydu'lláh entered Raqqáda in triumph and assumed the title of Commander of the Faithful. Tunis, where the Aghlabites had ruled since 800 A.D., was the cradle of Fáṭimid power, and here they built their capital, Mahdiyya, near the ancient Thapsus. Gradually advancing eastward, they conquered Egypt and Syria as far as Damascus (969–970 A.D.). At this

The Fáṭimid dynasty founded by the Mahdí 'Ubaydu'lláh (909 A.D.).

time the seat of government was removed to the newly-founded city of Cairo (*al-Qáhira*), which remained for two centuries the metropolis of the Fáṭimid Empire.[1]

The Shí'ite Anti-Caliphs maintained themselves in Egypt until 1171 A.D., when the famous Saladin (Ṣaláḥu 'l-Dín b. Ayyúb) took possession of that country and restored the Sunnite faith. He soon added Syria to his dominions, and "the fall of Jerusalem (in 1187) roused Europe to undertake the Third Crusade." The Ayyúbids were strictly orthodox, as behoved the champions of Islam against Christianity. They built and endowed many theological colleges. The Ṣúfí pantheist, Shihábu 'l-Dín Yaḥyá al-Suhrawardí, was executed at Aleppo by order of Saladin's son, Malik al-Ẓáhir, in 1191 A.D.

The Ayyúbids (1171–1250 A.D.).

The two centuries preceding the extinction of the 'Abbásid Caliphate by the Mongols witnessed the rise and decline of the Seljúq Turks, who "once more re-united Muḥammadan Asia from the western frontier of Afghanistan to the Mediterranean under one sovereign." Seljúq b. Tuqáq was a Turcoman chief. Entering Transoxania, he settled near Bukhárá and went over with his whole people to Islam. His descendants, Ṭughril Beg and Chagar Beg, invaded Khurásán, annexed the western provinces of the Ghaznevid Empire, and finally absorbed the remaining dominions of the Buwayhids. Baghdád was occupied by Ṭughril Beg in 1055 A.D. It has been said that the Seljúqs contributed almost nothing to culture, but this perhaps needs some qualification. Although Alp Arslán, who succeeded Ṭughril, and his son Malik Sháh devoted their energies in the first place to military affairs, the

The Seljúqs (1037–1300 A.D.).

[1] I regret that lack of space compels me to omit the further history of the Fáṭimids. Readers who desire information on this subject may consult Stanley Lane-Poole's *History of Egypt in the Middle Ages*; Wüstenfeld's *Geschichte der Faṭimiden-Chalifen* (Göttingen, 1881); and Professor Browne's *Lit. Hist. of Persia*, vol. ii, p. 196 sqq.

latter at least was an accomplished and enlightened monarch. "He exerted himself to spread the benefits of civilisation: he dug numerous canals, walled a great number of cities, built bridges, and constructed *ribáṭs* in the desert places."[1] He was deeply interested in astronomy, and scientific as well as theological studies received his patronage. Any shortcomings of Alp Arslán and Malik Sháh in this respect were amply repaired by their famous minister, Ḥasan b. 'Alí, the Niẓámu 'l-Mulk or 'Constable of the Empire,' to give him the title which he has made his own. Like so many great Viziers, he was a Persian, and his achievements must not detain us here, but it may be mentioned that he founded in Baghdád and Naysábúr the two celebrated academies which were called in his honour al-Niẓámiyya.

Arabia and Spain.

We have now taken a general, though perforce an extremely curtailed and disconnected, view of the political conditions which existed during the 'Abbásid period in most parts of the Muḥammadan Empire except Arabia and Spain. The motherland of Islam had long sunk to the level of a minor province: leaving the Holy Cities out of consideration, one might compare its inglorious destiny under the Caliphate to that of Macedonia in the empire which Alexander bequeathed to his successors, the Ptolemies and Seleucids. As regards the political history of Spain a few words will conveniently be said in a subsequent chapter, where the literature produced by Spanish Moslems will demand our attention. In the meantime we shall pass on to the characteristic literary developments of this period, which correspond more or less closely to the historical outlines.

The first thing that strikes the student of mediæval Arabic literature is the fact that a very large proportion of the leading writers are non-Arabs, or at best semi-Arabs, men whose fathers

[1] Ibn Khallikán, De Slane's translation, vol. iv, p. 441.

or mothers were of foreign, and especially Persian, race. They wrote in Arabic, because down to about 1000 A.D. that language was the sole medium of literary expression in the Muḥammadan world, a monopoly which it retained in scientific compositions until the Mongol Invasion of the thirteenth century. I have already referred to the question whether such men as Bashshár b. Burd, Abú Nuwás, Ibn Qutayba, Ṭabarí, Ghazálí, and hundreds of others should be included in a literary history of the Arabs, and have given reasons, which I need not repeat in this place, for considering their admission to be not only desirable but fully justified on logical grounds.[1] The absurdity of treating them as Persians—and there is no alternative, if they are not to be reckoned as Arabs—appears to me self-evident.

"It is strange," says Ibn Khaldún, "that most of the learned among the Moslems who have excelled in the religious or intellectual sciences are non-Arabs (*'Ajam*) with rare exceptions; and even those savants who claimed Arabian descent spoke a foreign language, grew up in foreign lands, and studied under foreign masters, notwithstanding that the community to which they belonged was Arabian and the author of its religion an Arab." The historian proceeds to explain the cause of this singular circumstance in an interesting passage which may be summarised as follows:—

Ibn Khaldún's explanation of the fact that learning was chiefly cultivated by the Persian Moslems.

The first Moslems were entirely ignorant of art and science, all their attention being devoted to the ordinances of the Koran, which they "carried in their breasts," and to the practice (*sunna*) of the Prophet. At that time the Arabs knew nothing of the way by which learning is taught, of the art of composing books, and of the means whereby knowledge is enregistered. Those, however, who could repeat the Koran and relate the Traditions of Muḥammad were called Readers (*qurrá*). This oral transmission continued until the reign of Hárún al-Rashíd, when the need of

[1] See the Introduction.

securing the Traditions against corruption or of preventing their total loss caused them to be set down in writing; and in order to distinguish the genuine Traditions from the spurious, every *isnád* (chain of witnesses) was carefully scrutinised. Meanwhile the purity of the Arabic tongue had gradually become impaired: hence arose the science of grammar; and the rapid development of Law and Divinity brought it about that other sciences, *e.g.*, logic and dialectic, were professionally cultivated in the great cities of the Muḥammadan Empire. The inhabitants of these cities were chiefly Persians, freedmen and tradesmen, who had been long accustomed to the arts of civilisation. Accordingly the most eminent of the early grammarians, traditionists, and scholastic theologians, as well as of those learned in the principles of Law and in the interpretation of the Koran, were Persians by race or education, and the saying of the Prophet was verified—"*If Knowledge were attached to the ends of the sky, some amongst the Persians would have reached it.*" Amidst all this intellectual activity the Arabs, who had recently emerged from a nomadic life, found the exercise of military and administrative command too engrossing to give them leisure for literary avocations which have always been disdained by a ruling caste. They left such studies to the Persians and the mixed race (*al-muwalladún*), which sprang from intermarriage of the conquerors with the conquered. They did not entirely look down upon the men of learning but recognised their services—since after all it was Islam and the sciences connected with Islam that profited thereby.[1]

Even in the Umayyad period, as we have seen, the maxim that Knowledge is Power was strikingly illustrated by the immense social influence which Persian divines exerted in the Muḥammadan community.[2] Nevertheless, true Arabs of the old type regarded these *Mawálí* and their learning with undisguised contempt. To the great majority of Arabs, who prided themselves on their noble lineage and were content to know nothing beyond the glorious traditions of heathendom and the virtues practised by their sires, all literary culture seemed petty and degrading. Their overbearing attitude

[1] Ibn Khaldún, *Muqaddima* (Beyrout, 1900), p. 543 seq.=De Slane, *Prolegomena*, vol iii, p. 296 sqq.

[2] *Cf.* Goldziher, *Muhamm. Studien*, Part I, p. 114 seq.

towards the *Mawálí*, which is admirably depicted in the first part of Goldziher's *Muhammedanische Studien*, met with a vigorous response. Non-Arabs and Moslem pietists alike appealed to the highest authority—the Koran; and since they required a more definite and emphatic pronouncement than was forthcoming from that source, they put in the mouth of the Prophet sayings like these: "He that speaks Arabic is thereby an Arab"; "whoever of the people of Persia accepts Islam is (as much an Arab as) one of Quraysh." This doctrine made no impression upon the Arabian aristocracy, but with the downfall of the Umayyads the political and social equality of the *Mawálí* became an accomplished fact. Not that the Arabs were at all disposed to abate their pretensions. They bitterly resented the favour which the foreigners enjoyed and the influence which they exercised. The national indignation finds a voice in many poems of the early 'Abbásid period, *e.g.*:—

"See how the asses which they used to ride
They have unsaddled, and sleek mules bestride!
No longer kitchen-herbs they buy and sell,[1]
But in the palace and the court they dwell;
Against us Arabs full of rage and spleen,
Hating the Prophet and the Moslem's *dín*.[2]

The side of the non-Arabs in this literary quarrel was vehemently espoused by a party who called themselves the Shu'úbites (*al-Shu'úbiyya*),[3] while their opponents gave them

[1] Read *masháráti 'l-buqúl* (beds of vegetables), not *musharát* as my rendering implies. The change makes little difference to the sense, but *masharat*, being an Aramaic word, is peculiarly appropriate here.

[2] *Aghání*, xii, 177, l. 5 sqq; Von Kremer, *Culturgesch. Streifzüge*, p. 32. These lines are aimed, as has been remarked by S. Khuda Bukhsh (*Contributions to the History of Islamic Civilisation*, Calcutta, 1905, p. 92), against Nabaṭæans who falsely claimed to be Persians.

[3] The name is derived from Koran, xlix, 13: "*O Men, We have created you of a male and a female and have made you into peoples* (shu'úban) *and tribes, that ye might know one another. Verily the noblest of you in*

the name of Levellers (*Ahlu 'l-Taswiya*), because they contended for the equality of all Moslems without regard to distinctions of race. I must refer the reader who seeks information concerning the history of the movement to Goldziher's masterly study,[1] where the controversial methods adopted by the Shu'úbites are set forth in ample detail. He shows how the bolder spirits among them, not satisfied with claiming an *equal* position, argued that the Arabs were absolutely inferior to the Persians and other peoples. The question was hotly debated, and many eminent writers took part in the fray. On the Shu'úbite side Abú 'Ubayda, Bírúní, and Ḥamza of Iṣfahán deserve mention. Jáḥiẓ and Ibn Durayd were the most notable defenders of their own Arabian nationality, but the 'pro-Arabs' also included several men of Persian origin, such as Ibn Qutayba, Baládhurí, and Zamakhsharí. The Shu'úbites directed their attacks principally against the racial pride of the Arabs, who were fond of boasting that they were the noblest of all mankind and spoke the purest and richest language in the world. Consequently the Persian genealogists and philologists lost no opportunity of bringing to light scandalous and discreditable circumstances connected with the history of the Arab tribes or of particular families. Arabian poetry, especially the vituperative pieces (*mathálib*), furnished abundant matter of this sort, which was adduced by the Shu'úbites as convincing evidence that the claims of the Arabs to superior nobility were absurd. At the same time the national view as to the unique and incomparable excellence of the Arabic language received some rude criticism.

The Shu'úbites.

So acute and irreconcilable were the racial differences between Arabs and Persians that one is astonished to see how thoroughly the latter became Arabicised in the course of a

the sight of God are they that do most fear Him." Thus the designation 'Shu'úbite' emphasises the fact that according to Muḥammad's teaching the Arab Moslems are no better than their non-Arab brethren.

[1] *Muhamm. Studien*, Part I, p. 147 sqq.

few generations. As clients affiliated to an Arab tribe, they assumed Arabic names and sought to disguise their foreign extraction by fair means or foul. Many provided themselves with fictitious pedigrees, on the strength of which they passed for Arabs. Such a pretence could have deceived nobody if it had not been supported by a complete assimilation in language, manners, and even to some extent in character. On the neutral ground of Muḥammadan science animosities were laid aside, and men of both races laboured enthusiastically for the common cause. When at length, after a century of bloody strife and engrossing political agitation, the great majority of Moslems found themselves debarred from taking part in public affairs, it was only natural that thousands of ardent and ambitious souls should throw their pent-up energies into the pursuit of wealth or learning. We are not concerned here with the marvellous development of trade under the first 'Abbásid Caliphs, of which Von Kremer has given a full and entertaining description in his *Culturgeschichte des Orients.* It may be recalled, however, that many commercial terms, *e.g.*, tariff, names of fabrics (muslin, tabby, &c.), occurring in English as well as in most European languages are of Arabic origin and were brought to Europe by merchants from Baghdád, Mosul, Baṣra, and other cities of Western Asia. This material expansion was accompanied by an outburst of intellectual activity such as the East had never witnessed before. It seemed as if all the world from the Caliph down to the humblest citizen suddenly became students, or at least patrons, of literature. In quest of knowledge men travelled over three continents and returned home, like bees laden with honey, to impart the precious stores which they had accumulated to crowds of eager disciples, and to compile with incredible industry those works of encyclopædic range and erudition from which modern Science, in the widest sense of the word, has derived far more than is generally supposed.

Assimilation of Arabs and Persians.

Enthusiasm for learning in the early 'Abbásid period.

The Revolution which made the fortune of the 'Abbásid House was a triumph for Islam and the party of religious reform. While under the worldly Umayyads the studies of Law and Tradition met with no public encouragement and were only kept alive by the pious zeal of oppressed theologians, the new dynasty drew its strength from the Muḥammadan ideas which it professed to establish, and skilfully adapted its policy to satisfying the ever-increasing claims of the Church. Accordingly the Moslem sciences which arose at this time proceeded in the first instance from the Koran and the Ḥadíth. The sacred books offered many difficulties both to provincial Arabs and especially to Persians and other Moslems of foreign extraction. For their right understanding a knowledge of Arabic grammar and philology was essential, and this involved the study of the ancient Pre-islamic poems which supplied the most authentic models of Arabian speech in its original purity. The study of these poems entailed researches into genealogy and history, which in the course of time became independent branches of learning. Similarly the science of Tradition was systematically developed in order to provide Moslems with practical rules for the conduct of life in every conceivable particular, and various schools of Law sprang into existence.

Development of the Moslem sciences.

Muḥammadan writers usually distinguish the sciences which are connected with the Koran and those which the Arabs learned from foreign peoples. In the former class they include the Traditional or Religious Sciences (*al-'Ulúm al-Naqliyya awi 'l-Shar'iyya*) and the Linguistic Sciences (*'Ulúmu 'l-Lisáni 'l-'Arabí*); in the latter the Intellectual or Philosophical Sciences (*al-'Ulúm al-'Aqliyya awi 'l-Ḥikmiyya*), which are sometimes called 'The Sciences of the Foreigners' (*'Ulúmu 'l-'Ajam*) or 'The Ancient Sciences' (*al-'Ulúm al-Qadíma*).

Their classification.

The general scope of this division may be illustrated by the following table:—

I. THE NATIVE SCIENCES.

1. Koranic Exegesis (*'Ilmu 'l-Tafsír*).
2. Koranic Criticism (*'Ilmu 'l-Qirá'át*).
3. The Science of Apostolic Tradition (*'Ilmu 'l-Ḥadíth*).
4. Jurisprudence (*Fiqh*).
5. Scholastic Theology (*'Ilmu 'l-Kalám*).
6. Grammar (*Naḥw*).
7. Lexicography (*Lugha*).
8. Rhetoric (*Bayán*).
9. Literature (*Adab*).

II. THE FOREIGN SCIENCES.

1. Philosophy (*Falsafa*).[1]
2. Geometry (*Handasa*).[2]
3. Astronomy (*'Ilmu 'l-Nujúm*).
4. Music (*Músíqí*).
5. Medicine (*Ṭibb*).
6. Magic and Alchemy (*al-Siḥr wa-'l-Kímiyá*).

The early 'Abbásid period favourable to free-thought.

The religious phenomena of the Period will be discussed in a separate chapter, and here I can only allude cursorily to their general character. We have seen that during the whole Umayyad epoch, except in the brief reign of 'Umar b. 'Abd al-'Azíz, the professors of religion were out of sympathy with the court, and that many of them withdrew from all participation in public affairs. It was otherwise when the 'Abbásids established themselves in power. Theology now dwelt in the shadow of the throne and directed the policy of the Government. Honours were showered on eminent jurists and divines, who frequently held official posts of high importance and stood in the most confidential and intimate relations to the Caliph ; a classical example is the friendship of the Cadi Abú Yúsuf and Hárún al-Rashíd. The century after the Revolution gave birth to the four great schools of Muḥammadan Law, which are still called by the

[1] The term *Falsafa* properly includes Logic, Metaphysics, Mathematics Medicine, and the Natural Sciences.

[2] Here we might add the various branches of Mathematics, such as Arithmetic, Algebra, Mechanics, &c.

names of their founders—Málik b. Anas, Abú Ḥanífa, Sháfi'í, and Aḥmad b. Ḥanbal. At this time the scientific and intellectual movement had free play. The earlier Caliphs usually encouraged speculation so long as it threatened no danger to the existing *régime*. Under Ma'mún and his successors the Mu'tazilite Rationalism became the State religion, and Islam seemed to have entered upon an era of enlightenment. Thus the first 'Abbásid period (750-847 A.D.) with its new learning and liberal theology may well be compared to the European Renaissance; but in the words of a celebrated Persian poet—

Khil'ati bas fákhir ámad 'umr 'aybash kútahíst.[1]

"Life is a very splendid robe: its fault is brevity."

The triumph of orthodoxy.

The Caliph Mutawakkil (847-861 A.D.) signalised his accession by declaring the Mu'tazilite doctrines to be heretical and by returning to the traditional faith. Stern measures were taken against dissenters. Henceforth there was little room in Islam for independent thought. The populace regarded philosophy and natural science as a species of infidelity. Authors of works on these subjects ran a serious risk unless they disguised their true opinions and brought the results of their investigations into apparent conformity with the text of the Koran. About the middle of the tenth century the reactionary spirit assumed a dogmatic shape in the system of Abu 'l-Ḥasan al-Ash'arí, the father of Muḥammadan Scholasticism, which is essentially opposed to intellectual freedom and has maintained its petrifying influence almost unimpaired down to the present time.

I could wish that this chapter were more worthy of the title which I have chosen for it, but the foregoing pages will have served their purpose if they have enabled my readers to form some idea of the politics of the Period and of the broad features marking the course of its literary and religious history.

[1] 'Abdu 'l-Raḥmán Jámí († 1492 A.D.).

CHAPTER VII

POETRY, LITERATURE, AND SCIENCE IN THE 'ABBÁSID PERIOD

The Pre-islamic poets regarded as classical

PRE-ISLAMIC poetry was the natural expression of nomad life. We might therefore have expected that the new conditions and ideas introduced by Islam would rapidly work a corresponding revolution in the poetical literature of the following century. Such, however, was far from being the case. The Umayyad poets clung tenaciously to the great models of the Heroic Age and even took credit for their skilful imitation of the antique odes. The early Muḥammadan critics, who were philologists by profession, held fast to the principle that Poetry in Pre-islamic times had reached a perfection which no modern bard could hope to emulate, and which only the lost ideals of chivalry could inspire.[1] To have been born after Islam was in itself a proof of poetical inferiority.[2] Linguistic considerations, of course, entered largely into this prejudice. The old poems were studied as repositories of the pure classical tongue and were estimated mainly from a grammarian's standpoint.

These ideas gained wide acceptance in literary circles and gradually biassed the popular taste to such an extent that learned pedants could boast, like Khalíl b. Aḥmad,

[1] I am deeply indebted in the following pages to Goldziher's essay entitled *Alte und Neue Poesie im Urtheile der Arabischen Kritiker* in his *Abhand. zur Arab. Philologie*, Part I, pp. 122–174.

[2] *Cf.* the remark made by Abú 'Amr b. al-'Alá about the poet Akhṭal (p. 242 *supra*).

the inventor of Arabic prosody, that it lay in their power to make or mar the reputation of a rising poet as they deemed fit. Originality being condemned in advance, those who desired the approval of this self-constituted Academy were obliged to waste their time and talents upon elaborate reproduction of the ancient masterpieces, and to entertain courtiers and citizens with borrowed pictures of Bedouin life in which neither they nor their audience took the slightest interest. Some, it is true, recognised the absurdity of the thing. Abú Nuwás († *circa* 810 A.D.) often ridicules the custom, to which reference has been made elsewhere, of apostrophising the deserted encampment (*aṭlál* or *ṭulúl*) in the opening lines of an ode, and pours contempt on the fashionable glorification of antiquity. In the passage translated below he gives a description of the desert and its people which recalls some of Dr. Johnson's sallies at the expense of Scotland and Scotsmen :—

Abú Nuwás as a critic.

"Let the south-wind moisten with rain the desolate scene
And Time efface what once was so fresh and green!
Make the camel-rider free of a desert space
Where high-bred camels trot with unwearied pace;
Where only mimosas and thistles flourish, and where,
For hunting, wolves and hyenas are nowise rare!
Amongst the Bedouins seek not enjoyment out:
What do they enjoy? They live in hunger and drought.
Let them drink their bowls of milk and leave them alone,
To whom life's finer pleasures are all unknown."[1]

Ibn Qutayba, who died towards the end of the ninth century A.D., was the first critic of importance to declare that ancients and moderns should be judged on their merits without regard to their age. He writes as follows in the Introduction

[1] *Diwan des Abu Nowas, Die Weinlieder*, ed. by Ahlwardt, No. 10, vv. 1–5.

to his 'Book of Poetry and Poets' (*Kitábu 'l-Shi'r wa-'l-Shu'ará*) :—[1]

Ibn Qutayba on ancient and modern poets.

"In citing extracts from the works of the poets I have been guided by my own choice and have refused to admire anything merely because others thought it admirable. I have not regarded any ancient with veneration on account of his antiquity nor any modern with contempt on account of his being modern, but I have taken an impartial view of both sides, giving every one his due and amply acknowledging his merit. Some of our scholars, as I am aware, pronounce a feeble poem to be good, because its author was an ancient, and include it among their chosen pieces, while they call a sterling poem bad though its only fault is that it was composed in their own time or that they have seen its author. God, however, did not restrict learning and poetry and rhetoric to a particular age nor appropriate them to a particular class, but has always distributed them in common amongst His servants, and has caused everything old to be new in its own day and every classic work to be an upstart on its first appearance."

Revolt against classicism.

The inevitable reaction in favour of the new poetry and of contemporary literature in general was hastened by various circumstances which combined to overthrow the prevalent theory that Arabian heathendom and the characteristic pagan virtues—honour, courage, liberality, &c.—were alone capable of producing poetical genius. Among the chief currents of thought tending in this direction, which are lucidly set forth in Goldziher's essay, pp. 148 sqq., we may note (*a*) the pietistic and theological spirit fostered by the 'Abbásid Government, and (*b*) the influence of foreign, pre-eminently Persian, culture. As to the former, it is manifest that devout Moslems would not be at all disposed to admit the exclusive pretensions made on behalf of the *Jáhiliyya* or to agree with those who exalted chivalry (*muruwwa*) above religion (*dín*). Were not the language and style of the Koran incomparably excellent? Surely the Holy Book was a more proper subject for study

[1] Ed. by De Goeje, p. 5, ll. 5-15.

than heathen verses. But if Moslems began to call Pre-islamic ideals in question, it was especially the Persian ascendancy resulting from the triumph of the 'Abbásid House that shook the old arrogant belief of the Arabs in the intellectual supremacy of their race. So far from glorying in the traditions of paganism, many people thought it grossly insulting to mention an 'Abbásid Caliph in the same breath with heroes of the past like Ḥátim of Ṭayyi' and Harim b. Sinán. The philosopher al-Kindí († about 850 A.D.) rebuked a poet for venturing on such odious comparisons. "Who are these Arabian vagabonds" (*ṣa'álíku 'l-'Arab*), he asked, "and what worth have they?"[1]

Critics in favour of the modern school.

While Ibn Qutayba was content to urge that the modern poets should get a fair hearing, and should be judged not chronologically or philologically, but *æsthetically*, some of the greatest literary critics who came after him do not conceal their opinion that the new poetry is superior to the old. Tha'álibí († 1038 A.D.) asserts that in tenderness and elegance the Pre-islamic bards are surpassed by their successors, and that both alike have been eclipsed by his contemporaries. Ibn Rashíq († *circa* 1070 A.D.), whose *'Umda* on the Art of Poetry is described by Ibn Khaldún as an epoch-making work, thought that the superiority of the moderns would be acknowledged if they discarded the obsolete conventions of the Ode. European readers cannot but sympathise with him when he bids the poets draw inspiration from nature and truth instead of relating imaginary journeys on a camel which they never owned, through deserts which they never saw, to a patron residing in the same city as themselves. This seems to us a very reasonable and necessary protest, but it must be remembered that the Bedouin *qaṣída* was not easily adaptable to the conditions of urban life, and needed complete remoulding rather than modification in detail.[2]

[1] *Cf.* the story told of Abú Tammám by Ibn Khallikán (De Slane's translation, vol. i, p. 350 seq.).

[2] See Nöldeke, *Beiträge*, p. 4.

"In the fifth century," says Goldziher—*i.e.*, from about 1000 A.D.—"the dogma of the unattainable perfection of the heathen poets may be regarded as utterly demolished." Henceforth popular taste ran strongly in the other direction, as is shown by the immense preponderance of modern pieces in the anthologies—a favourite and characteristic branch of Arabic literature—which were compiled during the 'Abbásid period and afterwards, and by frequent complaints of the neglect into which the ancient poetry had fallen. But although, for Moslems generally, Imru'u 'l-Qays and his fellows came to be more or less what Chaucer is to the average Englishman, the views first enunciated by Ibn Qutayba met with bitter opposition from the learned class, many of whom clung obstinately to the old philological principles of criticism, and even declined to recognise the writings of Mutanabbí and Abu 'l-'Alá al-Ma'arrí as poetry, on the ground that those authors did not observe the classical 'types' (*asálíb*).[1] The result of such pedantry may be seen at the present day in thousands of *qaṣídas*, abounding in archaisms and allusions to forgotten far-off things of merely antiquarian interest, but possessing no more claim to consideration here than the Greek and Latin verses of British scholars in a literary history of the Victorian Age.

Popularity of the modern poets.

Passing now to the characteristics of the new poetry which followed the accession of the 'Abbásids, we have to bear in mind that from first to last (with very few exceptions) it flourished under the patronage of the court. There was no organised book trade, no wealthy publishers, so that poets were usually dependent for their livelihood on the capricious bounty of the Caliphs and his favourites whom they belauded. Huge sums were paid

Characteristics of the new poetry.

[1] Ibn Khaldún, *Muqaddima* (Beyrout, 1900), p. 573, l. 21 seq.; *Prolegomena* of Ibn K., translated by De Slane, vol. iii, p. 380.

20

for a successful panegyric, and the bards vied with each other in flattery of the most extravagant description. Even in writers of real genius this prostitution of their art gave rise to a great deal of the false glitter and empty bombast which are often erroneously attributed to Oriental poetry as a whole.[1] These qualities, however, are absolutely foreign to Arabian poetry of the best period. The old Bedouins who praised a man only for that which was in him, and drew their images directly from nature, stand at the opposite pole to Tha'álibí's contemporaries. Under the Umayyads, as we have seen, little change took place. It is not until after the enthronement of the 'Abbásids, when Persians filled the chief offices at court, and when a goodly number of poets and eminent men of learning had Persian blood in their veins, that an unmistakably new note makes itself heard. One might be tempted to surmise that the high-flown, bombastic, and ornate style of which Mutanabbí is the most illustrious exponent, and which is so marked a feature in later Muḥammadan poetry, was first introduced by the Persians and Perso-Arabs who gathered round the Caliph in Baghdád and celebrated the triumph of their own race in the person of a noble Barmecide; but this would scarcely be true. The style in question is not specially Persian; the earliest Arabic-writing poets of Íránian descent, like Bashshár b. Burd and Abú Nuwás, are (so far as I can see) without a trace of it. What the Persians brought into Arabian poetry was not a grandiose style, but a lively and graceful fancy, elegance of diction, depth and tenderness of feeling, and a rich store of ideas.

The process of transformation was aided by other causes besides the influx of Persian and Hellenistic culture: for example, by the growing importance of Islam in public life and the diffusion of a strong religious spirit among the community at large—a spirit which attained its most perfect

[1] See Professor Browne's *Literary History of Persia*, vol. ii, p. 14 sqq.

expression in the reflective and didactic poetry of Abu 'l-'Atáhiya. Every change of many-coloured life is depicted in the brilliant pages of these modern poets, where the reader may find, according to his mood, the maddest gaiety and the shamefullest frivolity; strains of lofty meditation mingled with a world-weary pessimism; delicate sentiment, unforced pathos, and glowing rhetoric; but seldom the manly self-reliance, the wild, invigorating freedom and inimitable freshness of Bedouin song.

Five typical poets of the 'Abbásid period.

It is of course impossible to do justice even to the principal 'Abbásid poets within the limits of this chapter, but the following five may be taken as fairly representative: Muṭí' b. Iyás, Abú Nuwás, Abu 'l-'Atáhiya, Mutanabbí, and Abu 'l-'Alá al-Ma'arrí. The first three were in close touch with the court of Baghdád, while Mutanabbí and Abu 'l-'Alá flourished under the Ḥamdánid dynasty which ruled in Aleppo.

Muṭí' b. Iyás.

Muṭí' b. Iyás only deserves notice here as the earliest poet of the New School. His father was a native of Palestine, but he himself was born and educated at Kúfa. He began his career under the Umayyads, and was devoted to the Caliph Walíd b. Yazíd, who found in him a fellow after his own heart, "accomplished, dissolute, an agreeable companion and excellent wit, reckless in his effrontery and suspected in his religion."[1] When the 'Abbásids came into power Muṭí' attached himself to the Caliph Manṣúr. Many stories are told of the debauched life which he led in the company of *zindíqs*, or free-thinkers, a class of men whose opinions we shall sketch in another chapter. His songs of love and wine are distinguished by their lightness and elegance. The best known is that in which he laments his separation from the daughter of a *Dihqán* (Persian landed

[1] *Aghání*, xii, 80, l. 3.

proprietor), and invokes the two palm-trees of Ḥulwán, a town situated on the borders of the Jibál province between Hamadhán and Baghdád. From this poem arose the proverb, "Faster friends than the two palm-trees of Ḥulwán." [1]

THE YEOMAN'S DAUGHTER.

"O ye two palms, palms of Ḥulwán,
Help me weep Time's bitter dole!
Know that Time for ever parteth
Life from every living soul.

Had ye tasted parting's anguish,
Ye would weep as I, forlorn.
Help me! Soon must ye asunder
By the same hard fate be torn.

Many are the friends and loved ones
Whom I lost in days of yore.
Fare thee well, O yeoman's daughter!—
Never grief like this I bore.
Her, alas, mine eyes behold not,
And on me she looks no more!"

Abú Nuwás (†*circa* 810 A.D.).

By Europeans who know him only through the *Thousand and One Nights* Abú Nuwás is remembered as the boon-companion and court jester of "the good Haroun Alraschid," and as the hero of countless droll adventures and facetious anecdotes—an Oriental Howleglass or Joe Miller. It is often forgotten that he was a great poet who, in the opinion of those most competent to judge, takes rank above all his contemporaries and successors, including even Mutanabbí, and is not surpassed in poetical genius by any ancient bard.

[1] Freytag, *Arabum Proverbia*, vol. i, p. 46 seq., where the reader will find the Arabic text of the verses translated here. Rückert has given a German rendering of the same verses in his *Hamâsa*, vol. i, p. 311. A fuller text of the poem occurs in *Aghání*, xii, 107 seq.

Ḥasan b. Háni' gained the familiar title of Abú Nuwás (Father of the lock of hair) from two locks which hung down on his shoulders. He was born of humble parents, about the middle of the eighth century, in Aḥwáz, the capital of Khúzistán. That he was not a pure Arab the name of his mother, Jallabán, clearly indicates, while the following verse affords sufficient proof that he was not ashamed of his Persian blood :—

"Who are Tamím and Qays and all their kin?
The Arabs in God's sight are nobody." [1]

He received his education at Baṣra, of which city he calls himself a native,[2] and at Kúfa, where he studied poetry and philology under the learned Khalaf al-Aḥmar. After passing a 'Wanderjahr' among the Arabs of the desert, as was the custom of scholars at that time, he made his way to Baghdád and soon eclipsed every competitor at the court of Hárún the Orthodox. A man of the most abandoned character, which he took no pains to conceal, Abú Nuwás, by his flagrant immorality, drunkenness, and blasphemy, excited the Caliph's anger to such a pitch that he often threatened the culprit with death, and actually imprisoned him on several occasions ; but these fits of severity were brief. The poet survived both Hárún and his son, Amín, who succeeded him in the Caliphate. Age brought repentance—"the Devil was sick, the Devil a monk would be." He addressed the following lines from prison to Faḍl b. al-Rabí', whom Hárún appointed Grand Vizier after the fall of the Barmecides :—

"Faḍl, who hast taught and trained me up to goodness
(And goodness is but habit), thee I praise.
Now hath vice fled and virtue me revisits,
And I have turned to chaste and pious ways.

---

[1] *Díwán*, ed. by Ahlwardt, *Die Weinlieder*, No. 26, v. 4.
[2] Ibn Qutayba, *K. al-Shi'r wa-'l-Shu'ará*, p. 502, l. 13.

To see me, thou would'st think the saintly Baṣrite,
Ḥasan, or else Qatáda, met thy gaze,[1]
So do I deck humility with leanness,
While yellow, locust-like, my cheek o'erlays.
Beads on my arm; and on my breast the Scripture,
Where hung a chain of gold in other days."[2]

The Díwán of Abú Nuwás contains poems in many different styles—*e.g.*, panegyric (*madlḥ*), satire (*hijá*), songs of the chase (*ṭardiyyát*), elegies (*maráthí*), and religious poems (*zuhdiyyát*); but love and wine were the two motives by which his genius was most brilliantly inspired. His wine-songs (*khamriyyát*) are generally acknowledged to be incomparable. Here is one of the shortest:—

"Thou scolder of the grape and me,
  I ne'er shall win thy smile!
Because against thee I rebel,
  'Tis churlish to revile.

Ah, breathe no more the name of wine
  Until thou cease to blame,
For fear that thy foul tongue should smirch
  Its fair and lovely name!

Come, pour it out, ye gentle boys,
  A vintage ten years old,
That seems as though 'twere in the cup
  A lake of liquid gold.

And when the water mingles there,
  To fancy's eye are set
Pearls over shining pearls close strung
  As in a carcanet."[3]

---

[1] For the famous ascetic, Ḥasan of Baṣra, see pp. 225–227. Qatáda was a learned divine, also of Baṣra and contemporary with Ḥasan. He died in 735 A.D.

[2] These verses are quoted by Ibn Qutayba, *op. cit.*, p. 507 seq. 'The Scripture' (*al-maṣḥaf*) is of course the Koran.

[3] *Die Weinlieder*, ed. by Ahlwardt, No. 47.

Another poem begins—

"Ho! a cup, and fill it up, and tell me it is wine,
For I will never drink in shade if I can drink in shine!
Curst and poor is every hour that sober I must go,
But rich am I whene'er well drunk I stagger to and fro.
Speak, for shame, the loved one's name, let vain disguise alone:
No good there is in pleasures o'er which a veil is thrown." [1]

Abú Nuwás practised what he preached, and hypocrisy at any rate cannot be laid to his charge. The moral and religious sentiments which appear in some of his poems are not mere cant, but should rather be regarded as the utterance of sincere though transient emotion. Usually he felt and avowed that pleasure was the supreme business of his life, and that religious scruples could not be permitted to stand in the way. He even urges others not to shrink from any excess, inasmuch as the Divine mercy is greater than all the sins of which a man is capable:—

"Accumulate as many sins thou canst:
The Lord is ready to relax His ire.
When the day comes, forgiveness thou wilt find
Before a mighty King and gracious Sire,
And gnaw thy fingers, all that joy regretting
Which thou didst leave thro' terror of Hell-fire!" [2]

We must now bid farewell to Abú Nuwás and the licentious poets (*al-shuʿará al-mujján*) who reflect so admirably the ideas and manners prevailing in court circles and in the upper classes of society which were chiefly influenced by the court. The scenes of luxurious dissipation and refined debauchery which they describe show us, indeed, that Persian culture was not an unalloyed blessing to the Arabs any more

[1] *Ibid.*, No. 29, vv. 1–3.
[2] Ibn Khallikán, ed. by Wüstenfeld, No. 169, p. 100; De Slane's translation, vol. i, p. 393.

than were the arts of Greece to the Romans; but this is only the darker side of the picture. The works of a contemporary poet furnish evidence of the indignation which the libertinism fashionable in high places called forth among the mass of Moslems who had not lost faith in morality and religion.

Abu 'l-'Atáhiya, unlike his great rival, came of Arab stock. He was bred in Kúfa, and gained his livelihood as a young man by selling earthenware. His poetical talent, however, promised so well that he set out to present himself before the Caliph Mahdí, who richly rewarded him; and Hárún al-Rashíd afterwards bestowed on him a yearly pension of 50,000 dirhems (about £2,000), in addition to numerous extraordinary gifts. At Baghdád he fell in love with 'Utba, a slave-girl belonging to Mahdí, but she did not return his passion or take any notice of the poems in which he celebrated her charms and bewailed the sufferings that she made him endure. Despair of winning her affection caused him, it is said, to assume the woollen garb of Muḥammadan ascetics,[1] and henceforth, instead of writing vain and amatorious verses, he devoted his powers exclusively to those joyless meditations on mortality which have struck a deep chord in the hearts of his countrymen. Like Abu 'l-'Alá al-Ma'arrí and others who neglected the positive precepts of Islam in favour of a moral philosophy based on experience and reflection, Abu 'l-'Atáhiya was accused of being a freethinker (*zindíq*).[2] It was alleged that in his poems he often spoke of

Abu 'l-'Atáhiya (748-828 A.D.).

[1] *Cf. Díwán* (ed. of Beyrout, 1886), p. 279, l. 9, where he reproaches one of his former friends who deserted him because, in his own words, "I adopted the garb of a dervish" (*ṣirtu fí ziyyi miskíni*). Others attribute his conversion to disgust with the immorality and profanity of the court-poets amongst whom he lived.

[2] Possibly he alludes to these aspersions in the verse (*ibid.*, p. 153, l. 10): "*Men have become corrupted, and if they see any one who is sound in his religion, they call him a heretic*" (*mubtadi'*).

death but never of the Resurrection and the Judgment—a calumny which is refuted by many passages in his Díwán. According to the literary historian al-Ṣúlí († 946 A.D.), Abu 'l-'Atáhiya believed in One God who formed the universe out of two opposite elements which He created from nothing; and held, further, that everything would be reduced to these same elements before the final destruction of all phenomena. Knowledge, he thought, was acquired naturally (*i.e.*, without Divine Revelation) by means of reflection, deduction, and research.[1] He believed in the threatened retribution (*al-wa'íd*) and in the command to abstain from commerce with the world (*taḥrímu 'l-makásib*).[2] He professed the opinions of the Butrites,[3] a subdivision of the Zaydites, as that sect of the Shí'a was named which followed Zayd b. Alí b. Ḥusayn b. 'Alí b. Abí Ṭálib. He spoke evil of none, and did not approve of revolt against the Government. He held the doctrine of predestination (*jabr*).[4]

Abu 'l-'Atáhiya may have secretly cherished the Manichæan views ascribed to him in this passage, but his poems contain little or nothing that could offend the most orthodox Moslem. The following verse, in which Goldziher finds an allusion to Buddha,[5] is capable of a different interpretation. It rather

[1] Abu 'l-'Atáhiya declares that knowledge is derived from three sources, logical reasoning (*qiyás*), examination (*'iyár*), and oral tradition (*samá'*). See his *Díwán*, p. 158, l. 11.

[2] *Cf. Mání, seine Lehre und seine Schriften*, by G. Flügel, p. 281, l. 3 sqq. Abu 'l-'Atáhiya did not take this extreme view (*Díwán*, p. 270, l. 3 seq.).

[3] See Shahrastání, Haarbrücker's translation, Part I, p. 181 sqq. It appears highly improbable that Abu 'l-'Atáhiya was a Shí'ite. *Cf.* the verses (*Díwán*, p. 104, l. 13 seq.), where, speaking of the prophets and the holy men of ancient Islam, he says:—

"*Reckon first among them Abú Bakr, the veracious,*
And exclaim 'O 'Umar!' in the second place of honour.
And reckon the father of Ḥasan after 'Uthmán,
For the merit of them both is recited and celebrated."

[4] *Aghání*, iii, 128, l. 6 sqq.

[5] *Transactions of the Ninth Congress of Orientalists*, vol. ii. p. 114.

seems to me to exalt the man of ascetic life, without particular reference to any individual, above all others :—

> "If thou would'st see the noblest of mankind,
> Behold a monarch in a beggar's garb." [1]

But while the poet avoids positive heresy, it is none the less true that much of his Díwán is not strictly religious in the Muḥammadan sense and may fairly be called 'philosophical.' This was enough to convict him of infidelity and atheism in the eyes of devout theologians who looked askance on moral teaching, however pure, that was not cast in the dogmatic mould. The pretended cause of his imprisonment by Hárún al-Rashíd—namely, that he refused to make any more love-songs—is probably, as Goldziher has suggested, a popular version of the fact that he persisted in writing religious poems which were supposed to have a dangerous bias in the direction of free-thought.

His poetry breathes a spirit of profound melancholy and hopeless pessimism. Death and what comes after death, the frailty and misery of man, the vanity of worldly pleasures and the duty of renouncing them—these are the subjects on which he dwells with monotonous reiteration, exhorting his readers to live the ascetic life and fear God and lay up a store of good works against the Day of Reckoning. The simplicity, ease, and naturalness of his style are justly admired. Religious

[1] *Díwán*, p. 274, l. 10. *Cf.* the verse (p. 199, penultimate line) :—

> "*When I gained contentment, I did not cease* (*thereafter*)
> *To be a king, regarding riches as poverty.*"

The ascetic "lives the life of a king" (*ibid.*, p. 187, l. 5). Contented men are the noblest of all (p. 148, l. 2). So the great Persian mystic, Jalálu 'l-Dín Rúmí, says in reference to the perfect Ṣúfí (*Díván-i Shams-i Tabríz*, No. viii, v. 3 in my edition) : *Mard-i khudá sháh buvad zír-i dalq*, "the man of God is a king 'neath dervish-cloak ;" and eminent spiritualists are frequently described as "kings of the (mystic) path." I do not deny, however, that this metaphor may have been originally suggested by the story of Buddha.

poetry, as he himself confesses, was not read at court or by scholars who demanded rare and obscure expressions, but only by pious folk, traditionists and divines, and especially by the vulgar, "who like best what they can understand."[1] Abu 'l-'Atáhiya wrote for 'the man in the street.' Discarding conventional themes tricked out with threadbare artifices, he appealed to common feelings and matters of universal experience. He showed for the first and perhaps for the last time in the history of classical Arabic literature that it was possible to use perfectly plain and ordinary language without ceasing to be a poet.

Although, as has been said, the bulk of Abu 'l-'Atáhiya's poetry is philosophical in character, there remains much specifically Islamic doctrine, in particular as regards the Resurrection and the Future Life. This combination may be illustrated by the following ode, which is considered one of the best that have been written on the subject of religion, or, more accurately, of asceticism (*zuhd*) :—

"Get sons for death, build houses for decay!
All, all, ye wend annihilation's way.
For whom build we, who must ourselves return
Into our native element of clay?
O Death, nor violence nor flattery thou
Dost use, but when thou com'st, escape none may.
Methinks, thou art ready to surprise mine age,
As age surprised and made my youth his prey.
What ails me, World, that every place perforce
I lodge thee in, it galleth me to stay?
And, O Time, how do I behold thee run
To spoil me? Thine own gift thou tak'st away!
O Time! inconstant, mutable art thou,
And o'er the realm of ruin is thy sway.

[1] *Díwán*, p. 25, l. 3 sqq. Abu 'l-'Atáhiya took credit to himself for introducing 'the language of the market-place' into his poetry (*ibid.*, p. 12, l. 3 seq.).

What ails me that no glad result it brings
Whene'er, O World, to milk thee I essay?
And when I court thee, why dost thou raise up
On all sides only trouble and dismay?
Men seek thee every wise, but thou art like
A dream; the shadow of a cloud; the day
Which hath but now departed, nevermore
To dawn again; a glittering vapour gay.
This people thou hast paid in full: their feet
Are on the stirrup—let them not delay!
But those that do good works and labour well
Hereafter shall receive the promised pay.
As if no punishment I had to fear,
A load of sin upon my neck I lay;
And while the world I love, from Truth, alas,
Still my besotted senses go astray.
I shall be asked of all my business here:
What can I plead then? What can I gainsay?
What argument allege, when I am called
To render an account on Reckoning-Day?
Dooms twain in that dread hour shall be revealed,
When I the scroll of these mine acts survey:
Either to dwell in everlasting bliss,
Or suffer torments of the damned for aye!" [1]

I will now add a few verses culled from the Díwán which bring the poet's pessimistic view of life into clearer outline, and also some examples of those moral precepts and sententious criticisms which crowd his pages and have contributed in no small degree to his popularity.

"The world is like a viper soft to touch that venom spits.[2]"

"Men sit like revellers o'er their cups and drink,
From the world's hand, the circling wine of death."[3]

"Call no man living blest for aught you see
But that for which you blessed call the dead."[4]

---

[1] *Díwán* (Beyrout, 1886), p. 23, l. 13 *et seqq.*
[2] *Ibid.*, p. 51, l. 2.
[3] *Ibid.*, p. 132, l. 3.
[4] *Ibid.*, p. 46, l. 16.

FALSE FRIENDS.

"'Tis not the Age that moves my scorn,
But those who in the Age are born.
I cannot count the friends that broke
Their faith, tho' honied words they spoke;
In whom no aid I found, and made
The Devil welcome to their aid.
May I—so best we shall agree—
Ne'er look on them nor they on me!"[1]

"If men should see a prophet begging, they would turn and scout him.
Thy friend is ever thine as long as thou canst do without him;
But he will spew thee forth, if in thy need thou come about him."[2]

THE WICKED WORLD.

"'Tis only on the culprit sin recoils,
The ignorant fool against himself is armed.
Humanity are sunk in wickedness;
The best is he that leaveth us unharmed."[3]

"'Twas my despair of Man that gave me hope
God's grace would find me soon, I know not how."[4]

LIFE AND DEATH.

"Man's life is his fair name, and not his length of years;
Man's death is his ill-fame, and not the day that nears.
Then life to thy fair name by deeds of goodness give:
So in this world two lives, O mortal, thou shalt live."[5]

MAXIMS AND RULES OF LIFE.

"Mere falsehood by its face is recognised,
But Truth by parables and admonitions."[6]

---

[1] *Díwán*, p. 260, l. 11 *et seqq.*
[2] *Ibid.*, p. 295, l. 14 *et seqq.*
[3] *Ibid.*, p. 287, l. 10 seq.
[4] *Ibid.*, p. 119, l. 11.
[5] *Ibid.*, p. 259, penultimate line *et seq.*
[6] *Ibid.*, p. 115, l 4.

"I keep the bond of love inviolate
Towards all humankind, for I betray
Myself, if I am false to any man." [1]

"Far from the safe path, hop'st thou to be saved?
Ships make no speedy voyage on dry land." [2]

"Strip off the world from thee and naked live,
For naked thou didst fall into the world." [3]

"Man guards his own and grasps his neighbours' pelf,
And he is angered when they him prevent;
But he that makes the earth his couch will sleep
No worse, if lacking silk he have content." [4]

"Men vaunt their noble blood, but I behold
No lineage that can vie with righteous deeds." [5]

"If knowledge lies in long experience,
Less than what I have borne suffices me." [6]

"Faith is the medicine of every grief,
Doubt only raises up a host of cares." [7]

"Blame me or no, 'tis my predestined state:
If I have erred, infallible is Fate." [8]

Abu 'l-'Atáhiya found little favour with his contemporaries, who seem to have regarded him as a miserly hypocrite. He died, an aged man, in the Caliphate of Ma'mún.[9] Von

[1] *Díwán*, p. 51, l. 10. [2] *Ibid.*, p. 133, l. 5.
[3] *Ibid.*, p. 74, l. 4. [4] *Ibid.*, p. 149, l. 12 seq.
[5] *Ibid.*, p. 195, l. 9. *Cf.* p. 243, l. 4 seq.
[6] *Ibid.*, p. 274, l. 6. [7] *Ibid.*, p. 262, l. 4.
[8] *Ibid.*, p. 346, l. 11. *Cf.* p. 102, l. 11; p. 262, l. 1 seq.; p. 267, l. 7. This verse is taken from Abu 'l-'Atáhiya's famous didactic poem composed in rhyming couplets, which is said to have contained 4,000 sentences of morality. Several of these have been translated by Von Kremer in his *Culturgeschichte des Orients*, vol. ii, p. 374 sqq.
[9] In one of his poems (*Díwán*, p. 160, l. 11), he says that he has lived ninety years, but if this is not a mere exaggeration, it needs to be corrected. The words for 'seventy' and 'ninety' are easily confused in Arabic writing.

Kremer thinks that he had a truer genius for poetry than Abú Nuwás, an opinion in which I am unable to concur. Both, however, as he points out, are distinctive types of their time. If Abú Nuwás presents an appalling picture of a corrupt and frivolous society devoted to pleasure, we learn from Abu 'l-'Atáhiya something of the religious feelings and beliefs which pervaded the middle and lower classes, and which led them to take a more earnest and elevated view of life.

With the rapid decline and disintegration of the 'Abbásid Empire which set in towards the middle of the ninth century, numerous petty dynasties arose, and the hitherto unrivalled splendour of Baghdád was challenged by more than one provincial court. These independent or semi-independent princes were sometimes zealous patrons of learning—it is well known, for example, that a national Persian literature first came into being under the auspices of the Sámánids in Khurásán and the Buwayhids in 'Iráq—but as a rule the anxious task of maintaining, or the ambition of extending, their power left them small leisure to cultivate letters, even if they wished to do so. None combined the arts of war and peace more brilliantly than the Ḥamdánid Sayfu 'l-Dawla, who in 944 A.D. made himself master of Aleppo, and founded an independent kingdom in Northern Syria.

Tha'álibí's eulogy of Sayfu 'l-Dawla.

"The Ḥamdánids," says Tha'álibí, "were kings and princes, comely of countenance and eloquent of tongue, endowed with open-handedness and gravity of mind. Sayfu 'l-Dawla is famed as the chief amongst them all and the centre-pearl of their necklace. He was—may God be pleased with him and grant his desires and make Paradise his abode!—the brightest star of his age and the pillar of Islam: by him the frontiers were guarded and the State well governed. His attacks on the rebellious Arabs checked their fury and blunted their teeth and tamed their stubbornness and secured his subjects against their barbarity. His campaigns exacted vengeance from the Emperor of the Greeks, decisively broke their hostile onset, and had an excellent effect on Islam. His court was the goal of ambassadors, the dayspring of liberality, the horizon-point of hope, the end of journeys, a place where savants assembled and poets competed for the palm. It is said that after the Caliphs no prince gathered around him so many masters of poetry and men illustrious in literature as he did; and to a monarch's hall, as to a market, people bring only what is in demand. He was an accomplished scholar, a poet himself and a lover of fine poetry; keenly susceptible to words of praise."[1]

Sayfu 'l-Dawla's cousin, Abú Firás al-Ḥamdání, was a gallant soldier and a poet of some mark, who if space permitted would receive fuller notice here.[2] He, however, though superior to the common herd of court poets, is overshadowed by one who with all his faults—and they are not inconsiderable—made an extraordinary impression upon his contemporaries, and by the commanding influence of his reputation decided what should henceforth be the standard of poetical taste in the Muḥammadan world.

Mutanabbí (915–965 A.D.).

Abu 'l-Ṭayyib Aḥmad b. Ḥusayn, known to fame as al-Mutanabbí, was born and bred at Kúfa, where his father is said to have been a water-carrier. Following the admirable custom by which young men of promise were sent abroad to complete their education, he studied at Damascus and visited other towns in Syria, but also passed much of his time among the Bedouins, to whom he owed the singular knowledge and mastery of Arabic displayed in his poems. Here he came forward as a prophet (from which circumstance he was afterwards entitled al-Mutanabbí, *i.e.*, 'the pretender to prophecy'), and induced a great multitude to believe in him; but ere long he was captured by Lu'lu', the governor of Ḥimṣ (Emessa), and thrown into prison. After his release he

[1] Tha'álibí, *Yatímatu 'l-Dahr* (Damascus, 1304 A.H.), vol. i, p. 8 seq.

[2] See Von Kremer's *Culturgeschichte*, vol. ii, p. 381 sqq.; Ahlwardt, *Poesie und Poetik der Araber*, p. 37 sqq.; R. Dvorak, *Abú Firás, ein arabischer Dichter und Held* (Leyden, 1895).

wandered to and fro chanting the praises of all and sundry, until fortune guided him to the court of Sayfu 'l-Dawla at Aleppo. For nine years (948–957 A.D.) he stood high in the favour of that cultured prince, whose virtues he celebrated in a series of splendid eulogies, and with whom he lived as an intimate friend and comrade in arms. The liberality of Sayfu 'l-Dawla and the ingenious impudence of the poet are well brought out by the following anecdote:—

Mutanabbí on one occasion handed to his patron the copy of an ode which he had recently composed in his honour, and retired, leaving Sayfu 'l-Dawla to peruse it at leisure. The prince began to read, and came to these lines—

Aqil anil aqṭi' iḥmil 'alh salli a'id
zid hashshi bashshi tafaḍḍal adni surra ṣili.[1]

"Pardon, bestow, endow, mount, raise, console, restore,
Add, laugh, rejoice, bring nigh, show favour, gladden, give!"

Far from being displeased by the poet's arrogance, Sayfu 'l-Dawla was so charmed with his artful collocation of fourteen imperatives in a single verse that he granted every request. Under *pardon* he wrote 'we pardon thee'; under *bestow*, 'let him receive such and such a sum of money'; under *endow*, 'we endow thee with an estate,' which he named (it was beside the gate of Aleppo); under *mount*, 'let such and such a horse be led to him'; under *raise*, 'we do so'; under *console*, 'we do so, be at ease'; under *restore*, 'we restore thee to thy former place in our esteem'; under *add*, 'let him have such and such in addition'; under *bring nigh*, 'we admit thee to our intimacy'; under *show favour*, 'we have done so'; under *gladden*, 'we have made thee glad'[2]; under *give*, 'this we have already done.' Mutanabbí's rivals envied his good fortune, and one of them said to Sayfu 'l-Dawla—"Sire, you have done all that he asked, but when he uttered the words *laugh*, *rejoice*, why did not you answer, 'Ha, ha, ha'?" Sayfu 'l-Dawla laughed, and said, "You too, shall have your wish," and ordered him a donation.

---

[1] Mutanabbí, ed. by Dieterici, p. 493. Wáḥidí gives the whole story in his commentary on this verse.

[2] Mutanabbí, it is said, explained to Sayfu 'l-Dawla that by *surra* (gladden) he meant *surriyya*; whereupon the good-humoured prince presented him with a slave-girl.

Mutanabbí was sincerely attached to his generous master, and this feeling inspired a purer and loftier strain than we find in the fulsome panegyrics which he afterwards addressed to the negro Káfúr. He seems to have been occasionally in disgrace, but Sayfu 'l-Dawla could deny nothing to a poet who paid him such magnificent compliments. Nor was he deterred by any false modesty from praising himself: he was fully conscious of his power and, like Arabian bards in general, he bragged about it. Although the verbal legerdemain which is so conspicuous in his poetry cannot be reproduced in another language, the lines translated below may be taken as a favourable and sufficiently characteristic specimen of his style.

"How glows mine heart for him whose heart to me is cold,
Who liketh ill my case and me in fault doth hold!
Why should I hide a love that hath worn thin my frame?
To Sayfu 'l-Dawla all the world avows the same.
Tho' love of his high star unites us, would that we
According to our love might so divide the fee!
Him have I visited when sword in sheath was laid,
And I have seen him when in blood swam every blade:
Him, both in peace and war the best of all mankind,
Whose crown of excellence was still his noble mind.

Do foes by flight escape thine onset, thou dost gain
A chequered victory, half of pleasure, half of pain.
So puissant is the fear thou strik'st them with, it stands
Instead of thee, and works more than thy warriors' hands.
Unfought the field is thine: thou need'st not further strain
To chase them from their holes in mountain or in plain.
What! 'fore thy fierce attack whene'er an army reels,
Must thy ambitious soul press hot upon their heels?
Thy task it is to rout them on the battle-ground:
No shame to thee if they in flight have safety found.
Or thinkest thou perchance that victory is sweet
Only when scimitars and necks each other greet?

O justest of the just save in thy deeds to me!
Thou art accused and thou, O Sire, must judge the plea.

Look, I implore thee, well! Let not thine eye cajoled
See fat in empty froth, in all that glisters gold![1]
What use and profit reaps a mortal of his sight,
If darkness unto him be indistinct from light?

My deep poetic art the blind have eyes to see,
My verses ring in ears as deaf as deaf can be.
They wander far abroad while I am unaware,
But men collect them watchfully with toil and care.
Oft hath my laughing mien prolonged the insulter's sport,
Until with claw and mouth I cut his rudeness short.
Ah, when the lion bares his teeth, suspect his guile,
Nor fancy that the lion shows to you a smile.
I have slain the man that sought my heart's blood many a time,
Riding a noble mare whose back none else may climb,
Whose hind and fore-legs seem in galloping as one;
Nor hand nor foot requireth she to urge her on.
And O the days when I have swung my fine-edged glaive
Amidst a sea of death where wave was dashed on wave!
The desert knows me well, the night, the mounted men,
The battle and the sword, the paper and the pen!"[2]

Finally an estrangement arose between Mutanabbí and Sayfu 'l-Dawla, in consequence of which he fled to Egypt and attached himself to the Ikhshídite Káfúr. Disappointed in his new patron, a negro who had formerly been a slave, the poet set off for Baghdád, and afterwards visited the court of the Buwayhid 'Aḍudu 'l-Dawla at Shíráz. While travelling through Babylonia he was attacked and slain by brigands in 965 A.D.

The popularity of Mutanabbí is shown by the numerous commentaries[3] and critical treatises on his *Díwán*. By his countrymen he is generally regarded as one of the greatest of Arabian poets, while not a few would maintain that he ranks

[1] Literally, "Do not imagine fat in one whose (apparent) fat is (really) a tumour."

[2] *Díwán*, ed. by Dieterici, pp. 481–484.

[3] The most esteemed commentary is that of Wáḥidí († 1075 A.D.), which has been published by Fr. Dieterici in his edition of Mutanabbí (Berlin, 1858–1861).

absolutely first. Abu 'l-'Alá al-Ma'arrí, himself an illustrious poet and man of letters, confessed that he had sometimes wished to alter a word here and there in Mutanabbí's verses, but had never been able to think of any improvement. "As to his poetry," says Ibn Khallikán, "it is perfection." European scholars, with the exception of Von Hammer,[1] have been far from sharing this enthusiasm, as may be seen by referring to what has been said on the subject by Reiske,[2] De Sacy,[3] Bohlen,[4] Brockelmann,[5] and others. No doubt, according to our canons of taste, Mutanabbí stands immeasurably below the famous Pre-islamic bards, and in a later age must yield the palm to Abú Nuwás and Abu 'l-'Atáhiya. Lovers of poetry, as the term is understood in Europe, cannot derive much æsthetic pleasure from his writings, but, on the contrary, will be disgusted by the beauties hardly less than by the faults which Arabian critics attribute to him. Admitting, however, that only a born Oriental is able to appreciate Mutanabbí at his full worth, let us try to realise the Oriental point of view and put aside, as far as possible, our preconceptions of what constitutes good poetry and good taste. Fortunately we possess abundant materials for such an attempt in the invaluable work of Tha'álibí, which has been already mentioned.[6] Tha'álibí (961–1038 A.D.) was nearly contemporary with Mutanabbí. He began to write his *Yatíma* about thirty years after the poet's death, and while he bears witness to

[1] *Motenebbi, der grösste arabische Dichter* (Vienna, 1824).

[2] *Abulfedæ Annales Muslemici* (Hafniæ, 1789, &c.), vol. ii, p. 774. *Cf.* his notes on Ṭarafa's *Mu'allaqa*, of which he published an edition in 1742.

[3] *Chrestomathie Arabe* (2nd edition), vol. iii, p. 27 sqq. *Journal des Savans*, January, 1825, p. 24 sqq.

[4] *Commentatio de Motenabbio* (Bonn, 1824).

[5] *Geschichte der Arabischen Litteratur* (Weimar, 1898, &c.), vol. i, p. 86.

[6] I have made free use of Dieterici's excellent work entitled *Mutanabbi und Seifuddaula aus der Edelperle des Tsaâlibi* (Leipzig, 1847), which contains on pp. 49–74 an abstract of Tha'álibí's criticism in the fifth chapter of the First Part of the *Yatíma*.

the unrivalled popularity of the *Díwán* amongst all classes of society, he observes that it was sharply criticised as well as rapturously admired. Tha'álibí himself claims to hold the balance even. "Now," he says, "I will mention the faults and blemishes which critics have found in the poetry of Mutanabbí; for is there any one whose qualities give entire satisfaction ?—

Kafa 'l-mar'a faḍlan an tu'adda ma'áyibuh.

'Tis the height of merit in a man that his faults can be numbered.

Then I will proceed to speak of his beauties and to set forth in due order the original and incomparable characteristics of his style.

The radiant stars with beauty strike our eyes
Because midst gloom opaque we see them rise."

It was deemed of capital importance that the opening couplet (*maṭla'*) of a poem should be perfect in form and meaning, and that it should not contain anything likely to offend. Tha'álibí brings forward many instances in which Mutanabbí has violated this rule by using words of bad omen, such as 'sickness' or 'death,' or technical terms of music and arithmetic which only perplex and irritate the hearer instead of winning his sympathy at the outset. He complains also that Mutanabbí's finest thoughts and images are too often followed by low and trivial ones: "he strings pearls and bricks together" (*jama'a bayna 'l-durrati wa-'l-ájurrati*). "While he moulds the most splendid ornament, and threads the loveliest necklace, and weaves the most exquisite stuff of mingled hues, and paces superbly in a garden of roses, suddenly he will throw in a verse or two verses disfigured by far-fetched metaphors, or by obscure language and confused thought, or by extravagant affectation and excessive profundity, or by unbounded and absurd exaggeration, or by vulgar and commonplace diction, or by pedantry and grotesqueness resulting from the use of unfamiliar words." We need not follow Tha'álibí in his illustration of these and other weaknesses with which he justly reproaches Mutanabbí, since we shall be able to form a better idea of the prevailing taste from those points which he singles out for special praise.

In the first place he calls attention to the poet's skill in handling the customary erotic prelude (*nasíb*), and particularly to his brilliant descriptions of Bedouin women, which were celebrated all over the East. As an example of this kind he quotes the following piece, which "is chanted in the *salons* on account of the extreme beauty of its diction, the choiceness of its sentiment, and the perfection of its art":—

"Shame hitherto was wont my tears to stay,
But now by shame they will no more be stayed,
So that each bone seems through its skin to sob,
And every vein to swell the sad cascade.
She uncovered: pallor veiled her at farewell:
No veil 'twas, yet her cheeks it cast in shade.
So seemed they, while tears trickled over them,
Gold with a double row of pearls inlaid.
She loosed three sable tresses of her hair,
And thus of night four nights at once she made;
But when she lifted to the moon in heaven
Her face, two moons together I surveyed."[1]

The critic then enumerates various beautiful and original features of Mutanabbí's style, *e.g.*—

1. His consecutive arrangement of similes in brief symmetrical clauses, thus:—

"She shone forth like a moon, and swayed like a moringa-bough,
And shed fragrance like ambergris, and gazed like a gazelle."

[1] Mutanabbí, ed. by Dieterici, p. 182, vv. 3–9, omitting v. 5.

2. The novelty of his comparisons and images, as when he indicates the rapidity with which he returned to his patron and the shortness of his absence in these lines:—

> "I was merely an arrow in the air,
> Which falls back, finding no refuge there."

3. The *laus duplex* or 'two-sided panegyric' (*al-madḥ al-muwajjah*), which may be compared to a garment having two surfaces of different colours but of equal beauty, as in the following verse addressed to Sayfu 'l-Dawla:—

> "Were all the lives thou hast ta'en possessed by thee,
> Immortal thou and blest the world would be!"

Here Sayfu 'l-Dawla is doubly eulogised by the mention of his triumphs over his enemies as well as of the joy which all his friends felt in the continuance of his life and fortune.

4. His manner of extolling his royal patron as though he were speaking to a friend and comrade, whereby he raises himself from the position of an ordinary encomiast to the same level with kings.

5. His division of ideas into parallel sentences:—

> "We were in gladness, the Greeks in fear,
> The land in bustle, the sea in confusion."

From this summary of Tha'álibí's criticism the reader will easily perceive that the chief merits of poetry were then considered to lie in elegant expression, subtle combination of words, fanciful imagery, witty conceits, and a striking use of rhetorical figures. Such, indeed, are the views which prevail to this day throughout the whole Muḥammadan world, and it is unreasonable to denounce them as false simply because they do not square with ours. Who shall decide when nations disagree? If Englishmen rightly claim to be the best judges of Shakespeare, and Italians of Dante, the almost unanimous verdict of Mutanabbí's countrymen is surely not less authoritative—a verdict which places him at the head of all the poets born or made in Islam. And although the peculiar excellences indicated by Tha'álibí do not appeal to us, there are few poets that leave so distinct an impression of greatness. One might call Mutanabbí the Victor Hugo of the East, for he has the grand style whether he soars to sublimity or sinks to fustian. In the masculine vigour of his verse, in the sweep and splendour of his rhetoric, in the luxuriance and reckless audacity of his imagination we recognise qualities which inspired the oft-quoted lines of the elegist:—

> "Him did his mighty soul supply
> With regal pomp and majesty.
> A Prophet by his *diction* known;
> But in the *ideas*, all must own,
> His miracles were clearly shown."[1]

One feature of Mutanabbí's poetry that is praised by Tha'álibí should not be left unnoticed, namely, his fondness for sententious moralising on topics connected with human life; wherefore Reiske has compared him to Euripides. He is allowed to be a master of that proverbial philosophy in which Orientals delight and which is characteristic of the modern school beginning with Abu 'l-'Atáhiya, though some of the ancients had already cultivated it with success (*cf.* the verses of Zuhayr, p. 118 *supra*). The following examples are among those cited by Bohlen (*op. cit.*, p. 86 sqq.):—

> "When an old man cries 'Ugh!' he is not tired
> Of life, but only tired of feebleness."[2]

> "He that hath been familiar with the world
> A long while, in his eye 'tis turned about
> Until he sees how false what looked so fair."[3]

---

[1] The author of these lines, which are quoted by Ibn Khallikán in his article on Mutanabbí, is Abu 'l-Qásim b. al-Muẓaffar b. 'Alí al-Ṭabasí.

[2] Mutanabbí, ed. by Dieterici, p. 581, v. 27.

[3] *Ibid.*, p. 472, v. 5.

"The sage's mind still makes him miserable
In his most happy fortune, but poor fools
Find happiness even in their misery."[1]

The sceptical and pessimistic tendencies of an age of social decay and political anarchy are unmistakably revealed in the writings of the poet, philosopher, and man of letters, Abu 'l-'Alá al-Ma'arrí, who was born in 973 A.D. at Ma'arratu 'l-Nu'mán, a Syrian town situated about twenty miles south of Aleppo on the caravan road to Damascus. While yet a child he had an attack of small-pox, resulting in partial and eventually in complete blindness, but this calamity, fatal as it might seem to literary ambition, was repaired if not entirely made good by his stupendous powers of memory. After being educated at home under the eye of his father, a man of some culture and a meritorious poet, he proceeded to Aleppo, which was still a flourishing centre of the humanities, though it could no longer boast such a brilliant array of poets and scholars as were attracted thither in the palmy days of Sayfu 'l-Dawla. Probably Abu 'l-'Alá did not enter upon the career of a professional encomiast, to which he seems at first to have inclined: he declares in the preface to his *Saqṭu 'l-Zand* that he never eulogised any one with the hope of gaining a reward, but only for the sake of practising his skill. On the termination of his 'Wanderjahre' he returned in 993 A.D. to Ma'arra, where he spent the next fifteen years of his life, with no income beyond a small pension of thirty dínárs (which he shared with a servant), lecturing on Arabic poetry, antiquities, and philology, the subjects to which his youthful studies had been chiefly devoted. During this period his reputation was steadily increasing, and at last, to adapt what Boswell wrote of Dr. Johnson on a similar occasion, "he thought of trying his fortune in Baghdád, the great field of genius and

Abu 'l-'Alá al-Ma'arrí (973-1057 A.D.).

[1] Mutanabbí, ed. by Dieterici, p. 341, v. 8.

exertion, where talents of every kind had the fullest scope and the highest encouragement." Professor Margoliouth in the Introduction to his edition of Abu 'l-'Alá's correspondence supplies many interesting particulars of the literary society at Baghdád in which the poet moved. "As in ancient Rome, so in the great Muḥammadan cities public recitation was the mode whereby men of letters made their talents known to their contemporaries. From very early times it had been customary to employ the mosques for this purpose; and in Abu 'l-'Alá's time poems were recited in the mosque of al-Manṣúr in Baghdád. Better accommodation was, however, provided by the Mæcenates who took a pride in collecting savants and *littérateurs* in their houses." [1] Such a Mæcenas was the Sharíf al-Raḍí, himself a celebrated poet, who founded the Academy called by his name in imitation, probably, of that founded some years before by Abú Naṣr Sábúr b. Ardashír, Vizier to the Buwayhid prince, Bahá'u 'l-Dawla. Here Abu 'l-'Alá met a number of distinguished writers and scholars who welcomed him as one of themselves. The capital of Islam, thronged with travellers and merchants from all parts of the East, harbouring followers of every creed and sect—Christians and Jews, Buddhists and Zoroastrians, Ṣábians and Ṣúfís, Materialists and Rationalists—must have seemed to the provincial almost like a new world. It is certain that Abu 'l-'Alá, a curious observer who set no bounds to his thirst for knowledge, would make the best use of such an opportunity. The religious and philosophical ideas with which he was now first thrown into contact gradually took root and ripened. His stay in Baghdád, though it lasted only a year and a half (1009–1010 A.D.), decided the whole bent of his mind for the future.

His visit to Baghdád.

Whether his return to Ma'arra was hastened, as he says, by want of means and the illness of his mother, whom he tenderly loved, or by an indignity which he suffered at the

[1] Margoliouth's Introduction to the *Letters of Abu 'l-'Alá*, p. xxii.

hands of an influential patron,[1] immediately on his arrival he shut himself in his house, adopted a vegetarian diet and other ascetic practices, and passed the rest of his long life in comparative seclusion :—

> "Methinks, I am thrice imprisoned—ask not me
> Of news that need no telling—
> By loss of sight, confinement to my house,
> And this vile body for my spirit's dwelling." [2]

We can only conjecture the motives which brought about this sudden change of habits and disposition. No doubt his mother's death affected him deeply, and he may have been disappointed by his failure to obtain a permanent footing in the capital. It is not surprising that the blind and lonely man, looking back on his faded youth, should have felt weary of the world and its ways, and found in melancholy contemplation of earthly vanities ever fresh matter for the application and development of these philosophical ideas which, as we have seen, were probably suggested to him by his recent experiences. While in the collection of early poems, entitled *Saqṭu 'l-Zand* or 'The Spark of the Fire-stick' and mainly composed before his visit to Baghdád, he still treads the customary path of his predecessors,[3] his poems written after that time and generally known as the *Luzúmiyyát*[4] arrest attention by their boldness and originality as well as by the sombre and earnest tone which pervades them. This, indeed, is not the view of most Oriental critics, who dislike the poet's irreverence and fail to appreciate the fact that he stood considerably in advance of his age ; but in Europe he has received full justice and perhaps higher

[1] *Ibid.*, p. xxvii seq.

[2] *Luzúmiyyát* (Cairo, 1891), vol. i, p. 201.

[3] *I.e.*, his predecessors of the modern school. Like Mutanabbí, he ridicules the conventional types (*asálíb*) in which the old poetry is cast *Cf.* Goldziher, *Abhand. zur Arab. Philologie*, Part I, p. 146 seq.

[4] The proper title is *Luzúmu má lá yalzam*, referring to a technical difficulty which the poet unnecessarily imposed on himself with regard to the rhyme.

praise than he deserves. Reiske describes him as 'Arabice callentissimum, vasti, subtilis, sublimis et audacis ingenii'; [1] Von Hammer, who ranks him as a poet with Abú Tammám, Buḥturí, and Mutanabbí, also mentions him honourably as a philosopher; [2] and finally Von Kremer, who made an exhaustive study of the *Luzúmiyyát* and examined their contents in a masterly essay,[3] discovered in Abu 'l-'Alá, one of the greatest moralists of all time whose profound genius anticipated much that is commonly attributed to the so-called modern spirit of enlightenment. Here Von Kremer's enthusiasm may have carried him too far; for the poet, as Professor Margoliouth says, was unconscious of the value of his suggestions, unable to follow them out, and unable to adhere to them consistently. Although he builded better than he knew, the constructive side of his philosophy was overshadowed by the negative and destructive side, so that his pure and lofty morality leaves but a faint impression which soon dies away in louder, continually recurring voices of doubt and despair.

Abu 'l-'Alá is a firm monotheist, but his belief in God amounted, as it would seem, to little beyond a conviction that all things are governed by inexorable Fate, whose mysteries none may fathom and from whose omnipotence there is no escape. He denies the Resurrection of the dead, *e.g.*:—

"We laugh, but inept is our laughter;
We should weep and weep sore,
Who are shattered like glass, and thereafter
Re-moulded no more!" [4]

---

[1] *Abulfedæ Annales Muslemici*, ed. by Adler (1789–1794), vol. iii, p. 677.

[2] *Literaturgesch. der Araber*, vol. vi, p. 900 sqq.

[3] *Sitzungsberichte der Philosophisch-Historischen Classe der Kaiserlichen Akademie der Wissenschaften*, vol. cxvii, 6th Abhandlung (Vienna, 1889). Select passages admirably rendered by Von Kremer into German verse will be found in the *Z.D.M.G.*, vol. 29, pp. 304–312; vol. 30, pp. 40–52; vol. 31, pp. 471–483; vol. 38, pp. 499–529.

[4] *Z.D.M.G.*, vol. 38, p. 507; Margoliouth, *op. cit.*, p. 131, l. 15 of the Arabic text.

Since Death is the ultimate goal of mankind, the sage will pray to be delivered as speedily as possible from the miseries of life and refuse to inflict upon others what, by no fault of his own, he is doomed to suffer :—

> "Amends are richly due from sire to son :
> What if thy children rule o'er cities great?
> That eminence estranges them the more
> From thee, and causes them to wax in hate,
> Beholding one who cast them into Life's
> Dark labyrinth whence no wit can extricate." [1]

There are many passages to the same effect, showing that Abu 'l-'Alá regarded procreation as a sin and universal annihilation as the best hope for humanity. He acted in accordance with his opinions, for he never married, and he is said to have desired that the following verse should be inscribed on his grave :—

> "This wrong was by my father done
> To me, but ne'er by me to one." [2]

Hating the present life and weary of its burdens, yet seeing no happier prospect than that of return to non-existence, Abu 'l-'Alá can scarcely have disguised from himself what he might shrink openly to avow—that he was at heart, not indeed an atheist, but wholly incredulous of any Divine revelation. Religion, as he conceives it, is a product of the human mind, in which men believe through force of habit and education, never stopping to consider whether it is true.

"Sometimes you may find a man skilful in his trade, perfect in sagacity and in the use of arguments, but when he comes to religion he is found obstinate, so does he follow the old groove. Piety is implanted in human nature; it is deemed a sure refuge.

---

[1] *Z.D.M.G.*, vol. 29, p. 308.
[2] Margoliouth, *op. cit.*, p. 133 of the Arabic text.

To the growing child that which falls from his elders' lips is a lesson that abides with him all his life. Monks in their cloisters and devotees in the mosques accept their creed just as a story is handed down from him who tells it, without distinguishing between a true interpreter and a false. If one of these had found his kin among the Magians, he would have declared himself a Magian, or among the Ṣábians, he would have become nearly or quite like *them*."[1]

Religion, then, is "a fable invented by the ancients," worthless except to those unscrupulous persons who prey upon human folly and superstition. Islam is neither better nor worse than any other creed:—

> "Ḥanífs are stumbling,[2] Christians all astray,
> Jews wildered, Magians far on error's way.
> We mortals are composed of two great schools—
> Enlightened knaves or else religious fools."[3]

Not only does the poet emphatically reject the proud claim of Islam to possess a monopoly of truth, but he attacks most of its dogmas in detail. As to the Koran, Abu 'l-'Alá could not altogether refrain from doubting if it was really the Word of God, but he thought so well of the style that he accepted the challenge flung down by Muḥammad and produced a rival work (*al-Fuṣúl wa-'l-Gháyát*), which appears to have been a somewhat frivolous parody of the sacred volume, though in the author's judgment its inferiority was simply due to the fact that it was not yet polished by the tongues of four centuries of readers. Another work which must have sorely offended orthodox Muḥammadans is the *Risálatu 'l-Ghufrán* (Epistle of Forgiveness).[4] Here the Paradise of the Faithful becomes

[1] This passage occurs in Abu 'l-'Alá's *Risálatu 'l-Ghufrán* (see *infra*), *J.R.A.S.* for 1902, p. 351. *Cf.* the verses translated by Von Kremer in his essay on Abu 'l-'Alá, p. 23.

[2] For the term 'Ḥaníf' see p. 149 *supra*. Here it is synonymous with 'Muslim.'

[3] *Z.D.M.G.*, vol. 38, p. 513.

[4] This work, of which only two copies exist in Europe—one at Constantinople and another in my collection—has been described and partially translated in the *J.R.A.S.* for 1900, pp. 637–720, and for 1902, pp. 75–101, 337–362, and 813–847.

a glorified salon tenanted by various heathen poets who have been forgiven—hence the title—and received among the Blest. This idea is carried out with much ingenuity and in a spirit of audacious burlesque that reminds us of Lucian. The poets are presented in a series of imaginary conversations with a certain Shaykh 'Alí b. Manṣúr, to whom the work is addressed, reciting and explaining their verses, quarrelling with one another, and generally behaving as literary Bohemians. The second part contains a number of anecdotes relating to the *zindíqs* or freethinkers of Islam interspersed with quotations from their poetry and reflections on the nature of their belief, which Abu 'l- 'Alá condemns while expressing a pious hope that they are not so black as they paint themselves. At this time it may have suited him—he was over sixty—to assume the attitude of charitable orthodoxy. Like so many wise men of the East, he practised dissimulation as a fine art—

"I lift my voice to utter lies absurd,
But when I speak the truth, my hushed tones scarce are heard."[1]

In the *Luzúmiyyát*, however, he often unmasks. Thus he describes as idolatrous relics the two Pillars of the Ka'ba and the Black Stone, venerated by every Moslem, and calls the Pilgrimage itself 'a heathen's journey' (*riḥlatu jáhiliyy^in*). The following sentiments do him honour, but they would have been rank heresy at Mecca :—

"Praise God and pray,
Walk seventy times, not seven, the Temple round—
And impious remain !
Devout is he alone who, when he may
Feast his desires, is found
With courage to abstain."[2]

---

[1] Margoliouth, *op. cit.*, p. 132, last line of the Arabic text.
[2] *Z.D.M.G*, vol. 31, p. 483.

It is needless to give further instances of the poet's contempt for the Muḥammadan articles of faith. Considering that he assailed persons as well as principles, and lashed with bitter invective the powerful class of the *'Ulamá*, the clerical and legal representatives of Islam, we may wonder that the accusation of heresy brought against him was never pushed home and had no serious consequences. The question was warmly argued on both sides, and though Abu 'l-'Alá was pronounced by the majority to be a freethinker and materialist, he did not lack defenders who quoted chapter and verse to prove that he was nothing of the kind. It must be remembered that his works contain no philosophical system; that his opinions have to be gathered from the ideas which he scatters incoherently, and for the most part in guarded language, through a long succession of rhymes; and that this task, already arduous enough, is complicated by the not infrequent occurrence of sentiments which are blamelessly orthodox and entirely contradictory to the rest. A brilliant writer, familiar with Eastern ways of thinking, has observed that in general the conscience of an Asiatic is composed of the following ingredients: (1) an almost bare religious designation; (2) a more or less lively belief in certain doctrines of the creed which he professes; (3) a resolute opposition to many of its doctrines, even if they should be the most essential; (4) a fund of ideas relating to completely alien theories, which occupies more or less room; (5) a constant tendency to get rid of these ideas and theories and to replace the old by new.[1] Such phenomena will account for a great deal of logical inconsistency, but we should beware of invoking them too confidently in this case. Abu 'l- 'Alá with his keen intellect and unfanatical temperament was not the man to let himself be mystified. Still lamer is the explanation offered by some Muḥammadan critics, that his thoughts were decided by the

[1] De Gobineau, *Les religions et les philosophies dans l'Asie centrale*, p. 11 seq.

necessities of the difficult metre in which he wrote. It is conceivable that he may sometimes have doubted his own doubts and given Islam the benefit, but Von Kremer's conclusion is probably near the truth, namely, that where the poet speaks as a good Moslem, his phrases if they are not purely conventional are introduced of set purpose to foil his pious antagonists or to throw them off the scent. Although he was not without religion in the larger sense of the word, unprejudiced students of the later poems must recognise that from the orthodox standpoint he was justly branded as an infidel. The following translations will serve to illustrate the negative side of his philosophy :—

"Falsehood hath so corrupted all the world
That wrangling sects each other's gospel chide;
But were not hate Man's natural element,
Churches and mosques had risen side by side."[1]

"What is Religion? A maid kept close that no eye may view her;
The price of her wedding-gifts and dowry baffles the wooer.
Of all the goodly doctrine that I from the pulpit heard
My heart has never accepted so much as a single word!"[2]

"The pillars of this earth are four,
Which lend to human life a base;
God shaped two vessels, Time and Space,
The world and all its folk to store.

That which Time holds, in ignorance
It holds—why vent on it our spite?
Man is no cave-bound eremite,
But still an eager spy on Chance

He trembles to be laid asleep,
Tho' worn and old and weary grown.
We laugh and weep by Fate alone,
Time moves us not to laugh or weep;

[1] *Z.D.M.G.*, vol. 31, p. 477. [2] *Ibid.*, vol. 29, p. 311.

Yet we accuse it innocent,
  Which, could it speak, might us accuse,
  Our best and worst, at will to choose,
United in a sinful bent.[1]

"'The stars' conjunction comes, divinely sent,
And lo, the veil o'er every creed is rent.
No realm is founded that escapes decay,
The firmest structure soon dissolves away.'[2]
With sadness deep a thoughtful mind must scan
Religion made to serve the pelf of Man.
Fear thine own children: sparks at random flung
Consume the very tinder whence they sprung.
Evil are all men; I distinguish not
That part or this: the race entire I blot.
Trust none, however near akin, tho' he
A perfect sense of honour show to thee,
Thy self is the worst foe to be withstood:
Be on thy guard in hours of solitude.

*   *   *   *

Desire a venerable shaykh to cite
Reason for his doctrine, he is gravelled quite.
What! shall I ripen ere a leaf is seen?
The tree bears only when 'tis clad in green.'[3]

"How have I provoked your enmity?
Christ or Muḥammad, 'tis one to me.
No rays of dawn our path illume,
We are sunk together in ceaseless gloom.
Can blind perceptions lead aright,
Or blear eyes ever have clear sight?
Well may a body racked with pain
Envy mouldering bones in vain;
Yet comes a day when the weary sword
Reposes, to its sheath restored.

---

[1] *Z.D.M.G.* vol. 38, p. 522.

[2] According to De Goeje, *Mémoires sur les Carmathes du Bahrain*, p. 197, n. 1, these lines refer to a prophecy made by the Carmathians that the conjunction of Saturn and Jupiter, which took place in 1047 A.D. would herald the final triumph of the Fáṭimids over the 'Abbásids.

[3] *Z.D.M.G.*, vol. 38, p. 504.

Ah, who to me a frame will give
As clod or stone insensitive?—
For when spirit is joined to flesh, the pair
Anguish of mortal sickness share.
O Wind, be still, if wind thy name,
O Flame, die out, if thou art flame!"[1]

Pessimist and sceptic as he was, Abu 'l-'Alá denies more than he affirms, but although he rejected the dogmas of positive religion, he did not fall into utter unbelief; for he found within himself a moral law to which he could not refuse obedience.

"Take Reason for thy guide and do what she
Approves, the best of counsellors in sooth.
Accept no law the Pentateuch lays down:
Not there is what thou seekest—the plain truth."[2]

He insists repeatedly that virtue is its own reward.

"Oh, purge the good thou dost from hope of recompense
Or profit, as if thou wert one that sells his wares."[3]

His creed is that of a philosopher and ascetic. Slay no living creature, he says; better spare a flea than give alms. Yet he prefers active piety, active humanity, to fasting and prayer. "The gist of his moral teaching is to inculcate as the highest and holiest duty a conscientious fulfilment of one's obligations with equal warmth and affection towards all living beings."[4]

Abu 'l-'Alá died in 1057 A.D., at the age of eighty-four. About ten years before this time, the Persian poet and traveller, Náşir-i Khusraw, passed through Ma'arra on his way to Egypt. He describes Abu 'l-'Alá as the chief man in the town, very rich, revered by the inhabitants, and surrounded by more than two hundred students who came from all parts to attend his lectures on literature and

[1] *Z.D.M.G.*, vol. 31, p. 474.
[2] *Luzúmiyyát* (Cairo, 1891), i, 394.
[3] *Ibid.*, i, 312.
[4] Von Kremer, *op. cit.*, p. 38.

poetry.[1] We may set this trustworthy notice against the doleful account which Abu 'l-'Alá gives of himself in his letters and other works. If not among the greatest Muḥammadan poets, he is undoubtedly one of the most original and attractive. After Mutanabbí, even after Abu 'l-'Atáhiya, he must appear strangely modern to the European reader. It is astonishing to reflect that a spirit so unconventional, so free from dogmatic prejudice, so rational in spite of his pessimism and deeply religious notwithstanding his attacks on revealed religion, should have ended his life in a Syrian country-town some years before the battle of Senlac. Although he did not meddle with politics and held aloof from every sect, he could truly say of himself, "I am the son of my time" (*ghadawtu 'bna waqtí*).[2] His poems leave no aspect of the age untouched, and present a vivid picture of degeneracy and corruption, in which tyrannous rulers, venal judges, hypocritical and unscrupulous theologians, swindling astrologers, roving swarms of dervishes and godless Carmathians occupy a prominent place.[3]

Although the reader may think that too much space has been already devoted to poetry, I will venture by way of concluding the subject to mention very briefly a few well-known names which cannot be altogether omitted from a work of this kind.

Abú Tammám and Buḥturí.

Abú Tammám (Ḥabíb b. Aws) and Buḥturí, both of whom flourished in the ninth century, were distinguished court poets of the same type as Mutanabbí, but their reputation rests more securely on the anthologies which they compiled under the title of *Ḥamása* (see p. 129 seq.).

[1] *Safar-náma*, ed. by Schefer, p. 10 seq. = pp. 35–36 of the translation.

[2] *Luzúmiyyát*, ii, 280. The phrase does not mean "I am the child of my age," but "I live in the present," forgetful of the past and careless what the future may bring.

[3] See Von Kremer, *op. cit.*, p. 46 sqq.

Abu 'l-'Abbás 'Abdulláh, the son of the Caliph al-Mu'tazz, was a versatile poet and man of letters, who showed his originality by the works which he produced in two novel styles of composition. It has often been remarked that the Arabs have no great epos like the Iliad or the Persian *Sháhnáma*, but only prose narratives which, though sometimes epical in tone, are better described as historical romances. Ibnu 'l-Mu'tazz could not supply the deficiency. He wrote, however, in praise of his cousin, the Caliph Mu'taḍid, a metrical epic in miniature, commencing with a graphic delineation of the wretched state to which the Empire had been reduced by the rapacity and tyranny of the Turkish mercenaries. He composed also, besides an anthology of Bacchanalian pieces, the first important work on Poetics (*Kitábu 'l-Badí'*). A sad destiny was in store for this accomplished prince. On the death of the Caliph Muktafí he was called to the throne, but a few hours after his accession he was overpowered by the partisans of Muqtadir, who strangled him as soon as they discovered his hiding-place. Picturing the scene, one thinks almost inevitably of Nero's dying words, *Qualis artifex pereo!*

Ibnu 'l-Mu'tazz (861–908 A.D.).

The mystical poetry of the Arabs is far inferior, as a whole, to that of the Persians. Fervour and passion it has in the highest degree, but it lacks range and substance, not to speak of imaginative and speculative power. 'Umar Ibnu 'l-Fáriḍ, though he is undoubtedly the poet of Arabian mysticism, cannot sustain a comparison with his great Persian contemporary, Jalálu'l-Dín Rúmí († 1273 A.D.); he surpasses him only in the intense glow and exquisite beauty of his diction. It will be convenient to reserve a further account of Ibnu 'l-Fáriḍ for the next chapter, where we shall discuss the development of Ṣúfiism during this period.

'Umar Ibnu 'l-Fáriḍ (1181–1235 A.D.).

Finally two writers claim attention who owe their reputation to single poems—a by no means rare phenomenon in the history of Arabic literature. One of these universally celebrated odes is the *Lámiyyatu 'l-'Ajam* (the ode rhyming in *l* of the non-Arabs) composed in the year 1111 A.D. by Ṭughrá'í; the other is the *Burda* (Mantle Ode) of Búṣírí, which I take the liberty of mentioning in this chapter, although its author died some forty years after the Mongol Invasion.

Ḥasan b. 'Alí al-Ṭughrá'í was of Persian descent and a native of Iṣfahán.[1] He held the offices of *kátib* (secretary) and *munshí* or *ṭughrá'í* (chancellor) under the great Seljúq Sultans, Maliksháh and Muḥammad, and afterwards became Vizier to the Seljúqid prince Ghiyáthu 'l-Dín Mas'úd[2] in Mosul. He derived the title by which he is generally known from the royal signature (*ṭughrá*) which it was his duty to indite on all State papers over the initial *Bismilláh*. The *Lámiyyatu 'l-'Ajam* is so called with reference to Shanfará's renowned poem, the *Lámiyyatu 'l-'Arab* (see p. 79 seq.), which rhymes in the same letter; otherwise the two odes have only this in common,[3] that whereas Shanfará depicts the hardships of an outlaw's life in the desert, Ṭughrá'í, writing in Baghdád, laments the evil times on which he has fallen, and complains that younger rivals, base and servile men, are preferred to him, while he is left friendless and neglected in his old age.

Ṭughrá'í († *circa* 1120 A.D.).

The *Qaṣídatu 'l-Burda* (Mantle Ode) of al-Búṣírí[4] is a

[1] See the article on Ṭughrá'í in Ibn Khallikán, De Slane's translation, vol. i, p. 462.

[2] *Ibid.*, vol. iii, p. 355.

[3] The spirit of fortitude and patience (*ḥamása*) is exhibited by both poets, but in a very different manner. Shanfará describes a man of heroic nature. Ṭughrá'í wraps himself in his virtue and moralises like a Muḥammadan Horace. Ṣafadí, however, says in his commentary on Ṭughrá'í's ode (I translate from a MS. copy in my possession): "It is named *Lámiyyatu 'l-'Ajam* by way of comparing it with the *Lámiyyatu 'l-'Arab*, because it resembles the latter in its wise sentences and maxims."

[4] *I.e.*, the native of Abúṣír (Búṣír), a village in Egypt.

hymn in praise of the Prophet. Its author was born in Egypt in 1212 A.D. We know scarcely anything concerning his life, which, as he himself declares, was passed in writing poetry and in paying court to the great[1]; but his biographers tell us that he supported himself by copying manuscripts, and that he was a disciple of the eminent Ṣúfí, Abu 'l-'Abbás Aḥmad al-Marsí. It is said that he composed the *Burda* while suffering from a stroke which paralysed one half of his body. After praying God to heal him, he began to recite the poem. Presently he fell asleep and dreamed that he saw the Prophet, who touched his palsied side and threw his mantle (*burda*) over him.[2] "Then," said al-Búṣírí, "I awoke and found myself able to rise." However this may be, the Mantle Ode is held in extraordinary veneration by Muḥammadans. Its verses are often learned by heart and inscribed in golden letters on the walls of public buildings; and not only is the whole poem regarded as a charm against evil, but some peculiar magical power is supposed to reside in each verse separately. Although its poetical merit is no more than respectable, the *Burda* may be read with pleasure on account of its smooth and elegant style, and with interest as setting forth in brief compass the mediæval legend of the Prophet—a legend full of prodigies and miracles in which the historical figure of Muḥammad is glorified almost beyond recognition.

Búṣírí († *circa* 1296 A.D.).

Rhymed prose (*saj'*) long retained the religious associations which it possessed in Pre-islamic times and which were consecrated, for all Moslems, by its use in the Koran. About the middle of the ninth century it began to appear

[1] The *Burda*, ed. by C. A. Ralfs (Vienna, 1860), verse 140; *La Bordah traduite et commentée par René Basset* (Paris, 1894), verse 151.

[2] This appears to be a reminiscence of the fact that Muḥammad gave his own mantle as a gift to Ka'b b. Zuhayr, when that poet recited his famous ode, *Bánat Su'ád* (see p. 127 *supra*).

in the public sermons (*khuṭab*, sing. *khuṭba*) of the Caliphs and their viceroys, and it was still further developed by professional preachers, like Ibn Nubáta († 984 A.D.), and by official secretaries, like Ibráhím b. Hilál al-Ṣábí († 994 A.D.). Henceforth rhyme becomes a distinctive and almost indispensable feature of rhetorical prose.

Rhymed prose.

The credit of inventing, or at any rate of making popular, a new and remarkable form of composition in this style belongs to al-Hamadhání († 1007 A.D.), on whom posterity conferred the title *Badí'u 'l-Zamán*, *i.e.*, 'the Wonder or the Age.' Born in Hamadhán (Ecbatana), he left his native town as a young man and travelled through the greater part of Persia, living by his wits and astonishing all whom he met by his talent for improvisation. His *Maqámát* may be called a romance or literary Bohemianism. In the *maqáma* we find some approach to the dramatic style, which has never been cultivated by the Semites.[1] Hamadhání imagined as his hero a witty, unscrupulous vagabond journeying from place to place and supporting himself by the presents which his impromptu displays of rhetoric, poetry, and learning seldom failed to draw from an admiring audience. The second character is the *ráwí* or narrator, "who should be continually meeting with the other, should relate his adventures, and repeat his excellent compositions."[2] The *Maqámát* of Hamadhání

Badí'u 'l-Zamán al-Hamadhání († 1007 A.D.).

[1] *Maqáma* (plural, *maqámát*) is properly 'a place of standing'; hence, an assembly where people stand listening to the speaker, and in particular, an assembly for literary discussion. At an early period reports of such conversations and discussions received the name of *maqámát* (see Brockelmann, *Gesch. der Arab. Litteratur*, vol. i, p. 94). The word in its literary sense is usually translated by 'assembly,' or by the French '*séance*.'

[2] *The Assemblies of al-Ḥaríri*, translated from the Arabic, with an introduction and notes by T. Chenery (1867), vol. i, p. 19. This excellent work contains a fund of information on diverse matters connected with Arabian history and literature. Owing to the author's death it was left unfinished, but a second volume (including *Assemblies* 27–50) by F. Steingass appeared in 1898.

became the model for this kind of writing, and the types which he created survive unaltered in the more elaborate work of his successors. Each *maqáma* forms an independent whole, so that the complete series may be regarded as a novel consisting of detached episodes in the hero's life, a medley of prose and verse in which the story is nothing, the style everything.

Ḥarírí (1054–1122 A.D.).

Less original than Badí'u 'l-Zamán, but far beyond him in variety of learning and copiousness of language, Abú Muḥammad al-Qásim al-Ḥarírí of Baṣra produced in his *Maqámát* a masterpiece which for eight centuries "has been esteemed as, next to the Koran, the chief treasure of the Arabic tongue." In the Preface to his work he says that the composition of *maqámát* was suggested to him by "one whose suggestion is a command and whom it is a pleasure to obey." This was the distinguished Persian statesman, Anúshirwán b. Khálid,[1] who afterwards served as Vizier under the Caliph Mustarshid Billáh (1118–1135 A.D.) and Sultán Mas'úd, the Seljúq (1133–1152 A.D.); but at the time when he made Ḥarírí's acquaintance he was living in retirement at Baṣra and devoting himself to literary studies. Ḥarírí begged to be excused on the score that his abilities were unequal to the task, "for the lame steed cannot run like the strong courser."[2] Finally, however, he yielded to the request of Anúshirwán, and, to quote his own words—

"I composed, in spite of hindrances that I suffered
From dullness of capacity and dimness of intellect,
And dryness of imagination and distressing anxieties,
Fifty *Maqámát*, which contain serious language and lightsome,

---

[1] A full account of his career will be found in the Preface to Houtsma's *Recueil de textes relatifs à l'histoire des Seldjoucides*, vol. ii, p. 11 sqq. *Cf.* Browne's *Lit. Hist. of Persia*, vol. ii, p. 360.

[2] This is a graceful, but probably insincere, tribute to the superior genius of Hamadhání.

And combine refinement with dignity of style,
And brilliancies with jewels of eloquence,
And beauties of literature with its rarities,
Beside verses of the Koran wherewith I adorned them,
And choice metaphors, and Arab proverbs that I interspersed,
And literary elegancies and grammatical riddles,
And decisions based on the (double) meaning of words,
And original discourses and highly-wrought orations,
And affecting exhortations as well as entertaining jests:
The whole of which I have indited as by the tongue of Abú Zayd of Sarúj,
The part of narrator being assigned to Harith son of Hammám of Baṣra."[1]

Ḥarírí then proceeds to argue that his *Maqámát* are not mere frivolous stories such as strict Moslems are bound to reprobate in accordance with a well-known passage of the Koran referring to Naḍr b. Ḥárith, who mortally offended the Prophet by amusing the Quraysh with the old Persian legends of Rustam and Isfandiyár (Koran, xxxi, 5–6): "*There is one that buyeth idle tales that he may seduce men from the way of God, without knowledge, and make it a laughing-stock: these shall suffer a shameful punishment. And when Our signs are read to him, he turneth his back in disdain as though he heard them not, as though there were in his ears a deafness: give him joy of a grievous punishment!*" Ḥarírí insists that the *Assemblies* have a moral purpose. The ignorant and malicious, he says, will probably condemn his work, but intelligent readers will perceive, if they lay prejudice aside, that it is as useful and instructive as the fables of beasts, &c.,[2] to which no one has ever objected. That his fears of hostile criticism were not altogether groundless is shown by the

[1] The above passage is taken, with some modification, from the version of Ḥarírí published in 1850 by Theodore Preston, Fellow of Trinity College, Cambridge, who was afterwards Lord Almoner's Professor of Arabic (1855–1871).

[2] Moslems had long been familiar with the fables of Bidpai, which were translated from the Pehleví into Arabic by Ibnu 'l-Muqaffa' († *circa* 760 A.D.).

following remarks of the author of the popular history entitled *al-Fakhrí* († *circa* 1300 A.D.). This writer, after claiming that his own book is more useful than the *Ḥamása* of Abú Tammám, continues:—

"And, again, it is more profitable than the *Maqámát* on which men have set their hearts, and which they eagerly commit to

Maqámát criticised as immoral. memory; because the reader derives no benefit from *Maqámát* except familiarity with elegant composition and knowledge of the rules of verse and prose. Undoubtedly they contain maxims and ingenious devices and experiences; but all this has a debasing effect on the mind, for it is founded on begging and sponging and disgraceful scheming to acquire a few paltry pence. Therefore, if they do good in one direction, they do harm in another; and this point has been noticed by some critics of the *Maqámát* of Ḥarírí and Badí'u 'l-Zamán."[1]

Before pronouncing on the justice of this censure, we must consider for a moment the character of Abú Zayd, the hero of Ḥarírí's work, whose adventures are related by

The character of Abú Zayd. a certain Ḥárith b. Hammám, under which name the author is supposed to signify himself. According to the general tradition, Ḥarírí was one day seated with a number of savants in the mosque of the Banú Ḥarám at Baṣra, when an old man entered, footsore and travel-stained. On being asked who he was and whence he came, he answered that his name of honour was Abú Zayd and that he came from Sarúj.[2] He described in eloquent and moving terms how his native town had been plundered by the Greeks, who made his daughter a captive and drove him forth to exile and poverty. Ḥarírí was so struck with his wonderful powers of improvisation that on the same evening he began to compose the *Maqáma of the Banú Ḥarám*,[3] where Abú Zayd

---

[1] *Al-Fakhrí*, ed. by Derenbourg, p. 18, l. 4 sqq.

[2] A town in Mesopotamia, not far from Edessa. It was taken by the Crusaders in 1101 A.D. (Abu 'l-Fidá, ed. by Reiske, vol. iii, p. 332).

[3] The 48th *Maqáma* of the series as finally arranged.

is introduced in his invariable character: "a crafty old man, full of genius and learning, unscrupulous of the artifices which he uses to effect his purpose, reckless in spending in forbidden indulgences the money he has obtained by his wit or deceit, but with veins of true feeling in him, and ever yielding to unfeigned emotion when he remembers his devastated home and his captive child."[1] If an immoral tendency has been attributed to the *Assemblies* of Ḥaríri it is because the author does not conceal his admiration for this unprincipled and thoroughly disreputable scamp. Abú Zayd, indeed, is made so fascinating that we can easily pardon his knaveries for the sake of the pearls of wit and wisdom which he scatters in splendid profusion—excellent discourses, edifying sermons, and plaintive lamentations mingled with rollicking ditties and ribald jests. Modern readers are not likely to agree with the historian quoted above, but although they may deem his criticism illiberal, they can hardly deny that it has some justification.

Ḥaríri's rhymed prose might be freely imitated in English, but the difficulty of rendering it in rhyme with tolerable fidelity has caused me to abandon the attempt to produce a version of one of the *Assemblies* in the original form.[2] I will translate instead three poems which are put into the mouth of Abú Zayd. The first is a tender elegiac strain recalling far-off days of youth and happiness in his native land:—

"Ghassán is my noble kindred, Sarúj is my land of birth,
Where I dwelt in a lofty mansion of sunlike glory and worth,
A Paradise for its sweetness and beauty and pleasant mirth!

---

[1] Chenery, *op. cit.*, p. 23.

[2] This has been done with extraordinary skill by the German poet, Friedrich Rückert (*Die Verwandlungen des Abu Seid von Serug*, 2nd ed. 1837), whose work, however, is not in any sense a translation.

And oh, the life that I led there abounding in all delight!
I trailed my robe on its meadows, while Time flew a careless flight,
Elate in the flower of manhood, no pleasure veiled from my sight.

Now, if woe could kill, I had died of the troubles that haunt me here,
Or could past joy ever be ransomed, my heart's blood had not been dear,
Since death is better than living a brute's life year after year,

Subdued to scorn as a lion whom base hyenas torment.
But Luck is to blame, else no one had failed of his due ascent:
If she were straight, the conditions of men would never be bent."[1]

The scene of the eleventh *Assembly* is laid in Sáwa, a city lying midway between Hamadhán (Ecbatana) and Rayy (Rhages). "Ḥárith, in a fit of religious zeal, betakes himself to the public burial ground, for the purpose of contemplation. He finds a funeral in progress, and when it is over an old man, with his face muffled in a cloak, takes his stand on a hillock, and pours forth a discourse on the certainty of death and judgment. . . . He then rises into poetry and declaims a piece which is one of the noblest productions of Arabic literature. In lofty morality, in religious fervour, in beauty of language, in power and grace of metre, this magnificent hymn is unsurpassed."[2]

"Pretending sense in vain, how long, O light of brain, wilt thou heap sin and bane, and compass error's span?
Thy conscious guilt avow! The white hairs on thy brow admonish thee, and thou hast ears unstopt, O man!

---

[1] A literal translation of these verses, which occur in the sixth *Assembly*, is given by Chenery, *op. cit.*, p. 138.
[2] *Ibid.*, p. 163.

Death's call dost thou not hear? Rings not his voice full clear? Of parting hast no fear, to make thee sad and wise?

How long sunk in a sea of sloth and vanity wilt thou play heedlessly, as though Death spared his prize?

Till when, far wandering from virtue, wilt thou cling to evil ways that bring together vice in brief?

For thy Lord's anger shame thou hast none, but let maim o'ertake thy cherished aim, then feel'st thou burning grief.

Thou hail'st with eager joy the coin of yellow die, but if a bier pass by, feigned is thy sorry face;

Perverse and callous wight! thou scornest counsel right to follow the false light of treachery and disgrace.

Thy pleasure thou dost crave, to sordid gain a slave, forgetting the dark grave and what remains of dole;

Were thy true weal descried, thy lust would not misguide nor thou be terrified by words that should console.

Not tears, blood shall thine eyes pour at the great Assize, when thou hast no allies, no kinsman thee to save;

Straiter thy tomb shall be than needle's cavity: deep, deep thy plunge I see as diver's 'neath the wave.

There shall thy limbs be laid, a feast for worms arrayed, till utterly decayed are wood and bones withal,

Nor may thy soul repel that ordeal horrible, when o'er the Bridge of Hell she must escape or fall.

Astray shall leaders go, and mighty men be low, and sages shall cry, 'Woe like this was never yet.'

Then haste, my thoughtless friend, what thou hast marred to mend, for life draws near its end, and still thou art in the net.

Trust not in fortune, nay, though she be soft and gay; for she will spit one day her venom, if thou dote;

Abate thy haughty pride! lo, Death is at thy side, fastening, whate'er betide, his fingers on thy throat.

When prosperous, refrain from arrogant disdain, nor give thy tongue the rein: a modest tongue is best.

Comfort the child of bale and listen to his tale: repair thine actions frail, and be for ever blest.

Feather the nest once more of those whose little store has vanished: ne'er deplore the loss nor miser be;

With meanness bravely cope, and teach thine hand to ope, and spurn the misanthrope, and make thy bounty free.

Lay up provision fair and leave what brings thee care: for
sea the ship prepare and dread the rising storm.
This, friend, is what I preach expressed in lucid speech. Good
luck to all and each who with my creed conform!"

In the next *Maqáma*—that of Damascus—we find Abú Zayd, gaily attired, amidst casks and vats of wine, carousing and listening to the music of lutes and singing—

"I ride and I ride through the waste far and wide, and I fling
away pride to be gay as the swallow;
Stem the torrent's fierce speed, tame the mettlesome steed,
that wherever I lead Youth and Pleasure may follow.
I bid gravity pack, and I strip bare my back lest liquor I lack
when the goblet is lifted:
Did I never incline to the quaffing of wine, I had ne'er been
with fine wit and eloquence gifted.
Is it wonderful, pray, that an old man should stay in a well-
stored seray by a cask overflowing?
Wine strengthens the knees, physics every disease, and from
sorrow it frees, the oblivion-bestowing!
Oh, the purest of joys is to live sans disguise unconstrained
by the ties of a grave reputation,
And the sweetest of love that the lover can prove is when
fear and hope move him to utter his passion.
Thy love then proclaim, quench the smouldering flame, for
'twill spark out thy shame and betray thee to laughter:
Heal the wounds of thine heart and assuage thou the smart
by the cups that impart a delight men seek after;
While to hand thee the bowl damsels wait who cajole and
enravish the soul with eyes tenderly glancing,
And singers whose throats pour such high-mounting notes,
when the melody floats, iron rocks would be dancing!
Obey not the fool who forbids thee to pull beauty's rose when
in full bloom thou'rt free to possess it;
Pursue thine end still, tho' it seem past thy skill: let them say
what they will, take thy pleasure and bless it!
Get thee gone from thy sire, if he thwart thy desire; spread
thy nets nor enquire what the nets are receiving;
But be true to a friend, shun the miser and spend, ways of
charity wend, be unwearied in giving.
He that knocks enters straight at the Merciful's gate, so repent
or e'er Fate call thee forth from the living!"

The reader may judge from these extracts whether the *Assemblies* of Ḥaríri are so deficient in matter as some critics have imagined. But, of course, the celebrity of the work is mainly due to its consummate literary form—a point on which the Arabs have always bestowed singular attention. Ḥaríri himself was a subtle grammarian, living in Baṣra, the home of philological science;[1] and though he wrote to please rather than to instruct, he seems to have resolved that his work should illustrate every beauty and nicety of which the Arabic language is capable. We Europeans can see as little merit or taste in the verbal conceits—equivoques, paronomasias, assonances, alliterations, &c.—with which his pages are thickly studded, as in *tours de force* of composition which may be read either forwards or backwards, or which consist entirely of pointed or of unpointed letters; but our impatience of such things should not blind us to the fact that they are intimately connected with the genius and traditions of the Arabic tongue,[2] and therefore stand on a very different footing from those euphuistic extravagances which appear, for example, in English literature of the Elizabethan age. By Ḥaríri's countrymen the *Maqámát* are prized as an almost unique monument of their language, antiquities, and culture. One of the author's contemporaries, the famous Zamakhsharí, has expressed the general verdict in pithy verse—

"I swear by God and His marvels,
By the pilgrims' rite and their shrine:
Ḥaríri's *Assemblies* are worthy
To be written in gold each line."

---

[1] Two grammatical treatises by Ḥaríri have come down to us. In one of these, entitled *Durratu 'l-Ghawwáṣ* ('The Pearl of the Diver') and edited by Thorbecke (Leipzig, 1871), he discusses the solecisms which people of education are wont to commit.

[2] See Chenery, *op. cit.*, pp. 83–97.

Concerning some of the specifically religious sciences, such as Dogmatic Theology and Mysticism, we shall have more to say in the following chapter, while as to the science of Apostolic Tradition (*Ḥadíth*) we must refer the reader to what has been already said. All that can be attempted here is to take a passing notice of the most eminent writers and the most celebrated works of this epoch in the field of religion.

The religious literature of the period.

The place of honour belongs to the Imám Málik b. Anas of Medína, whose *Muwaṭṭa'* is the first great *corpus* of Muḥammadan Law. He was a partisan of the 'Alids, and was flogged by command of the Caliph Manṣúr in consequence of his declaration that he did not consider the oath of allegiance to the 'Abbásid dynasty to have any binding effect.

Málik b. Anas (713-795 A.D.).

The two principal authorities for Apostolic Tradition are Bukhárí († 870 A.D.) and Muslim († 875 A.D.), authors of the collections entitled *Ṣaḥíḥ*. Compilations of a narrower range, embracing only those traditions which bear on the *Sunna* or custom of the Prophet, are the *Sunan* of Abú Dáwúd al-Sijistání († 889 A.D.), the *Jámi'* of Abú 'Ísá Muḥammad al-Tirmidhí († 892 A.D.), the *Sunan* of al-Nasá'í († 915 A.D.), and the *Sunan* of Ibn Mája († 896 A.D.). These, together with the *Ṣaḥíḥs* of Bukhárí and Muslim, form the Six Canonical Books (*al-kutub al-sitta*), which are held in the highest veneration. Amongst the innumerable works of a similar kind produced in this period it will suffice to mention the *Maṣábíḥu 'l-Sunna* by al-Baghawí († *circa* 1120 A.D.). A later adaptation called *Mishkátu 'l-Maṣábíḥ* has been often printed, and is still extremely popular.

Bukhárí and Muslim.

The four *Sunan*.

Omitting the great manuals of Moslem Jurisprudence, which are without literary interest in the larger sense, we may pause for a moment at the name of al-Máwardí, a Sháfi'ite lawyer, who wrote a well-known treatise on politics—

the *Kitábu 'l-Aḥkám al-Sulṭániyya*, or 'Book of the Principles of Government.' His standpoint is purely theoretical. Thus he lays down that the Caliph should be elected by the body of learned, pious, and orthodox divines, and that the people must leave the administration of the State to the Caliph absolutely, as being its representative. Máwardí lived at Baghdád during the period of Buwayhid ascendancy, a period described by Sir W. Muir in the following words: "The pages of our annalists are now almost entirely occupied with the political events of the day, in the guidance of which the Caliphs had seldom any concern, and which therefore need no mention here."[1] Under the 'Abbásid dynasty the mystical doctrines of the Ṣúfís were systematised and expounded. Some of the most important Arabic works of reference on Ṣúfiism are the *Qútu 'l-Qulúb*, or 'Food of Hearts,' by Abú Ṭálib al-Makkí († 996 A.D.); the *Kitábu 'l-Ta'arruf li-Madhhabi ahli 'l-Taṣawwuf*, or 'Book of Enquiry as to the Religion of the Ṣúfís,' by Muḥammad b. Isḥáq al-Kalábádhí († *circa* 1000 A.D.); the *Ṭabaqátu 'l-Ṣúfiyya*, or 'Classes of the Ṣúfís,' by Abú 'Abd al-Raḥmán al-Sulamí († 1021 A.D.); the *Ḥilyatu 'l-Awliyá*, or 'Adornment of the Saints,' by Abú Nu'aym al-Iṣfahání († 1038 A.D.); the *Risálatu 'l-Qushayriyya*, or 'Qushayrite Tract,' by Abu 'l-Qásim al-Qushayrí of Naysábúr († 1074 A.D.); the *Iḥyá'u 'Ulúm al-Dín*, or 'Revivification of the Religious Sciences,' by Ghazálí († 1111 A.D.); and the *'Awárifu 'l-Ma'árif*, or 'Bounties of Knowledge,' by Shihábu 'l-Dín Abú Ḥafṣ 'Umar al-Suhrawardí († 1234 A.D.) —a list which might easily be extended. In Dogmatic Theology there is none to compare with Abú Ḥámid al-Ghazálí, surnamed 'the Proof of Islam' (*Ḥujjatu 'l-Islám*). He is a figure of such towering importance that some detailed account of his life and opinions must be inserted in a book like this,

Máwardí († 1058 A.D.).

Arabic authorities on Ṣúfiism.

Ghazálí († 1111 A.D.).

[1] *The Caliphate, its Rise, Decline, and Fall*, p. 573.

which professes to illustrate the history of Muḥammadan thought. Here, however, we shall only give an outline of his biography in order to pave the way for discussion of his intellectual achievements and his far-reaching influence.

Life of Ghazálí according to the *Shadharátu 'l-Dhahab.*

"In this year (505 A.H. = 1111 A.D.) died the Imám, who was the Ornament of the Faith and the Proof of Islam, Abú Ḥámid Muḥammad . . . of Ṭús, the Sháfi'ite. His death took place on the 14th of the Latter Jumádá at Ṭábarán, a village near Ṭús. He was then fifty-five years of age. Ghazzálí is equivalent to Ghazzál, like 'Aṭṭárí (for 'Aṭṭár) and Khabbází (for Khabbáz), in the dialect of the people of Khurásán[1]: so it is stated by the author of the *'Ibar.*[2] Al-Isnawí says in his *Ṭabaqát*[3]:—Ghazzálí is an Imám by whose name breasts are dilated and souls are revived, and in whose literary productions the ink-horn exults and the paper quivers with joy; and at the hearing thereof voices are hushed and heads are bowed. He was born at Ṭús in the year 450 A.H. = 1058–1059 A.D. His father used to spin wool (*yaghzilu 'l-ṣúf*) and sell it in his shop. On his death-bed he committed his two sons, Ghazzálí himself and his brother Aḥmad, to the care of a pious Ṣúfí, who taught them writing and educated them until the money left him by their father was all spent. 'Then,' says Ghazzálí, 'we went to the college to learn divinity (*fiqh*) so that we might gain our livelihood.' After studying there for some time he journeyed to Abú Naṣr al-Ismá'ílí in Jurján, then to the Imámu 'l-Ḥaramayn[4] at Naysábúr, under whom he studied with such assiduity that he became the best scholastic of his contemporaries (*ṣára anẓara ahli zamánihi*), and he lectured *ex*

[1] Another example is 'Umar al-Khayyámí for 'Umar Khayyám. The spelling Ghazzálí (with a double *z*) was in general use when Ibn Khallikán wrote his Biographical Dictionary in 1256 A.D. (see De Slane's translation, vol. i, p. 80), but according to Sam'ání the name is derived from Ghazála, a village near Ṭús; in which case Ghazálí is the correct form of the *nisba*. I have adopted 'Ghazalí' in deference to Sam'ání's authority, but those who write 'Ghazzálí' can at least claim that they err in very good company.

[2] Shamsu 'l-Dín al-Dhahabí († 1348 A.D.).

[3] 'Abdu 'l-Raḥím al-Isnawí († 1370 A.D.), author of a biographical work on the Sháfi'ite doctors. See Brockelmann, *Gesch. der Arab. Litt.*, vol. ii, p. 90.

[4] Abu 'l-Ma'álí al-Juwayní, a famous theologian of Naysábúr († 1085 A.D.), received this title, which means 'Imám of the Two Sanctuaries,' because he taught for several years at Mecca and Medína.

cathedrâ in his master's lifetime, and wrote books. . . . And on the death of his master he set out for the Camp[1] and presented himself to the Niẓámu 'l-Mulk, whose assembly was the alighting-place of the learned and the destination of the leading divines and savants; and there, as was due to his high merit, he enjoyed the society of the principal doctors, and disputed with his opponents and rebutted them in spite of their eminence. So the Niẓámu 'l-Mulk inclined to him and showed him great honour, and his name flew through the world. Then, in the year '84 (1091 A.D.) he was called to a professorship in the Niẓámiyya College at Baghdád, where a splendid reception awaited him. His words reached far and wide, and his influence soon exceeded that of the Emírs and Viziers. But at last his lofty spirit recoiled from worldly vanities. He gave himself up to devotion and dervishhood, and set out, in the year '88 (1095 A.D.), for the Ḥijáz.[2] On his return from the Pilgrimage he journeyed to Damascus and made his abode there for ten years in the minaret of the Congregational Mosque, and composed several works, of which the *Iḥyá* is said to be one. Then, after visiting Jerusalem and Alexandria, he returned to his home at Ṭús, intent on writing and worship and constant recitation of the Koran and dissemination of knowledge and avoidance of intercourse with men. The Vizier Fakhru 'l-Mulk,[3] son of the Niẓámu 'l-Mulk, came to see him, and urged him by every means in his power to accept a professorship in the Niẓámiyya College at Naysábúr.[4] Ghazzálí consented, but after teaching for a time, resigned the appointment and returned to end his days in his native town."

His principal works.

Besides his *magnum opus*, the already-mentioned *Iḥyá*, in which he expounds theology and the ethics of religion from the standpoint of the moderate Ṣúfí school, Ghazálí wrote a great number of important works, such as the *Munqidh mina 'l-Ḍalál*, or 'Deliverer from Error,' a sort of 'Apologia pro Vitâ Suâ'; the *Kímiyá'u 'l-Sa'ádat*, or 'Alchemy of Happiness,' which was

[1] *I.e.*, the camp-court of the Seljúq monarch Malikshâh, son of Alp Arslán.

[2] According to his own account in the *Munqidh*, Ghazálí on leaving Baghdád went first to Damascus, then to Jerusalem, and then to Mecca. The statement that he remained ten years at Damascus is inaccurate.

[3] The MS. has Fakhru 'l-Dín.

[4] Ghazálí's return to public life took place in 1106 A.D.

originally written in Persian; and the *Taháfutu 'l-Falásifa*, or 'Collapse of the Philosophers,' a polemical treatise designed to refute and destroy the doctrines of Moslem philosophy. This work called forth a rejoinder from the celebrated Ibn Rushd (Averroes), who died at Morocco in 1198–1199 A.D.

Shahrastání's 'Book of Religions and Sects.'

Here we may notice two valuable works on the history of religion, both of which are generally known as *Kitábu 'l-Milal wa-'l-Niḥal*,[1] that is to say, 'The Book of Religions and Sects,' by Ibn Ḥazm of Cordova († 1064 A.D.) and Abu 'l-Fatḥ al-Shahrastání († 1153 A.D.). Ibn Ḥazm we shall meet with again in the chapter which deals specially with the history and literature of the Spanish Moslems. Shahrastání, as he is named after his birthplace, belonged to the opposite extremity of the Muḥammadan Empire, being a native of Khurásán, the huge Eastern province bounded by the Oxus. Cureton, who edited the Arabic text of the *Kitábu 'l-Milal wa-'l-Niḥal* (London, 1842–1846), gives the following outline of its contents:—

After five introductory chapters, the author proceeds to arrange his book into two great divisions; the one comprising the Religious, the other the Philosophical Sects. The former of these contains an account of the various Sects of the followers of Muḥammad, and likewise of those to whom a true revelation had been made (the *Ahlu 'l-Kitáb*, or 'People of the Scripture'), that is, Jews and Christians; and of those who had a doubtful or pretended revelation (*man lahú shubhatu 'l-Kitáb*), such as the Magi and the Manichæans. The second division comprises an account of the philosophical opinions of the Sabæans (Ṣábians), which are mainly set forth in a very interesting dialogue between a Sabæan and an orthodox Muḥammadan; of the tenets of various Greek Philosophers and some of the Fathers of the Christian Church; and also of the Muḥammadan doctors, more particularly of the system of Ibn Síná or Avicenna, which the author explains at considerable length. The work terminates with an account of the tenets of the Arabs before the commencement of Islamism, and of the religion of the people of India.

---

[1] The correct title of Ibn Ḥazm's work is uncertain. In the Cairo ed. (1321 A.H.) it is called *Kitábu 'l-Fiṣal fí 'l-Milal wa 'l-Ahwá wa 'l-Niḥal*.

Grammar and philology.

The science of grammar took its rise in the cities of Baṣra and Kúfa, which were founded not long after Muḥammad's death, and which remained the chief centres of Arabian life and thought outside the peninsula until they were eclipsed by the great 'Abbásid capital. In both towns the population consisted of Bedouin Arabs, belonging to different tribes and speaking many different dialects, while there were also thousands of artisans and clients who spoke Persian as their mother-tongue, so that the classical idiom was peculiarly exposed to corrupting influences. If the pride and delight of the Arabs in their noble language led them to regard the maintenance of its purity as a national duty, they were equally bound by their religious convictions to take decisive measures for ensuring the correct pronunciation and interpretation of that "miracle of Divine eloquence," the Arabic Koran. To this latter motive the invention of grammar is traditionally ascribed. The inventor is related to have been Abu 'l-Aswad al-Du'ilí, who died at Baṣra during the Umayyad period. "Abu 'l-Aswad, having been asked where he had acquired the science of grammar, answered that he had learned the rudiments of it from 'Alí b. Abí Ṭálib. It is said that he never made known any of the principles which he had received from 'Alí till Ziyád[1] sent to him the order to compose something which might serve as a guide to the public and enable them to understand the Book of God. He at first asked to be excused, but on hearing a man recite the following passage out of the Koran, *anna 'lláha barí'un mina 'l-mushrikína wa-rasúluhu*,[2] which last word the reader pronounced *rasúlihi*, he exclaimed, 'I never thought that things would have come to this.' He then returned to Ziyád and

The invention of Arabic grammar.

[1] See p. 195 *supra*.

[2] Kor. ix, 3. The translation runs ("This is a declaration) *that God is clear of the idolaters, and His Apostle likewise*." With the reading *rasúlihi* it means that God is clear of the idolaters and also of His Apostle.

said, 'I will do what you ordered.'"[1] The Başra school of grammarians which Abu 'l-Aswad is said to have founded is older than the rival school of Kúfa and surpassed it in fame. Its most prominent representatives were Abú 'Amr b. al-'Alá († 770 A.D.), a diligent and profound student of the Koran, who on one occasion burned all his collections of old poetry, &c., and abandoned himself to devotion; Khalíl b. Aḥmad, inventor of the Arabic system of metres and author of the first Arabic lexicon (the *Kitábu 'l-'Ayn*), which, however, he did not live to complete; the Persian Síbawayhi, whose Grammar, entitled 'The Book of Síbawayhi,' is universally celebrated; the great Humanists al-Aṣma'í and Abú 'Ubayda who flourished under Hárún al-Rashid; al-Mubarrad, about a century later, whose best-known work, the *Kámil*, has been edited by Professor William Wright; his contemporary al-Sukkarí, a renowned collector and critic of old Arabian poetry; and Ibn Durayd († 934 A.D.), a distinguished philologist, genealogist, and poet, who received a pension from the Caliph Muqtadir in recognition of his services on behalf of science, and whose principal works, in addition to the famous ode known as the *Maqṣúra*, are a voluminous lexicon (*al-Jamhara fi 'l-Lugha*) and a treatise on the genealogies of the Arab tribes (*Kitábu 'l-Ishtiqáq*).

The philologists of Başra.

Against these names the school of Kúfa can set al-Kisá'í, a Persian savant who was entrusted by Hárún al-Rashíd with the education of his sons Amín and Ma'mún; al-Farrá († 822 A.D.), a pupil and compatriot of al-Kisá'í; al-Mufaḍḍal al-Ḍabbí, a favourite of the Caliph Mahdí, for whom he compiled an excellent anthology of Pre-islamic poems (*al-Mufaḍḍaliyyát*), which has already been noticed[2]; Ibnu 'l-Sikkít, whose outspoken partiality for the House of 'Alí b. Abí Ṭálib caused him to be brutally trampled to death by the Turkish

The philologists of Kúfa.

[1] Ibn Khallikan, De Slane's translation, vol. i, p. 663.

[2] See p. 128.

guards of the tyrant Mutawakkil (858 A.D.); and Tha'lab, head of the Kúfa school in his time († 904 A.D.), of whose rivalry with al-Mubarrad many stories are told. A contemporary, Abú Bakr b. Abi 'l-Azhar, said in one of his poems:—

> "Turn to Mubarrad or to Tha'lab, thou
> That seek'st with learning to improve thy mind!
> Be not a fool, like mangy camel shunned:
> All human knowledge thou with them wilt find.
> The science of the whole world, East and West,
> In these two single doctors is combined."[1]

Reference has been made in a former chapter to some of the earliest Humanists, *e.g.*, Ḥammád al-Ráwiya († 776 A.D.) and his slightly younger contemporary, Khalaf al-Aḥmar, to their inestimable labours in rescuing the old poetry from oblivion, and to the unscrupulous methods which they sometimes employed.[2] Among their successors, who flourished in the Golden Age of Islam, under the first 'Abbásids, the place of honour belongs to Abú 'Ubayda († about 825 A.D.) and al-Aṣma'í († about 830 A.D.).

Abú 'Ubayda.

Abú 'Ubayda Ma'mar b. al-Muthanná was of Jewish-Persian race, and maintained in his writings the cause of the Shu'úbites against the Arab national party, for which reason he is erroneously described as a Khárijite.[3] The rare expressions of the Arabic language, the history of the Arabs and their conflicts were his predominant study—"neither in heathen nor Muḥammadan times," he once boasted, "have two horses met in battle but that I possess information about them and their riders"[4]; yet, with all his learning, he was not always able to recite a verse without mangling it; even in reading the Koran, with the book

[1] Ibn Khallikán, No. 608; De Slane's translation, vol. iii, p. 31.
[2] See pp. 131–134, *supra*.
[3] Goldziher, *Muhammedanische Studien*, Part I, p. 197.
[4] *Ibid.*, p. 195.

before his eyes, he made mistakes.[1] Our knowledge of Arabian antiquity is drawn, to a large extent, from the traditions collected by him which are preserved in the *Kitábu 'l-Aghání* and elsewhere. He left nearly two hundred works, of which a long but incomplete catalogue occurs in the *Fihrist* (pp. 53–54). Abú 'Ubayda was summoned by the Caliph Hárún al-Rashíd to Baghdád, where he became acquainted

Aṣmaʻí.

with Aṣmaʻí. There was a standing feud between them, due in part to difference of character[2] and in part to personal jealousies. 'Abdu 'l-Malik b. Qurayb al-Aṣmaʻí was, like his rival, a native of Baṣra. Although he may have been excelled by others of his contemporaries in certain branches of learning, none exhibited in such fine perfection the varied literary culture which at that time was so highly prized and so richly rewarded. Whereas Abú 'Ubayda was dreaded for his sharp tongue and sarcastic humour, Aṣmaʻí had all the accomplishments and graces of a courtier. Abú Nuwás, the first great poet of the 'Abbásid period, said that Aṣmaʻí was a nightingale to charm those who heard him with his melodies. In court circles, where the talk often turned on philological matters, he was a favourite guest, and the Caliph would send for him to decide any abstruse question connected with literature which no one present was able to answer. Of his numerous writings on linguistic and antiquarian themes several have come down to us, *e.g.*, 'The Book of Camels' (*Kitábu 'l-Ibil*), 'The Book of Horses' (*Kitábu 'l-Khayl*), and 'The Book of the Making of Man' (*Kitábu Khalqi 'l-Insán*), a treatise which shows that the Arabs of the desert had acquired a considerable knowledge of human anatomy. His work as editor, commentator, and critic of Arabian poetry forms (it has been said) the basis of nearly all that has since been written on the subject.

[1] Ibn Qutayba, *Kitábu 'l-Maʻárif*, p. 269.

[2] While Abú 'Ubayda was notorious for his free-thinking proclivities, Aṣmaʻí had a strong vein of pietism. See Goldziher, *loc. cit.*, p. 199 and *Abh. zur Arab. Philologie*, Part I, p. 136.

Belles-lettres (*Adab*) and literary history are represented by a whole series of valuable works. Only a few of the most important can be mentioned here, and that in a very summary manner. The Persian Rúzbih, better known as 'Abdulláh Ibnu 'l-Muqaffa', who was put to death by order of the Caliph Manṣúr, made several translations from the Pehleví or Middle-Persian literature into Arabic. We possess a specimen of his powers in the famous *Book of Kalíla and Dimna*, which is ultimately derived from the Sanscrit *Fables of Bidpai*. The Arabic version is one of the oldest prose works in that language, and is justly regarded as a model of elegant style, though it has not the pungent brevity which marks true Arabian eloquence. Ibn Qutayba, whose family came from Merv, held for a time the office of Cadi at Dínawar, and lived at Baghdád in the latter half of the ninth century. We have more than once cited his 'Book of General Knowledge' (*Kitábu 'l-Ma'árif*)[1] and his 'Book of Poetry and Poets,' (*Kitábu 'l-Shi'r wa-'l-Shu'ará*), and may add here the *Adabu 'l-Kátib*, or 'Accomplishments of the Secretary,'[2] a manual of stylistic, dealing with orthography, orthoepy, lexicography, and the like; and the *'Uyúnu 'l-Akhbár*, or 'Choice Histories,'[3] a work in ten chapters, each of which is devoted to a special theme such as Government, War, Nobility, Friendship, Women, &c.

Ibnu 'l-Muqaffa' († *circa* 760 A.D.).

Ibn Qutayba († 889 A.D.).

'Amr b. Baḥr al-Jáḥiẓ of Baṣra was a celebrated freethinker, and gave his name to a sect of the Mu'tazilites (*al-Jáḥiẓiyya*).[4] He composed numerous books of an anecdotal and entertaining character. Ibn Khallikán singles out as his finest and most instructive works the *Kitábu 'l-Ḥayawán* ('Book of Animals'), and the

Jáḥiẓ († 869 A.D.).

[1] Professor Browne has given a *résumé* of the contents in his *Lit. Hist. of Persia*, vol. i, p. 387 seq.

[2] Ed. by Max Grünert (Leyden, 1900).

[3] Vol. i ed. by C. Brockelmann (Weimar and Strassburg, 1898–1908).

[4] The epithet *jáḥiẓ* means 'goggle-eyed.'

Kitábu 'l-Bayán wa-'l-Tabyín ('Book of Eloquence and Exposition'), which is a popular treatise on rhetoric. It so happens—and the fact is not altogether fortuitous—that extremely valuable contributions to the literary history of the Arabs were made by two writers connected with the Umayyad House. Ibn 'Abdi Rabbihi of Cordova, who was descended from an enfranchised slave of the Spanish Umayyad Caliph, Hishám b. 'Abd al-Raḥmán (788–796 A.D.), has left us a miscellaneous anthology entitled *al-'Iqd al-Faríd*, or 'The Unique Necklace,' which is divided into twenty-five books, each bearing the name of a different gem, and "contains something on every subject." Though Abu 'l-Faraj 'Alí, the author of the *Kitábu 'l-Aghání*, was born at Iṣfahán, he was an Arab of the Arabs, being a member of the tribe Quraysh and a lineal descendant of Marwán, the last Umayyad Caliph. Coming to Baghdád, he bent all his energies to the study of Arabian antiquity, and towards the end of his life found a generous patron in al-Muhallabí, the Vizier of the Buwayhid sovereign, Mu'izzu 'l-Dawla. His minor works are cast in the shade by his great 'Book of Songs.' This may be described as a history of all the Arabian poetry that had been set to music down to the author's time. It is based on a collection of one hundred melodies which was made for the Caliph Hárún al-Rashíd, but to these Abu 'l-Faraj has added many others chosen by himself. After giving the words and the airs attached to them, he relates the lives of the poets and musicians by whom they were composed, and takes occasion to introduce a vast quantity of historical traditions and anecdotes, including much ancient and modern verse. It is said that the Ṣáḥib Ibn 'Abbád,[1] when travelling, used to take thirty camel-loads of books about with him, but on receiving the *Aghání* he con-

Ibn 'Abdi Rabbihi († 940 A.D.).

Abu 'l-Faraj al-Iṣfahání († 967 A.D.).

[1] See p. 267.

tented himself with this one book and dispensed with all the rest.[1] The chief man of letters of the next generation was Abú Manṣúr al-Tha'álibí (the Furrier) of Naysábúr. Notwithstanding that most of his works are unscientific compilations, designed to amuse the public rather than to impart solid instruction, his famous anthology of recent and contemporary poets—the *Yatímatu 'l-Dahr*, or 'Solitaire of the Time'—supplies indubitable proof of his fine scholarship and critical taste. Successive continuations of the *Yatíma* were written by al-Bákharzí († 1075 A.D.) in the *Dumyatu 'l-Qaṣr*, or 'Statue of the Palace'; by Abu 'l-Ma'álí al-Ḥaẓírí († 1172 A.D.) in the *Zínatu 'l-Dahr*, or 'Ornament of the Time'; and by the favourite of Saladin, 'Imádu 'l-Dín al-Kátib al-Iṣfahání († 1201 A.D.), in the *Kharídatu 'l-Qaṣr*, or 'Virgin Pearl of the Palace.' From the tenth century onward the study of philology proper began to decline, while on the other hand those sciences which formerly grouped themselves round philology now became independent, were cultivated with brilliant success, and in a short time reached their zenith.

Tha'álibí († 1037 A.D.).

The elements of History are found (1) in Pre-islamic traditions and (2) in the *Ḥadíth* of the Prophet, but the idea of historical composition on a grand scale was probably suggested to the Arabs by Persian models such as the Pehleví *Khudáy-náma*, or 'Book of Kings,' which Ibnu 'l-Muqaffa' turned into Arabic in the eighth century of our era under the title of *Siyaru Mulúki 'l-'Ajam*, that is, 'The History of the Kings of Persia.'

History.

Under the first head Hishám Ibnu 'l-Kalbí († 819 A.D.) and his father Muḥammad deserve particular mention as painstaking and trustworthy recorders.

Historical traditions relating to the Prophet were put in

[1] Ibn Khallikán, De Slane's translation, vol. ii, p. 250.

writing at an early date (see p. 247). The first biography of Muḥammad (*Síratu Rasúli 'lláh*), compiled by Ibn Isḥáq, who died in the reign of Manṣúr (768 A.D.), has come down to us only in the recension made by Ibn Hishám († 834 A.D.). This work as well as those of al-Wáqidí († 823 A.D.) and Ibn Sa'd († 845 A.D.) have been already noticed.

Histories of the Prophet and his Companions.

Other celebrated historians of the 'Abbásid period are the following.

Aḥmad b. Yaḥyá al-Baládhurí († 892 A.D.), a Persian, wrote an account of the early Muḥammadan conquests (*Kitábu Futúḥi 'l-Buldán*), which has been edited by De Goeje, and an immense chronicle based on genealogical principles, 'The Book of the Lineages of the Nobles' (*Kitábu Ansábi 'l-Ashráf*), of which two volumes are extant.[1]

Baládhurí.

Abú Ḥánífa Aḥmad al-Dínawarí († 895 A.D.) was also of Íránian descent. His 'Book of Long Histories' (*Kitábu 'l-Akhbár al-Ṭiwál*) deals largely with the national legend of Persia, and is written throughout from the Persian point of view.

Dínawarí.

Ibn Wáḍiḥ al-Ya'qúbí, a contemporary of Dínawarí, produced an excellent compendium of universal history, which is specially valuable because its author, being a follower of the House of 'Alí, has preserved the ancient and unfalsified Shí'ite tradition. His work has been edited in two volumes by Professor Houtsma (Leyden, 1883).

Ya'qúbí.

The Annals of Ṭabarí, edited by De Goeje and other European scholars (Leyden, 1879–1898), and the Golden Meadows[2] (*Murúju 'l-Dhahab*) of Mas'údí, which Pavet de

[1] One of these, the eleventh of the complete work, has been edited by Ahlwardt: *Anonyme Arabische Chronik* (Greifswald, 1883). It covers part of the reign of the Umayyad Caliph, 'Abdu 'l-Malik (685–705 A.D.).

[2] The French title is *Les Prairies d'Or*. Brockelmann, in his shorter

Courteille and Barbier de Meynard published with a French translation (Paris, 1861–1877), have been frequently cited in the foregoing pages; and since these two authors are not only the greatest historians of the Muḥammadan East but also (excepting, possibly, Ibn Khaldún) the most eminent of all who devoted themselves to this branch of Arabic literature, we must endeavour to make the reader more closely acquainted with them.

Ṭabarí (838–923 A.D.).

Abú Ja'far Muḥammad b. Jarír was born in 838–839 A.D. at Ámul in Ṭabaristán, the mountainous province lying along the south coast of the Caspian Sea; whence the name, Ṭabarí, by which he is usually known.[1] At this time 'Iráq was still the principal focus of Muḥammadan culture, so that a poet could say:—

"I see a man in whom the secretarial dignity is manifest,
One who displays the brilliant culture of 'Iráq."[2]

Thither the young Ṭabarí came to complete his education. He travelled by way of Rayy to Baghdád, visited other neighbouring towns, and extended his tour to Syria and Egypt. Although his father sent him a yearly allowance, it did not always arrive punctually, and he himself relates that on one occasion he procured bread by selling the sleeves of his shirt. Fortunately, at Baghdád he was introduced to 'Ubaydulláh b. Yaḥyá, the Vizier of Mutawakkil, who engaged him as tutor for his son. How long he held this post is uncertain, but he was only twenty-three years of age when his patron went out of office. Fifteen years later we find him, penniless once more, in Cairo

Hist. of Arabic Literature (Leipzig, 1901), p. 110, states that the correct translation of *Murúju 'l-Dhahab* is 'Goldwäschen.'

[1] Concerning Ṭabarí and his work the reader should consult De Goeje's Introduction (published in the supplementary volume containing the Glossary) to the Leyden edition, and his excellent article on Ṭabarí and early Arab Historians in the *Encyclopædia Britannica*.

[2] Abu 'l-Maḥásin, ed. by Juynboll, vol. i, p. 608.

(876–877 A.D.). He soon, however, returned to Baghdád, where he passed the remainder of his life in teaching and writing. Modest, unselfish, and simple in his habits, he diffused his encyclopædic knowledge with an almost superhuman industry. During forty years, it is said, he wrote forty leaves every day. His great works are the *Ta'ríkhu 'l-Rusul wa-'l-Mulúk*, or 'Annals of the Apostles and the Kings,' and his *Tafsír*, or 'Commentary on the Koran.' Both, even in their present shape, are books of enormous extent, yet it seems likely that both were originally composed on a far larger scale and were abbreviated by the author for general use. His pupils, we are told, flatly refused to read the first editions with him, whereupon he exclaimed: "Enthusiasm for learning is dead!" The History of Ṭabarí, from the Creation to the year 302 A.H.=915 A.D., is distinguished by "completeness of detail, accuracy, and the truly stupendous learning of its author that is revealed throughout, and that makes the Annals a vast storehouse of valuable information for the historian as well as for the student of Islam."[1] It is arranged chronologically, the events being tabulated under the year (of the Muḥammadan era) in which they occurred. Moreover, it has a very peculiar form. "Each important fact is related, if possible, by an eye-witness or contemporary, whose account came down through a series of narrators to the author. If he has obtained more than one account of a fact, with more or less important modifications, through several series of narrators, he communicates them all to the reader *in extenso*. Thus we are enabled to consider the facts from more than one point of view, and to acquire a vivid and clear notion of them."[2] According to modern ideas, Ṭabarí's compilation is not so much a history as a priceless collection of original documents placed side by side without any attempt to construct a critical

[1] *Selection from the Annals of Tabari*, ed. by M. J. de Goeje (Leyden, 1902), p. xi.

[2] De Goeje's Introduction to Ṭabarí, p. xxvii.

and continuous narrative. At first sight one can hardly see the wood for the trees, but on closer study the essential features gradually emerge and stand out in bold relief from amidst the multitude of insignificant circumstances which lend freshness and life to the whole. Ṭabarí suffered the common fate of standard historians. His work was abridged and popularised, the *isnáds* or chains of authorities were suppressed, and the various parallel accounts were combined by subsequent writers into a single version.[1] Of the Annals, as it left the author's hands, no entire copy exists anywhere, but many odd volumes are preserved in different parts of the world. The Leyden edition is based on these scattered MSS., which luckily comprise the whole work with the exception of a few not very serious lacunæ.

Mas'údí († 956 A.D.).

'Alí b. Ḥusayn, a native of Baghdád, was called Mas'údí after one of the Prophet's Companions, 'Abdulláh b. Mas'úd, to whom he traced his descent. Although we possess only a small remnant of his voluminous writings, no better proot can be desired of the vast and various erudition which he gathered not from books alone, but likewise from long travel in almost every part of Asia. Among other places, he visited Armenia, India, Ceylon, Zanzibar, and Madagascar, and he appears to have sailed in Chinese waters as well as in the Caspian Sea. "My journey," he says, "resembles that of the sun, and to me the poet's verse is applicable :—

"'We turn our steps toward each different clime,
Now to the Farthest East, then West once more ;
Even as the sun, which stays not his advance
O'er tracts remote that no man durst explore.'"[2]

---

[1] Al-Bal'amí, the Vizier of Manṣúr I, the Sámánid, made in 963 A.D. a Persian epitome of which a French translation by Dubeux and Zotenberg was published in 1867–1874.

[2] *Murúju 'l-Dhahab*, ed. by Barbier de Meynard, vol. i, p. 5 seq.

He spent the latter years of his life chiefly in Syria and Egypt —for he had no settled abode—compiling the great historical works,[1] of which the *Murúju 'l-Dhahab* is an epitome. As regards the motives which urged him to write, Mas'údí declares that he wished to follow the example of scholars and sages and to leave behind him a praiseworthy memorial and imperishable monument. He claims to have taken a wider view than his predecessors. "One who has never quitted his hearth and home, but is content with the knowledge which he can acquire concerning the history of his own part of the world, is not on the same level as one who spends his life in travel and passes his days in restless wanderings, and draws forth all manner of curious and precious information from its hidden mine."[2]

Mas'údí has been named the 'the Herodotus of the Arabs,' and the comparison is not unjust.[3] His work, although it lacks the artistic unity which distinguishes that of the Greek historian, shows the same eager spirit of enquiry, the same open-mindedness and disposition to record without prejudice all the marvellous things that he had heard or seen, the same ripe experience and large outlook on the present as on the past. It is professedly a universal history beginning with the Creation and ending at the Caliphate of Muṭí', in 947 A.D., but no description can cover the immense range of topics which are discussed and the innumerable digressions with which the author delights or irritates his readers, as the case may be.[4] Thus, to pick

The *Murúju 'l-Dhahab.*

[1] The *Akhbáru 'l-Zamán* in thirty volumes (one volume is extant at Vienna) and the *Kitáb al-Awsaṭ*.

[2] *Murúju 'l-Dhahab*, p. 9 seq.

[3] It may be noted as a coincidence that Ibn Khaldún calls Mas'údí *imám^{an} lil-mu'arrikhín*, "an Imám for all the historians," which resembles, though it does not exactly correspond to, "the Father of History."

[4] Mas'údí gives a summary of the contents of his historical and religious works in the Preface to the *Tanbíh wa-'l-Ishráf*, ed. by De Goeje, p. 2 sqq. A translation of this passage by De Sacy will be found in Barbier de Meynard's edition of the *Murúju 'l-Dhahab*, vol. ix, p. 302 sqq.

a few examples at random, we find a dissertation on tides (vol. i, p. 244); an account of the *tinnín* or sea-serpent (*ibid.*, p. 267); of pearl-fishing in the Persian Gulf (*ibid.*, p. 328); and of the rhinoceros (*ibid.*, p. 385). Mas'údí was a keen student and critic of religious beliefs, on which subject he wrote several books.[1] The *Murúju 'l-Dhahab* supplies many valuable details regarding the Muḥammadan sects, and also regarding the Zoroastrians and Ṣábians. There is a particularly interesting report of a meeting which took place between Aḥmad b. Ṭúlún, the governor of Egypt (868–877 A.D.), and an aged Copt, who, after giving his views as to the source of the Nile and the construction of the Pyramids, defended his faith (Christianity) on the ground of its manifest errors and contradictions, arguing that its acceptance, in spite of these, by so many peoples and kings was decisive evidence of its truth.[2] Mas'údí's account of the Caliphs is chiefly remarkable for the characteristic anecdotes in which it abounds. Instead of putting together a methodical narrative he has thrown off a brilliant but unequal sketch of public affairs and private manners, of social life and literary history. Only considerations of space have prevented me from enriching this volume with not a few pages which are as lively and picturesque as any in Suetonius. His last work, the *Kitábu 'l-Tanbíh wa-'l-Ishráf* ('Book of Admonition and Recension'),[3] was intended to take a general survey of the field which had been more fully traversed in his previous compositions, and also to supplement them when it seemed necessary.

We must pass over the minor historians and biographers of this period—for example, 'Utbí († 1036 A.D.), whose

[1] See *Murúj*, vol. i, p. 201, and vol. iii, p. 268.
[2] *Ibid.*, vol. ii, p. 372 sqq.
[3] De Sacy renders the title by 'Le Livre de l'Indication et de l'Admonition ou l'Indicateur et le Moniteur'; but see De Goeje's edition of the text (Leyden, 1894), p. xxvii.

Kitáb al-Yamíní celebrates the glorious reign of Sultan Mahmúd of Ghazna; Khaṭíb of Baghdád († 1071 A.D.), who composed a history of the eminent men of that city; 'Imádu 'l-Dín of Iṣfahán († 1201 A.D.), the biographer of Saladin; Ibnu 'l-Qifṭí († 1248 A.D.), born at Qifṭ (Coptos) in Upper Egypt, whose lives of the philosophers and scientists have only come down to us in a compendium entitled *Ta'ríkhu 'l-Ḥukamá*; Ibnu 'l-Jawzí († 1200 A.D.), a prolific writer in almost every branch of literature, and his grandson, Yúsuf († 1257 A.D.)—generally called Sibṭ Ibn al-Jawzí—author of the *Mir'átu 'l-Zamán*, or 'Mirror of the Time'; Ibn Abí Uṣaybi'a († 1270 A.D.), whose history of physicians, the *'Uyúnu 'l-Anbá*, has been edited by A. Müller (1884); and the Christian, Jirjis (George) al-Makín († 1273 A.D.), compiler of a universal chronicle—named the *Majmú' al-Mubárak*—of which the second part, from Muḥammad to the end of the 'Abbásid dynasty, was rendered into Latin by Erpenius in 1625.

Minor historians.

A special notice, brief though it must be, is due to 'Izzu 'l-Dín Ibnu 'l-Athír (†1234 A.D.). He was brought up at Mosul in Mesopotamia, and after finishing his studies in Baghdád, Jerusalem, and Syria, he returned home and devoted himself to reading and literary composition. Ibn Khallikán, who knew him personally, speaks of him in the highest terms both as a man and as a scholar. "His great work, the *Kámil*,[1] embracing the history of the world from the earliest period to the year 628 of the Hijra (1230–1231 A.D.), merits its reputation as one of the best productions of the kind."[2] Down to the year 302 A.H. the author has merely abridged the Annals of Ṭabarí with occasional additions from other sources. In

Ibnu 'l-Athír († 1234 A.D.).

[1] The full title is *Kitábu 'l-Kámil fi 'l-Ta'ríkh*, or 'The Perfect Book of Chronicles.' It has been edited by Tornberg in fourteen volumes (Leyden, 1851–1876).

[2] Ibn Khallikán, De Slane's translation, vol. ii, p. 289.

the first volume he gives a long account of the Pre-islamic battles (*Ayyámu 'l-'Arab*) which is not found in the present text of Ṭabarí; but De Goeje, as I learn from Professor Bevan, thinks that this section was included in Ṭabarí's original draft and was subsequently struck out. Ibnu 'l-Athír was deeply versed in the science of Tradition, and his *Usdu 'l-Ghába* ('Lions of the Jungle') contains biographies of 7,500 Companions of the Prophet.

Geographers.

An immense quantity of information concerning the various countries and peoples of the 'Abbásid Empire has been preserved for us by the Moslem geographers, who in many cases describe what they actually witnessed and experienced in the course of their travels, although they often help themselves liberally and without acknowledgment from the works of their predecessors. The following list, which does not pretend to be exhaustive, may find a place here.[1]

Ibn Khurdádbih.

1. The Persian Ibn Khurdádbih (first half of ninth century) was postmaster in the province of Jibál, the Media of the ancients. His *Kitábu 'l-Masálik wa-'l-Mamálik* ('Book of the Roads and Countries'), an official guide-book, is the oldest geographical work in Arabic that has come down to us.

Iṣṭakhri and Ibn Ḥawqal.

2. Abú Isḥáq al-Fárisí, a native of Persepolis (Iṣṭakhr)—on this account he is known as Iṣṭakhrí—wrote a book called *Masáliku 'l-Mamálik* ('Routes of the Provinces'), which was afterwards revised and enlarged by Ibn Ḥawqal. Both works belong to the second half of the tenth century and contain "a careful description

[1] An excellent account of the Arab geographers is given by Guy Le Strange in the Introduction to his *Palestine under the Moslems* (London, 1890). De Goeje has edited the works of Ibn Khurdádbih, Iṣṭakhrí, Ibn Ḥawqal, and Muqaddasí in the *Bibliotheca Geographorum Arabicorum* (Leyden, 1870, &c.)

of each province in turn of the Muslim Empire, with the chief cities and notable places."

Muqaddasí.

3. Al-Muqaddasí (or al-Maqdisí), *i.e.*, 'the native of the Holy City', was born at Jerusalem in 946 A.D. In his delightful book entitled *Aḥsanu 'l-Taqásím fí ma'rifati 'l-Aqálím* he has gathered up the fruits of twenty years' travelling through the dominions of the Caliphate.

Yáqút.

4. Omitting the Spanish Arabs, Bakrí, Idrísí, and Ibn Jubayr, all of whom flourished in the eleventh century, we come to the greatest of Moslem geographers, Yáqút b. 'Abdalláh (1179–1229 A.D.). A Greek by birth, he was enslaved in his childhood and sold to a merchant of Baghdád. His master gave him a good education and frequently sent him on trading expeditions to the Persian Gulf and elsewhere. After being enfranchised in consequence of a quarrel with his benefactor, he supported himself by copying and selling manuscripts. In 1219–1220 A.D. he encountered the Tartars, who had invaded Khwárizm, and "fled as naked as when he shall be raised from the dust of the grave on the day of the resurrection." Further details of his adventurous life are recorded in the interesting notice by Ibn Khallikán.[1] His great Geographical Dictionary (*Mu'jamu 'l-Buldán*) has been edited in six volumes by Wüstenfeld (Leipzig, 1866), and is described by Mr. Le Strange as "a storehouse of geographical information, the value of which it would be impossible to over-estimate." We possess a useful epitome of it, made about a century later, viz., the *Maráṣidu 'l-Iṭṭilá'*. Among the few other extant works of Yáqút, attention may be called to the *Mushtarik*—a lexicon of places bearing the same name—and the *Mu'jamu 'l-Udabá*, or 'Dictionary of Littérateurs,' which has been edited by Professor Margoliouth for the Trustees of the Gibb Memorial Fund.

[1] De Slane's translation, vol. iv, p. 9 sqq.

As regards the philosophical and exact sciences the Moslems naturally derived their ideas and material from Greek culture, which had established itself in Egypt, Syria, and Western Asia since the time of Alexander's conquests. When the Syrian school of Edessa was broken up by ecclesiastical dissensions towards the end of the fifth century of our era, the expelled savants took refuge in Persia at the Sásánian court, and Khusraw Anúshirwán, or Núshírwán (531–578 A.D.)—the same monarch who welcomed the Neo-platonist philosophers banished from Athens by Justinian—founded an Academy at Jundé-shápúr in Khúzistán, where Greek medicine and philosophy continued to be taught down to 'Abbásid days. Another centre of Hellenism was the city of Ḥarrán in Mesopotamia. Its inhabitants, Syrian heathens who generally appear in Muḥammadan history under the name of 'Ṣábians,' spoke Arabic with facility and contributed in no small degree to the diffusion of Greek wisdom. The work of translation was done almost entirely by Syrians. In the monasteries of Syria and Mesopotamia the writings of Aristotle, Galen, Ptolemy, and other ancient masters were rendered with slavish fidelity, and these Syriac versions were afterwards retranslated into Arabic. A beginning was made under the Umayyads, who cared little for Islam but were by no means indifferent to the claims of literature, art, and science. An Umayyad prince, Khálid b. Yazíd, procured the translation of Greek and Coptic works on alchemy, and himself wrote three treatises on that subject. The accession of the 'Abbásids gave a great impulse to such studies, which found an enlightened patron in the Caliph Manṣúr. Works on logic and medicine were translated from the Pehleví by Ibnu 'l-Muqaffa' († about 760 A.D.) and others. It is, however, the splendid reign of Ma'mún (813–833 A.D.) that marks the full vigour of this Oriental Renaissance. Ma'mún was no ordinary man. Like a true Persian, he threw himself heart and soul into

The foreign sciences.

Translations from the Greek.

theological speculations and used the authority of the Caliphate to enforce a liberal standard of orthodoxy. His interest in science was no less ardent. According to a story told in the *Fihrist*,[1] he dreamed that he saw the venerable figure of Aristotle seated on a throne, and in consequence of this vision he sent a deputation to the Roman Emperor (Leo the Armenian) to obtain scientific books for translation into Arabic. The Caliph's example was followed by private individuals. Three brothers, Muḥammad, Aḥmad, and Ḥasan, known collectively as the Banú Músá, "drew translators from distant countries by the offer of ample rewards[2] and thus made evident the marvels of science. Geometry, engineering, the movements of the heavenly bodies, music, and astronomy were the principal subjects to which they turned their attention; but these were only a small number of their acquirements."[3] Ma'mún installed them, with Yaḥyá b. Abí Manṣúr and other scientists, in the House of Wisdom (*Baytu 'l-Ḥikma*) at Baghdád, an institution which comprised a well-stocked library and an astronomical observatory. Among the celebrated translators of the ninth century, who were themselves conspicuous workers in the new field, we can only mention the Christians Qusṭá b. Lúqá and Ḥunayn b. Isḥáq, and the Ṣábian Thábit b. Qurra. It does not fall within the scope of this volume to consider in detail the achievements of the Moslems in science and philosophy. That in some departments they made valuable additions to existing knowledge must certainly be granted, but these discoveries count for little in comparison with the debt which we owe to the Arabs as pioneers of learning and bringers of light to mediæval Europe.[4] Meanwhile it is only

Ma'mún's encouragement of the New Learning.

[1] P. 243.

[2] The translators employed by the Banú Músá were paid at the rate of about 500 dínárs a month (*ibid.*, p. 43, l. 18 sqq.).

[3] *Ibid.*, p. 271; Ibn Khallikán, De Slane's translation, vol. iii, p. 315.

[4] A chapter at least would be required in order to set forth adequately the chief material and intellectual benefits which European civilisation

possible to enumerate a few of the most eminent philosophers and scientific men who lived during the 'Abbásid age. The reader will observe that with rare exceptions they were of foreign origin.

The leading spirits in philosophy were :—

Kindí.

1. Ya'qúb b. Isḥáq al-Kindí, a descendant of the princely family of Kinda (see p. 42). He was distinguished by his contemporaries with the title *Faylasúfu 'l-'Arab*, 'The Philosopher of the Arabs.' He flourished in the first half of the ninth century.

Fárábí.

2. Abú Naṣr al-Fárábí († 950 A.D.), of Turkish race, a native of Fáráb in Transoxania. The later years of his life were passed at Aleppo under the patronage of Sayfu 'l-Dawla. He devoted himself to the study of Aristotle, whom Moslems agree with Dante in regarding as "il maestro di color che sanno."

Ibn Síná.

3. Abú 'Alí Ibn Síná (Avicenna), born of Persian parents at Kharmaythan, near Bukhárá, in the year 980 A.D. As a youth he displayed extraordinary talents, so that "in the sixteenth year of his age physicians of the highest eminence came to read medicine with him and to learn those modes of treatment which he had discovered by his practice." [1] He was no quiet student, like Fárábí, but a pleasure-loving, adventurous man of the world who travelled from court to court, now in favour, now in disgrace, and always writing indefatigably. His system

has derived from the Arabs. The reader may consult Von Kremer's *Culturgeschichte des Orients*, vol. ii, chapters 7 and 9; Diercks, *Die Araber im Mittelalter* (Leipzig, 1882); Sédillot, *Histoire générale des Arabes*; Schack, *Poesie und Kunst der Araber in Spanien und Sicilien*; Munk, *Mélanges de Philosophie Juive et Arabe*; De Lacy O'Leary, *Arabic Thought and its Place in History* (1922); and Campbell, *Arabian Medicine and its Influence on the Middle Ages* (1926). A volume entitled *The Legacy of the Islamic World*, ed. by Sir T. W. Arnold and Professor A. Guillaume, is in course of publication.

[1] Ibn Khallikán, De Slane's translation, vol. i, p. 440.

of philosophy, in which Aristotelian and Neo-platonic theories are combined with Persian mysticism, was well suited to the popular taste, and in the East it still reigns supreme. His chief works are the *Shifá* (Remedy) on physics, metaphysics, &c., and a great medical encyclopædia entitled the *Qánún* (Canon). Avicenna died in 1037 A.D.

4. The Spanish philosophers, Ibn Bájja (Avempace), Ibn Ṭufayl, and Ibn Rushd (Averroes), all of whom flourished in the twelfth century after Christ.

The most illustrious name beside Avicenna in the history of Arabian medicine is Abú Bakr al-Rází (Rhazes), a native of Rayy, near Teheran († 923 or 932 A.D.). Jábir b. Ḥayyán of Tarsus († about 780 A.D.)—the Geber of European writers—won equal renown as an alchemist. Astronomy went hand in hand with astrology. The reader may recognise al-Farghání, Abú Ma'shar of Balkh († 885 A.D.) and al-Battání, a Ṣábian of Ḥarrán († 929 A.D.), under the names of Alfraganus, Albumaser, and Albategnius, by which they became known in the West. Abú 'Abdalláh al-Khwárizmí, who lived in the Caliphate of Ma'mún, was the first of a long line of mathematicians. In this science, as also in Medicine and Astronomy, we see the influence of India upon Muḥammadan civilisation—an influence, however, which, in so far as it depended on literary sources, was more restricted and infinitely less vital than that of Greece. Only a passing reference can be made to Abú Rayḥán al-Bírúní, a native of Khwárizm (Khiva), whose knowledge of the sciences, antiquities, and customs of India was such as no Moslem had ever equalled. His two principal works, the *Áthár al-Báqiya*, or 'Surviving Monuments,' and the *Ta'ríkhu 'l-Hind*, or 'History of India,' have been edited and translated into English by Dr. Sachau.[1]

Medicine, Astronomy, and Mathematics.

Bírúní 973–1048 A.D.)

Some conception of the amazing intellectual activity of the

[1] *The Chronology of Ancient Nations* (London, 1879) and *Alberuni's India* (London, 1888).

Moslems during the earlier part of the ʽAbbásid period, and also of the enormous losses which Arabic literature has suffered through the destruction of thousands of books that are known to us by nothing beyond their titles and the names of their authors, may be gained from the *Fihrist*, or 'Index' of Muḥammad b. Isḥáq b. Abí Yaʽqúb al-Nadím al-Warráq al-Baghdádí († 995 A.D.). Regarding the compiler we have no further information than is conveyed in the last two epithets attached to his name: he was a copyist of MSS., and was connected with Baghdád either by birth or residence; add that, according to his own statement (p. 349, l. 14 sqq.), he was at Constantinople (*Dáru 'l-Rúm*) in 988 A.D., the same year in which his work was composed. He may possibly have been related to the famous musician, Isḥáq b. Ibráhím al-Nadím of Mosul († 849–850 A.D.), but this has yet to be proved. At any rate we owe to his industry a unique conspectus of the literary history of the Arabs to the end of the fourth century after the Flight. The *Fihrist* (as the author explains in his brief Preface) is "an Index of the books of all nations, Arabs and foreigners alike, which are extant in the Arabic language and script, on every branch of knowledge; comprising information as to their compilers and the classes of their authors, together with the genealogies of those persons, the dates of their birth, the length of their lives, the times of their death, the places to which they belonged, their merits and their faults, since the beginning of every science that has been invented down to the present epoch: namely, the year 377 of the Hijra." As the contents of the *Fihrist* (which considerably exceed the above description) have been analysed in detail by G. Flügel (*Z.D.M.G.*, vol. 13, p. 559 sqq.) and set forth in tabular form by Professor Browne in the first volume of his *Literary History of Persia*,[1] I need only indicate the general arrangement and scope of the work. It is divided into ten

The *Fihrist*.

[1] P. 384 sqq.

discourses (*maqálát*), which are subdivided into a varying number of sections (*funún*). Ibnu 'l-Nadím discusses, in the first place, the languages, scripts, and sacred books of the Arabs and other peoples, the revelation of the Koran, the order of its chapters, its collectors, redactors, and commentators. Passing next to the sciences which, as we have seen, arose from study of the Koran and primarily served as handmaids to theology, he relates the origin of Grammar, and gives an account of the different schools of grammarians with the treatises which they wrote. The third discourse embraces History, Belles-Lettres, Biography, and Genealogy; the fourth treats of Poetry, ancient and modern. Scholasticism (*Kalám*) forms the subject of the following chapter, which contains a valuable notice of the Ismá'ílís and their founder, 'Abdulláh b. Maymún, as also of the celebrated mystic, Ḥusayn b. Manṣúr al-Ḥalláj. From these and many other names redolent of heresy the author returns to the orthodox schools of Law—the Málikites, Ḥanafites, Sháfi'ites and Ẓáhirites; then to the jurisconsults of the Shí'a, &c. The seventh discourse deals with Philosophy and 'the Ancient Sciences,' under which head we find some curious speculations concerning their origin and introduction to the lands of Islam; a list of translators and the books which they rendered into Arabic; an account of the Greek philosophers from Thales to Plutarch, with the names of their works that were known to the Moslems; and finally a literary survey of the remaining sciences, such as Mathematics, Music, Astronomy, and Medicine. Here, by an abrupt transition, we enter the enchanted domain of Oriental fable—the *Hazár Afsán*, or Thousand Tales, Kalíla and Dimna, the Book of Sindbád, and the legends of Rustam and Isfandiyár; works on sorcery, magic, conjuring, amulets, talismans, and the like. European savants have long recognised the importance of the ninth discourse,[1] which is

[1] The passages concerning the Ṣábians were edited and translated, with copious annotations, by Chwolsohn in his *Ssabier und Ssabismus* (St.

devoted to the doctrines and writings of the Ṣábians and the Dualistic sects founded by Manes, Bardesanes, Marcion, Mazdak, and other heresiarchs. The author concludes his work with a chapter on the Alchemists (*al-Kímiyá'ún*).

Petersburg, 1856), vol. ii, p. 1–365, while Flügel made similar use of the Manichæan portion in *Mani, seine Lehre und seine Schriften* (Leipzig, 1862).

CHAPTER VIII

ORTHODOXY, FREE-THOUGHT, AND MYSTICISM

The 'Abbásids and Islam.

WE have already given some account of the great political revolution which took place under the 'Abbásid dynasty, and we have now to consider the no less vital influence of the new era in the field of religion. It will be remembered that the House of 'Abbás came forward as champions of Islam and of the oppressed and persecuted Faithful. Their victory was a triumph for the Muḥammadan over the National idea. "They wished, as they said, to revive the dead Tradition of the Prophet. They brought the experts in Sacred Law from Medína, which had hitherto been their home, to Baghdád, and always invited their approbation by taking care that even political questions should be treated in legal form and decided in accordance with the Koran and the Sunna. In reality, however, they used Islam only to serve their own interest. They tamed the divines at their court and induced them to sanction the most objectionable measures. They made the pious Opposition harmless by leading it to victory. With the downfall of the Umayyads it had gained its end and could now rest in peace."[1] There is much truth in this view of the matter, but notwithstanding the easy character of their religion, the 'Abbásid Caliphs were sincerely devoted to the cause of Islam and zealous to maintain its principles in public life. They regarded themselves as the

[1] Wellhausen, *Das Arabische Reich*, p. 350 seq.

sovereign defenders of the Faith; added the Prophet's mantle (*al-burda*) to those emblems of Umayyad royalty, the sceptre and the seal; delighted in the pompous titles which their flatterers conferred on them, *e.g.*, 'Vicegerent of God,' 'Sultan of God upon the Earth,' 'Shadow of God,' &c.; and left no stone unturned to invest themselves with the attributes of theocracy, and to inspire their subjects with veneration.[1] Whereas the Umayyad monarchs ignored or crushed Muḥammadan sentiment, and seldom made any attempt to conciliate the leading representatives of Islam, the 'Abbásids, on the other hand, not only gathered round their throne all the most celebrated theologians of the day, but also showed them every possible honour, listened respectfully to their counsel, and allowed them to exert a commanding influence on the administration of the State.[2] When Málik b. Anas was summoned by the Caliph Hárún al-Rashíd, who wished to hear him recite traditions, Málik replied, "People come to seek knowledge." So Hárún went to Málik's house, and leaned against the wall beside him. Málik said, "O Prince of the Faithful, whoever honours God, honours knowledge." Al-Rashíd arose and seated himself at Málik's feet and spoke to him and heard him relate a number of traditions handed down from the Apostle of God. Then he sent for Sufyán b. 'Uyayna, and Sufyán came to him and sat in his presence and recited traditions to him. Afterwards al-Rashíd said, "O Málik, we humbled ourselves before thy knowledge, and profited thereby, but Sufyán's knowledge humbled itself to us, and we got no good from it."[3] Many instances might be given of the high favour which theologians enjoyed at this time, and of the lively interest with which religious topics were debated by the

Influence of theologians.

[1] See Goldziher, *Muhamm. Studien*, Part II, p. 53 sqq.

[2] *Ibid.*, p. 70 seq.

[3] *Fragmenta Historicorum Arabicorum*, ed. by De Goeje and De Jong, p. 298.

Caliph and his courtiers. As the Caliphs gradually lost their temporal sovereignty, the influence of the *'Ulamá*—the doctors of Divinity and Law—continued to increase, so that ere long they formed a privileged class, occupying in Islam a position not unlike that of the priesthood in mediæval Christendom.

It will be convenient to discuss the religious phenomena of the 'Abbásid period under the following heads:—

I. Rationalism and Free-thought.

II. The Orthodox Reaction and the rise of Scholastic Theology.

III. The Ṣúfí Mysticism.

Rationalism and Free-thought.

I. The first century of 'Abbásid rule was marked, as we have seen, by a great intellectual agitation. All sorts of new ideas were in the air. It was an age of discovery and awakening. In a marvellously brief space the diverse studies of Theology, Law, Medicine, Philosophy, Mathematics, Astronomy, and Natural Science attained their maturity, if not their highest development. Even if some pious Moslems looked askance at the foreign learning and its professors, an enlightened spirit generally prevailed. People took their cue from the court, which patronised, or at least tolerated,[1] scientific research as well as theological speculation.

The Mu'tazilites and their opponents.

These circumstances enabled the Mu'tazilites (see p. 222 sqq.) to propagate their liberal views without hindrance, and finally to carry their struggle against the orthodox party to a successful issue. It was the same conflict that divided Nominalists and Realists in the days of Thomas Aquinas, Duns Scotus, and Occam. As often happens when momentous principles are at stake, the whole

[1] There are, of course, some partial exceptions to this rule, *e.g.*, Mahdí and Hárún al-Rashíd.

controversy between Reason and Revelation turned on a single question—"Is the Koran created or uncreated?" In other terms, is it the work of God or the Word of God? According to orthodox belief, it is uncreated and has existed with God from all eternity, being in its present form merely a transcript of the heavenly archetype.[1] Obviously this conception of the Koran as the direct and literal Word of God left no room for exercise of the understanding, but required of those who adopted it a dumb faith and a blind fatalism. There were many to whom the sacrifice did not seem too great. The Mu'tazilites, on the contrary, asserted their intellectual freedom. It was possible, they said, to know God and distinguish good from evil without any Revelation at all. They admitted that the Koran was God's work, in the sense that it was produced by a divinely inspired Prophet, but they flatly rejected its deification. Some went so far as to criticise the 'inimitable' style, declaring that it could be surpassed in beauty and eloquence by the art of man.[2]

The Mu'tazilite controversy became a burning question in the reign of Ma'mún (813–833 A.D.), a Caliph whose scientific enthusiasm and keen interest in religious matters we have already mentioned. He did not inherit the orthodoxy of his father, Hárún al-Rashíd; and it was believed that he was at heart a *zindíq*. His liberal tendencies would have been wholly admirable if they had not been marred by excessive intolerance towards those who held opposite views to his own. In 833 A.D., the year of his death, he promulgated a decree which bound all Moslems to accept the Mu'tazilite doctrine as to the creation of the Koran on pain of losing their civil rights, and at the same time he established an inquisition (*miḥna*) in order to obtain the assent of

[1] See p. 163, note.

[2] Several freethinkers of this period attempted to rival the Koran with their own compositions. See Goldziher, *Muhamm. Studien*, Part II, p. 401 seq.

the divines, judges, and doctors of law. Those who would not take the test were flogged and threatened with the sword.

Rationalism adopted and put in force by the Caliph Ma'mún.

After Ma'mún's death the persecution still went on, although it was conducted in a more moderate fashion. Popular feeling ran strongly against the Mu'tazilites. The most prominent figure in the orthodox camp was the Imám Aḥmad b. Ḥanbal, who firmly resisted the new dogma from the first. "But for him," says the Sunnite historian, Abu 'l-Maḥásin, "the beliefs of a great number would have been corrupted."[1] Neither threats nor entreaties could shake his resolution, and when he was scourged by command of the Caliph Mu'taṣim, the palace was in danger of being wrecked by an angry mob which had assembled outside to hear the result of the trial. The Mu'tazilite dogma remained officially in force until it was abandoned by the Caliph Wáthiq and once more declared heretical by the cruel and bigoted Mutawakkil (847 A.D.). From that time to this the victorious party have sternly suppressed every rationalistic movement in Islam.

Mutawakkil returns to orthodoxy.

According to Steiner, the original Mu'tazilite heresy arose in the bosom of Islam, independently of any foreign influence, but, however that may be, its later development was largely affected by Greek philosophy. We need not attempt to follow the recondite speculations of Abú Hudhayl al-'Alláf († about 840 A.D.) of his contemporaries, al-Naẓẓám, Bishr b. al-Mu'tamir, and others, and of the philosophical schools of Baṣra and Baghdád in which the movement died away. Vainly they sought to replace the Muḥammadan idea of God as will by the Aristotelian conception of God as law. Their efforts to purge the Koran of anthropomorphism made no impression on the faithful, who ardently hoped to see God in Paradise face to face. What they actually achieved was little enough. Their weapons of

The end of the Mu'tazilites.

[1] *Al-Nujúm al-Záhira*, ed. by Juynboll, vol. i, p. 639.

logic and dialectic were turned against them with triumphant success, and scholastic theology was founded on the ruins of Rationalism. Indirectly, however, the Mu'tazilite principles leavened Muḥammadan thought to a considerable extent and cleared the way for other liberal movements, like the Fraternity of the *Ikhwánu 'l-Ṣafá*, which endeavoured to harmonise authority with reason, and to construct a universal system of religious philosophy.

These 'Brethren of Purity,'[1] as they called themselves, compiled a great encyclopædic work in fifty tractates (*Rasá'il*). Of the authors, who flourished at Baṣra towards the end of the tenth century, five are known to us by name: viz., Abú Sulaymán Muḥammad b. Ma'shar al-Bayusti or al-Muqaddasí (Maqdisí), Abu 'l-Ḥasan 'Alí b. Hárún al-Zanjání, Abú Aḥmad al-Mihrajání, al-'Awfí, and Zayd b. Rifá'a. "They formed a society for the pursuit of holiness, purity, and truth, and established amongst themselves a doctrine whereby they hoped to win the approval of God, maintaining that the Religious Law was defiled by ignorance and adulterated by errors, and that there was no means of cleansing and purifying it except philosophy, which united the wisdom of faith and the profit of research. They held that a perfect result would be reached if Greek philosophy were combined with Arabian religion. Accordingly they composed fifty tracts on every branch of philosophy, theoretical as well as practical, added a separate index, and entitled them the 'Tracts of the Brethren of Purity' (*Rasá'ilu Ikhwán al-Ṣafá*). The authors of this work concealed their names, but circulated it among the booksellers and gave it to the public. They filled their pages with devout phraseology, religious parables, metaphorical expressions, and figurative turns of style."[2]

The Ikhwánu 'l-Ṣafá.

[1] This is the literal translation of *Ikhwánu 'l-Ṣafá*, but according to Arabic idiom 'brother of purity' (*akhu 'l-ṣafá*) simply means 'one who is pure or sincere,' as has been shown by Goldziher, *Muhamm. Studien*, Part I, p. 9, note. The term does not imply any sort of brotherhood.

[2] Ibnu 'l-Qifṭí, *Ta'ríkhu 'l-Ḥukamá* (ed. by Lippert), p. 83, l. 17 sqq.

Nearly all the tracts have been translated into German by Dieterici, who has also drawn up an epitome of the whole encyclopædia in his *Philosophie der Araber im X Jahrhundert.* It would take us too long to describe the system of the *Ikhwán*, but the reader will find an excellent account of it in Stanley Lane-Poole's *Studies in a Mosque*, 2nd ed., p. 176 sqq. The view has recently been put forward that the Brethren of Purity were in some way connected with the Ismá'ílí propaganda, and that their eclectic idealism represents the highest teaching of the Fáṭimids, Carmathians, and Assassins. Strong evidence in support of this theory is supplied by a MS. of the Bibliothèque Nationale (No. 2309 in De Slane's Catalogue), which contains, together with fragments of the *Rasá'il*, a hitherto unknown tract entitled the *Jámi'a* or 'Summary.'[1] The latter purports to be the essence and crown of the fifty *Rasá'il*, it is manifestly Ismá'ílite in character, and, assuming that it is genuine, we may, I think, agree with the conclusions which its discoverer, M. P. Casanova, has stated in the following passage :—

The doctrines of the Brethren of Purity identical with the esoteric philosophy of the Ismá'ílís.

"Surtout je crois être dans le vrai en affirmant que les doctrines philosophiques des Ismaïliens sont contenues tout entières dans les Epîtres des Frères de la Pureté. Et c'est ce qui explique 'la séduction extraordinaire que la doctrine exerçait sur des hommes sérieux.'[2] En y ajoutant la croyance en l' *imám caché* (*al-imám al-mastúr*) qui doit apparaître un jour pour établir le bonheur universel, elle réalisait la fusion de toutes les doctrines idéalistes, du messianisme et du platonisme. Tant que l' imám restait caché, il s'y mêlait encore une saveur de mystère qui attachait les esprits les plus élevés. . . . En tous cas, on peut affirmer que les Carmathes et les Assassins ont été profondément calomniés quand ils ont été accusés par leurs adversaires d'athéisme et de débauche. Le fetwa d' Ibn Taimiyyah, que j'ai cité plus haut, prétend que leur dernier degré dans l' initiation (*al-balágh al-akbar*) est la négation même du Créateur. Mais la *djâmi'at* que nous avons découverte est, comme

---

[1] *Notice sur un manuscrit de la secte des Assassins*, by P. Casanova in the *Journal Asiatique* for 1898, p. 151 sqq.

[2] De Goeje, *Mémoire sur les Carmathes*, p. 172.

tout l'indique, le dernier degré de la science des Frères de la Pureté et des Ismaïliens ; il n'y a rien de fondé dans une telle accusation. La doctrine apparait très pure, très élevée, très simple même : je repète que c'est une sorte de panthéisme mécaniste et esthétique qui est absolument opposé au scepticisme et au matérialisme, car il repose sur l' harmonie générale de toutes les parties du monde, harmonie voulue par le Créateur parce qu'elle est la beauté même.

"Ma conclusion sera que nous avons là un exemple de plus dans l'histoire d' une doctrine très pure et très élevée en théorie, devenue, entre les mains des fanatiques et des ambitieux, une source d'actes monstrueux et méritant l'infamie qui est attachée a ce nom historique d'Assassins."

Besides the Mu'tazilites, we hear much of another class of heretics who are commonly grouped together under the name of *Zindiqs*.

The *Zindiqs*.

"It is well known," says Goldziher,[1] "that the earliest persecution was directed against those individuals who managed more or less adroitly to conceal under the veil of Islam old Persian religious ideas. Sometimes indeed they did not consider any disguise to be necessary, but openly set up dualism and other Persian or Manichæan doctrines, and the practices associated therewith, against the dogma and usage of Islam. Such persons were called *Zindiqs*, a term which comprises different shades of heresy and hardly admits of simple definition. Firstly, there are the old Persian families incorporated in Islam who, following the same path as the Shu'úbites, have a *national interest* in the revival of Persian religious ideas and traditions, and from this point of view react against the *Arabian* character of the Muḥammadan system. Then, on the other hand, there are freethinkers, who oppose in particular the stubborn dogma of Islam, reject *positive religion*, and acknowledge only the moral law. Amongst the latter there is developed a monkish

[1] *Ṣâliḥ b. 'Abd al-Quddûs und das Zindîḳthum während der Regierung des Chalifen al-Mahdí* in *Transactions of the Ninth Congress of Orientalists*, vol. ii, p. 105 seq.

asceticism extraneous to Islam and ultimately traceable to Buddhistic influences."

The 'Abbásid Government, which sought to enforce an official standard of belief, was far less favourable to religious liberty than the Umayyads had been. Orthodox and heretic alike fell under its ban. While Ma'mún harried pious Sunnites, his immediate predecessors raised a hue and cry against *Zindíqs*. The Caliph Mahdí distinguished himself by an organised persecution of these enemies of the faith. He appointed a Grand Inquisitor (*Ṣáḥibu 'l-Zanádiqa* [1] or *'Aríf u 'l-Zanádiqa*) to discover and hunt them down. If they would not recant when called upon, they were put to death and crucified, and their books [2] were cut to pieces with knives.[3] Mahdí's example was followed by Hádí and Hárún al-Rashíd. Some of the 'Abbásids, however, were less severe. Thus Khaṣíb, Manṣúr's physician, was a *Zindíq* who professed Christianity,[4] and in the reign of Ma'mún it became the mode to affect Manichæan opinions as a mark of elegance and refinement.[5]

Persecution of *Zindíqs*.

The two main types of *zandaqa* which have been described above are illustrated in the contemporary poets, Bashshár b. Burd and Ṣáliḥ b. 'Abd al-Quddús. Bashshár was born stone-blind. The descendant of a noble Persian family—though his father, Burd, was a slave—he cherished strong national sentiments and did not attempt to conceal his sympathy with the Persian clients (*Mawálí*), whom he was accused of stirring up against their Arab lords. He may also have had leanings towards Zoroastrianism, but Professor Bevan has observed that there is no real

Bashshár b. Burd.

[1] Ṭabarí, iii, 522, 1.

[2] *I.e.* the sacred books of the Manichæans, which were often splendidly illuminated. See Von Kremer, *Culturgesch. Streifzüge*, p. 39.

[3] *Cf.* Ṭabarí, iii, 499, 8 sqq.

[4] *Ibid.*, iii, 422, 19 sqq.

[5] *Cf.* the saying "*Aẓrafu mina 'l-Zindíq*" (Freytag, *Arabum Proverbia*, vol. i, p. 214).

evidence for this statement,[1] though Zoroastrian or Manichæan views are probably indicated by the fact that he used to dispute with a number of noted Moslem theologians in Baṣra, *e.g.*, with Wáṣil b. 'Aṭá, who started the Mu'tazilite heresy, and 'Amr b. 'Ubayd. He and Ṣáliḥ b. 'Abd al-Quddús were put to death by the Caliph Mahdí in the same year (783 A.D.).

This Ṣáliḥ belonged by birth or affiliation to the Arab tribe of Azd. Of his life we know little beyond the circumstance that he was for some time a street-preacher at Baṣra, and afterwards at Damascus. It is possible that his public doctrine was thought dangerous, although the preachers as a class were hand in glove with the Church and did not, like the Lollards, denounce religious abuses.[2] His extant poetry contains nothing heretical, but is wholly moral and didactic in character. We have seen, however, in the case of Abu 'l-'Atáhiya, that Muḥammadan orthodoxy was apt to connect 'the philosophic mind' with positive unbelief; and Ṣáliḥ appears to have fallen a victim to this prejudice. He was accused of being a dualist (*thanawí*), *i.e.*, a Manichæan. Mahdí, it is said, conducted his examination in person, and at first let him go free, but the poet's fate was sealed by his confession that he was the author of the following verses :—

Ṣáliḥ b. 'Abd al-Quddús.

"The greybeard will not leave what in the bone is bred
Until the dark tomb covers him with earth o'erspread;
For, tho' deterred awhile, he soon returns again
To his old folly, as the sick man to his pain."[3]

---

[1] As Professor Bevan points out, it is based solely on the well-known verse (*Aghání*, iii, 24, l. 11), which has come down to us without the context :—

"*Earth is dark and Fire is bright,*
And Fire has been worshipped ever since Fire existed."

[2] These popular preachers (*quṣṣáṣ*) are admirably described by Goldziher, *Muhamm. Studien*, Part II, p. 161 sqq.

[3] The Arabic text of these verses will be found in Goldziher's monograph, p. 122, ll. 6–7.

Abu 'l-'Alá al-Ma'arrí, himself a bold and derisive critic of Muḥammadan dogmas, devotes an interesting section of his *Risálatu 'l-Ghufrán* to the *Zindíqs*, and says many hard things about them, which were no doubt intended to throw dust in the eyes of a suspicious audience. The wide scope of the term is shown by the fact that he includes under it the pagan chiefs of Quraysh; the Umayyad Caliph Walíd b. Yazíd; the poets Di'bil, Abú Nuwás, Bashshár, and Ṣáliḥ b. 'Abd al-Quddús; Abú Muslim, who set up the 'Abbásid dynasty; the Persian rebels, Bábak and Mázyár; Afshín, who after conquering Bábak was starved to death by the Caliph Mu'taṣim; the Carmathian leader al-Jannábí; Ibnu 'l-Ráwandí, whose work entitled the *Dámigh* was designed to discredit the 'miraculous' style of the Koran; and Ḥusayn b. Manṣúr al-Ḥalláj, the Ṣúfí martyr. Most of these, one may admit, fall within Abu 'l-'Alá's definition of the *Zindíqs*: "they acknowledge neither prophet nor sacred book." The name *Zindíq*, which is applied by Jáḥiẓ († 868 A.D.) to certain wandering monks,[1] seems in the first instance to have been used of Manes (*Mání*) and his followers, and is no doubt derived, as Professor Bevan has suggested, from the *zaddíqs*, who formed an elect class in the Manichæan hierarchy.[2]

Abu 'l-'Alá al-Ma'arrí on the *Zindíqs*.

II. The official recognition of Rationalism as the State religion came to an end on the accession of Mutawakkil in 847 A.D. The new Caliph, who owed his throne to the

[1] See a passage from the *Kitábu 'l-Ḥayawán*, cited by Baron V. Rosen in *Zapiski*, vol. vi, p. 337, and rendered into English in my *Translations from Eastern Poetry and Prose*, p. 53. Probably these monks were Manichæans, not Buddhists.

[2] *Zaddíq* is an Aramaic word meaning 'righteous.' Its etymological equivalent in Arabic is *ṣiddíq*, which has a different meaning, namely, 'veracious.' *Zaddíq* passed into Persian in the form *Zandík*, which was used by the Persians before Islam, and *Zindíq* is the Arabicised form of the latter word. For some of these observations I am indebted to Professor Bevan. Further details concerning the derivation and meaning of *Zindíq* are given in Professor Browne's *Literary Hist. of Persia* (vol. i, p. 159 sqq.), where the reader will also find a lucid account of the Manichæan doctrines.

Turkish Prætorians, could not have devised a surer means of making himself popular than by standing forward as the avowed champion of the faith of the masses. He persecuted impartially Jews, Christians, Mu'tazilites, Shí'ites, and Ṣúfís—every one, in short, who diverged from the narrowest Sunnite orthodoxy. The Vizier Ibn Abí Du'ád, who had shown especial zeal in his conduct of the Mu'tazilite Inquisition, was disgraced, and the bulk of his wealth was confiscated. In Baghdád the followers of Aḥmad b. Ḥanbal went from house to house terrorising the citizens,[1] and such was their fanatical temper that when Ṭabarí, the famous divine and historian, died in 923 A.D., they would not allow his body to receive the ordinary rites of burial.[2] Finally, in the year 935 A.D., the Caliph Ráḍí issued an edict denouncing them in these terms: "Ye assert that your ugly, ill-favoured faces are in the likeness of the Lord of Creation, and that your vile exterior resembles His, and ye speak of the hand, the fingers, the feet, the golden shoes, and the curly hair (of God), and of His going up to Heaven and of His coming down to Earth. . . . The Commander of the Faithful swears a binding oath that unless ye refrain from your detestable practices and perverse tenets he will lay the sword to your necks and the fire to your dwellings."[3] Evidently the time was ripe for a system which should reconcile the claims of tradition and reason, avoiding the gross anthropomorphism of the extreme Ḥanbalites on the one side and the pure rationalism of the advanced Mu'tazilites (who were still a power to be reckoned with) on the other. It is a frequent experience that great intellectual or religious movements rising slowly and invisibly, in response, as it were, to some incommunicable want, suddenly find a distinct interpreter with whose name they are henceforth associated for ever. The man, in this case, was Abu 'l-Ḥasan al-Ash'arí. He belonged to a noble and traditionally orthodox family of

The Orthodox Reaction.

[1] Ibnu 'l-Athír, vol. viii, p. 229 seq. (anno 323 A.H.=934–935 A.D.).

[2] *Ibid.*, p. 98.

[3] *Ibid.*, p. 230 seq.

Yemenite origin. One of his ancestors was Abú Músá al-Ash'arí, who, as the reader will recollect, played a somewhat inglorious part in the arbitration between 'Alí and Mu'áwiya after the battle of Ṣiffín.[1] Born in 873–874 A.D. at Baṣra, a city renowned for its scientific and intellectual fertility, the young Abu 'l-Ḥasan deserted the faith of his fathers, attached himself to the freethinking school, and until his fortieth year was the favourite pupil and intimate friend of al-Jubbá'í († 915 A.D.), the head of the Mu'tazilite party at that time. He is said to have broken with his teacher in consequence of a dispute as to whether God always does what is best (*aṣlaḥ*) for His creatures. The story is related as follows by Ibn Khallikán (De Slane's translation, vol. ii, p. 669 seq.) :—

Abu 'l-Ḥasan al-Ash'arí.

Ash'arí proposed to Jubbá'í the case of three brothers, one of whom was a true believer, virtuous and pious ; the second an infidel, a debauchee and a reprobate ; and the third an infant : they all died, and Ash'arí wished to know what had become of them. To this Jubbá'í answered: "The virtuous brother holds a high station in Paradise; the infidel is in the depths of Hell, and the child is among those who have obtained salvation."[2] "Suppose now," said Ash'arí, "that the child should wish to ascend to the place occupied by his virtuous brother, would he be allowed to do so?" "No," replied Jubbá'í, "it would be said to him : 'Thy brother arrived at this place through his numerous works of obedience towards God, and thou hast no such works to set forward.'" "Suppose then," said Ash'arí, "that the child say: 'That is not my fault; you did not let me live long enough, neither did you give me the means of proving my obedience.'" "In that case," answered Jubbá'í, "the Almighty would say: 'I knew that if I had allowed thee to live, thou wouldst have been disobedient and incurred the severe punishment (of Hell); I therefore acted for thy advantage.'" "Well," said Ash'arí, "and suppose the infidel brother were to say: 'O God of the universe! since you knew what awaited him, you must have known what

Story of the three brothers.

[1] See p. 192.

[2] *I.e.*, he is saved from Hell but excluded from Paradise.

awaited me; why then did you act for his advantage and not for mine?" Jubbá'í had not a word to offer in reply.

Soon afterwards Ash'arí made a public recantation. One Friday, while sitting (as his biographer relates) in the chair from which he taught in the great mosque of Baṣra, he cried out at the top of his voice: "They who know me know who I am: as for those who do not know me I will tell them. I am 'Alí b. Ismá'íl al-Ash'arí, and I used to hold that the Koran was created, that the eyes of men shall not see God, and that we ourselves are the authors of our evil deeds. Now I have returned to the truth; I renounce these opinions, and I undertake to refute the Mu'tazilites and expose their infamy and turpitude."[1]

Ash'arí's conversion to orthodoxy.

These anecdotes possess little or no historical value, but illustrate the fact that Ash'arí, having learned all that the Mu'tazilites could teach him and having thoroughly mastered their dialectic, turned against them with deadly force the weapons which they had put in his hands. His doctrine on the subject of free-will may serve to exemplify the method of *Kalám* (Disputation) by which he propped up the orthodox creed.[2] Here, as in other instances, Ash'arí took the central path—*medio tutissimus*—between two extremes. It was the view of the early Moslem Church—a view justified by the Koran and the Apostolic Traditions—that everything was determined in advance and inscribed, from all eternity, on the Guarded Tablet (*al-Lawḥ al-Maḥfúẓ*), so that men had no choice but to commit the actions decreed by destiny. The Mu'tazilites, on the

Ash'arí as the founder of Scholastic Theology.

[1] Ibn Khallikán, ed. by Wüstenfeld, No. 440; De Slane's translation, vol. ii, p. 228.

[2] The clearest statement of Ash'arí's doctrine with which I am acquainted is contained in the Creed published by Spitta, *Zur Geschichte Abu 'l-Ḥasan al-Ash'arí's* (Leipzig, 1876), p. 133, l. 9 sqq.; German translation, p. 95 sqq. It has been translated into English by D. B. Macdonald in his *Muslim Theology*, p. 293 and foll.

contrary, denied that God could be the author of evil and insisted that men's actions were free. Ash'arí, on his part, declared that all actions are created and predestined by God, but that men have a certain subordinate power which enables them to acquire the actions previously created, although it produces no effect on the actions themselves. Human agency, therefore, was confined to this process of acquisition (*kasb*). With regard to the anthropomorphic passages in the Koran, Ash'arí laid down the rule that such expressions as "*The Merciful has settled himself upon His throne*," "*Both His hands are spread out*," &c., must be taken in their obvious sense without asking 'How?' (*bilá kayfa*). Spitta saw in the system of Ash'arí a successful revolt of the Arabian national spirit against the foreign ideas which were threatening to overwhelm Islam,[1] a theory which does not agree with the fact that most of the leading Ash'arites were Persians.[2] Von Kremer came nearer the mark when he said "Ash'arí's victory was simply a clerical triumph,"[3] but it was also, as Schreiner has observed, "a victory of reflection over unthinking faith."

The victory, however, was not soon or easily won.[4] Many of the orthodox disliked the new Scholasticism hardly less than the old Rationalism. Thus it is not surprising to read in the *Kámil* of Ibnu 'l-Athír under the year 456 A.H. = 1063–4 A.D., that Alp Arslán's Vizier, 'Amídu 'l-Mulk al-Kundurí, having obtained his master's permission to have curses pronounced against the Ráfiḍites (Shí'ites) from the pulpits of Khurásán, included the Ash'arites in the same malediction, and that the famous Ash'arite doctors, Abu 'l-Qásim al-Qushayrí and the Imámu 'l-Ḥaramayn Abu 'l-Ma'álí al-Juwayní, left the country in consequence. The great Niẓámu 'l-Mulk

[1] *Op. cit.*, p. 7 seq.

[2] Schreiner, *Zur Geschichte des Ash'aritenthums* in the *Proceedings of the Eighth International Congress of Orientalists* (1889), p. 5 of the *tirage à part.*

[3] *Z.D.M.G.*, vol. 31, p. 167.

[4] See Goldziher in *Z.D.M.G.*, vol. 41, p. 63 seq., whence the following details are derived.

exerted himself on behalf of the Ash'arites, and the Niẓámiyya College, which he founded in Baghdád in the year 1067 A.D., was designed to propagate their system of theology. But the man who stamped it with the impression of his own powerful genius, fixed its ultimate form, and established it as the universal creed of orthodox Islam, was Abú Ḥámid al-Ghazálí (1058–1111 A.D.). We have already sketched the outward course of his life, and need only recall that he lectured at Baghdád in the Niẓámiyya College for four years (1091–1095 A.D.).[1] At the end of that time he retired from the world as a Ṣúfí, and so brought to a calm and fortunate close the long spiritual travail which he has himself described in the *Munqidh mina 'l-Ḍalál*, or 'Deliverer from Error.'[2] We must now attempt to give the reader some notion of this work, both on account of its singular psychological interest and because Ghazálí's search for religious truth exercised, as will shortly appear, a profound and momentous influence upon the future history of Muḥammadan thought. It begins with these words:—

Ghazálí's autobiography.

"In the name of God, the Merciful, the Compassionate. Praise be to God by the praise of whom every written or spoken discourse is opened! And blessings on Muḥammad, the Elect, the Prophet and Apostle, as well as on his family and his companions who lead us forth from error! To proceed: You have asked me, O my brother in religion, to explain to you the hidden meanings and the ultimate goal of the sciences, and the secret bane of the different doctrines, and their inmost depths. You wish me to relate all that I have endured in seeking to recover the truth from amidst the confusion of sects with diverse ways and paths, and how I have dared to raise myself from the abyss of blind belief in authority to the height of discernment. You desire to know what benefits I have derived in the first place from Scholastic Theology, and what I have appropriated, in the second

---

[1] See p. 339 seq.

[2] I have used the Cairo edition of 1309 A.H. A French translation by Barbier de Meynard was published in the *Journal Asiatique* (January, 1877), pp. 9–93.

place, from the methods of the Ta'límites[1] who think that truth can be attained only by submission to the authority of an Imám; and thirdly, my reasons for spurning the systems of philosophy; and, lastly, why I have accepted the tenets of Ṣúfiism: you are anxious, in short, that I should impart to you the essential truths which I have learned in my repeated examination of the (religious) opinions of mankind."

In a very interesting passage, which has been translated by Professor Browne, Ghazálí tells how from his youth upward he was possessed with an intense thirst for knowledge, which impelled him to study every form of religion and philosophy, and to question all whom he met concerning the nature and meaning of their belief.[2] But when he tried to distinguish the true from the false, he found no sure test. He could not trust the evidence of his senses. The eye sees a shadow and declares it to be without movement; or a star, and deems it no larger than a piece of gold. If the senses thus deceive, may not the mind do likewise? Perhaps our life is a dream full of phantom thoughts which we mistake for realities—until the awakening comes, either in moments of ecstasy or at death. "For two months," says Ghazálí, "I was actually, though not avowedly, a sceptic." Then God gave him light, so that he regained his mental balance and was able to think soundly. He resolved that this faculty must guide him to the truth, since blind faith once lost never returns. Accordingly, he set himself to examine the foundations of belief in four classes of men who were devoted to the search for truth, namely, Scholastic Theologians, Ismá'ílís (*Báṭiniyya*), Philosophers, and Ṣúfís. For a long while he had to be content with wholly negative results. Scholasticism was, he admitted, an excellent purge against heresy, but it could not cure the disease from which he was suffering. As for the philosophers, all of them—Materialists (*Dahriyyún*), Naturalists (*Ṭabí'iyyún*),

[1] These are the Ismá'ílís or Báṭinís (including the Carmathians and Assassins). See p. 271 sqq.

[2] *A Literary History of Persia*, vol. ii, p. 295 seq.

and Theists (*Iláhiyyún*)—"are branded with infidelity and impiety." Here, as often in his discussion of the philosophical schools, Ghazálí's religious instinct breaks out. We cannot imagine him worshipping at the shrine of pure reason any more than we can imagine Herbert Spencer at Lourdes. He next turned to the Ta'límites (Doctrinists) or Báṭinites (Esoterics), who claimed that they knew the truth, and that its unique source was the infallible Imám. But when he came to close quarters with these sectaries, he discovered that they could teach him nothing, and their mysterious Imám vanished into space. Ṣúfiism, therefore, was his last hope. He carefully studied the writings of the mystics, and as he read it became clear to him that now he was on the right path. He saw that the higher stages of Ṣúfiism could not be learned by study, but must be realised by actual experience, that is, by rapture, ecstasy, and moral transformation. After a painful struggle with himself he resolved to cast aside all his worldly ambition and to live for God alone. In the month of Dhu 'l-Qa'da, 488 A.H. (November, 1095 A.D.), he left Baghdád and wandered forth to Syria, where he found in the Ṣúfí discipline of prayer, praise, and meditation the peace which his soul desired.

Mr. Duncan B. Macdonald, to whom we owe the best and fullest life of Ghazálí that has yet been written, sums up his work and influence in Islam under four heads [1] :—

First, he led men back from scholastic labours upon theological dogmas to living contact with, study and exegesis of, the Word and the Traditions.

Second, in his preaching and moral exhortations be re-introduced the element of fear.

Third, it was by his influence that Ṣúfiism attained a firm and assured position within the Church of Islam.

[1] *The Life of al-Ghazzālī* in the *Journal of the American Oriental Society*, vol. xx (1899), p. 122 sqq.

Fourth, he brought philosophy and philosophical theology within the range of the ordinary mind.

"Of these four phases of al-Ghazzālī's work," says Macdonald, "the first and third are undoubtedly the most important. He made his mark by leading Islam back to its fundamental and historical facts, and by giving a place in its system to the emotional religious life. But it will have been noticed that in none of the four phases was he a pioneer. He was not a scholar who struck out a new path, but a man of intense personality who entered on a path already trodden and made it the common highway. We have here his character. Other men may have been keener logicians, more learned theologians, more gifted saints; but he, through his personal experiences, had attained so overpowering a sense of the divine realities that the force of his character—once combative and restless, now narrowed and intense—swept all before it, and the Church of Islam entered on a new era of its existence."

Ghazálí's work and influence.

III. We have traced the history of Mysticism in Islam from the ascetic movement of the first century, in which it originated, to a point where it begins to pass beyond the sphere of Muḥammadan influence and to enter on a strange track, of which the Prophet assuredly never dreamed, although the Ṣúfís constantly pretend that they alone are his true followers. I do not think it can be maintained that Ṣúfiism of the theosophical and speculative type, which we have now to consider, is merely a development of the older asceticism and quietism which have been described in a former chapter. The difference between them is essential and must be attributed in part, as Von Kremer saw,[1] to the intrusion of some extraneous, non-Islamic, element. As to the nature of this new element there are several conflicting theories, which have been so clearly and fully stated by Professor Browne in his *Literary History of Persia* (vol. i, p. 418 sqq.) that I need not dwell upon them here. Briefly it is claimed—

Ṣúfiism in the 'Abbásid period.

[1] *Herrschende Ideen*, p. 67.

(*a*) That Ṣúfiism owes its inspiration to Indian philosophy, and especially to the Vedanta.

(*b*) That the most characteristic ideas in Ṣúfiism are of Persian origin.

(*c*) That these ideas are derived from Neo-platonism.

Instead of arguing for or against any of the above theories, all of which, in my opinion, contain a measure of truth, I propose in the following pages to sketch the historical evolution of the Súfí doctrine as far as the materials at my disposal will permit. This, it seems to me, is the only possible method by which we may hope to arrive at a definite conclusion as to its origin. Since mysticism in all ages and countries is fundamentally the same, however it may be modified by its peculiar environment, and by the positive religion to which it clings for support, we find remote and unrelated systems showing an extraordinarily close likeness and even coinciding in many features of verbal expression. Such resemblances can prove little or nothing unless they are corroborated by evidence based on historical grounds. Many writers on Ṣúfiism have disregarded this principle; hence the confusion which long prevailed. The first step in the right direction was made by Adalbert Merx,[1] who derived valuable results from a chronological examination of the sayings of the early Ṣúfís. He did not, however, carry his researches beyond Abú Sulaymán al-Dárání († 830 A.D.), and confined his attention almost entirely to the doctrine, which, according to my view, should be studied in connection with the lives, character, and nationality of the men who taught it.[2] No doubt the origin and growth of mysticism in Islam, as in all other religions, *ultimately* depended on general causes and conditions, not on external

[1] *Idee und Grundlinien einer allgemeiner Geschichte der Mystik*, an academic oration delivered on November 22, 1892, and published at Heidelberg in 1893.

[2] The following sketch is founded on my paper, *An Historical Enquiry concerning the Origin and Development of Ṣúfiism* (*J.R.A.S.*, April, 1906, p. 303 sqq.).

circumstances. For example, the political anarchy of the Umayyad period, the sceptical tendencies of the early 'Abbásid age, and particularly the dry formalism of Moslem theology could not fail to provoke counter-movements towards quietism, spiritual authority, and emotional faith. But although Ṣúfiism was not called into being by any impulse from without (this is too obvious to require argument), the influences of which I am about to speak have largely contributed to make it what it is, and have coloured it so deeply that no student of the history of Ṣúfiism can afford to neglect them.

Ma'rúf al-Karkhí († 815 A.D.).

Towards the end of the eighth century of our era the influence of new ideas is discernible in the sayings of Ma'rúf al-Karkhí († 815 A.D.), a contemporary of Fuḍayl b. 'Iyáḍ and Shaqíq of Balkh. He was born in the neighbourhood of Wásiṭ, one of the great cities of Mesopotamia, and the name of his father, Fírúz, or Fírúzán, shows that he had Persian blood in his veins. Ma'rúf was a client (*mawlá*) of the Shí'ite Imám, 'Alí b. Músá al-Riḍá, in whose presence he made profession of Islam; for he had been brought up as a Christian (such is the usual account), or, possibly, as a Ṣábian. He lived during the reign of Hárún al-Rashíd in the Karkh quarter of Baghdád, where he gained a high reputation for saintliness, so that his tomb in that city is still an object of veneration. He is described as a God-intoxicated man, but in this respect he is not to be compared with many who came after him. Nevertheless, he deserves to stand at the head of the mystical as opposed to the ascetic school of Ṣúfís. He defined Ṣúfiism as "the apprehension of Divine realities and renunciation of human possessions."[1] Here are a few of his sayings:—

"Love is not to be learned from men; it is one of God's gifts and comes of His grace.

[1] This, so far as I know, is the oldest extant definition of Ṣúfiism.

"The Saints of God are known by three signs: their thought is of God, their dwelling is with God, and their business is in God.

"If the gnostic (*'árif*) has no bliss, yet he himself is in every bliss.

"When you desire anything of God, swear to Him by me."

From these last words, which Ma'rúf addressed to his pupil Sarí al-Saqaṭí, it is manifest that he regarded himself as being in the most intimate communion with God.

Abú Sulaymán al-Dáraní († 830 A.D.).

Abú Sulaymán († 830 A.D.), the next great name in the Ṣúfí biographies, was also a native of Wásiṭ, but afterwards emigrated to Syria and settled at Dárayá (near Damascus), whence he is called 'al-Dárání.' He developed the doctrine of gnosis (*ma'rifat*). Those who are familiar with the language of European mystics—*illuminatio*, *oculus cordis*, &c.—will easily interpret such sayings as these:—

"None refrains from the lusts of this world save him in whose heart there is a light that keeps him always busied with the next world.

"When the gnostic's spiritual eye is opened, his bodily eye is shut: they see nothing but Him.

"If Gnosis were to take visible form, all that looked thereon would die at the sight of its beauty and loveliness and goodness and grace, and every brightness would become dark beside the splendour thereof.[1]

"Gnosis is nearer to silence than to speech."

Dhu 'l-Nún al-Miṣrí († 860 A.D.).

We now come to Dhu 'l-Nún al-Miṣrí († 860 A.D.), whom the Ṣúfís themselves consider to be the primary author of their doctrine.[2] That he at all events was among the first of those who helped to give it permanent shape is a fact which is amply attested by the collection of his sayings preserved in 'Aṭṭár's *Memoirs of the*

[1] It is impossible not to recognise the influence of Greek philosophy in this conception of Truth as Beauty.

[2] Jámí says (*Nafaḥátu 'l-Uns*, ed. by Nassau Lees, p. 36): "He is the head of this sect: they all descend from, and are related to, him."

Saints and in other works of the same kind.[1] It is clear that the theory of gnosis, with which he deals at great length, was the central point in his system ; and he seems to have introduced the doctrine that true knowledge of God is attained only by means of ecstasy (*wajd*). "The man that knows God best," he said, "is the one most lost in Him." Like Dionysius, he refused to make any positive statements about the Deity. "Whatever you imagine, God is the contrary of that." Divine love he regarded as an ineffable mystery which must not be revealed to the profane. All this is the very essence of the later Ṣúfiism. It is therefore desirable to ascertain the real character of Dhu 'l-Nún and the influences to which he was subjected. The following account gives a brief summary of what I have been able to discover; fuller details will be found in the article mentioned above.

His name was Abu 'l-Fayḍ Thawbán b. Ibráhím, Dhu 'l-Nún (He of the Fish) being a sobriquet referring to one of his miracles, and his father was a native of Nubia, or of Ikhmím in Upper Egypt. Ibn Khallikán describes Dhu 'l-Nún as 'the nonpareil or his age' for learning, devotion, communion with the Divinity (*ḥál*), and acquaintance with literature (*adab*) ; adding that he was a philosopher (*ḥakím*) and spoke Arabic with elegance. The people of Egypt, among whom he lived, looked upon him as a *zindíq* (freethinker), and he was brought to Baghdád to answer this charge, but after his death he was canonised. In the *Fihrist* he appears among "the philosophers who discoursed on alchemy," and Ibnu 'l-Qifṭí brackets him with the famous occultist Jábir b. Ḥayyán. He used to wander (as we learn from Mas'údí)[2] amidst the ruined Egyptian monuments, studying the inscriptions and endeavouring to decipher the mysterious figures which were thought to hold the key to the

[1] See 'Aṭṭár's *Tadhkiratu 'l-Awliyá*, ed. by Nicholson, Part I, p. 114 ; Jámí's *Nafaḥát*, p. 35 ; Ibn Khallikán, De Slane's translation, vol. i, p. 291.

[2] *Murúju 'l-Dhahab*, vol. ii, p. 401 seq.

lost sciences of antiquity. He also dabbled in medicine, which, like Paracelsus, he combined with alchemy and magic.

Let us see what light these facts throw upon the origin or the Şúfí theosophy. Did it come to Egypt from India, Persia, or Greece?

The origin of theosophical Şúfiism.

Considering the time, place, and circumstances in which it arose, and having regard to the character of the man who bore a chief part in its development, we cannot hesitate, I think, to assert that it is largely a product of Greek speculation. Ma'rúf al-Karkhí, Abú Sulaymán al-Dárání, and Dhu 'l-Nún al-Mişrí all three lived and died in the period (786–861 A.D.) which begins with the accession of Hárún al-Rashíd and is terminated by the death of Mutawakkil. During these seventy-five years the stream of Hellenic culture flowed unceasingly into the Moslem world. Innumerable works of Greek philosophers, physicians, and scientists were translated and eagerly studied. Thus the Greeks became the teachers of the Arabs, and the wisdom of ancient Greece formed, as has been shown in a preceding chapter, the basis of Muḥammadan science and philosophy. The results are visible in the Mu'tazilite rationalism as well as in the system of the *Ikhwánu 'l-Şafá*. But it was not through literature alone that the Moslems were imbued with Hellenism. In 'Iráq, Syria, and Egypt they found themselves on its native soil, which yielded, we may be sure, a plentiful harvest of ideas—Neo-platonic, Gnostical, Christian, mystical, pantheistic, and what not? In Mesopotamia, the heart of the 'Abbásid Empire, dwelt a strange people, who were really Syrian heathens, but who towards the beginning of the ninth century assumed the name of Şábians in order to protect themselves from the persecution with which they were threatened by the Caliph Ma'mún. At this time, indeed, many of them accepted Islam or Christianity, but the majority clung to their old pagan beliefs, while the educated class continued to profess a religious philosophy which, as it is described by Shahrastání and other Muḥammadan writers, is simply the Neo-platonism of Proclus and Iamblichus. To return to Dhu 'l-Nún, it is incredible that a mystic and natural philosopher living in the first half of the ninth century in Egypt should have derived his doctrine directly from India. There may be Indian elements in Neo-platonism and Gnosticism, but this possibility does not affect my contention that the immediate source of the Ṣúfí theosophy is to be sought in Greek and Syrian speculation. To define its origin more narrowly is not, I think, practicable in the present state of our knowledge. Merx, however, would trace it to Dionysius, the Pseudo-Areopagite, or rather to his master, a certain "Hierotheus," whom Frothingham has identified with the Syrian mystic, Stephen bar Sudaili (*circa* 500 A.D.). Dionysius was of course a Christian Neo-platonist. His works certainly laid the foundations of mediæval mysticism in Europe, and they were also popular in the East at the time when Ṣúfiism arose.

Ṣúfiism composed of many different elements.

When speaking of the various current theories as to the origin of Ṣúfiism, I said that in my opinion they all contained a measure of truth. No single cause will account for a phenomenon so widely spread and so diverse in its manifestations. Ṣúfiism has always been thoroughly eclectic, absorbing and transmuting whatever 'broken lights' fell across its path, and consequently it gained adherents amongst men of the most opposite views—theists and pantheists, Mu'tazilites and Scholastics, philosophers and divines. We have seen what it owed to Greece, but the Perso-Indian elements are not to be ignored. Although the theory "that it must be regarded as the reaction of the Aryan mind against a Semitic religion imposed on it by force" is inadmissible—Dhu 'l-Nún, for example, was a Copt or Nubian—the fact remains that there was at the time a powerful anti-Semitic reaction, which expressed itself, more or less consciously, in Ṣúfís of Persian race. Again, the literary influence of India upon Muḥammadan thought before 1000 A.D.

was greatly inferior to that of Greece, as any one can see by turning over the pages of the *Fihrist*; but Indian religious ideas must have penetrated into Khurásán and Eastern Persia at a much earlier period.

These considerations show that the question as to the origin of Ṣúfiism cannot be answered in a definite and exclusive way. None of the rival theories is completely true, nor is any of them without a partial justification. The following words of Dr. Goldziher should be borne in mind by all who are interested in this subject:—

Goldziher on the character of Ṣúfiism.

"Ṣúfiism cannot be looked upon as a regularly organised sect within Islam. Its dogmas cannot be compiled into a regular system. It manifests itself in different shapes in different countries. We find divergent tendencies, according to the spirit of the teaching of distinguished theosophists who were founders of different schools, the followers of which may be compared to Christian monastic orders. The influence of different environments naturally affected the development of Ṣúfiism. Here we find mysticism, there asceticism the prevailing thought."[1]

The four principal foreign sources of Ṣúfiism are undoubtedly Christianity, Neo-platonism, Gnosticism, and Indian asceticism and religious philosophy. I shall not attempt in this place to estimate their comparative importance, but it should be clearly understood that the speculative and theosophical side of Ṣúfiism, which, as we have seen, was first elaborated in 'Iráq, Syria, and Egypt, bears unmistakable signs of Hellenistic influence.

The early Ṣúfís are particularly interested in the theory of mystical union (*faná wa-baqá*) and often use expressions which it is easy to associate with pantheism, yet none of them can fairly be called a pantheist in the true sense. The step from theosophy

[1] *The Influence of Buddhism upon Islam*, by I. Goldziher (Budapest, 1903). As this essay is written in Hungarian, I have not been able to consult it at first hand, but have used the excellent translation by Mr. T. Duka, which appeared in the *J.R.A.S.* for January, 1904, pp. 125–141.

to pantheism was not, I think, made either by Ḥalláj († 922 A.D.) or by the celebrated Abú Yazíd, in Persian Báyazíd († 874–75 A.D.), of Bisṭám, a town in the province of Qúmis situated near the south-eastern corner of the Caspian Sea. While his father, Surúshán, was a Zoroastrian, his master in Ṣúfiism seems to have been connected with Sind (Scinde), where Moslem governors had been installed since 715 A.D. Báyazíd carried the experimental doctrine of *faná* (dying to self) to its utmost limit, and his language is tinged with the peculiar poetic imagery which was afterwards developed by the great Ṣúfí of Khurásán, Abú Sa'íd b. Abi 'l-Khayr († 1049 A.D.). I can give only a few specimens of his sayings. Their genuineness is not above suspicion, but they serve to show that if the theosophical basis of Ṣúfiism is distinctively Greek, its mystical extravagances are no less distinctively Oriental.

Báyazíd of Bisṭám.

"Creatures are subject to 'states' (*aḥwál*), but the gnostic has no 'state,' because his vestiges are effaced and his essence is annihilated by the essence of another, and his traces are lost in another's traces.

"I went from God to God until they cried from me in me, 'O Thou I!'

"Nothing is better for Man than to be without aught, having no asceticism, no theory, no practice. When he is without all, he is with all.

"Verily I am God, there is no God except me, so worship me!

"Glory to me! how great is my majesty!

"I came forth from Báyazíd-ness as a snake from its skin. Then I looked. I saw that lover, beloved, and love are one, for in the world of unification all can be one.

"I am the wine-drinker and the wine and the cup-bearer."

Thus, in the course of a century, Ṣúfiism, which at first was little more than asceticism, became in succession mystical and theosophical, and even ran the risk of being confused with pantheism. Henceforward the term *Taṣawwuf* unites all these varying shades. As a rule, however, the great Ṣúfís of the third century A.H. (815–912 A.D.) keep their antinomian enthusiasm under control. Most of them agreed with Junayd of Baghdád († 909 A.D.), the leading theosophist of his time, in preferring "the path of sobriety," and in seeking to reconcile the Law (*sharí'at*) with the Truth (*ḥaqíqat*). "Our principles," said Sahl b. 'Abdulláh al-Tustarí († 896 A.D.), "are six: to hold fast by the Book of God, to model ourselves upon the Apostle (Muḥammad), to eat only what is lawful, to refrain from hurting people even though they hurt us, to avoid forbidden things, and to fulfil obligations without delay." To these articles the strictest Moslem might cheerfully subscribe. Ṣúfiism in its ascetic, moral, and devotional aspects was a spiritualised Islam, though it was a very different thing essentially. While doing lip-service to the established religion, it modified the dogmas of Islam in such a way as to deprive them of their original significance. Thus Allah, the God of mercy and wrath, was in a certain sense depersonalised and worshipped as the One absolutely Real (*al-Ḥaqq*). Here the Ṣúfís betray their kinship with the Mu'tazilites, but the two sects have little in common except the Greek philosophy.[1] It must never be forgotten that Ṣúfiism was the expression of a profound religious feeling—"hatred of the world and love of the Lord."[2] "*Taṣawwuf*," said Junayd, "is this: that God should make thee die to thyself and should make thee live in Him."

The further development of Ṣúfiism may be indicated in a few words.

What was at first a form of religion adopted by individuals and communicated to a small circle of companions gradually became a monastic system, a school for saints, with rules of discipline and devotion which the novice (*muríd*) learned from his spiritual director (*pír* or *ustádh*), to whose guidance he

[1] It was recognised by the Ṣúfís themselves that in some points their doctrine was apparently based on Mu'tazilite principles. See Sha'rání, *Lawáqiḥu 'l-Anwár* (Cairo, 1299 A.H.), p. 14, l. 21 sqq.

[2] This definition is by Abu 'l-Ḥusayn al-Núrí († 907–908 A.D.).

submitted himself absolutely. Already in the third century after Muḥammad it is increasingly evident that the typical Ṣúfí adept of the future will no longer be a solitary ascetic shunning the sight of men, but a great Shaykh and hierophant, who appears on ceremonial occasions attended by a numerous train of admiring disciples. Soon the doctrine began to be collected and embodied in books. Some of the most notable Arabic works of reference on Ṣúfiism have been mentioned already. Among the oldest are the *Kitábu 'l-Luma'* by Abú Naṣr al-Sarráj († 988 A.D.) and the *Qútu 'l-Qulúb* by Abú Ṭálib al-Makkí († 996 A.D.). The twelfth century saw the rise of the Dervish Orders. 'Adí al-Hakkárí († 1163 A.D.) and 'Abdu 'l-Qádir al-Jílí († 1166 A.D.) founded the fraternities which are called 'Adawís and Qádirís, after their respective heads. These were followed in rapid succession by the Rifá'ís, the Shádhilís, and the Mevlevís, of whom the last named owe their origin to the Persian poet and mystic, Jalálu 'l-Dín Rúmí († 1273 A.D.). By this time, mainly through the influence of Ghazálí, Ṣúfiism had won for itself a secure and recognised position in the Muḥammadan Church. Orthodoxy was forced to accept the popular Saint-worship and to admit the miracles of the *Awliyá*, although many Moslem puritans raised their voices against the superstitious veneration which was paid to the tombs of holy men, and against the prayers, sacrifices, and oblations offered by the pilgrims who assembled. Ghazálí also gave the Ṣúfí doctrine a metaphysical basis. For this purpose he availed himself of the terminology, which Fárábí (also a Ṣúfí) and Avicenna had already borrowed from the Neo-platonists. From his time forward we find in Ṣúfí writings constant allusions to the Plotinian theories of emanation and ecstasy.

The development of Ṣúfiism.

Mysticism was more congenial to the Persians than to the Arabs, and its influence on Arabic literature is not to be compared with the extraordinary spell which it has cast over the Persian mind since the eleventh century of the

Christian era to the present day. With few exceptions, the great poets of Persia (and, we may add, of Turkey) speak the allegorical language and use the fantastic imagery of which the quatrains of the Persian Ṣúfí, Abú Sa'íd b. Abi 'l-Khayr,[1] afford almost the first literary example. The Arabs have only one mystical poet worthy to stand beside the Persian masters.

'Umar Ibnu 'l-Fáriḍ.

This is Sharafu 'l-Dín 'Umar Ibnu 'l-Fáriḍ, who was born in Cairo (1181 A.D.) and died there in 1235. His *Díwán* was edited by his grandson 'Alí, and the following particulars regarding the poet's life are extracted from the biographical notice prefixed to this edition[2]:—

"The Shaykh 'Umar Ibnu 'l-Fáriḍ was of middle stature; his face was fair and comely, with a mingling of visible redness; and when he was under the influence of music (*samá'*) and rapture (*wajd*), and overcome by ecstasy, it grew in beauty and brilliancy, and sweat dropped from his body until it ran on the ground under his feet. I never saw (so his son relates) among Arabs or foreigners a figure equal in beauty to his, and I am the likest of all men to him in form. . . . And when he walked in the city, the people used to press round him asking his blessing and trying to kiss his hand, but he would not allow any one to do so, but put his hand in theirs. . . . 'Umar Ibnu 'l-Fáriḍ said: 'In the beginning of my detachment (*tajríd*) from the world I used to beg permission of my father and go up to the Wádi 'l-Mustaḍ'afín on the second mountain of al-Muqaṭṭam. Thither I would resort and continue in this hermit life (*siyáḥa*) night and day; then I would return to my father, as bound in duty to cherish his affection. My father was at that time Lieutenant of the High Court (*khalífatu 'l-ḥukmi 'l-'azíz*) in Qáhira and Miṣr,[3] the two guarded cities, and was one of the men most eminent for learning and affairs. He was wont to be glad when I returned, and he frequently let me sit with him in the chambers of the court and in the colleges of law. Then I would long for "detachment," and beg leave to return to the life of

[1] See Professor Browne's *Lit. Hist. of Persia*, vol. ii, p. 261 sqq.

[2] The *Díwán of 'Umar Ibnu 'l-Fáriḍ*, ed. by Rushayyid al-Daḥdáḥ (Marseilles, 1853).

[3] *I.e.*, New and Old Cairo.

a wandering devotee, and thus I was doing repeatedly, until my father was asked to fill the office of Chief Justice (*Qáḍi 'l-Quḍát*), but refused, and laid down the post which he held, and retired from society, and gave himself entirely to God in the preaching-hall (*qá'atu 'l-khiṭába*) of the Mosque al-Azhar. After his death I resumed my former detachment, and solitary devotion, and travel in the way of Truth, but no revelation was vouchsafed to me. One day I came to Cairo and entered the Sayfiyya College. At the gate I found an old grocer performing an ablution which was not prescribed. First he washed his hands, then his feet; then he wiped his head and washed his face. "O Shaykh," I said to him, "do you, after all these years, stand beside the gate of the college among the Moslem divines and perform an irregular ablution?" He looked at me and said, "O 'Umar, nothing will be vouchsafed to thee in Egypt, but only in the Ḥijáz, at Mecca (may God exalt it!); set out thither, for the time of thy illumination hath come." Then I knew that the man was one of God's saints and that he was disguising himself by his manner of livelihood and by pretending to be ignorant of the irregularity of the ablution. I seated myself before him and said to him, "O my master, how far am I from Mecca! and I cannot find convoy or companions save in the months of Pilgrimage." He looked at me and pointed with his hand and said, "Here is Mecca in front of thee"; and as I looked with him, I saw Mecca (may God exalt it!); and bidding him farewell, I set off to seek it, and it was always in front of me until I entered it. At that moment illumination came to me and continued without any interruption. . . . I abode in a valley which was distant from Mecca ten days' journey for a hard rider, and every day and night I would come forth to pray the five prayers in the exalted Sanctuary, and with me was a wild beast of huge size which accompanied me in my going and returning, and knelt to me as a camel kneels, and said, "Mount, O my master," but I never did so.'"

When fifteen years had elapsed, 'Umar Ibnu 'l-Fáriḍ returned to Cairo. The people venerated him as a saint, and the reigning monarch, Malik al-Kámil, wished to visit him in person, but 'Umar declined to see him, and rejected his bounty. "At most times," says the poet's son, "the Shaykh was in a state of bewilderment, and his eyes stared fixedly. He neither heard nor saw any one speaking to him. Now he would stand, now sit, now repose on his side, now lie on his back wrapped up like a dead man ; and thus would he pass ten consecutive days, more or less, neither eating nor drinking nor speaking nor stirring." In 1231 A.D. he made the pilgrimage to Mecca, on which occasion he met his famous contemporary, Shihábu' l-Dín Abú Ḥafṣ 'Umar al-Suhrawardí. He died four years later, and was buried in the Qaráfa cemetery at the foot of Mount Muqaṭṭam.

The poetry of Ibnu 'l-Fáriḍ.

His *Díwán* of mystical odes, which were first collected and published by his grandson, is small in extent compared with similar works in the Persian language, but of no unusual brevity when regarded as the production of an Arabian poet.[1] Concerning its general character something has been said above (p. 325). The commentator, Ḥasan al-Búríní († 1615 A.D.), praises the easy flow (*insijám*) of the versification, and declares that Ibnu 'l-Fáriḍ "is accustomed to play with ideas in ever-changing forms, and to clothe them with splendid garments."[2] His style, full of verbal subtleties, betrays the influence of Mutanabbí.[3] The longest piece in the *Díwán* is a Hymn of Divine Love, entitled *Naẓmu 'l-Sulúk* ('Poem on the Mystic's Progress'), and often called *al-Tá'iyyatu 'l-Kubrá* ('The Greater Ode rhyming in *t*'), which has been edited with a German verse-translation by Hammer-Purgstall (Vienna, 1854). On account of this poem the author was accused of favouring the doctrine of *ḥulúl*, *i.e.*, the incarnation of God in human beings. Another celebrated ode is the *Khamriyya*, or Hymn of Wine.[4]

[1] The *Díwán*, excluding the *Tá'iyyatu 'l-Kubrá*, has been edited by Rushayyid al-Daḥdáḥ (Marseilles, 1853).

[2] *Díwán*, p. 219, l. 14 and p. 213, l. 18.

[3] Ibnu 'l-Fáriḍ, like Mutanabbí, shows a marked fondness for diminutives. As he observes (*Díwán*, p. 552) :—

má qultu ḥubayyibí mina 'l-taḥqíri
bal ya'dhubu 'smu 'l-shakhṣi bi-'l-taṣghíri.

"*Not in contempt I say 'my darling.' No !*
By 'diminution' names do sweeter grow."

[4] *Díwán*, p. 472 sqq. A French rendering will be found at p. 41 of Grangeret de Lagrange's *Anthologie Arabe* (Paris, 1828).

The following versions will perhaps convey to English readers some faint impression of the fervid rapture and almost ethereal exaltation which give the poetry of Ibnu 'l-Fáriḍ a unique place in Arabic literature :—

" Let passion's swelling tide my senses drown !
Pity love's fuel, this long-smouldering heart,
Nor answer with a frown,
When I would fain behold Thee as Thou art,
'*Thou shalt not see Me.*'[1] O my soul, keep fast
The pledge thou gav'st : endure unfaltering to the last !
For Love is life, and death in love the Heaven
Where all sins are forgiven.
To those before and after and of this day,
That witnesseth my tribulation, say,
'By me be taught, me follow, me obey,
And tell my passion's story thro' wide East and West.'
With my Beloved I alone have been
When secrets tenderer than evening airs
Passed, and the Vision blest
Was granted to my prayers,
That crowned me, else obscure, with endless fame,
The while amazed between
His beauty and His majesty
I stood in silent ecstasy,
Revealing that which o'er my spirit went and came.
Lo ! in His face commingled
Is every charm and grace ;
The whole of Beauty singled
Into a perfect face
Beholding Him would cry,
'There is no God but He, and He is the most High !'"[2]

Here are the opening verses of the *Tá'iyyatu 'l-Ṣughrá*, or 'The Lesser Ode rhyming in *t*,' which is so called in order to distinguish it from the *Tá'iyyatu 'l-Kubrá* :—

" Yea, in me the Zephyr kindled longing, O my loves, for you ;
Sweetly breathed the balmy Zephyr, scattering odours when it blew ;

[1] The words of God to Moses (Kor. vii, 139). [2] *Díwán*, p. 257 sqq.

Whispering to my heart at morning secret tales of those who dwell
(How my fainting heart it gladdened!) nigh the water and the well;
Murmuring in the grassy meadows, garmented with gentleness,
Languid love-sick airs diffusing, healing me of my distress.
When the green slopes wave before thee, Zephyr, in my loved Ḥijáz,
Thou, not wine that mads the others, art my rapture's only cause.
Thou the covenant eternal[1] callest back into my mind,
For but newly thou hast parted from my dear ones, happy Wind!
Driver of the dun-red camels that amidst acacias bide,
Soft and sofa-like thy saddle from the long and weary ride!
Blessings on thee, if descrying far-off Túḍiḥ at noon-day,
Thou wilt cross the desert hollows where the fawns of Wajra play,
And if from 'Urayḍ's sand-hillocks bordering on stony ground
Thou wilt turn aside to Ḥuzwá, driver for Suwayqa bound,
And Ṭuwayli''s willows leaving, if to Sal' thou thence wilt ride—
Ask, I pray thee, of a people dwelling on the mountain-side!
Halt among the clan I cherish (so may health attend thee still!)
And deliver there my greeting to the Arabs of the hill.
For the tents are basking yonder, and in one of them is She
That bestows the meeting sparely, but the parting lavishly.
All around her as a rampart edge of sword and point of lance,
Yet my glances stray towards her when on me she deigns to glance.
Girt about with double raiment—soul and heart of mine, no less—
She is guarded from beholders, veiled by her unveiledness.
Death to me, in giving loose to my desire, she destineth;
Ah, how goodly seems the bargain, and how cheap is Love for Death![2]

Ibnu 'l-Fáriḍ came of pure Arab stock, and his poetry is thoroughly Arabian both in form and spirit. This is not

[1] This refers to Kor. vii, 171. God drew forth from the loins of Adam all future generations of men and addressed them, saying, "*Am not I your Lord?*" They answered, "*Yes,*" and thus, according to the Ṣúfí interpretation, pledged themselves to love God for evermore.

[2] *Díwán*, p. 142 sqq.

the place to speak of the great Persian Ṣúfís, but Ḥusayn b. Manṣúr al-Ḥalláj, who was executed in the Caliphate of Muqtadir (922 A.D.), could not have been omitted here but for the fact that Professor Browne has already given an admirable account of him, to which I am unable to add anything of importance.[1] The Arabs, however, have contributed to the history of Ṣúfiism another memorable name—Muḥyi 'l-Dín Ibnu 'l-'Arabí, whose life falls within the final century of the 'Abbásid period, and will therefore fitly conclude the present chapter.[2]

Ibnu 'l-'Arabí.

Muḥyi 'l-Dín Muḥammad b. 'Alí Ibnu 'l-'Arabí (or Ibn 'Arabí)[3] was born at Mursiya (Murcia) in Spain on the 17th of Ramaḍán, 560 A.H. = July 29, 1165 A.D. From 1173 to 1202 he resided in Seville. He then set out for the East, travelling by way of Egypt to the Ḥijáz, where he stayed a long time, and after visiting Baghdád, Mosul, and Asia Minor, finally settled at Damascus, in which city he died (638 A.H. = 1240 A.D.). His tomb below Mount Qásiyún was thought to be "a piece of the gardens of Paradise," and was called the Philosophers' Stone.[4] It is now enclosed in a mosque which bears the name of Muḥyi 'l-Dín, and a cupola rises over it.[5] We know little concerning the events of his life, which seems to have been passed chiefly in travel and conversation with Ṣúfís and in the composition of his

[1] See *A Literary History of Persia*, vol. i, p. 428 sqq. But during the last twenty years a great deal of new light has been thrown upon the character and doctrines of Ḥalláj. See Appendix.

[2] The best-known biography of Ibnu 'l-'Arabí occurs in Maqqarí's *Nafḥu 'l-Ṭíb*, ed. by Dozy and others, vol. i, pp. 567–583. Much additional information is contained in a lengthy article, which I have extracted from a valuable MS. in my collection, the *Shadharátu 'l-Dhahab*, and published in the *J.R.A.S.* for 1906, pp. 806–824. *Cf.* also Von Kremer's *Herrschende Ideen*, pp. 102–109.

[3] Muḥyi 'l-Dín means 'Reviver of Religion.' In the West he was called Ibnu 'l-'Arabí, but the Moslems of the East left out the definite article (*al*) in order to distinguish him from the Cadi Abú Bakr Ibnu 'l-'Arabí of Seville (†1151 A.D.).

[4] *Al-Kibrít al-aḥmar* (literally, 'the red sulphur').

[5] See Von Kremer, *op. cit.*, p. 108 seq.

voluminous writings, about three hundred in number according to his own computation. Two of these works are especially celebrated, and have caused Ibnu 'l-'Arabí to be regarded as the greatest of all Muḥammadan mystics—the *Futúḥát al-Makkiyya*, or 'Meccan Revelations,' and the *Fuṣúṣu 'l-Ḥikam*, or 'Bezels of Philosophy.' The *Futúḥát* is a huge treatise in five hundred and sixty chapters, containing a complete system of mystical science. The author relates that he saw Muḥammad in the World of Real Ideas, seated on a throne amidst angels, prophets, and saints, and received his command to discourse on the Divine mysteries. At another time, while circumambulating the Ka'ba, he met a celestial spirit wearing the form of a youth engaged in the same holy rite, who showed him the living esoteric Temple which is concealed under the lifeless exterior, even as the eternal substance of the Divine Ideas is hidden by the veils of popular religion—veils through which the lofty mind must penetrate, until, having reached the splendour within, it partakes of the Divine nature and beholds what no mortal eye can endure to look upon. Ibnu 'l-'Arabí immediately fell into a swoon. When he came to himself he was instructed to contemplate the visionary form and to write down the mysteries which it would reveal to his gaze. Then the youth entered the Ka'ba with Ibnu 'l-'Arabí, and resuming his spiritual aspect, appeared to him on a three-legged steed, breathed into his breast the knowledge of all things, and once more bade him describe the heavenly form in which all mysteries are enshrined.[1] Such is the reputed origin of the 'Meccan Revelations,' of which the greater portion was written in the town where inspiration descended on Muḥammad six hundred years before. The author believed, or pretended to believe, that every word of them was dictated to him by supernatural means. The

[1] The above particulars are derived from an abstract of the *Futúḥát* made by 'Abdu 'l-Wahháb al-Sha'rání († 1565 A.D.), of which Fleischer has given a full description in the *Catalogue of Manuscripts in the Leipzig Univ. Library* (1838), pp. 490–495.

Fúṣúṣ, a short work in twenty-seven chapters, each of which is named after one of the prophets, is no less highly esteemed, and has been the subject of numerous commentaries in Arabic, Persian, and Turkish.

Curiously enough, Ibnu 'l-'Arabí combined the most extravagant mysticism with the straitest orthodoxy "He was a Ẓáhirite (literalist) in religion and a Báṭinite (spiritualist) in his speculative beliefs."[1] He rejected all authority (*taqlíd*). "I am not one of those who say, 'Ibn Ḥazm said so-and-so, Aḥmad[2] said so-and-so, al-Nu'mán[3] said so-and-so,'" he declares in one of his poems. But although he insisted on punctilious adherence to the letter of the sacred law, we may suspect that his refusal to follow any human authority, analogy, or opinion was simply the overweening presumption of the seer who regards himself as divinely illuminated and infallible. Many theologians were scandalised by the apparently blasphemous expressions which occur in his writings, and taxed him with holding heretical doctrines, *e.g.*, the incarnation of God in man (*ḥulúl*) and the identification of man with God (*ittiḥád*). Centuries passed, but controversy continued to rage over him. He found numerous and enthusiastic partisans, who urged that the utterances of the saints must not be interpreted literally nor criticised at all. It was recognised, however, that such high mysteries were unsuitable for the weaker brethren, so that many even of those who firmly believed in his sanctity discouraged the reading of his books. They were read nevertheless, publicly and privately, from one end of the Muḥammadan world to the other; people copied them for the sake of obtaining the author's blessing, and the manuscripts were eagerly bought. Among the distinguished men who wrote in his defence we can mention here only Majdu 'l-Dín al-Fírúzábádí († 1414 A.D.), the author of the great Arabic lexicon entitled *al-Qámús*; Jalálu 'l-Dín al-Suyúṭí († 1445 A.D.); and 'Abdu 'l-Wahháb al-Sha'rání († 1565 A.D.). The funda-

[1] Maqqarí, i, 569, 11. [2] Aḥmad b. Ḥanbal. [3] Abú Ḥanífa.

mental principle of his system is the Unity of Being (*waḥdatu 'l-wujúd*). There is no real difference between the Essence and its attributes or, in other words, between God and the universe. All created things subsist eternally as ideas (*a'yán thábita*) in the knowledge of God, and since being is identical with knowledge, their "creation" only means His knowing them, or Himself, under the aspect of actuality; the universe, in fact, is the concrete sum of the relations of the Essence as subject to itself as object. This pantheistic monism puts on an Islamic mask in the doctrine of "the Perfect Man" (*al-Insán al-Kámil*), a phrase which Ibnu 'l-'Arabí was the first to associate with it. The Divine consciousness, evolving through a series of five planes (*ḥaḍarát*), attains to complete expression in Man, the microcosmic being who unites the creative and creaturely attributes of the Essence and is at once the image of God and the archetype of the universe. Only through him does God know Himself and make Himself known; he is the eye of the world whereby God sees His own works. The daring paradoxes of Ibnu 'l-'Arabí's dialectic are illustrated by such verses as these:—

The doctrine of the Perfect Man.

He praises me (by manifesting my perfections and creating me in His form),
And I praise Him (by manifesting His perfections and obeying Him).
How can He be independent when I help and aid Him?
(because the Divine attributes derive the possibility of manifestation from their human correlates).
For that cause God brought me into existence,
And I know Him and bring Him into existence (in my knowledge and contemplation of Him).[1]

Thus it is the primary function of Man to reveal and realise his Divine nature; and the Perfect Men, regarded individually,

[1] *Fuṣúṣu 'l-Ḥikam* (Cairo, A.H. 1321), p. 78. The words within brackets belong to the commentary of 'Abdu 'l-Razzáq al-Káshání which accompanies the text.

are the prophets and saints. Here the doctrine—an amalgam of Manichæan, Gnostic, Neo-platonic and Christian speculations—attaches itself to Muḥammad, "the Seal of the prophets." According to Moslem belief, the pre-existent Spirit or Light of Muḥammad (*Núr Muḥammadí*) became incarnate in Adam and in the whole series of prophets, of whom Muḥammad is the last. Muḥammad, then, is the Logos,[1] the Mediator, the Vicegerent of God (*Khalífat Allah*), the God-Man who has descended to this earthly sphere to make manifest the glory of Him who brought the universe into existence.

But, of course, Ibnu 'l-'Arabí's philosophy carries him far beyond the realm of positive religion. If God is the "self" of all things sensible and intelligible, it follows that He reveals Himself in every form of belief in a degree proportionate to the pre-determined capacity of the believer; the mystic alone sees that He is One in all forms, for the mystic's heart is all-receptive: it assumes whatever form God reveals Himself in, as wax takes the impression of the seal.

"My heart is capable of every form,
A cloister for the monk, a fane for idols,
A pasture for gazelles, the pilgrim's Ka'ba,
The Tables of the Torah, the Koran.
Love is the faith I hold: wherever turn
His camels, still the one true faith is mine."[2]

The vast bulk of Ibnu 'l-'Arabí's writings, his technical and scholastic terminology, his recondite modes of thought, and the lack of method in his exposition have, until recently, deterred European Orientalists from bestowing on him the attention

[1] Ibnu 'l-'Arabí uses the term "Idea of ideas" (*Ḥaqíqatu 'l-ḥaqá'iq*) as equivalent to λόγος ἐνδιάθετος, while "the Idea of Muḥammad" (*al-Ḥaqíqatu 'l-Muḥammadiyya*) corresponds to λόγος προφορικός.

[2] The Arabic text of these verses will be found in the collection of Ibnu 'l-'Arabí's mystical odes, entitled *Tarjumánu 'l-Ashwáq*, which I have edited (Oriental Translation Fund, New Series, vol. xx, p. 19, vv. 13–15).

which he deserves.[1] In the history of Ṣúfiism his name marks an epoch: it is owing to him that what began as a profoundly religious personal movement in Islam ends as an eclectic and definitely pantheistic system of philosophy. The title of "The Grand Master" (*al-Shaykh al-Akbar*), by which he is commonly designated, bears witness to his supremacy in the world of Moslem mysticism from the Mongol Invasion to the present day. In Persia and Turkey his influence has been enormous, and through his pupil, Ṣadru 'l-Dín of Qóniya, he is linked with the greatest of all Ṣúfí poets, Jalálu 'l-Dín Rúmí, the author of the *Mathnawí*, who died some thirty years after him. Nor did all those who borrowed his ideas call themselves Moslems. He inspired, amongst other mediæval Christian writers, "the Illuminated Doctor" Raymond Lull, and probably Dante.[2]

[1] Ibnu 'l-'Arabí has been studied by Asin Palacios, Professor of Arabic at Madrid, whose books are written in Spanish, and H. S. Nyberg (*Kleinere Schriften des Ibn al-'Arabí*, Leiden, 1919). A general view may be obtained from my *Studies in Islamic Mysticism*, pp. 77–142 and pp. 149–161.

[2] See Asin Palacios, *Islam and the Divine Comedy*, London, 1926.

CHAPTER IX

THE ARABS IN EUROPE

It will be remembered that before the end of the first century of the Hijra, in the reign of the Umayyad Caliph, Walíd b. 'Abd al-Malik (705–715 A.D.), the Moslems under Ṭáriq and Músá b. Nuṣayr, crossed the Mediterranean, and having defeated Roderic the Goth in a great battle near Cadiz, rapidly brought the whole of Spain into subjection. The fate of the new province was long doubtful. The Berber insurrection which raged in Africa (734–742 A.D.) spread to Spain and threatened to exterminate the handful of Arab colonists; and no sooner was this danger past than the victors began to rekindle the old feuds and jealousies which they had inherited from their ancestors of Qays and Kalb. Once more the rival factions of Syria and Yemen flew to arms, and the land was plunged in anarchy.

'Abdu 'l-Raḥmán, the Umayyad.

Meanwhile 'Abdu 'l-Raḥmán b. Mu'áwiya, a grandson of the Caliph Hishám, had escaped from the general massacre with which the 'Abbásids celebrated their triumph over the House of Umayya, and after five years of wandering adventure, accompanied only by his faithful freedman, Badr, had reached the neighbourhood of Ceuta, where he found a precarious shelter with the Berber tribes. Young, ambitious, and full of confidence in his destiny, 'Abdu 'l-Raḥmán conceived the bold plan of throwing himself into Spain and of winning a kingdom with the help of the Arabs, amongst whom, as he well knew, there were many clients of his own family. Accordingly in 755 A.D. he sent Badr across the sea on a secret mission. The envoy accomplished even more than was expected of him. To gain over the clients was easy, for 'Abdu 'l-Raḥmán was their natural chief, and in the event of his success they would share with him the prize. Their number, however, was comparatively small. The pretender could not hope to achieve anything unless he were supported by one of the great parties, Syrians or Yemenites. At this time the former, led by the feeble governor, Yúsuf b. 'Abd al-Raḥmán al-Fihrí, and his cruel but capable lieutenant, Ṣumayl b. Ḥátim, held the reins of power and were pursuing their adversaries with ruthless ferocity. The Yemenites, therefore, hastened to range themselves on the side of 'Abdu 'l-Raḥmán, not that they loved his cause, but inspired solely by the prospect of taking a bloody vengeance upon the Syrians. These Spanish Moslems belonged to the true Bedouin stock!

A few months later 'Abdu 'l-Raḥmán landed in Spain, occupied Seville, and, routing Yúsuf and Ṣumayl under the walls of Cordova, made himself master of the capital. On the same evening he presided, as Governor of Spain, over the citizens assembled for public worship in the great Mosque (May, 756 A.D.).

During his long reign of thirty-two years 'Abdu 'l-Rahmán was busily employed in defending and consolidating the empire which more than once seemed to be on the point of slipping from his grasp. The task before him was arduous in the extreme. On the one hand, he was confronted by the unruly Arab aristocracy, jealous of their independence and regarding the monarch as their common foe. Between him and them no permanent compromise was possible, and since they could only be kept in check by an armed force stronger than themselves, he was compelled to rely on mercenaries, for the most part Berbers imported from Africa. Thus, by a fatal necessity the Moslem Empire in the West gradually assumed that despotic and Prætorian character which we have learned to associate with the 'Abbásid Government in the period of its decline, and the results were in the end hardly less disastrous. The monarchy had also to reckon with the fanaticism of its Christian subjects and with a formidable Spanish national party eager to throw off the foreign yoke. Extraordinary energy and tact were needed to maintain authority over these explosive elements, and if the dynasty founded by 'Abdu 'l-Raḥmán not only survived for two centuries and a half but gave to Spain a more splendid era of prosperity and culture than she had ever enjoyed, the credit is mainly due to the bold adventurer from whom even his enemies could not withhold a tribute of admiration. One day, it is said, the Caliph Manṣúr asked his courtiers, "Who is the Falcon of Quraysh?" They replied, "O Prince of the Faithful, that title belongs to you who have vanquished mighty kings and have put an end to civil war." "No," said the Caliph, "it is not I." "Mu'áwiya, then, or 'Abdu 'l-Malik?" "No," said Manṣúr, "the Falcon of Quraysh is 'Abdu 'l-Raḥmán b. Mu'áwiya, he who traversed alone the deserts of Asia and Africa, and without an army to aid him sought his fortune in an unknown country beyond the sea. With no weapons except judgment and resolution he subdued his enemies, crushed the rebels, secured his frontiers, and founded a great empire. Such a feat was never achieved by any one before."[1]

Of the Moslems in Spain the Arabs formed only a small minority, and they, moreover, showed all the indifference towards religion and contempt for the laws of Islam

[1] Abridged from Ibnu 'l-'Idhárí, *al-Bayán al-Mughrib*, ed. by Dozy, vol. ii, p. 61 seq.

which might be expected from men imbued with Bedouin traditions whose forbears had been devotedly attached to the world-loving Umayyads of Damascus. It was otherwise with the Spanish converts, the so-called 'Renegades' or *Muwalladún* (Affiliati) living as clients under protection of the Arab nobility, and with the Berbers. These races took their adopted religion very seriously, in accordance with the fervid and sombre temperament which has always distinguished them. Hence among the mass of Spanish Moslems a rigorous orthodoxy prevailed. The Berber, Yaḥyá b. Yaḥyá († 849 A.D.), is a typical figure. At the age of twenty-eight years he travelled to the East and studied under Málik. b Anas, who dictated to him his celebrated work known as the *Muwaṭṭa'*. Yaḥyá was one day at Málik's lecture with a number of fellow-students, when some one said, "Here comes the elephant!" All of them ran out to see the animal, but Yaḥyá did not stir. "Why," said Málik, "do you not go out and look at it? Such animals are not to be seen in Spain." To this Yaḥyá replied, "I left my country for the purpose of seeing you and obtaining knowledge under your guidance. I did not come here to see the elephant." Málik was so pleased with this answer that he called him the most intelligent (*'âqil*) of the people of Spain. On his return to Spain Yaḥyá exerted himself to spread the doctrines of his master, and though he obstinately refused, on religious grounds, to accept any public office, his influence and reputation were such that, as Ibn Ḥazm says, no Cadi was ever appointed till Yaḥyá had given his opinion and designated the person whom he preferred.[1] Thus the Málikite system, based on close adherence to tradition, became the law of the land. "The Spaniards," it is observed by a learned writer or the tenth century, "recognise only the Koran and the

Islam in Spain.

Yaḥya b. Yaḥyá.

[1] Ibn Khallikán, ed. by Wüstenfeld, No. 802; De Slane's translation, vol. iv, p. 29 sqq.

Muwaṭṭa'; if they find a follower of Abú Ḥanífa or Sháfi'í, they banish him from Spain, and if they meet with a Mu'tazilite or a Shí'ite or any one of that sort, they often put him to death."[1] Arrogant, intensely bigoted, and ambitious of power, the Muḥammadan clergy were not disposed to play a subordinate rôle in the State. In Hishám (788–796 A.D.), the successor of 'Abdu 'l-Raḥmán, they had a prince after their own heart, whose piety and devotion to their interests left nothing to be desired. Ḥakam (796–822 A.D.) was less complaisant. He honoured and respected the clergy, but at the same time he let them see that he would not permit them to interfere in political affairs. The malcontents, headed by the fiery Yaḥyá b. Yaḥyá, replied with menaces and insults, and called on the populace of Cordova—especially the 'Renegades' in the southern quarter (*rabaḍ*) of the city—to rise against the tyrant and his insolent soldiery. One day in Ramaḍán, 198 A.H. (May, 814 A.D.), Ḥakam suddenly found himself cut off from the garrison and besieged in his palace by an infuriated mob, but he did not lose courage, and, thanks to his coolness and skilful strategy, he came safely out of the peril in which he stood. The revolutionary suburb was burned to the ground and those of its inhabitants who escaped massacre, some 60,000 souls, were driven into exile. The real culprits went unpunished. Ḥakam could not afford further to exasperate the divines, who on their part began to perceive that they might obtain from the prince by favour what they had failed to wring from him by force. Being mostly Arabs or Berbers, they had a strong claim to his consideration. Their power was soon restored, and in the reign of 'Abdu 'l-Raḥmán II (822–852 A.D.) Yaḥyá himself, the ringleader of the mutiny, directed ecclesiastical policy and dispensed judicial patronage as he pleased.

The Revolt of the Suburb.

[1] Muqaddasí (ed. by De Goeje), p. 236, cited by Goldziher, *Die Záhiriten* p. 114.

The Revolt of the Suburb was only an episode in the long and sanguinary struggle between the Spaniards, Moslem or Christian, on the one hand, and the monarchy of Cordova on the other—a struggle complicated by the rival Arab tribes, which sometimes patched up their own feuds in order to defend themselves against the Spanish patriots, but never in any circumstances gave their support to the detested Umayyad Government. The hero of this war of independence was 'Umar b. Ḥafṣún. He belonged to a noble family of West-Gothic origin which had gone over to Islam and settled in the mountainous district north-east of Malaga. Hot-blooded, quarrelsome, and ready to stab on the slightest provocation, the young man soon fell into trouble. At first he took shelter in the wild fastnesses of Ronda, where he lived as a brigand until he was captured by the police. He then crossed the sea to Africa, but in a short time returned to his old haunts and put himself at the head of a band of robbers. Here he held out for two years, when, having been obliged to surrender, he accepted the proposal of the Sultan of Cordova that he and his companions should enlist in the Imperial army. But 'Umar was destined for greater glory than the Sultan could confer upon him. A few contemptuous words from a superior officer touched his pride to the quick, so one fine day he galloped off with all his men in the direction of Ronda. They found an almost impregnable retreat in the castle of Bobastro, which had once been a Roman fortress. From this moment, says Dozy, 'Umar b. Ḥafṣún was no longer a brigand-chief, but leader of the whole Spanish race in the south. The lawless and petulant free-lance was transformed into a high-minded patriot, celebrated for the stern justice with which he punished the least act of violence, adored by his soldiers, and regarded by his countrymen as the champion of the national cause. During the rest of his life (884–917 A.D.) he conducted the guerilla with untiring energy and made himself a terror to the

'Umar b. Ḥafṣún.

Arabs, but fortune deserted him at the last, and he died—*felix opportunitate mortis*—only a few years before complete ruin overtook his party. The Moslem Spaniards, whose enthusiasm had been sensibly weakened by their leader's conversion to Christianity, were the more anxious to make their peace with the Government, since they saw plainly the hopelessness of continuing the struggle.

In 912 A.D. 'Abdu 'l-Raḥmán III, the Defender of the Faith (*al-Náṣir li-díni 'lláh*), succeeded his grandfather, the Amír 'Abdulláh, on the throne of Cordova. The character, genius, and enterprise of this great monarch are strikingly depicted in the following passage from the pen of an eloquent historian whose work, although it was published some fifty years ago, will always be authoritative[1] :—

'Abdu 'l-Raḥmán III (912–961 A.D.).

"Amongst the Umayyad sovereigns who have ruled Spain the first place belongs incontestably to 'Abdu 'l-Raḥmán III. What he accomplished was almost miraculous. He had found the empire abandoned to anarchy and civil war, rent by factions, parcelled amongst a multitude of heterogeneous princes, exposed to incessant attacks from the Christians of the north, and on the eve of being swallowed up either by the Léonnese or the Africans. In spite of innumerable obstacles he had saved Spain both from herself and from the foreign domination. He had endowed her with new life and made her greater and stronger than she had ever been. He had given her order and prosperity at home, consideration and respect abroad. The public treasury, which he had found in a deplorable condition, was now overflowing. Of the Imperial revenues, which amounted annually to 6,245,000 pieces of gold, a third sufficed for ordinary expenses; a third was held in reserve, and 'Abdu 'l-Raḥmán devoted the remainder to his buildings. It was calculated that in the year 951 he had in his coffers the enormous sum of 20,000,000 pieces of gold, so that a traveller not without judgment in matters of finance assures us that 'Abdu 'l-Raḥmán and the Ḥamdánid (Náṣiru 'l-Dawla), who was then reigning over Mesopotamia, were the wealthiest princes of that epoch. The state of the country was in

[1] Dozy, *Histoire des Musulmans d'Espagne* (Leyden, 1861), vol. iii, p. 90 sqq.

keeping with the prosperous condition of the treasury. Agriculture, industry, commerce, the arts and the sciences, all flourished. . . . Cordova, with its half-million inhabitants, its three thousand mosques, its superb palaces, its hundred and thirteen thousand houses, its three hundred bagnios, and its twenty-eight suburbs, was inferior in extent and splendour only to Baghdád, with which city the Cordovans loved to compare it. . . . The power of 'Abdu 'l-Raḥmán was formidable. A magnificent fleet enabled him to dispute with the Fáṭimids the empire of the Mediterranean, and secured him in the possession of Ceuta, the key of Mauritania. A numerous and well-disciplined army, perhaps the finest in the world, gave him superiority over the Christians of the north. The proudest sovereigns solicited his alliance. The emperor of Constantinople, the kings of Germany, Italy, and France sent ambassadors to him.

"Assuredly, these were brilliant results; but what excites our astonishment and admiration when we study this glorious reign is not so much the work as the workman: it is the might of that comprehensive intelligence which nothing escaped, and which showed itself no less admirable in the minutest details than in the loftiest conceptions. This subtle and sagacious man, who centralises, who founds the unity of the nation and of the monarchy, who by means of his alliances establishes a sort of political equilibrium, who in his large tolerance calls the professors of another religion into his councils, is a modern king rather than a mediæval Caliph."[1]

In short, 'Abdu 'l-Raḥmán III made the Spanish Moslems one people, and formed out of Arabs and Spaniards a united Andalusian nation, which, as we shall presently see, advanced with incredible swiftness to a height of culture that was the envy of Europe and was not exceeded by any contemporary State in the Muḥammadan East. With his death, however, the decline of the Umayyad dynasty began. His son, Ḥakam II († 976 A.D.), left as heir-apparent a boy eleven years old, Hishám II, who received the title of Caliph while the government was carried on by his mother Aurora and the ambitious minister Muḥammad b. Abí 'Ámir. The latter was virtually monarch of Spain, and whatever may be thought of the means by which he rose to eminence, or of his treatment of the unfortunate Caliph whose

Regency of Manṣúr Ibn Abí 'Ámir (976–1002 A.D.).

[1] 'Abdu 'l-Raḥmán III was the first of his line to assume this title.

mental faculties he deliberately stunted and whom he condemned to a life of monkish seclusion, it is impossible to deny that he ruled well and nobly. He was a great statesman and a great soldier. No one could accuse him of making an idle boast when he named himself 'Al-Manṣúr' ('The Victorious'). Twice every year he was accustomed to lead his army against the Christians, and such was the panic which he inspired that in the course of more than fifty campaigns he scarcely ever lost a battle. He died in 1002 A.D. A Christian monk, recording the event in his chronicle, adds, "he was buried in Hell," but Moslem hands engraved the following lines upon the tomb of their champion :—

> "His story in his relics you may trace,
> As tho' he stood before you face to face.
> Never will Time bring forth his peer again,
> Nor one to guard, like him, the gaps of Spain."[1]

His demise left the Prætorians masters of the situation. Berbers and Slaves[2] divided the kingdom between them, and

[1] Maqqarí, vol. i, p. 259. As Maqqarí's work is our principal authority for the literary history of Moslem Spain, I may conveniently give some account of it in this place. The author, Aḥmad b. Muḥammad al-Tilimsání al-Maqqarí († 1632 A.D.) wrote a biography of Ibnu 'l-Khaṭíb, the famous Vizier of Granada, to which he prefixed a long and discursive introduction in eight chapters : (1) Description of Spain ; (2) Conquest of Spain by the Arabs ; (3) History of the Spanish dynasties ; (4) Cordova ; (5) Spanish-Arabian scholars who travelled in the East ; (6) Orientals who visited Spain ; (7) Miscellaneous extracts, anecdotes, poetical citations, &c., bearing on the literary history of Spain ; (8) Reconquest of Spain by the Christians and expulsion of the Arabs. The whole work is entitled *Nafḥu 'l-Ṭíb min ghuṣni 'l-Andalusi 'l-raṭíb wa-dhikri wazírihá Lisáni 'l-Dín Ibni 'l-Khaṭíb*. The introduction, which contains a fund of curious and valuable information—"a library in little"—has been edited by Dozy and other European Arabists under the title of *Analectes sur l'Histoire et la Littérature des Arabes d'Espagne* (Leyden, 1855–1861).

[2] The name of Slaves (*Ṣaqáliba*) was originally applied to prisoners of war, belonging to various northern races, who were sold to the Arabs of Spain, but the term was soon widened so as to include all foreign slaves serving in the harem or the army, without regard to their nationality. Like the Mamelukes and Janissaries, they formed a privileged corps under the

amidst revolution and civil war the Umayyad dynasty passed away (1031 A.D.).

It has been said with truth that the history of Spain in the eleventh century bears a close resemblance to that of Italy in the fifteenth. The splendid empire of 'Abdu 'l-Raḥmán III was broken up, and from its ruins there emerged a fortuitous conglomeration of petty states governed by successful condottieri. Of these Party Kings (*Mulúku 'l-Ṭawá'if*), as they are called by Muḥammadan writers, the most powerful were the 'Abbádids of Seville. Although it was an age of political decay, the material prosperity of Spain had as yet suffered little diminution, whilst in point of culture the society of this time reached a level hitherto unequalled. Here, then, we may pause for a moment to review the progress of literature and science during the most fruitful period of the Moslem occupation of European soil.

The Party Kings (*Mulúku 'l-Ṭawá'if*).

Whilst in Asia, as we have seen, the Arab conquerors yielded to the spell of an ancient culture infinitely superior to their own, they no sooner crossed the Straits of Gibraltar than the rôles were reversed. As the invaders extended their conquests to every part of the peninsula, thousands of Christians fell into their hands, who generally continued to live under Moslem protection. They were well treated by the Government, enjoyed religious liberty, and often rose to high offices in the army or at court. Many of them became rapidly imbued with Moslem civilisation, so that as early as the middle of the ninth century we find Alvaro, Bishop of Cordova, complaining that his co-religionists read the poems and romances of the Arabs, and studied the writings of Muḥammadan theologians and philosophers, not in

Influence of Arabic culture on the Spaniards.

patronage of the palace, and since the reign of 'Abdu 'l-Raḥmán III their number and influence had steadily increased. *Cf.* Dozy, *Hist. des Mus. d'Espagne*, vol. iii, p. 58 sqq.

order to refute them but to learn how to express themselves in Arabic with correctness and elegance. "Where," he asks, "can any one meet nowadays with a layman who reads the Latin commentaries on the Holy Scriptures? Who studies the Gospels, the Prophets, the Apostles? Alas, all young Christians of conspicuous talents are acquainted only with the language and writings of the Arabs; they read and study Arabic books with the utmost zeal, spend immense sums of money in collecting them for their libraries, and proclaim everywhere that this literature is admirable. On the other hand, if you talk with them of Christian books, they reply contemptuously that these books are not worth their notice. Alas, the Christians have forgotten their own language, and amongst thousands of us scarce one is to be found who can write a tolerable Latin letter to a friend; whereas very many are capable of expressing themselves exquisitely in Arabic and of composing poems in that tongue with even greater skill than the Arabs themselves."[1]

However the good bishop may have exaggerated, it is evident that Muḥammadan culture had a strong attraction for the Spanish Christians, and equally, let us add, for the Jews, who made numerous contributions to poetry, philosophy, and science in their native speech as well as in the kindred Arabic idiom. The 'Renegades,' or Spanish converts to Islam, became completely Arabicised in the course of a few generations; and from this class sprang some of the chief ornaments of Spanish-Arabian literature.

Considered as a whole, the poetry of the Moslems in Europe shows the same characteristics which have already been noted in the work of their Eastern contemporaries. The paralysing conventions from which the laureates of Baghdád and Aleppo could not emancipate themselves remained in full force at Cordova and

The poetry of the Spanish Arabs.

[1] Dozy, *op. cit.*, vol. ii, p. 103 seq.

Seville. Yet, just as Arabic poetry in the East was modified by the influences of Persian culture, in Spain also the gradual amalgamation of Aryans with Semites introduced new elements which have left their mark on the literature of both races. Perhaps the most interesting features of Spanish-Arabian poetry are the tenderly romantic feeling which not infrequently appears in the love-songs, a feeling that sometimes anticipates the attitude of mediæval chivalry; and in the second place an almost modern sensibility to the beauties of nature. On account of these characteristics the poems in question appeal to many European readers who do not easily enter into the spirit of the *Mu'allaqát* or the odes of Mutanabbí, and if space allowed it would be a pleasant task to translate some of the charming lyric and descriptive pieces which have been collected by anthologists. The omission, however, is less grave inasmuch as Von Schack has given us a series of excellent versions in his *Poesie und Kunst der Araber in Spanien and Sicilien* (2nd ed., Stuttgart, 1877).

"One of its marvels," says Qazwíní, referring to the town of Shilb (Silves) in Portugal, "is the fact, which innumerable persons have mentioned, that the people living there, with few exceptions, are makers of verse and devoted to belles-lettres; and if you passed by a labourer standing behind his plough and asked him to recite some verses, he would at once improvise on any subject that you might demand."[1] Of such folk-songs the *zajal* and *muwashshaḥ* were favourite types.[2] Both forms were invented in Spain, and their structure is very similar, consisting of several stanzas in which the rhymes are so arranged that the master-rhyme ending each stanza and running through the whole poem like a refrain is continually interrupted by a various succession of subordinate rhymes, as is shown in the following scheme:—

Folk-songs.

[1] Qazwíní, *Átháru 'l-Bilád*, ed. by Wüstenfeld, p. 364, l. 5 sqq.

[2] See Schack, *op. cit.*, vol. ii, p. 46 sqq.

aa
bbba
ccca
ddda.

Many of these songs and ballads were composed in the vulgar dialect and without regard to the rules of classical prosody. The troubadour Ibn Quzmán († 1160 A.D.) first raised the *zajal* to literary rank. Here is an example of the *muwashshaḥ* :—

"Come, hand the precious cup to me,
And brim it high with a golden sea!
Let the old wine circle from guest to guest,
While the bubbles gleam like pearls on its breast,
So that night is of darkness dispossessed.
How it foams and twinkles in fiery glee!
'Tis drawn from the Pleiads' cluster, perdie.

Pass it, to music's melting sound,
Here on this flowery carpet round,
Where gentle dews refresh the ground
And bathe my limbs deliciously
In their cool and balmy fragrancy.

Alone with me in the garden green
A singing-girl enchants the scene:
Her smile diffuses a radiant sheen.
I cast off shame, for no spy can see,
And 'Hola,' I cry, 'let us merry be!'"[1]

True to the traditions of their family, the Spanish Umayyads loved poetry, music, and polite literature a great deal better than the Koran. Even the Falcon of Quraysh, 'Abdu 'l-Raḥmán I, if the famous verses on the Palm-tree are really by him, concealed something of the softer graces under his grim exterior. It is

Verses by 'Abdu 'l-Raḥmán I.

[1] The Arabic original occurs in the 11th chapter of the *Ḥalbatu 'l-Kumayt*, a collection of poems on wine and drinking by Muḥammad b. Ḥasan al-Nawájí († 1455 A.D.), and is also printed in the *Anthologie Arabe* of Grangeret de Lagrange, p. 202.

said that in his gardens at Cordova there was a solitary date-palm, which had been transplanted from Syria, and that one day 'Abdu 'l-Raḥmán, as he gazed upon it, remembered his native land and felt the bitterness of exile and exclaimed :—

"O Palm, thou art a stranger in the West,
Far from thy Orient home, like me unblest.
Weep! But thou canst not. Dumb, dejected tree,
Thou art not made to sympathise with me.
Ah, thou wouldst weep, if thou hadst tears to pour,
For thy companions on Euphrates' shore;
But yonder tall groves thou rememberest not,
As I, in hating foes, have my old friends forgot."[1]

Ziryáb the musician.

At the court of 'Abdu 'l-Raḥmán II (822–852 A.D.) a Persian musician was prime favourite. This was Ziryáb, a client of the Caliph Mahdí and a pupil of the celebrated singer, Isḥáq al-Mawṣilí.[2] Isḥáq, seeing in the young man a dangerous rival to himself, persuaded him to quit Baghdád and seek his fortune in Spain. 'Abdu 'l-Raḥmán received him with open arms, gave him a magnificent house and princely salary, and bestowed upon him every mark of honour imaginable. The versatile and accomplished artist wielded a vast influence. He set the fashion in all things appertaining to taste and manners; he fixed the toilette, sanctioned the cuisine, and prescribed what dress should be worn in the different seasons of the year. The kings of Spain took him as a model, and his authority was constantly invoked and universally recognised in that country down to the last days of Moslem rule.[3] Ziryáb was only one

[1] *Al-Ḥullat al-Siyará* of Ibnu 'l-Abbár, ed. by Dozy, p. 34. In the last line instead of "foes" the original has "the sons of 'Abbás." Other verses addressed by 'Abdu 'l-Raḥmán to this palm-tree are cited by Maqqarí, vol. ii, p. 37.

[2] Full details concerning Ziryáb will be found in Maqqarí, vol. ii, p. 83 sqq. *Cf.* Dozy, *Hist. des Mus. d'Espagne*, vol. ii, p. 89 sqq.

[3] Maqqari, *loc. cit.*, p. 87, l. 10 sqq.

of many talented and learned men who came to Spain from the East, while the list of Spanish savants who journeyed "in quest of knowledge" (*fí ṭalabi 'l-'ilm*) to Africa and Egypt, to the Holy Cities of Arabia, to the great capitals of Syria and 'Iráq, to Khurásán, Transoxania, and in some cases even to China, includes, as may be seen from the perusal of Maqqarí's fifth chapter, nearly all the eminent scholars and men of letters whom Moslem Spain has produced. Thus a lively exchange of ideas was continually in movement, and so little provincialism existed that famous Andalusian poets, like Ibn Hání and Ibn Zaydún, are described by admiring Eastern critics as the Buḥturís and Mutanabbís of the West.

The tenth century of the Christian era is a fortunate and illustrious period in Spanish history. Under 'Abdu 'l-Raḥmán III and his successor, Ḥakam II, the nation, hitherto torn asunder by civil war, bent its united energies to the advancement of material and intellectual culture. Ḥakam was an enthusiastic bibliophile. He sent his agents in every direction to purchase manuscripts, and collected 400,000 volumes in his palace, which was thronged with librarians, copyists, and bookbinders. All these books, we are told, he had himself read, and he annotated most of them with his own hand. His munificence to scholars knew no bounds. He made a present of 1,000 dínárs to Abu 'l-Faraj of Iṣfahán, in order to secure the first copy that was published of the great 'Book of Songs' (*Kitábu 'l-Aghání*), on which the author was then engaged. Besides honouring and encouraging the learned, Ḥakam took measures to spread the benefits of education amongst the poorest of his subjects. With this view he founded twenty-seven free schools in the capital and paid the teachers out of his private purse. Whilst in Christian Europe the rudiments of learning were confined to the clergy, in Spain almost every one could read and write.

The Library of Ḥakam II.

"The University of Cordova was at that time one of the most celebrated in the world. In the principal Mosque, where the lectures were held, Abú Bakr b. Mu'áwiya, the Qurayshite, discussed the Traditions relating to Muḥammad. Abú 'Alí al-Qálí of Baghdád dictated a large and excellent miscellany which contained an immense quantity of curious information concerning the ancient Arabs, their proverbs, their language, and their poetry. This collection he afterwards published under the title of *Amálí*, or 'Dictations.' Grammar was taught by Ibnu 'l-Qúṭiyya, who, in the opinion of Abú 'Alí al-Qálí, was the leading grammarian of Spain. Other sciences had representatives no less renowned. Accordingly the students attending the classes were reckoned by thousands. The majority were students of what was called *fiqh*, that is to say, theology and law, for that science then opened the way to the most lucrative posts." [1]

The University of Cordova.

Among the notable savants of this epoch we may mention Ibn 'Abdi Rabbihi († 940 A.D.), laureate of 'Abdu 'l- Raḥmán III and author of a well-known anthology entitled *al-'Iqd al-Faríd*; the poet Ibn Hání of Seville († 973 A.D.), an Ismá'ílí convert who addressed blasphemous panegyrics to the Fáṭimid Caliph Mu'izz;[2] the historians of Spain, Abú Bakr al-Rází († 937 A.D.), whose family belonged to Rayy in Persia, and Ibnu 'l-Qúṭiyya († 977 A.D.), who, as his name indicates, was the descendant of a Gothic princess; the astronomer and mathematician Maslama b. Aḥmad of Madrid († 1007 A.D.); and the great surgeon Abu 'l-Qásim al-Zahráwí of Cordova, who died about the same time, and who became known to Europe by the name of Albucasis.

The fall of the Spanish Umayyads, which took place in the first half of the eleventh century, left Cordova a republic and a merely provincial town; and though she might still claim to be regarded as the literary metropolis of Spain, her ancient glories were overshadowed by the independent dynasties which

[1] Dozy *Histoire des Musulmans d'Espagne*, vol. iii, p. 107 sqq.
[2] See the verses cited by Ibnu 'l-Athír, vol. viii, p. 457

now begin to flourish in Seville, Almeria, Badajoz, Granada, Toledo, Malaga, Valencia, and other cities. Of these rival princedoms the most formidable in arms and the most brilliant in its cultivation of the arts was, beyond question, the family of the 'Abbádids, who reigned in Seville. The foundations of their power were laid by the Cadi Abu 'l-Qásim Muḥammad. "He acted towards the people with such justice and moderation as drew on him the attention of every eye and the love of every heart," so that the office of chief magistrate was willingly conceded to him. In order to obtain the monarchy which he coveted, the Cadi employed an audacious ruse. The last Umayyad Caliph, Hishám II, had vanished mysteriously: it was generally supposed that, after escaping from Cordova when that city was stormed by the Berbers (1013 A.D.), he fled to Asia and died unknown; but many believed that he was still alive. Twenty years after his disappearance there suddenly arose a pretender, named Khalaf, who gave out that he was the Caliph Hishám. The likeness between them was strong enough to make the imposture plausible. At any rate, the Cadi had his own reasons for abetting it. He called on the people, who were deeply attached to the Umayyad dynasty, to rally round their legitimate sovereign. Cordova and several other States recognised the authority of this pseudo-Caliph, whom Abu 'l-Qásim used as a catspaw. His son 'Abbád, a treacherous and bloodthirsty tyrant, but an amateur of belles-lettres, threw off the mask and reigned under the title of al-Mu'taḍid (1042–1069 A.D.). He in turn was succeeded by his son, al-Mu'tamid, whose strange and romantic history reminds one of a sentence frequently occurring in the *Arabian Nights*: "Were it graven with needle-gravers upon the eye-corners, it were a warner to whoso would be warned." He is described as "the most liberal, the most hospitable, the most munificent, and the most powerful of all the princes who ruled in Spain. His court was the halting-place of travellers, the rendezvous

The 'Abbádids (1023–1091 A.D.).

of poets, the point to which all hopes were directed, and the haunt of men of talent."[1] Mu'tamid himself was a poet of rare distinction. "He left," says Ibn Bassám, "some pieces of verse beautiful as the bud when it opens to disclose the flower; and had the like been composed by persons who made of poetry a profession and a merchandise, they would still have been considered charming, admirable, and singularly original."[2] Numberless anecdotes are told of Mu'tamid's luxurious life at Seville: his evening rambles along the banks of the Guadalquivir; his parties of pleasure; his adventures when he sallied forth in disguise, accompanied by his Vizier, the poet Ibn 'Ammár, into the streets of the sleeping city; and his passion for the slave-girl I'timád, commonly known as Rumaykiyya, whom he loved all his life with constant devotion.

Mu'tamid of Seville (1069–1091 A.D.).

Meanwhile, however, a terrible catastrophe was approaching. The causes which led up to it are related by Ibn Khallikán as follows[3]:—

"At that time Alphonso VI, the son of Ferdinand, the sovereign of Castile and king of the Spanish Franks, had become so powerful that the petty Moslem princes were obliged to make peace with him and pay him tribute. Mu'tamid Ibn 'Abbád surpassed all the rest in greatness of power and extent of empire, yet he also paid tribute to Alphonso. After capturing Toledo (May 29, 1085 A.D.) the Christian monarch sent him a threatening message with the demand that he should surrender his fortresses; on which condition he might retain the open country as his own. These words provoked Mu'tamid to such a degree that he struck the ambassador and put to death all those who accompanied him.[4] Alphonso, who was marching on Cordova,

The Almoravides in Spain.

[1] Ibn Khallikán, No. 697; De Slane's translation, vol. iii, p. 186.

[2] Ibn Khallikán, *loc. cit.*

[3] *Loc. cit.*, p. 189. For the sake of clearness I have slightly abridged and otherwise remodelled De Slane's translation of this passage.

[4] A somewhat different version of these events is given by Dozy, *Histoire des Musulmans d'Espagne*, vol. iv, p. 189 sqq.

no sooner received intelligence of this event than he returned to Toledo in order to provide machines for the siege of Seville. When the Shaykhs and doctors of Islam were informed of this project they assembled and said: 'Behold how the Moslem cities fall into the hands of the Franks whilst our sovereigns are engaged in warfare against each other! If things continue in this state the Franks will subdue the entire country.' They then went to the Cadi (of Cordova), 'Abdulláh b. Muḥammad b. Adham, and conferred with him on the disasters which had befallen the Moslems and on the means by which they might be remedied. Every person had something to say, but it was finally resolved that they should write to Abú Ya'qúb Yúsuf b. Táshifín, the king of the *Mulaththamún*[1] and sovereign of Morocco, imploring his assistance. The Cadi then waited on Mu'tamid, and informed him of what had passed. Mu'tamid concurred with them on the expediency of such an application, and told the Cadi to bear the message himself to Yúsuf b. Táshifín. A conference took place at Ceuta. Yúsuf recalled from the city of Morocco the troops which he had left there, and when all were mustered he sent them across to Spain, and followed with a body of 10,000 men. Mu'tamid, who had also assembled an army, went to meet him; and the Moslems, on hearing the news, hastened from every province for the purpose of combating the infidels. Alphonso, who was then at Toledo, took the field with 40,000 horse, exclusive of other troops which came to join him. He wrote a long and threatening letter to Yúsuf b. Táshifín, who inscribed on the back of it these words: '*What will happen thou shalt see!*' and returned it. On reading the answer Alphonso was filled with apprehension, and observed that this was a man of resolution. The two armies met at Zalláqa, near Badajoz. The Moslems gained the victory, and Alphonso fled with a few others, after witnessing the complete destruction of his army. This year was adopted in Spain as the commencement of a new era, and was called the year of Zalláqa."

Battle of Zalláqa (October 23, 1086 A.D.).

Mu'tamid soon perceived that he had "dug his own grave"—to quote the words used by himself a few years afterwards—when he sought aid from the perfidious Almoravide. Yúsuf

[1] The term *Mulaththamún*, which means literally 'wearers of the *lithám*' (a veil covering the lower part of the face), is applied to the Berber tribes of the Sahara, the so-called Almoravides (*al-Murábiṭún*), who at this time ruled over Northern Africa.

could not but contrast the beauty, riches, and magnificent resources of Spain with the barren deserts and rude civilisation of Africa. He was not content to admire at a distance the enchanting view which had been dangled before him. In the following year he returned to Spain and took possession of Granada. He next proceeded to pick a quarrel with Mu'tamid. The Berber army laid siege to Seville, and although Mu'tamid displayed the utmost bravery, he was unable to prevent the fall of his capital (September, 1091 A.D.). The unfortunate prince was thrown into chains and transported to Morocco. Yúsuf spared his life, but kept him a prisoner at Aghmát, where he died in 1095 A.D. During his captivity he bewailed in touching poems the misery of his state, the sufferings which he and his family had to endure, and the tragic doom which suddenly deprived him of friends, fortune, and power. "Every one loves Mu'tamid," wrote an historian of the thirteenth century, "every one pities him, and even now he is lamented."[1] He deserved no less, for, as Dozy remarks, he was "the last Spanish-born king (*le dernier roi indigène*), who represented worthily, nay, brilliantly, a nationality and culture which succumbed, or barely survived, under the dominion of barbarian invaders."[2]

Captivity and death of Mu'tamid.

The Age of the Tyrants, to borrow from Greek history a designation which well describes the character of this period, yields to no other in literary and scientific renown. Poetry was cultivated at every Andalusian court. If Seville could point with just pride to Mu'tamid and his Vizier, Ibn 'Ammár, Cordova claimed a second pair almost equally illustrious—Ibn Zaydún (1003–1071 A.D.) and Walláda, a daughter of the Umayyad Caliph al-Mustakfí. Ibn Zaydún entered upon a political career and became the confidential agent of Ibn Jahwar, the chief

Ibn Zaydún.

[1] Ibnu 'l-Abbár (Dozy, *Loci de Abbadidis*, vol. ii, p. 63).
[2] *Histoire des Musulmans d'Espagne*, vol. iv, p. 287.

magistrate of Cordova, but he fell into disgrace, probably on account of his love for the beautiful and talented princess, who inspired those tender melodies which have caused the poet's European biographers to link his name with Tibullus and Petrarch. In the hope of seeing her, although he durst not show himself openly, he lingered in al-Zahrá, the royal suburb of Cordova built by 'Abdu 'l-Raḥmán III. At last, after many wanderings, he found a home at Seville, where he was cordially received by Mu'taḍid, who treated him as an intimate friend and bestowed on him the title of *Dhu 'l-Wizáratayn.*[1] The following verses, which he addressed to Wallada, depict the lovely scenery of al-Zahrá and may serve to illustrate the deep feeling for nature which, as has been said, is characteristic of Spanish-Arabian poetry in general.[2]

"To-day my longing thoughts recall thee here;
The landscape glitters, and the sky is clear.
So feebly breathes the gentle zephyr's gale,
In pity of my grief it seems to fail.
The silvery fountains laugh, as from a girl's
Fair throat a broken necklace sheds its pearls.
Oh, 'tis a day like those of our sweet prime,
When, stealing pleasures from indulgent Time,
We played midst flowers of eye-bewitching hue,
That bent their heads beneath the drops of dew.
Alas, they see me now bereaved of sleep;
They share my passion and with me they weep.
Here in her sunny haunt the rose blooms bright,
Adding new lustre to Aurora's light;
And waked by morning beams, yet languid still,
The rival lotus doth his perfume spill.

---

[1] *I.e.*, 'holder of the two vizierships'—that of the sword and that of the pen. See De Slane's translation of Ibn Khallikán, vol. iii, p. 130, n. 1.

[2] The Arabic text of this poem, which occurs in the *Qalá'idu 'l-'Iqyán* of Ibn Kháqán, will be found on pp. 24–25 of Weyers's *Specimen criticum exhibens locos Ibn Khacanis de Ibn Zeidouno* (Leyden, 31).

All stirs in me the memory of that fire
Which in my tortured breast will ne'er expire.
Had death come ere we parted, it had been
The best of all days in the world, I ween;
And this poor heart, where thou art every thing,
Would not be fluttering now on passion's wing.
Ah, might the zephyr waft me tenderly,
Worn out with anguish as I am, to thee!
O treasure mine, if lover e'er possessed
A treasure! O thou dearest, queenliest!
Once, once, we paid the debt of love complete
And ran an equal race with eager feet.
How true, how blameless was the love I bore,
Thou hast forgotten; but I still adore!"

Ibn Ḥazm (994–1064 A.D.).

The greatest scholar and the most original genius of Moslem Spain is Abú Muḥammad 'Alí Ibn Ḥazm, who was born at Cordova in 994 A.D. He came of a 'Renegade' family, but he was so far from honouring his Christian ancestors that he pretended to trace his descent to a Persian freedman of Yazíd b. Abí Sufyán, a brother of the first Umayyad Caliph, Mu'áwiya; and his contempt for Christianity was in proportion to his fanatical zeal on behalf of Islam. His father, Aḥmad, had filled the office of Vizier under Manṣúr Ibn Abí 'Ámir, and Ibn Ḥazm himself plunged ardently into politics as a client—through his false pedigree—of the Umayyad House, to which he was devotedly attached. Before the age of thirty he became prime minister of 'Abdu 'l-Raḥmán V (1023–1024 A.D.), but on the fall of the Umayyad Government he retired from public life and gave himself wholly to literature. Ibn Bashkuwál, author of a well-known biographical dictionary of Spanish celebrities entitled *al-Ṣila fí akhbári a'immati 'l-Andalus*, speaks of him in these terms: "Of all the natives of Spain Ibn Ḥazm was the most eminent by the universality and the depth of his learning in the sciences cultivated by the Moslems; add to this his profound acquaintance with the Arabic tongue, and his vast abilities as an elegant writer, a poet, a biographer, and an historian; his son possessed about 400 volumes, containing nearly 80,000 leaves, which Ibn Ḥazm had composed and written out."[1] It is recorded that he said, "My only desire in seeking knowledge was to attain a high scientific rank in this world and the next."[2] He got little encouragement from his contemporaries. The mere fact that he belonged to the Ẓáhirite school of theology would not have mattered, but the caustic style in which he attacked the most venerable religious authorities of Islam aroused such bitter hostility that he was virtually excommunicated by the orthodox divines. People were warned against having anything to do with him, and at Seville his writings were solemnly committed to the flames. On this occasion he is said to have remarked—

> "The paper ye may burn, but what the paper holds
> Ye cannot burn: 'tis safe within my breast: where I
> Remove, it goes with me, alights when I alight,
> And in my tomb will lie."[3]

'The Book of Religions and Sects.'

After being expelled from several provinces of Spain, Ibn Ḥazm withdrew to a village, of which he was the owner, and remained there until his death. Of his numerous writings only a few have escaped destruction, but fortunately we possess the most valuable of them all, the 'Book of Religions and Sects' (*Kitábu 'l-Milal wa-'l-Niḥal*),[4] which was recently printed in Cairo for the first time. This work treats in controversial fashion (1) of the non-Muḥammadan religious systems, especially Judaism, Christianity, and Zoroastrianism, and (2) of Islam and its dogmas, which are of course regarded from the Ẓáhirite

[1] Cited by Ibn Khallikán in his article on Ibn Ḥazm (De Slane's translation, vol. ii, p. 268).

[2] Maqqarí, vol. i, p. 511, l. 21.

[3] Maqqarí, *loc. cit.* p. 515, l. 5 seq.

[4] See p. 341, note 1.

standpoint, and of the four principal Muḥammadan sects, viz., the Mu'tazilites, the Murjites, the Shí'ites, and the Khárijites. The author maintains that these sects owed their rise to the Persians, who sought thus to revenge themselves upon victorious Islam.[1]

The following are some of the most distinguished Spanish writers of this epoch: the historian, Abú Marwán Ibn Ḥayyán of Cordova († 1075 A.D.), whose chief works are a colossal history of Spain in sixty volumes entitled *al-Matín* and a smaller chronicle (*al-Muqtabis*), both of which appear to have been almost entirely lost;[2] the jurisconsult and poet, Abu 'l-Walíd al-Bájí († 1081 A.D.); the traditionist Yúsuf Ibn 'Abd al-Barr († 1071 A.D.); and the geographer al-Bakrí, a native of Cordova, where he died in 1094 A.D. Finally, mention should be made of the famous Jews, Solomon Ibn Gabirol (Avicebron) and Samuel Ha-Levi. The former, who was born at Malaga about 1020 A.D., wrote two philosophical works in Arabic, and his *Fons Vitae* played an important part in the development of mediæval scholasticism. Samuel Ha-Levi was Vizier to Bádís, the sovereign of Granada (1038–1073 A.D.). In their admiration of his extraordinary accomplishments the Arabs all but forgot that he was a Jew and a prince (*Naghíd*) in Israel.[3] Samuel, on his part, when he wrote letters of State, did not scruple to employ the usual Muḥammadan formulas, "Praise to Allah!" "May Allah bless our Prophet Muḥammad!"

Literature in Spain in the eleventh century.

Samuel Ha-Levi.

[1] The contents of the *Kitábu 'l-Milal wa-'l-Niḥal* are fully summarised by Dozy in the Leyden Catalogue, vol. iv, pp. 230–237. *Cf.* also *Zur Komposition von Ibn Ḥazm's Milal wa'n-Niḥal*, by Israel Friedlaender in the *Nöldeke-Festschrift* (Giessen, 1906), vol. i, p. 267 sqq.

[2] So far as I am aware, the report that copies are preserved in the great mosque at Tunis has not been confirmed.

[3] His Arabic name is Ismá'íl b. Naghdála. See the Introduction to Dozy's ed. of Ibnu 'l-'Idhárí, p. 84, n. 1.

and to glorify Islam quite in the manner of a good Moslem. He had a perfect mastery of Hebrew and Arabic; he knew five other languages, and was profoundly versed in the sciences of the ancients, particularly in astronomy. With all his learning he was a supple diplomat and a man of the world. Yet he always preserved a dignified and unassuming demeanour, although in his days (according to Ibnu 'l-'Idhárí) "the Jews made themselves powerful and behaved arrogantly towards the Moslems."[1]

During the whole of the twelfth, and well into the first half of the thirteenth, century Spain was ruled by two African dynasties, the Almoravides and the Almohades, which originated, as their names denote, in the religious fanaticism of the Berber tribes of the Sahara. The rise of the Almoravides is related by Ibnu 'l-Athír as follows:—[2]

Rise of the Almoravides.

"In this year (448 A.H. = 1056 A.D.) was the beginning of the power of the *Mulaththamún*.[3] These were a number of tribes descended from Ḥimyar, of which the most considerable were Lamtúna, Jadála, and Lamṭa. . . . Now in the above-mentioned year a man of Jadála, named Jawhar, set out for Africa[4] on his way to the Pilgrimage, for he loved religion and the people thereof. At Qayrawán he fell in with a certain divine—Abú 'Imrán al-Fásí, as is generally supposed—and a company of persons who were studying theology under him. Jawhar was much pleased with what he saw of their piety, and on his return from Mecca he begged Abú 'Imrán to send back with him to the desert a teacher who should instruct the ignorant Berbers in the laws of Islam. So Abú 'Imrán sent

---

[1] An interesting notice of Samuel Ha-Levi is given by Dozy in his *Hist. des Mus. d'Espagne*, vol. iv, p. 27 sqq.

[2] *Kámil* of Ibnu 'l-Athír, ed. by Tornberg, vol. ix, p. 425 sqq. The following narrative (which has been condensed as far as possible) differs in some essential particulars from the accounts given by Ibn Khaldún (*History of the Berbers*, De Slane's translation, vol. ii, p. 64 sqq.) and by Ibn Abí Zar' (Tornberg, *Annales Regum Mauritaniæ*, p. 100 sqq. of the Latin version). *Cf.* A. Müller, *Der Islam*, vol. ii, p. 611 sqq.

[3] See note on p. 423.

[4] The province of Tunis.

with him a man called 'Abdulláh b. Yásín al-Kuzúlí, who was an excellent divine, and they journeyed together until they came to the tribe of Lamtúna. Then Jawhar dismounted from his camel and took hold of the bridle of 'Abdulláh b. Yásín's camel, in reverence for the law of Islam; and the men of Lamtúna approached Jawhar and greeted him and questioned him concerning his companion. 'This man,' he replied, 'is the bearer of the Sunna of the Apostle of God: he has come to teach you what is necessary in the religion of Islam.' So they bade them both welcome, and said to 'Abdulláh, 'Tell us the law of Islam,' and he explained it to them. They answered, 'As to what you have told us of prayer and alms-giving, that is easy; but when you say, "He that kills shall be killed, and he that steals shall have his hand cut off, and he that commits adultery shall be flogged or stoned," that is an ordinance which we will not lay upon ourselves. Begone elsewhere!' . . . And they came to Jadála, Jawhar's own tribe, and 'Abdulláh called on them and the neighbouring tribes to fulfil the law, and some consented while others refused. Then, after a time, 'Abdulláh said to his followers, 'Ye must fight the enemies of the Truth, so appoint a commander over you.' Jawhar answered, 'Thou art our commander,' but 'Abdulláh declared that he was only a missionary, and on his advice the command was offered to Abú Bakr b. 'Umar, the chief of Lamtúna, a man of great authority and influence. Having prevailed upon him to act as leader, 'Abdulláh began to preach a holy war, and gave his adherents the name of Almoravides (*al-Murábiṭún*)."[1]

The Almoravide Empire (1056–1147 A.D.).

The little community rapidly increased in numbers and power. Yúsuf b. Táshifín, who succeeded to the command in 1069 A.D., founded the city of Morocco, and from this centre made new conquests in every direction, so that ere long the Almoravides ruled over the whole of North-West Africa from Senegal to Algeria. We have already seen how Yúsuf was invited by

[1] *Murábiṭ* is literally 'one who lives in a *ribáṭ*,' *i.e.*, a guardhouse or military post on the frontier. Such buildings were often occupied, in addition to the garrison proper, by individuals who, from pious motives, wished to take part in the holy war (*jihád*) against the unbelievers. The word *murábiṭ*, therefore, gradually got an exclusively religious signification, 'devotee' or 'saint,' which appears in its modern form, *marabout*. As applied to the original Almoravides, it still retains a distinctly military flavour.

the ʻAbbádids to lead an army into Spain, how he defeated Alphonso VI at Zalláqa and, returning a few years later, this time not as an ally but as a conqueror, took possession of Granada and Seville. The rest of Moslem Spain was subdued without much trouble: laity and clergy alike hailed in the Berber monarch a zealous reformer of the Faith and a mighty bulwark against its Christian enemies. The hopeful prospect was not realised. Spanish civilisation enervated the Berbers, but did not refine them. Under the narrow bigotry of Yúsuf and his successors free thought became impossible, culture and science faded away. Meanwhile the country was afflicted by famine, brigandage, and all the disorders of a feeble and corrupt administration.

The empire of the Almoravides passed into the hands of another African dynasty, the Almohades.[1] Their founder, Muḥammad Ibn Túmart, was a native of the mountainous district of Sús which lies to the south-west of Morocco. When a youth he made the Pilgrimage to Mecca (about 1108 A.D.), and also visited Baghdád, where he studied in the Niẓámiyya College and is said to have met the celebrated Ghazálí. He returned home with his head full of theology and ambitious schemes. We need not dwell upon his career from this point until he finally proclaimed himself as the Mahdí (1121 A.D.), nor describe the familiar methods—some of them disreputable enough—by which he induced the Berbers to believe in him. His doctrines, however, may be briefly stated. "In most questions," says one of his biographers,[2] "he followed the system of Abu 'l-Ḥasan al-Ashʻarí, but he agreed with the Muʻtazilites in their denial of the Divine Attributes and in a few matters besides; and he

Ibn Túmart.

[1] See Goldziher's article *Materialien zur Kenntniss der Almohadenbewegung in Nordafrika* (*Z.D.M.G.*, vol. 41, p. 30 sqq.).

[2] ʻAbdu 'l-Wáḥid, *History of the Almohades*, ed. by Dozy, p. 135, l. 1 sqq.

was at heart somewhat inclined to Shí'ism, although he gave it no countenance in public."[1] The gist of his teaching is indicated by the name *Muwaḥḥid* (Unitarian), which he bestowed on himself, and which his successors adopted as their dynastic title.[2] Ibn Túmart emphasised the Unity of God; in other words, he denounced the anthropomorphic ideas which prevailed in Western Islam and strove to replace them by a purely spiritual conception of the Deity. To this main doctrine he added a second, that of the Infallible Imám (*al-Imám al-Ma'ṣúm*), and he naturally asserted that the Imám was Muḥammad Ibn Túmart, a descendant of 'Alí b. Abí Ṭálib.

The Almohades (1130–1269 A.D.).

On the death of the Mahdí (1130 A.D.) the supreme command devolved upon his trusted lieutenant, 'Abdu 'l-Mu'min, who carried on the holy war against the Almoravides with growing success, until in 1158 A.D. he "united the whole coast from the frontier of Egypt to the Atlantic, together with Moorish Spain, under his sceptre."[3] The new dynasty was far more enlightened and favourable to culture than the Almoravides had been. Yúsuf, the son of 'Abdu 'l-Mu'min, is described as an excellent scholar, whose mind was stored with the battles and traditions and history of the Arabs before and after Islam. But he found his highest pleasure in the study and patronage of philosophy. The great Aristotelian, Ibn Ṭufayl, was his Vizier and court physician; and Ibn Rushd (Averroes) received flattering honours both from him and from his successor, Ya'qúb al-Manṣúr, who loved to converse with the philosopher on scientific topics, although in a fit of orthodoxy he banished him for a time.[4] This curious mixture

[1] The Berbers at this time were Sunnite and anti-Fáṭimid.
[2] Almohade is the Spanish form of *al-Muwaḥḥid.*
[3] Stanley Lane-Poole, *The Mohammadan Dynasties*, p. 46.
[4] Renan, *Averroès et l'Averroïsme*, p. 12 sqq.

of liberality and intolerance is characteristic of the Almohades. However they might encourage speculation in its proper place, their law and theology were cut according to the plain Ẓáhirite pattern. "The Koran and the Traditions of the Prophet—or else the sword!" is a saying of the last-mentioned sovereign, who also revived the autos-da-fé, which had been prohibited by his grandfather, of Málikite and other obnoxious books.[1] The spirit of the Almohades is admirably reflected in Ibn Ṭufayl's famous philosophical romance, named after its hero, *Ḥayy ibn Yaqẓán, i.e.*, 'Alive, son of Awake,'[2] of which the following summary is given by Mr. Duncan B. Macdonald in his excellent *Muslim Theology* (p. 253):—

The story of Ḥayy b. Yaqẓán.

"In it he conceives two islands, the one inhabited and the other not. On the inhabited island we have conventional people living conventional lives, and restrained by a conventional religion of rewards and punishments. Two men there, Salámán and Asál,[3] have raised themselves to a higher level of self-rule. Salámán adapts himself externally to the popular religion and rules the people; Asál, seeking to perfect himself still further in solitude, goes to the other island. But there he finds a man, Ḥayy ibn Yaqẓán, who has lived alone from infancy and has gradually, by the innate and uncorrupted powers of the mind, developed himself to the highest philosophic level and reached the Vision of the Divine. He has passed through all the stages of knowledge until the universe lies clear before him, and now he finds that his philosophy thus reached, without prophet or revelation, and the purified religion of Asál are one and the same. The story told by Asál of the people of the other island sitting in darkness stirs his soul, and he goes forth to them as a missionary. But he soon learns that the method of Muḥammad was the true one

[1] See a passage from 'Abdu 'l-Wáḥid's *History of the Almohades* (p. 201, l. 19 sqq.), which is translated in Goldziher's *Ẓâhiriten*, p. 174.

[2] The Arabic text, with a Latin version by E. Pocock, was published in 1671, and again in 1700, under the title *Philosophus Autodidactus*. An English translation by Simon Ockley appeared in 1708, and has been several times reprinted.

[3] The true form of this name is Absál, as in Jámí's celebrated poem. *Cf.* De Boer, *The History of Philosophy in Islam*, translated by E. R. Jones, p. 144.

for the great masses, and that only by sensuous allegory and concrete things could they be reached and held. He retires to his island again to live the solitary life."

Literature under the Almoravides and Almohades (1100–1250 A.D.).

Of the writers who flourished under the Berber dynasties few are sufficiently important to deserve mention in a work of this kind. The philosophers, however, stand in a class by themselves. Ibn Bájja (Avempace), Ibn Rushd (Averroes), Ibn Ṭufayl, and Músá b. Maymún (Maimonides) made their influence felt far beyond the borders of Spain : they belong, in a sense, to Europe. We have noticed elsewhere the great mystic, Muḥyi 'l-Dín Ibnu 'l-'Arabí († 1240 A.D.); his fellow-townsman, Ibn Sab'ín († 1269 A.D.), a thinker of the same type, wrote letters on philosophical subjects to Frederick II of Hohenstaufen. Valuable works on the literary history of Spain were composed by Ibn Kháqán († 1134 A.D.), Ibn Bassám († 1147 A.D.), and Ibn Bashkuwál († 1183 A.D.). The geographer Idrísí († 1154 A.D.) was born at Ceuta, studied at Cordova, and found a patron in the Sicilian monarch, Roger II; Ibn Jubayr published an interesting account of his pilgrimage from Granada to Mecca and of his journey back to Granada during the years 1183–1185 A.D.; Ibn Zuhr (Avenzoar), who became a Vizier under the Almoravides, was the first of a whole family of eminent physicians; and Ibnu 'l-Bayṭár of Malaga († 1248 A.D.), after visiting Egypt, Greece, and Asia Minor in order to extend his knowledge of botany, compiled a Materia Medica, which he dedicated to the Sultan of Egypt, Malik al-Kámil.

Reconquest of Spain by Ferdinand III.

We have now taken a rapid survey of the Moslem empire in Spain from its rise in the eighth century of our era down to the last days of the Almohades, which saw the Christian arms everywhere triumphant. By 1230 A.D. the Almohades had been driven out of the peninsula, although they continued to rule Africa for about forty years after this date. Amidst the general wreck one spot remained where the Moors could find shelter. This was Granada. Here, in 1232 A.D., Muḥammad Ibnu 'l-Aḥmar assumed the proud title of 'Conqueror by Grace of God' (*Ghálib billáh*) and founded the Naṣrid dynasty, which held the Christians at bay during two centuries and a half. That the little Moslem kingdom survived so long was not due to its own strength, but rather to its almost impregnable situation and to the dissensions of the victors. The latest bloom of Arabic culture in Europe renewed, if it did not equal, the glorious memories of Cordova and Seville. In this period arose the world-renowned Alhambra, *i.e.*, 'the Red Palace' (al-Ḥamrá) of the Naṣrid kings, and many other superb monuments of which the ruins are still visible. We must not, however, be led away into a digression even upon such a fascinating subject as Moorish architecture. Our information concerning literary matters is scantier than it might have been, on account of the vandalism practised by the Christians when they took Granada. It is no dubious legend (like the reputed burning of the Alexandrian Library by order of the Caliph 'Umar),[1] but a well-ascertained fact that the ruthless Archbishop Ximenez made a bonfire of all the Arabic manuscripts on which he could lay his hands. He wished to annihilate the record of seven centuries of Muḥammadan culture in a single day.

The Naṣrids of Granada (1232–1492 A.D.).

The names of Ibnu 'l-Khaṭíb and Ibn Khaldún represent the highest literary accomplishment and historical comprehension of which this age was capable. The latter, indeed, has no parallel among Oriental historians.

Lisánu 'l-Dín Ibnu 'l-Khaṭíb[2] played a great figure in the

[1] Jurjí Zaydán, however, is disposed to regard the story as being not without foundation. See his interesting discussion of the evidence in his *Ta'ríkhu 'l-Tamaddun al-Islámí* ('History of Islamic Civilisation'), Part III, pp. 40–46.

[2] The life of Ibnu 'l-Khaṭíb has been written by his friend and contemporary, Ibn Khaldún (*Hist. of the Berbers*, translated by De Slane, vol. iv.

politics of his time, and his career affords a conspicuous example of the intimate way in which Moslem poetry and literature are connected with public life. "The Arabs did not share the opinion widely spread nowadays, that poetical talent flourishes best in seclusion from the tumult of the world, or that it dims the clearness of vision which is required for the conduct of public affairs. On the contrary, their princes entrusted the chief offices of State to poets, and poetry often served as a means to obtain more brilliant results than diplomatic notes could have procured."[1] A young man like Ibnu 'l-Khaṭíb, who had mastered the entire field of belles-lettres, who improvised odes and rhyming epistles with incomparable elegance and facility, was marked out to be the favourite of kings. He became Vizier at the Naṣrid court, a position which he held, with one brief interval of disgrace, until 1371 A.D., when the intrigues of his enemies forced him to flee from Granada. He sought refuge at Fez, and was honourably received by the reigning Sultan, 'Abdu 'l-'Azíz; but on the accession of Abu 'l-'Abbás in 1374 A.D. the exiled minister was incarcerated and brought to trial on the charge of heresy (*zandaqa*). While the inquisition was proceeding a fanatical mob broke into the gaol and murdered him. Maqqarí relates that Ibnu 'l-Khaṭib suffered from insomnia, and that most of his works were composed during the night, for which reason he got the nickname of *Dhu 'l-'Umrayn*, or 'The man of two lives.'[2] He was a prolific writer in various branches of literature, but, like so many of his countrymen, he excelled in History. His monographs on the sovereigns and savants of Granada (one of which includes an autobiography) supply interesting details concerning this obscure period.

Ibnu 'l-Khaṭíb (1313–1374 A.D.).

p. 390 sqq.), and forms the main subject of Maqqarí's *Nafḥu 'l-Ṭíb* (vols. iii and iv of the Buláq edition).

[1] Schack, *op. cit.*, vol. i, p. 312 seq.

[2] Cited in the *Shadharátu 'l-Dhahab*, a MS. in my collection. See *J.R.A.S.* for 1899, p. 911 seq., and for 1906, p. 797.

Some apology may be thought necessary for placing Ibn Khaldún, the greatest historical thinker of Islam, in the present chapter, as though he were a Spaniard either by birth or residence. He descended, it is true, from a family, the Banú Khaldún, which had long been settled in Spain, first at Carmona and afterwards at Seville; but they migrated to Africa about the middle of the thirteenth century, and Ibn Khaldún was born at Tunis. Nearly the whole of his life, moreover, was passed in Africa—a circumstance due rather to accident than to predilection; for in 1362 A.D. he entered the service of the Sultan of Granada, Abú 'Abdalláh Ibnu 'l-Aḥmar, and would probably have made that city his home had not the jealousy of his former friend, the Vizier Ibnu 'l-Khaṭíb, decided him to leave Spain behind. We cannot give any account of the agitated and eventful career which he ended, as Cadi of Cairo, in 1406 A.D. Ibn Khaldún lived with statesmen and kings: he was an ambassador to the court of Pedro of Castile, and an honoured guest of the mighty Tamerlane. The results of his ripe experience are marvellously displayed in the Prolegomena (*Muqaddima*), which forms the first volume of a huge general history entitled the *Kitábu 'l-'Ibar* ('Book of Examples').[1] He himself has stated his idea of the historian's function in the following words:—

Ibn Khaldún (1332–1406 A.D.).

"Know that the true purpose of history is to make us acquainted with human society, *i.e.*, with the civilisation of the world, and with its natural phenomena, such as savage life, the softening of manners, attachment to the family and the tribe, the various kinds of superiority which one people gains over another, the kingdoms and diverse dynasties which arise in this way, the different trades and laborious occupations to

Ibn Khaldún as a philosophical historian.

---

[1] The Arabic text of the Prolegomena has been published by Quatremère in *Notices et extraits des manuscrits de la Bibliothèque Impériale*, vols. 16–18, and at Beyrout (1879, 1886, and 1900). A French translation by De Slane appeared in *Not. et Extraits*, vols. 19–21.

which men devote themselves in order to earn their livelihood, the sciences and arts; in fine, all the manifold conditions which naturally occur in the development of civilisation."[1]

Ibn Khaldún argues that History, thus conceived, is subject to universal laws, and in these laws he finds the only sure criterion of historical truth.

His canons of historical criticism.

"The rule for distinguishing what is true from what is false in history is based on its possibility or impossibility: that is to say, we must examine human society (civilisation) and discriminate between the characteristics which are essential and inherent in its nature and those which are accidental and need not be taken into account, recognising further those which cannot possibly belong to it. If we do this we have a rule for separating historical truth from error by means of a demonstrative method that admits of no doubt. . . . It is a genuine touchstone whereby historians may verify whatever they relate."[2]

Here, indeed, the writer claims too much, and it must be allowed that he occasionally applied his principles in a pedantic fashion, and was led by purely *a priori* considerations to conclusions which are not always so warrantable as he believed. This is a very trifling matter in comparison with the value and originality of the principles themselves. Ibn Khaldún asserts, with justice, that he has discovered a new method of writing history. No Moslem had ever taken a view at once so comprehensive and so philosophical; none had attempted to trace the deeply hidden causes of events, to expose the moral and spiritual forces at work beneath the surface, or to divine the immutable laws of national progress and decay. Ibn Khaldún owed little to his predecessors, although he mentions some of them with respect. He stood far above his age, and his own countrymen have admired rather than followed him. His intellectual descendants are the great

[1] *Muqaddima* (Beyrout ed. of 1900), p. 35, l. 5 sqq. = Prolegomena translated by De Slane, vol. i, p. 71.

[2] *Muqaddima*, p. 37, l. 4 fr. foot = De Slane's translation, vol. i, p. 77.

mediæval and modern historians of Europe—Machiavelli and Vico and Gibbon.

Ibn Khaldún's theory of historical evolution.

It is worth while to sketch briefly the peculiar theory of historical development which Ibn Khaldún puts forward in his Prolegomena—a theory founded on the study of actual conditions and events either past or passing before his eyes.[1] He was struck, in the first place, with the physical fact that in almost every part of the Muḥammadan Empire great wastes of sand or stony plateaux, arid and incapable of tillage, wedge themselves between fertile domains of cultivated land. The former were inhabited from time immemorial by nomad tribes, the latter by an agricultural or industrial population; and we have seen, in the case of Arabia, that cities like Mecca and Ḥíra carried on a lively intercourse with the Bedouins and exerted a civilising influence upon them. In Africa the same contrast was strongly marked. It is no wonder, therefore, that Ibn Khaldún divided the whole of mankind into two classes—Nomads and Citizens. The nomadic life naturally precedes and produces the other. Its characteristics are simplicity and purity of manners, warlike spirit, and, above all, a loyal devotion to the interests of the family and the tribe. As the nomads become more civilised they settle down, form states, and make conquests. They have now reached their highest development. Corrupted by luxury, and losing the virtues which raised them to power, they are soon swept away by a ruder people. Such, in bare outline, is the course of history as Ibn Khaldún regards it; but we must try to give our readers some further account of the philosophical ideas

[1] Von Kremer has discussed Ibn Khaldún's ideas more fully than is possible here in an admirably sympathetic article, *Ibn Chaldun und seine Culturgeschichte der islamischen Reiche*, contributed to the *Sitz. der Kais. Akad. der Wissenschaften*, vol. 93 (Vienna, 1879). I have profited by many of his observations, and desire to make the warmest acknowledgment of my debt to him in this as in countless other instances.

underlying his conception. He discerns, in the life of tribes and nations alike, two dominant forces which mould their destiny. The primitive and cardinal force he calls *'aṣabiyya*, the *binding* element in society, the feeling which unites members of the same family, tribe, nation, or empire, and which in its widest acceptation is equivalent to the modern term, Patriotism. It springs up and especially flourishes among nomad peoples, where the instinct of self-preservation awakens a keen sense of kinship and drives men to make common cause with each other. This *'aṣabiyya* is the vital energy of States: by it they rise and grow; as it weakens they decline; and its decay is the signal for their fall. The second of the forces referred to is Religion. Ibn Khaldún hardly ascribes to religion so much influence as we might have expected from a Moslem. He recognises, however, that it may be the only means of producing that solidarity without which no State can exist. Thus in the twenty-seventh chapter of his *Muqaddima* he lays down the proposition that "the Arabs are incapable of founding an empire unless they are imbued with religious enthusiasm by a prophet or a saint."

In History he sees an endless cycle of progress and retrogression, analogous to the phenomena of human life. Kingdoms are born, attain maturity, and die within a definite period which rarely exceeds three generations, *i.e.*, 120 years.[1] During this time they pass through five stages of development and decay.[2] It is noteworthy that Ibn Khaldún admits the moral superiority of the Nomads. For him civilisation necessarily involves corruption and degeneracy. If he did not believe in the gradual advance of mankind towards some higher goal, his pessimism was justified by the lessons of experience and by the mournful plight of the Muḥammadan world, to which his view was restricted.[3]

[1] *Muqaddima*, Beyrout ed., p. 170 = De Slane's translation, vol. i, p. 347 sqq.

[2] *Muqaddima*, p. 175 = De Slane's translation, vol. i, p. 356 sqq.

[3] An excellent appreciation of Ibn Khaldún as a scientific historian will

In 1492 A.D. the last stronghold of the European Arabs opened its gates to Ferdinand and Isabella, and "the Cross supplanted the Crescent on the towers of Granada." The victors showed a barbarous fanaticism that was the more abominable as it violated their solemn pledges to respect the religion and property of the Moslems, and as it utterly reversed the tolerant and liberal treatment which the Christians of Spain had enjoyed under Muḥammadan rule. Compelled to choose between apostasy and exile, many preferred the latter alternative. Those who remained were subjected to a terrible persecution, until in 1609 A.D., by order of Philip III, the Moors were banished *en masse* from Spanish soil.

The fall of Granada (1492 A.D.).

Spain was not the sole point whence Moslem culture spread itself over the Christian lands. Sicily was conquered by the Aghlabids of Tunis early in the ninth century, and although the island fell into the hands of the Normans in 1071 A.D., the court of Palermo retained a semi-Oriental character. Here in the reign of Frederick II of Hohenstaufen (1194–1250 A.D.) might be seen "astrologers from Baghdád with long beards and waving robes, Jews who received princely salaries as translators of Arabic works, Saracen dancers and dancing-girls, and Moors who blew silver trumpets on festal occasions."[1] Both Frederick himself and his son Manfred were enthusiastic Arabophiles, and scandalised Christendom by their assumption of 'heathen' manners as well as by the attention which they devoted to Moslem philosophy and science. Under their auspices Arabic learning was communicated to the neighbouring towns of Lower Italy.

The Arabs in Sicily.

be found in Robert Flint's *History of the Philosophy of History*, vol. i, pp. 157–171.

[1] Schack, *op. cit.*, vol. ii, p. 151.

CHAPTER X

FROM THE MONGOL INVASION TO THE PRESENT DAY

General characteristics of the period.

BEFORE proceeding to speak of the terrible catastrophe which filled the whole of Western Asia with ruin and desolation, I may offer a few preliminary remarks concerning the general character of the period which we shall briefly survey in this final chapter. It forms, one must admit, a melancholy conclusion to a glorious history. The Caliphate, which symbolised the supremacy of the Prophet's people, is swept away. Mongols, Turks, Persians, all in turn build up great Muḥammadan empires, but the Arabs have lost even the shadow of a leading part and appear only as subordinate actors on a provincial stage. The chief centres of Arabian life, such as it is, are henceforth Syria and Egypt, which were held by the Turkish Mamelukes until 1517 A.D., when they passed under Ottoman rule. In North Africa the petty Berber dynasties (Ḥafṣids, Ziyánids, and Marínids) gave place in the sixteenth century to the Ottoman Turks. Only in Spain, where the Naṣrids of Granada survived until 1492 A.D., in Morocco, where the Sharífs (descendants of ʻAlí b. Abí Ṭálib) assumed the sovereignty in 1544 A.D., and to some extent in Arabia itself, did the Arabs preserve their political independence. In such circumstances it would be vain to look for any large developments of literature and culture worthy to rank with those of the past. This is an age of imitation and compilation. Learned men abound, whose erudition embraces every subject under the sun. The mass of writing shows no visible diminution, and much of it is valuable and meritorious work. But with one or two conspicuous exceptions—*e.g.* the historian Ibn Khaldún and the mystic Sha'rání—we cannot point to any new departure, any fruitful ideas, any trace of original and illuminating thought. The fifteenth and sixteenth centuries "witnessed the rise and triumph of that wonderful movement known as the Renaissance, . . . but no ripple of this great upheaval, which changed the whole current of intellectual and moral life in the West, reached the shores of Islam."[1] Until comparatively recent times, when Egypt and Syria first became open to European civilisation, the Arab retained his mediæval outlook and habit of mind, and was in no respect more enlightened than his forefathers who lived under the 'Abbásid Caliphate. And since the Mongol Invasion I am afraid we must say that instead of advancing farther along the old path he was being forced back by the inevitable pressure of events. East of the Euphrates the Mongols did their work of destruction so thoroughly that no seeds were left from which a flourishing civilisation could arise; and, moreover, the Arabic language was rapidly extinguished by the Persian. In Spain, as we have seen, the power of the Arabs had already begun to decline; Africa was dominated by the Berbers, a rude, unlettered race, Egypt and Syria by the blighting military despotism of the Turks. Nowhere in the history of this period can we discern either of the two elements which are most productive of literary greatness: the quickening influence of a higher culture or the inspiration of a free and vigorous national life.[2]

Between the middle of the eleventh century and the end

[1] E. J. W. Gibb, *A History of Ottoman Poetry*, vol. ii, p. 5.

[2] The nineteenth century should have been excepted, so far as the influence of modern civilisation has reacted on Arabic literature.

of the fourteenth the nomad tribes dwelling beyond the Oxus burst over Western Asia in three successive waves. First came the Seljúq Turks, then the Mongols under Chingíz Khan and Húlágú, then the hordes, mainly Turkish, of Tímúr. Regarding the Seljúqs all that is necessary for our purpose has been said in a former chapter. The conquests of Tímúr are a frightful episode which I may be pardoned for omitting from this history, inasmuch as their permanent results (apart from the enormous damage which they inflicted) were inconsiderable; and although the Indian empire of the Great Moguls, which Bábur, a descendant of Tímúr, established in the first half of the sixteenth century, ran a prosperous and brilliant course, its culture was borrowed almost exclusively from Persian models and does not come within the scope of the present work. We shall, therefore, confine our view to the second wave of the vast Asiatic migration, which bore the Mongols, led by Chingíz Khan and Húlágú, from the steppes of China and Tartary to the Mediterranean.

The Mongol Invasion.

In 1219 A.D. Chingíz Khan, having consolidated his power in the Far East, turned his face westward and suddenly advanced into Transoxania, which at that time formed a province of the wide dominions of the Sháhs of Khwárizm (Khiva). The reigning monarch, 'Alá'u 'l-Dín Muḥammad, was unable to make an effective resistance; and notwithstanding that his son, the gallant Jalálu 'l-Dín, carried on a desperate guerilla for twelve years, the invaders swarmed over Khurásán and Persia, massacring the panic-stricken inhabitants wholesale and leaving a wilderness behind them. Hitherto Baghdád had not been seriously threatened, but on the first day of January, 1256 A.D.—an epoch-marking date—Húlágú, the grandson of Chingíz Khan, crossed the Oxus, with the intention of occupying the 'Abbásid capital. I translate the following

Chingíz Khan and Húlágú.

narrative from a manuscript in my possession of the *Ta'ríkh al-Khamís* by Diyárbakrí († 1574 A.D.) :—

In the year 654 (A.H. = 1256 A.D.) the stubborn tyrant, Húlágú, the destroyer of the nations (*Mubídu 'l-Umam*), set forth and took the castle of Alamút from the Ismá'ílís[1] and slew them and laid waste the lands of Rayy. . . . And in the year 655 there broke out at Baghdád a fearful riot between the Sunnís and the Shí'ites, which led to great plunder and destruction of property. A number of Shí'ites were killed, and this so incensed and infuriated the Vizier Ibnu 'l-'Alqamí that he encouraged the Tartars to invade 'Iráq, by which means he hoped to take ample vengeance on the Sunnís.[2] And in the beginning of the year 656 the tyrant Húlágú b. Túlí b. Chingíz Khán, the Moghul, arrived at Baghdád with his army, including the Georgians (*al-Kurj*) and the troops of Mosul. The Dawídár[3] marched out of the city and met Húlágú's vanguard, which was commanded by Bájú.[4] The Moslems, being few, suffered defeat; whereupon Bájú advanced and pitched his camp to the west of Baghdád, while Húlágú took up a position on the eastern side. Then the Vizier Ibnu 'l-'Alqamí said to the Caliph Musta'ṣim Billáh: "I will go to the Supreme Khán to arrange peace." So the hound[5] went and obtained security for himself, and on his return said to the Caliph: "The Khán desires to marry his daughter to your son and to render homage to you, like the Seljúq kings, and then to depart." Musta'ṣim set out, attended by the nobles of

Húlágú before Baghdád (1258 A.D.).

---

[1] These Ismá'ílís are the so-called Assassins, the terrible sect organised by Ḥasan b. Ṣabbáḥ (see Professor Browne's *Literary History of Persia*, vol. ii, p. 201 sqq.), and finally exterminated by Húlágú. They had many fortresses, of which Alamút was the most famous, in the Jibál province, near Qazwín.

[2] The reader must be warned that this and the following account of the treacherous dealings of Ibnu 'l-'Alqamí are entirely contradicted by Shí'ite historians. For example, the author of *al-Fakhrí* (ed. by Derenbourg, p. 452) represents the Vizier as a far-seeing patriot who vainly strove to awaken his feeble-minded master to the gravity of the situation.

[3] Concerning the various functions of the Dawídár (literally Inkstand-holder) or Dawádár, as the word is more correctly written, see Quatremère, *Histoire des Sultans Mamlouks*, vol. i, p. 118, n. 2.

[4] The MS. writes Yájúnas.

[5] *Al-kalb*, the Arabic equivalent of the Persian *sag* (dog), an animal which Moslems regard as unclean.

his court and the grandees of his time, in order to witness the contract of marriage. The whole party were beheaded except the Caliph, who was trampled to death. The Tartars entered Baghdád and distributed themselves in bands throughout the city. For thirty-four days the sword was never sheathed. Few escaped. The slain amounted to 1,800,000 and more. Then quarter was called. . . . Thus it is related in the *Duwalu 'l-Islám.*[1] . . . And on this wise did the Caliphate pass from Baghdád. As the poet sings:—

Sack of Baghdád.

"Khalati 'l-manábiru wa-'l-asirratu minhumú
wa-'alayhimú ḥatta 'l-mamáti salámú."

"The pulpits and the thrones are empty of them;
I bid them, till the hour of death, farewell!"

It seemed as if all Muḥammadan Asia lay at the feet of the pagan conqueror. Resuming his advance, Húlágú occupied Mesopotamia and sacked Aleppo. He then returned to the East, leaving his lieutenant, Ketboghá, to complete the reduction of Syria. Meanwhile, however, an Egyptian army under the Mameluke Sultan Muẓaffar Quṭuz was hastening to oppose the invaders. On Friday, the 25th of Ramaḍán, 658 A.H., a decisive battle was fought at 'Ayn Jálút (Goliath's Spring), west of the Jordan. The Tartars were routed with immense slaughter, and their subsequent attempts to wrest Syria from the Mamelukes met with no success. The submission of Asia Minor was hardly more than nominal, but in Persia the descendants of Húlágú, the Íl-Kháns, reigned over a great empire, which the conversion of one of their number, Gházán (1295–1304 A.D.), restored to Moslem rule. We are not concerned here with the further history of the Mongols in Persia nor with that of the Persians themselves. Since the days of Húlágú the lands east and west of the Tigris are separated by an ever-widening gulf. The two races—Persians and Arabs—to whose co-operation the mediæval

Battle of 'Ayn Jálút (September, 1260 A.D.).

[1] By Shamsu 'l-Dín al-Dhahabí († 1348 A.D.).

world, from Samarcand to Seville, for a long time owed its highest literary and scientific culture, have now finally dissolved their partnership. It is true that the cleavage began many centuries earlier, and before the fall of Baghdád the Persian genius had already expressed itself in a splendid national literature. But from this date onward the use of Arabic by Persians is practically limited to theological and philosophical writings. The Persian language has driven its rival out of the field. Accordingly Egypt and Syria will now demand the principal share of our attention, more especially as the history of the Arabs of Granada, which properly belongs to this period, has been related in the preceding chapter.

Arabic ceases to be the language of the whole Moslem world.

The dynasty of the Mameluke[1] Sultans of Egypt was ounded in 1250 A.D. by Aybak, a Turkish slave, who commenced his career in the service of the Ayyúbid, Malik Ṣáliḥ Najmu 'l-Dín. His successors[2] held sway in Egypt and Syria until the conquest of these countries by the Ottomans. The Mamelukes were rough soldiers, who seldom indulged in any useless refinement, but they had a royal taste for architecture, as the visitor to Cairo may still see. Their administration, though disturbed by frequent mutinies and murders, was tolerably prosperous on the whole, and their victories over the Mongol hosts, as well as the crushing blows which they dealt to the Crusaders, gave Islam new prestige. The ablest of them all was Baybars, who richly deserved his title Malik al-Ẓáhir, *i.e*, the Victorious King. His name has passed into the legends of the people, and his warlike exploits into

The Mamelukes of Egypt (1250–1517 A.D.).

Sultan Baybars (1260–1277 A.D.).

[1] Mameluke (Mamlúk) means 'slave.' The term was applied to the mercenary troops, Turks and Kurds for the most part, who composed the bodyguard of the Ayyúbid princes.

[2] There are two Mameluke dynasties, called respectively Baḥrí (River) Mamelukes and Burjí (Tower) Mamelukes. The former reigned from 1250 to 1390, the latter from 1382 to 1517.

romances written in the vulgar dialect which are recited by story-tellers to this day.[1] The violent and brutal acts which he sometimes committed—for he shrank from no crime when he suspected danger—made him a terror to the ambitious nobles around him, but did not harm his reputation as a just ruler. Although he held the throne in virtue of having murdered the late monarch with his own hand, he sought to give the appearance of legitimacy to his usurpation. He therefore recognised as Caliph a certain Abu 'l-Qásim Aḥmad, a pretended scion of the 'Abbásid house, invited him to Cairo, and took the oath of allegiance to him in due form. The Caliph on his part invested the Sultan with sovereignty over Egypt, Syria, Arabia, and all the provinces that he might obtain by future conquests. This Aḥmad, entitled al-Mustanṣir, was the first of a long series of mock Caliphs who were appointed by the Mameluke Sultans and generally kept under close surveillance in the citadel of Cairo. There is no authority for the statement, originally made by Mouradgea d'Ohsson in 1787 and often repeated since, that the last of the line bequeathed his rights of succession to the Ottoman Sultan Selím I, thus enabling the Sultans of Turkey to claim the title and dignity of Caliph.[2]

The 'Abbásid Caliphs of Egypt.

The poets of this period are almost unknown in Europe, and until they have been studied with due attention it would be premature to assert that none of them rises above mediocrity. At the same time my own impression (based, I confess, on a very desultory and imperfect acquaintance with their work) is that the best among them are merely elegant and accomplished artists, playing brilliantly with words and phrases, but doing little else. No doubt extreme artificiality may coexist with poetical genius of a high order, provided that it has behind it Mutanabbí's power, Ma'arrí's earnestness, or Ibnu 'l-Fáriḍ's enthusiasm. In the absence of these

Arabic poetry after the Mongol Invasion.

[1] See Lane, *The Modern Egyptians*, ch. xxii.

[2] See Sir T. W. Arnold, *The Caliphate*, p. 146.

qualities we must be content to admire the technical skill with which the old tunes are varied and revived. Let us take, for example, Ṣafiyyu 'l-Dín al-Ḥillí, who was born at Ḥilla, a large town on the Euphrates, in 1278 A.D., became laureate of the Urtuqid dynasty at Máridín, and died in Baghdád about 1350. He is described as "the poet of his age absolutely," and to judge from the extracts in Kutubí's *Fawátu 'l-Wafayát*[1] he combined subtlety of fancy with remarkable ease and sweetness of versification. Many of his pieces, however, are *jeux d'esprit*, like his ode to the Prophet, in which he employs 151 rhetorical figures, or like another poem where all the nouns are diminutives.[2] The following specimen of his work is too brief to do him justice:—

Ṣafiyyu 'l-Dín al-Ḥillí.

"How can I have patience, and thou, mine eye's delight,
All the livelong year not one moment in my sight?
And with what can I rejoice my heart, when thou that art a joy
Unto every human heart, from me hast taken flight?
I swear by Him who made thy form the envy of the sun
(So graciously He clad thee with lovely beams of light):
The day when I behold thy beauty doth appear to me
As tho' it gleamed on Time's dull brow a constellation bright.
O thou scorner of my passion, for whose sake I count as naught
All the woe that I endure, all the injury and despite,
Come, regard the ways of God! for never He at life's last gasp
Suffereth the weight to perish even of one mite!"[3]

We have already referred to the folk-songs (*muwashshaḥ* and *zajal*) which originated in Spain. These simple ballads,

[1] Ed. of Buláq (1283 A.H.), pp. 356–366.

[2] *Ibid.*, p. 358.

[3] These verses are cited in the *Ḥadíqatu 'l-Afráḥ* (see Brockelmann's *Gesch. d. Arab. Litt.*, ii, 502), Calcutta, 1229 A.H., p. 280. In the final couplet there is an allusion to Kor. iv, 44: "*Verily God will not wrong any one even the weight of an ant*" (mithqála dharratin).

with their novel metres and incorrect language, were despised by the classical school, that is to say, by nearly all Moslems with any pretensions to learning; but their popularity was such that even the court poets occasionally condescended to write in this style. To the *zajal* and *muwashshaḥ* we may add the *dúbayt*, the *mawáliyyá*, the *kánwakán*, and the *ḥimáq*, which together with verse of the regular form made up the 'seven kinds of poetry' (*al-funún al-sab'a*). Ṣafiyyu 'l-Dín al-Ḥillí, who wrote a special treatise on the Arabic folk-songs, mentions two other varieties which, he says, were invented by the people of Baghdád to be sung in the early dawn of Ramaḍán, the Moslem Lent.[1] It is interesting to observe that some few literary men attempted, though in a timid fashion, to free Arabic poetry from the benumbing academic system by which it was governed and to pour fresh life into its veins. A notable example of this tendency is the *Hazzu 'l-Quḥúf*[2] by Shirbíní, who wrote in 1687 A.D. Here we have a poem in the vulgar dialect of Egypt, but what is still more curious, the author, while satirising the uncouth manners and rude language of the peasantry, makes a bitter attack on the learning and morals of the Muḥammadan divines.[3] For this purpose he introduces a typical Fellah named Abú Shádúf, whose rôle corresponds to that of Piers the Plowman in Longland's *Vision*. Down to the end of the nineteenth century, at any rate, such isolated offshoots had not gone far to found a living school of popular poetry. Only the future can show whether the Arabs are capable of producing a genius who will succeed in doing for the national folk-songs what Burns did for the Scots ballads.

Popular poetry.

1 Hartmann, *Das Muwaššaḥ* (Weimar, 1897), p. 218.

2 Literally, 'The Shaking of the Skull-caps,' in allusion to the peasants' dance.

3 See Vollers, *Beiträge zur Kenntniss der lebenden arabischen Sprache in Aegypten*, *Z.D.M.G.*, vol. 41 (1887), p. 370.

Biography and History were cultivated with ardour by the savants of Egypt and Syria. Among the numerous compositions of this kind we can have no hesitation in awarding the place of honour to the *Wafayátu 'l-A'yán*, or 'Obituaries of Eminent Men,' by Shamsu 'l-Dín Ibn Khallikán, a work which has often been quoted in the foregoing pages. The author belonged to a distinguished family descending from Yaḥyá b. Khálid the Barmecide (see p. 259 seq.), and was born at Arbela in 1211 A.D. He received his education at Aleppo and Damascus (1229–1238) and then proceeded to Cairo, where he finished the first draft of his Biographical Dictionary in 1256. Five years later he was appointed by Sultan Baybars to be Chief Cadi of Syria. He retained this high office (with a seven years' interval, which he devoted to literary and biographical studies) until a short time before his death. In the Preface to the *Wafayát* Ibn Khallikán observes that he has adopted the alphabetical order as more convenient than the chronological. As regards the scope and character of his Dictionary, he says :—

Ibn Khallikán (1211–1282 A.D.).

"I have not limited my work to the history of any one particular class of persons, as learned men, princes, emírs, viziers, or poets; but I have spoken of all those whose names are familiar to the public, and about whom questions are frequently asked; I have, however, related the facts I could ascertain respecting them in a concise manner, lest my work should become too voluminous; I have fixed with all possible exactness the dates of their birth and death; I have traced up their genealogy as high as I could; I have marked the orthography of those names which are liable to be written incorrectly; and I have cited the traits which may best serve to characterise each individual, such as noble actions, singular anecdotes, verses and letters, so that the reader may derive amusement from my work, and find it not exclusively of such a uniform cast as would prove tiresome; for the most effectual inducement to reading a book arises from the variety of its style."[1]

His Biographical Dictionary.

[1] Ibn Khallikán, De Slane's translation, vol. i, p. 3.

Ibn Khallikan might have added that he was the first Muḥammadan writer to design a Dictionary of National Biography, since none of his predecessors had thought of comprehending the lives of eminent Moslems of every class in a single work.[1] The merits of the book have been fully recognised by the author's countrymen as well as by European scholars. It is composed in simple and elegant language, it is extremely accurate, and it contains an astonishing quantity of miscellaneous historical and literary information, not drily catalogued but conveyed in the most pleasing fashion by anecdotes and excerpts which illustrate every department of Moslem life. I am inclined to agree with the opinion of Sir William Jones, that it is the best general biography ever written; and allowing for the difference of scale and scope, I think it will bear comparison with a celebrated English work which it resembles in many ways—I mean Boswell's *Johnson.*[2]

Historians of the Mameluke period.

To give an adequate account of the numerous and talented historians of the Mameluke period would require far more space than they can reasonably claim in a review of this kind. Concerning Ibn Khaldún, who held a professorship as well as the office of Cadi in Cairo under Sultan Barqúq (1382–1398 A.D.), we have already spoken at some length. This extraordinary genius discovered principles and methods which might have been

[1] It should be pointed out that the *Wafayát* is very far from being exhaustive. The total number of articles only amounts to 865. Besides the Caliphs, the Companions of the Prophet, and those of the next generation (*Tábi'ún*), the author omitted many persons of note because he was unable to discover the date of their death. A useful supplement and continuation of the *Wafayát* was compiled by al-Kutubí († 1363 A.D.) under the title *Fawátu 'l-Wafayát.*

[2] The Arabic text of the *Wafayát* has been edited with variants and indices by Wüstenfeld (Göttingen, 1835–1850). There is an excellent English translation by Baron MacGuckin de Slane in four volumes (1842–1871).

expected to revolutionise historical science, but neither was he himself capable of carrying them into effect nor, as the event proved, did they inspire his successors to abandon the path of tradition. I cannot imagine any more decisive symptom of the intellectual lethargy in which Islam was now sunk, or any clearer example of the rule that even the greatest writers struggle in vain against the spirit of their own times. There were plenty of learned men, however, who compiled local and universal histories. Considering the precious materials which their industry has preserved for us, we should rather admire these diligent and erudite authors than complain of their inability to break away from the established mode. Perhaps the most famous among them is Taqiyyu 'l-Dín al-Maqrízí (1364–1442 A.D.). A native of Cairo, he devoted himself to Egyptian history and antiquities, on which subject he composed several standard works, such as the *Khiṭaṭ*[1] and the *Sulúk*.[2] Although he was both unconscientious and uncritical, too often copying without acknowledgment or comment, and indulging in wholesale plagiarism when it suited his purpose, these faults which are characteristic of his age may easily be excused. "He has accumulated and reduced to a certain amount of order a large quantity of information that would but for him have passed into oblivion. He is generally painstaking and accurate, and always resorts to contemporary evidence if it is available. Also he has a pleasant and lucid style, and writes without bias and apparently with distinguished impartiality."[3] Other well-known works belonging to this

Maqrízí.

[1] The full title is *al-Mawá'iẓ wa-'l-I'tibár fí dhikri 'l-Khiṭaṭ wa-'l-Athár.* It was printed at Buláq in 1270 A.H.

[2] *Al-Sulúk li-ma'rifati Duwali 'l-Mulúk*, a history of the Ayyúbids and Mamelukes. The portion relating to the latter dynasty is accessible in the excellent French version by Quatremère (*Histoire des Sultans Mamlouks de l'Égypte*, Paris, 1845).

[3] A. R. Guest, *A List of Writers, Books, and other Authorities mentioned by El Maqrīzī in his Khiṭaṭ*, *J.R.A.S.* for 1902, p. 106.

epoch are the *Fakhrí* of Ibnu 'l-Ṭiqṭaqá, a delightful manual of Muḥammadan politics[1] which was written at Mosul in 1302 A.D.; the epitome of universal history by Abu 'l-Fidá, Prince of Ḥamát († 1331); the voluminous Chronicle of Islam by Dhahabí († 1348); the high-flown Biography of Tímúr entitled *'Ajá'ibu 'l-Maqdúr*, or 'Marvels of Destiny,' by Ibn 'Arabsháh († 1450); and the *Nujúm al-Záhira* ('Resplendent Stars') by Abu 'l-Maḥásin b. Taghríbirdí († 1469), which contains the annals of Egypt under the Moslems. The political and literary history of Muḥammadan Spain by Maqqarí of Tilimsán († 1632) was mentioned in the last chapter.[2]

Jalálu 'l-Dín al-Suyúṭí (1445-1505 A.D.).

If we were asked to select a single figure who should exhibit as completely as possible in his own person the literary tendencies of the Alexandrian age of Arabic civilisation, our choice would assuredly fall on Jalálu 'l-Dín al-Suyúṭí, who was born at Suyúṭ (Usyúṭ) in Upper Egypt in 1445 A.D. His family came originally from Persia, but, like Dhahabí, Ibn Taghríbirdí, and many celebrated writers of this time, he had, through his mother, an admixture of Turkish blood. At the age of five years and seven months, when his father died, the precocious boy had already reached the *Súratu 'l-Taḥrím* (Súra of Forbidding), which is the sixty-sixth chapter of the Koran, and he knew the whole volume by heart before he was eight years old. He prosecuted his studies under the most renowned masters in every branch of Moslem learning, and on finishing his education held one Professorship after another at Cairo until 1501, when he was deprived of his post in consequence of malversation of the bursary monies in his charge. He died

[1] The *Fakhrí* has been edited by Ahlwardt (1860) and Derenbourg (1895). The simplicity of its style and the varied interest of its contents have made it deservedly popular. Leaving the Koran out of account, I do not know any book that is better fitted to serve as an introduction to Arabic literature.

[2] See p. 413, n. 1.

four years later in the islet of Rawḍa on the Nile, whither he had retired under the pretence of devoting the rest of his life to God. We possess the titles of more than five hundred separate works which he composed. This number would be incredible but for the fact that many of them are brief pamphlets displaying the author's curious erudition on all sorts of abstruse subjects—*e.g.*, whether the Prophet wore trousers, whether his turban had a point, and whether his parents are in Hell or Paradise. Suyúṭí's indefatigable pen travelled over an immense field of knowledge—Koran, Tradition, Law, Philosophy and History, Philology and Rhetoric. Like some of the old Alexandrian scholars, he seems to have taken pride in a reputation for polygraphy, and his enemies declared that he made free with other men's books, which he used to alter slightly and then give out as his own. Suyúṭí, on his part, laid before the Shaykhu 'l-Islám a formal accusation of plagiarism against Qasṭallání, an eminent contemporary divine. We are told that his vanity and arrogance involved him in frequent quarrels, and that he was 'cut' by his learned brethren. Be this as it may, he saw what the public wanted. His compendious and readable handbooks were famed throughout the Moslem world, as he himself boasts, from India to Morocco, and did much to popularise the scientific culture of the day. It will be enough to mention here the *Itqán* on Koranic exegesis; the *Tafsíru 'l-Jalálayn*, or 'Commentary on the Koran by the two Jaláls,' which was begun by Jalálu 'l-Dín al-Maḥallí and finished by his namesake, Suyúṭí; the *Muzhir* (*Mizhar*), a treatise on philology; the *Ḥusnu 'l-Muḥáḍara*, a history of Old and New Cairo; and the *Ta'ríkhu 'l-Khulafá*, or 'History of the Caliphs.'

To dwell longer on the literature of this period would only be to emphasise its scholastic and unoriginal character. A passing mention, however, is due to the encyclopædists Nuwayrí (†1332), author of the *Nihdyatu 'l-Arab*, and Ibnu 'l-Wardí

(†1349). Ṣafadí (†1363) compiled a gigantic biographical dictionary, the *Wáfí bi 'l-Wafayát*, in twenty-six volumes, and the learned traditionist, Ibn Ḥajar of Ascalon (†1449), has left a large number of writings, among which it will be sufficient to name the *Iṣába fí tamyíz al-Ṣaḥába*, or Lives of the Companions of the Prophet.[1] We shall conclude this part of our subject by enumerating a few celebrated works which may be described in modern terms as standard text-books for the Schools and Universities of Islam. Amidst the host of manuals of Theology and Jurisprudence, with their endless array of abridgments, commentaries, and supercommentaries, possibly the best known to European students are those by Abu 'l-Barakát al-Nasafí (†1310), 'Aḍudu 'l-Dín al-Íjí (†1355), Sídí Khalíl al-Jundí (†1365), Taftázání (†1389), Sharíf al-Jurjání (†1413), and Muḥammad b. Yúsuf al-Sanúsí (†1486). For Philology and Lexicography we have the *Alfiyya*, a versified grammar by Ibn Málik of Jaen (†1273); the *Ájurrúmiyya* on the rudiments of grammar, an exceedingly popular compendium by Ṣanhájí (†1323); and two famous Arabic dictionaries, the *Lisánu 'l-'Arab* by Jamálu 'l-Dín Ibn Mukarram (†1311), and the *Qámús* by Fírúzábádí (†1414). Nor, although he was a Turk, should we leave unnoticed the great bibliographer Ḥájjí Khalífa (†1658), whose *Kashfu 'l-Ẓunún* contains the titles, arranged alphabetically, of all the Arabic, Persian, and Turkish books of which the existence was known to him.

Other scholars of the period.

The Mameluke period gave final shape to the *Alf Layla wa-Layla*, or 'Thousand and One Nights,' a work which is far more popular in Europe than the Koran or any other masterpiece of Arabic literature. The modern title, 'Arabian Nights,' tells only a part of the truth. Mas'údí (†956 A.D.) mentions

[1] *A Biographical Dictionary of Persons who knew Mohammad*, ed. by Sprenger and others (Calcutta, 1856–1873).

an old Persian book, the *Hazár Afsána* ('Thousand Tales') which "is generally called the Thousand and One Nights; it is the story of the King and his Vizier, and of the Vizier's daughter and her slave-girl: Shírázád and Dínázád."[1] The author of the *Fihrist*, writing in 988 A.D., begins his chapter "concerning the Story-Tellers and the Fabulists and the names of the books which they composed" with the following passage (p. 304):—

The 'Thousand and One Nights.'

"The first who composed fables and made books of them and put them by in treasuries and sometimes introduced animals as speaking them were the Ancient Persians. Afterwards the Parthian kings, who form the third dynasty of the kings of Persia, showed the utmost zeal in this matter. Then in the days of the Sásánian kings such books became numerous and abundant, and the Arabs translated them into the Arabic tongue, and they soon reached the hands of philologists and rhetoricians, who corrected and embellished them and composed other books in the same style. Now the first book ever made on this subject was the Book of the Thousand Tales (*Hazár Afsán*), on the following occasion: A certain king of Persia used to marry a woman for one night and kill her the next morning. And he wedded a wise and clever princess, called Shahrázád, who began to tell him stories and brought the tale at daybreak to a point that induced the king to spare her life and ask her on the second night to finish her tale. So she continued until a thousand nights had passed, and she was blessed with a son by him. . . . And the king had a stewardess (*qahramána*) named Dínárzád, who was in league with the queen. It is also said that this book was composed for Ḥumání, the daughter of Bahman, and there are various traditions concerning it. The truth, if God will, is that Alexander (the Great) was the first who heard stories by night, and he had people to make him laugh and divert him with tales; although he did not seek amusement therein, but only to store and preserve them (in his memory). The kings who came after him used the 'Thousand Tales' (*Hazár Afsán*) for this

Persian origin of the 'Thousand and One Nights.'

The *Hazár Afsán.*

[1] *Murúju 'l-Dhahab*, ed. by Barbier de Meynard, vol. iv. p. 90. The names Shírázád and Dínázád are obviously Persian. Probably the former is a corruption of Chihrázád, meaning 'of noble race,' while Dínázád signifies 'of noble religion.' My readers will easily recognise the familiar Scheherazade and Dinarzade.

purpose. It covers a space of one thousand nights, but contains less than two hundred stories, because the telling of a single story often takes several nights. I have seen the complete work more than once, and it is indeed a vulgar, insipid book (*kitáb^un ghathth^un báridu'l-ḥadíth*).[1]

Abú 'Abdalláh Muḥammad b. 'Abdús al-Jahshiyárí (†942–943 A.D.), the author of the 'Book of Viziers,' began to compile a book in which he selected one thousand stories of the Arabs, the Persians, the Greeks, and other peoples, every piece being independent and unconnected with the rest. He gathered the story-tellers round him and took from them the best of what they knew and were able to tell, and he chose out of the fable and story-books whatever pleased him. He was a skilful craftsman, so he put together from this material 480 nights, each night an entire story of fifty pages, more or less, but death surprised him before he completed the thousand tales as he had intended."

Different sources of the collection.

Evidently, then, the *Hazár Afsán* was the kernel of the 'Arabian Nights,' and it is probable that this Persian archetype included the most finely imaginative tales in the existing collection, *e.g.*, the 'Fisherman and the Genie,' 'Camaralzamán and Budúr,' and the 'Enchanted Horse.' As time went on, the original stock received large additions which may be divided into two principal groups, both Semitic in character : the one belonging to Baghdád and consisting mainly of humorous anecdotes and love romances in which the famous Caliph 'Haroun Alraschid' frequently comes on the scene ; the other having its centre in Cairo, and marked by a roguish, ironical pleasantry as well as by the mechanic supernaturalism which is perfectly illustrated in 'Aladdin and the Wonderful Lamp.' But, apart from these three sources, the 'Arabian Nights' has in the course of centuries accumulated and absorbed an immense number of Oriental folk-tales of every description, equally various in origin and style. The oldest translation by Galland (Paris, 1704–1717) is a charming

[1] Strange as it may seem, this criticism represents the view of nearly all Moslem scholars who have read the 'Arabian Nights.'

paraphrase, which in some respects is more true to the spirit of the original than are the scholarly renderings of Lane and Burton.

The 'Romance of 'Antar' (*Síratu 'Antar*) is traditionally ascribed to the great philologist, Aṣma'í,[1] who flourished in the reign of Hárún al-Rashíd, but this must be considered as an invention of the professional reciters who sit in front of Oriental cafés and entertain the public with their lively declamations.[2] According to Brockelmann, the work in its present form apparently dates from the time of the Crusades.[3] Its hero is the celebrated heathen poet and warrior, 'Antara b. Shaddád, of whom we have already given an account as author of one of the seven *Mu'allaqát*. Though the Romance exhibits all the anachronisms and exaggerations of popular legend, it does nevertheless portray the unchanging features of Bedouin life with admirable fidelity and picturesqueness. Von Hammer, whose notice in the *Mines de l'Orient* (1802) was the means of introducing the *Síratu 'Antar* to European readers, justly remarks that it cannot be translated in full owing to its portentous length. It exists in two recensions called respectively the Arabian (*Ḥijáziyya*) and the Syrian (*Shámiyya*), the latter being very much curtailed.[4]

The 'Romance of 'Antar.'

While the decadent state of Arabic literature during all

[1] Many episodes are related on the authority of Aṣma'í, Abú 'Ubayda, and Wahb b. Munabbih.

[2] Those who recite the *Síratu 'Antar* are named *'Anátira*, sing. *'Antarí*. See Lane's *Modern Egyptians*, ch. xxiii.

[3] That it was extant in some shape before 1150 A.D. seems to be beyond doubt. *Cf.* the *Journal Asiatique* for 1838, p. 383; Wüstenfeld, *Gesch. der Arab. Aerzte*, No. 172.

[4] *Antar, a Bedoueen Romance*, translated from the Arabic by Terrick Hamilton (London, 1820), vol. i, p. xxiii seq. See, however, Flügel's Catalogue of the Kais. Kön. Bibl. at Vienna, vol. ii, p. 6. Further details concerning the 'Romance of 'Antar' will be found in Thorbecke's *'Antarah* (Leipzig, 1867), p. 31 sqq. The whole work has been published at Cairo in thirty-two volumes.

these centuries was immediately caused by unfavourable social and political conditions, the real source of the malady lay deeper, and must, I think, be referred to the spiritual paralysis which had long been creeping over Islam and which manifested itself by the complete victory of the Ash'arites or Scholastic Theologians about 1200 A.D. Philosophy and Rationalism were henceforth as good as dead. Two parties remained in possession of the field —the orthodox and the mystics. The former were naturally intolerant of anything approaching to free-thought, and in their principle of *ijmá'*, *i.e.*, the consensus of public opinion (which was practically controlled by themselves), they found a potent weapon against heresy. How ruthlessly they sometimes used it we may see from the following passage in the *Yawáqít* of Sha'rání. After giving instances of the persecution to which the Ṣúfís of old—Báyazíd, Dhu 'l-Nún, and others—were subjected by their implacable enemies, the *'Ulamá*, he goes on to speak of what had happened more recently [1] :—

Orthodoxy and mysticism.

"They brought the Imám Abú Bakr al-Nábulusí, notwithstanding his merit and profound learning and rectitude in religion, from the Maghrib to Egypt and testified that he was a heretic (*zindíq*). The Sultan gave orders that he should be suspended by his feet and flayed alive. While the sentence was being carried out, he began to recite the Koran with such an attentive and humble demeanour that he moved the hearts of the people, and they were near making a riot. And likewise they caused Nasímí to be flayed at Aleppo.[2] When he silenced them by

Persecution of heretics.

---

[1] Sha'rání, *Yawáqít* (ed. of Cairo, 1277 A.H.), p. 18.

[2] In 1417 A.D. The reader will find a full and most interesting account of Nasímí, who is equally remarkable as a Turkish poet and as a mystic belonging to the sect of the Ḥurúfís, in Mr. E. J. W. Gibb's *History of Ottoman Poetry*, vol. i, pp. 343–368. It is highly improbable that the story related here gives the true ground on which he was condemned: his pantheistic utterances afford a sufficient explanation, and the Turkish biographer, Laṭífí, specifies the verse which cost him his life. I may add that the author of the *Shadharátu 'l-Dhahab* calls him Nasímu 'l-Dín of

his arguments, they devised a plan for his destruction, thus: They wrote the *Súratu 'l-Ikhláṣ*[1] on a piece of paper and bribed a cobbler of shoes, saying to him, 'It contains only love and pleasantness, so place it inside the sole of the shoe.' Then they took that shoe and sent it from a far distance as a gift to the Shaykh (Nasímí), who put it on, for he knew not. His adversaries went to the governor of Aleppo and said: 'We have sure information that Nasímí has written, *Say, God is One,* and has placed the writing in the sole of his shoe. If you do not believe us, send for him and see!' The governor did as they wished. On the production of the paper, the Shaykh resigned himself to the will of God and made no answer to the charge, knowing well that he would be killed on that pretext. I was told by one who studied under his disciples that all the time when he was being flayed Nasímí was reciting *muwashshaḥs* in praise of the Unity of God, until he composed five hundred verses, and that he was looking at his executioners and smiling. And likewise they brought Shaykh Abu 'l-Ḥasan al-Shádhilí[2] from the West to Egypt and bore witness that he was a heretic, but God delivered him from their plots. And they accused Shaykh 'Izzu 'l-Dín b. 'Abd al-Salám[3] of infidelity and sat in judgment over him on account of some expressions in his *'Aqída* (Articles of Faith) and urged the Sultan to punish him; afterwards, however, he was restored to favour. They denounced Shaykh Táju 'l-Dín al-Subkí[4] on the same charge, asserting that he held it lawful to drink wine and that he wore at night the badge (*ghiyár*) of the unbelievers and the zone (*zunnár*)[5]; and they brought him, manacled and in chains, from Syria to Egypt."

This picture is too highly coloured. It must be admitted for the credit of the *'Ulamá*, that they seldom resorted to violence. Islam was happily spared the horrors of an organised Inquisition. On the other hand, their authority was

Tabríz (he is generally said to be a native of Nasím in the district of Baghdád), and observes that he resided in Aleppo, where his followers were numerous and his heretical doctrines widely disseminated.

[1] The 112th chapter of the Koran. See p. 164.

[2] Founder of the Shádhiliyya Order of Dervishes. He died in 1258 A.D.

[3] A distinguished jurist and scholar who received the honorary title, 'Sultan of the Divines.' He died at Cairo in 1262 A.D.

[4] An eminent canon lawyer († 1370 A.D.).

[5] It was the custom of the Zoroastrians (and, according to Moslem belief, of the Christians and other infidels) to wear a girdle round the waist.

now so firmly established that all progress towards moral and intellectual liberty had apparently ceased, or at any rate only betrayed itself in spasmodic outbursts. Ṣúfiism in some degree represented such a movement, but the mystics shared the triumph of Scholasticism and contributed to the reaction which ensued. No longer an oppressed minority struggling for toleration, they found themselves side by side with reverend doctors on a platform broad enough to accommodate all parties, and they saw their own popular heroes turned into Saints of the orthodox Church. The compromise did not always work smoothly—in fact, there was continual friction—but on the whole it seems to have borne the strain wonderfully well. If pious souls were shocked by the lawlessness of the Dervishes, and if bigots would fain have burned the books of Ibnu 'l-'Arabí and Ibnu 'l-Fáriḍ, the divines in general showed a disposition to suspend judgment in matters touching holy men and to regard them as standing above human criticism.

As typical representatives of the religious life of this period we may take two men belonging to widely opposite camps—Taqiyyu 'l-Dín Ibn Taymiyya and 'Abdu 'l-Wahháb al-Sha'rání.

Ibn Taymiyya (1263—1328 A.D.).

Ibn Taymiyya was born at Ḥarrán in 1263 A.D. A few years later his father, fleeing before the Mongols, brought him to Damascus, where in due course he received an excellent education. It is said that he never forgot anything which he had once learned, and his knowledge of theology and law was so extensive as almost to justify the saying, "A tradition that Ibn Taymiyya does not recognise is no tradition." Himself a Ḥanbalite of the deepest dye—holding, in other words, that the Koran must be interpreted according to its letter and not by the light of reason—he devoted his life with rare courage to the work of religious reform. His aim, in short, was to restore the primitive monotheism taught by the Prophet and to purge Islam of the heresies and corruptions which threatened to destroy it. One may imagine what a hornet's nest he was attacking. Mystics, philosophers, and scholastic theologians, all fell alike under the lash of his denunciation. Bowing to no authority, but drawing his arguments from the traditions and practice of the early Church, he expressed his convictions in the most forcible terms, without regard to consequences. Although several times thrown into prison, he could not be muzzled for long. The climax was reached when he lifted up his voice against the superstitions of the popular faith—saint-worship, pilgrimage to holy shrines, vows, offerings, and invocations. These things, which the zealous puritan condemned as sheer idolatry, were part of a venerable cult that was hallowed by ancient custom, and had engrafted itself in luxuriant overgrowth upon Islam. The mass of Moslems believed, and still believe implicitly in the saints, accept their miracles, adore their relics, visit their tombs, and pray for their intercession. Ibn Taymiyya even declared that it was wrong to implore the aid of the Prophet or to make a pilgrimage to his sepulchre. It was a vain protest. He ended his days in captivity at Damascus. The vast crowds who attended his funeral—we are told that there were present 200,000 men and 15,000 women—bore witness to the profound respect which was universally felt for the intrepid reformer. Oddly enough, he was buried in the Cemetery of the Ṣúfís, whose doctrines he had so bitterly opposed, and the multitude revered his memory—as a saint! The principles which inspired Ibn Taymiyya did not fall to the ground, although their immediate effect was confined to a very small circle. We shall see them reappearing victoriously in the Wahhábite movement of the eighteenth century.

Notwithstanding the brilliant effort of Ghazálí to harmonise dogmatic theology with mysticism, it soon became clear that the two parties were in essence irreconcilable. The orthodox clergy who held fast by the authority of the Koran and the

Traditions saw a grave danger to themselves in the esoteric revelation which the mystics claimed to possess; while the latter, though externally conforming to the law of Islam, looked down with contempt on the idea that true knowledge of God could be derived from theology, or from any source except the inner light of heavenly inspiration. Hence the antithesis of *faqíh* (theologian) and *faqír* (dervish), the one class forming a powerful official hierarchy in close alliance with the Government, whereas the Ṣúfís found their chief support among the people at large, and especially among the poor. We need not dwell further on the natural antagonism which has always existed between these rival corporations, and which is a marked feature in the modern history of Islam. It will be more instructive to spend a few moments with the last great Muḥammadan theosophist, 'Abdu 'l-Wahháb al-Sha'rání, a man who, with all his weaknesses, was an original thinker, and exerted an influence strongly felt to this day, as is shown by the steady demand for his books. He was born about the beginning of the sixteenth century. Concerning his outward life we have little information beyond the facts that he was a weaver by trade and resided in Cairo. At this time Egypt was a province of the Ottoman Empire. Sha'rání contrasts the miserable lot of the peasantry under the new *régime* with their comparative prosperity under the Mamelukes. So terrible were the exactions of the tax-gatherers that the fellah was forced to sell the whole produce of his land, and sometimes even the ox which ploughed it, in order to save himself and his family from imprisonment; and every lucrative business was crushed by confiscation. It is not to be supposed, however, that Sha'rání gave serious attention to such sublunary matters. He lived in a world of visions and wonderful experiences. He conversed with angels and prophets, like his more famous predecessor, Muḥyi 'l-Dín Ibnu 'l-'Arabí, whose *Meccan Revelations* he studied and epitomised. His autobiography entitled *Laṭá'ifu 'l-Minan*

Sha'rání († 1565 A.D.).

displays the hierophant in full dress. It is a record of the singular spiritual gifts and virtues with which he was endowed, and would rank as a masterpiece of shameless self-laudation, did not the author repeatedly assure us that all his extraordinary qualities are Divine blessings and are gratefully set forth by their recipient *ad majorem Dei gloriam*. We should be treating Sha'rání very unfairly if we judged him by this work alone. The arrogant miracle-monger was one of the most learned men of his day, and could beat the scholastic theologians with their own weapons. Indeed, he regarded theology (*fiqh*) as the first step towards Ṣúfiism, and endeavoured to show that in reality they are different aspects of the same science. He also sought to harmonise the four great schools of law, whose disagreement was consecrated by the well-known saying ascribed to the Prophet: "The variance of my people is an act of Divine mercy" (*ikhtiláfu ummatí raḥmat*^{un}). Like the Arabian Ṣúfís generally, Sha'rání kept his mysticism within narrow bounds, and declared himself an adherent of the moderate section which follows Junayd of Baghdád († 909–910 A.D.). For all his extravagant pretensions and childish belief in the supernatural, he never lost touch with the Muḥammadan Church.

In the thirteenth century Ibn Taymiyya had tried to eradicate the abuses which obscured the simple creed of Islam. He failed, but his work was carried on by others and was crowned, after a long interval, by the Wahhábite Reformation.[1]

Muḥammad b. 'Abd al-Wahháb,[2] from whom its name is

[1] See *Materials for a History of the Wahabys*, by J. L. Burckhardt, published in the second volume of his *Notes on the Bedouins and Wahabys* (London, 1831). Burckhardt was in Arabia while the Turks were engaged in re-conquering the Ḥijáz from the Wahhábís. His graphic and highly interesting narrative has been summarised by Dozy, *Essai sur l'histoire de l'Islamisme*, ch. 13.

[2] Following Burckhardt's example, most European writers call him simply 'Abdu 'l-Wahháb.

derived, was born about 1720 A.D. in Najd, the Highlands of Arabia. In his youth he visited the principal cities of the East, "as is much the practice with his countrymen even now,"[1] and what he observed in the course of his travels convinced him that Islam was thoroughly corrupt. Fired by the example of Ibn Taymiyya, whose writings he copied with his own hand,[2] Ibn 'Abd al-Wahháb determined to re-establish the pure religion of Muḥammad in its primitive form. Accordingly he returned home and retired with his family to Ḍira'iyya at the time when Muḥammad b. Sa'úd was the chief personage of the town. This man became his first convert and soon after married his daughter. But it was not until the end of the eighteenth century that the Wahhábís, under 'Abdu 'l-'Azíz, son of Muḥammad b. Sa'úd, gained their first great successes. In 1801 they sacked Imám-Ḥusayn,[3] a town in the vicinity of Baghdád, massacred five thousand persons, and destroyed the cupola of Ḥusayn's tomb; the veneration paid by all Shí'ites to that shrine being, as Burckhardt says, a sufficient cause to attract the Wahhábí fury against it. Two years later they made themselves masters of the whole Ḥijáz, including Mecca and Medína. On the death of 'Abdu 'l-'Azíz, who was assassinated in the same year, his eldest son, Sa'úd, continued the work of conquest and brought the greater part of Arabia under Wahhábite rule. At last, in 1811, Turkey despatched a fleet and army to recover the Holy Cities. This task was accomplished by Muḥammad 'Alí, the Pasha of Egypt (1812–13), and after five years' hard fighting the war ended in favour of the Turks, who in 1818 inflicted a severe defeat on the Wahhábís and took their capital, Ḍira'iyya, by storm. The sect, however, still maintains

Muḥammad b. 'Abd al-Wahháb and his successors.

[1] Burckhardt, *op. cit.*, vol. ii, p. 96.

[2] MSS. of Ibn Taymiyya copied by Ibn 'Abd al-Wahháb are extant (Goldziher in *Z.D.M.G.*, vol. 52, p. 156).

[3] This is the place usually called Karbalá or Mashhad Ḥusayn.

its power in Central Arabia, and in recent times has acquired political importance.

The Wahhábís were regarded by the Turks as infidels and authors of a new religion. It was natural that they should appear in this light, for they interrupted the pilgrim-caravans, demolished the domes and ornamented tombs of the most venerable Saints (not excepting that of the Prophet himself), and broke to pieces the Black Stone in the Ka'ba. All this they did not as innovators, but as reformers. They resembled the Carmathians only in their acts. Burckhardt says very truly: "Not a single new precept was to be found in the Wahaby code. Abd el Waháb took as his sole guide the Koran and the Sunne (or the laws formed upon the traditions of Mohammed); and the only difference between his sect and the orthodox Turks, however improperly so termed, is, that the Wahabys rigidly follow the same laws which the others neglect, or have ceased altogether to observe."[1] "The Wahhábites," says Dozy, "attacked the idolatrous worship of Mahomet; although he was in their eyes a Prophet sent to declare the will of God, he was no less a man like others, and his mortal shell, far from having mounted to heaven, rested in the tomb at Medína. Saint-worship they combated just as strongly. They proclaimed that all men are equal before God; that even the most virtuous and devout cannot intercede with Him; and that, consequently, it is a sin to invoke the Saints and to adore their relics."[2] In the same puritan spirit they forbade the smoking of tobacco, the wearing of gaudy robes, and praying over the rosary. "It has been stated that they likewise prohibited the drinking of coffee; this, however, is not the fact: they have always used it to an immoderate degree."[3]

The Wahhábite Reformation.

The Wahhábite movement has been compared with the

[1] *Op. cit.*, vol. ii, p. 112.

[2] *Essai sur l'histoire de l'Islamisme*, p. 416.

[3] Burckhardt, *loc. laud.*, p. 115.

Protestant Reformation in Europe; but while the latter was followed by the English and French Revolutions, the former has not yet produced any great political results. It has borne fruit in a general religious revival throughout the world of Islam and particularly in the mysterious Sanúsiyya Brotherhood, whose influence is supreme in Tripoli, the Sahara, and the whole North African Hinterland, and whose members are reckoned by millions. Muḥammad b. 'Alí b. Sanúsí, the founder of this vast and formidable organisation, was born at Algiers in 1791, lived for many years at Mecca, and died at Jaghbúb in the Libyan desert, midway between Egypt and Tripoli, in 1859. Concerning the real aims of the Sanúsís I must refer the reader to an interesting paper by the Rev. E. Sell (*Essays on Islam*, p. 127 sqq.). There is no doubt that they are utterly opposed to all Western and modern civilisation, and seek to regenerate Islam by establishing an independent theocratic State on the model of that which the Prophet and his successors called into being at Medína in the seventh century after Christ.

The Sanúsís in Africa.

Since Napoleon showed the way by his expedition to Egypt in 1798, the Moslems in that country, as likewise in Syria and North Africa, have come more and more under European influence.[1] The above-mentioned Muḥammad 'Alí, who founded the Khedivial dynasty, and his successors were fully alive to the practical benefits which might be obtained from the superior culture of the West, and although their policy in this respect was marked by greater zeal than discretion, they did not exert themselves altogether in vain. The introduction of the printing-press in 1821 was an epoch-making measure. If, on the one hand, the publication of

Islam and modern civilisation.

[1] I cannot enter into details on this subject. A review of modern Arabic literature is given by Brockelmann, *Gesch. der Arab. Litt.*, vol. ii, pp. 469–511, and by Huart, *Arabic Literature*, pp. 411–443.

many classical works, which had well-nigh fallen into oblivion, rekindled the enthusiasm of the Arabs for their national literature, the cause of progress—I use the word without prejudice—has been furthered by the numerous political, literary, and scientific journals which are now regularly issued in every country where Arabic is spoken.[1] Besides these ephemeral sheets, books of all sorts, old and new, have been multiplied by the native and European presses of Cairo, Búláq, and Beyrout. The science and culture of Europe have been rendered accessible in translations and adaptations of which the complete list would form a volume in itself. Thus, an Arab may read in his own language the tragedies of Racine, the comedies of Molière,[2] the fables of La Fontaine, 'Paul and Virginia,' the 'Talisman,' 'Monte Cristo' (not to mention scores of minor romances), and even the Iliad of Homer.[3] Parallel to this imitative activity, we see a vigorous and growing movement away from the literary models of the past. "Neo-Arabic literature is only to a limited extent the heir of the old 'classical' Arabic literature, and even shows a tendency to repudiate its inheritance entirely. Its leaders are for the most part men who have drunk from other springs and look at the world with different eyes. Yet the past still plays a part in their intellectual background, and there is a section amongst them upon whom that past retains a hold scarcely shaken by newer influences. For many decades the partisans of the 'old' and the 'new' have engaged in a struggle for the soul of the Arabic world, a struggle in which the victory of one side over the other is even yet not assured. The protagonists are (to classify them roughly for practical purposes) the European-educated classes of Egyptians and Syrians on the one hand, and those in Egypt and the less advanced Arabic lands whose education has followed traditional

[1] See M. Hartmann, *The Arabic Press of Egypt* (London, 1899).

[2] Brockelmann, *loc. cit.*, p. 476.

[3] Translated into Arabic verse by Sulaymán al-Bistání (Cairo, 1904). See Professor Margoliouth's interesting notice of this work in the *J.R.A.S.* for 1905, p. 417 sqq.

lines on the other. Whatever the ultimate result may be, there can be no question that the conflict has torn the Arabic world from its ancient moorings, and that the contemporary literature of Egypt and Syria breathes in its more recent developments a spirit foreign to the old traditions."[1]

Hitherto Western culture has only touched the surface of Islam. Whether it will eventually strike deeper and penetrate the inmost barriers of that scholastic discipline and literary tradition which are so firmly rooted in the affections of the Moslem peoples, or whether it will always remain an exotic and highly-prized accomplishment of the enlightened and emancipated few, but an object of scorn and detestation to Muḥammadans in general—these are questions that may not be fully solved for centuries to come.

Meanwhile the Past affords an ample and splendid field of study.

"*Man lam ya'i 'l-ta'ríkha fí ṣadrihí*
Lam yadri ḥulwa 'l-'ayshi min murrihí
Wa-man wa'á akhbára man qad maḍá
Aḍáfa a'már^an^ *ilá 'umrihí.*"

"He in whose heart no History is enscrolled
Cannot discern in life's alloy the gold.
But he that keeps the records of the Dead
Adds to his life new lives a hundredfold."

[1] H. A. R. Gibb, *Studies in contemporary Arabic literature*, Bulletin of the School of Oriental Studies, vol. iv, pt. 4, p. 746; cf. also vol. v, pt. 2, p. 311 foll. Mr Gibb has given references to the chief works on the subject, but for the sake of those who do not read Arabic or Russian it may be hoped that he will continue and complete his own survey, to which there is nothing *simile aut secundum* in English.

APPENDIX

P. xxii, l. 2. Arabic begins to appear in North Arabian inscriptions in the third century A.D. Perhaps the oldest yet discovered is one, of which the probable date is 268 A.D., published by Jaussen and Savignac (*Mission archéologique en l'Arabie*, vol. i, p. 172). Though it is written in Aramaic characters, nearly all the words are Arabic, as may be seen from the transcription given by Professor Horovitz in *Islamic Culture* (Hyderabad, Deccan), April 1929, vol. iii, No. 2, p. 169, note 2.

P. 4 foll. Concerning the Sabaeans and the South Arabic inscriptions a great deal of valuable information will be found in the article *Saba'* by J. Tkatsch in the *Encyclopædia of Islam*. The writer points out the special importance of the epigraphic discoveries of E. Glaser, who, in the course of four journeys (1882–94), collected over 2000 inscriptions. See also D. Nielsen, *Handbuch der altarabischen Altertumskunde*, vol. i (Copenhagen and Paris, 1927).

P. 13, note 2. Excerpts from the *Shamsu 'l-'Ulúm* relating to South Arabia have been edited by Dr 'Azímu'ddín Aḥmad (E. J. W. Gibb Memorial Series, vol. xxiv).

P. 26 foll. For contemporary and later Christian accounts of the martyrdom of the Christians of Najrán, see the fragmentary *Book of the Himyarites* (Syriac text and English translation), ed. by A. Moberg in 1924, and cf. Tor Andrae, *Der Ursprung des Islams und das Christentum* (Uppsala, 1926), pp. 10–13.

P. 31. The collection of Arabic proverbs, entitled *Kitábu 'l-Fákhir*, by Mufaḍḍal b. Salama of Kúfa, is now available in the excellent edition of Mr C. A. Storey (Leyden, 1915).

P. 32, note 1. An edition of the *Aghání* with critical notes is in course of publication at Cairo.

P. 52, l. 9 foll. The battle mentioned here cannot be the battle of 'Ayn Ubágh, which took place between Ḥárith, the son of Ḥárith b. Jabala, and Mundhir IV of Ḥíra about 583 A.D. (Guidi, *L'Arabie antéislamique*, p. 27).

P. 127, l. 16. The ode *Bánat Su'ád* is rendered into English in my *Translations of Eastern Poetry and Prose*, pp. 19–23.

P. 133. As regards the authenticity of the Pre-islamic poems which have come down to us, the observations of one of the greatest authorities on the subject, the late Sir Charles J. Lyall, seem to me to be eminently judicious (Introduction to the

Mufaḍḍalīyāt, vol. ii, pp. xvi–xxvi). He concludes that "upon the whole, the impression which a close study of these ancient relics gives is that we must take them, generally speaking, as the production of the men whose names they bear." All that can be urged against this view has been said with his usual learning by Professor Margoliouth (*The Origins of Arabic Poetry, J.R.A.S.*, 1925, p. 417 foll.).

P. 145, l. 2. The oldest extant commentary on the Koran is that of Bukhárí in ch. 65 of the *Ṣaḥíḥ*, ed. Krehl, vol. iii, pp. 193–390.

P. 146, note 2. Recent investigators (Caetani and Lammens) are far more sceptical. Cf. Snouck Hurgronje, *Mohammedanism*, p. 22 foll.

P. 152, note 5. As suggested by Mr Richard Bell (*The Origin of Islam in its Christian environment*, p. 88), the word *rujz* is in all likelihood identical with the Syriac *rugza*, wrath, so that this verse of the Koran means, "Flee from the wrath to come."

P. 170, l. 2 foll. This is one of the passages I should have liked to omit. Even in its present form, it maintains a standpoint which I have long regarded as mistaken.

P. 184, l. 4 foll. Professor Snouck Hurgronje (*Mohammedanism*, p. 44) asks, "Was Mohammed conscious of the universality of his mission?" and decides that he was not. I now agree that "in the beginning he conceived his work as merely the Arabian part of a universal task"—in which case *dhikr*[un] *li 'l-'álamín* in the passage quoted will mean "a warning to all the people (of Mecca or Arabia)." But similar expressions in Súras of the Medina period carry, I think, a wider significance. The conception of Islam as a world-religion is implied in Mohammed's later belief—he only came to it gradually—that the Jewish and Christian scriptures are corrupt and that the Koran alone represents the original Faith which had been preached in turn by all the prophets before him. And having arrived at that conviction, he was not the man to leave others to act upon it.

P. 223, l. 9. In an article which appeared in the *Rivista degli studi orientali*, 1916, p. 429 foll., Professor C. A. Nallino has shown that this account of the origin of the name "Mu'tazilite" is erroneous. The word, as Mas'údí says (*Murúju 'l-Dhahab*, vol. vi, p. 22, and vol. vii, p. 234), is derived from *i'tizál*, *i.e.* the doctrine that anyone who commits a capital sin has thereby withdrawn himself (*i'tazala*) from the true believers and taken a position (described as *fisq*, impiety) midway between them and the infidels. According to the Murjites, such a person was still a true believer, while their opponents, the Wa'ídites, and also the Khárijites, held him to be an unbeliever.

P. 225, l. 1. The Ḥadíth, "No monkery (*rahbániyya*) in Islam," probably dates from the third century of the Hijra. According to the usual interpretation of Koran, LVII, 27, the *rahbániyya* practised by Christian ascetics is condemned as an innovation not authorised by divine ordinance; but Professor Massignon (*Essai sur les origines du lexique technique de la mystique musulmane*, p. 123 foll.) shows that by some of the early Moslem commentators and also by the Ṣúfís of the third century A.H. this verse of the Koran was taken as justifying and commending those Christians who devoted themselves to the ascetic life, except in so far as they had neglected to fulfil its obligations.

P. 225, l. 6 from foot. For the life and doctrines of Ḥasan of Baṣra, see Massignon, *op. cit.*, p. 152 foll.

P. 228 foll. It can now be stated with certainty that the name "Ṣúfí" originated in Kúfa in the second century A.H. and was at first confined to the mystics of 'Iráq. Hence the earliest development of Ṣúfiism, properly so called, took place in a hotbed of Shí'ite and Hellenistic (Christian and Gnostic) ideas.

P. 233, l. 4 from foot. In *Rābi'a the Mystic* (Cambridge, 1928) Miss Margaret Smith has given a scholarly and sympathetic account of the life, legend, and teaching of this celebrated woman-saint. The statement that she died and was buried at Jerusalem is incorrect. Moslem writers have confused her with an earlier saint of the same name, Rábi'a bint Ismá'íl († 135).

P. 313 foll. The text and translation of 332 extracts from the *Luzúmiyyát* will be found in ch. ii of my *Studies in Islamic Poetry*, pp. 43–289.

P. 318, l. 12. Since there is no warrant for the antithesis of "knaves" and "fools," these verses are more faithfully rendered (*op. cit.*, p. 167):

They all err—Moslems, Christians, Jews, and Magians;
Two make Humanity's universal sect:
One man intelligent without religion,
And one religious without intellect.

P. 318, l. 7 from foot. *Al-Fuṣúl wa 'l-Ghäyát.* No copy of this work was known before 1919, when the discovery of the first part of it was announced (*J.R.A.S.*, 1919, p. 449).

P. 318, note 2. An edition of the *Risálatu 'l-Ghufrán* by Shaykh Ibráhím al-Yáziji was published at Cairo in 1907.

P. 319, l. 6. The epistle of 'Alí b. Manṣúr al-Ḥalabí (Ibnu 'l-Qáriḥ), to which the *Risálatu 'l-Ghufrán* is the reply, has been published in *Rasá'ilu 'l-Bulaghá*, ed. Muḥammad Kurd 'Alí (Cairo, 1913).

P. 332, note 2. For rhymed prose renderings of the 11th and 12th *Maqámas*, see *Translations of Eastern Poetry and Prose*, pp. 116–124.

P. 367, l. 7 from foot. New light has recently been thrown upon the character of the Mu'tazilite movement by the publication of the Mu'tazilite al-Khayyáṭ's *Kitábu 'l-Intiṣár* (ed. H. S. Nyberg, Cairo, 1926), a third (ninth) century polemical work directed against the Shí'ite freethinker Ibnu 'l-Ráwandí (cf. p. 375 *supra*). It is now evident that this "heretical" sect played an active part as champions of Islam, not only in the early controversies which arose between Moslems and Christians in Syria but also against the more dangerous attacks which proceeded in the first hundred years of the 'Abbásid period from the Manichæans and other "*zanádiqa*" in Persia and especially in 'Iráq (cf. I. Guidi, *La Lotta tra l'Islam e il Manicheismo* (Rome, 1927)). In order to meet these adversaries on equal terms, the Mu'tazilites made themselves acquainted with Greek philosophy and logic, and thus laid the foundations of an Islamic scholasticism. Cf. H. H. Schaeder, *Der Orient und die Griechische Erbe* in W. Jaeger's *Die Antike*, vol. iv, p. 261 foll.

P. 370, l. 3 foll. From what has been said in the preceding note it follows that this view of the relation between the Mu'tazilites and the *Ikhwánu 'l-Ṣafá* requires considerable modification. Although, in contrast to their orthodox opponents, the Mu'tazilites may be described as "rationalists" and "liberal theologians," their principles were entirely opposed to the anti-Islamic eclecticism of the *Ikhwán*.

P. 375, note 2. Professor Schaeder thinks that Middle Persian *zandík* has nothing to do with the Aramaic *zaddíq* (*Z.D.M.G.*, vol. 82, Heft 3–4, p. lxxx).

Pp. 383–393. During the last twenty years our knowledge of early Ṣúfiism has increased, chiefly through the profound researches of Professor Massignon, to such an extent as to render the account given in these pages altogether inadequate. The subject being one of great difficulty and unsuitable for detailed exposition in a book of this kind, I must content myself with a few illustrative remarks and references, which will enable the student to obtain further information.

P. 383. Massignon's view is that Ṣúfiism (down to the fourth century A.H.) owed little to foreign influences and was fundamentally Islamic, a product of intensive study of the Koran and of inward meditation on its meaning and essential nature. There is great force in his argument, though I cannot help believing that the development of mysticism, like that of other contemporary branches of Moslem thought, must have been vitally affected by contact with the ancient Hellenistic culture of the Sásánian and Byzantine empires on its native soil. Cf. A. J. Wensinck, *The Book of the Dove* (Leyden, 1919) and *Mystic Treatises by Isaac of Niniveh* (Amsterdam, 1923).

P. 384, l. 1. The identity of third-century Ṣúfiism with the doctrines of the Vedanta is maintained by M. Horten (*Indische Strömungen in der Islamischen Mystik*, Heidelberg, 1927–8). Few, however, would admit this. The conversion of Ṣúfiism into a monistic philosophy was the work of Ibnu 'l-'Arabí (1165–1240 A.D.). See p. 402 foll.

P. 384, l. 5. The so-called "Theology of Aristotle," translated from Syriac into Arabic about 830 A.D., is mainly an abstract of the *Enneads* of Plotinus. There is an edition with German translation by Dieterici.

P. 385, l. 11. All previous accounts of the development of mystical doctrines in Islam during the first three centuries after the Hijra have been superseded by Massignon's intimate analysis (*Essai*, chs. iv and v, pp. 116–286), which includes biographies of the eminent Ṣúfís of that period and is based upon an amazingly wide knowledge of original and mostly unpublished sources of information. A useful summary of these two chapters is given by Father Joseph Maréchal in his *Studies in the Psychology of the Mystics*, tr. Thorold (1927), pp. 241–9.

P. 386, l. 6 from foot. For Dhu 'l-Nún, see Massignon, *op. cit.*, p. 184 foll.

P. 389, l. 12. *The Book of the Holy Hierotheos* has recently been edited in Syriac for the first time, with English translation, by F. S. Marsh (Text and Translation Society, 1927).

P. 391. For Báyazíd of Bisṭám, see Massignon, *op. cit.*, p. 243 foll. The oldest complete Arabic version of his "Ascension" (*Mi'ráj*)—a spiritual dream-experience—has been edited and translated into English in *Islamica*, vol. ii, fasc. 3, p. 402 foll.

P. 396, l. 8. See my essay on the Odes of Ibnu 'l-Fáriḍ (*Studies in Islamic Mysticism*, pp. 162–266), which comprises translations of the *Khamriyya* and three-fourths of the *Tá'iyyatu 'l-Kubrá*.

P. 399, note 1. With Ḥalláj, thanks to the monumental work of Massignon (*La Passion d'al-Ḥalláj*, 2 vols., Paris, 1922), we are now better acquainted than with any other Moslem mystic. His doctrine exhibits some remarkable affinities with Christianity and bears no traces of the pantheism attributed to him by later Ṣúfís as well as by Von Kremer and subsequent European writers. Cf. the summary given by Father Joseph Maréchal, *op. cit.*, pp. 249–281, and *The Idea of Personality in Ṣúfism* (Cambridge, 1922), pp. 26–37.

P. 402, l. 9. For Ibnu 'l-'Arabí's theory of the Perfect Man, see Tor Andrae, *Die Person Muhammeds*, p. 339 foll., and for the same theory as expounded by 'Abdu 'l-Karím al-Jílí († circ. 1410 A.D.), a follower of Ibnu 'l-'Arabí, in his famous treatise entitled *al-Insán al-Kámil*, cf. *Studies in Islamic Mysticism*, pp. 77–142.

P. 456, l. 1 foll. Here, though he is out of place in such an academic company, mention should have been made of Ibn Baṭṭúṭa of Tangier († 1377), whose frank and entertaining story of his almost world-wide travels, entitled *Tuḥfatu 'l-Nuẓẓár*, is described by its latest translator, Mr H. A. R. Gibb, as "an authority for the social and cultural history of post-Mongol Islam."

P. 465, last line. For a summary of the doctrines and history of the Wahhábís, see the article *Wahhābīs* by Professor D. S. Margoliouth in Hastings' *Encyclopædia of Religion and Ethics*.

P. 469. *La littérature arabe au xix*ᵉ *siècle*, by L. Cheikho (Beyrouth, 1908–10), which deals chiefly with the literature produced by the Christian Arabs of Syria, deserves mention as one of the few works on the subject written in a European language. The influence of Western ideas on Moslem theology may be studied in the *Risálatu 'l-tauḥíd* of the great Egyptian divine, Muḥammad 'Abduh (1842–1905), which has been translated into French by B. Michel and Mustapha 'Abd el Razik (Paris, 1925).

BIBLIOGRAPHY OF WORKS BY EUROPEAN AUTHORS

THE following list is intended to give students of Arabic as well as those who cannot read that language the means of obtaining further information concerning the various topics which fall within the scope of a work such as this. Since anything approaching to a complete bibliography is out of the question, I have mentioned only a few of the most important translations from Arabic into English, French, German, and Latin; and I have omitted (1) monographs on particular Arabic writers, whose names, together with the principal European works relating to them, will be found in Brockelmann's great History of Arabic Literature, and (2) a large number of books and articles which appeal to specialists rather than to students. Additional information is supplied by E. G. Browne in his *Literary History of Persia*, vol. i, pp. 481–496, and D. B. Macdonald in his *Development of Muslim Theology, etc.* (London, 1903), pp. 358–367, while the Appendix to H. A. R. Gibb's *Arabic Literature* (Oxford University Press, 1926) contains a well-chosen list of books of reference and translations. Those who require more detailed references may consult the *Bibliographie des ouvrages arabes ou relatifs aux Arabes publ. dans l'Europe chrétienne de* 1810 *à* 1885, by V. Chauvin (Liège, 1892–1903), the *Orientalische Bibliographie*, edited by A. Müller, E. Kuhn, and L. Scherman (Berlin, 1887—), the *Handbuch der Islam-Litteratur*, by D. G. Pfannmüller (Berlin and Leipzig, 1923), and the *Catalogue of the Arabic Books in the British Museum*, by A. G. Ellis, 2 vols. (London, 1894–1902) with the *Supplementary Catalogue*, by A. S. Fulton and A. G. Ellis (London, 1926).

As a rule, titles of monographs and works of a specialistic character which have been already given in the footnotes are not repeated in the Bibliography.

I

PHILOLOGY.

1. *Die Semitischen Sprachen*, by Th. Nöldeke (2nd ed. Leipzig, 1899).

An improved and enlarged reprint of the German original of his article, 'Semitic Languages,' in the *Encyclopædia Britannica* (9th edition).

2. *A Grammar of the Arabic Language*, by W. Wright, 3rd ed., revised by W. Robertson Smith and M. J. de Goeje, 2 vols. (Cambridge, 1896–98).

The best Arabic grammar for advanced students. Beginners may prefer to use the abridgment by F. du Pre Thornton, *Elementary Arabic: a Grammar* (Cambridge University Press, 1905).

3. *Arabic-English Lexicon*, by E. W. Lane, 8 parts (London, 1863–93).

This monumental work is unfortunately incomplete. Among other lexica those of Freytag (Arabic and Latin, 4 vols, Halle, 1830–37), A. de Biberstein Kazimirski (Arabic and French, 2 vols., Paris, 1846–60, and 4 vols., Cairo, 1875), and Dozy's *Supplément aux Dictionnaires arabes*, 2 vols. (Leyden, 1881), deserve special notice. Smaller dictionaries, sufficient for ordinary purposes, have been compiled by Belot (*Dictionnaire arabe-français*, Beyrout, 1928), and Wortabet and Porter (*Arabic-English Dictionary*, 3rd ed., Beyrout, 1913).

4. *Abhandlungen zur Arabischen Philologie*, by Ignaz Goldziher, Part I (Leyden, 1896).

Contains masterly studies on the origins of Arabic Poetry and other matters connected with literary history.

5. *Die Rhetorik der Araber*, by A. F. Mehren (Copenhagen, 1853).

II

GENERAL WORKS ON ARABIAN HISTORY, BIOGRAPHY, GEOGRAPHY, LITERATURE, ETC.

6. *The Encyclopædia of Islam* (Leyden, 1913—).

A great number of Orientalists have contributed to this invaluable work, of which the first half (A–L) is now completed.

7. *Chronique de Ṭabarí, traduite sur la version persane de... Bel'amí*, by H. Zotenberg, 4 vols. (Paris, 1867–74).

8. The *Murúju 'l-Dhahab* of Mas'údí (*Maçoudi: Les Prairies d'Or*), Arabic text with French translation by Barbier de Meynard and Pavet de Courteille, 9 vols. (Paris, 1861–77).

The works of Ṭabarí and Mas'údí are the most ancient and celebrated Universal Histories in the Arabic language.

9. *Abulfedæ Annales Muslemici arabice et latine*, by J. J. Reiske, 5 vols. (Hafniæ, 1789–94).

10. *Der Islam im Morgen- und Abendland*, by August Müller, 2 vols. (Berlin, 1885–87).

11. *Histoire des Arabes*, by C. Huart, 2 vols. (Paris, 1912).
12. *A Short History of the Saracens*, by Syed Ameer Ali (London, 1921).
13. *Essai sur l'histoire de l'Islamisme*, by R. Dozy, translated from the Dutch by Victor Chauvin (Leyden and Paris, 1879).
14. *The Preaching of Islam, a History of the Propagation of the Muslim Faith*, by T. W. Arnold (2nd ed., London, 1913).
15. *Sketches from Eastern History*, by Th. Nöldeke, translated by J. S. Black (London, 1892).
16. *The Mohammadan Dynasties*, by Stanley Lane-Poole (London, 1894).
    Indispensable to the student of Moslem history.
17. *Genealogische Tabellen der Arabischen Stämme und Familien mit historischen und geographischen Bemerkungen in einem alphabetischen Register*, by F. Wüstenfeld (Göttingen, 1852–53).
18. *Ibn Khallikán's Biographical Dictionary*, translated from the Arabic by Baron MacGuckin de Slane, 4 vols. (Oriental Translation Fund, 1842–71).
    One of the most characteristic, instructive, and interesting books in Arabic literature.
19. *Géographie d'Aboulféda, traduite de l'arabe*, by Reinaud and Guyard, 2 vols. (Paris, 1848–83).
20. *Travels in Arabia Deserta*, by C. M. Doughty, 2 vols. (Cambridge, 1888).
    Gives a true and vivid picture of Bedouin life and manners.
21. *Personal Narrative of a Pilgrimage to al-Madinah and Meccah*, by Sir R. F. Burton, 2 vols. (London, 1898).
22. *The Penetration of Arabia: a record of the development of Western knowledge concerning the Arabian Peninsula*, by D. G. Hogarth (London, 1905).
23. Ḥájjí Khalífa, *Lexicon bibliographicum et encyclopædicum*, Arabic text and Latin translation, by G. Flügel, 7 vols. (Leipzig and London, 1835–58).
24. *Die Geschichtschreiber der Araber und ihre Werke* (aus dem xxviii. und xxix. Bande der Abhand. d. Königl. Ges. d. Wiss. zu Göttingen), by F. Wüstenfeld (Göttingen, 1882).
25. *Litteraturgeschichte der Araber bis zum Ende des 12. Jahrhunderts der Hidschret*, by J. von Hammer-Purgstall, 7 vols. (Vienna, 1850–56).
    A work of immense extent, but unscientific and extremely inaccurate.
26. *Geschichte der Arabischen Litteratur*, by Carl Brockelmann, 2 vols. (Weimar, 1898–1902).
    Invaluable for bibliography and biography.

27. *A Literary History of Persia*, by E. G. Browne, vol. i from the earliest times to Firdawsí (London, 1902), and vol. ii down to the Mongol Invasion (London, 1906).
The first volume in particular of this well-known work contains much information concerning the literary history of the Arabs.
28. *A History of Arabic Literature*, by Clément Huart (London, 1903).
The student will find this manual useful for purposes of reference.
29. *Arabic Literature: an Introduction*, by H. A. R. Gibb (London, 1926).
A trustworthy outline of the subject.
30. *Arabum Proverbia*, Arabic text with Latin translation, by G. W. Freytag, 3 vols. (Bonn, 1838–43).
31. *Arabic Proverbs*, by J. L. Burckhardt (2nd ed., London, 1875).

III

PRE-ISLAMIC HISTORY, LITERATURE, AND RELIGION.

32. *Essai sur l'histoire des Arabes avant l'Islamisme*, by A. P. Caussin de Perceval, 3 vols. (Paris, 1847–48).
Affords an excellent survey of Pre-islamic legend and tradition.
33. *Geschichte der Perser und Araber zur Zeit der Sasaniden*, translated from the Annals of Ṭabarí, by Th. Nöldeke (Leyden, 1879).
The ample commentary accompanying the translation is valuable and important in the highest degree.
34. *Fünf Mo'allaqât übersetzt und erklärt*, by Th. Nöldeke (Vienna, 1899–1901).
The omitted *Mu'allaqas* are those of Imru'u 'l-Qays and Ṭarafa.
35. *The Seven Golden Odes of Pagan Arabia*, translated from the original Arabic by Lady Anne Blunt and done into English verse by Wilfrid Scawen Blunt (London, 1903).
36. *Hamâsa oder die ältesten arabischen Volkslieder übersetzt und erläutert*, by Friedrich Rückert, 2 vols. (Stuttgart, 1846).
Masterly verse-translations of the old Arabian poetry.
37. *Translations of ancient Arabian poetry, chiefly Pre-islamic*, with an introduction and notes, by C. J. Lyall (London, 1885).
38. *Beiträge zur Kenntniss der Poesie der alten Araber*, by Th. Nöldeke (Hannover, 1864).

39. *Studien in arabischen Dichtern*, Heft iii, *Altarabisches Beduinenleben nach den Quellen geschildert*, by G. Jacob (Berlin, 1897).
40. *Kinship and Marriage in Early Arabia*, by W. Robertson Smith (2nd ed., London, 1903).
41. *Lectures on the Religion of the Semites*, First Series, by W. Robertson Smith, 3rd ed., revised by S. A. Cook (London, 1927).
42. *Reste Arabischen Heidentums*, by J. Wellhausen (2nd ed., Berlin, 1897).

IV

MUḤAMMAD AND THE KORAN.

43. *Das Leben Mohammed's*, translated from the Arabic biography of Ibn Hishám by G. Weil, 2 vols. (Stuttgart, 1864).
44. *Muhammed in Medina*, by J. Wellhausen (Berlin, 1882).
An abridged translation of Wáqidí's work on Muḥammad's Campaigns.
45. *Das Leben und die Lehre des Moḥammad*, by A. Sprenger, 3 vols. (Berlin, 1861–65).
46. *Life of Mahomet*, by Sir W. Muir, ed. by T. H. Weir (Edinburgh, 1923).
47. *Das Leben Muhammed's nach den Quellen populär dargestellt*, by Th. Nöldeke (Hannover, 1863).
48. *The Spirit of Islam*, by Syed Ameer Ali (London, 1922).
49. *Mohammed*, by H. Grimme, 2 vols. (Münster, 1892–95).
50. *Die weltgeschichtliche Bedeutung Arabiens: Mohammed*, by H. Grimme (Munich, 1904).
51. *Mohammed and the Rise of Islam*, by D. S. Margoliouth in 'Heroes of the Nations' Series (London and New York, 1905).
52. *Mohammed and Islam*, by A. A. Bevan in *The Cambridge Mediæval History*, vol. ii, ch. 10 (Cambridge, 1913).
53. *Die Person Muhammeds in Lehre und Glauben seiner Gemeinde*, by Tor Andrae (Uppsala, 1918).
54. *The origin of Islam in its Christian environment*, by R. Bell (London, 1926).
55. *Annali dell' Islām*, by Leone Caetani, Principe di Teano, vol. i (Milan, 1905).
Besides a very full and readable historical introduction this magnificent work contains a detailed account of Muḥammad's life during the first six years after the Hijra (622–628 A.D.).

56. *The Koran*, translated into English with notes and a preliminary discourse, by G. Sale (London, 1734).

Sale's translation, which has been frequently reprinted, is still serviceable. Mention may also be made of the English versions by J. M. Rodwell (London and Hertford, 1861) and by E. H. Palmer (the best from a literary point of view) in vols. vi and ix of 'The Sacred Books of the East' (Oxford, 1880); reprinted in *The World's Classics*, vol. 328.

57. *Geschichte des Qorâns*, by Th. Nöldeke, 2nd ed., revised by F. Schwally (Leipzig, 1909–19).

Cf. Nöldeke's essay, 'The Koran,' in *Sketches from Eastern History*, pp. 21–59, or his article in the *Encyclopædia Britannica* (11th ed.).

58. *The Teaching of the Qur'ān*, by H. W. Stanton (London, 1920).

V

THE HISTORY OF THE CALIPHATE.

59. *The Caliphate*, by T. W. Arnold (Oxford, 1924).

60. *Geschichte der Chalifen*, by G. Weil, 3 vols. (Mannheim, 1846–51).

Completed by the same author's *Geschichte des Abbasiden-Chalifats in Egypten*, 2 vols. (Stuttgart, 1860–62).

61. *Annals of the Early Caliphate*, by Sir W. Muir (London, 1883).

62. *The Caliphate, its rise, decline, and fall*, by Sir W. Muir (2nd ed., London, 1924).

63. *The Arab Conquest of Egypt and the last thirty years of Roman dominion*, by A. J. Butler (London, 1902).

64. *Das Arabische Reich und sein Sturz*, by J. Wellhausen (Berlin, 1902).

An excellent history of the Umayyad dynasty based on the Annals of Ṭabarí.

65. *The Eclipse of the Abbasid Caliphate*, by H. F. Amedroz and D. S. Margoliouth, 7 vols. (Oxford, 1920–1).

Arabic texts and translations valuable for the history of the fourth century A.H.

66. *The life and times of 'Alí b. 'Ísâ, the Good Vizier*, by H. Bowen (Cambridge, 1928).

67. *Geschichte der Fatimiden-Chalifen, nach arabischen Quellen*, by F. Wüstenfeld (Göttingen, 1881).

VI

THE HISTORY OF MOSLEM CIVILISATION.

68. *Prolégomènes d'Ibn Khaldoun*, a French translation of the *Muqaddima* or Introduction prefixed by Ibn Khaldún to his Universal History, by Baron MacGuckin de Slane, 3 vols. (in *Notices et Extraits des Manuscrits de la Bibliothèque Impériale*, vols. xix–xxi, Paris, 1863–68).

69. *Culturgeschichte des Orients unter den Chalifen*, by A. von Kremer, 2 vols. (Vienna, 1875–77).

70. *Culturgeschichtliche Streifzüge auf dem Gebiete des Islams*, by A. von Kremer (Leipzig, 1873).

This work has been translated into English by S. Khuda Bukhsh in his *Contributions to the History of Islamic Civilization* (Calcutta, 1905; 2nd ed., 1929).

71. *Geschichte der herrschenden Ideen des Islams*, by A. von Kremer (Leipzig, 1868).

A celebrated and most illuminating book.

72. *La civilisation des Arabes*, by G. Le Bon (Paris, 1884).

73. *Muhammedanische Studien*, by Ignaz Goldziher (Halle, 1888–90).

This book, which has frequently been cited in the foregoing pages, should be read by every serious student of Moslem civilisation.

74. *Islamstudien*, vol. i, by C. H. Becker (Leipzig, 1924).

75. *Umayyads and 'Abbásids*, being the Fourth Part of Jurji Zaydán's *History of Islamic Civilisation*, translated by D. S. Margoliouth (E. J. W. Gibb Memorial, vol. iv, 1907).

76. *Die Renaissance des Islams*, by A. Mez (Heidelberg, 1922).

77. *Baghdad during the Abbasid Caliphate*, by G. le Strange (Oxford, 1900).

78. *A Baghdad Chronicle*, by R. Levy (Cambridge, 1929).

79. *The Lands of the Eastern Caliphate*, by G. le Strange (Cambridge, 1905).

80. *Palestine under the Moslems*, by G. le Strange (London, 1890).

81. *Painting in Islam*, by T. W. Arnold (Oxford, 1928).

82. *Moslem Architecture*, by G. T. Rivoira, translated by G. M. Rushforth (Oxford, 1919).

83. *Arabian Society in the Middle Ages*, by E. W. Lane, edited by Stanley Lane-Poole (London, 1883).

84. *Die Araber im Mittelalter und ihr Einfluss auf die Cultur Europa's*, by G. Diercks (2nd ed., Leipzig, 1882).

85. *An account of the Manners and Customs of the Modern Egyptians*, by E. W. Lane (5th ed., London, 1871).

VII

MUḤAMMADAN RELIGION, THEOLOGY, JURISPRUDENCE, PHILOSOPHY, AND MYSTICISM.

86. *Development of Muslim Theology, Jurisprudence, and Constitutional Theory,* by Duncan B. Macdonald (London, 1903).
The best general sketch of the subject.

87. *Asch-Schahrastâni's Religionspartheien und Philosophen-Schulen,* translated by T. Haarbrücker (Halle, 1850–51).

88. *The Traditions of Islam,* by A. Guillaume (Oxford, 1924).
See also No. 73, Pt. ii.

89. *Les traditions islamiques trad. de l'arabe,* by O. Houdas and W. Marçais (Paris, 1903–14).
A translation of the celebrated collection of Traditions by Bukhárí.

90. *A Handbook of early Muhammadan Tradition,* by A. J. Wensinck (Leyden, 1927).

91. *Mohammedanism,* by C. Snouck Hurgronje (American lectures on the history of religions, 1916).

92. *Vorlesungen über den Islam,* by I. Goldziher (Heidelberg, 1910; 2nd ed., 1925).

93. *The Early Development of Mohammedanism,* by D. S. Margoliouth (London, 1914; re-issued, 1927).

94. *L'Islam, croyances et institutions,* by H. Lammens (Beyrout, 1926); translation by E. Denison Ross (London, 1929).

95. *The Islamic Faith,* by T. W. Arnold (Benn's Sixpenny Library, No. 42).

96. *The History of Philosophy in Islam,* by T. J. de Boer, translated by E. R. Jones (London, 1903).

97. *Die Mutaziliten oder die Freidenker im Islam,* by H. Steiner (Leipzig, 1865).

98. *Die Philosophie der Araber im X. Jahrhundert n. Chr. aus den Schriften der lautern Brüder herausgegeben,* by F. Dieterici (Berlin and Leipzig, 1861–79).

99. *Averroes et l'Averroisme,* by E. Renan (Paris, 1861).

100. *Mélanges de Philosophie Juive et Arabe,* by S. Munk (Paris, 1859).

101. *Fragments, relatifs à la doctrine des Ismaélîs,* by S. Guyard (Paris, 1874).

102. *Exposé de la Religion des Druzes,* by Silvestre de Sacy, 2 vols. (Paris, 1838).

103. *The Mystics of Islam,* by R. A. Nicholson (London, 1914).

104. *The Religious Attitude and Life in Islam,* by D. B. Macdonald (Chicago, 1909).

105. *Essai sur les origines du lexique technique de la mystique musulmane*, by L. Massignon (Paris, 1922).
106. *La Passion d'al-Halláj*, by L. Massignon, 2 vols. (Paris, 1922).
107. *Al-Ḳuschairîs Darstellung des Ṣûfîtums*, by Richard Hartmann (Berlin, 1914).
108. *Kleinere Schriften des Ibn al-'Arabī*, by H. S. Nyberg (Leiden, 1919).
109. *Studies in Islamic Mysticism*, by R. A. Nicholson (Cambridge, 1921).
110. *The Idea of Personality in Ṣúfism*, by R. A. Nicholson (Cambridge, 1923).
111. *The Dervishes or Oriental Spiritualism*, by John P. Brown, ed. by H. A. Rose (London, 1927).
112. *Les Confréries religieuses musulmanes*, by O. Depont and X. Coppolani (Algiers, 1897).

VIII

THE HISTORY AND LITERATURE OF THE MOORS.

113. *Histoire des Musulmans d'Espagne jusqu'à la conquête de l'Andalusie par les Almoravides* (711–1110 A.D.), by R. Dozy, 4 vols. (Leyden, 1861). Translated into English under the title *Spanish Islam* by F. G. Stokes (London, 1913).
114. *History of the Moorish Empire in Europe*, by S. P. Scott, 3 vols. (New York, 1904).
115. *The Moriscos of Spain, their conversion and expulsion*, by H. C. Lea (Philadelphia, 1901).
116. *History of the Mohammedan dynasties of Spain*, translated from the *Nafḥ al-Ṭíb* of Maqqarí by Pascual de Gayangos, 2 vols. (London, Oriental Translation Fund, 1840–43).
117. *The History of the Almohades*, by 'Abdu 'l-Wáḥid al-Marrákoshí, translated by E. Fagnan (Algiers, 1893).
118. *Recherches sur l'histoire et la littérature de l'Espagne pendant le moyen âge*, by R. Dozy, 2 vols. (3rd ed., Leyden, 1881).
119. *Poesie und Kunst der Araber in Spanien und Sicilien*, by A. F. von Schack, 2 vols. (2nd ed., Stuttgart, 1877).
120. *Moorish remains in Spain*, by A. F. Calvert (London, 1905).
121. *Storia dei musulmani di Sicilia*, by M. Amari (Firenze, 1854–72). A revised edition is in course of publication.

IX

THE HISTORY OF THE ARABS FROM THE MONGOL INVASION IN THE THIRTEENTH CENTURY TO THE PRESENT DAY.

122. *Histoire des Sultans Mamlouks de l'Égypte, écrite en arabe par Taki-eddin Ahmed Makrizi, traduite en français...par* M. Quatremère, 2 vols. (Oriental Translation Fund, 1845).
123. *The Mameluke or Slave dynasty of Egypt*, by Sir W. Muir (London, 1896).
124. *Histoire de Bagdad depuis la domination des Khans mongols jusqu'au massacre des Mamlouks*, by C. Huart (Paris, 1901).
125. *History of the Egyptian revolution from the period of the Mamelukes to the death of Mohammed Ali*, by A. A. Paton, 2 vols. (London, 1870).
126. *The Shaikhs of Morocco in the XVIth century*, by T. H. Weir (Edinburgh, 1904).
127. *The Arabic Press of Egypt*, by M. Hartmann (London, 1899).
128. *Neuarabische Volkspoesie gesammelt und uebersetzt*, by Enno Littmann (Berlin, 1902).

INDEX

In the following Index it has been found necessary to omit the accents indicating the long vowels, and the dots which are used in the text to distinguish letters of similar pronunciation. On the other hand, the definite article *al* has been prefixed throughout to those Arabic names which it properly precedes: it is sometimes written in full, but is generally denoted by a hyphen, *e.g.*-'Abbas for al-'Abbas. Names of books, as well as Oriental words and technical terms explained in the text, are printed in italics. Where a number of references occur under one heading, the more important are, as a rule, shown by means of thicker type.

A

Aaron, 215, 273
'Abbad, 421
'Abbadid dynasty, the, 414, 421–424, 431
-'Abbas, 146, 249, 250, 251
-'Abbas b. -Ahnaf (poet), 261
'Abbasa, 261
'Abbasid history, two periods of, 257
'Abbasid propaganda, the, 249–251
'Abbasids, the, xxviii, xxix, xxx, 65, 181, **182**, 193, 194, 220, **249–253**, **254–284**, 287–291, **365–367**, 373
'Abdullah, father of the Prophet, xxvii, 146, 148, 250
'Abdullah, brother of Durayd b. -Simma, 83
'Abdullah, the Amir (Spanish Umayyad), 411
'Abdullah b. -'Abbas, 145, 237, 249
'Abdullah b. Hamdan, 269
'Abdullah b. Ibad, 211
'Abdullah b. Mas'ud, 352
'Abdullah b. Maymun al-Qaddah, 271–274, 363
'Abdullah b. Muhammad b. Adham, 423
'Abdullah b. -Mu'tazz. See *Ibnu 'l-Mu'tazz*
'Abdullah b. Saba, 215, 216
'Abdullah b. Tahir, 129
'Abdullah b. Ubayy, 172
'Abdullah b. Yasin al-Kuzuli, 430
'Abdullah b. -Zubayr, 198, 199, 200, 202
'Abdu 'l-'Aziz (Marinid), 436
'Abdu 'l-'Aziz, brother of 'Abdu 'l-Malik, 200
'Abdu 'l-'Aziz, son of Muhammad b. Sa'ud, 466
'Abdu 'l-Ghani al-Nabulusi, 402
'Abdu 'l-Hamid, 267
'Abdu 'l-Malik (Umayyad Caliph), **200–202**, 206, 209, 224, 240, 242, 244, 247, 349, 407
'Abd Manaf, 146
'Abdu 'l-Mu'min (Almohade), 432
'Abdu 'l-Muttalib, 66–68, 146, 148, 154, 250
'Abdu 'l-Qadir al-Baghdadi, 131
'Abdu 'l-Qadir al-Jili, 393
'Abd al-Qays (tribe), 94
'Abdu 'l-Rahman I, the Umayyad, 253, 264, **405–407**, 417, 418
'Abdu 'l-Rahman II (Spanish Umayyad), 409, 418
'Abdu 'l-Rahman III (Spanish Umayyad), **411–412**, 420, 425
'Abdu 'l-Rahman V (Spanish Umayyad), 426
'Abdu 'l-Rahman b. 'Awf, 186
'Abdu 'l-Razzaq-Kashani, 402
'Abd Shams, 146
'Abd Shams Saba, 14
'Abdu 'l-'Uzza, 159
'Abdu 'l-Wahhab, founder of the Wahhabite sect. See *Muhammad b. 'Abd al-Wahhab.*
'Abdu 'l-Wahhab al-Sha'rani. See *-Sha'rani*
'Abdu 'l-Wahid of Morocco (historian), 431, 433
'Abid b. -Abras (poet), 39, 44, 86, 101
'Abid b. Sharya, 13, 19, 247
'Abida b. Hilal, 239
'Abir, xviii
'Abla, 115
-Ablaq (name of a castle), 84
Ablutions, the ceremonial, incumbent on Moslems, 149
-Abna, 29
Abraha, 6, 15, **28**, **65–68**
Abraham, xviii, 22, 62, 63, 66, 149, 150, 165, 172, 177
Abraham, the religion of, 62, 149, 177
'Abs (tribe), **xix**, 61, 88, 114–117
Absal, 433
Abu 'l-'Abbas (Marinid), 436
Abu 'l-'Abbas Ahmad al-Marsi, 327
Abu 'l-'Abbas al-Nami (poet), 270
Abu 'l-'Abbas-Saffah, 182, 253. See *-Saffah*
Abu 'Abdallah Ibnu 'l-Ahmar (Nasrid), 437
Abu 'Abd al-Rahman al-Sulami, 338
Abu Ahmad al-Mihrajani, 370
Abu 'l-'Ala al-Ma'arri, 166, 167, 206, 271, 289, 291, 296, 308, **313–324**, **375**, 448
Abu 'Ali al-Qali, 131, 420
Abu 'Ali b. Sina, 265. See *Ibn Sina*
Abu 'Amir, the Monk, 170
Abu 'Amr b. al-'Ala, 242, 285, **343**
Abu 'l-Aswad al-Du'ili, 342, 343
Abu 'l-'Atahiya (poet), 261, 291, **296–303**, 308, 312, 324, 374
Abu Ayman (title), 14
Abu Bakr (Caliph), xxvii, 142, 153, 175, 180, **183**, 185, 210, 214, 215, 257, 268, 297
Abu Bakr b. Abi 'l-Azhar, 344
Abu Bakr Ibnu 'l-'Arabi of Seville, 399
Abu Bakr b. Mu'awiya, 420
Abu Bakr al-Nabulusi, 460
Abu Bakr al-Razi (physician), 265. See *-Razi*
Abu Bakr b. 'Umar, 430
Abu 'l-Darda, 225
Abu Dawud al-Sijistani, 337
Abu 'l-Faraj of Isfahan, 32, 123, 131, 270, **347**, 419. See *Kitabu 'l-Aghani*
Abu 'l-Faraj al-Babbagha (poet), 270
Abu 'l-Fida (historian), 308, 316, 331, **454**
Abu Firas al-Hamdani (poet), 270, 304
Abu Ghubshan, 65
Abu Hanifa, 222, 284, 402, 408
Abu 'l-Hasan 'Ali b. Harun al-Zanjani, 370
Abu 'l-Hasan al-Ash'ari, **284**. See *-Ash'ari*

N

T